RIVALS

Rivals

Legendary Matchups
That Made Sports History

EDITED BY

DAVID K. WIGGINS
AND R. PIERRE RODGERS

The University of Arkansas Press
Fayetteville
2010

Copyright © 2010 by The University of Arkansas Press

All rights reserved
Manufactured in the United States of America

ISBN-10: (cloth) 1-55728-920-4
ISBN-13: (cloth) 978-1-55728-920-9

ISBN-10: (paper) 1-55728-921-2
ISBN-13: (paper) 978-1-55728-921-6

13   12   11   10   09   5   4   3   2   1

Designed by Liz Lester

♾ The paper used in this publication meets the minimum requirements of the American
National Standard for Permanence of Paper for Printed Library Materials Z39.48–1984.

LIBRARY OF CONGRESS CATALOGING-IN-PUBLICATION DATA

Rivals : legendary matchups that made sports history / edited by David K. Wiggins
    and R. Pierre Rodgers.
        p.   cm.
    Includes bibliographical references and index.
        ISBN 978-1-55728-920-9 (casebound : alk. paper) — ISBN 978-1-55728-921-6
    (pbk. : alk. paper)
        1. Sports rivalries—History. 2. Sports—History. 3.Athletes—History.
    I. Wiggins, David Kenneth, 1951–   II. Rodgers, R. Pierre.
        GV571.R58   2010
        796.09—dc22

                                                2009053650

To the memory of Lyle I. Olsen (1929–2000),
the most voracious reader and lover of sport I have ever known.
—DKW

To the memory of Cyril E. Griffith (1929–1994) who made
African and African American history come alive; Richard B. Gregg
(1936–2001) who scored in football and debate; and Lawrence (Larry)
Hugenberg (1953–2008) who rubbed, raced, and educationally
communicated with the best of them.
—RPR

CONTENTS

III. Wide, Wide World

PREFACE

The intent of this book is to provide insights and a more complete understanding of some of the more famous sport rivalries. Although it is impossible to include every sport rivalry that has ever existed, it is our hope that the ones we have chosen to include in this volume will provide a more thorough picture of how and why people are fascinated with athletic competitions between equally matched opponents who have decidedly different backgrounds and styles and personalities. It is also our hope that this volume will provide additional insights into the institution of sport and how it is connected to the economy, the media, politics, education, and other crucial spheres of social life. It is our hope, moreover, that this volume on sport rivalries will furnish additional insights into how sports affect people's ideas about such things as femininity and race and are connected to social relations and the changing nature of power among individuals and groups.

This book, like most others, took much time to complete and involved a good number of people who need to be acknowledged. We would like to express our appreciation to all of the contributors who worked diligently to ensure that their manuscripts were completed on time and with the utmost care. We would also like to thank Lisa Reeves for taking time out from her already busy schedule to type portions of the manuscript and to compile materials necessary for its completion. A big thank you as well to Larry Malley, who offered us sage advice, guidance, and encouragement.

INTRODUCTION

This book provides detailed information and an analysis of sixteen famous sport rivalries. Not intended to be exhaustive by covering each and every sport rivalry that has ever existed, the sport rivalries chosen for inclusion in this book deal with a wide variety of sports, both individual and team competitions, and male and female athletes of various races and cultural backgrounds. The chapters are written by scholars—many of them with worldwide reputations and long lists of quality publications dealing with various aspects of sport—who were asked to address four specific questions: (1) What was the origin of the rivalry? (2) What were the societal conditions that gave rise to the rivalry? (3) How was the rivalry maintained? and (4) What did the rivalry come to represent for both participants and fans? These questions were posed in an effort to help us understand more fully the essence and meaning of sport rivalries.

What is immediately apparent from all sixteen chapters is that sport rivalries are only possible and remain significant if the opponents are evenly matched and there is uncertainty as to who will win the game, match, or athletic contest. In addition to equality of competition, sport rivalries are only possible if there are significant contrasts and differences between opponents. These contrasts and differences may revolve around variations in race and culture, political and societal ideologies, individual style and personality, and geography and religious traditions. Importantly, sport rivalries are followed with great interest by fans, typically hyped by the media to engender additional interest, and often result in outstanding athletic performances because of the intensity of the competition and comparable talent of the two opponents. Sport rivalries, moreover, embody obvious symbolic qualities represented through athletic contests between two evenly matched and decidedly different opponents. At their most basic level, they publicly express larger issues and concerns and interests.

What is also immediately apparent from all sixteen chapters is that sport rivalries often result in genuine friendships and respect between opponents. Although the intensity of competition and the high stakes involved in contests between two opponents sometimes result in bitter disputes and antagonisms, mutual admiration and respect also frequently occur between athletes and teams fighting to outduel one another. Ultimately, the opponents in sport rivalries seemingly understand that their contests are about defining one another through athletic competitions as much as anything else. This fact often results in a special relationship between the two opponents that can be found in few places other than sport.

The first section of the book, "One-on-One," includes six chapters devoted to noted rivalries between famous athletes representing a number of different sports. In chapter 1, "The Purest of Rivalries: Rafer Johnson, C. K. Yang, and the 1960 Olympic Decathlon," Joseph M. Turrini analyzes the rivalry between track and field athletes Rafer Johnson and C. K. Yang. The two men, friends who competed at the intercollegiate level at the University of California at Los Angeles, fashioned a relatively brief yet important rivalry which was made all the more interesting by their different racial backgrounds and by virtue of the fact that their ultimate competition took place on the international stage. In dramatic style, Johnson, an African American from California, bettered his previous best time in the last event (1,500-meter run) to beat Yang, a native of Taiwan, for the decathlon title at the 1960 Olympic Games in Rome.

The enormously intense competition between Johnson and Yang at the 1960 Olympic Games did not fracture their relationship. In fact, the two men remained close friends and part of each other's lives until Yang passed away in 2007. Fortunately, Johnson's post-athletic career was far more successful than the one enjoyed by Yang. Perhaps, noted Johnson in his autobiography, "If Yang had won gold, his life would have been much easier and far more prosperous."

The relationship between Johnson and Yang was far different than the one between the legendary golfers Arnold Palmer and Jack Nicklaus. As George B. Kirsch makes clear in chapter 2, "The King and the Bear: The Arnold Palmer–Jack Nicklaus Rivalry and the Rise of Modern Golf," the two giants of the sport had a complicated relationship and were extraordinarily competitive on and off the golf course. The intense rivalry between the two great athletes with decidedly different personalities and playing styles would, as noted by Kirsch, contribute to both of their reputations while also promoting the growth of golf as a mainstream sport in America. Perhaps unlike any other individual athletic rivalry in history, Palmer and Nicklaus took their intense competition off the golf course and into the marketplace. Both men parlayed their name recognition and utilized the great wealth they had accumulated through their many victories on the tour to create vast business empires that were frequently in competition with each other. One of the most intense competitions of this type was over golf course designs.

The rivalry between Muhammad Ali and Joe Frazier had nothing to do with business empires and golf course design. As Gerald Early makes clear in chapter 3, "The Mortality of Kings: Ali versus Frazier," the rivalry between Ali and Frazier was about two "remarkably different men who fought each other savagely in the ring while outside the ring one theatrically disparaged the other, which the other deeply despised and openly resented." However, as Early also notes, "Frazier needed Ali almost as much as Ali needed Frazier." The two great fighters, while having an acrimonious personal relationship, defined one another in three classic bouts that garnered worldwide attention among boxing aficionados and the lay public alike. Similar to other well-known rivalries in the sport, including Jack Dempsey's famous bouts against Gene Tunney, Sugar Ray Robinson's fights against Jake LaMotta, and Joe Louis's fights against Max Schmeling, the pugilistic encounters between Ali and Frazier were fraught with political symbolism and perhaps unparalleled drama.

The hatred between Ali and Frazier was nowhere to be found in the rivalry between Magic Johnson and Larry Bird. As pointed out by Daniel A. Nathan in chapter 4, "'We Were about Winning': Larry Bird, Magic Johnson, and the Rivalry That Remade the NBA," the rivalry between Bird, the great white forward from French Lick, Indiana, and Johnson, the enormously talented black guard from Lansing, Michigan, was "characterized by mutual admiration and respect." The rivalry between the two celebrated hoopsters, which began when they starred for their respective universities in the famous 1979 National Collegiate Athletic Association title game in Salt Lake City, Utah, "represented," explains Nathan, "deeply entrenched cultural values and tensions, and it continues to resonate." Although never competing directly against one another because of their participation in a team game, the rivalry between Bird and Johnson helped reignite the rivalry between their respective franchises, the Boston Celtics and Los Angeles Lakers, and helped renew the popularity of the National Basketball Association, which had experienced an assortment of problems during the 1970s. Like so many other sport rivalries, the media accentuated the differences and pointed out the contrasts rather than the similarities between Johnson and Bird because that is what sells and is most marketable. Finally, like many other sport rivalries, race was one of the defining factors in the rivalry between Johnson and Bird, the two great players, particularly Bird, carrying "the unwanted burden of racial symbolism" as a white man in a league that was predominantly black.

Unlike the Johnson and Bird rivalry, Martina Navratilova and Chris Evert directly battled one another on the tennis court eighty times over a span of sixteen years. Remarkably, Navratilova won forty-three of these confrontations and Evert won thirty-seven, a difference of just three matches. This parity, notes Mary Jo Festle in chapter 5, "Friendly Rivals: Martina Navratilova and Chris Evert," combined with their different styles of play and personalities, contributed to the heightened interest and fascination that people had with the Navratilova and Evert rivalry. Though they were always respectful of one another and eventually became good friends, the media, in an effort to heighten interest in the rivalry, played up the contrasts between Navratilova and Evert. Navratilova, born in Czechoslovakia during the days of communism, was a muscular left-handed server and volleyer who was, both on and off the tennis court, "impulsive, passionate, and a risk-taker. She could be warm and generous, was ready for fun and open to new ideas and things to do." Evert, on the other hand, was a native of Florida who played the game from the baseline with a steely resolve and expressionless demeanor that intimidated many of her opponents. She always emphasized her femininity and spoke of love and interest in getting married and having children. These differences between Navratilova and Evert were good theater and, along with their superb athletic skills and closely fought and exciting matches, generated enormous interest and a wide following among tennis fans everywhere.

A far less well known rivalry was that between Debi Thomas and Katerina Witt. As Alison M. Wrynn and Annette R. Hofmann point out in chapter 6, "The Battle of the Carmens: Debi Thomas versus Katerina

Witt," America's Thomas and East Germany's Witt only skated against each other four times between 1984 and 1988, with Witt being victorious on three of those occasions. The contests between the two great skaters, however, were always high drama with the Western media in particular contributing to the rivalry by carefully pointing out the differences between Thomas and Witt in regards to race, performance, style, and cultural background. Importantly, Wrynn and Hofmann make clear that while Thomas and Witt "were inexorably linked by their decision to both skate their long programs to the music of Bizet's 'Carmen' in the 1988 Calgary Games" and were "fierce competitive rivals on the ice," the most important rivalry that both skaters perhaps "needed to overcome was the pressure within themselves and from their respective cultures."

The second section of the book, "Team Games," includes six chapters devoted to well-known rivalries between various teams representing different levels of competition. In chapter 7 Ryan King-White analyzes the highly publicized and hotly contested rivalry between the New York Yankees and Boston Red Sox. King-White explains in his aptly titled chapter, "Bitter Foes, but Marketing Pros: The Red Sox–Yankees Rivalry," that to a large extent the rivalry between two of major league baseball's most historic franchises has been a media creation. While always bitter opponents, the rivalry has grown more serious over the recent past because of the relatively equal competition between the two teams and the fact that the media takes every opportunity to perpetuate this competition so as to create additional fan interest and "garner more capital." Examples of this media coverage are on the Entertainment and Sports Network (ESPN), which airs year-long programs of the two teams, and the Yankees' and Red Sox's own local cable channels, Yankees Entertainment and Sport Network (YES) and New England Sport Network (NESN), which saturate the market with public-interest stories about their respective organizations. This coverage is very selective and often disregards the "historical and contextual realities" of the rivalry while at once fostering contentious relationships between the followers of both clubs.

There are few sport rivalries better known than the one between the Toronto Maple Leafs and Montreal Canadiens. In chapter 8, "A Tale of Two Cities: The Toronto Maple Leafs versus the Montreal Canadiens," Brian P. Soebbing and Daniel S. Mason provide an analysis of the ice hockey rivalry in the context of the two cities in which the historic franchises are located. The Maple Leafs and Canadiens, representing two cities that "have developed identities that are rooted in their differences from one another" and "vie for status as Canada's preeminent economic and cultural center," both joined the National Hockey League (NHL) in its first season in 1917 and began their rivalry twenty-nine years later when Franke Selke Sr. left the Maple Leafs and became general manager of the Canadiens. Although the rivalry has waned recently because of Toronto's lack of success on the ice, the two longtime opponents are more successful than any other teams in the NHL, with the Canadiens capturing twenty-three Stanley Cups compared to thirteen Stanley Cups for the Maple Leafs. In head-to-head competition, the two teams faced off 690 times from 1917 through the 2008–2009 season, with the Canadiens winning 328 of those contests.

In chapter 9, "Like Cats and Dogs: The Massillon–Canton McKinley Football Rivalry," Lawrence W. Hugenberg and Brian C. Pattie discuss the only high school football game listed on the betting line in Las Vegas. Utilizing an assortment of primary and secondary source materials, Hugenberg and Pattie detail the various reasons for the enormous popularity of the Massillon–Canton McKinley football rivalry and why it has generated such fervor and enthusiasm since its beginnings in 1894. Ultimately, the annual game between the two schools has evolved into a culturally significant event that seemingly involves every citizen in Massillon and Canton and engenders unparalleled community pride and enthusiasm. This pride and enthusiasm are reflected in large booster associations, spirit wear, victory parades, alumni involvement, and media attention. Perhaps no game in the series was more important than the one hundredth meeting between the two schools in 1994, featured in an article in *Sports Illustrated*. Massillon defeated Canton McKinley 42–41 as a result of a missed extra point in overtime by Canton McKinley.

There is no more important rivalry in women's college basketball than the one between the University of Connecticut and the University of Tennessee. In chapter 10, "A Rivalry for the Ages: Tennessee-UConn Women's Basketball," Jaime Schultz examines the rivalry between the two major powerhouses in the women's game at the intercollegiate level of competition. Through an examination of a wide range of primary and secondary source materials, including *ESPN the Magazine*, *Sports Illustrated*, and *Women's Basketball*, Schultz persuasively argues that the intense and often heated rivalry between the women's basketball teams from Connecticut and Tennessee resulted from the success of the two programs, the prominence and personalities of the school's longtime coaches, Pat Summitt and Geno Auriemma, and the influence of both the print and electronic media. Of these three, the intense personal competition and antagonism between Connecticut's Auriemma and Tennessee's Summitt is perhaps the most fascinating story line of the rivalry. Importantly, the contrasting personalities of the two coaches, which helped fuel the rivalry, was apparently the same thing that helped account for Summitt's decision in 2007 not to renew the contract to continue playing Connecticut during the regular season. For now, fans of women's college basketball can only hope that the two schools meet each year in post-season play.

One of the oldest, most contentious, and most highly publicized rivalries in college sports is the annual gridiron battle between the University of Michigan and Ohio State University. In chapter 11, "Three Yards and a Pool of Blood: Ohio State versus Michigan," Brad Austin examines the over one-hundred-year-old football rivalry between two of the most prominent state institutions of higher learning in the country. Convincingly arguing that it is the "most consistently meaningful game for the longest span," Austin makes clear that the rivalry began in earnest during the decade of the 1920s as a result of the more equitable competition between the two institutions, promotional efforts of school officials, and influence of radio and newspaper coverage. The rivalry would become even more heated and significant with the advent of television and Ohio State's hiring of the legendary coach Woody Hayes in the 1950s, and it escalated in 1969 into what is termed the "ten-year war" with Michigan's hiring of equally legendary coach Bo Schembechler. During the next ten years, Ohio State and Michigan either won or shared the Big Ten title, resulting in a league that some termed the "Big Two and Little Eight."

One of the most well known of all the rivalries in professional football is between the Dallas Cowboys and Washington Redskins. In fact, in chapter 11, "Corporate Cowboys and Blue-Collar Bureaucrats: The Dallas-Washington Football Rivalry," Stephen H. Norwood makes plain that no other professional sport rivalry since 1960 "has been sustained between teams so geographically distant." This sustained rivalry resulted from a myriad of factors, including the commitment of each franchise to pageantry, the decided differences between the two cities, the quality of the teams' quarterbacks, the teams' contrasting approaches during the various players' strikes, and conflicting team identities and images. Of the above, it is perhaps the conflicting team identities and images of the Cowboys and Redskins that provide the most intriguing explanation for the level and intensity of the rivalry. The citizens of Dallas, writes Norwood, "many of whom attended Cowboys games wearing the ten-gallon hats and high boots of a mythic West and arriving in pickup trucks, derided Washingtonians as pallid bureaucrats, confined to cubicles, lacking any connection to the great outdoors." On the other hand, the fans of the Redskins, "a significant proportion of whom were federal employees, tended to view Dallas as culturally unsophisticated, populated by crass and garish newly rich oil barons and western rubes."

The third section of the book, "Wide, Wide World," includes four chapters devoted to well-known rivalries involving athletes from the United States and those from other countries. In chapter 13, "Imperial Rivalries: America versus Britain for the Davis Cup," S. W. Pope analyzes the Davis Cup tennis matches. The brainchild of Dwight F. Davis, a Harvard University tennis player, the first Davis Cup tennis match was held in 1900 and pitted the United States against Great Britain. Eventually, teams from other countries began to participate and it became a truly international event marked by stiff competition and nationalistic pride. This stiff competition, writes Pope, "emerged within the context of raging imperial rivalries and as such provided a prominent venue for Western imperialist players to symbolically contest and validate their respective national and sporting prowess." This attempt at validation was certainly evident in the many challenges launched by the United States against Great Britain on "various cultural and political fronts," including Davis Cup competitions.

The Ryder Cup golf matches, analyzed by John Nauright in chapter 14, "This Has Nothing to Do with Money: The Ryder Cup and International Rivalry in Golf," have been held since 1927. Named after Samuel Ryder, a wealthy merchant who put forth the money for a specially designed gold chalice trophy, the Ryder Cup was for many years a competition between professional golfers from the United States and their counterparts from Great Britain. In 1977, however, Jack Nicklaus proposed that the team from Great Britain be expanded to professional players from continental Europe in order to equalize competition and improve the quality of the matches. The proposal was approved, and in 1979 professional players from the United States began competing for the first time against professional players from continental Europe. It is the post-1979 period, since 1982 to be exact, that is the focus of Nauright's analysis of the Ryder Cup. He persuasively argues that the European team's more recent success in the Ryder Cup can partly be explained by the fact that "this is the one time that a pan-European team is produced to challenge the United States, and thus the Ryder Cup provides a focus for European identity from Spain to Sweden and from Ireland to Italy, where Ryder Cup golfers have originated and where golf is now widely played." Other possible reasons for European success in the Ryder Cup have to do with the "differing spectator cultures of the United States and Europe" and the fact that Europeans seemingly have "a better ability to understand the team approach and how to lift themselves up as a group, which goes hand in hand with their supporters, who have fun in victory or defeat."

Chris Elzey provides important insights into the highly intense sports rivalry between the United States and the Soviet Union via a detailed examination of the first track and field meet held between the two countries in 1958. Elzey explains in chapter 15, "The Match of the Century: the U.S.-USSR Rivalry in Sports," that the 1958 track and field meet between the two countries, like any of the sporting competitions between the super powers during the Cold War, was about "defeating one's ideological foe" and "attempting to prove the advantages of their economic and social systems." The "Match of the Century" and the other athletic competitions between the United States and the Soviet Union were never about "just games and contests," but about "capitalism against communism, West against East, us against them." Tellingly, when the Soviet Union collapsed in 1991, the decades-long "Cold War rivalry in sports evaporated too."

Lindsey J. Meân provides the final examination of rivalries in chapter 16, "Dare to Dream: U.S. Women's Soccer versus the World." As is true in so many of the chapters in this volume, Meân makes clear that the media is crucial to an understanding of the place of women's soccer in the world and the rivalries that are constructed in the sport. The powerful media networks, while being a major impediment to the success of soccer in the United States and as a women's sport, have selectively created, nonetheless, rivalries between the United States women's soccer team and those from foreign countries based on more than equitable talent level and skill. Much of the media construction of women's soccer rivalries has to do with political ideology and hegemony. A prime example is the failure of the U.S. media to commodify the United States and Norway rivalry because of a lack of ideological differences between the two countries and the fact that the Norwegian women's players do not fulfill the typical representational practices of women athletes as either "big and unfeminine" or "reproducers of hegemonic beauty." Conversely, the U.S. media has constructed a rivalry between the U.S. women's soccer team and the Chinese women's soccer team around contrasting styles and political and cultural differences.

RIVALS

I
One-on-One

Rafer Johnson and C. K. Yang, the two great decathletes and close friends who won the gold and silver medals in the 1960 Olympic decathlon, with their coach, Elvin "Ducky" Drake. *From left to right,* Yang, Drake, and Johnson. *Courtesy of the Bancroft Library, University of California Library.*

one

The Purest of Rivalries
Rafer Johnson, C. K. Yang, and the 1960 Olympic Decathlon

JOSEPH M. TURRINI

This was such an exciting decathlon the people in the stands at the end of the 1,500, the people were chanting—the Italian people—"Give both of them a gold medal!" That's the way I felt about it too.

—UCLA track coach, Elvin "Ducky" Drake

Rafer Johnson and Yang Chuan-Kwang (C. K. Yang) were rivals forever linked by their classic decathlon battle at the 1960 Olympic Games in Rome.[1] *Track and Field News* called it "one of the greatest man-to-man battles in the history of track and field."[2] The event is still routinely included in Olympic and track and field histories.[3] The 1960 decathlon was the pinnacle of a unique rivalry between two great athletes known equally for the support they provided each other as for the intensity of the close athletic competitions. Yang and Johnson competed against each other in only four decathlons over a four-year span. They clashed at the 1956 Olympic Games, at the Amateur Athletic Union (AAU) national decathlon championships in 1958 and 1960, and at the 1960 Olympic Games. Johnson beat Yang in all four of the contests. (see chart 1) The distinctive conditions under which the 1960 Olympic decathlon developed and the relationship between C. K. Yang and Rafer Johnson explain the continued interest in the 1960 Olympic decathlon.

The Rafer Johnson and C. K. Yang battle at the 1960 Olympic Games is the most remembered decathlon for a number of reasons. First, it was fiercely contested throughout the two-day competition with the outcome

CHART 1: Rafer Johnson and C. K. Yang's Decathlon Competitions

DATE	COMPETITION	LOCATION
November 29–30, 1956	1956 Olympic Games	Melbourne, Australia
July 4–5, 1958	AAU Championship	Palmyra, New Jersey
July 8–9, 1960	AAU Championship (also Olympic Trials)	Eugene, Oregon
September 5–6, 1960	1960 Olympic Games	Rome, Italy

Source: The information in this table was compiled from charts in Frank Zarnowski, *The Decathlon: A Colorful History of Track and Field's Most Challenging Event* (Champaign: Leisure Press, 1989), 88, 97.

uncertain until the completion of the last event, the 1,500-meter race. Rarely are decathlons this close; usually a clear winner emerges well before the last event. Decathlon historian Frank Zarnowski maintains that the Johnson and Yang tilt was "the most dramatic finish in Olympic decathlon history."[4] Second, in the two years prior to the 1960 Olympic Games, Yang and Johnson had become close friends. They trained together daily and helped each other develop their fitness and improve their techniques. They both competed, although not at the same time, on the University of California at Los Angeles (UCLA) track team and they shared the same coach, Elvin "Ducky" Drake. Their close relationship heightened the tense competition. Third, the Cold War served as a backdrop to the competition, enhancing the political and social meaning of the athletic success of Yang and Johnson. Rafer Johnson, an educated and successful African American, became a model of an integrated America. He symbolized, however inaccurately in many regards, the country's advances in racial equality and opportunity. The career of C. K. Yang, on the other hand, demonstrated the continued battle over the geographic and political boundaries of China and the identity of Chinese people after Mao Tse Tung's communist revolution in China in 1949. A native of Taiwan, Yang's national identity became embroiled in the confusion caused by the battle between Chinese nationalists who fled to Taiwan, led by deposed leader Chiang Kai-shek, and Mao's Communist China. The competing claims of Mao and Chiang Kai-shek to represent all of China and Taiwan seeped into international sport and at times created problems for the athletes. The participation of Taiwanese athletes like Yang in international sporting events, such as the

R. J.'S SCORE	R. J.'S PLACE	C. K.'S SCORE	C. K.'S PLACE
7,587	2	6,521	8
7,754	1	7,625	2
8,636	1	8,426	2
8,392	1	8,334	2

Asian Games and the Olympics, influenced international politics. Finally, the modern decathlon has been an exceptionally popular Olympic event ever since being introduced at the 1912 Games in Stockholm, Sweden. It is a unique and grueling competition that consists of ten running (100 meters, 400 meters, 1,500 meters, and 110-meter high hurdles), throwing (discus, shot put, and javelin), and jumping (high jump, long jump, and pole vault) events. It requires athletes to develop speed, strength, and stamina as well as to master a variety of throwing and jumping techniques. The winner garners the unofficial title of world's greatest athlete.

The Making of a Decathlete: Rafer Johnson

Rafer Johnson spent most of his first decade growing up poor in racially segregated Texas. He was born the first child of Lewis and Alma (Gibson) Johnson in the midst of the Great Depression (August 18, 1935) in Hillsboro, Texas, a small farming town about sixty miles south of Dallas. Johnson's father followed New Deal farm work to Oklahoma for a brief period, then quickly returned the family to Texas, settling in Oak Cliff, a dismal, impoverished, and rigorously segregated neighborhood west of downtown Dallas. The family home lacked indoor plumbing and electricity. The grinding poverty and segregation in Oak Cliff posed serious limitations to the opportunities of its poor African American inhabitants like Rafer Johnson.[5] Just prior to the 1960 Olympic Games, Johnson recounted, "If my family had stayed in Texas, I not only wouldn't be representing the U.S. in the Olympic Games—I wouldn't even have gone to college."[6]

The Johnson family fled the poverty and segregation of Texas and moved to California in 1944 when Rafer was nine years old. They settled in Kingsburg, a small town in central California's San Joaquin Valley. Kingsburg had been settled by Swedes, but by the mid-1940s, its twenty-five hundred inhabitants included a small mixture of recently immigrated Italians, Latinos, Armenians, and Japanese. Although they were the only African American family in town, the Johnson clan found Kingsburg an exceptional place to raise their five children. It lacked the debilitating poverty and racial segregation they had encountered in Texas and had minimal racial conflict.[7] Johnson recalled Kingsburg "with great affection as a Norman Rockwell painting come to life, a peaceful, harmonious place where people were treated with decency."[8]

Johnson's athletic and leadership skills matured in Kingsburg. A popular and active student, Johnson was elected to numerous class offices, including student body president at Roosevelt Elementary School, president of his sophomore class, and, during his senior year, student body president of Kingsburg Joint Union High School (KJUHS). His athletic career almost derailed before it even began. When Johnson was ten years old his left foot got caught in a conveyor belt while playing at a Del Monte cannery facility near his house. Doctors thought the injury might cause Johnson permanent physical limitations; but he recovered to become a multi-sport star athlete, earning eleven varsity letters (baseball, basketball, football, and track) at KJUHS.[9] The young star favored track and field. Murl Dodson, Johnson's high school track coach, encouraged Johnson to pursue the decathlon. In July 1952, between his sophomore and junior years, Dodson drove Johnson twenty-five miles to nearby Tulare, the hometown of 1948 (and soon to be 1952) Olympic decathlon gold medalist and then world record holder Bob Mathias, to see the 1952 decathlon Olympic Trials. A few months later, the two traveled back to Tulare for the parade celebrating Mathias's 1952 Olympic win. Mathias's victory and parade captivated Johnson.[10] For the next eight years he devoted his athletic career and ambitions to becoming a decathlon gold medalist and world record holder.

Johnson jumped into the event quickly, competing in a number of decathlons prior to entering college. High school athletes rarely compete in decathlons, and it is unlikely that Johnson would have if not for his high school coach's interest and urging. He won in his first attempt at the event at a high school invitational just weeks after Mathias's victory parade and then captured the California state high school decathlon meet in 1953 and 1954.[11] *Track and Field News* referred to Johnson as "as good a decathlon prospect as Tulare's Bob Mathias."[12] Soon after graduating from high school in 1954, Johnson competed in the national Amateur Athletic Union (AAU) decathlon championship in Atlantic City, New Jersey. The always supportive Kingsburg residents raised the money to fly Johnson and coach Dodson to the meet.[13] Johnson finished third, behind Bob Richards and Aubrey Lewis.[14]

Johnson was highly recruited out of high school in both football and track and field. Craig Dixon, a former UCLA track star, bronze medalist in the 1948 Olympic 110-meter high hurdles, and then assistant track coach at UCLA, recruited Johnson. Dixon told Johnson that UCLA was a "major university with a well-rounded educational institution, which had no prejudices."[15] Johnson recalled that one of the reasons he chose UCLA was its "long-standing commitment to racial equality." Two of his childhood heroes, Jackie Robinson and Ralph Bunche, had both competed in athletics and graduated from UCLA. While visiting the campus Johnson also noticed that one of UCLA's past student body presidents was an African American.[16] This turned out to be prophetic as Johnson would be elected student body president during his senior year at UCLA.[17] The National Association for the Advancement of Colored People agreed with Johnson's conclusion that UCLA was an excellent institution for African American athletes when it bestowed the UCLA Athletic Department with an award for "fielding teams without regard to race or color," during Johnson's freshman year.[18]

Johnson quickly began fulfilling his own ambitious athletic goals and the lofty public expectations that followed him to UCLA.[19] He won the Pan-American Games gold medal in Mexico City in March 1955 and, just three months later (June 1955), broke Bob Mathias's decathlon world record by a 96-point margin at the central coast AAU decathlon championship meet in front of an excited Kingsburg crowd.[20] Johnson's 7,985 points left him a mere 15 points shy of the 8,000 point mark. Johnson also performed yeoman service for the UCLA freshman track squad (affectionately called the Brubabes), regularly competing in four, five, and as many as six events in dual meets.[21] Johnson, for example, had five first-place finishes and one second-place finish in the team's victory over traditional powerhouse and cross town rival, the University of Southern California (USC); this was only the second time the

Brubabes had beaten the USC freshman squad in the previous sixteen dual meets.[22]

Johnson's contributions were critical to the success of the UCLA varsity track team during his sophomore season. He used dual track meets to improve his technique in multiple events, but also to gain valuable points for the team. For instance, he competed in five events and was the meet's high point scorer (16 points) while leading the Bruins to a 2.5 point victory (69.5 to 67.0) over perennial champions USC at the 1956 Pacific Conference Championships. The *UCLA Daily Bruin* enthusiastically reported, "Southern California's [USC] stranglehold on the Pacific Coast Conference track championship crumbled after 28 long years."[23] His second-place finishes in both the 110-meter high hurdles and the broad jump at the 1956 NCAA championship meet paced UCLA to its first national track and field championship, a 55- to 50-point victory over second-place University of Kansas.[24] Johnson was awarded the Dr. Edward S. Ruth trophy for amassing the most points (129.5) in the 1956 track season for UCLA.[25]

Although committed to the success of the UCLA Bruin track team, the 1956 Olympic decathlon remained Johnson's primary goal. Commentators declared Johnson the overwhelming favorite to win the decathlon at Melbourne.[26] Plagued by a lingering knee injury and a pulled stomach muscle, Johnson finished second to Milt Campbell, the outstanding football and track athlete from Indiana University. Always a gracious competitor, Johnson acknowledged that he "lost to a good man."[27] But like many successful athletes, he "despised" losing.[28] Most assume that Johnson would have won if not for the injuries; but perhaps more credit should be given to Campbell, who was also an excellent athlete.[29] Campbell only decided to compete in the decathlon after finishing a disappointing fourth place in the Olympic Trials in the 110-meter high hurdles, narrowly missing qualifying in his preferred event. Campbell scored the second highest point total (7,937) ever, just 48 points behind Johnson's world record. The second-place finish stung Johnson, who, according to his coach, Ducky Drake, "felt he had let a lot of people down."[30] Years later Johnson recalled the frustration: "I don't think I've ever been as disappointed as after losing to Milt Campbell at the 1956 Olympic Games."[31] Allison Danzig reported that "Milton Campbell took his place with Jim Thorpe and Bob Mathias on the pedestal where Rafer Johnson was expected to be enshrined as the world's finest all around athlete."[32] Unhappy with his silver medal, Johnson vowed that he would redeem himself with a gold medal at the 1960 Olympics.[33]

Johnson recovered after a lengthy period of recuperation from knee surgery and triumphed in a much heralded battle against Vasiliy Kuznyetsov at the first U.S.-USSR dual track meet in 1958. Kuznyetsov had become the top-ranked decathlete in the world while Johnson convalesced from knee surgery in 1957. The Soviet star bested Johnson's world record six weeks before (May 1958) the U.S.-USSR meet, becoming the first decathlete to amass more than 8,000 points.[34] The decathlon battle between the former and the current world record holder was the most anticipated event in the most important dual track meet in American history.[35] Johnson recalled the competition as "not just man-on-man for the unofficial title of World's Greatest Athlete, it was Communism vs. the Free World."[36] Johnson established a new world record (8,302 points) in route to beating Kuznyetsov. Track and field journalist and historian R. L. Quercetani thought his performance "was no doubt the most spectacular feat in the history of the decathlon since the days of Jim Thorpe."[37]

Politicians and other observers imbued Johnson's athletic successes with political and social meaning. He became a symbol of the achievements of African Americans, successful racial integration in the United States, and the superiority of capitalism over communism. His success was used to counter the racial segregation, racism, and civil rights battles that pervaded much of the news through the 1950s. His rise from a rather humble background—the poverty, segregation, and racism of Texas to UCLA graduate, student body president, world record holder, and Olympic medalist—was trumpeted as an American success story that helped to disprove the disturbing daily news from Montgomery, Birmingham, and other parts of the South. For example, the Amateur Athlete reported, "No matter what they [USSR] had read about the shame of Little Rock, here was the real symbol of America standing before them."[38]

Johnson was patriotic, and a thoughtful supporter of integration and a somewhat ill-defined American way of life. Being on the victory stand and seeing the American flag raised at the Pan-American Games was Johnson's biggest thrill in track to that point.[39] When he received Sports Illustrated's Athlete of the Year Award in 1958, Johnson proudly avowed that he had one "goal in life: To live like an American."[40] Johnson stated just prior to the 1960 Olympic Games that he wanted to work for the State Department after the Olympics so he could "show them how we live in America."[41] But he was also well aware of the limitations that racism and segregation imposed on many African Americans, like his neighbors in Texas as a youth. He strove through his actions to counter these problems and remained optimistic that progress was being made.[42] Johnson recalled that he "was fully aware of the irony that a black man was an emissary of a nation where discrimination raged and racists still got away with lynchings. I found myself affected by the political overtones despite my efforts to ignore them."[43]

Unknown to Johnson and Kuznyetsov, a third athlete, the not yet recognized C. K. Yang, was about to burst onto the international scene, complicating their tidy East versus West duel. Yang had finished second to Johnson by 129 points at the 1958 AAU decathlon championship. He would become a much more important competitor and companion than Johnson's Soviet rival. Johnson recalled that he "had no way of knowing at the time, but Yang would soon become [his] close friend, training partner, and costar in the most dramatic decathlon in Olympic history."[44]

The Asian Iron Man Comes to America

Yang's path to UCLA and the 1960 Olympic decathlon was less direct than Johnson's. Yang was born into an aboriginal Taiwanese family on July 10, 1933, in Taitung, Taiwan.[45] A baseball player as a youth, he found modest athletic success after turning to track and field, competing in the high jump and the broad jump. Recognizing he was a versatile athlete, Taiwan athletic officials coaxed a reluctant Yang into competing in the decathlon at the 1954 Asian Games, despite his initial objections and dislike of events like the pole vault and the 1,500-meter race. Yang had limited experience in most of the decathlon events and no understanding of how the decathlon was scored. The neophyte managed, however, to win the decathlon with 5,300 points at the 1954 Asian Games held in Manila, Philippines.[46] A 1955 U.S. State Department–sponsored goodwill tour visit from American decathlon great Bob Mathias further encouraged Yang's newfound interest in the decathlon. Mathias worked on Yang's technique in a number of events, including the javelin. Mathias left a much coveted steel-tipped javelin with the excited youngster, who did not have access to this kind of equipment.[47]

During the 1950s, Taiwan remained embroiled in political turmoil, making it an unlikely place to train for international track and field. Japan controlled Taiwan, an island off the coast of China, sometimes called Formosa, when Yang was born in 1933.[48] Japan yielded control of Taiwan to China (Republic of China) after World War II. This lasted four years, until Mao Tse-Tung's Communist Party gained control of mainland China and declared the People's Republic of China (PRC) in 1949. The deposed rulers in the Nationalist Party (Kuomintang), led by the American-supported Chiang Kai-shek, fled to Taiwan with somewhere between 1.5 and 2 million other Chinese exiles and established political control on the small island, which they referred to as the Republic of China (ROC). The Chinese immigrants included most of the ROC's Olympic Committee, who claimed to represent all of China, both Taiwan (ROC) and mainland China (PRC), in the Olympic movement.[49] Two of the three Chinese members of the International Olympic Committee (IOC) also fled to Taiwan.[50] Many countries, including the United States, did not acknowledge Mao's rule in Communist China. Instead, they recognized the Chiang regime in Taipei as the rightful political government of all of China.[51] Not surprisingly, the Soviet Union recognized Mao's rule in China and considered Chiang's government as illegitimate. Cold War conflicts such as these increased the political importance of IOC decisions because political leaders, like those in both Communist China and Taiwan, "linked membership in the Olympic movement with political legitimacy."[52] Which political entities would be recognized by the IOC, what geographic areas they covered, and what they would be called, all came to have important diplomatic consequences. By 1954, the IOC recognized mainland Communist China (Olympic Committee of the Chinese Republic[53]) and Taiwan (Chinese Olympic Committee) as independent entities.[54] The "two-China" solution pleased no one. Between 1954 and 1958 leaders in Communist China and Taiwan both stubbornly claimed they were the only appropriate representative to the Olympic movement for the entire geographic area of the two entities.[55] The PRC attempted to force the IOC to expel Taiwan from the 1956 Olympic Games and, when unsuccessful, opted out of the games. The conflict between Taiwan and Communist China would beleaguer the IOC for almost three decades.[56] Given the political machinations and social upheaval, it is no surprise that sport remained a low priority in Taiwan, which lacked facilities, resources, and coaching.[57]

Yang trained and improved despite the obstacles. He scored 6,521 points and finished in eighth place in just his second decathlon at the 1956 Olympics. He had an exceptional year in 1958 when he bested 7,100 points in all five of the decathlons in which he competed.[58] Yang advanced from being an unranked and relatively unknown decathlete in 1957, with a career best of 6,478 points, to the third-ranked decathlete in the world in 1958, with a top score of 7,625.[59] His second-place finish to Johnson at the 1958 AAU championship meet was Yang's most important competition of the year, not only because it was his best performance to date, but also because it facilitated his move to the United States and admission to UCLA. In 1958, Taiwanese athletic officials decided that Yang's full potential would not likely be realized if he stayed in his home country. They wanted Yang to train in the United States, which had much better facilities, coaching, and competitive opportunities.[60] UCLA track coach Ducky Drake met Dr. Wei Chun-wu, Yang's coach in Taiwan, at the 1958 AAU decathlon meet. Dr. Wei was trying to find a way for Yang, who spoke no English and knew no one in the United States, to train in the United States for a lengthy period of time. Yang initially planned on attending USC but changed his mind after visiting UCLA and meeting Coach Drake.[61]

Yang and Johnson Become Fast Friends

Johnson and Yang became immediate friends and training partners after Yang moved to Los Angeles in mid-1958. Johnson recalled that "from the first day we met, we were friends."[62] Johnson "always liked to be around C. K. Yang." Yang remembered Johnson as "a very warm person" who helped him adjust to his new environment. They developed a close bond that continued until Yang's death in 2007.[63] But they were never actually teammates at UCLA. Johnson's last year of track eligibility was in the spring of 1958, before Yang moved to the country. After graduating in 1958, Johnson stayed at UCLA, taking graduate courses, assisting with the UCLA track team, and training on campus. Yang enrolled in extension courses to learn English in the latter half of 1958, but he was not eligible for track until the 1959–1960 school year. Yang's freshman year of track at UCLA was in the spring of 1960, two years after Johnson's senior year of track. One of Johnson's younger brothers, Jimmy Johnson, an excellent hurdler who won the NCAA national championship in the 110-meter high hurdles (1960) and played professional football for the San Francisco Forty-Niners (1961–1976), was Yang's teammate on the UCLA track team.[64] Although never technically teammates, after Yang moved to Los Angeles the two trained together daily with Coach Drake and Assistant Coach Dixon.

Throughout their two years training together Yang and Johnson had the same objective, a gold medal in the decathlon at the 1960 Olympic Games. Johnson sacrificed greatly to continue his quest for an Olympic gold medal after graduating from UCLA in 1958. He had numerous professional offers. For example, the Los Angeles Rams drafted him and he was offered roles in important Hollywood movies, such as *Spartacus,* which starred Kirk Douglas and Laurence Oliver.[65] He rejected these and other lucrative offers to maintain his amateur status with the goal of capturing the gold medal he failed to win in 1956. Yang had moved to the United States, where he did not speak the language and had no family or friends, with the hope of winning the first gold medal ever for his country. They both had invested a good deal of their lives into this single-minded pursuit in which only one could ultimately succeed. They both also felt significant external pressure to succeed, Johnson to rectify his silver medal in 1956 and Yang to bring the first gold medal to his country. A wealthy Taiwanese benefactor paid for Yang's tuition and living expenses to improve the chances of his athletic success. But the competition for the gold never got in the way of their friendship nor their desire to help each other develop into successful athletes and to do the best they could at the Olympics.

Yang and Johnson both pointed out that training together for the 1960 Olympic Games made them much better athletes and better prepared for the decathlon. Having another highly skilled athlete to train with helped Yang and Johnson complete their workouts at a high level and gain an advanced level of fitness. They had very different strengths and weaknesses as athletes, and they helped improve each other's weaknesses. The bulkier Johnson performed better and helped Yang with the strength field events, like the discus, shot put, and javelin. The much thinner Yang excelled in the jumping events, like the high jump and the pole vault.[66] Yang was an excellent technician. Johnson recalled that having Yang around "was like having another coach" because he was "at the time and even today . . . the most knowledgeable athlete about what he does."[67] Johnson also credited Yang with increasing his strength. UCLA assistant coach Dixon introduced Yang to weight lifting in an effort to help the lean athlete increase his strength and his performance in the weight events. The emphasis on weight training was uncommon at the time. When Johnson found out that Yang lifted weights, he began tagging along, which helped him improve his already impressive showing in the weight events.[68] Johnson claimed, "Without C. K.'s help I would not have beaten him in 1960."[69] They labored daily to make each other better, sharing advice and encouraging each other, knowing that they were also improving their competition and thereby making it more difficult to achieve their own ambitions.

Both Yang and the Soviet star, Kuznyetsov, trained hard and improved while Johnson recovered from an unfortunate back injury sustained in a car accident in early June of 1959.[70] Kuznyetsov broke Johnson's world record by 55 points with an impressive 8,367 points at a regional Soviet meet in Moscow on May 16–17, 1959.[71] Yang won a closely contested 1959 AAU decathlon championship over American Dave Edstrom by a razor-thin 5-point margin (7,549 to 7,544). An injured Johnson "fidgeted in his hometown stands, kept from defending his title because of a bad back," as his training partner and close friend won the national decathlon title.[72] Yang then improved his personal best to 7,835 at the southern pacific AAU decathlon later that year.[73] The press, fans, and amateur sport officials were disappointed that Johnson's back injury prevented him from competing in the second U.S.-USSR meet against the new world record holder.[74] At the meet Kuznyetsov scored 8,350, just 7 points under his recently established world record, despite bad weather and a lack of competition. *Track and Field News* thought he would have easily broken his own world record if not for the dire weather and argued that the Soviet great "had no weaknesses."[75] A month later Kuznyetsov broke the 8,000-point barrier for an astonishing third time in 1959.[76] Although Yang had made substantial progress, as 1959 ended and the Olympic year began, Kuznyetsov appeared the biggest threat to Johnson's chances to win the gold medal.

The Battle in Rome: The 1960 Olympic Decathlon

The decathlon was one of the most anticipated track events at the 1960 Olympics. Johnson had successfully recovered from his back injury and resumed serious training in early 1960. He demonstrated excellent condition when he once again broke Kuznyetsov's world record at the AAU championship meet with a 8,683-point performance. Unnoticed by many at the time, Yang scored 8,426 points while finishing second to Johnson's world record–breaking effort at the same meet.[77] Johnson's 1,500 heat ran before Yang's at the meet. In a demonstration which characterized the athletes' support for each other, Johnson urged Yang on during his heat, even though Yang could have won the meet and bested

Johnson's world record if he had run a good 1,500.[78] Yang was now the second best decathlete ever. But most still thought the Olympic decathlon would be a replay of the classic battle between Kuznyetsov and Johnson at the 1958 U.S.-USSR meet. Johnson continued to have a good deal of respect for Kuznyetsov. When asked about the Soviet star, Johnson responded that he knew "three things about him. He's a fine athlete. He's a gentleman. And he's a fine competitor."[79] But to the surprise of many journalists, Johnson insisted that his training partner C. K. Yang would be his toughest competition.[80] While preparing for the Rome Olympics, Coach Drake, who attended the games as a coach for Taiwan, told the athletes that they would finish first and second, but which one would finish first and which one would finish second would be decided during the two-day competition: "We never talked about who would win—C. K. or Rafer. We always talked about when we get to Rome we're going to get first and second."[81]

Johnson remained extremely popular with the press and among U.S. Olympic officials in the lead up to the games. Johnson was attractive, bright, educated, and thoughtful. He remained very competitive and confident of his talents without being arrogant. At six feet three inches and two hundred pounds of chiseled fitness, Johnson had an imposing physical presence that combined with a disarming smile. Journalists regularly trumpeted Johnson's character, intelligence, physical characteristics, and accomplishments on and off the track. The media used terms like "handsome," "an athlete of world renown," "polite and articulate," and "a man of the highest character" to describe Johnson.[82] According to the press, Johnson was the ultimate athlete and Olympian. He possessed "monastic dedication to sport that would please the most spiritual of Olympic enthusiasts."[83] Of course, accounts also regularly identified Johnson as a "Negro," a common reference at the time. It surprised no one when the U.S. Olympic Committee chose Johnson to carry the American flag during the opening ceremony. He was the first African American to have this honor.[84] Johnson was also the captain of the men's track team and arguably the most respected athlete and person on the team. His continued success as an athlete and student and as a likeable person made Johnson an ideal representative.

Politics threatened Yang's participation in the Olympic Games even though Communist China had pulled out of the Olympic movement in 1958 in response to Taiwan's continued presence.[85] At the Soviet Union's urging, the IOC insisted that Taiwan not include China in its name because it did not represent nor include athletes from mainland Communist China.[86] Taiwan vigorously objected and sought to have China somehow included in its name, whether it be the Chinese National Olympic Committee, Committee of the Republic of China, or some other variation.[87] In 1958 and 1959 the issue "sent the IOC into a political paroxysm that would not abate even during the Summer Games [1960]."[88] One of the American members on the IOC, John Garland, thought that "they [Taiwan] should be called ROC [Republic of China] as they are in the UN."[89] The American press and government strongly supported Taiwan.[90] A furious Taiwanese government reluctantly consented to IOC demands, in large part because Yang would likely earn a medal.[91] The potential to win a medal in track and field took precedence over the value of withdrawing from the games in protest. But Chiang Kai-shek and other nationalists were determined to make their objections known.[92] At the Olympics' opening ceremony parade the Taiwanese delegation whipped "out a hand-painted banner" that read "Under Protest" as they marched in the stadium to show their displeasure.[93] IOC leaders thought that the protest was "inelegant, political-minded, and an offence to the dignity which should prevail in the Olympic Games."[94] According to the *New York Times,* the "International Olympic Committee was the first world body to tell it [Taiwan] it no longer represented China and to march as Formosa or go home."[95]

Yang was popular with the American media, but the political situation complicated the media's characterization of him. Its inconsistent approach to Yang's national identity mirrored the problems encountered by the IOC and the uncertain future of Taiwan's relationship with Mao's China. The American press referred to Yang and his country of origin in a variety of different ways which changed from day to day. The press referred to Yang as Chinese, Taiwanese, Asian, Formosan, Chinese Nationalist, and even as "the Chinaman."[96] The press reported his country of origin inconsistently as China, Republic of China, free China, nationalist China, Formosa, and Taiwan, for example.[97] The press rarely attempted to explain exactly what the difference in terminology meant or why a particular name was chosen over another. But the choice of name at times possessed political meaning in the United States, whose government supported Chiang Kai-shek's claim to be the legitimate political government covering all of China.

Yang remained extremely popular in the United States. Given the American government and press support of Taiwan and Yang's training in the country, this should not be surprising. By all accounts he was also a hard-working and talented athlete and an exceptionally likable person. But coming from Taiwan also made him an appealing symbol of non-communist Asia, a counterpoint to Mao's Communist China. *Sports Illustrated*, for example, reported,

> That the Chinese [Yang] in question is a citizen of Chiang Kai-Shek's Republic of China (11 million people) rather than Mao Tse-Tung's People's Republic of China (670 million) is an irony that must delight the one China as much as it galls the other, though it seems certain that on the Communist mainland all but the most thoroughly brainwashed will feel a surge of national pride when the name of C. K. Yang—or Yang Chuan-Kwang, to give it its proper Chinese form—leads all the rest.[98]

The conflict between Communist China and Taiwan encouraged Yang's support in the United States and further complicated the political meaning of the competitions. Johnson, Yang, and Kuznyetsov, the three athletes expected to compete for the gold medal in the highly anticipated 1960 decathlon, remained aware of the politics that surrounded their participation and success in international track and field. Through the years of international meets they became friends who respected each other as athletes and people, even at times providing assistance to each other during competitions. They were far more concerned with the athletic competition than the political uses of their victories. It was ultimately the competition that made the 1960 decathlon memorable.

The Rome decathlon turned into a two-man battle between Yang and Johnson during a dismal rain-delayed first day of competition, which started with the 100-meter race at 7:00 AM and did not conclude until fourteen hours later at 11:00 PM. Kuznyetsov had incurred a nagging ankle injury while pole vaulting during the summer and was not in top condition in Rome.[99] He ran a disappointing 11.1 seconds in the 100 meters, the first event, and never challenged the leaders.[100] Yang grabbed an early 130-point lead after besting Johnson in the first two events, the 100-meter race and the long jump. But Johnson heaved the shot put an impressive 51 feet 10¾ inches to gain a massive 273 points over Yang (43 feet 8¾ inches) in the third event. This erased Yang's lead and gave Johnson a 143-point lead after the third event. Importantly, Yang had a throw of 47 feet, but he fouled and it did not count. This was Yang's biggest setback of the first day.[101] Torrential rains flooded the track and forced the delay of the meet for hours in the middle of the high jump, the fourth event of the day. After the competition resumed, Yang whittled Johnson's first-day margin down to a 55-point advantage when he beat Johnson by small margins in the high jump and the 400 meters, the fourth and fifth events on the first day. Yang (48.1 seconds) bested Johnson (48.3 seconds) by a mere 0.2 seconds in a "thrilling 400 on the wet track."[102] Only fifteen hundred spectators remained to witness the 400-meter heats concluded under powerful temporary floodlights at 11:00 PM. Yang had bested Johnson in four of the first five events, but Johnson's margin in the one event he won, the shot put, was so large that he held a small lead of 55 points going into the second day of competition. Johnson thought that the first day's competition occurred "under the most difficult conditions I could ever imagine."[103] It had been an exhausting first day for the athletes who, because of the late finish, would have much less time to rest for the second day than usual.

The weather cleared for day two of the decathlon and all eyes focused on the battle between the two friends and training partners. Neither athlete gained a decisive lead during the tense second day of competition. Yang regained the lead (128 points) after easily beating Johnson in the 110-meter high hurdles, the sixth event. Yang ran the race in 14.6 seconds while Johnson hit a hurdle and clocked a disappointing 15.3, well below his best of 13.8.[104] Coach Drake thought it was "the poorest flight of hurdles he [Rafer] had ever run since he was in high school."[105] Johnson had only once run slower in a 110-meter high-hurdle race during a decathlon, his first one in 1954 when he was just out of high school.[106] Drake had told his two athletes that "the one that didn't make a mistake would be the winner."[107] Both Yang and Johnson had now both made significant mistakes, Yang in the shot put and Johnson in the hurdles. Johnson regained the lead in the seventh event, the discus, one of his best events, with a 159 feet 1 inch toss. Johnson had a 144-point advantage after Yang managed just 130 feet 8 inches. The eighth event, the pole vault, was one of Yang's better events and one of Johnson's weakest. The pole vault was a critical turning point in the competition. Yang gained 120 points and reduced Johnson's lead to 24 points when he vaulted 14 feet 1¼ inches to Johnson's 13 feet 5¼ inches. But Yang expected a much larger increase. It was easily Johnson's best vault ever, and he got far more points than anticipated. Moreover, Yang barely missed at a 14 feet 9 inches attempt which would have garnered him a substantial lead going into the ninth event, the javelin, another strong event for Johnson. Johnson gained 43 more points in the javelin, which nudged his lead to 67 points going into the final event, the dreaded 1,500-meter race.

The 1960 decathlon would be decided by the last event, the 1,500-meter race. Virtually all decathletes agree on one thing: they dislike the 1,500-meter race. One journalist explained that "track people figure Satan himself must have thought up the idea of running nearly a mile after having performed nine other events."[108] An exhausted Johnson told reporters at the end of the long first day of competition that he hoped the decathlon "would be all wrapped up before the 1,500 meters. I never want to settle one in that thing."[109] In his previous decathlons Johnson was usually so far ahead prior to the last event that he was assured victory with minimal effort in the 1,500. But not this time. Yang and Johnson were in the same heat, adding to the drama. All eyes were cast upon the duo and everyone knew that Yang needed to beat Johnson by ten seconds to overtake Johnson's slim 67-point margin and win Taiwan's first track and field gold medal. Johnson needed to finish within ten seconds of his close friend to win the gold medal that eluded him in 1956. According to Coach Drake, Johnson and Yang had helped each other throughout the two-day, twenty-six-hour competition. But now, completely exhausted, with the competition down to the last event, they had finally stopped talking to each other. Drake recalled the tension: "There they are with their heads turned away from each other. They've quit helping each other because the competition is so tough that either one of them can win."[110] Yang, not surprisingly, given his smaller frame, was a much better 1,500-meter runner than the larger Johnson. Yang's best 1,500 was 4:36.9 while Johnson's was 4:54.2. But Yang's best 1,500 meter during a decathlon was a much less impressive 4:51. Both athletes approached Coach Drake for last-minute instructions, and he told them separately what they should do to win. Coach Drake insisted, "Even though I was coaching both boys I was for both of them doing the very best they could. I could not have a favorite."[111] Jack Tobin sat next to Drake during the competition and later claimed that he still did not know who Drake wanted to win.[112] Drake told Johnson to trail closely behind Yang from the start and shadow him the entire race. Yang would attempt to lose him during the race, Drake told Johnson, but he needed to stay within a few yards of Yang at all times. Coach Drake instructed Yang that Johnson would try to follow him closely throughout the race.

Chart 2: Rafer Johnson's and C. K. Yang's 1960 Olympic Decathlon Scores

NAME	100	LJ	SP	HJ	400
Rafer Johnson	10.9	24' 1¼"	51' 10¾"	6' ¾"	48.3
	948	906	976	832	985
	948	1,854	2,830	3,662	4,647
C. K. Yang	10.7	24' 5¾"	43' 8¾"	6' 2¾"	48.1
	1,034	950	703	900	1,005
	1,034	1,984	2,687	3,587	4,592
	7,989	8,334			
Running Score	CK +86	CK +130	RJ +143	RJ +75	RJ +55

Source: Compiled from Track and Field News, September 1960, 16–17.
Note: First line is event performance. The second line is the points gained for that event. The third line is the total points at the end of that event.

Yang would need to make a strong enough surge to break the determined Johnson well before the final sprint if he was going to win by more than ten seconds. An exhausted Yang made a valiant effort to break away from Johnson, but he failed. Johnson grimly pursued Yang through the 3¾ laps. Yang beat Johnson, but only by four yards and 1.2 seconds. Johnson ran 4:49.7, his fastest 1,500 ever, and Yang completed the distance in 4:48.5. Johnson won the decathlon by a meager 58 points (see chart 2).

Rafer Johnson had won what is still considered the greatest decathlon competition against his training partner and best friend. It was the highlight of the 1960 Olympic Games. Yang had, somewhat astonishingly, beaten Johnson in seven of the ten events. Johnson outdid Yang in only the three weight events, the shot put, discus, and the javelin. But he won the shot put and discus by large margins. Johnson accumulated a combined 545 points—273 in the shot put and 272 in the discus—over Yang in those two events. At the end of the competition a spent Johnson told reporters that "victory obliterates fatigue."[113] But, as Yang, Johnson, and Drake knew for the previous two years while preparing for this day, there could be only one victor. Johnson was thrilled to have won; he "wanted this one real bad."[114] But Johnson also recalled the mixed feelings of beating his friend: "As good as I felt about winning, I felt equally bad that my friend [Yang] had lost."[115] A dejected and fatigued Yang graciously congratulated Johnson with a "nice going Rafe" after the 1,500.[116] Yang vacillated between accepting defeat and questioning his performance. He said,

110 HH	DIS	PV	JAV	1500		TOTAL
15.3	159' 1"	228' 10½"	13' 5¼"	4:49.7		
730	894	795	980		336	8,392
5,387	6,281	7,076	8,056			
14.6	130' 8"	14' 1¼"	223' 9½"	4:48.5		
923	622	915	937	345		
5,515	6,137	7,052				
CK +128	RJ +144	RJ +24	RJ +67	RJ +58		

"There was nothing I could do. Rafer was the better man. Near the end I had little or nothing left." The silver medalist, however, tortured himself, thinking that he "should have done better in the pole vault. I keep thinking that if I had only done better in the pole vault, I might have the gold medal right now."[117] The 1960 decathlon was the end of Johnson's athletic career; immediately after winning the champion stated emphatically, "I never want to go through that again. . . . Never."[118] Like Johnson four years earlier, Yang quickly decided that he would continue and go for the gold medal four years later in Toyko. The past two decathlon silver medalists—Milt Campbell (1952) and Rafer Johnson (1956)—both returned four years later to win gold. If recent history was any indicator, Yang would win the gold in 1964.

Tough Times for C. K. Yang: Life after the 1960 Olympic Games

Yang continued competing and had fantastic athletic success in the four years after the 1960 Olympic Games, but he failed in his attempt to win a decathlon gold medal in 1964. In 1963 he set a briefly held indoor pole-vault world record and a decathlon world record, breaking the 9,000-point barrier. *Track and Field News* named him the athlete of the year for his efforts in 1963. His pole vault success contributed to his decathlon improvement, but it also led to changes in his competitive focus and in the event that spoiled his chances for a gold medal in the decathlon in the 1964 games.

The new fiberglass pole made the pole vault an extremely popular event in 1963 and 1964 as world records fell with unusual regularity and athletes soared higher and higher into the stratosphere. The event was extremely popular with fans and the media, and meet directors high-lighted it to gain publicity.[119] Yang was an early convert to the new fiber-glass pole technology. On January 26, 1963, Yang cleared 16 feet 3¼ inches to break the indoor world record that Dave Tork had established just twenty-four hours earlier.[120] Although Yang only held the record for one week, he welcomed and exploited the popularity gained from his pole-vaulting success. The event came to dominate his competitive schedule and, one might assume, his training as well in 1963 and much of 1964. In 1961 and 1962, Yang, similar to Johnson, often competed in multiple events at most UCLA track meets, assiduously honing and per-fecting all of the decathlon events.[121] But his pole vault success altered his competitive schedule. Yang now much more often competed in a single event, a highly publicized marquee pole-vault competition, at invi-tational meets throughout the country, as opposed to three, four, or five events.[122] He appears to have become fixated on the pole vault after his indoor world record.[123]

His pole vault success initially helped advance his decathlon score. Yang established a world decathlon record and became the first person to best 9,000 points when he scored 9,121 at the Mount San Antonio College Relays in 1963. This was partly because his vaults exceeded the highest pole vault mark in the decathlon scoring tables, which topped out at 1,515 points for a 15 feet 9½ inch vault. Yang now easily earned the 1,515 point maximum in the pole vault in the decathlon as he vaulted in excess of 16 feet. This was an unprecedented feat: no athlete had ever beaten the top listed mark in the decathlon table.[124] Thus, the pole vault was initially a great boon for Yang, who argued that the decathlon scor-ing tables needed to be changed to accommodate his higher vaults. Yang argued he should be able to get far more than 1,515 points because the table should go higher. He envisioned vaulting as high as 17 feet and get-ting as much as 2,000 points.[125] Yang was correct. The decathlon scoring tables had not been adjusted in over a decade and this needed to be done. But when the International Amateur Athletic Federation (IAAF) altered the decathlon scoring tables, which went into effect just prior to the 1964

Olympic Games, instead of raising the point total for the higher pole vaults, the IAAF adjusted the pole vault points downward. They altered the scoring so that Yang would get fewer points for his higher vaults, not more. The new table, for example, required an astonishing 18 feet 4 inches to get the maximum 1,515 points. The new tables also downgraded a number of other events in which Yang excelled. The new scoring tables hurt Yang far more than any other competitive international decathlete. They reduced Yang's 9,121 world record by more than 1,000 points, to 8,089.[126] Many thought that the introduction of the new scoring tables immediately before the Olympic Games was decidedly unfair to Yang.[127] Yang went from being the favorite to one of a handful of athletes who would battle for a medal.

Yang felt substantial pressure to win his country's first track and field Olympic gold medal in 1964. In late 1963 Yang explained that he had "one obligation: to win a gold medal for China in the Olympics. That's the only thing, the main thing." Yang insisted, "I must win at Tokyo. And that will be my last competition."[128] A sympathetic Coach Drake thought that Yang was "a young man with the weight of a continent on his shoulders."[129] Drake saw what many others did not, that Yang was "doing a great thing for all the young athletes of Asia, not just Taiwan. He's got millions of people to drive him on. He carries a load nobody knows about, and for people who don't know about sports. He has the greatest desire of any athlete I've known."[130] Yang was exceptionally popular in Taiwan and he desperately wanted to win a gold medal for his country. But Yang's desire to win could not overcome the new scoring tables and a nagging injury at the 1964 Olympic Games. A disappointed Yang finished in fifth place in his third and last Olympic decathlon in Tokyo, Japan, in 1964. He retired from competitive track and field after the 1964 Olympic Games.

Yang's post-athletic career was at times difficult. He recalled after the 1964 Olympic Games, "[I] was lost. I didn't know what to do." He sold insurance and acted in a few movies in the United States. He returned to Taiwan and coached and served as the president of an underfunded graduate school in Taiwan.[131] He was a member of the Taiwan Olympic Committee and coached Taiwan at the 1976 Olympic Games in Montreal, where Taiwan once again engaged in a conflict with the PRC after the country returned to Olympic competition. This turned into a controversy that threatened the team's participation. Yang recalled, "It has been like this for many, many Olympics. I always cross my fingers and they [amateur sport officials] always solve the problems."[132]

Political parties exploited Yang's enormous popularity in Taiwan during a brief and troubled political career. He was first elected to the legislature in 1983 as part of the Kuomintang (KMT). But rumors that Yang planned to defect to the People's Republic of China dogged him and, according to Rick Chu, "he was maliciously cast aside" by the KMT after his "propaganda value" had been thoroughly used.[133] In 1989, Yang ran for a local office after joining the opposition Democratic Progressive Party (DPP). Most thought that the DPP, which wanted Yang to sell his silver medal to help finance the campaign, was taking advantage of Yang. Chu argued that "everyone regarded his candidacy as a farce. And everyone knew that honest, straight forward Yang was being intentionally used by someone again. Once more he had become a political tool of other people."[134] Yang continued to drift in and out of various opportunities until he died in 2007.

Movies and Politics:
Rafer Johnson after the 1960 Olympic Games

Rafer Johnson has had a varied and successful post-athletic career. Within weeks of the Olympic Games Johnson signed a long-term acting contract with 20th Century Fox, where he was assigned a role in *Journey into Danger* as his first movie.[135] He acted in a slew of movies and made a number of appearances as an actor on television shows in the 1960s.[136] He tried his hand at broadcasting for a few years.[137] Johnson later worked for fifteen years as a vice president of personnel (later community affairs) at Continental Telephone. The position allowed him substantial freedom to devote time to a variety of public service activities.[138] Although he never ran for political office, Johnson became active in Democratic Party politics. He established a close connection with the Kennedy family as a result of his involvement in the federal government's People-To-People sports program and his early support of John F. Kennedy's Peace Corps.[139] He supported and traveled with Bobby Kennedy during his campaign for the presidential nomination in 1968. Johnson stood next to Kennedy as he was shot and killed by Sirhan Sirhan after the California Democratic Party primary in June 1968. Johnson and football star Rosey Grier wrestled the gun from the assailant's hand.[140] Johnson has used his celebrity to gain attention for a number of charities in which he has been active, most prominently the Special Olympics and the Hershey Track and Field for Youth Program.[141] Whenever he appears on television, radio, or in newspaper interviews to promote these events, the 1960 Olympic Games and his battle with Yang emerge as the central point of discussion.[142]

Johnson and Yang remained close friends until Yang died in 2007. After the 1960 Olympic Games, Johnson was Yang's most confident and enthusiastic booster, predicting that Yang would break his world record and win a gold medal at the 1964 Olympic Games.[143] Johnson presented Yang the inaugural Rafer Johnson Award in 1963 and gave track clinics in Yang's homeland.[144] The two friends stayed in close contact after Yang retired from track following the 1964 Olympic Games. For example, Yang served as an usher at Johnson's 1971 wedding.[145] Twenty years after the 1960 decathlon, Coach Drake stressed that Johnson and Yang "still have a great friendship. They love each other, those two."[146] Assistant Coach Dixon fondly recalled golfing in 1990 with Yang and Johnson at his country club.[147] Whenever Yang visited the United States, Johnson was the first person he called.[148] It troubled Johnson that winning the gold had provided him with opportunities that his close friend Yang never had. In his 1998 autobiography Johnson noted sorrowfully that had Yang "won Gold, his life would have been much easier and far more prosperous."[149] The close friendship affected not only the competition, but also how the athletes and others viewed the competition decades later.

Documentaries, Olympic history books, and newspaper and magazine articles continue to recount the 1960 Olympic decathlon as one of the most memorable athletic contests in sport history. Neither Rafer Johnson nor C .K. Yang appeared upset that they were most often remembered and forever connected by their epic competition. Although a good deal of political turmoil at the time provided increased importance to the contest, it was their camaraderie, mutual respect, friendship, competitiveness, and talent that defined it. Yang and Johnson demonstrated, through their actions before, during, and after the 1960 Olympics, the good in competitive athletics, and this is what ultimately continues to draw people to the 1960 decathlon. Both athletes desperately wanted to win the gold medal; the intensity of the competition attests to this fact. But they also respected one another as friends and wanted the other to succeed. It was, as Johnson recalled thirty-eight years later, "the purest of rivalries: We each wanted the other guy to do well, but we wanted even more to win."[150]

Arnold Palmer (*left*) and Jack Nicklaus shaking hands during the 1962 National Open Tournament. *Courtesy of Getty Images.*

two

The King and the Bear
The Arnold Palmer–Jack Nicklaus Rivalry and the Rise of Modern Golf

GEORGE B. KIRSCH

On Wednesday afternoon, June 2, 1993, fifteen hundred golf fans gathered in a drenching rain around the eighteenth green at the Muirfield Village Golf Club in Dublin, Ohio, to pay tribute to Arnold Palmer, that year's honoree of Jack Nicklaus's Memorial Tournament. Previously, the committee that chose the recipient had selected a person who had long since retired or was deceased. But this time, at the suggestion of Nicklaus, it skipped the waiting period and honored Palmer for his lifetime achievements and especially for his contributions to golf. The program featured written tributes from President George Bush and celebrities and speeches from fellow golfers and friends, but what made the occasion especially poignant was the homage paid by Nicklaus to his longtime archrival. Nicklaus reflected: "When I turned pro in 1961, this was the guy you had to take aim at. He was the big winner. We've always competed against each other, but we've always been friends."[1] After thirty years, Nicklaus was widely recognized as the greatest golfer of the post–World War II era, but Palmer was still beloved by the public as the game's "King." The event that rainy springtime afternoon celebrated the career of Arnold Palmer, but it was also at least indirectly a testament to the rivalry between Palmer and Nicklaus that elevated both of their reputations and promoted golf as a mainstream sport in the United States.

During the fifteen years that followed World War II American golf celebrated its second golden age, as the sport's growing popularity exceeded its progress achieved during the flush times of the 1920s. Although many commentators have attributed this boom to President Dwight D. Eisenhower's obsession with the game during the mid-1950s, in fact it began a few years before his first inauguration in 1953 and resulted from several more influential factors. Among these were the prosperity of the period that generated a rising standard of living for blue- and white-collar workers, new rounds of suburbanization and the extension of resort and retirement communities, the promotion of golf by media celebrities (especially Bing Crosby and Bob Hope), the advent of golf cars (today called "carts"), popular heroes (especially Sam Snead, Ben Hogan, and Arnold Palmer), and the rise of television. While some of these forces (most notably the economy, residential trends, and the role of champions) had shaped golf's fortunes during earlier eras and were cyclical, others (especially the introduction of golf cars and television) were unique to this period.

As Arnold Palmer began his ascendancy to the pinnacle of American golf, Snead and Hogan were in the twilight of their long careers that stretched back to the 1930s. Snead's humble origins, folksy, homespun humor, and early success made him a darling of the media. Although he never won the U.S. Open, over forty-two years of tournament golf on the regular and senior PGA Tours he compiled a remarkable record of 135 titles, including eighty-two PGA events (nine more than Jack Nicklaus) and seven major championships. Hogan became a legendary figure during the post–World War II period because of the character and courage he displayed in recovering from a near fatal automobile accident in 1949 and because of his dramatic victories in major championships. His two PGA titles in 1946 and 1948 and his first U.S. Open crown in 1948 preceded his car crash, but after his rehabilitation he stunned the golfing world with wins at the U.S. Open in 1950 and the Masters and the U.S. Open again in 1951. But it was his heroic performances in 1953 that elevated him to the ranks of golf's immortals, as he captured the championships of the Masters, the U.S. Open, and the British Open.

The rise of Palmer, golf's newest superstar, during the late 1950s coincided with the first attempts to televise the sport across the nation, and Palmer's aggressive style of play and charismatic personality perfectly suited the new medium. Earlier in the decade local radio and television golf shows that combined instruction and consumer information with some commentary by professionals and celebrities enjoyed a modest success with audiences. But network producers hoped that they could achieve high viewer ratings with broadcasts of major tournaments and also packaged (or "canned") series of edited matches presented weekly. The first golf telecasts demonstrated their potential to attract large audiences, despite a few early mishaps, their excessive costs, and the logistical and technical problems of following numerous contestants and of showing the ball in flight. Television clearly was the critical factor in the PGA's decision in 1958 to change its championship's format from match play to four rounds of stroke play, which gave more players the opportunity to win on the final day and thus generated more excitement for the viewers. By 1960 it was obvious that golf and television strongly boosted each other, as the new medium showcased the game and its cast of characters while the sport provided viewers with dramatic and sometimes thrilling entertainment.

The man who would be celebrated as the "King" of golf was born on September 10, 1929, in Latrobe in western Pennsylvania. Arnold Palmer was the son of the greenkeeper and professional at the Latrobe Country Club. His father, Deacon, taught him to play the game at the age of five, and during his youth he became the star of his high school team and a junior champion in his region. A collegiate player at Wake Forest College between 1947 and 1950, he left school for three years of service in the U.S. Coast Guard. His victory in the 1954 U.S. Amateur championship marked his arrival on the national golfing scene. The following year he turned professional and won the Canadian Open with a 265, the second-lowest score in the tournament's forty-six year history. In 1958 he achieved one of his life's goals by winning a major title—the Masters. Just short of the age of thirty, he had become one of the world's best golfers with a relentless, attacking, and bold approach to the game off the tees and fairways and even on the greens.[2]

In 1960 Palmer achieved the status of a golfing superstar with two spectacular triumphs in major championships—the Masters and the U.S. Open. At Augusta in April he came to the last two holes on the final day needing a birdie to tie and two birdies to win. On the seventeenth green he sank a twenty-seven-foot putt for his birdie, and on the eighteenth his six-iron approach stopped five feet from the pin. He calmly drained the putt, took one stride, and then jumped for joy. Writing for *Sports Illustrated,* Herbert Warren Wind called Palmer "an authentic and unforgettable hero." Two months later at Cherry Hills in Denver Palmer began his final round seven shots behind the leader, Mike Souchak. But after a run of six birdies out of the first seven holes and one birdie on the final nine he carded a 65 for the lowest final round ever shot by the winner of the U.S. Open to that date. His four-day total of 280 was two strokes better than the runner-up, Jack Nicklaus, a twenty-year-old national amateur champion who would soon challenge Palmer for supremacy in the world of golf. In extolling Palmer's achievement Wind labeled Palmer "a marvelous golfer" and "destiny's favorite."[3]

Palmer's come-from-behind heroics in these and other tournaments gained him a huge following among spectators on the courses and television viewers at home. "Arnie's Army"—the crowds that thronged around him on the links—loved his hard-hitting ball striking and his penchant for taking chances when his errant shots landed in the rough or in the trees. He fed off of the energy of his fans as they yelled "Charge!" to urge him onward toward victory. Unlike the stoic and detached Hogan, he openly showed his emotions, from jubilation over a brilliant stroke or putt to agony over a costly blunder. A handsome man with an engaging smile, he was polite, pleasant, and articulate with golf writers and broadcasters. On January 9, 1961, *Sports Illustrated* named him its "Sportsman of the Year" for 1960, proclaiming: "With his golf credo— 'Hit it hard'—that horrifies traditionalists, his boyish enthusiasm, his athletic good looks and irrepressible will to win, he has dominated the game as no one has since the heyday of Ben Hogan nearly a decade ago. Thus he has ended his sport's long wait for a fresh, vibrant personality, bringing a new age to golf: The Palmer Era."[4] Jack Nicklaus, Gary Player, Tom Watson, and other stars would match or eclipse his record during the following three decades, but none of them would equal his popularity with America's golfing masses.

Although Arnold Palmer did not win the most major championships during the 1960s and 1970s, he was the era's dominant personality because of his charismatic qualities and his extensive business interests that generated enormous income and influence far beyond his earnings and record on the links. After winning the Masters in 1958 and both the Masters and the U.S. Open in 1960, he set his sights on the British Open. He failed in his first try in 1960 at the Old Course at St. Andrews, Scotland, finishing one stroke behind Kel Nagle. But the following year he carried off the Claret Jug, emblematic of the championship of that venerable tournament, defeating Dai Reese by one stroke on the Royal Birkdale links on the Lancashire coast of England. 1962 proved to be another magical year for Palmer, beginning with back-to-back victories at Palm Springs and Phoenix, followed by his third Masters title in April and three consecutive triumphs at the Texas Open, the Tournament of Champions, and the Colonial. But that season was also marred by his disappointing loss to the upstart Jack Nicklaus in the U.S. Open at Oakmont, only about forty miles from his hometown in Pennsylvania.

Born on January 21, 1940, in Columbus, Ohio, the son of a middle-class pharmacist, Nicklaus was a talented all-around athlete who had spectacular success as a young golfer and was National Amateur champion in 1959 and 1961. As a thirteen-year-old at Toledo, Ohio, in 1953 Nicklaus watched from a hillside as Palmer practiced nine-irons while preparing to defend his Ohio Amateur championship. He later recalled, "I kept wondering 'How's this Palmer guy going to do?'"[5] Palmer first met Nicklaus at an exhibition match held in Athens, Ohio, in the fall of 1958 to honor Dow Finsterwald. In his autobiography Palmer described his first impressions of Nicklaus as a "muscular, somewhat pudgy" teenager who exhibited great power and an "eerie composure under fire." Four years later at Oakmont he warned the writers, "Everybody says I'm the favorite, but you'd better watch the fat boy."[6] He later explained that he did not intend to insult Nicklaus, but that he was merely mimicking those reporters who were highlighting Nicklaus's extra poundage. Those words turned out to be prophetic, because he and Nicklaus wound up tied after four rounds. In his autobiography Nicklaus recalled that just prior to their playoff on Father's Day Palmer wished him good luck and offered to split the combined purse money for first and second place. Nicklaus replied: "No, Arn, you don't want to do that, that's not fair to you, let's just go and play." In his own memoir Palmer stated that he did not remember the incident, but admitted that it might have happened.[7] Nicklaus won the playoff by three strokes. Over the five rounds Palmer had outplayed his youthful challenger from tee to green; his downfall resulted from thirteen three-putts, compared to only one by the champion.

The 1962 U.S. Open at Oakmont was also memorable for some unruly crowd behavior and poor sportsmanship by members of Palmer's highly partisan Arnie's Army. Although Palmer didn't witness many of these incidents firsthand, he later heard of instances when a few of his fans "called

out unflatteringly to Jack and even cheered when he . . . missed a shot."
Members of Nicklaus's family were especially upset to hear fans heckling
Nicklaus and to see them waving offensive signs, including one that proclaimed, "Nicklaus is a Pig." But Nicklaus remained poised and unflap-
pable under the pressure. Although he later learned about the bad
behavior from some of the spectators, he recalled: "Nobody talked to me
about it at the time and it did not penetrate my intense concentration during play. So far as I was concerned, the noise was just that—noise."[8]

After his win Nicklaus was gracious in proclaiming that Palmer was
"still the greatest," and Palmer's record for the remainder of the year
bore out that testimony. Palmer bounced back to capture the British
Open for the second year in a row, this time at Troon, Scotland, shooting
a record-breaking 276. In early September Nicklaus recaptured some of
the limelight by defeating Palmer and Gary Player in the first televised
"World Series of Golf" at the Firestone Country Club in Akron, Ohio.
But at year's end Palmer was the PGA's leading money winner and was
voted its Player of the Year.[9]

The Palmer-Nicklaus rivalry heated up over the next few years, until
Nicklaus ultimately established his supremacy by the end of the decade.
Nicklaus strengthened his claim to fame in 1963 by winning both the
Masters and the PGA titles. At the Masters in April Nicklaus made it
clear that he was poised to dethrone Palmer as the ruler of American
golf. Palmer wrote: "As if taking a U.S. Open trophy out from under me
and my Army at Oakmont wasn't enough, Jack Nicklaus now had the
temerity to stroll onto the hallowed grounds at Augusta National as Tour
sophomore and simply lay waste to the course in a devastating display
of shotmaking not seen in that part of Dixie since a fellow named
Sherman made his way from Atlanta to Savannah."[10] In August Nicklaus
survived intense heat at the Dallas Athletic Club to claim his first PGA
crown. Although Palmer did not win any of the four major tournaments, he did record nine victories and finished the 1963 campaign as
the PGA Tour's leading money winner for the second consecutive year.

Palmer's fourth Masters green jacket in 1964 raised his lifetime total
of major championships to seven, but otherwise he was able to win only
one other tournament that year (the Oklahoma City Open). Nicklaus
did not win a major title that season, but according to Palmer his rivalry
with Nicklaus reached "fever pitch" in November when both flew to

Lafayette, Louisiana, to compete in the final PGA Tour event of 1964—
the Cajun Classic. What was at stake was the PGA Tour's yearly money
winner's title. Palmer was holding a slim lead of $318.87 and wanted to
add a fifth title to those he had captured in 1958, 1960, 1962, and 1963.
But Palmer finished behind Nicklaus, who tied for second place but
earned enough to edge out Palmer for the 1964 prize money crown.[11]

Palmer's 1964 Masters triumph would prove to be his last major
tournament championship, but his remarkable run of stirring victories
over a six-year span secured his place in sports history for all time. After
his victory at Augusta National in 1964, a *New York Times* columnist proclaimed: "Palmer is a hero to all, the darling of an era in which television
has put golf into millions of homes. The man in the street finds a sense
of identification with him . . . [and] he discovers a little of himself in this
athlete of athletes. . . . He has also captivated the public perhaps as no
other athlete since Babe Ruth or Jack Dempsey. He is golf's finest showpiece."[12] While golf fans most remember Palmer for his thrilling come-
from-behind victories, he also suffered several agonizing defeats. Perhaps
the most memorable came in 1966, when he blew a seven-shot lead with
nine holes to play in the final round of the U.S. Open, and then lost the
playoff to Billy Casper. But win or lose, Palmer touched the hearts of
his adoring legions. On July 8, 1966, a writer for the *Wall Street Journal*
explained: "His intense competitiveness, daring style of play, expressive
features and what has been called an 'All-American' appearance have
captivated galleries. He is that rare champion whom spectators root for
like an underdog." At tournaments adoring fans in Arnie's Army cheered
him on (and often were rude or hostile to other contestants) because
they felt personally connected with his performance. In the words of
one psychologist, "He looks and acts like a regular guy, and at the same
time he does the kind of things others wish they could do. His expres-
siveness makes his spectators feel they are part of his game; he looks as
though he needs their help, and they respond."[13]

Given Palmer's enormous popularity, any serious rival would likely
be cast as a villain in the eyes of his adoring fans, especially a golfer who
displayed such prodigious talent. But during the early to mid-1960s
Nicklaus also was plagued by a negative public image, partly because he
was perceived to be overweight. As a student at Ohio State he was
known as "Blob-O" or "Whaleman"; as a professional he was "Ohio

Fats," "Baby Beef," or "Fat Jack." During the 1963 World Series of Golf
at the Firestone course in Akron, Ohio, Nicklaus was upset when members of the gallery rooted for his ball to wind up in sand traps. In January
1964 a journalist for *Golf* magazine remarked on Nicklaus's "frozen face
and lumbering stride," his "state prison stare," and his irritating, slow
and deliberate style of play. In October 1966 a psychologist writing for
Golf Digest interviewed gallery members concerning their feelings about
Nicklaus. He concluded that many golf fans shared four negative impressions of him. In their view he was too mechanical, methodical, even
robotic in his play; his build resembled a football player; he was too aloof,
too cool, too disconnected from spectators; he was an anti-hero in his
threat to their idol, Palmer.[14]

In his autobiography Nicklaus acknowledged his image problem as
a young golfer. A fierce competitor, he aimed to defeat Palmer, and he
explained that if that meant "also toppling a legend and throwing half
the population into deep depression, well, so long as it was done fairly
and squarely, fine and dandy." But as he reflected back on his early battles
with Palmer, Nicklaus realized, "I was in the entertainment business as
much as the golf-playing business. And it was this, I'm sure, that made
me such a black hat to so many of those fans for so many of those years."
He conceded: "Sure, I was overweight and crew-cut, and sure, I dressed
like a guy painting a porch, and sure, I had a squeaky voice and didn't
laugh and joke a lot in public, and sure, I often lacked tact and diplomacy
in my public utterances." But he also believed that golf fans would have
forgiven all of those failings if he had downplayed his will to win—
"including, particularly, trying to knock the game's best-loved idol off
his throne. And the best thing I remember about it all was that, hard as
I sometimes had to fight Arnold's galleries, the only way I ever had to
fight him was with my golf clubs."[15]

From 1965 to the end of the decade Nicklaus's sparkling performances won over the hearts of more fans, even when he battled Palmer
head-to-head. He was buoyed by a more supportive, even enthusiastic
reaction from spectators at the Masters in 1965. He responded in kind with
a rare show of emotion and later recalled: "I was no longer golf's Black
Hat. . . . I just had to show how much I appreciated this sudden and unexpected about-face. It was a moving experience, and I now realize, one of
the great turning points in my career."[16] The cheering crowds lifted him

to victory and a record-setting total score of 271 strokes (which Raymond Floyd would equal in 1976 and Tiger Woods would surpass by one stroke in 1997). Two years later he won his second U.S. Open championship at the Baltusrol Golf Club in Springfield, New Jersey. Tied with Palmer after three rounds of intense play in front of galleries dominated by Arnie's Army, Nicklaus struck a legendary one-iron on the eighteenth hole and sank a long putt for a final round score of 65 and a record setting total of 275 (which he would lower with a 272 in 1980 and which would be equaled by Lee Janzen in 1993, Tiger Woods in 2000, and Jim Furyk in 2003). By the end of the 1960s the golfing community had finally accepted Nicklaus as a great champion and genuine hero who had become more warm and relaxed. In an interview in *Golf Digest* in July 1971 Nicklaus attributed his increased popularity to weight loss, longer hair, and more stylish clothing. But overall he concluded that as he grew older people were more open to admiring him for his achievements. While he denied that he had done anything to change his image deliberately, he thought that more than anything else maturity helped boost his public persona. Now he was beloved as the "Golden Bear."[17]

A powerful driver and accurate iron player with a deft touch on the greens, Nicklaus had a flair for the dramatic and a capacity to intimidate and demoralize opponents. Between the 1960s and 1980s he earned a reputation as the sport's best golfer, capturing eighteen major titles. These included six Masters (1963, 1965, 1966, 1972, 1975, 1986); four U.S. Opens (1962, 1967, 1972, 1980); three British Opens (1966, 1970, 1978); and five PGAs (1963, 1971, 1973, 1975, 1980). His record for peak performance over a long career separates him from all previous legendary golfers. With the exception of the British Open, he won each major championship in three different decades. Perhaps equally remarkable were his nineteen second-place finishes in major competitions. As the years rolled by he turned back challenges from such upstarts as Lee Trevino, Johnny Miller, and Tom Watson, who threatened to replace him as the premier golfer in the world. Among the young lions Watson was the only one who could regularly defeat Nicklaus, most notably at the 1982 U.S. Open at Pebble Beach in California when he chipped into the seventeenth hole from the rough, thereby depriving Nicklaus of his fifth U.S. Open title.

Nicklaus also made major contributions to international golf through his willingness to travel and through his proposal for a change in the format for the Ryder Cup competition, which traditionally had matched golfers from the United States against those from Britain and, after 1973, Ireland. Between 1927 and 1977 the U.S. team won nineteen of the twenty-three matches (one ended in a tie). During the 1977 match in England Nicklaus asked Lord Derby, the president of the British PGA, to consider making the event more competitive by broadening the membership of the British side to include leading European players. Although the British officials were at first reluctant to part with tradition, the following year they agreed that for the 1979 contest a few Europeans would join the British and Irish contestants, and that their side would be renamed "Europe." As a result the balance has tipped toward the European side, especially since 1995. Between 1979 and 2006 the European team won seven of the fourteen events, with one tie. Since 1995 the Europeans have dominated the Americans, wining five of the next six matches through 2006.

During the 1960s and 1970s Gary Player shared the golfing limelight with Palmer and Nicklaus, earning fame and fortune by winning nine major championships, including the Masters in 1961, 1974, and 1978; the U.S. Open in 1965; the British Open in 1959, 1968, and 1974; and the PGA in 1962 and 1972. Short in stature but strong in physical training and superb in skill, Player became close friends with his two rivals and shared lucrative exhibitions and television shows with them. Known as the "Black Knight" because of his preference for golf attire of that color, the media honored him as one of the "Big Three." But as time passed, despite his achievements he did not retain his charmed place alongside the two titans of golf, perhaps because he was a foreigner or because he lacked the charisma of Palmer and the trophies of Nicklaus. A very proud man, decades after his prime Player expressed annoyance that he did not receive the respect paid to Palmer and Nicklaus. Commenting on a Golf Channel documentary on Palmer, he told a reporter: "All they did was speak about Arnold and Jack . . . and they said, 'There's Gary lurking in the background.' I won more majors than Arnold. More money. More tournaments around the world. More senior tournaments. More majors on the senior tour. . . . You've got to be fair in life." He added that media "would just never realize what my record was. Maybe it's the pride of the American journalists."[18]

• • •

During the 1960s, as the Palmer-Nicklaus rivalry intensified on the fairways and greens, the two golfers also collaborated in a variety of endeavors that boosted each of their careers as both sportsmen and businessmen. On the links as partners they combined to win four Canada/World Cups and three national team championships together. With Palmer leading the way, they also took the field of sports marketing to a new level, and they used their collective influence to force important changes in the PGA Tour. In the late 1950s Palmer joined into a partnership with Mark McCormack, a lawyer from Cleveland, Ohio, and founder of International Management Group (IMG). Together the two men parlayed Palmer's success on the links into a business empire that included a company that manufactured golf equipment and another that handled golf franchises, sportswear licenses, golf books and pamphlets, and television and radio shows and exhibitions. Other interests included a dry-cleaning franchise business and insurance. One business executive whose company had a licensing contract with Palmer described his magic: "When you buy the Palmer name you buy quality, goodness, honesty and sincerity. . . . People love him; they want to do things for him."[19] Decades later McCormack explained that Palmer had five qualities that enhanced his marketability. He was handsome, came from a family of modest means, played an aggressive style of golf, won major televised tournaments with exciting final rounds, and had excellent interpersonal skills.[20] Later Palmer would add a lucrative corporation that designed golf courses. His success on the Senior PGA Tour kept his name in the public eye, so that decades after his last major title he was still reaping millions from endorsement and course construction deals.

When Nicklaus decided to turn professional late in 1961, Palmer introduced him to McCormack, who became his business manager for the next nine years. Initially, Nicklaus remembered, "The prospect of being in the same stable with Arnie was very appealing."[21] With the rise of Gary Player (another IMG client) the "Big Three" all benefited from McCormack's management, especially through lucrative personal appearances, exhibitions, and endorsements. But by the end of the decade Nicklaus had become disenchanted with his connection to McCormack and IMG. McCormack thought that the divorce resulted from Nicklaus's jealousy over his relationship with Palmer, adding, "Arnold was getting all the press adulation in those days and Jack, starting in sixty-two, was beating Arnold most of the time." But in Nicklaus's view, McCormack made business mistakes with him: "He didn't make me any money to start off with, and I was second fiddle to Arnold and Gary."[22] After the death of his father, Nicklaus parted company with IMG in July 1970, forming Golden Bear, Inc., a conglomerate composed of companies which specialized in advertising, golf equipment and clothing, golf course design, real estate, leasing, travel, media, and other businesses.

As the business empires founded by Palmer and Nicklaus competed with each other for clients during the 1970s, especially in the field of golf course design, each also launched signature annual golf tournaments. Nicklaus took the lead in that enterprise, with the inaugural Memorial tournament in May 1976 at the Muirfield Village Golf Club in Dublin, Ohio, close to his native city of Columbus. Widely recognized as the premier golfer in the world and as one of the sport's all-time greatest champions, Nicklaus hoped to further secure his reputation by following the example of Bobby Jones and his role in promoting the Augusta National Golf Club and especially the Masters Invitational tournament. To further commemorate golf's history, Nicklaus planned to dedicate each event to one of the sport's immortals, with the first honor going to Jones. According to a *New York Times* preview, although Nicklaus avoided direct comparisons, he hinted indirectly that his new tournament "will establish itself as a northern Masters, with all of the class and prestige of the original. He hopes it will also surpass the Masters in excellence of management." The reporter praised the course itself as "at once an esthetic wonder, pleasing to the eye and to the lover of golf, and a technical achievement, the first venue especially developed for golf tournaments and spectators."[23] Palmer competed in the Memorial until he missed the cut in 1984, but he returned in 1993 as the event's honoree. While the Memorial tournament never seriously threatened to surpass the Masters as the premier invitational event in American golf, it did become an important stop on the PGA Tour.

By comparison, when Palmer organized his PGA tournament he did not begin with the grandiose plans and great expectations that characterized Nicklaus's venture. In the mid-1960s Palmer established a winter residence near Orlando in central Florida, and in 1969 he signed a lease and an option to purchase the Bay Hill Club and Lodge. In March 1979 he welcomed an offer to move the ailing Florida Citrus Open to the Bay Hill Club. Although Nicklaus trimmed his schedule that year to attend to his business interests, he agreed to participate. Referring to Palmer's project, he told the press, "I know he's trying to build a good tournament, and I think he needs the support."[24] In 1984 the tournament shifted from an open format to a more elite invitational field. After that year Nicklaus stopped attending, which some observers interpreted as a response to Palmer's absence from the Memorial in 1985. But Nicklaus returned to the Bay Hill event in 1993, in appreciation for Palmer's acceptance of the invitation to be the honoree at his Memorial tournament that year.[25] Renamed the "Arnold Palmer Invitational" in 2007, it remains a feature event on the winter circuit of the PGA Tour.

Palmer and Nicklaus also worked together in the creation of the modern PGA Tour during the late 1960s, facilitating a key transformation in the development of professional golf as a multi-million-dollar business in the United States. It resulted from a long-standing controversy within the PGA between club and tournament professionals. Most of the 6,300 members of the PGA were employed at country clubs or public courses and were chiefly concerned with instruction, renting carts, scheduling events, and selling merchandise and equipment at their shops. One or two hundred of them were skilled enough to compete in national tournaments, and they resented restrictions imposed on them by the PGA. In particular, many demanded their own commissioner to replace the PGA's Tournament Committee, control over the negotiation of television contracts and the scheduling of tournaments, and a looser affiliation with the parent organization. In his autobiography, Palmer conceded that "as crass as it sounds, the issue was really money—more precisely television money." In Nicklaus's words, "the bottom line was money. In a nutshell, as the rewards of the tour grew, the players saw less and less reason why non-competitors should profit from it." But Palmer also insisted that he and his peers were increasingly annoyed and frustrated over numerous PGA regulations, including one that barred a tour rookie from accepting any tournament prize money for the first six months of his career and another that mandated a five-year waiting period before a player was eligible to participate in the PGA Championship.[26]

The criticism of the PGA by prominent touring professionals intensified during the mid-1960s and escalated into outright rebellion in August of 1968. They resolved to take action after they learned that the PGA had negotiated contracts for the television rights to the World

Series of Golf and Shell's Wonderful World of Golf without consulting the players and that it had also decided to put all of the proceeds into its general fund. A dissident group then announced the formation of a new organization—the American Professional Golfers (APG). Palmer supported the APG (which some PGA officials and supporters derisively called the "Arnold Palmer Golfers"), but he also kept a low profile and eventually worked to negotiate a settlement with the PGA. The APG's leadership committee featured such stars as Jack Nicklaus, Gardner Dickinson, Frank Beard, Doug Ford, Billy Casper, and Jerry Barber. Dickinson explained, "What we want is the right to cast the deciding vote over such matters as where, how, and under what conditions we will play." Although Warren Orlick, treasurer of the PGA, insisted that the quarrel had "nothing to do with money," in fact, hundreds of thousands of dollars of television contracts were at stake. The PGA went to court to obtain a temporary restraining order blocking the APG from signing contracts with sponsors for future tournaments.[27]

The standoff between the two warring parties lasted through the annual meeting of the PGA in November, but in mid-December attorneys representing both sides reached an agreement. The "Declaration of Principles" created a new Tournament Players Division (TPD) within the PGA (later renamed the PGA Tour) and a ten-member tournament policy board composed of three PGA officials, four players, and three prominent business leaders. That committee established all policy concerning PGA competitions, including schedules, purses, television commitments, disciplinary actions, and all other matters pertaining to the tour. One month later the policy board announced the appointment of Joseph C. Dey Jr., executive director of the U.S. Golf Association (USGA), as the new commissioner of the TPD. Dey served until 1974, when he was replaced by Deane R. Beman, whose term of service ended in 1994. Under Dey and Beman tournament purses and revenues skyrocketed from the hundreds of thousands to the hundreds of millions of dollars as golf reached new heights of popularity in the nation. Meanwhile, the PGA concentrated on its rank-and-file membership, helping club professionals serve their members and turn a profit at their home shops.[28]

One of the highlights of Beman's first decade as commissioner of the PGA Tour was the creation of the Senior PGA Tour in 1980. It grew out of the popularity of Liberty Mutual's *Legends of Golf* television series, which debuted in 1978. On January 16, 1980, a group of aging former champions that included Sam Snead, Julius Boros, Dan Sikes, Bob Goalby, Gardner Dickinson, and Dan January met with Beman and persuaded him to back the idea of founding a senior tour for men over the age of fifty. The gathering also agreed to recruit star performers to help sell the concept to the public and especially to potential sponsors and television networks. The support of Palmer turned out to be critical, for he was not only famous but also well connected with the corporate world. The new senior tour also gained more exposure and credibility after Palmer won both the 1980 PGA Seniors' Championship and the 1981 Senior U.S. Open title (after the USGA lowered the age restriction from fifty-five to fifty for that event). The Senior PGA Tour flourished partly because of Palmer's heroic exploits, but also because Gary Player, Chi Chi Rodriguez, Raymond Floyd, Billy Casper, Lee Trevino, Nicklaus, and other big names of the golf world turned fifty during the 1980s and 1990s. It became perhaps the most successful venture in all of American professional sports during the 1980s, growing from a modest experiment of two co-sponsored events with prize money of $250,000 in 1980 to thirty tournaments with purses totaling more than $52 million at its twenty-fifth anniversary.[29]

Although the PGA Tour enjoyed spectacular growth under Beman's leadership, during the early 1980s he did survive a challenge from Nicklaus, Palmer, Tom Watson, and a few other premier players over his policies. In their view, Beman placed the interests of all of the touring professionals ahead of those of the elite contestants. In part he did this by selling naming rights of tournaments to corporate sponsors. In a few cases companies then dropped endorsement deals with individual professionals in favor of signing deals directly with the PGA Tour. Nicklaus wrote that Beman "saw generating cash and other benefits for the players *collectively* not only as his principal mission but as the best way of establishing and sustaining his power base." Nicklaus applauded Beman's efforts "to increase purses, lock in solid sponsors and cut rich television deals," with the resulting funds "dispersed strictly according to player ability." But he and the other star performers strongly objected to his other revenue-generating projects, in particular, the construction of PGA Tour courses and the signing of PGA Tour endorsement deals. In the end Beman refused to follow the suggestions of Palmer and Nicklaus, partly because he had the solid backing of the PGA Tour's rank-and-file members. Nicklaus concluded that "if push came to shove, the collective as represented by the commissioner would easily defeat the 'names' as represented by Palmer, Watson, Nicklaus, etc." Beman prevailed in his showdown with the tour superstars and later concluded in an interview with Howard Sounes, "They're not interested in the PGA Tour and golf, they're interested in what's best for *them*."[30]

While Palmer and Nicklaus collaborated in their campaigns to reform the PGA to suit their financial and business interests, they were fierce competitors for product endorsements and especially golf course design projects. Over the decades both experienced several real estate failures, but in the long run Palmer proved to be the better golf entrepreneur. In the late 1990s, as Palmer approached the age of seventy, he still ranked near the top of the list of highest paid sportsmen in the world, earning approximately $18 million in 1998–99. By contrast, during that decade Nicklaus's Golden Bear Golf went through a financial collapse that its namesake was fortunate to survive. He then asked Mark McCormack to manage his business interests again, three decades after he left IMG. In the field of golf course design, Palmer has delegated much of the work to staff architects—especially longtime collaborator Ed Seay. Nicklaus has applied a more "hands-on" approach to his projects. Arnold Palmer Course Design in Florida has constructed more facilities than Nicklaus's Golden Bear Golf, but in 2001 the Golf Research Group ranked Nicklaus's "Signature" courses superior to those designed by Palmer's company.[31] In 2001 the two men co-designed the King and Bear course at World Golf Village in St. Augustine, Florida, which reflected both of their principles of course layouts. At the beginning of the project Palmer explained: "We are going to do some things that probably neither one of us would do alone. On the other hand, we're going to totally cooperate, so it will have both styles incorporated." Before groundbreaking, Nicklaus reported: "Arnold and I were competitive every time we teed it up. We stayed competitive in everything we have done. One wins one time; the other guy wins another time. This time we are both going to win."[32]

In the twilight of their golfing careers Palmer and Nicklaus continued to attract huge crowds as they competed in major tournaments. Such was the case at the 1980 Masters, when the two legends of golf were paired together for the final round. Now fifty years old, Palmer carded a 69 for a total of 288—finishing three shots ahead of the forty-year-old Nicklaus. Both were far back of the winner, Severiano Ballesteros. Afterwards,

Palmer reflected: "I don't think Jack and I have ever played together and not competed against each other. Whether it's for first place in the national Open or for first place in the Masters, or for last place in the Masters. And we will always compete until Jack gets too old."[33] Sometimes when they were paired together they lost sight of the rest of the field, costing them a chance to win. Palmer later remembered: "Our rivalry became so intense that it often worked to our detriment. There were many times when he and I were so focused on one another that we wound up in the locker room surprised to find out someone had come along and beaten us both." Nicklaus agreed: "That happened a lot. When two guys spend so much time together, their competitive juices flow. They try to whip each other."[34] Their personal battle very likely kept them out of the playoff at the Medinah Open in 1975. But Nicklaus did get the last laugh, as he won the 1986 Masters at the age of forty-six. By the turn of the twenty-first century both had concluded play on both the PGA Tour and the Senior (Champions) Tour. Their records show Nicklaus far ahead of his longtime rival, with seventy-three victories on the PGA Tour out of 450 tournaments played (winning 16 percent) and eighteen major titles. As a senior on the Champions Tour, Nicklaus compiled ten titles, including eight majors. Palmer's record shows sixty-two PGA Tour titles out of 478 events (13 percent) and seven majors. As a senior he also captured ten titles, including five majors.

A final assessment of the legacies of Palmer and Nicklaus must extend beyond their respective achievements on fairways and greens. It requires an evaluation of their personal relationship and their impact on golf in America and throughout the world. In 1993, writing for *Golf Digest,* Tom Callahan asked, "How Much Did They Really Love Each Other?" He acknowledged that "golf's most complicated relationship included at times a measure of real warmth and an element of authentic affection." He explained: "It was never permitted to stray very far from the principle on which it was founded: mutual jealousy. Arnie envied Jack's ability; Jack envied Arnie's lovability. Grace came easily to Palmer; golf came easily to Nicklaus." They also enjoyed needling each other. Sometimes it got physical. Nicklaus recalled: "I remember one night, we got to kicking each other's shins under the table. I don't know why. I kicked him. He kicked me. Neither would give. We ended up with the biggest damned bruises. We used to do the stupidest stuff."[35]

In their respective autobiographies the two titans of golf paid tribute to each other and testified to their rivalry and a friendship that at times had a testy edge to it. Nicklaus wrote that early in his career he gained and learned a lot from Palmer and that the good feelings counted more than any ill will between them. He remarked: "So, as hard as we tried to whip each other in competition and relentlessly as we needled each other . . . Arnie and I became good friends, our wives became friends, we traveled together, we ate dinner together, we played cards together, we won four Canada / World Cups and three national team championships together. In short, we established a bond that has lasted for many years."[36]

Palmer was more expansive and reflective in his life story in characterizing his complicated relationship with Nicklaus, whom he labeled "his greatest competition in golf, both on the course during my peak years and off it years later as our separate interests evolved in the business world." His view of their impact on golf in the United States has been echoed by countless sportswriters and historians. Palmer wrote: Our rivalry . . . happened at a time when golf was beginning to take root in the broader American sports psyche, and the intensity of our competition, as well as the distinct differences in our personalities, created tremendous natural drama and a fan interest in the professional game that had never been seen before." He also underscored the growing commercialization of the game: "The fans and sponsors . . . were the beneficiaries of our fierce but gentlemanly thirty-five-year competition on the links. Tournament gates doubled, even tripled, I'm told, when it was announced that Jack and I would be playing in the same field. . . . We knew we were good theater— and we enjoyed it at least as much as the fans and reporters did." He admitted that both "had a lot of fun being the center of that attention," but he also emphasized that "most of all, we wanted to beat each other to a pulp." Perhaps for that reason, he admitted that he and Nicklaus never became "pals off the golf course" and that he stills feels a surge of competitiveness whenever his company loses a contract or a course design project to Nicklaus's firm.[37]

The Palmer-Nicklaus rivalry surpassed all other celebrated duels between champions in golf, tennis, boxing, bowling, or other individual sports in the United States. As the sporting public became enthralled with their epic battles, the two men became rich and famous, but they also elevated their sport to unprecedented heights of popularity. Both contributed mightily to the growth of the PGA Tour, founded signature tournaments, and established golf course design companies that built hundreds of superior new facilities. In addition, Palmer and Nicklaus also transformed the business of sports by demonstrating the power of product endorsements by superstar athletes.

During the final third of the twentieth century, the Age of Palmer, the "King," gave way to the Age of Nicklaus, the "Golden Bear," but both facilitated the rise of golf's new superstar, who was destined to surpass both in fortune and very likely ultimately in championships won and enduring fame. On Wednesday afternoon, April 10, 1996, Palmer and Nicklaus played a practice round in preparation for the Masters Tournament at the Augusta National Golf Club. Thirty-two years had passed since Palmer's fourth and final Masters victory; a decade earlier, at the age of forty-six, Nicklaus had earned his sixth green jacket. Joining these two legends of American (and world) golf on the first tee was a twenty-year-old Stanford sophomore, Eldrick "Tiger" Woods. Although the young man did not play especially well that day, Nicklaus and Palmer were impressed with his game and predicted great performances from Woods in the future. "Arnold and I both agreed," said Nicklaus, "you probably could take Arnold's Masters and my Masters and add them together, and this kid should win more than that." He continued: "This kid is the most fundamentally sound golfer that I've ever seen at almost any age. And he is a nice kid. He's got great composure. He handles himself very, very well. Hits the ball nine million miles."[38] Surely Nicklaus was engaging in some hyperbole both in estimating the distance of his drives and in his prospects for winning eleven Masters titles. But he and Palmer did see something special in Woods, even though that year he failed to make the cut over the next two days of the competition. That spring and summer, Woods won the NCAA individual men's championship and his record third consecutive U.S. Amateur title. After turning professional in late August he won two tournaments before the end of the year. The following April he began to fulfill Nicklaus's prophecy when at twenty-one he became the youngest Masters champion with the lowest score in tournament history and a record twelve-shot margin of victory. It was an auspicious start in his quest to surpass the legends of Arnold Palmer and Jack Nicklaus.

Muhammad Ali throwing a left jab at Joe Frazier in their heavyweight fight at Madison Square Garden on January 28, 1974. Ali won in twelve rounds in this second of three fights between the two great boxing champions. *Courtesy of Getty Images.*

three

The Mortality of Kings
Ali *versus* Frazier

GERALD EARLY ———

As with all sports, boxing's drama depends on great matches between evenly matched opponents. But rivalries in the sport depend on more than just this. Opponents must have faced each other more than once, for a rivalry must be a series of encounters in order to constitute a true test of the fighters' abilities: the fighters must know each other well. The creation of rivalry in boxing is even more deeply appreciated than in many other sports as boxers can pick and choose their opponents and, thus, try to avoid difficult fights unless there is a high reward. A good fighter does not wish to fight another good fighter unless he has to in order to make a great deal of money or to gain the prestige of a title. Of course, in this warrior sport, the idea of proving one's masculine mettle against a tough opponent is also a motivation. In the past, rematches were more common, so rivalries were easier to construct and maintain.

Among the great rivalries in boxing were Jack Johnson's non-championship fights against black fighters like Sam McVea, Denver Ed Martin, and Joe Jeanette, all of whom he fought several times. These were, without question, among his toughest contests, far more so than his major championship victories against white opponents like Tommy Burns, Jim Jeffries, and Stanley Ketchel, as black boxers felt they had something to prove among themselves and often were forced to fight each other to make a living as white fighters avoided them. Other key rivalries in the sport include Jack Dempsey's contests against Gene Tunney, Sugar Ray Robinson's fights against Jake LaMotta, and Sugar Ray Leonard's bouts against Roberto Duran and Thomas Hearns. Joe Louis's fights against Max Schmeling intensified the sense of rivalry because the two men came to represent something symbolic, both

racially and as nationalities. This heightened sense of symbolism, something which boxing frequently tries to exploit if the fighters offer that possibility, makes such matches dramas not only for enthusiasts of the sport
but typically for the general public as well. It was such political symbolism
that characterized the rivalry between Muhammad Ali and Joe Frazier,
two of the greatest heavyweights of their era (the 1960s and 1970s),
remarkably different men who fought each other savagely in the ring,
while outside the ring one theatrically disparaged the other, which the
other deeply despised and openly resented.

Joe Frazier would likely have been recognized as the greatest heavyweight of the 1960s had he not been overshadowed by Muhammad Ali.
When he first fought Ali in 1971, he had won a gold medal in the 1964
Olympics and amassed a professional record of twenty-seven victories, no
defeats, and twenty-four knockouts, a higher knockout percentage than
Ali or, for that matter, any other ranked heavyweight of the day. He was
a fearsome puncher with a devastating left hook, who applied relentless
pressure against his opponents. At five feet, eleven and one-half inches,
his achievement was the more remarkable as he was, for his era, a short
heavyweight, stumpy arms with a short reach and heavy legs. His bobbing
and weaving in the ring made him appear even shorter than he was.

Frazier was born on January 12, 1944, in Laurel Bay, near Beaufort,
South Carolina. He was the last of eleven children. Mark Kram describes
the area where Frazier grew up as "the other-worldly low country that
was the oldest and most historical settlement of the slave culture in the
nation."[1] The people there were Gullah, spoke a dialect or mixture of an
African language and English, and were in their way isolated in the hin-
terlands. Northern African Americans pejoratively called these people
and other country people from the South "Geechees." Frazier grew up
in an area that was much like a location in a Zora Neale Hurston novel:
conjuring, root doctors, hoodoo; in other words, a strong African
American folk culture, not much different from the slave folk culture of
plantation days that permeated Frazier's childhood and youth. It was also
an area of the Big Boss White Man. The blacks of Beaufort were, by and
large, unskilled agricultural workers, treated as near-peons under the
harsh racist regime. Frazier found it difficult to adapt to this and, being
fired by his white boss for complaining to his fellow workers about the
boss beating a black child, felt he had to leave: "I knew it was time for me

to leave this place where I'd been raised up. There wasn't nothing ahead but bad times and a low-rent life for a man like me," Frazier writes in his autobiography.[2] This was quite different from the cultural atmosphere that shaped young Muhammad Ali as a child, although both men were born in the South and experienced segregation. If anything, the difference between the two men was rather like the difference between the Town Negro and the Country Negro, and the public drama that played out between them as professional athletes was something like a variation of this.

Frazier left Beaufort in 1959, first, for New York, and then to live with relatives in Philadelphia, where he worked in a kosher slaughterhouse. He began working out at PAL boxing gym, not only to lose weight, but also to fulfill his dream of becoming the next Joe Louis, the fighter he grew up idolizing. He grew up a tough country kid, good with his hands. He had little education and little desire for it: "While I felt a restlessness about what my future held," Frazier wrote about his childhood, "I never saw school as holding the answer."[3] The tough black neighborhoods of north Philadelphia exposed Frazier to urban black life, with its street violence, drug addiction, poor housing, and broken families. It was a great credit to his character and to the strength of his family that Frazier never succumbed to any of this and had not Ali overshadowed, Frazier likely would have been revered for it. Although Frazier was sometimes clumsy, he worked out in the gym with manic dedication and was willing to learn, as he understood that he was not "a natural." Unlike many other young men in the gym, he seemed determined; he was willing to sacrifice to get what he wanted. A tough, loud-mouthed trainer named Yank Durham, whose day job was welding for the Pennsylvania Railroad, noticed him, saw that he had the drive of a champion athlete, and took him under his wing. Unlike with most young fighters, Durham had to discourage his young protégé from over-training, had to tell him to lay off from coming to the gym so much. The two men became very close and no one was more responsible than Durham for shaping Frazier, devising the relentless, straight-ahead style about which Frazier at first was skeptical; no one was more responsible than Durham for guiding Frazier to the championship.

Frazier won the Mid-Atlantic Golden Gloves heavyweight championship in 1962, 1963, and 1964. In fact, his only loss as an amateur was to Buster Mathis (a loss Frazier would avenge when both men became professionals), who beat him in the Olympic Trials. But Mathis injured his hand in an exhibition on an army base and Frazier replaced him on the team, bringing back the gold medal in 1964 as a heavyweight. (Ali had won the gold as a light heavyweight, and Floyd Patterson as a middleweight. Frazier became the first Olympic gold heavyweight to become the heavyweight champion of the world.)

A question has arisen in recent years if Frazier was legally blind in one eye throughout his boxing career, like his sparring partner and running buddy, flashy Philly welterweight Gypsy Joe Harris. There is little doubt that at the end of his career Frazier was suffering severe problems with his left eye that he hid from boxing officials. Whether he was so afflicted all his life is unclear. In his autobiography, Frazier says that he developed a cataract in his left eye in 1964. Frazier said he faked his eye examinations for his fights. If he fought his entire professional career with an impaired left eye, his achievements are all the more remarkable.

Frazier did not immediately benefit from winning the gold medal. He severely damaged his thumb in his Olympic fights. No sponsors would bankroll him, thinking him a poor risk for a professional career. He was unable to work at the slaughterhouse because of his injury, his growing family depending on his wife's income as a bagger at Sears Roebuck. (At this point, Frazier had children by both his wife, Florence, and a girlfriend in Beaufort named Rosetta. He married Florence in Philadelphia in 1963.) A special Christmas appeal in the local papers prevented the Fraziers from enduring a bleak Christmas in 1964. Frazier began his pro career in August 1965 with a first-round knockout of Woody Goss. In December 1965, a group of prominent Philadelphia businessmen formed Coverlay to sponsor Frazier, much like the group of white Louisville businessmen who originally sponsored Muhammad Ali when he returned from the Olympic Games in Rome in 1960. On the whole, Frazier faced much more difficulty in getting his pro career started, but he began ripping through the opponents with whom Yank Durham matched him, most of them journeymen fighters at best. Among his most noted opponents before his first fight with Ali were Eddie Machen, Doug Jones (who gave Ali a great deal of trouble early in Ali's career; Frazier dispatched him in five rounds), George Chuvalo, Buster Mathis, Jerry Quarry, and Jimmy Ellis, all among the better heavyweights of the era. The fighter who gave Frazier the most difficulty was the bull-like Argentine Oscar Bonavena, whom he was unable to knock out in two fights. (Ali knocked him out in the fifteenth round of their 1970 fight.)

It is likely that Frazier would have fought Ali a few years sooner than the two men wound up meeting, perhaps in 1968 or 1969, had not Ali refused induction in the U.S. Army in 1967. As a result of Ali's conviction in federal court of violation of the Selective Service Act, he was sentenced to five years in prison and stripped of his boxing license everywhere in the country. Every sanctioning body in the sport declared the heavyweight title officially vacant. Frazier opted out of the World Boxing Association (WBA) elimination matches, instead fighting for the New York State Athletic Commission Championship against old nemesis Buster Mathis, whom he knocked out in eleven rounds. On February 16, 1970, he unified the titles by beating WBA champion Jimmy Ellis in five rounds. By the summer of 1970, like Alexander the Great at the height of his moment in history, Frazier had no more worlds to conquer, except fighting Ali, a man he had come to know and who had not fought since 1967 but whose return to the ring was more imminent than people suspected at the time.

There have been few athletes in the history of American amateur or professional sports that had either the fame or the cultural impact of heavyweight boxing champion Muhammad Ali. He was born Cassius Marcellus Clay Jr. on January 17, 1942, in Louisville, Kentucky. He was the older of two brothers. His father, Cassius Clay Sr., was a sign painter and something of a frustrated artist, and his mother, Odessa Grady Clay, was a domestic.

Young Clay began to take boxing lessons in October 1954 at the age of twelve because someone had stolen his bicycle and he was determined to exact revenge against the perpetrators. He never discovered who stole his bike but he did blossom as a young fighter, taking instruction from Louisville policeman Joe Martin. His brother, Rudolph Arnette Clay (Rudolph Valentino Clay in some sources, later Rahaman Ali), also took up boxing but, lacking his brother's talent, never became a significant presence in the sport. He eventually became part of his brother's circle of hangers-on, assistants, sycophants, hustlers, and Muslim strongmen who surrounded him in his glory days like a miasma. Perhaps some form of sibling rivalry inspired Cassius; his relationship with his brother was not always easy to understand.

Clay became a gym rat, feeling that he could succeed in boxing, as he never could in school. Although he showed no special ability in his first few years, he was, like Frazier, extraordinarily determined. "Cassius Clay," Joe Martin said, "when he first began coming around, looked no better or worse than the majority. . . . He was just ordinary, and I doubt whether any scout would have thought much of him in his first year." But Martin went on: "He was a kid willing to make the sacrifices necessary to achieve something worthwhile in sports. I realized that it was almost impossible to discourage him. He was easily the hardest worker of any kid I ever taught."[4]

Clay was a mediocre student, graduating from Central High School with a D- average, ranking 376 out of a class of 391. Clay could barely read and write, and although his high school progress report showed his intelligence as average,[5] on official IQ tests he actually recorded below-average intelligence. It was clear that a combination of temperament, natural inclination, and little aptitude signaled that he was not likely to succeed in any profession that would require attaining a great deal of education or a high degree of literacy. Another reason, therefore, that he threw himself into boxing. There were, moreover, models in the sport to inspire him as they inspired Frazier. But whereas Frazier's hero was Joe Louis, Clay's idol was the magnificent middleweight champion Sugar Ray Robinson.

Cassius Clay eventually became one of the most impressive amateur boxers in the country, winning six Kentucky Golden Gloves championships. He became the National Amateur Athletic Union (AAU) champion in 1959 and 1960 and won a gold medal as a light-heavyweight in the 1960 Rome Olympics, although he almost didn't go because he was afraid to fly on an airplane. At this point, Clay was already famous, having been occasionally televised locally as an amateur and, of course, having been on national television during the Olympics. He enormously enjoyed the attention. One point of dispute has been what happened to Clay's gold medal. In his autobiography, *The Greatest: My Own Story*, Clay claims to have thrown it in the Ohio River after he returned from the Olympics and experienced racist treatment in his hometown:[6] He was refused a meal at a restaurant and chased by a gang of white motorcyclists. This has been vigorously disputed by some who say this incident never happened.[7] While in Rome, Clay was asked about the American race situation by a reporter from the Soviet Union, to whom he replied: "Tell your readers we've got qualified people working on that problem, and I'm not worried about the outcome. To me, the U.S.A. is still the best country in the world, counting yours. It may hard to get something to eat sometimes, but anyhow I ain't fighting alligators and living in a mud hut."[8] Clay began visiting the temples of the Nation of Islam in 1959, so it may be safe to say that while he was intrigued by the group at this stage, the Muslims did not seem to have made an impression upon his political views. That would come later.

Clay's boyish good looks, his outgoing personality, combined with the gimmicks of his poetry and his good-natured bragging, sustained his fame after the Olympics, as he received a great deal more media attention than most amateur fighters. He turned professional immediately after returning from Rome and was managed by a syndicate of eleven Louisville businessmen led by William Faversham. At first, he was placed under the guidance of light-heavyweight champion Archie Moore, but the two men could not get along. Clay resented Moore's advice and training regimen. He returned to Louisville from Moore's camp in California and was taken on by trainer Angelo Dundee. Skillfully guided by the wily Dundee, a highly experienced boxing man who did not try to change Clay's unorthodox style, which had always infuriated most of the old heads of boxing, Clay, like most highly touted young fighters, won all of his early fights against either second- or third-rate opponents or noted fighters whose skills had deteriorated, like Archie Moore, his short-lived tutor, whom he knocked out in four rounds on November 15, 1962, in Los Angeles. His most difficult fight of this "contender" stage was against Doug Jones, in which Clay won a ten-round decision on May 13, 1963, in New York, although many at ringside thought he lost the fight. Four years later, Frazier knocked out Jones, but he was not the caliber of fighter he was when he fought Clay. Clay's relationship with Dundee was different than that of most between a boxer and a trainer: Dundee never spoke for Clay as Yank Durham did for Frazier, never scripted his answers with the press, never advised him in any way in his personal life, never, in fact, seemed to advise him about boxing itself. Clay always spoke for himself, never through an intermediary, and he seemed never to take advice from anyone, not even Drew "Bundini" Brown, who was probably closer to Clay as a trainer throughout his career than Dundee was. Clay, in fact, throughout his entire career, always gave the impression that he trained himself, that he managed himself, that he created himself. He, thus, gave the impression that he had more power as a boxer than any previous fighter ever had in the sport. In fame and public reach, in creating his own persona and voicing his own views, this was certainly true. It was not true in his relation to the commercial powers that ran the sport. He was, in that regard, as controlled as any other fighter in the history of the sport. To be sure, with his constant bragging, his poetry, and his zany antics, he won a national following, even appearing briefly in the 1962 film version of Rod Serling's "Requiem for a Heavyweight."

At 6 feet 3 inches and over two hundred pounds, Clay astonished sportswriters with his hand and foot speed, his reluctance never to take a punch to the body or to fight in close, his ability to defend himself while holding his hands at his waist, and his insistence on avoiding punches by moving his head backward instead of moving to the side. Clay modeled much of his style after his idol Sugar Ray Robinson. But it seemed an inappropriate style for a heavyweight and a style that Archie Moore thought would only prolong his fights, much to Clay's detriment in the long run. He thought Clay was big enough and strong enough to knock out his opponents quickly and he intended to teach Clay how to do that. One of the reasons the men fell out was that Clay was resistant to learning to fight in that way. But no heavyweight before Clay ever possessed such speed, quickness, or grace. He could succeed with the style he had because of his physical gifts and his ring savvy. "People said I held my hands too low and did other things wrong, but when I was young, my defense was my legs. My style in the ring was to keep my distance, don't get too close, stay just out of range, get in just enough to punch, and get out."[9] Clay attracted a great many people to boxing who would normally have had little interest in it simply because they were enthralled with the lyricism of his style.

On February 25, 1964, in Miami, Clay fought as a heavy underdog (7 to 1) for the heavyweight title against Charles Sonny Liston, an ex-convict who grew up in rural Arkansas among twenty-four brothers and sisters (he served time in prison in Jefferson City, Missouri, for armed robbery), who was thought by many to be virtually invincible because of his devastating one-round knockouts of former champion Floyd Patterson, the last heavyweight champion to weigh under two hundred pounds. He beat Patterson on September 25, 1962, to win the championship, a fight he had a difficult time getting because he was an ex-convict, and a fight that most of the public wanted to see him lose. He retained the title when he beat Patterson again on July 22, 1963. So few thought that the bragging Clay had a chance that rumors circulated that he would not even show up for the fight. Most thought the young fighter had no punch, no chin, and would hardly be able to withstand the hard-punching Liston. Clay, for his part, had been harassing Liston during most of the period before the fight, taunting him by calling him "the Bear" (a word for Liston he borrowed from Patterson's trainer Cus D'Amato) and "ugly," banging on Liston's front door in the early morning hours, demanding that he fight him then and there. It was unclear how afraid Clay might actually have been of Liston; fear plays an important part in the psychological makeup of a fighter, and most fighters enter the ring with some fear of both their opponents and of failing, of being physically punished. Liston once slapped a taunting Clay in the face in a Las Vegas casino and sent him meekly on his way.[10] The weigh-in ceremony the morning of the fight was part theater of the absurd, part screwball comedy, and part, no doubt, Clay trying to work up his courage against a formidable opponent. (After all, as a professional fighter, Clay knew very well how well Liston could fight and he had no reason to believe that Liston would do anything less than his best.) At the weigh-in, Clay, wearing a robe that said "Bear Hunting," seemed as if he wanted to attack Liston and gave the appearance of being completely out of control. It was, apparently, all an act on Clay's part to gain a psychological edge over his opponent. But yet it is unlikely that this greatly affected Liston, unless it was to make him overconfident. Liston was already convinced that Clay was afraid of him.

What was more ominous, from the perspective of the fight's promoters and most of the general public, were rumors coming out of Miami that Clay was being seen with Malcolm X, the charismatic minister of the Nation of Islam (NIO), probably the most feared and misunderstood religious cult of the time and certainly one of the most militant black organizations to emerge since the Great Depression. Clay had already joined the controversial group, but he did not announce this until after the fight with Liston, in part because he did not want the fight cancelled because of his religious conversion and in part because the Muslims did not want to be overly embarrassed by his defeat, which nearly all in the organization thought would happen, including the NOI's leader, Elijah Muhammad. Indeed, Muhammad himself was not very pleased with having Clay as a member. He thought very little of prizefighters (dumb guys who participated in a politically incorrect sport) and was particularly unimpressed with Clay's antics, quite out of keeping with the somber, stern demeanor of the group. Clay was not fully aware at the time of how little the Muslim leadership thought of him and how little confidence they had in his abilities to beat Liston. Malcolm X, however, was confident that Clay would win, convincing the young boxer that the fight was a jihad, a symbolic war that was both political and religious between the crescent and the cross or between the black man who was for his people and the black man who represented white interests, a psychological device that Clay nearly always—and his opponents occasionally, particularly Floyd Patterson— was to use to dramatize virtually all the major fights of his career, turning them into contesting forms of black political propaganda. He used this technique with particular success in his first fight against Joe Frazier. Some of Clay's denigration of his opponents was distinctly not funny, not illuminating, not fair, and, as his career went along, seemed to become especially tiresome by the middle-1970s. It was the denigration of his opponents that would lead to the bitter hatred that Frazier would develop for Ali.

Clay stunned the sporting world by defeating the aging Liston fairly easily in seven rounds. After the fight, Clay announced that he had not only joined the Nation of Islam but had a new name, Muhammad Ali. The response from the boxing establishment, the sporting press, and the white public generally was hostile, even vitriolic. The NOI was largely seen, mistakenly so, as an anti-white hate group, something on the order of the Ku Klux Klan, with its beliefs in complete racial separation, white racial inferiority, and Allah's ultimate descent into human history to right all racial wrongs, ending in a massive, supernaturally induced, white genocide. Although there had been a few black jazz musicians who had converted to Islam, such as Ahmad Jamal, Art Blakey, and Dakota Staton (they were not members of the Nation of Islam), most of the public, either black or white, knew little about the religion; and the NOI's highly racialized distortion of the religion diminished further what little understanding most Americans had. Never was an athlete so pilloried by the public as Ali was. Most sports journalists ridiculed his religion and refused to call him by his new name. Former champion Floyd Patterson went on a personal crusade against the NOI in his fight against Ali on November 22, 1965, which Patterson lost, in part because he simply lacked the skills and in part because he injured his back and was virtually unable to throw a meaningful punch in the fight. Patterson was particularly outraged that Ali would condemn America as he did and that he would permit himself to be taken over by the Muslims. (Ali fired his white syndicate, and Herbert Muhammad, one of Elijah Muhammad's sons, became his manager.) Patterson later became one of the few fighters to defend Ali publicly during his years of exile.

After winning his rematch with Sonny Liston in Lewiston, Maine, on May 25, 1965, in a bizarre first-round knockout caused by a punch no one saw thrown, just two months after Malcolm X was gunned down in Harlem by members of the NOI, Ali, probably one of the most unpopular fighters in history, spent most of the next year abroad, beating George Chuvalo in Toronto, Henry Cooper in London, and Karl Mildenberger in Germany. He also defeated Ernie Terrell in Houston, one of his few American fights during this period.

While Ali was abroad, the Selective Service changed his draft status from 1-Y (unfit for military service because of his low score on army intelligence tests; in high school, Ali only scored an 83 on standardized intelligence tests, which means that he had a score that was about one standard deviation below average intelligence) to 1-A (qualified for induction). Many saw this change as a direct response to intense negative public opinion concerning Ali's political views. In fact, after the August 1964 Gulf of Tonkin incident that produced the Gulf of Tonkin Resolution that gave President Lyndon Johnson broad powers to escalate the war in Vietnam without an official declaration of war from the Congress, the passing score on the U.S. Army intelligence tests was lowered so that many other men besides Ali were affected. Ali refused to serve in the military on the grounds that it violated his religious beliefs. Elijah Muhammad, leader of the NOI, had served time in prison during World War II for refusing to serve in the armed services and for sympathizing with the Japanese. (There was greater, and misplaced, sympathy for the Japanese among many blacks during the 1930s and into World War II because they were a "colored" nation standing up to European

and white American power.) Wallace Muhammad, son of Elijah, also
served time for refusing military service. Yet it was unclear how Ali saw
himself as being exempted from service: Islam is not a pacifist religion,
and Muslims have served in the American military. Ali himself made his
money in a violent profession where it was possible he could permanently maim or kill an opponent, so he lived by no personal principal of
pacifism like, say, Bayard Rustin or people associated with the Peace or
War Resisters Movement. He claimed to be a Muslim preacher, one of
his claims for exemption, yet he was never formally put in charge of any
mosque, nor did he regularly preach for the Muslims anywhere. He
never had the status in the organization that Malcolm X had and was
never referred to, as Malcolm was, as a minister. Part of his claim of
exemption was also that there were no blacks on his local draft board at
the time his change in status occurred, and thus it was not a reflection
of the local community. It must be understood that during the 1960s
most men served in the military and thought it was something that
everyone should be willing to do. Most veterans of the Korean War and
World War II were alive and actively shaped American public opinion at
the time. These men could not understand why Ali would be opposed
to serving in the military, why he was unpatriotic and how this had anything to do with his race. Joe Louis had served honorably during World
War II. Why not Ali now? If anything, despite racism and entrenched
segregation before the Korean War, the military was largely seen as an
attractive career by many black men. But blacks had a troubled history
with the military and many were not eager to serve. Some felt that society itself was so stacked against them that serving in the military was
virtually the only option they had, short of a life on the margins of the
criminal world. For his part, Ali was afraid to join the military because
he thought he might be killed by some overly patriotic white (a not
unrealistic possibility as Ali's opposition to military service and his membership in the NOI had stirred up plenty of racial hatred in an age when
there was a great deal of violence committed against public figures). He
also saw the war in racial terms and was not convinced that he should
risk his life to fight for whites, as he saw it, against "colored" people (the
Vietnamese) who had done nothing to him or anything to his country,
as far as he could discern. The Vietnam War was seen as a race war by

the American left and by many younger, more militant blacks. Naturally, the refusal to serve on the part of such a prominent and charismatic black person was bound to affect other young blacks, at least, to make people look upon resistance of this sort as something heroic, something principled.

In June 1967, Ali was convicted in federal court of violation of the Selective Service Act and sentenced to five years in prison and fined $10,000. He was immediately stripped of his boxing title and every state athletic commission stripped him of his boxing license. For the next three and one-half years, Ali, free on bond while appealing his case (which he eventually won unanimously on appeal to the U.S. Supreme Court on a technicality on June 28, 1971), was prohibited from boxing. He spoke on college campuses (because he needed the money, although his conservative views about race, sex, and morality were often met with skepticism, if not outright disapproval); became a darling of the anti-war movement because he was, as was often pointed out, sacrificing the best years of his athletic life for his beliefs (but so were athletes who had chosen to fight in wars and who had to endure the rigors of combat to boot); and inspired other black athletes such as Harry Edwards, who tried to organize a black boycott of the 1968 Mexico City Olympics. Medal-winning track stars Tommie Smith and John Carlos gave a clenched-fist salute during the playing of the national anthem at those Olympic Games and were promptly sent home.

Despite the college lectures, Ali had little money during his exile years and he desperately wanted to get back into the ring. He wanted not only the money but also the adulation of the crowd. Besides, he enjoyed boxing: it was something he did better than virtually anyone else in his profession. Frazier apparently lent Ali money during Ali's time out of the ring and publicly supported his return to boxing, not an altogether altruistic move, as Frazier needed Ali as much as Ali needed Frazier. How much Frazier revered Ali is unclear. Mark Kram suggests that it was nearly blind hero-worship: Frazier was even willing to have a 50–50 split of the purse should he and Ali fight.[11] But even Frazier admits the two men were friendly for a time during Ali's exile. At the time, Ali was living in Cherry Hill, New Jersey, a stone's throw from Philadelphia, Frazier's stomping ground. Frazier writes in his autobiography, "In those days, we were on a friendly basis—rivals who could talk to each other in a reasonable way. That was mostly when there were no crowds, microphones, or cameras. Once Clay had an audience, he was like the comedian who opened the refrigerator and, seeing the light go on, had to do ten minutes of his best material. That was goddamn Clay—a nonstop promoter. The sucker had fifty-seven varieties of bullshit—and he needed it all. With a legal bill reported to be around $280,000, Clay was hustling the buck on the lecture circuit, talking up the Black Muslims and his favorite subject, himself."[12] The real rupture between the two came in 1969 when Ali, on a Philadelphia radio talk program, called Frazier an "Uncle Tom," someone who was fighting for the white man, "a coward," "flat-footed, and ugly" and challenged Frazier to meet him at the PAL North Philadelphia gym where Frazier trained. Ali was there, yelling, when Frazier, in a fury, stripping off his shirt, ready to fight. As the gym was so packed with people, Ali challenged Frazier to go across the street to fight him in Fairmount Park. Frazier declined, as Ali, like the pied piper, led the crowd out of the gym. Frazier was humiliated by all of this occurring in his hometown. He felt that Ali had disrespected him. For Ali, this was theater, ramping up the voltage of a fight between them that would eventually happen; for Frazier, Ali simply seemed to be using him as a foil, defining him for the public as the politically incorrect dragon that the heroic political rebel Ali had to slay. If Ali loved black people so much as he professed, how could he do this to another black man? This was a perfectly reasonable way for Frazier to interpret the situation and especially so as a high-level boxer with an intense degree of masculine honor. Frazier's regard for Ali turned to pure hatred.

In 1970, with public opinion strongly against the Vietnam War, and aided by growing black political power in several southern state governments, Ali was given a license to fight in Georgia, led by the efforts of African American state senator Leroy Johnson, despite the fact that segregationist Lester Maddox was governor, something made possible by the very civil rights movement, the push for integration that, as a Black Muslim, Ali condemned. He returned to the ring on October 26 and defeated journeyman Jerry Quarry in three rounds; the fight stopped because Quarry had sustained a terrible cut over his left eye. Otherwise Quarry had not been hurt, so it is difficult to say what might have happened had Quarry not been cut and had the fight lasted longer. Although

Ali was still a brilliant fighter, the long layoff had clearly eroded his skills to some degree. He took more punishment in the ring when he returned than before. Ali's next fight was against Oscar Bonavena on December 7 in New York City. Ali stopped Bonavena in the fifteenth round, something that Frazier could not do in two fights against the tough Latin American, but it was a dull fight that at times resembled a sparring session. Because Ali's draft case was still pending on appeal, he was unsure how much time he might have before he would have to go to prison, as it was hardly a certainty that the lower court verdict would be overturned. Therefore, knowing that Frazier, now the champion, was the only real big money fight available and the man Ali would have to defeat to get his title back, Ali decided he would dispense with the tune-ups. So, there was no doubt now that Ali and Frazier would finally meet in the ring.

The first Ali-Frazier fight, held in Madison Square Garden, was one of the biggest, most hyped fights in the history of the sport. For instance, Norman Mailer covered the fight for *Life* magazine, and Frank Sinatra took the photos that accompanied the piece. All the glitterati of the time showed up, from Diana Ross and Sidney Poitier to Gene Kelly and Michael Caine. Both fighters were paid a guaranteed fee of $2.5 million each, an unheard of purse for a professional boxing match at the time. Featured on close-circuit outlets throughout the country, the fight made millions for promoters Jack Kent Cooke and Jerry Perenchio, so much so that Ali and Frazier would have made much more money had they chosen to take a percentage of the gate. On March 8, 1971, Joe Frazier extracted some measure of revenge by beating archrival Ali in a fifteen-round decision. Ali lost rounds by clowning and lying on the ropes and having Frazier punch at his midsection, a strategy that would work better later against George Foreman. Frazier was relentless in his attack, battering Ali with sizzling left hooks, but took a severe beating himself, hammered by Ali's jabs and right crosses. Frazier sealed the fight by staggering Ali in the eleventh round and knocking him down in the fifteenth. The fight was so brutal that both men were hospitalized after, Frazier for several weeks, deathly ill. It was Ali's first defeat. But he almost turned it into a victory by saying afterward that he felt that he had won nine rounds of the fight and that Frazier had been far more severely beaten that he had been. For Frazier, his boxing career was to go down-hill from this moment. For Ali there were greater moments to come.

Ali won the North American Boxing Federation title, a significant but lesser honor than the world's championship, in July 1971 by beating former sparring partner Jimmy Ellis. He lost again in March 1973 against ex-marine Ken Norton in a twelve-round decision where Ali's jaw was broken late in the fight. (It was said that Ali slept with two women the night before this fight.[13] It was during Ali's return to the ring in the 1970s that his womanizing grew legendary, uncontrollable.) Ali regained his North American Boxing Federation title from Norton in a highly dis-puted twelve-round decision six months later. If Ali had lost that fight, his career might have been finished. But clearly Ali was struggling as a fighter at this point, no longer the brilliant, unbeatable golden boy of his pre-exile days.

Frazier, if anything, was faring worse than Ali. He defended his title again on January 15, 1972, easily beating a tomato-can fighter named Terry Daniels in four rounds. In May, he knocked out another tomato can, Ron Stander, in five rounds. These unimpressive fights did not make him appear a great champion. After the Ali fight, Yank Durham was han-dling him very carefully. Then, Frazier made his biggest mistake, going against Durham's advice; he met young George Foreman, gold medal heavyweight of the 1968 Olympics, on January 22, 1973, in Kingston, Jamaica. Foreman knocked him down six times and stopped him in two rounds, winning the title. Durham died later in 1973 and Eddie Futch took over as Frazier's trainer. Frazier was never to be champion again.

On January 28, 1974, Ali and Frazier fought again at Madison Square Garden in a non-title fight. When they had met three years earlier, both men were undefeated and both could claim to be champions, princes of the realm. Now, both were hanging on, their skills clearly reduced, des-perately needing a win in the hope of gaining another title shot as age crept on them inexorably. This time Ali won a close twelve-round deci-sion, having learned much from their first fight. Ali smothered Frazier's attack by holding him; he did not clown around, giving away rounds. Indeed, Ali hurt Frazier badly in the second round and may have been able to knock him out had referee Tony Perez not mistakenly stopped the round several seconds early, thinking he heard the bell ring. Frazier came back to have some good rounds, but Ali controlled the fight and contained Frazier's attacks, taking full advantage of his superior height and reach. Frazier complained bitterly about Ali's holding, feeling that Perez did not properly referee the fight.

The two men met for a third and final time in the Philippines on September 30, 1975. Ali had regained the title in Kinshasa, Zaire, on October 30, 1974, when he knocked out Foreman in the eighth round of a fight where he was a decided underdog, most of the public thinking that Ali, at thirty-two, had passed his prime, the fight that made the expression "rope-a-dope" famous. Since their second fight, Frazier had two impressive fights, stopping Jerry Quarry and Jimmy Ellis in five and nine rounds, respectively. But the four-plus years since their first meeting had taken their toll: the men were older (Ali was thirty-three, and Frazier thirty-one), heavier (Ali weighed in for their last fight at 224½ pounds, Frazier at 215½ pounds), more shop worn, more diminished by their fights and their gym wars. They were lesser versions of themselves in every respect. Ali was, if anything, even crueler in promoting the fight, calling Frazier a gorilla and an Uncle Tom. Frazier complained that his children were viciously teased in school. Ali's turbulent personal life caught up with him at this fight as he publicly presented another woman, Veronica Porsche, as his wife, much to chagrin of his real wife, Belinda, who immediately flew to the Philippines to confront Ali on the matter. The marriage did not survive. (Neither man was a paragon of marital virtue: Frazier was to divorce Florence and father eleven children with both her and other women; Ali would marry four times and father eight children by wives and other women.)

The fight itself was the last great hurrah for both men, although Ali would go on to have other important fights against Ken Norton, Ernie Shavers, and Leon Spinks. Ali stopped Frazier when the latter was unable to answer the bell for the fifteenth round. Both men endured a terrific beating. Ali was fiercely beaten in the body and Frazier's face was a swollen mess, his eyes punched shut (which was why the fight was stopped: Frazier couldn't see anymore). Ali himself was close to quitting the fight himself and may not have survived the fifteenth round had the fight continued. Frazier's hatred seemed to fuel his body onward, relentlessly, frighteningly absorbing punishing blows in order to deliver them. Ali said afterwards that the fight was the closest he had come to death itself. Frazier was upset that his trainer, Eddie Futch, had stopped it, although it was clear to everyone that he did it out of regard for Frazier's health, realizing that in his current condition it was impossible for Frazier to continue. The fight did little to settle things between the two men: Ali had won two of the three encounters convincingly but painfully. There is no question that Frazier was the most difficult fighter Ali ever faced: the man whom he brutalized in the ring more than any other. For Frazier, his blind hatred of Ali continued unabated, even to the point of believing that he actually won all three fights. Frazier has, in fact, said some cruel things about Ali over the years, especially since their retirements from the ring. (Both men fought their last fight in 1981.) For instance, Frazier stated publicly that he wished Ali had immolated himself when, trembling with Parkinson's disease, the former champion lit the Olympic flame in 1996 for the Atlanta games. Doubtless, Frazier was jealous and angry that he had not been invited to light the flame for that or any other Olympics, as he himself, like Ali, was an Olympic gold medalist. Sportswriters were shocked by the depth and persistence of Frazier's hatred; perhaps his clinging to it was a sign of psychological unbalance. But who is entitled to tell Frazier to forgive his enemy? How are we to judge the measure of what Frazier endured when Ali was at the height of his popularity and mercilessly taunted Frazier, far beyond what was necessary to build public interest in their fights? On the other hand, Frazier has much to be proud of in his career, and it would be a shame if he were to ruin his standing with the public by clinging to a pointless hatred, the cultural context of which has long passed by. After all, to the public today both are simply old men in bad health who, to many, lost more than they gained by becoming professional fighters.

At the end of his autobiography, Frazier writes:

> Truth is, I'd like to rumble with that sucker again—beat him up piece by piece and mail him back to Jesus. No, I ain't forgiven him for what he said and did. I stood up for him when few others did. Told the boxing officials, "Let the man fight." Then, when he got what he needed, he turned on me and said everything bad that he could. Called me the white man's champion to get the black men to turn on me. Called me a Tom and an ignoramus to demean me

in public. Now people ask me if I feel bad for him, now that things aren't going so well for him. Nope. I don't. Fact is, I don't give a damn. They want me to love him, but I'll open up the graveyard and bury his ass when the Lord chooses to take him.[14]

Muhammad Ali put it more succinctly: "We went to Manila as champions, Joe and me, and we came back as old men."[15] I would not be surprised at all if the last words Ali mutters on this earth are "Joe Frazier."

Larry Bird and Magic Johnson battling for a rebound in one of their many confrontations on the court. *Courtesy of Steve Lipofsky.*

— four

"We Were about Winning"

Larry Bird, Magic Johnson, and the Rivalry That Remade the NBA

DANIEL A. NATHAN ——————

On the eve of the 2008 National Basketball Association (NBA) playoffs, almost two months before the finals, *Sports Illustrated* featured Kobe Bryant of the Los Angeles Lakers and Kevin Garnett of the Boston Celtics on its cover. "There's a long way to go, of course," mused senior writer Jack McCallum, "but the idea of a Celtics-Lakers title showdown, which hasn't happened since the Reagan Administration, is the most tantalizing postseason prospect to come along in years for the league, its network partners and fans starved for a rivalry that evokes the NBA's glory days."[1] Depending upon whom one asks, "the NBA's glory days" might be the 1960s, when coach Red Auerbach and center Bill Russell led the Celtics to nine championships, beating the Lakers six times. Or it might be the 1980s, when Larry Bird of the Celtics and Earvin "Magic" Johnson of the Lakers reinvigorated the rivalry between the franchises, and, arguably, the NBA itself.

Perhaps responding to *Sports Illustrated,* or to the widespread hope that the Lakers and the Celtics, the teams with the best records in their respective conferences, would meet in the finals, Harvey Araton of the *New York Times* reminisced, "Lakers-Celtics, or at least the anticipation of another Bird-Johnson showdown, had been the league's meal ticket for the better part of a decade, with beloved team-first superstars from opposite coasts: one black, one white, by then fraternal soul brothers, headlining a basketball Cosby Show."[2] Araton was right, for while the Lakers-Celtics rivalry obviously preceded and has outlasted the Bird-Johnson competition, the latter was sui generis for many reasons, including that it was a valued commodity. At the same time, the Bird-Johnson rivalry represented deeply entrenched cultural values and tensions, and it continues to resonate.

Indeed, few American sports rivalries were and remain as celebrated and symbolic as the one between Larry Bird and Magic Johnson. Tremendously talented, successful basketball players, whose lengthy careers were intertwined with one another dating back to their final college game, Bird and Johnson played with passion, intelligence, and creativity. "They'll always be linked," declared Johnson's former coach, Pat Riley: "They were just smarter than the other players in the league. Spiritually. Mentally. I think of four words to describe them: Respect. Dignity. Integrity. Trust."[3] During the 1980s and early 1990s, Bird and Johnson were NBA superstars of the highest order and their teams were perennial championship contenders. Collectively, they won eight titles in twelve years: Bird's Celtics, three; Johnson's Lakers, five. "We weren't about stats," Johnson later explained. "We were about winning."[4]

Because of their winning ways, different styles, public personas, and racial identities, and because of the tremendous media attention they received and the cultural moment in which they played, Bird and Johnson "enthralled fans (and players), literally, across the globe" and contributed to taking the NBA from its popular and commercial nadir to somewhere close to its zenith.[5] This certainly explains much about the duo's continued importance and iconicity. Yet the Bird-Johnson rivalry was about more than the NBA's renaissance. It was, in fact, about more than basketball; when understood in its multiple contexts—historical, social, and political—it was a rivalry rife with cultural meaning, one that reflected and helped define an era.

A brief word on the nature of sports rivalries and on Bird and Johnson's, in particular, is in order. Essentially, rivalries work or are meaningful because of contrast and genuine competition. The rivals need to be different in some significant way: say, geographically (proximity usually breeds hostility) or in terms of temperament (cool versus fiery), strategic philosophy (innovation versus tradition), aesthetics (baroque versus minimalist), or politics (conservative versus progressive)—or some combination of these characteristics. The operative idea here is *difference*. If the difference takes on obvious symbolic qualities—consider the cultural salience of the National Football League's Dallas Cowboys–Washington Redskins rivalry—all the better. It is also important for the rivals to be relatively evenly matched; the outcome of the competition cannot be obvious; there needs to be doubt about who will win, about who is better. If over time the results become consistently lopsided—if one competitor usually crushes the other or if one wins most of the contests—the rivalry diminishes in importance. In tennis, when Chris Evert's skills began to slip and she was no longer Martina Navratilova's toughest opponent—"the swashbuckling serve-and-volleyer" (Navratilova) defeated "the methodical baseliner" (Evert) thirty-one times in their final forty matches—the rivalry lost its vitality.[6]

But since basketball is a team game, Bird and Johnson did not compete directly against each other; they were not rivals in the same way that Evert and Navratilova or Muhammad Ali and Joe Frazier were. Moreover, as sportswriter Bob Ryan correctly notes, "They were never directly matched up. Bird was a forward. Magic was a guard. They might occasionally meet as the result of a defensive switch, or cross paths if one of them was back defending against a fast break, but they never *guarded* each other."[7] Ryan adds: "This was not [Bill] Russell versus [Wilt] Chamberlain, a nose-to-nose, navel-to-navel war. Bird and Magic's battle instead took on a can-you-top-this flavor."[8] Still, it was a stimulating rivalry for fans, the media, and the athletes themselves. "When the new schedule would come out each year," Johnson said, "I'd grab it and circle the Boston games. To me it was The Two and the other 80. During the season I'd check out Larry's line first thing. If he had a triple double, I knew what I'd want that night." Bird had the same mindset: "The first thing I would do every morning during the season," Bird explained, "was look at the box scores to see what Magic did. I didn't care about anything else."[9] Except winning.

• • •

The Larry Bird–Magic Johnson rivalry began on March 26, 1979. That night, in Salt Lake City, Utah, Johnson's Michigan State University Spartans played Bird's number-one-ranked, undefeated Indiana State University Sycamores for the National Collegiate Athletic Association (NCAA) championship.[10] It was the only time Johnson and Bird played against each other as collegians, which made it all the more memorable.[11]

The game was highly anticipated nationally, not just for fans in East Lansing, Michigan, and Terre Haute, Indiana. To many, it seemed like a David-and-Goliath affair, with the small, over-achieving Indiana State being the stone thrower, despite its 33-0 record going into the contest.[12]

For others, it was an interesting match-up because of the teams' stars, with their stellar games and contrasting personalities.

Johnson was an ebullient, flashy, 6-foot 8-inch sophomore point guard whom *Sports Illustrated* had presciently featured on the cover of its college basketball preview issue the previous November. A standout at Everett High School in Lansing, the son of stable, hard-working parents, Johnson was, the magazine reported, "the first three-time all-state player in Michigan history and an attraction of staggering dimensions in his hometown," in part because he led Everett to a 27-1 record and a state championship his senior year.[13] After having played just one season of college ball, Johnson already had professional basketball executives gushing. One called him "the most exciting college player I've ever seen. I can't believe God created a 6'8" man who can handle the ball like that."[14] Months later, after Johnson led MSU to a 25-6 record and advanced his team to the NCAA championship game, the *New York Times* pre-game scouting report noted: "His ability to control a team and hit the open man, and his overall court sense, are already legend. Everything he does on the court, in his smooth, controlled fashion, is absolutely superb. Although he frequently makes tremendous passes, he rarely forces a play."[15] Unselfish and exuberant, Johnson was, in spite of his youth (he was only nineteen years old), also team co-captain, a leader, "setting up his team, shouting instructions, leading celebrations."[16] As one of his teammates remarked, "He's got a personality that's like Muhammad Ali. It's classy, not conceited or anything. He would be running down the floor, and he's telling jokes. He's always smiling, always laughing. Never a frown on his face. Everyone likes a guy like that."[17]

Bird, too, was popular, despite his reticent public persona. A 6-foot 9-inch senior forward, Bird was a superb shooter, rebounder, and passer. He was a two-time All-American, the College Player of the Year, and had been drafted by the Boston Celtics in 1978 but chose to return to school for his senior year.[18] Unlike Johnson, though, Bird had taken a more circuitous route to the NCAA finals. Laconic and lanky, Bird was from a small town, French Lick (population approximately 2,200), in southern Indiana, and an impoverished family. Years later, sportswriter Ralph Wiley noted that Bird was "born and raised hardscrabble, with hardscrabble expectations."[19] After starring at Springs Valley High School, Bird enrolled at Indiana University, where Bobby Knight coached one of the country's premier basketball programs. Bird, however, never played there. "Shy, intimidated off the court, a desultory student still given to bad grammar," sportswriter Frank Deford explained, Bird left Indiana, not due to the mercurial Knight, but because he was "defeated by the size of the place and his confident suburban classmates with their fancy mall wardrobes. He slunk back to French Lick, to a job on a garbage truck and a bitter, failed marriage."[20] Eventually, Bird was recruited by and enrolled at the more modestly sized and less renowned Indiana State. "Four years later," *Newsweek* reported a month before the NCAA finals, "Bird is the hottest property in college basketball."[21] The magazine declared that the twenty-two-year-old Bird "stirs pleasant memories for basketball purists: not only can he shoot and rebound as well as the game's legendary forwards; he is an old-fashioned playmaker who can look one way and hit the open man breaking to the hoop."[22] The same *New York Times* scouting report that lauded Johnson said of his soon-to-be rival: "Surprisingly there are other players comparable to Larry Bird in basic skills. The one ingredient that sets him apart is his remarkable court sense. He utilizes his skills at the right times with an awareness that is unusual for anyone playing so complicated and quick-moving a game."[23] Johnson did likewise.

Clearly, Johnson and Bird were two of the most talented and interesting college players in the country; and just as clearly, contrasts were being drawn between them, some of which were real, some of which were exaggerated. Whereas Johnson was extroverted and enjoyed the spotlight, Bird was introverted and retreated from it.[24] Johnson was urban, flamboyant, a point guard with extraordinary vision and, because of his unprecedented size for his position, fundamentally different than any predecessor; Bird was small-town, self-made, "old-fashioned," a throwback, fundamentally sound, do-it-all forward. While never explicit, these media representations and popular understandings were tinged with not-so-subtle racial politics and coding, subtexts that made it plain that Johnson and Bird were raced subjects, somehow black and white archetypes, despite being spectacularly exceptional. "In 1979," Frank Deford reminisced many years later,

> when Bird at Indiana State (where?) and Johnson at Michigan State met in the NCAA championship, basketball was already accepted as a black game. The old snapshot of the freckle-faced farm boy hurling

set shots at the barnyard hoop had been replaced by ghetto boyz
dunking at the playground. The '70s had produced some white players who were preeminent for a while—[Jerry] West, [John] Havlicek
and [Rick] Barry at their peaks, [Bill] Walton for his whole comet
career—but Bird, from French Lick, Ind. (where?), loomed up out
of nowhere, make-believe, a cross between the Devil's own Shoeless
Joe from Hannibal, Mo., in "Damn Yankees" and Elvis, taking
rhythm-and-blues crossover.[25]

Like some of the aforementioned players, Bird did creatively blend different basketball styles. Yet in reality, Bird and Johnson had a great deal
in common. They were both Midwesterners who did not stray far from
home. They were physically similar, roughly the same size and not
blessed with exceptional physical gifts; neither was particularly strong
nor fast, but both were supremely coordinated, well conditioned, and
had extraordinary vision and basketball intelligence. They both worked
tirelessly on their games. They were both coachable, students of the
game, disciplined. And they both were unselfish and made their teammates better. For all of his fundamental soundness, Bird was also an
exciting, creative player. "You can't take your eyes off him one second,"
said one of his Indiana State teammates, "or he'll hit you in the face with
the ball."[26] Johnson's teammates often said the same thing. For all of his
flashiness, Johnson was also well schooled in the game's fundamentals
and stuck to coach Jud Heathcote's game plans. Perhaps most important,
they were both intensely competitive, driven, with an almost obsessive
desire to win.

At the time of the national championship game, neither the media
nor the principals focused on what they had in common. The preternat-
urally cheerful Johnson was mildly annoyed at the comparisons between
his personality and Bird's.[27] Meanwhile, Bird emphasized the differences
between the two young men. "He is more of a passer, and I'm more of
a scorer," Bird said before the game. "And to me it's a very serious game.
I can't be laughing like he does out there. I just hope when it's over he
ain't laughing at me."[28] A gracious sportsman, Johnson didn't.

In some ways the game was anticlimactic. David did not slay Goliath;
Indiana State never got closer than 6 points in the second half and
Michigan State won, 75–64. Johnson was spectacular; he led his team,
scored 24 points, and was named the tournament's Most Outstanding

Player. He also had more help than Bird did. Greg Kelser, a senior All-American forward (and a future NBA player), was on the receiving end of many of Johnson's passes and played well, offensively and defensively, as did several other less-heralded Spartans. Bird was stifled by Michigan State's tough defense and finished with only 19 points (on 7-of-21 field-goal shooting), well below his career and NCAA tournament averages. "Michigan State grounded The Bird with a touch of Magic and a magnificent zone defense," the *New York Times* explained.[29] "They are an excellent team," Bird acknowledged. "Give them credit, they played very tough defense and they had a real good zone. The ball just wouldn't drop for us and we missed too many free throws."[30] After the game—which earned the highest television ratings ever for a NCAA championship final and was watched by an estimated 40 million people—Johnson and his teammates cut down the nets. Bird sat on the bench, despondent, quietly crying into a towel.[31] Johnson noticed. "While half the arena was screaming with joy," Johnson writes in his autobiography, *My Life* (1992), "Larry Bird was sitting there with his face buried in a towel. He was obviously crying, and my heart went out to him. As happy as I was, I knew that if things had gone just a little differently, *I* would have been the one sitting there with his face in a towel."[32] Respect and empathy would be defining features of their rivalry in the years to come—although at this point neither man could have imagined how their careers would be intertwined.[33]

• • •

Looking back at 1979, American society was undergoing some dramatic and disorientating transitions—political, economic, and cultural—and was on the cusp of a new era, which may help explain why the Bird-Johnson rivalry was meaningful to so many people. "The 1970s was a paradoxical decade that defies easy categorization, for divergent and seemingly contradictory trends unfolded simultaneously," observes historian Paul Boyer. "Self-absorbed narcissism, for example, coexisted alongside relentlessly churning activist energies."[34] Famously dubbed "The Me Decade" by writer Tom Wolfe, by which he meant that millions of Americans seemed increasingly committed to different forms of self-exploration and self-expression, the 1970s has also been described as "the runt of decades," a neglected era sandwiched between the tumultuous 1960s and the conservatism of the 1980s, when President Ronald

Reagan (and others) steered the country and culture to the Right.[35] Despite (or perhaps because of) the country's embarrassing, disastrous defeat in Vietnam and the disillusionment of Watergate, the "resurgence of old American strains began to appear: ideological certitude; patriotism; nationalism; America's God-given mission in the world."[36] At the same time, many of the political issues and cultural concerns that garnered so much attention in the 1960s and fueled various social movements persisted throughout the 1970s and well beyond: civil rights, feminist, gay liberation, and environmental activists continued to challenge the status quo and worked for social justice.

That is, when Bird and Johnson initiated their rivalry the national mood was conflicted and divisive, and it would remain so into the 1980s. Politically, the country was certainly moving to the Right, but just as certainly there was no consensus; everything was contested. Economically, the country was suffering double-digit inflation, coupled with high interest and unemployment rates and a growing federal budget deficit.[37] Culturally, the country was moving in myriad directions simultaneously, as witnessed by "the agonies of busing, the shake of disco, the new power and consciousness of the elderly, the rise of the Sunbelt, and the brie, chardonnay, and BMWs of yuppies."[38] For many people, writes historian Bruce J. Schulman, it was simply "an era of bad clothes, bad hair, and bad music."[39]

It was also an era of bad professional basketball, despite the brilliant play of individuals like Kareem Abdul-Jabbar, Rick Barry, Julius Erving, Walt Frazier, Pete Maravich, Earl Monroe, David Thompson, and others. By all accounts, the pro game was in the midst of a crisis in the mid and late 1970s. After resolving a costly bidding war with the upstart American Basketball Association (ABA) in 1976, the newly expanded NBA (it added four former ABA teams) suffered many problems, including competitive parity and on-court violence. With regard to the former, there were eight different champions in the 1970s, the most in any ten-year period, and no team defended its title; the most glaring example of the latter was when the Los Angeles Lakers' Kermit Washington punched and almost killed the Houston Rockets' Rudy Tomjanovich during a 1977 game.[40] There were other problems, too. "The NBA of the '70s was the enclave of the selfish and the satisfied," sportswriter Jack McCallum contends, "a place where individual talent flourished at the expense of team play. That's the way the average fan saw it, anyway, and there was more than a little truth in that perception."[41] The NBA was also widely perceived by many white middle-class fans and corporate advertisers as "drug-infested, too black, and too regional" and thus suffered financially and was on the verge of contracting.[42] As sport studies scholar David Andrews explains, during the late 1970s the NBA

> was stuck in a quagmire of paltry game attendances, minuscule television audiences, a poor national television contract, torpid licensed merchandising sales, and negligible corporate sponsorships for the league, franchises, and individual players alike. All of the above combined to produce annual league and franchise revenues that barely exceeded expenditures. In sum, the NBA faced its impending demise. At that time, much of the NBA's problems were attributable to the widespread negative perception of the league. The public saw the NBA as a space of racial threat (over 70% of the players were African American) and criminal menace (a moral panic about players' recreational drug use dominated press coverage of the league).[43]

It was, in other words, a propitious time for new, wholesome hardwood heroes, "saviors" who could help generate enthusiasm for the NBA and the game itself.

Their considerable individual athletic skills notwithstanding, Bird and Johnson were extremely fortunate to join the Celtics and Lakers, something over which they had little control.[44] It is hard to imagine that their rivalry would have been as exciting or meaningful had they been on other teams. In fact, one of the things that made the Bird-Johnson rivalry interesting was that it evoked and reignited a rivalry between their franchises, the two most successful in league history. In the late 1940s and early 1950s, the Lakers, then still in Minneapolis and led by center George Mikan, won five NBA championships in six years. Soon thereafter, the Celtics began an unprecedented run of success, winning eleven NBA titles in thirteen years (1957–1969), including eight consecutively (1959–1966).[45] During the 1960s, the Lakers (the team moved to Los Angeles in 1960) had the more impressive individual players—guard Jerry West, forward Elgin Baylor, and center Wilt Chamberlain—but the Celtics had the better teams, largely due to Bill Russell's defensive presence, rebounding, and leadership.[46] "Boston and Los Angeles met in the

NBA finals six times in the 1960s," notes sportswriter Peter May. "The Celtics won them all," although it should be noted that the series went to seven games three times (1962, 1966, and 1969).[47] When Bird and Johnson joined the NBA, the Celtics and Lakers had not faced each other in the finals in ten years, but the bicoastal rivalry had not been completely extinguished. Bird and Johnson would eventually restore it.

• • •

Because Larry Bird and Magic Johnson loom so large in basketball lore, NBA history, American culture, and many memories, it is surprising to note that as professionals they only played against each other thirty-seven times during the twelve years their careers overlapped: more specifically, eighteen regular season and nineteen playoff games.[48] Prior to the much-anticipated 1984 NBA Finals between Boston and Los Angeles, Bird and Johnson had competed against each other a mere seven times (with the Lakers winning four games). Then again, Bird and Johnson accomplished a great deal prior to their first finals showdown.

The season before Larry Bird joined the Celtics, the team won just twenty-nine regular season games, its worst record since 1950 and a far cry from the teams that had won twelve titles between 1957 and 1974. Boston also won the NBA championship in 1976, but had declined dramatically by the time Bird arrived. The Celtics, their fans, and the media (especially in Boston) all expected Bird to have a major impact on the team. Even though he did not have much interest in professional basketball growing up in Indiana,[49] Bird quickly recognized the significance of being a Celtic and took it upon himself to uphold the team's great tradition.[50] As a rookie, Bird started all eighty-two games, led the team in scoring (with 23.8 points per game [ppg]) and rebounding (10.4 per game), and won the league's Rookie of the Year award. Guided by first-year Boston coach Bill Fitch, Bird meshed well with veterans Dave Cowens and Nate "Tiny" Archibald. The team went 61-21 and finished first in the Atlantic Division. At the time, the thirty-two-game swing was the best single-season improvement in league history.[51] After winning a playoff series, the Celtics were beaten by the Philadelphia 76ers in the Eastern Conference Finals.[52] Nevertheless, Bird managed to restore Celtic pride and earned the respect and affection of Boston fans via his hard work, hustle, and unselfishness. His creative passing and clutch shooting helped, too. Rustic and reserved, a self-described "intensely private person," Bird was immediately appealing by virtue of his on-court style, effort, and dedication.[53] There was more to it, though. "In Larry Bird," argues critic Jeffrey Lane, "Boston fans, like white sports buffs nationwide, reveled in the union of two vanishing icons in one sports hero: the blue-collar factory man and the white athlete."[54] And of course there was all of the winning.

By building on the previous season's success, and by trading for veteran center Robert Parish and drafting rookie forward Kevin McHale (both of whom would become Hall of Famers), the Bird-led Celtics went 62-20 and made the NBA Finals in 1981, where they met the Houston Rockets. In game one of the series, in what is now an iconic moment, Bird took a jump shot and, anticipating that it was going to miss, "raced to the right baseline, grabbed the rebound with his right hand, switched the ball into his left hand as his momentum was taking him out of bounds and somehow laid it in the basket. Red Auerbach called it the greatest play he had ever seen, both for Bird's physical ability to make the shot and his basketball instinct to get into position for the rebound."[55] The Celtics won the game and subsequently the series, 4–2.[56] It was the franchise's record-setting fourteenth NBA championship. Bostonians were thrilled. More than 2,500 of them met the team at Logan airport, "bedecked in green and many drowned in beer," reported *Sports Illustrated;* "Bostonians, beleaguered as they are with a severe municipal financial crisis and a corresponding collapse of civic morale, were clearly starved for a winner."[57] Bird did not do it alone, of course; in fact, veteran forward Cedric "Cornbread" Maxwell was named the Most Valuable Player (MVP) of the finals. But Bird was a first team All-NBA selection and the best player on the best team in the league that year.

While Larry Bird was the primary impetus for the Celtics' resurgence, Magic Johnson reinvigorated a veteran Los Angeles Lakers team, albeit one that had made the playoffs the year before. As a twenty-year-old rookie, Johnson came to a team fashioned around 7-foot 2-inch All-Star center Kareem Abdul-Jabbar, who had already won five league MVP awards. The victims of injuries and contract disputes as well as a largely apathetic public, the Lakers needed a boost. The cheerful, ever-smiling Johnson provided it. Lakers forward Jamaal Wilkes explained Johnson's impact in terms of his boundless energy and love for the game: "His enthusiasm was something out of this world, something I had never seen prior to him and something I haven't seen since. It just kind of gave everyone a shot in the arm."[58] In addition to enthusiasm, Johnson brought an unprecedented range of skills to the Lakers, often hitting big shots, starting fast breaks with his rebounding, and making seemingly impossible passes appear mundane. "Never had the league seen quite such a multi-faceted offensive weapon packaged in the body of a single superior player," writes basketball historian Peter C. Bjarkman. "Elgin Baylor and perhaps Oscar Robertson had come close, but the methodical game of their day had not given free reign to their full athletic potential."[59] Along with fellow guard Norm Nixon, Johnson formed one of the best backcourts in the league, opened up the middle for Abdul-Jabbar, and thrilled Lakers fans.

With the benefit of new talent, chemistry, and energy, Los Angeles finished the regular season with a 60-22 record and won the Pacific Division. Like Bird, Johnson had a strong first season, averaging 18 points, 7.3 assists, and 7.7 rebounds per game (rpg).[60] Johnson also put up impressive numbers throughout the playoffs and facilitated Abdul-Jabbar's resurgent play as the Lakers marched to a 3–2 lead over the Philadelphia 76ers in the 1980 NBA Finals. Abdul-Jabbar injured his ankle in game five and was forced to watch the next game from his home in Los Angeles. Most observers thought game six was a foregone conclusion without Abdul-Jabbar. However, playing all five positions at one time or another, the precocious rookie Johnson dazzled the crowd and confounded the 76ers with a truly transcendent performance. The Lakers won the game, 123–107, and the title; Johnson finished with 42 points, 15 rebounds, 7 assists, three steals, and a block. It was not a one-man show, of course; Jamaal Wilkes added a career-high 37 points and several role players had big games on the way to the Lakers' first championship since 1972. After the game, Johnson gushed, "The N.C.A.A. was a great championship, but this is greater." Not forgetting his absent teammate Abdul-Jabbar, he added, talking into the television microphones, "I did it for you. I know your ankle hurts, but I want you to get up and dance."[61] In the other locker room, 76ers guard Doug Collins remarked: "Magic was outstanding. Unreal. I knew he was good, but I never realized he was great."[62] Now everyone knew (well, almost everyone, since CBS showed the game late at night via tape delay rather than live). "I am in total shock," said Lakers team owner Jerry Buss, who bought the team the year before. "I can't believe it. You have just witnessed a miracle, a magical ride by our Magical Man."[63] Not quite miraculous, it was remarkable: both his performance that night and that over four seasons Johnson had won championships in high school, college, and the pros.

The success continued. With essentially the same cast, the multi-talented Lakers won the NBA title in 1982, once again beating the Philadelphia 76ers; Johnson was the NBA Finals MVP for a second time. But because of injuries (Johnson missed forty-five games during the 1980–81 season due to a torn cartilage in his left knee) and the ascendance of the 76ers, who were led by acrobatic forward Julius "Dr. J" Erving and rugged center Moses Malone, Bird and Johnson did not meet in the NBA Finals until 1984.

By then, Ronald Reagan was president of the United States and David Stern was commissioner of the NBA. Both represented important features of the 1980s, but one can hardly imagine different leaders: one was avuncular, embodied conservative, Midwestern values, and made his name in Hollywood; the other was the son of a Jewish New York City deli owner, a creative attorney with a zeal for marketing. Yet both, like Bird and Johnson, projected self-assurance and got things done, in different ways. Of Reagan, historian Garry Wills asked: "Is he bright, shallow, complex, simple, instinctively shrewd, plain dumb? He is all these things and more."[64] Stern, a Columbia Law School graduate and formerly the NBA's general counsel and later its executive vice president, had many of the same traits, minus the pejoratives; no one, not even his harshest critics, ever accused Stern of being shallow, simple, or dumb. Despite this difference, both Reagan and Stern greatly contributed to shifting the substance and the image of the institutions they led. If the 1980s was "a new era of American history—the triumphant conservatism of Reagan, Rambo and retrenchment"—it was also a new era for the NBA: the triumphant excellence of Larry Bird, Magic Johnson, and David Stern, whose leadership, acumen, and entrepreneurial vision contributed to the league's popular, financial, and cultural success.[65]

During the five years before the Celtics and Lakers met in the 1984 NBA Finals, Bird and Johnson were prolific, constantly improving their already impressive skills (and quietly comparing themselves to one another from afar); and in the process they made their teammates and teams better. After his second season, Bird's scoring average steadily improved and he averaged more than 10 rebounds and 5 assists per game (apg). He was also durable: missing only eleven games in his first five seasons. Bird played in all five annual All-Star games and was the game's MVP in 1982. He was also a four-time All-NBA first team selection and was the league MVP runner-up for three straight years (1981–83). Bird was also a terrific team-mate whose creative, unselfish passing created opportunities for others, and whose hustle and work ethic were inspiring. As a result, the Celtics won the Atlantic Division four times during Bird's first five seasons and had a league-best .741 winning percentage. Johnson was similarly superb. He twice the led the league in assists ('83 and '84) and steals ('81 and '82) per game. As a point guard, Johnson scored less than Bird (he averaged 18.5 ppg to Bird's 22.6), but he rebounded extremely well for a guard: 8.4 per game, just slightly less than the 7-foot 2-inch Kareem Abdul-Jabbar's average (8.92) over the same time span. Johnson played against Bird in four All-Star games and was a three-time All-NBA first team selection. Despite some bad publicity in 1981 over his role in the firing of Lakers coach Paul Westhead (who was replaced by Assistant Coach Pat Riley), "he proved himself to be a leader, a great teammate, a player who was admired and loved."[66] The winning helped: the Lakers won the Pacific Division four times during Johnson's first five years and had a .698 winning percentage. Against each other—that is, in the seven games they played before the 1984 NBA Finals—Bird and Johnson performed in ways that were consis-tent with their career averages: Bird outscored (19.7 to 15.1 ppg) and out-rebounded Johnson (9.4 to 8.4 rpg), and Johnson handed out more assists (9.1 to 6.4 apg).[67]

• • •

This brings us to the heart of the Larry Bird–Magic Johnson rivalry: the three NBA Finals between the Celtics and the Lakers during the mid-1980s.

At the conclusion of the 1983–84 regular season, the Celtics and Lakers had the best records in the league. Piloted by first-year coach K. C. Jones, who played for the Celtics during the team's glory years, Boston was also led by Bird, who was twenty-seven-years old and in his prime (after the playoffs, he would win his first NBA MVP award). With

Bird, Robert Parish, and Kevin McHale, the Celtics had what many considered to be the best frontcourt in basketball history.[68] The Celtics also had newly acquired guard Dennis Johnson, a defensive stalwart and clutch shooter with a lot of playoff experience. Coach Pat Riley and Magic Johnson, who had led the league in assists per game, guided Los Angeles. Like the Celtics, the Lakers had several exceptional players, such as the thirty-seven-year-old Kareem Abdul-Jabbar and second-year forward James Worthy, who was the first pick in the 1982 NBA draft, and outstanding role players, like sinewy guard Michael Cooper and hustling forward Kurt Rambis. When the two teams wound their way to the NBA Finals, it was "the first time in 15 years two players who are arguably the best in the game have squared off in a championship series," wrote Bruce Newman of *Sports Illustrated*. "The last great summit meeting occurred in 1969, which was also the last time Boston and L.A. met in a title series, when centers Wilt Chamberlain of the Lakers and Bill Russell of the Celtics renewed their historic rivalry."[69]

However, more so than Chamberlain-Russell, the Bird-Johnson rivalry featured mutual appreciation and respect.[70] As one would expect, before the 1984 series many people assessed, compared, and contrasted Bird and Johnson, including the two rivals themselves. "We both do the same things," Bird said at the outset of the finals, "but we're not the same type player. When you think of the impact we have on a game, with me it's usually scoring, but with him it's always his passing. He's got his hands on the ball more than I do, so he has more control of the situation. You really can't compare us. He's more flashy and can make more things happen than me, make them happen quicker. Magic is just beyond description. I think of him as one of the three top players in the game today, maybe the best. He's a perfect player."[71] Johnson returned the compliment. "He's definitely the best player at this time," Johnson said of Bird. "But it's no personal battle—me against him. We never let it be personal, trying to outdo each other. Because that's going to be hard to do. He's the best, so you've got to bring your best. The boy is bad."[72]

It was a dramatic, hard-fought series with some memorable moments. After losing game 1 in Boston, the Celtics needed a steal and layup by guard Gerald Henderson with fourteen seconds left to send game 2 into overtime, before winning 124–121.[73] Game 4 was played in Los Angeles, with the Lakers up 2–1. In the third quarter, with the Lakers leading by six, Kevin McHale clotheslined the bespectacled Kurt Rambis as he was in midair on a fast-break layup attempt.[74] Both benches emptied but no punches were thrown. The game became increasingly rough, and the Celtics again came from behind to send the contest into overtime, winning this time 129–125, to tie the series at 2-2. The Celtics won game 5 in the stifling heat of the Boston Garden and the Lakers won the next one in L.A., to force a deciding game 7. On June 12, the largest television audience in NBA history saw Boston prevail, 111–102.[75] Bird was named NBA Finals MVP after averaging 27.4 points, 14 rebounds, 3.2 assists, and 2 steals per game.[76] It had been a grueling, emotional series, and the eighth time in as many meetings that the Celtics had beaten the Lakers in the finals. In the Celtics' champagne-drenched locker room, CBS sportscaster Brent Musberger asked Bird, "Does this get you even with Magic for what happened between Michigan State and Indiana State all those years ago?" Bird responded, "I don't worry about that, we're professionals now, but I won this one for Terre Haute."[77] Years later in his autobiography, Bird explained: "The fans had been so great to me when I was at Indiana State and we had come so close to winning that NCAA title for them. Dedicating this NBA title to them was the best I could do to make up for the loss to Michigan State. In their eyes at least, I had finally beaten Magic."[78]

That summer, far from the media glare, Bird and Johnson met again, in French Lick, Indiana, where Bird spent the off-season, to shoot a Converse shoe commercial. It was an important moment in their collegial but to that point not especially friendly relationship; this is understandable, as they had not spent much time together and when they did they were intense competitors on a public stage. As Bird explains in *Drive*, "we really didn't know each other until he came to French Lick to do a Converse commercial with me."[79] Apparently Johnson did not have high expectations for the experience. "Johnson went there thinking he was going to be spending [one of] the longest days of his life," reports sportswriter Leigh Montville. "He wound up loving the time. He and Larry talked. He and Larry talked some more. He and Larry kept talking."[80] Sitting in Bird's living room and four-wheeling around his property, the two men found they had a lot in common and enjoyed each other's company. "It didn't take us long to realize that all of the supposed hostility between us had no real substance," reminisced Johnson in *My*

Life. "It was a creation of the press, and nothing more. It had been going on for five years, but it took us only an hour to see that there was nothing to it."[81] Bird realized that if they "had grown up together or if we were teammates, I think we'd have been best friends. I have always admired the way Magic handles himself. I feel he's the greatest all-around team player in basketball. I have always looked up to him because *he knows how to win.* I've always put him a step ahead of me."[82]

That sense of admiration commingled with competition comes across in the Converse commercial they made. The ad features a limousine (with California "LA 32" license plates, Johnson's jersey number) on a country road (French Lick, Indiana, appears briefly at the bottom of the screen). Bird is alone on an outdoor basketball court when the car pulls up. Through the limo's rear window, Johnson, who is wearing his Lakers uniform, says, with some snap in his voice, "I heard Converse made a pair of Bird shoes [cut to the shoes on Bird's feet] for last year's MVP." The laconic Bird says, "Yup." As Johnson gets out of the car he declares, "Well, they made a pair of Magic shoes [cut to Johnson's shoes] for *this* year's MVP." Standing in front of his adversary, Johnson then rips off his yellow warm-up pants and Bird (wearing a white Converse T-shirt) says, "OK, Magic, show me what you've got," as he tosses him a basketball and the two play one-on-one. Finally, a narrator intones: "The Bird shoe, the Magic shoe. Chose your weapon, from Converse." Obviously, the commercial promotes conventional images of the rivals: it is glamorous Hollywood Magic versus homespun Hoosier Larry Legend. In reality, the process of making the commercial brought the men together and helped forge a meaningful personal relationship. Thereafter, Johnson notes, "Everything was different between us. We were still rivals, of course. But now there was a warmth that made our competition much more fun."[83]

The following NBA season must have been both fun and rewarding for Johnson and Bird. Their teams had exemplary 1984–85 regular seasons: Los Angeles went 62-20 and Boston was 63-19, the best records in their respective conferences. And as usual, Johnson and Bird were terrific, especially Bird, who scored a career-high (to that point) 28.7 ppg to go with his 10.5 rebounds and 6.6 assists per game. Meanwhile, Johnson improved his shooting and continued his brilliant playmaking, averaging 12.6 apg. Both were named to the All-NBA first team and Bird was later awarded the league's MVP for the second consecutive year, making him only the sixth player to win the honor multiple times (the others were Kareem Abdul-Jabbar, Wilt Chamberlain, Moses Malone, Bob Pettit, and Bill Russell).[84]

In May, the Lakers and Celtics cruised through the playoffs and thus squared off again in the NBA Finals, to the delight of their fans and the media, particularly CBS, which broadcasted the games. Much like the year before, it was a hard-fought, physical series. After being crushed in game 1, 148–114 (which was quickly dubbed the "Memorial Day Massacre" because it was played on that holiday), the Lakers rebounded to win two in a row and took a 2–1 series lead, thanks in large part to the inspired play of the thirty-eight-year-old Kareem Abdul-Jabbar. A last-second, game-winning jump shot by Celtics guard Dennis Johnson in game 4 evened the series, 2–2, and thereby negated Johnson's "triple double" of 20 points, 12 assists, and 11 rebounds. Nonetheless, the defending champion Celtics were in trouble. Bird was ailing (he had an injured finger and elbow, which he refused to talk about with the media) and the Lakers simply played a tougher, more resilient brand of basketball than the previous year, responding to the Celtics' physicality with their own.[85] They also had a deeper, more talented bench than the Celtics, and the benefit of playing the critical game 5 at home due to the NBA's new 2-3-2 format.[86] They did not squander the advantage or disappoint their fans, winning game 5, 120–111, behind Johnson's 26 points and 17 assists and Abdul-Jabbar's 36 points. Game 6 was in Boston. The weary Celtics played hard and Kevin McHale (32 points) played well, but Bird struggled, despite scoring 28 points (on only 12-for-29 shooting); the Lakers were relentless, better, and won, 111–100. "Big Game James" Worthy scored 28 points, Johnson accumulated 14 points, 14 assists, and 10 rebounds, and Abdul-Jabbar had 29 points and was unanimously voted the NBA Finals MVP.[87] The victory marked the first time the Lakers had defeated the Celtics in the finals, putting an end to their eight consecutive championship losses to Boston, which dated back to 1959.[88] It was also the first time the Celtics had ever lost a NBA Final on their home court. "When you lose, you're a failure," a disappointed Bird explained. "Your goal is to win a championship, and if you don't win it, you're a failure. Today we played like a bunch of guys who failed."[89] Johnson, on the other hand, was understandably jubilant and felt redeemed after making some costly mistakes in the finals the year before. "Everybody said we couldn't beat them here," Johnson said after the game. "But we outworked them. We beat them to the loose balls, everything we should have done last season."[90] The passage of time did not diminish Johnson's enthusiasm. "What a great series it was!" Johnson gushes in *My Life*. "The level of play was even better than it had been a year earlier, and the atmosphere was much more positive. Maybe it was because Larry and I had finally become friends the previous summer. Or maybe it was because the Lakers had become a more physical team. Whatever the reason, there were no cheap shots and no unnecessary roughness. There was just great basketball."[91] In his autobiography, Bird put the matter plainly: "There was no question we had lost to a better team."[92]

For those interested in the rubber match between Larry Bird's Celtics and Magic Johnson's Lakers, the 1986 NBA Finals were a disappointment: Boston made it, Los Angeles did not. The Celtics gambled that injury-plagued center Bill Walton (who was acquired in September 1985 by trading Cedric Maxwell, a popular player and an important contributor to Boston's championships teams, to the Los Angeles Clippers) would stay healthy enough to make a meaningful contribution playing limited minutes as Robert Parish's backup. He did: Walton played in eighty games, averaged 7.6 points and 6.8 rebounds per game, passed well, played solid defense, and earned the NBA Sixth Man Award.[93] Bird had yet another brilliant all-around season (he led the Celtics in points, rebounds, and assists, and was awarded his third consecutive league MVP trophy).[94] Kevin McHale emerged as a star in his own right (21.3 ppg), and the Celtics won a club-record 67 games against only 15 losses (and had an amazing 40-1 record at home) before tearing through the Eastern Conference playoffs, losing only one game en route to the NBA Finals. The Lakers also had an excellent regular season, going 62-20 and winning the Pacific Division by 22 games. Johnson, like Bird, once again earned All-NBA first team honors. But his season was unexpectedly derailed when the Houston Rockets, led by former Celtics coach Bill Fitch and featuring 7-foot 4-inch Ralph Sampson and 7-foot Hakeem Olajuwon, eliminated the Lakers in the Western Conference Finals. The fifth and final game of the series was decided by a desperation, buzzer-beating, turnaround touch shot by Sampson in Los Angeles that defeated and shocked the defending champions.[95] Another Bird-Johnson showdown would have to wait. In the meantime, the Celtics beat the Rockets in six games to win their sixteenth NBA championship. It was Bird's third title in seven years. Red Auerbach claimed that the 1986 Celtics was "one of the greatest, if not the greatest team I have ever been associated with."[96] Bird left those kinds of assessments to others, and focused on the immediate future: "I got a lot of work to do this summer," he said. "We want to repeat."[97] It was an ambitious goal: no NBA team had defended its title since 1969.

The Celtics' drive to repeat was dealt a terrible blow before the season even began. Just two days after the NBA draft, on June 19, 1986, the team's first-round selection (and the number two pick overall), University of Maryland All-American forward Len Bias, died from a drug overdose. "It's the cruelest thing I've ever heard," said a stunned Bird.[98] It was a tragic loss, and perhaps a bad portent. The aging Celtics struggled all year with injuries (Bill Walton appeared in only 10 games, and late in the season Kevin McHale played on a broken right foot and with torn ankle ligaments) and a weak bench. Still, Boston had the best record in the Eastern Conference, 59-23, largely due to Bird's 28.1 ppg and leadership. Getting to the NBA Finals, however, was a challenge, as the Milwaukee Bucks and the Detroit Pistons both pushed the Celtics to seven games before they prevailed. In game 5 of the Celtics-Pistons series, the ever-alert Bird made perhaps the most famous play of his career. Boston was trailing 107–106 with five seconds left when Bird stole Isiah Thomas's inbounds pass near Detroit's basket and found Dennis Johnson cutting down the lane for a game-winning layup and a 3-2 series lead.[99] The Lakers, meanwhile, rolled to a NBA-best 65-17 regular season record and the twenty-seven-year-old Johnson had the best season of his eight-year career: he scored 23.9 ppg, led the league with 12.2 apg, and was the first guard in twenty-three years to win the NBA's MVP award. The Lakers were talented, experienced, deep (the mid-season acquisition of forward Mychal Thompson enhanced an already talented reserve corps), motivated, and healthy; as a result, they lost just one playoff game before the finals.

In Los Angeles, the favored Lakers quickly ran out to a 2-0 series lead, beating the wounded and worn-out Celtics, 126–113 (Johnson had 29 points, 13 assists, 8 rebounds, and no turnovers; Bird scored 32 points) and 141–122 (Johnson tallied 22 points and 20 assists, while Bird went for 23 points and 10 rebounds). The Celtics, however, did not quit. They won game 3 in Boston, 109–103, behind Bird's 30 points and some inspired defense and rebounding by seldom-used backup center Greg Kite; Johnson finished with 32 points, 11 rebounds, and 9 assists.[100] Game 4 was a thriller. The Celtics had a 16-point lead in the third quarter. But the Lakers fought back and tied the game midway through the fourth quarter. The score went back and forth until the Celtics led 106–105 with seven seconds left, thanks to a 3-point field goal by Bird. On the game's penultimate play, Johnson received a sideline inbounds pass from Michael Cooper, drove left to right and lofted a running hook shot over the outstretched hands of Robert Parish and Kevin McHale. He made it, with two seconds remaining. The Celtics called a timeout and got Bird the ball; his jump shot from the corner missed and the Lakers won 107–106. "I could have shot the jumper," Johnson explained after the game, "but I'm not a jump shooter. If I would have tried it, McHale might have blocked it. When you have a big man on you, it's always a good idea to take the ball to him and that's what I did before I hooked it over him."[101] Johnson later called it "the biggest basket of my life."[102] Stunned to have blown a lead at home and a chance to even the series, Bird admonished his teammates, "If they [the Lakers] want to celebrate, let's not let them do it on the parquet."[103] Because the inspired, prideful Celtics won game 5, 123–108, there was no dancing on the Boston Garden's famous floor and the series returned to Los Angeles. The Celtics led game 6 by 6 points at halftime, but were eventually run off the court. The forty-year-old Kareem Abdul-Jabbar scored a season-high 32 points and had 4 blocks, James Worthy added 22 points, and Johnson had 16 points, 19 assists, and 8 rebounds in the Lakers' 106–93 win. It was Los Angeles' fourth NBA championship in eight years; and Johnson, who averaged 26.2 points, 13 assists, and 8 rebounds, was the NBA Finals MVP for an unprecedented third time.[104] The Celtics were beaten by the Lakers' athleticism, defense, and its team-first, clutch-shooting point guard. Bird was dejected yet impressed, with the Lakers and Johnson. "I guess this is the best team I've ever played against," Bird conceded, still smarting from the loss. "In '85, they were good. In '84, I really thought they should have beaten us. I don't know if this team's better than they were, but I guess they are."[105] When it came to Johnson, Bird was unequivocal: "Magic plays basketball the way you *should* play the game," he said. "He's the greatest all-around team player in basketball."[106]

Bird and Johnson never met again in the NBA Finals (for a variety of reasons, such as Bird's nagging injuries and gradual decline and the rise of the "Bad Boys" Detroit Pistons), and they only played against each other five more times over the next four seasons. So in a sense, although the two men could not have known it at the time, the Larry Bird–Magic Johnson on-court rivalry essentially ended in June 1987 when the Lakers beat the Celtics in the NBA Finals for the second time in three years. Nevertheless, their careers continued, their relationship deepened, and they remained linked in many different and important ways, as athletes, people, and cultural icons.

• • •

Larry Bird's basketball career, like his ailing body, slowly deteriorated, and so did the Celtics. After the 1987–88 season, in which he scored a career-high 29.9 ppg, Bird was never again an All-NBA first team selection. The next year, he only played six games due to ankle and heel injuries that required surgery, and the Detroit Pistons swept the Celtics in the play-offs.[107] During the final three years of his career, Bird played an average of sixty games a season and Boston failed to make the NBA Finals. Magic Johnson and the Lakers, on the other hand, continued to have a great deal of success. Just as Coach Pat Riley had guaranteed in 1987, Los Angeles repeated as NBA champions in 1988, becoming the first team to do so since the 1969 Celtics. The Lakers also reached the NBA Finals in 1989 and 1991, but lost to the Pistons and then to the Michael Jordan–led Chicago Bulls. Unlike Bird, Johnson stayed healthy and played at a high level during the last four years of his career: his scoring average for three of these seasons was better than his career average, his assists per game remained among the league leaders, he was named to four more All-NBA first teams, and he won two consecutive league MVP awards (1989 and 1990). In terms of individual success, Bird may have gotten off to a faster start as a professional, winning three MVP trophies before Johnson had any, but his friend and competitor eventually won three of his own and was able to maintain his level of excellence longer.

Unfortunately, Johnson's basketball career ended abruptly. On November 7, 1991, the thirty-two-year-old Johnson calmly announced at a press conference that he had tested positive for HIV (human immuno-deficiency virus), which causes AIDS (acquired immunodeficiency syndrome), and as a result he was retiring from the NBA.[108] It was sad, shocking news and quickly spread across the country and the world.[109] "Johnson is," reported the *New York Times* on its front page the next day,

> by far the most famous sports figure to be infected by the AIDS virus. In the 1980's his team won five league championships, and his name and face have been used to sell everything from Diet Pepsi to Converse sneakers.
>
> And because his fame spread through all levels of society from schoolyard courts to giant sports arenas, the impact of his announcement is likely to be felt by millions of people whose lives have not been touched by the disease.[110]

For many, Johnson's condition changed the face of the AIDS plague, demonstrating that those afflicted with the disease were not just gay men, intravenous drug users, or sub-Saharan Africans. In addition, Johnson vowed to become a spokesperson in the fight against HIV-AIDS. "Magic Johnson is the most powerful symbol of AIDS that has ever been created," editorialized one news magazine, "a sports hero of uncommon gentleness and grace, [he] is well slotted to address the failures and penetrate the denial of the epidemic."[111] In an article he co-wrote for *Sports Illustrated,* Johnson explained that before his press conference he shared the news with his teammates and "five of my closest friends," which included Larry Bird, who cried.[112] "The whole thing was so incredibly mind-boggling to me," Bird reminisced. "I kept trying to shake this sick feeling I had, but I couldn't. I got to the [Boston] Garden for the game, and everyone wanted to know how I felt and did I talk to Magic? I wouldn't talk to any of them except to say that my heart and prayers were with Magic and his family."[113] Like many people at the time, Bird did not know much about HIV-AIDS and was fearful that Johnson would die soon: "It was so hard to believe that someone that fun, someone that alive, could be so sick."[114]

Three months later, during halftime of the Lakers' game against the Celtics, Johnson had a retirement ceremony at the Los Angeles Forum. It was an emotional evening. One of its highlights was when a banner with Johnson's uniform number was hung in the rafters, joining those of Kareem Abdul-Jabbar, Wilt Chamberlain, Elgin Baylor, and Jerry West, all of whom were in attendance. The *Los Angeles Times* reported that Larry Bird made the cross-country trip "to be with his longtime adversary even though a bad back prevented" him from playing in the game.[115] Among the many gifts Johnson received that night was a piece of the Boston Garden's parquet floor that Bird presented. "It was an honor to have the guy there who'd brought out the best in me," Johnson explained later, "who'd really made me the player I became."[116] Not yet fully resigned to being retired, Johnson apparently said to Bird, "Let's both suit up and run out and play the last five minutes."[117] At the ceremony's conclusion, Johnson reminded everyone of his plans to play for the U.S. national team, the so-called "Dream Team," at the Summer Olympics in Barcelona, Spain, where his career-long rival would be a teammate.[118]

If the Bird-Johnson rivalry was sui generis, so was the 1992 Dream Team.[119] More than just one of most impressive collections of athletic talent ever assembled (in 1996, ten of the twelve men on the team were named among the fifty greatest players in NBA history),[120] the original Dream Team was a transnational cultural phenomenon. It was the subject of intense American and international media and popular attention well before it won the Olympic gold medal, beating teams by an average of almost 44 points along the way.[121] "It was," said the team's coach, Chuck Daly, "like Elvis and the Beatles put together. Traveling with the Dream Team was like traveling with 12 rock stars."[122] And like rock stars, many of the players had groupies, some of whom "stumbled all over each other with felt-tip pens and pocket cameras to touch the heart and hem of Magic Johnson," reported *U.S. News and World Report*. "He is the modern world's figure, the ultimate star of the Olympics: young, rich and HIV positive. Some dreams are confusing, and heartbreaking."[123] Be that as it may, Johnson played well and thus demonstrated that being HIV positive did not affect his athletic ability or the quality of his life. Bird, meanwhile, played in all eight games, but not many minutes, due partly to his chronically bad back; he later said, "Being part of that Olympic team was one of the best times I've ever had."[124]

By this point, Michael Jordan was approaching his prime, as an athlete and global marketing icon. According to sportswriter Jack McCallum, "on the most star-studded team in history, Jordan was, simply, the star stud."[125] Still, Larry Bird and Magic Johnson were named the Dream Team's co-captains. The recently retired Johnson "was impressed that our teammates, who are all leaders on their own teams, were able to defer to us. They gave us their respect, and whenever possible, we gave them the ball."[126] That was generous and judicious, confirmation that Bird and

Johnson were, as ever, team oriented and committed to winning, had high basketball IQs, and, as writer David Halberstam put it, were "still the respected champions, credited by their peers not just for their greatness but for their pioneer roles in bringing the league to a new position of wealth and popularity."[127] In the end, the rivals were teammates, sharing a victory podium.[128] It was "the symbolic denouement of their careers," writes McCallum, who covered the 1992 Olympics for *Sports Illustrated*. "Neither the 35-year-old Celtic nor the 33-year-old Laker was the sublime talent he had once been, but that wasn't the point. Without the dual influence of Bird and Magic, there might not have been a Dream Team. Or, for that matter, an NBA as we know it today."[129] It was and remains a widely held perspective.[130]

Barely off the Olympic medal stand, Johnson and Bird were asked about their basketball-playing futures. Johnson hedged, saying he needed a few weeks to decide whether to un-retire and return to the NBA. Bird needed more time, too, but added that playing in the Olympics was "a great way to end a career."[131] Ten days later, Bird announced his retirement. It was not a surprise, considering his failing health, which was partly the result of "a Pete Rose head-first recklessness that probably cost him a couple of years."[132] Bird's decision deeply affected the Celtics, of course, who languished without him. Predictably, the Boston media spent a great deal of time and energy reflecting on and celebrating Bird's accomplishments and legacy. One local editorial noted: "What makes Bird a legend and not merely a star is the sheer tenacity with which he played the game. For the past four seasons, Bird has been hampered by a series of painful injuries, yet he always somehow managed to pull off one more dazzling trick for the greedy Celtic faithful. Always publicity-shy, he chose to prove himself on the court and maintained a dignified, reticent air off the court."[133]

Many people who were not Celtics partisans also sang Bird's praises. Pat Riley, the former Lakers coach, said: "He was one of a kind, unique. Not just the best of the best, but the only one who ever did what he did. He was a true warrior. I will never forget the Celtics-Lakers battles."[134] Reiterating sentiments that he had expressed many times over the years, Magic Johnson remarked that Bird "was the only player in the league that I feared and he was the smartest player I ever played against. I always enjoyed competing against him because he brought out the best in me.

Even when we weren't going head to head I would follow his game because I always used his play as a measuring stick against mine."[135] Moreover, many commentators noted the role that Bird and Johnson, "the greatest duet the N.B.A. has ever heard," played in reviving the league (a theme to which I will return).[136] *USA Today* writer Mike Dodd put the matter simply: Bird "entered the pros with the Lakers' Magic Johnson in 1979 and together they rejuvenated a sagging NBA."[137] Another sportswriter predicted that Bird and Johnson would "forever be linked, for during their era, attendance soared, TV money ballooned, salaries skyrocketed and basketball once again became a game of five players a side."[138] Frank Deford was particularly effusive, and historically minded, arguing that "Bird has been a consequential figure quite beyond his talents," adding that no one "in football has ever played the role that Bird and Magic Johnson did together in basketball. Babe Ruth assayed it for baseball, while Jackie Robinson and Billie Jean King were society's instruments for American sport. But it's rare. No, certainly professional basketball wouldn't have closed up shop without Bird and Magic appearing as *dei ex machina,* but, yes, they changed history and made a lot of other folks rich."[139] Deford was right, yet the riches that Bird and Johnson generated were not just financial. They came in other forms, too.

Many of them were expressed on Larry Bird Night, which took place on February 4, 1993, in Boston. Rather than sandwich Bird's retirement ceremony between the halves of a regular season game, as the Lakers did with Magic Johnson the year before, the Celtics hosted a stand-alone event to retire Bird's number and hang it in Boston Garden's rafters. It was, writes journalist Peter May, "an elaborate yet tasteful two-and-a-half hour extravaganza that raised more than $1 million for charity."[140] Broadcaster Bob Costas hosted the event, which featured videos, speeches, gifts, a laser show, and several standing ovations.[141] Celtics past and present, former teammates and coaches and a few legends, like John Havlicek and Red Auerbach, honored Bird and regaled him and the crowd of fifteen thousand with testimonials. The highlight of the evening was when Magic Johnson, his "lifelong hardcourt brother," joined Bird on the stage, and the two reflected on their rivalry and the past.[142] "It was tough times in the beginning for both of us, being the competitors that we are," said Johnson, who was wearing a Lakers warm-up suit (with a Celtics T-shirt underneath). "But making that [Converse] commercial, I got a chance to go to Ma Bird's house and we had a chance to have a conversation for the first time. We found out we were much alike. We started a friendship that will last forever."[143] As usual, Johnson was respectful, appreciative, and charming, even when teasing his former rival. "You know what I love the most about you," Johnson said to Bird, "is that most guys talk trash and talk stuff but don't back it up. But Mr. Bird, you know you can back your trash."[144] Bird reciprocated the praise: "Magic is the best player I've seen and played against. Magic came in and won an NBA title his first year and there was pressure on me to win a championship, a lot of pressure, and I don't think I could have achieved that unless there was always somebody looking out to see what I was doing. I knew he was watching me because I was watching him."[145] They exchanged commemorative Olympic rings and "vowed they would be forever linked."[146] Johnson reveled in the moment and did not want it to end; he concluded by saying to Bird, "I love you, respect you and admire you."[147] Less emotive, Bird seemed to feel the same way. "We had a great time," Bird told Johnson. "And it's all over, buddy."[148]

Except that it was not—and is not. If playing together and winning the gold medal at the 1992 Olympics as members of the Dream Team was "the symbolic denouement" of Bird's and Johnson's playing careers, their induction into the Naismith Memorial Basketball Hall of Fame was its formal conclusion. Bird was elected to the Hall of Fame in June 1998 and inducted that October.[149] Because Johnson made a brief comeback with the Lakers in 1996, he was not eligible for the Hall of Fame until 2002, when he was elected and inducted.[150] That Bird and Johnson were elected in their first year of eligibility was unsurprising, as they obviously had magnificent careers. Nor was it surprising that when each man was inducted the other one and their relationship was a subject of public conversation. Reflecting on the ways in which Bird "was, and always will be, the personification of the sport, the one whose game was a microcosm of all the sport has to offer," sportswriter Bob Ryan added, "The only other person who has ever seen what Larry saw and knew deep inside what Larry knew was, of course, Magic Johnson, his great friend and rival."[151] Repeating a familiar refrain, sports columnist Harvey Araton wrote that Bird and Johnson "created a basketball renaissance that began during a college title showdown in Salt Lake City and spread worldwide, like an infectious smile."[152] Of course, it was Johnson, not

Bird, who did most of the smiling; as sports columnist Michael Wilbon once commented: "Bird was Magic without the smile."[153]

The Bird-Johnson references were even more pronounced four years later when Johnson was enshrined. The fact that Johnson chose Bird (rather than Julius Erving, his boyhood idol, or Kareem Abdul-Jabbar, his teammate for nine seasons) to be his presenter had a lot to do with it.[154] At the induction ceremony, Mike Wise reported, Johnson and Bird "told their homespun tales of competitiveness" and talked "about their careers, lives and legacies."[155] Living with HIV, Johnson was especially thankful to have been enshrined in the Hall of Fame, "because," he said, "11 years ago I didn't know whether I'd be here to accept this honor."[156] Johnson said to Bird, the rival whom he used to fear: "Larry, you're just what a basketball player should be. I'm glad I got to know you not only as a player, but as the man that you are."[157] Bird said that his friend and fellow Hall of Famer "played the game like I always wanted to play the game. To be able to control the ball and make plays. That's how I always envisioned a basketball player."[158] For many, seeing the old rivals together, listening to them reminisce about their glory days and pass compliments back and forth like a well-executed give-and-go play, promoted fond memories and contributed to the NBA's preferred narrative of the 1980s as an era of revitalization. That Johnson and Bird became friends, well, that "was an added gift for the NBA," wrote *Los Angeles Times* sportswriter Mark Heisler, "turning the Laker-Celtic rivalry, which was already glamorous and bitter, into one built on mutual respect."[159] The Hall of Fame inductions gave closure to Johnson's and Bird's lengthy, brilliant playing careers. In a sense, though, there is no definitive conclusion to this rivalry; it is ongoing in many memories, the media, and American culture.

•   •   •

When considering or debating a rivalry, someone usually calls the question, Who was better? In this particular case, the Bird-Johnson rivalry, it is not a subject that particularly matters or interests me. It is like asking, Who was better: Ted Williams or Joe DiMaggio? Hemingway or Faulkner? Beethoven or Mozart? Of course, people have opinions, oftentimes well-informed, nuanced, thoughtful opinions. These are obviously irresolvable debates—which can be engaging, revealing, and they remind me of something the painter John Currin once said: "I find it very difficult to argue with esthetic criticism of my work. It's like arguing with a woman who doesn't find you attractive, and you say, 'C'mon! You've *got* to find me attractive!' It's not really a logical process. You love certain things because you love them—the way you love your kids or something."[160] With sports rivalries, however, there is usually a statistical record to make comparisons and contrasts. If the competitors are from different historical eras, these comparisons and contrasts usually do not make much sense. Rules and playing conditions change, so comparing, say, John Unitas's career statistics to Peyton Manning's is not especially meaningful. That said, as contemporaries, Larry Bird and Magic Johnson did accumulate statistical records that can be justifiably compared, contrasted, and assessed. So perhaps it is worth looking at that record, if only briefly.

The numbers are impressive, but not conclusive (see chart 1 below). Both men played in the NBA for thirteen years, twelve of them overlapping. (Bird played one season after Johnson retired, but in 1996 Johnson made an abbreviated comeback, for thirty-two regular season and four playoff games.) They played in roughly the same number of regular season games; Johnson played in more playoff games. Bird was the more prolific scorer and rebounder; Johnson handed out more assists.[161] Their teams won a lot of regular season games and in every year of the 1980s either the Celtics or the Lakers played for the NBA title, but Johnson's teams won more championships and beat the Celtics more often than they lost. So who was better? "I once believed that he [Bird] was, at the very least, the outstanding player of his generation," Jack McCallum avers, "but I now give that nod to Magic, Bird's old sparring mate who also entered the NBA in 1979. You can line up their statistics, side by side, and stare at them all night, but the fact remains that Johnson, who led the Lakers into the 1991 Finals, was a great player over a longer period of time than was Bird, whose career began to be measured in medical reports rather than scouting reports as early as 1988."[162] Longevity has its place, to be sure. Sometimes, however, brilliance is short lived: think James Dean, Sandy Koufax, and Jimi Hendrix. Harvey Araton agrees with McCallum, but for different reasons: "The annals of the sport don't lie. Magic won five NBA titles to Bird's three. Counting the NCAA final, Magic beat Bird three of four in championship showdowns. For fans black and white, Magic made basketball matter in a way it never had before. He was a revolutionary player, a six-nine point guard who embodied the game at its multitasking best, who could simultaneously please with individual panache but always within the context of the team."[163] Bird, too, played "with individual panache" and "within the context of the team." As for the number of championships, this demonstrates that most of Johnson's *teams* were superior to Bird's. So who was better? They both were selected among the fifty greatest players in NBA history, were Olympic gold medalists, and were elected to Basketball Hall of Fame in their first year of eligibility. So who won the rivalry? The NBA and basketball fans everywhere.

Writers won, too, for Bird, Johnson, and their rivalry were and remain rich subjects.[164] Many writers, ranging from journalist David Halberstam to novelist John Edgar Wideman to critic Chuck Klosterman, have reflected on the Bird-Johnson rivalry, thought about what made it special and what it meant and means.[165] There are obviously differences of opinion about what these men (as athletes and cultural icons) and their relationship signify. At the same time, when the articles, essays, and books about these subjects are read collectively, themes emerge.

From the beginning, the media—that is, primarily journalists and broadcasters, but also advertisers—tended to accentuate the differences between Bird and Johnson; more often than not, they drew contrasts rather than comparisons, based primarily on race and temperament. More uncommon—and interesting, at least to me—were those few who were able to see beyond the obvious (and in many ways superficial) differences between the two men. Sportswriter Leigh Montville, for instance, notes that Bird and Johnson "had the same Midwestern ideals. They had the same work habits, the same senses of humor, the same competitive fires. The same talent. That was most important of all. They had the same talent, one step above everyone else who played their game, two men linked first by the talent and then by everything else."[166] In *Hoop Roots: Basketball, Race, and Love* (2001), John Edgar Wideman, a former Penn basketball player and Rhodes Scholar, goes hard at the conventional ways in which Bird and Johnson were represented and used by the media. "It's no coincidence that pro hoop's explosive rise to popularity coincided with the emergence of a Great White Hope in the person of Larry Bird and his old-school Boston Celtics to do battle with Magic Johnson's Los Angeles Lakers, West Coast wise-guy kings of shake-and-bake," Wideman muses:

Chart 1: Comparison of Larry Bird and Magic Johnson

	LARRY BIRD	MAGIC JOHNSON
Years	13 (1979–92)	13 (1979–91, '96)
Regular season games	897	906
Points	21,791	17,707
Points per game	24.3	19.5
Field goal percentage	.496	.520
Three-point field goal percentage	.376	.303
Free throw percentage	.886 (10th all-time)	.848
Rebounds	8,974	6,559
Rebounds per game	10	7.2
Assists	5,695	10,141 (3rd all-time)
Assists per game	6.3	11.2 (1st all-time)
Steals	1,556	1,724
Blocks	755	374
NBA MVP awards	1984, '85, '86	1987, '89, '90
Times All-NBA first team selection	9 (1980–88)	9 (1983–91)
Playoff games	164	190
NBA championships	1981, '84, '86	1980, '82, '85,' 87, '88
NBA Finals	1981,' 84, '85, '86, '87	1980, '82, '83, '84, '85, '87, '88, '89, '91
NBA Finals MVP awards	1984, '86	1980, '82, '87
Wins against each others' teams	15	22
Playoff wins against each others' teams	8	11

Source: NBA.com and *Sports Illustrated,* December 14, 1992.

Never mind that Magic's grin and Bird's tight-lipped Yankee sto-
icism were both masks disguising many identical features. Never
mind that both were products of endless hard work, ruthless determination, love of the game, supreme court intelligence and vision,
the willpower to jujitsu certain not very extraordinary physical
endowments into strengths. Never mind that both men constantly
learned from each other, appropriating the other's skills and tricks,
flattering each other by sincere imitation.[167]

Wideman understands better than most (or maybe he is just willing to say
it) that when it came to Johnson and Bird "what played in the media was
the masks. Showtime versus lunch-pail ethic. Pleasure versus duty. Helter-
skelter versus planning. Athletic ability versus intelligence. Nature versus
nurture. Ego versus teamwork. Grin versus scowl."[168] Perhaps this is a cultural predilection, but it seems like a choice. It did not have to be this way.
Thus Wideman argues, "The media could have examined how Magic and
Bird created each other, how they are inseparable, an amalgamation, how
together they achieved something more, probably better than either could
have managed alone. Unfortunately, such a treatment doesn't sell sneakers
or cars or beer."[169] Put differently, rivalries sell, they move products (indeed,
they are themselves a kind of commodity), and rivalries are predicated on
difference, contrast.

This sense that Bird and Johnson were and are inseparable or indelibly
connected is another common theme that emerges in discussions of their
rivalry; certainly the former adversaries themselves often stress this idea.
For many, it is almost as if Larry-Bird-and-Magic-Johnson is one word.
"The two men are now inextricably linked," wrote David Halberstam, the
Pulitzer prize–winning journalist, after the 1987 NBA Finals, stressing their
similarities and dominance. "They played against each other in the NCAA
championship game of 1979, the year they both came into the league.
Each has improved his game significantly every season since. Each has the
rare gift of the truly great basketball player—the ability to make other
players better—and each has played a crucial role in making his team a
perennial contender."[170] There is no doubt that their careers ran on para-
llel, sometimes intersecting tracks. Yet even though Halberstam noted
their commonalities, he also stressed the contrast between Bird and
Johnson, in this case melding their racial and personality differences:

when Bird and Johnson entered the league as rookies, it was Magic
who had an instinct—a virtual homing device—for the media, particularly television, and Bird who was warier and more suspicious
and who rejected the media's glare. Johnson was about basketball
and the media; Bird was about basketball. He largely regarded the
media as an unwanted intrusion. That was a reversal of the normal
racial order, in which white journalists are far more comfortable
with white players than with black players, and white players are
more comfortable with (or less suspicious of) the white media than
are blacks. From the start, Magic seemed to love the hype, which
came principally from network television. CBS, desperate to create
rivalries in a league savaged by expansion, seized on both him and
Bird from the very beginning. After a dozen years in which black
athletes had seemed alternately resentful and political, after endless
dour interviews with Kareem, here was a charming, ebullient
young black athlete who seemed to like the game, like the camera
and even like white people. One's first sight of Magic Johnson was
of a pleasant young man with television journalists fawning all over
him. The remaining impression of him from those early years is
that he seemed to be teamed in the backcourt not so much with
Norm Nixon as with Brent Musburger.[171]

It is this version of Johnson—extroverted, ever-smiling, likable, telegenic
—that critic Todd Boyd is referring to when he describes him as "acceptable, nonthreatening," essentially Bill Cosby–esque.[172] Here we see one
athlete constructed as a self-conscious cultural performer and self-
promoter and the other preferring to be merely an athlete, a camera-
shy one at that. In addition, Halberstam seems to use the discourse of
race to explain this phenomenon. He was not alone.

Again, from the outset, race was part of the Johnson-Bird rivalry,
sometimes explicitly (more than one journalist described the ballplayers
as "Ebony and Ivory"), sometimes subtly. For many commentators and
fans, race was and is one of the primary ways of making sense of this
rivalry.[173] "The black versus white element of the [Celtics-Lakers] rivalry
in the '80s was just as important as anything geographical or basketball-
related. That's what made a sports event transcend athletics and enter
into America's social structure," argues ESPN sports columnist Scoop
Jackson. "Race—built on the Bird/Magic non-basketball dynamic—was

the core reason we all were galvanized and fascinated."[174] This important theme needs to be addressed cautiously, for the subject of race and basketball is a "minefield" strewn with stereotypes.[175] Moreover, to suggest that the rivalry was *primarily* racial, featuring Bird the hard-working Great White Hope and Johnson the flashy showman with the "magnetic smile," may be to fall prey to what critic Carlo Rotella describes as the "race, race, race" fallacy.[176] According to Rotella, "race, race, race" is a too limited way of conceptualizing some subjects and "often proves to be a graveyard of analytical thinking. Americans in general and commentators on culture in particular have grown overused to assuming that when you have reduced a subject to 'race, race, race' your work is done and there is no need to devote further thought to the matter—a bad habit that prevents an argument from even attempting to do justice to its subject's full complexity."[177] In other words, it is appropriate to consider the racial politics of the Bird-Johnson rivalry, yet we need to be mindful that "as an analytical tool, 'race, race, race' is a stepping stone, a midpoint and not an endpoint."[178] To further complicate matters, racial meanings are not fixed or stable, rather they are constantly being contested and reconfigured.

During the 1980s, when racial tensions intensified, the Reagan-led "federal government reversed itself and switched sides on racial policy," and some white people (particularly many working-class men) felt frustrated by increased American deindustrialization and what they perceived to be the unfair advantages of affirmative action, the Bird-Johnson rivalry took on racial symbolism.[179] "Magic and Bird's significance," asserts Todd Boyd, "to the game and the culture at large is tied to the way that their presence on the scene could be read as symbolic of the racial and cultural difficulties still circulating through America, especially in the conservative heyday of the Reagan '80s."[180] Johnson and Bird did not intentionally promote this symbolism. To one another, they were basketball players, and later friends.[181] Bird, in particular, as a white superstar in a league dominated by African Americans, carried the unwanted burden of racial symbolism. Described as "torch carrier for his race," Bird was, writes Harvey Araton, "hailed as white players too often were—scrappier and smarter, the hardest worker. In a sport where athleticism was myopically defined by one's end-to-end speed and vertical leap, Bird's physical assets—his soft hands, amazing peripheral vision, and ambidexterity—were routinely underplayed."[182] Of course, Magic Johnson had basically the same skill set (minus the outside sharpshooting) and was far from one of the league's fastest or highest jumping players. "To be as slow and earthbound as Bird in this age of elevation," writes Nelson George in *Elevating the Game: Black Men and Basketball* (1992), "then to dominate African-American skywalkers for a decade testifies to his greatness. It's not Bird's fault that he was pale by birth and that a sporting press, desperate for white sporting hopes, heaped more praise on him than Isiah Thomas or Karl Malone or Charles Barkley."[183] Nor was it his fault that some bigoted white fans and members of the media endowed him with racial symbolism; as Jeffrey Lane puts it, "Bird neither asked for nor embraced the part of white savior."[184] Not that it mattered much. It was ascribed to him and so he lived with it. But it helped that Johnson often defused the rivalry's racial politics. When asked why some African Americans did not properly respect Bird, a disappointed Johnson replied: "It's sad, really sad. You don't see the players doing that. Anybody who had to play against him would have better sense than to say that. It's sad that race blinds people to the point that they can't see what they're supposed to see. Ain't nobody like Larry Bird and you can believe what I'm telling you."[185] Johnson saw Bird clearly, and vice versa, of course. On another occasion, though, Johnson explained that sometimes his vision of Bird was colored by their similarities: "It's hard to look at a white man and see black, but when I looked at Larry, that's what I saw. I saw myself."[186] Then again, Johnson's vision was special.

If it is difficult to ignore how race informed and continues to influence understandings (and representations) of Bird and Johnson, it is impossible to avoid the question, Did they and their rivalry save or remake the NBA? Apparently, most people think the answer is yes. Examples abound. "The NBA was stalled in 1979," asserts journalist Tom Callahan, "before Johnson and Bird got to Los Angeles and Boston. The finest players always lift the skills of their teammates, but these two raised the entire sport with the intelligence of their play and the sincerity of their pleasure."[187] As early as 1984, claims Peter May, "Bird and Magic Johnson were already ensconced as the game's dual saviors. History will always remember the 1980s as the Bird/Magic Era."[188] History, which is a kind of discourse, does not really remember anything; rather, people do, and the people who write history are generally historians. So it is noteworthy that sport historian Peter Bjarkman contends: "The mano-a-mano duels of Magic and Larry Bird revitalized a wandering sport and brought it straight into the television age."[189] "If Magic Johnson and Larry Bird did not save the NBA," Jack McCallum notes, "they most certainly performed CPR on it."[190] Raising, revitalizing, saving, call it what you will. These judgments, and many others like them, constitute the conventional wisdom, namely, that Bird and Johnson had a causal effect on the NBA's renaissance during the 1980s. Yet conventional wisdom is not always wise or nuanced. Yes, Bird and Johnson, by dint of their on-court excellence and (media-hyped) rivalry, greatly contributed to the NBA's reinvigoration, its revival. But these claims are more often repeated than convincingly demonstrated. Part of the explanation for this can be traced to the *post hoc, prompter hoc* fallacy, that is, "the mistaken idea that if event *B* happened after event *A*, it happened because of event *A*."[191] In this context, event *B* is the NBA's resurgence and event *A* is Bird and Johnson entering the league and being tremendously successful. The problem with this explanation is that it ignores other important factors that contributed to the league's metamorphosis during the 1980s, such as the hiring of an aggressive, visionary commissioner, new policies and marketing strategies, and burgeoning cable networks like TBS and ESPN.

"Over the years, it has become axiomatic to say that the NBA renaissance began the minute Magic and Bird arrived in the fall of 1979," observes Harvey Araton in *Crashing the Borders: How Basketball Won the World and Lost Its Soul at Home* (2005). "That was not the case, far from it. While the fan bases quickly revved up in Boston and Los Angeles, while the media quickly seized on the racial subtext of the charismatic black man orchestrating Showtime in Hollywood against the taciturn white man invigorating blue-collar Boston, the NBA as a national entity still lagged far behind the popularity of baseball and football."[192] With time and hard work that would change, and pro basketball would become more prominent and profitable as well as culturally important in the United States and globally. Seemingly indefatigable, David Stern, who was hired as NBA commissioner in 1984, did much of that work. Without question, the self-effacing Stern had a positive impact on the league's ascent during the 1980s and 1990s. Creative and proactive, Stern is "arguably the most influential figure in the process of popularizing the NBA," David Andrews contends. "Stern adopted a revolutionary approach to professional sport management, which while proving abhorrent to many Corinthian traditionalists, subsequently became the blueprint for profit-oriented sport organizations throughout the world."[193] It is a blueprint that includes tough, smart labor negotiations (which over the years included instituting a salary cap, revenue sharing with the players, and an improved drug policy), the skillful promotion of specific players into celebrities, aggressive global expansion (both in terms of recruiting athletes and opening markets), and, more recently, the innovative use of the Internet and digital technology to promote the league.

Of course, before the Internet, there was television. And before cable television became a cultural force, the Stern-led NBA partnered with CBS and then NBC to market Larry Bird, Magic Johnson, and their rivalry. It was a reciprocal relationship, mutually beneficial, which is why Peter Bjarkman claims that "no small part of the rivalry would be due to the magic of television itself."[194] Thanks to network and later cable TV, especially highlight-centric ESPN, the NBA in the 1980s achieved "unimagined prominence," asserts journalist Mark Starr. "The NBA was a league that had seen its finals booted from prime time and relegated to late-night tape delay. But the league was changing and TV embraced its speed, soaring elegance and urban edge—kind of a precursor to 'Miami Vice'—as well as its holy trinity of Magic, Larry and Michael. It turned pro basketball into the hippest game in town and the NBA into a burgeoning commercial empire."[195] The lucrative deals between the NBA and its television partners testify to this.[196] Via television's broadcasts and repeatedly aired commercials, fans across the country and the world came to know, appreciate, care about, and, in some cases, even love Bird and Johnson; some established "parasocial relationships" with them and many basked in their reflected glory.[197] In the process, the two men became meaningful, something more than basketball players: they became cultural icons. Nevertheless, the point is that while Larry Bird and Magic Johnson certainly *contributed* to the league's revitalization and popular and economic growth, they did not and could not rescue or remake the NBA by themselves. To their credit, Bird and Johnson never suggested that they did.[198]

Even so, popular perception sometimes becomes a kind of reality. People often believe what they need to believe and ascribe complicated processes to the deeds of heroic individuals—or in this case, to a dynamic duo. "Larry and Magic revived the NBA with their talent, their court sense, their commitment and, most of all, with their personal competition," reflects Jackie MacMullan. "Their triumphs and their travails, their epic battles for championship crowns, read like a novel you could not put down."[199] The rivalry was a gripping narrative, with unexpected twists and turns, subplots and supporting characters, all of which were enriched if one knew its history and read it closely. For many sports fans and commentators, there was indeed something sublime about the Bird-Johnson rivalry, something transcendent about it. It was about the "selfless and stylish" way they played basketball, to be sure, yet it also had to do with their respect for the game and each other, their sense of sportsmanship, their work ethics and acute desire to win, but not at any cost.[200] "The honest admiration Magic and Bird expressed for each other gave their competition all the trappings of fable," reflect sportswriter Robert Lipsyte and historian Peter Levine.[201] And like many fables, this one resonates because it touches something deep and enduring in American culture.

•   •   •

As fate would have it, in early June 2008, as many people had hoped, Los Angeles and Boston did meet in the NBA Finals. It was a matchup that reactivated many memories. In addition, because it was the first time the two teams played against each other for a championship since Magic Johnson's Lakers beat Larry Bird's Celtics in 1987, the pairing led to comparisons and contrasts between the past and the present. For example, ESPN.com ranked the top ten moments in Celtics-Lakers postseason history, five of which were from the 1980s.[202] By way of creating context for the 2008 NBA Finals, *USA Today* explained: "A trilogy of Celtics-Lakers battles in the '80s reinvigorated not only the Boston–Los Angeles rivalry but the league. At the forefront were Earvin 'Magic' Johnson and [Larry] Bird."[203] The *Boston Globe* reminded its older readers and informed its younger ones that the rivalry between the teams "evolved in the 1980s into a culture clash, with Larry Bird's Celtics epitomizing the lunchpail [sic] ethos of Boston's longshoremen and Magic Johnson's Lakers channeling Hollywood's celluloid heroes as they created a flashy, fast-paced, often-breathtaking rendition of the game famously known as Showtime."[204] *Sports Illustrated* featured Larry Bird and Magic Johnson on its cover, with the headline: "The Greatest Rivalry Returns." A week later, Jack McCallum quipped that the current finals have "conjured up more 1980s history than a documentary on Ronald Reagan."[205] As one would expect, Bird and Johnson were back in the limelight and held a press conference to talk about the past and to promote the games. Eventually, both men agreed that the focus should be on the active players, not the retired ones. "It's not really about Larry and I now," said Johnson. "It's about what we, of course, have built over the years, but now this is their stage."[206] Before Bird and Johnson left it, they made one more commercial together. It was part of the NBA's "There Can Only Be One" promotional campaign, which featured split screens of two contemporary players from rival teams, up close and looking directly into the camera, reciting the same script about things like believing in one's self, respect, fear, hard work, and the dream of winning a championship. Directed by filmmakers Jonathan Dayton and Valerie Faris, the ads were customized to correspond with the teams playing against each other in the playoffs.[207] So, when the Lakers and the Celtics reached the NBA Finals, it made historical, cultural, and business sense for Magic Johnson and Larry Bird to appear on screen together, in their old jerseys, and to say in unison:

> Rivalries are born, but they never die.
>
> Rivalries live on.
>
> The names and the stories may change.
>
> But the feeling remains.
>
> What matters so much then, matters now.
>
> Rivalries never die.[208]

It is an effective ad, even if some rivalries are, in fact, ephemeral. A time will come when the Larry Bird–Magic Johnson rivalry will be as remote as those of Bill Russell–Wilt Chamberlain and Jack Dempsey–Gene Tunney and others that are now forgotten. For the time being, though, almost twenty years after Bird and Johnson last played against each other, this rivalry lives on, in the media, memories, and imaginations.

Martina Navratilova (*left*) and Chris Evert hug following Navratilova's victory in the women's 1978 singles final at Wimbledon. *Courtesy of Getty Images.*

— five

Friendly Rivals

Martina Navratilova and Chris Evert

I'll miss playing Martina. My biggest thrills came in beating her.
Yet when I lost to Martina, I was disappointed but never devas-
tated. If I couldn't win the tournament, I wanted her to win it. I
could feel the rivalry emanating not only from us but from the
crowds around the world as well. The excitement and the tension
were everywhere.

—Chris Evert

There will never be another Chris and Martina show. There never
was another like it and there never will be another.

—Martina Navratilova

Theirs was an amazing rivalry. It stands out first because each was so talented. Less than two years apart in age, each dominated women's tennis
for a time. Chris Evert occupied the top spot at the beginning of their
careers and Martina Navratilova at the end, but one never knew who
might win one of their fiercely contested matches. They faced one another
across the net an amazing eighty times over the course of sixteen years, a
lengthy, grueling, direct competition between top stars that may be
unmatched in individual sports. Yet the rivalry never grew old because
each of them changed over time. Their competition was fascinating in
part because of their contrasts—both in terms of style of play and personality. Indeed, as the quote from Martina suggests, they had reached the
level of fame in which they were recognized by just their first names, and

they were quite aware that the world watched their "show" closely. Spectators found their rivalry compelling, probably because the media magnified their differences and because their lives dramatized important wider social and political issues being discussed in the 1970s and 1980s. Finally, as Chris Evert's quote suggests, their rivalry was also special because of their relationship with one another. While at times it proved difficult, in general, their intense, long-lasting, respectful competition proved quite beneficial for them, their sport, and for society.

Chris and Martina were in the public eye from the time they were teenagers. The world watched them grow up and witnessed their many growing pains along the way. In the beginning they were scared, lonely, and socially awkward adolescents, precociously talented but ill-equipped to answer serious questions the press asked about tennis, careers, gender, competition, and politics. Their early experiences in love and subsequent breakups made headlines, as did changes in their appearances. But over the years both matured and eventually found themselves, growing confident about their success, ambition, and competitive nature; comfortable in their strength and beauty; and more certain about their values, political views, and the balance between their public and private lives.

At the very same time, American society was also experiencing growing pains. In particular, protests for equality and freedom, starting with the black civil rights movement, had shaken the status quo. Feminists pushed for greater opportunities for women, including the right to work outside the home, earn equal pay, and expand gender roles. Women wanted freedom to choose their destiny, fulfill their potential, and strengthen their minds and bodies. Gay rights activists began asking for an end to discrimination and the acceptance of consensual same-sex relationships. Although the Cold War raged on, young Americans questioned the need to fight a war against Communism in Vietnam, and some nations in the Communist bloc, like Czechoslovakia, angled for more freedom within the Soviet system. Many arenas of life were politicized, including sports, as seen in Olympic protests and tense opposition to Title IX. At the same time, television made the drama of sports more popular than ever.

Tennis was in the midst of its own upheaval in the late 1960s and early 1970s. After decades of being a country club game reserved for amateurs, in 1968 tennis authorities finally gave in to pressure and changed the rules to allow prize money and welcome professionals into all the old, esteemed tournaments. That opened the gates to many new tournaments as well. "Open tennis" was a revolution, but one that primarily benefited men. The vast majority of the purse at each tournament was reserved for male players, and the ratio was getting worse instead of better. Angered by the injustice, Billie Jean King and some other women insisted on a larger share. When their requests were met with laughter and scorn, they organized an independent tour for women in 1970. Tennis authorities suspended them a number of times. They persisted, though, and playfully alluded to women's lib(eration) by calling their tour, sponsored by Virginia Slims, "Women's Lob." For the next couple years, these players worked hard and creatively to win audiences —personally handing out tickets, holding placards on the road, dressing in short, wild dresses, visiting with spectators in the stands and attending cocktail parties with corporate sponsors—and they successfully proved that women players could attract an audience independent of men. The Virginia Slims tour did better each year, organizing more tournaments and dramatically increasing the prize money available. For a brief period, two women's tennis tours existed, as the United States Lawn Tennis Association (USLTA) tried to put the militants out of business. Eventually, the two compromised and merged, and by 1973, it was looking very likely that female stars would be able to have careers as professional tennis players.[1]

Chris Evert appeared on the scene just in time to take advantage of the new opportunities available. Born in 1954, she started playing as a small child under the tutelage of her father, who was the teaching pro at a large municipal tennis facility in Fort Lauderdale, Florida. Evert was raised in a fairly conservative middle-class Catholic family, typical in just about every way except for the amount of tennis she played. A reserved child, she lacked confidence and occasionally resented having to give up other activities for tennis, but eventually tennis became a way to express herself. She became well known for a precise, consistent, two-handed backhand, which she developed as a youngster since the racket was too heavy. This stroke was unique, but everything else about her form was perfect—her footwork, her racket preparation, and her strokes. Her father taught her to play consistently well from the baseline. "Be patient, be steady, let your opponent make the error. The player who makes the least amount of errors will eventually win the match."[2] This appeared to be a fairly defensive style of tennis, but, in fact, Evert was a master at maneuvering her opponents from side to side, changing the pace of volleys, working the angles, and preventing her opponent from controlling the point. It worked for her in part because of her amazing concentration, discipline, and perfectionism. "From the time I was six years old," she recalled, "my father drilled in me the importance of being controlled on the court."[3] This control extended beyond the style of her game to her behavior. She was taught never to show any emotion—whether it was disappointment at a point lost or anger at a bad call—since that might give hope to an opponent. This imperviousness intimidated other players, one of whom said it was "like playing against a blank wall."[4] She rose through the junior ranks of American tennis, winning the national fourteen-and-under singles title in 1968.

Evert quickly took the adult women's tennis world by storm. At age fifteen, she stunned French star Francoise Durr and the world's top-ranked player, Margaret Court, making it to the semifinals of a small tournament in Charlotte, North Carolina. She earned invitations to the American Wightman Cup team and the 1971 U.S. Open, where she also made it to the semifinals. As a sixteen-year-old, she won the U.S. Clay Court Championship and made it to the semifinals of both Wimbledon and the U.S. Open. The next year she earned the number two ranking in the world, and in 1974 she won sixteen of the twenty-three tournaments she entered, including the French Open, Italian Open, U.S. Clay Court Championship, and Wimbledon. By 1975, she'd become the number one player in the world after winning 35 straight matches and 94 of the 100 she played. She finished each subsequent year with the number one ranking until 1979. Virtually unstoppable on clay courts, she won 125 matches in a row on that surface. Although others were surprised by the success of the pony-tailed youngster, Chris took it in stride. "It seemed quite natural for me to be number 1 in the world because I'd always been number 1 in the juniors," she reported in an autobiography.[5] She expected to win, craved winning, and suffered greatly in the wake of her rare defeats.

In the beginning, though, Evert didn't quite fit in with the other players. She was shy and chaperoned by her mother, and while the adults on the tour were worrying about making a living, she played for her father's approval and worried about getting her first menstrual period. The older pros were threatened by her obvious talent and the possible embarrassment of an amateur defeating them. (She finished high school a semester early so she could turn professional on her eighteenth birthday.) And because her father decided that she should participate in the USLTA-sponsored tour instead of the Virginia Slims tour, some players viewed her as a union-busting "scab." Traveling, eating, worrying, celebrating, and building a profession together, the women on the tour made up a fairly close community. Chris, on the other hand, felt she was "an outsider, adored by spectators . . . but unwelcome in the sorority." In fact, she asserted, "Beating me became a community project."[6] But Billie Jean King convinced the other players that as a future mainstay of the tour, Chris should be welcomed. Over time Evert developed more friendships and eventually was elected by her peers as president of the Women's Tennis Association many times, but it was primarily on the court that Evert made her mark. In the mid-1970s, she was winning about 94 percent of her matches.

Spectators embraced Evert from the moment she entered the national stage, cheering her enthusiastically. Part of her appeal in the beginning was undoubtedly her youth; she was an unknown schoolgirl and an underdog, defeating older, more established international stars. Evert looked the part of a little girl, wearing cute dresses, jewelry, makeup, and ribbons in her ponytail that matched the trim of the dress. The press gave her nicknames that noted her girl-next-door appearance, such as Little Miss America, Miss Apple Pie, Cinderella in Sneakers, and America's Sweetheart.[7] In stark contrast to how they wrote about male athletes, sportswriters paid an enormous amount of attention to how Evert looked. After describing her fingernails, earrings, necklace, hair, tan, eyelashes, and how prettily she perched on a folding chair, Dave Anderson of the *New York Times* concluded, "Some queens don't look as good on a throne." He asserted that part of her appeal was "that she always looks like a female."[8] "Chrissie" (the diminutive form of Christine that Evert used in her youth) became a household name. "Men liked to watch her; women liked to watch her; girls wanted to be like her," observed tennis analyst Mary Carillo. She became a role model. "She was the definition of girlhood," recalled sportswriter Sally Jenkins, who grew up rooting for her. "She's what you wanted to act like and what

you wanted to look like. You wanted to wear her eye shadow. You studied her earrings." [9]

Evert's popularity came with great rewards. She became a celebrity
whose life, love interests, and style graced magazines like *People* and
more than just the sports section of newspapers. She wrote two autobiographies by the time she was thirty-two years old. While at times it
was difficult for her life (especially her love life) to be scrutinized, all the
attention led to financial benefits. In the early 1980s, on top of the annual
average of $500,000 in tournament prize money, she earned another
$500,000 from exhibition matches and special events and another $2 million in endorsements from corporate sponsors, including Wilson rack-
ets, Ellesse clothes, Converse shoes, Lipton tea, Cirrus Banking, Rolex
watches, and British Airways.[10]

But as Evert won more and more matches, a bit of the shine wore off.
A few reporters began portraying her less flatteringly as "Cool Chris" and
"The Ice Maiden." Evert won, as one writer said, "precisely because she
was the underside of the iceberg, colder and harder than anyone suspected."[11] *Time* reported that "her steely reserve, unblinking will and emotionless court demeanor—together with a seemingly automatic baseline
game—left the fans unmoved." [12] While never as negative as the portrayal
of some other players (including Navratilova), the revised response to
Chris seemed to reflect societal discomfort with her "unfeminine" competitive drive. This portrayal never entirely replaced the goody-two-shoes,
clean-cut, all-American girl-next-door image from which she benefited.
Still, Evert disliked the ice maiden perception and countered it. "I project
cool on the court because my game demands total concentration. I'm not
cold and indifferent," she asserted.[13] If she didn't seem warm to the press
at first, she said it was because she was terrified. In fact, she felt that she
had been handed a personality before she'd had a chance to develop one
of her own. For a long time, she actually would think, "What would Chris
Evert do?" before speaking.[14] Over time she became more comfortable
with the press corps, who in turn became familiar with the Evert that her
friends knew, the one who was witty and loved telling dirty jokes. "The
public doesn't really know who I am. . . . I'm not as goody two shoes as
people think. . . . I guess I felt a little uncomfortable with my image when
it got to be squeaky clean because I know I'm no angel."[15] The image persisted even after retirement.

Even today when I do corporate appearances, people always say to me, "My God, I had no idea you had a sense of humor!" They're so surprised. But I couldn't play my best tennis if I let everything out. It would have been nice to be free and loose on the court, to have that exchange with the crowd that Billie Jean or Martina had. But I couldn't. So my control became associated with winning. But it was also one of the things that allowed people to put me in little boxes that were hard to escape. And it hurt.[16]

In retrospect, some of the responses to Evert reflected traditional discomfort with powerful women athletes. For example, when Chris was just in her mid-teens she was asked how long she planned to play tennis; it was a decades-old question that implied it was odd for a grown woman to participate in sports. She replied, "No longer than twenty-one. Then for sure, I want to get married and have kids."[17] Evert's answers seemed to contrast some of the other players on the tour, most of whom were over twenty-one and some of whom were feminists fighting for the right for women to be independent, to have careers, and to be judged by more than the men with whom they were associated. The more conservative Evert distanced herself from feminists.[18] She and her family were not comfortable with new ideas about careers for woman and felt ambivalent about her being a strong, successful athlete. Though the existence of such professional opportunities for women in sports was new, such ambivalence about female athletes was not new. For much of the century, female athletes had been forced to battle unflattering stereotypes and the notion that sports were unfeminine. And unfeminine often translated to "masculine," "abnormal," "lesbian," and the worst things a woman could be. Over the years, women who loved sports had adopted a variety of apologetic behaviors intended to compensate for their unfeminine behavior and preserve their reputation as good, normal women. Examples of apologetic behavior included downplaying the importance of their sport and their ambition; emphasizing the importance of femininity, marriage, and family; and dressing in ways that exaggerated traditional femininity, even while competing on the field or court.[19]

Evert displayed just about every type of apologetic behavior possible. She downplayed the importance of the game to her when she famously said, "No point is worth falling down over." She also said, "Tennis is fun now but the penalties you must pay in your social life must eventually tell

on you. I'd rather be known in the end as a woman than a tennis player."
[20] She intentionally wore very traditionally feminine dresses, hair ribbons,
bright nail polish, hoop earrings, and a lot of makeup during her matches:
"I thought it would make me look more attractive and feminine for the
spectators."[21] She regularly underscored the importance of traditional
norms to her, as when early in her career she described the appeal of
women's tennis: "That's the one thing women's tennis has, is femininity.
If women looked like men or played like men it would be boring. I know
some women who lift weights. . . . But even if it made me stronger I'd
never do it. It's important to look feminine.."[22] Throughout her career,
Evert insisted (to the annoyance of other players, whom she implicitly
criticized) that she personally brought femininity to women's tennis.
"Right from the start," she asserted, "I was sort of different from the
stereotypical woman athlete."[23] Rewriting the history of a sport that had
been always been extremely feminine and which actually took off at precisely the time when players became more assertive, athletic, and brash,
she regularly gave herself credit for helping save the sport. "Women's tennis badly needed a young fresh face," she claimed, and she also said that
she helped inspire girls by proving "you didn't have to look like a masculine
freak to become an athlete."[24]

But despite the apologetic words that suggested she wasn't quite
comfortable with her role as a strong woman, Evert's *actions* demonstrated her love of the game and the makeup of a champion. While still
insisting that love and marriage were very important, she kept putting
off her retirement date. Indeed, despite falling head over heels in love
with male pro Jimmy Connors, in what the press portrayed as a storybook "Love Match," she decided to cancel the wedding—in part because
Connors wanted her to quit playing once they married. In the mid-1970s,
she wrote in her diary the following entries.

> There's nothing that would make me happier than to get married
> to someone and retire from tennis—but *not now*. I know tennis and
> my freedom are the most important things to me now. I love tennis,
> I love the competition, the sheer challenge of playing to perfection.
> Always striving to hit a better shot, to be more aggressive, to hit with
> more power. I'm playing for myself now. I'm experiencing sensations
> in tennis I've never experienced before. No pressure or nerves. Loose,

aggressive, daring, gutty, confident. On the tennis court, I'm my own person. I'm expressing my inner desires and personality. I love tennis. How can I give it up? It's my life.[25]

In her 1982 autobiography, Evert shared these entries with an interested public, which probably included millions of women who shared Evert's initial hesitations about new gender roles and, like her, had gradually come to accept them. Over time, Evert shifted her political views on the acceptability of being a "career woman" instead of "just a full-time mother" and mentioned that her father had changed as well.[26] Evert enjoyed a storybook wedding to British pro John Lloyd (which Martina attended), but she confessed in her second (1985) autobiography that she struggled with how to balance support of her tennis-playing husband with her own ambitions. When to have children was another dilemma, since she hadn't taken the path she'd always assumed she would. And finally, like other women affected by the changing times, she employed apologetic behavior less frequently. She stopped wearing makeup on the court because it "runs in about five minutes and it's ridiculous and impractical to wear" and later laughed with embarrassment, "Why, I've been falling down and sweating for a couple years now."[27] It appears that her consciousness had been raised. She admitted that "the nail polish, the ruffles on my bloomers, not wearing socks—all of that was very important to me, to compensate. I would not be the stereotyped jock." She came to realize that she had unquestioningly accepted demeaning stereotypes of "women athletes as freaks, and I used to hate myself."[28] Presumably she was now trying to accept herself. By 1980, Evert was even lifting weights. That was not because of feminist enlightenment, however, but because at that time she had a serious rival who had not only caught up, but passed her.

Although she shared the same tennis ambitions, from the beginning Martina Navratilova differed drastically from Chris Evert. Born in Czechoslovakia in 1956 to a family whose lands and house had been seized and divided up by the government, the shadow of Communism hung over her early life. The nation had been ruled by the USSR since the end of World War II, but when Czech leaders tried to open up their society, Soviet tanks re-invaded the country in 1968. Most Czechs were unhappy about this response, including Martina, since she was at a tennis tournament that was cancelled. Her parents refused to join the Communist Party, but otherwise remained apolitical. Martina inherited athletic ability and a passion for tennis from her mother and grandmother, and her stepfather helped her dream of someday playing at Wimbledon. Although she was not as fortunate as Chris in many ways, she did have one advantage. In Czechoslovakia, there was not the same stereotypical notion that female athletes were unfeminine or odd. "I learned my lesson from my mother at an early age: sports are good for young women. It's good to compete, good to run, good to sweat, good to get dirty, good to feel tired and healthy and refreshed. We had no idea of tomboys—there's no word for it in the Czech language. Women played sports and had families and jobs. That simple. My mother was my role model."[29] Martina didn't escape all self-consciousness, but she was encouraged to direct her substantial energy and athletic ability into tennis.

Even though she too grew up on clay courts, the left-handed Navratilova always felt most comfortable rushing the net, and her serve and volley style contrasted with Evert's. "I didn't believe in playing conservatively," she observed. "My game was rushing the net, playing aggressively, playing for fun, playing to win."[30] Early on, her forehand was good and her backhand passable, but from the very beginning her serve was hard and strong, and her aggressive style forced her opponents out of sync. Her personality could not have differed more from Chris's. Martina wore her emotions on her sleeve, both on and off the court. Observers knew in an instant when Martina was enraged by a line call, pleased with a shot, or disappointed in her own performance. "She always cries when she loses," reported Billie Jean King. "She cries easier than anybody."[31] Yet after she cried, she let go of defeats and didn't let them undermine her ultimate confidence in her ability. In fact, for years many people thought she was more confident than her performance deserved. She had a reputation for losing matches that she shouldn't have because she let things bother or distract her. In tennis and in life, Martina was impulsive, passionate, and a risk-taker. She could be warm and generous, was ready for fun and open to new ideas and things to do. She was ever-changing.

While she was a young player, other people made decisions for Martina, just as they had for Chris, but in this case the authority figure was the state. The Czech tennis federation permitted only a couple players to compete each year in international tournaments, and even then, officials limited who they would associate with, where they would go, and how much prize money they could keep. Martina rebelled from the start. In her first trip to the United States, she was amazed by the material goods—cars, magazines, clothes, and jewelry—and she gained twenty pounds consuming fast-food delights and ice cream. More important, though, was the freedom available. "I always felt I could be me, the real Martina, from the first time I came to the States."[32] Each time she returned home, she was battling Czech officials, who thought she was becoming too Americanized.[33] When permitted to travel, she sometimes broke the rules, and she even engaged an American business manager to help her obtain a higher percentage of her winnings. Czech officials were torn; angered by her defiance, they considered prohibiting her from traveling altogether, but they also wanted to bask in the fame that would result from her success. So scrutiny tightened. She talked secretly with her family about whether she should defect, and her stepfather made it clear that if she did, she should tell no one of her plans, ignore her family's pleas for her return (which might result from coercion), and assume she would never see them again. It is astonishing to contemplate an eighteen-year-old making such a momentous decision, but despite its difficulty and perhaps because she was so young and confident, she took the plunge. In the middle of the U.S. Open in 1975, she approached American immigration officials and applied for asylum. After some cloak-and-dagger negotiations involving FBI protection and threats from Czech representatives, Navratilova was given a green card, permitting her to stay in the United States. (As soon as she could, she would become a naturalized citizen.) Her defection made front-page news, and for some time afterwards she was regularly asked how she felt about the decision. She always told the press that she was quite happy and that her parents were fine, but in actuality the adjustment was difficult. A teenager torn from her support system, she was sometimes lonely and overwhelmed, and she feared her parents were being punished for her actions.[34]

The newly independent Martina enjoyed success on the tour, though. By the end of 1975, her third year on the tour, she had earned the number four world ranking and was winning 81 percent of her matches. By 1977, she was advancing farther in tournaments and had moved up to number three. Navratilova was friendly with many players, including Chris Evert, who "stood for everything I admired in this country: poise, ability, sportsmanship, money, style."[35] In 1976 Evert invited Navratilova to be her doubles partner, and the pair won a Wimbledon title together. They were friends who discussed many subjects, shared advice, practiced together, and even went on a double-date together.[36] At that point, the top-ranked Evert was regularly defeating Navratilova. In 1975, they played eleven times, and Evert won all but two. In 1976, they faced one another three times, and Evert won two. In 1977, Evert took five of six. In all, Evert won twenty of the first twenty-four matches the two played and was clearly the superior player. Many people believed Martina could beat Evert, but she was not yet playing to her potential.

In the mid-1970s, pro golfer Sandra Haynie took Martina under her wing. Although Haynie didn't know much about tennis, she knew Martina did not yet have the habits of a champion. Although Martina loved sports, she had always hated exercise and relied too much on her natural ability. Haynie convinced her that she needed to work out much harder, and soon Navratilova was running wind sprints, lifting weights, and playing racquetball. Haynie also knew Martina needed to learn to control her temper. As a result of their work together, Navratilova dropped thirty pounds and became more stable. Evert noticed the change and decided not to play doubles with her anymore. Privately, she admitted, "I couldn't handle it. Martina was a threat. With all the practicing we were doing together, I felt she was getting a little too good of a read on my game."[37] In her autobiography, Evert described the difficulty of keeping "a close friend and rival" as a doubles partner. "How could I sustain intensity for an important [singles] match against someone I cared for, someone I might be clowning with in a doubles final or going out to dinner with afterward?"[38] She did have cause for worry, because by 1978, Martina had clearly narrowed the gap between them, taking two of their five matches. "This is a new Martina," Evert acknowledged. "But it's good. It gets my game up."[39] One of Navratilova's victories included the coveted championship at Wimbledon. Evert was upset, but didn't show it outwardly; instead she showed good sportsmanship, fondly patting Martina on the head after the victory.

Increasingly confident that the hard work was paying off, Martina continued looking for ways to go even farther. For the first time in her professional career, she hired coaches who were experienced tennis players. The choice of Renee Richards, the first transsexual many people had ever heard of, raised eyebrows. Later former pro Mike Estep joined what became known as "Team Navratilova," the not-always-unanimous off-beat collection of Navratilova supporters. Richards and Estep were surprised by Martina's lack of mental preparation for individual matches. They improved a few of her strokes and worked on her strategizing. They encouraged her to stop trying to beat Evert at her own game and go with her natural, very effective serve and volley style. Another advisor employed a computer to track her shots in order to analyze the tendencies of her and her opponents, a technique new to the tour. At a crucial period in her career, Navratilova's training was supervised by Nancy Lieberman. A collegiate All-American, Olympian, and professional basketball player who lived with Navratilova, Lieberman felt Martina should not only practice her tennis harder, but become stronger both physically and mentally. Lieberman had Martina lifting more weights, running more, and playing basketball. Navratilova also employed a nutritionist and radically changed her diet. Eventually, she eliminated all excess body fat, which, when combined with the building of her muscles, resulted in her trademark forearm vein standing out. Feeling better about her looks, Navratilova eventually changed her hair color and paid more attention to achieving a stylish appearance. Her lean sculpted body was now an impressive physical specimen. Later women would aspire to hers as a new, fitter ideal of female beauty, but to many people at that time it was shocking. The final step was to become as mentally strong as Chris. Lieberman believed that Evert had an amazing desire to win, much greater than that of Martina, who wanted to win but was held back by her desire to be nice and to be a friend. Lieberman insisted, "Chris wants what you want and you've got to take it away from her."[40]

At the end of the decade, the reformed Navratilova started taking tournament trophies away from Chris more and more frequently. In 1979, Martina won five of their seven matches, again defeating Chris in the finals at Wimbledon. Things were more even in 1980 when they split their matches, with Chris beating Martina in the semifinals at Wimbledon. Then through the early 1980s, the two were extraordinarily close, and their matches fascinating. One or the other was seeded number one, and they often met in finals. They knew exactly what to expect and understood the meaning of every movement of the other. While casual spectators thought Evert didn't display her emotions on the court, Navratilova knew otherwise. Evert had a look that meant she was furious and was about to raise her game another notch. "I'd be out there on one side of the net and I'd see those eyes squinting and I'd say, 'Oh, no.' I knew she would not make a mistake. She'd whip that two-handed backhand at me. I'd hit the ball back to her, and she would squint again and set her mouth and hit the two-hander, just a little differently this time. . . . She never quit on a ball, so you knew you could never quit, either. You'd always have to tell yourself, 'This is Chris. Don't give up.'"[41] Observers rightfully emphasized the differences in their games, but their absolute determination—to achieve the same goal, which only one of them could achieve and could only be done by preventing the other—meant that in one important way the two were mirror images. "Playing against Chris was always like battling part of your own nature," explained Martina. "You know it so well but you can't give in to it."[42]

Navratilova put it all together in the mid-1980s. Her winning percentage rose higher and higher each year, and she won more and more Grand Slam events. She had wanted desperately to win the championship of her adopted nation, but the U.S. Open had proven to be her nemesis. The more pressure she put on herself to win it, the more difficult it became, and she was aware of the whispers that she might "choke." In a fitting final in 1983, she faced Evert in their thirty-ninth head-to-head meeting. At that point their career mark against one another was tied at nineteen victories each. Before the match Navratilova's knees were knocking and she thought, "I want to win so bad, I'll die if I don't."[43] With more of the twenty thousand fans energetically cheering for Chris, Martina held it together and defeated Chris with relative ease, 6–1 and 6–3. It was a huge weight off her mind, but not surprising to anyone who'd been watching her play. Navratilova swept Evert in 1983 and did so again in 1984, defeating her thirteen times in a row, including the championship at the French Open, on the clay surface that Evert preferred. It wasn't just Evert who struggled against Martina in those days; no one could touch her. In 1982, Navratilova won ninety of the ninety-three matches she played. In the entire calendar year in 1983, she played eighty-seven times and lost *only one match*. She only dropped a handful in each of 1985 and 1986. As tennis analyst Mary Carillo put it, "Martina went from somebody who got nervous and thought, 'I can be up a set and a break and still lose' to someone who thought, 'This shouldn't take more than forty-five minutes.' That's an *incredible* mind change."[44]

All was not smooth sailing for Navratilova off the court, though. Martina had a number of intense relationships and breakups, but since her partners were women, she had an additional burden. Her inclination was to be open and honest about her lesbianism, and her relationships were known on the tour, but circumstances meant she was not immediately open with the wider world. One concern was her application to become a citizen. Her lawyers had warned her that homosexuality could lead to it being turned down. In addition, the Women's Tennis Association was extremely worried about the specter of lesbianism. In 1981, the *Los Angeles Times* revealed that the still-married Billie Jean King had had an affair with a woman, and its revelation had rocked the tour. The major tour sponsor declined to renew its contract, King herself lost hundreds of thousands of dollars in endorsements, and gossip rags reportedly were offering money to players who would "out" other lesbians. In a significant show of support, though, Chris Evert wrote a guest editorial in *World Tennis* that sympathized with King about the invasion of her privacy and asked, "Who are we to knock it if someone is gay?"[45]

In this atmosphere of paranoia, Navratilova initially gave off contradictory messages. She had given an honest interview to a reporter with details about the end of her relationship with lesbian novelist Rita Mae Brown, but then asked him not to publish it. He held off for a while, but then used the story. Afterwards, Martina held a press conference insisting that while she was bisexual, Nancy Lieberman was straight and her relationship with Lieberman was non-sexual. Even the admission of being bisexual was bombshell, however. "You have to remember," said sportswriter George Vecsey, "in 1981, '82, '83, '84, it was still a pretty serious thing for anybody on any occasion to be out. It just wasn't much done."[46] The admission meant she would always encounter some boos and would not be rewarded with corporate deals, but to her, it was worth the cost. "Although my candor about my sexuality has cost me millions of dollars in sponsorships and endorsements, that's only money. . . . Could I play as well if I were living a lie?"[47] It also meant a lot to the legions who appreciated her courage and honesty. "Martina was the first legitimate superstar who literally came out while she was a superstar," noted the Women's Sports Foundation's Donna Lopiano. "She exploded the barrier by putting it on the table. She basically said this part of my life doesn't have anything to do with me as a tennis player. Judge me for who I am."[48] Over time, Navratilova became more confident discussing

gay issues, eventually embracing a role as activist and leader. She once
explained to a smirking reporter that the pink triangle symbol harkened
back to the persecution of homosexuals during the Holocaust; she spoke
out against a Colorado anti-gay rights referendum; she helped raise money
for gay causes; and she attended the 1993 March on Washington for
Lesbian, Gay, and Bi Equal Rights and Liberation. There she was invited
to speak; and when she did so, she encouraged others to "come out."

> If we want others to give us respect, we must first be willing to give
> ourselves respect. We must be proud of who we are. And we cannot
> do that if we hide. We have to make ourselves palpable. Touchable.
> Real. Then we have the opportunity to show the world what we are
> all about: happy, intelligent, giving people. We can show our whole
> strength, our dignity and character. We can show our joy and sorrow,
> our heartaches and our pain. Then we can just be.[49]

Martina had done just that—allowed herself to be palpable, allowed the
public to see both her strength and pain—and she found that being open
freed her to care less about public perceptions.

Not surprisingly, media coverage of Navratilova differed rather dramatically from that of Evert. Navratilova had too many characteristics
that put her in the category of "Other." Early in her career, she was overweight (Bud Collins even referred to her as "The Great Wide Hope"). She
was foreign, and although she became a naturalized American citizen,
reporters continued to call her Czech. Despite the fact that she rejected
Communism and loved the United States as perhaps only naturalized citizens can, as one scholar put it, Navratilova "never lost the foreign association that linked her with Communism."[50] Her sexual orientation was a
second strike. *Sports Illustrated*'s Frank Deford referred to her as "the
bleached blonde Czech bisexual defector." The contrast to Chris Evert
couldn't have been starker, as seen in Frank Deford's recollection of the
days "when one of them was a frilly 18-year-old princess from Florida and
the other a wide-eyed 16-year-old butterball from Prague."[51] An ESPN
series on the greatest athletes of the twentieth century illustrated the contrast. The episode on Chris Evert portrayed her as America's sweetheart,
shown with children reciting the pledge of allegiance in the background
and images of her moving from an innocent child at the foot of her father
to a happy wife and mother. The episode on Martina, on the other hand,

had an undertone of threat. She was raised by Communists who targeted her for excellence, and then she became a model of physical strength and discipline with a "muscularity that made people uncomfortable." The show's commentators announced that while Evert displayed feminine grace and showed the world that "true womanhood combined softness and strength," Martina made people realize "that women's sports is not just the girl next door."[52]

Treatment of Martina became even less flattering when she began her victorious streak. Winning was a third strike against her—so serious that some actually suggested she was no longer even a woman. *Sports Illustrated* called her "the distaff beast . . . [who] annihilated the field."[53] Snide comments about her being programmed and whispers that she took steroids made her feel as though she was being described as a "robot" or a "monster."[54] At the U.S. Open, a fan yelled to Evert, "Come on Chris, I want a real woman to win."[55] Though they had never done so to Evert when she dominated the tour, the press corps speculated about whether it was unfair for Navratilova to win so much. After her 1983 Wimbledon victory, someone asked, "Do you think you're just too good for the women?"[56] Even Chris acknowledged the unfairness of the portrayals.

> It was as if Martina became the bully to some people, and I was the person who could silence the bully. People didn't even know us . . . and yet if I met somebody then, it was often like, "Oh, I never liked that Martina. She's so tough." I'd say, "You know what? She's a kitten. She really is. I'm the hard one. I was ruthless." And they'd always say, "No, no, not you—you're so frail and feminine. We always felt sorry for you." It was like Martina was the villain. And I was the fragile lamb, the little slaughtered lamb.[57]

And yet if the majority of fans seemed to pull for Chris—whether she was favorite or underdog—there were some who stuck by Martina. "I have friends who were tomboys or jocks when they were kids," noted sportswriter Grace Lichtenstein, "and to this day they will tell you that they never liked what Chris Evert 'stood for,' because she was adored because she was feminine and not because she was a champion."[58]

Martina sometimes felt aggrieved by the negative press and the relative lack of love she got from spectators at tournaments and said so.

On occasion, she pointed out double standards, tried to convince reporters to refer to her as an American, and, in her typical forthright fashion, even let them know she felt snubbed by *Sports Illustrated* not putting her on its cover until 1983. "The corporate big shots would rather have a model in a bathing suit on the cover than the best woman tennis player in the world." As for the question about whether it was unfair for her to win so much, she retorted, "They [my opponents] can do everything I do: all the line drills, the quarter-miles on the track, the full-court basketball games. . . . If they want to, they can do it. I know I'm blessed with talent and genes, but so are a lot of other people. I've put in the work. I'm a size eight [same size as Evert]; the only thing big about me are my feet. How is it unfair?"[59]

But she recognized the many factors that contributed to her less favorable reception, including the fact that she was automatically contrasted to Evert. "She played 'feminine' tennis and I played 'masculine' tennis; and she looked the part and I looked the part."[60] She also knew that her outspokenness played a role. "Chris has always been able to live up to her sweetheart image, knowing what to say and when to say it. I didn't know how to do that when I arrived, and I still don't. I say what I feel."[61] Although at times she desperately wished for fan approval, she didn't want it enough to change. "I wanted to be liked by everybody, but I wasn't willing to do what it took to be liked—which is to say absolutely nothing."[62]

When Martina was so dominant in the mid-1980s, some suggested it was time for Chris to retire. "She wasn't just beating me," Evert admitted later. "She was killing me. There was a stretch when I lost to her before I even took the court. I was intimidated."[63] Instead, though, Evert rededicated herself to reaching the top—and set her sights on Martina.[64] At age twenty-nine, when most tennis players had already peaked or quit, Evert began working out more intensely than ever and in new ways. She added training techniques to improve her footwork, stamina, and jumping and began lifting weights, jogging distances, and running stadium stairs. She practiced against left-handers and switched to a new midsize graphite racket. Perhaps most dramatically, she worked hard on coming to the net and volleying. And when the press suggested Martina was too good, she defended herself. "I'm head and shoulders above anybody else, except for Martina."[65] She used every tool at her disposal, including trying to psyche out Martina, repeatedly suggested to the press that while Martina was strong, she still lacked Evert's mental toughness and might choke if the match were close or long.

Evert achieved her goal at the French Open in 1985. The French Open in 1985 matched the newly buff, focused Evert against the woman who had won fifteen of their last sixteen meetings. It was a classic. For almost three hours, they battled through long points, with the momentum shifting back and forth. The crowd gasped as they broke one another's serves and then lost their own—neither able to take control. Evert took the first set, but Navratilova won the second. They took turns playing fearlessly and tentatively, with Martina celebrating narrow escapes and Chris studiously ignoring her displays and not showing any emotion until one time near the end when she raised clenched fists. It went to 5–5 in the third. At that point Evert made the shots that took the match, and Navratilova met her at the net with a hug. "It's too bad someone had to win," said Martina. "It was one of those matches that should go on forever."[66] Their rivalry went on for three more years and fifteen more matches, and while Navratilova won two-thirds of those contests, no longer was it an automatic victory.

Evert retired after the 1988 season, saying it was time to move on to the other things in life, including motherhood. She was given a farewell deserving of the queen of the game, including fond receptions and articles summarizing her classy reign as champion. She retired with her husband, skier Andy Mill, to Aspen, Colorado, where they subsequently raised three children. She also served as a media tennis analyst and helped found a tennis academy. Quickly she was inducted into the International Tennis Hall of Fame. Navratilova, a year and a half younger and slower to reach her prime, played half a decade longer before retiring in 1994. It turned out that her retirement was only from singles, since the lure of tennis proved too strong, and after a few years she resumed playing doubles. She had always been an energetic and effective doubles player, having won the most women's matches ever at the time of her induction into the Hall of Fame, including twenty Grand Slam titles with partner Pam Shriver. In 2003 she won mixed doubles titles at the Australian Open and Wimbledon, becoming, at forty-six, the oldest player to win a Grand Slam title. Perhaps because other players were now capable of defeating her and because society's views about women and gays had changed dramatically, she was met by fonder, more appreciative crowds.

Navratilova outlasted Evert, who played quite a long time herself at an extraordinarily high level, and Martina was the better doubles player as well; but who was the better singles player? Their record in head-to-head matches ended up quite close. Martina won forty-three and Evert won thirty-seven, meaning there was just a three-match difference. Evert entered fifty-six Grand Slam events in her career and won eighteen of them, which is the same number of Grand Slam singles titles Navratilova won. Defenders of Evert point out that they played less frequently on the clay surfaces on which Evert excelled. They also point out that Evert's astonishing overall winning percentage is unmatched; she won 90 percent of the matches she played. Not only that, but Evert was consistently excellent throughout her entire career: out of the fifty-six Grand Slam events she entered, Evert made it to the semifinal round fifty-two times. That 93 percent rate "is not just one of the great accomplishments in all of tennis history," maintained sportswriter Mike Lupica, "it is one of the great individual accomplishments in sports history."[67] Martina's loyalists point out that in addition to winning more of the overall head-to-head contests, Navratilova occupied the number one ranking more total weeks than Evert did (331 to 262). (Other viewers note that Steffi Graf, who dominated the game after Martina, actually occupied the top spot longer than either one at 377 weeks.) Since Martina played longer and more matches, it is not surprising that her overall singles winning percentage of 87 percent is slightly lower than Evert's, but she won 167 women's singles titles, the most ever. Navratilova also won a record seventy-four matches in a row and won six Grand Slam tournament championships in a row, both amazing feats.

The answer to who was better isn't clear cut, and it doesn't really matter. A bounce here or there, the ball dropping half an inch in or out, a linesman's call, a moment of concentration, a risky shot taken or not—any of those might have resulted in a slightly different record. Both women excelled, and their accomplishments are more impressive because they each had to face such stiff competition. Indeed, they took turns at the top and rarely shared the position with others. Perhaps the most impressive statistic is that one or the other was ranked number one for twelve years straight. Significantly, each appreciated the symbiotic nature of their rivalry. "I made Martina more disciplined. She made me more physically fit," said Evert. " . . . We pushed each other and, in the end, made the other one a much better player," said Evert.[68] Navratilova similarly observed, "Being on the court with an opponent is a strange business. You're totally out for yourself, to win a match, yet you're dependent on your opponent to some degree for the type of match it is and how well you play. You need the opponent; without her you do not exist."[69] Their impact was not just on one another. Even if their professional and private lives did not always play out in the manner the overly image-conscious Women's Tennis Association would have preferred, they were the faces of women's tennis from the mid-1970s through the mid-1980s, at a pivotal developmental stage for the sport. If their fans were polarized, it was quite important for the game that they were so passionate.

It is not surprising that at times during their long careers there were tensions between two such fierce competitors. This was true especially during the period when Nancy Lieberman tried to convince Martina to see Chris as her enemy and give her the cold shoulder. Evert referred to it as Lieberman's "Kill Chris" campaign, and Martina admitted it created a wedge between them. During this "low point" in their relationship, Evert, too, became less sympathetic. "One week, I might see Martina crying in the locker room after our match and my heart would go out to her. So I felt sorry for her, and the next week she knocked my block off. And now I don't feel sorry for her; now I say that I reacted vulnerably to the situation."[70] After Martina stopped working with Lieberman, things improved, but at times there were "petty jealousies or ill feelings," Chris admitted.[71] These might be related to behavior on the court or public comments instigated by media eager to provoke conflicts, and when they discussed their accomplishments, Navratilova noticed, things got "a little touchy on both sides."[72] At times in their careers and with other players as well, both struggled to figure out how to balance friendship and competition and to separate ruthlessness and selfishness on the court with kindness off of it.

Despite bumps along the way, their friendship endured. Even in the exultation of victory and the heartbreak of defeat, neither forgot how her opponent felt. For example, after Martina won the 1985 Australian Open championship and kept Chris from regaining the number one ranking, Evert cried in the locker room. Seeing her, Martina broke down, too. "I know how you feel, so I can't enjoy this," she cried. "Don't worry about me," replied Chris.[73] Evert reported that Martina regularly sought her out to console her if she lost a match and called to congratulate her on the wins. "We have an incredible bond," Chris said. "I trust her more than any other player, and she's the most compassionate, giving person I know."[74] The friends did meaningful things for one another. Evert ignored a knee injury and accompanied Martina on her first trip back to Czechoslovakia to play for the American Federation Cup team.[75] She stood beside her, and when she noticed Navratilova's tears as the national anthem played, she put her arm around her shoulder. And when Evert was despondent over her divorce from John Lloyd, Navratilova invited her to her home for the holidays. There she introduced her to the man who would eventually become her husband. In fact, the two even retired to the same community in Aspen, Colorado, where they sometimes still practiced together and knew they could depend on one another. Perhaps the most significant gesture was that the more conservative Evert never said a negative word about Navratilova's sexual orientation. While she may have exaggerated her own importance in feminizing women's tennis, her support of and friendship with Martina, the famous lesbian, may well have been very influential in encouraging people to look beyond stereotypes and fears.

Their fondness and respect for one another was obvious to the fans. They always demonstrated the height of sportsmanship and graciousness on the court—shown through a pat on the head, a hug, tousling the other's hair, or walking off arm in arm. It's hard to say why they were capable of this. Navratilova speculated that it was because of shared experiences. "No matter how catty we get with each other in private or public, I still have a closeness with [Chris] that I will never have with another human being because of what we went through together, on and off the court."[76] It was true that there were few people who truly understood what each went through—the pressure of the quest to strive for and achieve the top ranking, the increasing number of strong young players, the stereotypes of female athletes, the constant hounding from the media about both their games and personal lives. Maybe it was also related to the fact that they were of the right age to have learned from the first women's tennis pioneers the importance of unity between players. Whatever the case, certainly not all athletic rivals are able to negotiate the difficult terrain as admirably, compassionately, and professionally as Chris and Martina did. Ultimately, we must give credit to each as a person who made choices about how to behave. And like the lessons they were teaching the world about how a woman could maintain a professional career and be both strong and beautiful, it was important for Evert and Navratilova to demonstrate that it is possible for women to be extremely competitive and also decent human beings.

Individually and together they had an impact beyond the tennis courts. Evert served as a role model as she grew from a one-dimensional champ for whom winning came easily to an elite athlete who responded to challenges by adapting her training and style of play. She also grew as a person who grappled with how to buck some traditional expectations while retaining others; and she very publicly lived out a personal struggle about whether it was possible to do some "unfeminine" things and still be loved and considered normal. As she decided the answer was yes, so did millions of others. Navratilova also grew both as an athlete and as a person. Along with Chris, she vividly demonstrated what one can achieve through extremely hard work as she virtually remade both her body and her mental approach. In addition, she served as a role model for people desiring freedom. She inspired athletes in Communist bloc nations, and her defection convinced the Czech government to give more freedom to its athletes.[77] At the same time, Martina's appreciation of her new life served as a reminder to Americans of the value of their democratic system; and like Chris, one of the most important lessons she learned and spread was that of accepting oneself. Her forthrightness about her sexual orientation was path-breaking, and if few star athletes have had the courage to follow in her footsteps, millions in other walks of life have done so. Chris and Martina accepted and appreciated one another despite being rivals. They pushed and supported one another along the difficult road to championships, and that fact was good for us all.

Debi Thomas and Katarina Witt getting ready for their practice session prior to the ladies free skate program at the 1988 Winter Olympic Games in Calgary. *Courtesy of Getty Images.*

six

The Battle of the Carmens
Debi Thomas versus Katarina Witt

ALISON M. WRYNN AND
ANNETTE R. HOFMANN

Graceful figures gliding effortlessly across the ice—Who would think that this type of activity would elicit stark competitive fire? How could rivalries emerge in a sport where throughout most of its history the competitors met only once a year at the World Championships—and National or European Championships, if they were from the same nation or continent—and once every four years in the Winter Olympics? Women's figure skating, however, has given us some of the fiercest rivalries in the sporting world. From Tenley Albright and Carol Heiss to Nancy Kerrigan and Tonya Harding and beyond, in the words of male figure-skating champion Brian Boitano, "[The] girls are ruthless."[1]

The first Ladies Figure Skating World Championship competition was held in 1906 in Davos, Switzerland. Olympic competition preceded the establishment of the 1924 Winter Games in Chamonix with contests in 1908 in London and 1920 in Antwerp during the Summer Games. British skater Madge Syers entered the men's figure-skating World Championships in 1902 and placed second. Syers and others pushed the International Skating Union (ISU) to include women, which they finally did in 1906.[2]

Women's figure skating in the late 1920s and through most of the 1930s was dominated by Norwegian Sonja Henie, who won ten World Championships in a row as well as three Olympic gold medals. World War II interrupted international competition for much of the 1940s, but following the war Canadian Barbara Ann Scott captured two world gold medals and one Olympic gold medal. In the 1950s women's figure skating saw a competitive rivalry bloom between Americans Tenley Albright and Carol Heiss. Albright was viewed as the more athletic of the two, but she still was considered an artistic skater in the era before triple jumps made us consider the athleticism of female figure skaters. Over the span of four years, however, Heiss was only able to defeat Albright once, in the 1956 World Championships.[3]

In the 1960s an international skating rivalry flourished among the Netherlands' Sjoukje Dijkstra, the German Democratic Republic's Gabriele Seyfert, and American Peggy Fleming. Among the three of them they captured all but one World Championship gold medal in the decade and both the 1964 and 1968 Olympic gold (Dijkstra and Fleming, respectively). Fleming's Olympic victory in Grenoble was the first to be televised in color, bringing the visual appeal of figure skating to more viewers then ever before.[4]

According to Gina Daddario, as recently as the late 1980s, television executives still considered the athletic successes of women athletes as trivial.[5] Daddario contends that it was at the 1992 Olympic Winter Games in Albertville, France, that television executives finally fully realized the potential of the female viewer/consumer and began to provide broadcasts aimed directly at this demographic; and the centerpiece of this coverage was women's gymnastics in the Summer Olympic Games and figure skating during the Winter Olympic Games.

Figure skating moved beyond its popularity as an Olympic event to a sensationalist news story in 1994. You do not need to be a figure-skating aficionado to remember the drama between American figure skaters Tonya Harding and Nancy Kerrigan that year. Kerrigan was attacked as she left the ice following a practice session at the National Championships. The bruising and swelling to her right knee made her unable to continue in the competition. This left the door open for Harding, who won the event for the first time since 1991. As we now know, Harding's husband and his close friends were behind the attack on Kerrigan. Harding, however, was able to keep knowledge of her involvement in the plot quiet long enough to compete in the 1994 Winter Games. At Lillehammer, Kerrigan skated well enough to win, but her performance was outshined by Russian Oksana Baiul, who captured the gold. Harding, who continued her theatrics at the Winter Games with a broken skate lace, finished a distant eighth.[6]

"Sex Komma Null für Kati": Sex and Skating

It should come as no surprise that the media has promoted a competitive event for women that is considered to be "sex-appropriate."[7] The women who compete in figure skating are exceptional athletes; however, their sport requires them to display a sense of grace and style that is most closely associated with the feminine ideal of the late twentieth- and early twenty-first-century Western world. Throughout the history of figure skating, rivalry lines have habitually been drawn between a skater who was considered "athletic" and another who was "graceful" and more feminine. These distinctions have been intensified by the increased media focus on figure skating in the last three decades.

Ellyn Kestnbaum maintains that the media discourse about figure skating frequently focuses on these types of issues as the media knows this will engage a broader public.[8] The juxtaposition of artistry and athleticism as well as international rivalries were at play in the Debi Thomas and Katarina Witt rivalry of the late 1980s. Debi Thomas grew up in the San Jose, California, area, where she lived with her mother. She began figure-skating lessons at age nine and by the age of twelve was medaling at a number of national and international competitions for novice-level figure skaters.[9] She won a silver medal in the U.S. Championships at the age of seventeen. She is one of a very few African American figure skaters and the only one to win national and international medals at the senior level.[10] Throughout her competitive career, Thomas remained a full-time student, beginning as a pre-med student at Stanford University in 1986.[11] Following the end of her amateur career in 1988 Thomas began skating in professional ice shows.[12] She finally retired from full-time skating to pursue medical school and her career as a physician. Today Thomas is a successful orthopedic surgeon who resides in Southern California with her husband, Chris Bequette, and son, Luc.[13]

Katarina Witt—or "the prettiest face of socialism," as she continues to be called by the press—was an East German showpiece athlete who grew up in Karl-Marx Stadt, today's Chemnitz.[14] Witt is unclear about when she first took up figure skating; according to her autobiography it was between the ages of five and six. Her parent's encouraged her skating, and at seven years of age she won her first competition, and by the age of nine her talent was recognized by Frau Jutta Müller, the most successful East German figure-skating coach, who accompanied Witt throughout her amateur skating life. The victories they celebrated together include eight national and four world championships and Witt´s Olympic gold medals in 1984 and 1988. In 1994, at the age of twenty-eight, Witt competed again at the Olympics, although she only placed seventh at Lillehammer. After her amateur career she turned professional and skated at various ice shows. Besides her skating career she is an actress and business woman.[15] In 1990 she received an Emmy Award for the movie "Carmen on Ice" and five years later the Jim Thorpe Pro Sports Award. In 1991 and 1992 she was chosen as one of the "most beautiful people in the world."[16]

From 1984 to 1988, at the height of their competitive careers, Thomas and Witt only skated against each other four times; Witt won three of the four. In the 1986 World Figure Skating Championships Thomas defeated the two-time World Champion and 1984 Olympic Champion Witt. This was the eighteen-year-old Thomas's second competition on the international stage.[17] Thomas was the only skater in the world to defeat Witt from 1984 to 1988.[18]

The two skaters were inexorably linked by their decision to both skate their long programs to the music of Georges Bizet's *Carmen* in the 1988 Calgary Games. This common thread allowed the media and fans, with their limited knowledge of the technical side of figure skating, to focus on other stories. They were not only in the same event, but they were also using the same basic story—what an opportunity for comparison! One skater was from the Eastern Bloc, the other the West; one was defined as artistic and ultra feminine, the other as athletic; one was white and the other black.[19] These dichotomies created built-in story lines for the media leading up to the 1988 Winter Games in Calgary.

Thomas was driven by the need to defend her 1986 World title in 1987 and then go for the gold in 1988 in Calgary. In 1987 she was back at Stanford for her sophomore year as a pre-med student. Calgary would be Thomas's final amateur competition no matter what the results as she wanted to focus on her academics.[20] Witt defeated Thomas the next year at the 1987 World Championships that were held in Cincinnati, Ohio. Thomas came in second and was said to have been slowed by Achilles' tendonitis in both ankles. Witt skated to selections from *West Side Story*. The drama was increased as Thomas and Witt were the final two skaters for the evening and both performed flawlessly, with Witt edging Thomas out for the victory.[21]

Witt captured the short program in the 1988 Olympic Games in Calgary, but still was second to Thomas heading into the freestyle program as Thomas had the better score in compulsories. Thomas's coach, Alex McGowan, was concerned that the judges were swayed by Witt's appearance as six of the judges were male. Witt wore a short, sequined dress—and a tiara—while Thomas wore a body suit with sequins. Thomas's artistic scores were lower than Witt's.[22] Witt's costumes would eventually lead the International Skating Union (ISU) to rule that costumes could not be "excessively theatrical." Most in the figure-skating world referred to this as the "Katrina Rule," as Witt routinely appeared at competitions in dramatic costumes that pushed the limits of what the rules allowed.[23]

Sixty million viewers tuned into the Witt-Thomas skating drama, during the deciding moments of their competition the ratings rose from a 26.4 to 35.7.[24] In the end it came down to performance. Witt, the drama student, did not skate spectacularly, but with emotion and dramatic flair, and she avoided mistakes. She left the door open for Thomas, who skated after her, but Thomas faltered on two jumps, enough that she dropped to third place after an outstanding free-skate performance by Canada's Elizabeth Manley. Thomas failed to recover from her early error in the freestyle skate and skated the remainder of her program with uncertainty.[25] Following her performance Thomas suggested that she was uncomfortable with the focus on the rivalry between her and Witt.[26] As silver medalist Manley told interviewers later, "I haven't felt a lot of pressure—it's been the Debi and Katarina story here."[27] In fact, Thomas at first told reporters that she would not skate in the upcoming World Figure Skating Championships in Budapest. She later changed her mind, telling one interviewer, "I owe it to my coach . . . to show him I'm not a complete screw-up . . . I need to compete for my piece of mind."[28] The final act of their rivalry came in 1988 at the World Championships, with exactly the same results as the Calgary Games. Both Witt and Thomas were retiring from amateur competitions after this contest, and Thomas seemed relieved that it was all over.[29]

Thomas and Witt's rivalry is of interest on a number of levels. Except for the Olympics and the World Championships, they did not see or compete against each other. According to Witt, "We have no personal relationship really; our basic relationship is in sports."[30] One was from a socialist country, the other from a capitalist power, at the beginning of the end of the German Democratic Republic. "In the early years of the Winter Olympics, the most successful athletes were . . . from the northern European belt. . . . Then the Soviet Union joined the Olympic movement and started winning Olympic medals. Then East Germany did the same."[31]

Battle of the Systems

For East Germany Witt was a showpiece athlete. It was not unusual for athletes to be used as "diplomats in sweat suits." That she represented one of them can be seen from a quote Witt made in a 1988 article in the East German sport newspaper *Deutsche Sportecho*, "I agree with our politics," she said. She especially praised the "constant endeavor of her country to preserve peace and guarantee the right to work."[32] According to her, both were essential parts of human rights.[33]

High-performance sports were of great importance to the ideology of the German Democratic Republic (GDR, East Germany). The state had elaborated sports as politics, viewed as an instrument of power. High-performance sports were hierarchically structured and kept under close surveillance, and the government provided enormous financial support to ensure success in world and Olympic championships.[34] Those sports in which they were able to beat public enemies (among them the Federal Republic of Germany and other Western countries) were robustly supported and nurtured beginning in the late 1950s. Through their success in sport the GDR hoped to win international prestige, demonstrate the superiority of socialism, and strengthen the self-confidence of its inhabitants. Their plan appeared to be a success as the GDR—with only 17 million inhabitants—beat the United States in the Olympic medal count in 1976. Even greater was the success concerning the rivalry with West Germany. Beginning in 1968 East Germany regularly managed to beat its Western counterpart by winning more medals in Olympic competitions.

To be that successful, the East German state had a very detailed plan and invested a lot of money in it. Talented children were coached in the Kinder-und Jugendsportschulen (KJS), special boarding schools for children and youth in which they could not only be trained, but also educated to embody the typical ideal of the socialist personality. Sport scientists also had to orient themselves to the necessities of elite sports and enable a scientific and psychologically based optimal development of the athletes.[35] As Reinhart notes, the elite sports of the GDR were characterized by comprehensive recruiting mechanisms, spatial and social insularity, the full support of athletes, massive physical and psychological analyses, and Stasi (the state police of the GDR) monitoring.[36]

After the Sarajevo Olympics in 1984, Egon Krenz, member of the politbureau and secretary of the Central Committee of the East German party SED (Sozialistische Einheitspartei Deutschland), responsible for sports, welcomed the successful GDR Olympic team in Berlin. He emphasized that through their success they contributed to the thirty-fifth birthday of their nation: "It expresses a close relationship between the athletes and the working-class party, between the athletes and our GDR, our socialist fatherland."[37]

Four years later Witt officially announced that in a capitalist country she would have been unable to become such a great ice skater because she would not have been able to afford it financially.[38] Later on she also proclaimed that "[because she was] from East Germany—even after winning my first Olympic Gold medal—I was still able to successfully manage my time. There were no endorsement deals to distract me. It was forbidden."[39]

Debi Thomas's path to Olympic ice was decidedly different than Witt's. Without the state support provided by a socialist nation, Thomas's opportunities were based on the support provided by her family. Thomas's mother and father both worked in the computer industry in the Silicon Valley. After her parent's divorce her mother took the lead in supporting her figure-skating endeavors. Initially, Thomas took the path many young American figure skaters followed and completed the eighth grade via correspondence. However, she and her mother quickly realized that her skating, while important, would have to take a back seat to her education. Thomas entered high school and began the intensive physical training as well as the rigorous academic preparation that would lead her to the Olympics and Stanford University.[40] Despite the financial constraints of being a single parent, Thomas's mother found a way to meet the expense of elite coach Alex McGowan to boost Thomas's chances for success in the international skating arena.[41]

The Western Media Constructs a Rivalry

Throughout its history, figure skating has been a mostly white sport. Part of this has to do with the economics of skating, and race and socio-economic status are closely linked in the United States. In addition, figure skating has a strong tradition of European influences, including ballet and classical music; the introduction of new types of movement or music are strongly resisted.[42] In the 1940s, African American figure-skater Mabel Fairbanks was said to be the equal of Sonja Henie. She was unable to procure professional coaching; however, she did perform in several skating exhibitions.[43] A number of Asian American women have been very successful in figure skating, including Thomas's and Witt's contemporary Tiffany Chin. Chin's ethnicity was frequently discussed in the media. She was labeled a "China Doll" and her mother was called a "Dragon Lady."[44]

The American media habitually discussed Thomas's status as an African American in skating, both overtly and covertly. On a regular basis, Thomas had to answer questions about her race and what it meant to be successful in a sport that had few other African American competitors. She claimed that for her race was not an issue. "I don't want to be remem-bered as the best black skater in history, I want to be the best skater."[45] Early in her career it was noted that Thomas skated to the music of African American jazz musician Duke Ellington in her finals routine. Meanwhile, Witt skated to songs from West Side Story, most notably, "I feel pretty." Thomas was "exciting" but Witt was "dramatic."[46] The American press also referred to Thomas's disadvantage against skaters from socialist nations, claiming that Thomas had to come up with the approximately $25,000 per year it cost to train in figure skating while her rivals, like Witt, were supported as full-time athletes by their government.[47]

For the West German press the issues of ethnicity and race did not play a role in the rivalry between Witt and Thomas. It was more a matter of the Western athlete versus a skater with a socialist background. Especially during the Calgary Olympics in 1988 the newspapers Frankfurter Allgemeine and Stuttgarter Zeitung focused their reports on the competitions themselves, whereas the tabloid Bild started to make up stories between the two figure skaters toward the end of the ice-skating event. Headlines such as "Jubilance for Katherine the Great" or "Kati or Debi—who gets gold?" were intended to catch the eye of the reader.[48] Nevertheless, their duel never made it to the front page in any of these newspapers. A few days before the two women competed, *Bild* tried to reveal more about Witt and Thomas. "Debi versus Kati—entirely private. Men, fashion and music."[49] The article was based on questions that gave insight into the personal lives of the two opponents. Besides their political positions, information on their careers, relationships, favorite music and clothes, cars and vacation, they were also asked about each other. While Thomas, according to *Bild,* stated that she liked Witt and was learning German at night to be able to talk to her, Witt stated that she did not have any relationship with Thomas. In her biography, however, Witt provides a different perspective on their relationship.

> "She was one of the athletes I most respected, a strong, athletic skater and determined competitor—someone who got her act together when it mattered. She was also an honest and straightforward person. She wasn't fake. She showed what she felt. . . . She was never one of the typical skaters who tried to smile when they didn't feel like smiling. What you saw is what you got with Debi, and I never considered her my enemy the way our rivalry was sometimes described in the press. There was no personal animosity between us. We weren't friends because both of us so strongly wanted to win."[50]

As in the West German press, race did not play a role at all in the East German periodical *Sportecho.* Not once was it noted that Thomas was African American. In general, all the articles on the ice-skating event were focused on Witt and her performance, and her opponents were hardly mentioned. However, after her gold medal in Calgary a note that criticized the West German press, especially *Bild,* can be found in *Sportecho.* The author complained that *Bild* called the competition between Thomas and Witt a "war of two worlds."[51] He continued that from a socialist point of view, the Olympic arena was a "showplace of peaceful coexistence." Then he focused on the quarrel between socialism and imperialism. He agreed with *Bild* that the "Olympic Games are in fact one of those areas, where the better should be proven. However, not in the individual case—otherwise it wouldn't be a sport of many surprises with winners and losers—but rather in the amount of wins."

Here he was clearly referring to the leading position of his country in the Olympic medal count. Witt is described as a "talent of the people who is equipped with all liberties and assets of socialism." He also called her a trademark for the GDR "by which the perception of the east in North America" was changed.[52]

Change was coming to the Olympics as the 1988 games would be perhaps the last games with the patina of some amateurism upon them. Thomas was allowed to have income from commercials put into a "trust fund" to aid in her training expenses. Witt, however, was already a "pro" in the state-sponsored system of East Germany. Her life was controlled by the government as *New York Times* sportswriter Dave Anderson contended that the government would never allow her to capitalize on her skills—as Witt was a "National Treasure."[53] In addition, Thomas skated as a part-time venture, with the exception of her preparation for the 1988 Olympic Games, while pursuing her pre-med studies at Stanford University.

As mentioned previously, Witt was one of the GDR's showcase athletes. In many interviews she praised socialism, as was also noted in the magazine *FAZ*. "For the GDR and the working class party, Katarina Witt on occasion sings choruses of praise. After all, she is a companion in making and since November 1985 a candidate for the SED."[54] Her status in the GDR, where she had many privileges (for example, she drove a car, a Lada, which only very few of the citizens had), is described by *FAZ* journalist Zorn as "capitalistically tinted social status and socialistically dyed (extra-) class consciousness."[55] But he also noted that she convinced with her smile and aura.

> "She is only allowed to be [an] advertiser on her own account and for the good of her patron, the GDR. Katharina Witt—within one's reach but yet so far, a fairy tale character of sports. Seducible, 'western' habit, open—but yet bound to the brazen rules of her community, when the outward projected self-conception of socialist ideals are at stake. At the same time she is a fairytale character on call. If she ends her career, which could happen any year, she might have to go back to the pleasant surroundings of Karl-Marx-Stadt. Even for her, liberty is not boundless."[56]

However, when Witt announced after her victory in 1988 in Calgary that she would become a professional and skate at American ice shows, it proved to be a great shock for her fellow GDR countrymen and women. She experienced rejection at a rock concert in Berlin that she was emceeing. Her decision was seen by many as a betrayal of their perfect ideas of an athlete, in addition to her rejection of the socialist system that had nurtured and supported her, for the capitalist West.[57]

After the fall of the Berlin Wall a few years later, Witt's freedom would prove to be unlimited. She became a popular and famous figure for the broader public and in the media. But she was not only important for the Western-orientated TV shows. Witt still publicly showed her affection for the GDR past by being a central icon of an "Ostalgie-Welle," a wave of remembrances of the former East Germany in the mid 1990s, during which time Witt moderated "Ostalgie-Shows" on private TV. To achieve this popularity among both the West and East German population might be explained by the fact that she was never involved in any doping scandals or affairs of the East German police for the security of the homeland (Stasi). On the other hand, like many athletes in socialist countries, close tabs were kept on Witt when she traveled outside of East Germany. It later became public knowledge that the present-day German ice-skating coach, Ingo Steuer, spied on her. Her ice-skating career officially came to an end in 2008.

Conclusion

The final time that Thomas and Witt faced each other was in the 1988 World Championships in Budapest. But the performance that will link them forever was the 1988 Olympic long program three weeks earlier, where they both performed to the music from *Carmen*. The two skaters chose different sections of the music to skate to and had different interpretations. For Thomas, Carmen lived at the end, while Witt's Carmen died. Who chose to skate to "Carmen" first? In early 1986, in an interview for *Sports Illustrated,* Witt's interest in flamenco dancing and the movie *Carmen* were mentioned. Thomas came up with her routine in the spring of 1987 and performed it for the first time at a pre-Olympic competition in Calgary in late 1987 that Witt did not attend.[58]

Thomas's and Witt's performances in the short program at the Calgary Games drew the dichotomy between sexualized beauty and the athlete. Witt was criticized by one official of the International Skating

Union (ISU) for wearing a revealing outfit for her routine while the judges questioned Thomas's selection of trendy music by the group Dead or Alive. The music, according to one judge, made it "hard [for Thomas] to look pretty [skating] to that."[59]

Who knew in 1988 that such dramatic change was to come? In 1989 the Berlin Wall would fall and German reunification came in 1990. But during the 1988 Olympic Games the U.S. Olympic Committee (USOC) was concerned about the poor showing by the U.S. Olympic team in Calgary and pointed to the success of Eastern Bloc countries. Robert Helmick, then president of the USOC, contended, "Even with our political-social-economic system, there's no reason why we can't do better, much better."[60] Thomas's disappointing bronze-medal performance, compared with Witt's second gold, was certainly a part of his concern.

Much of this rivalry was constructed by the American press; little was made of it in the East and West German media. Although there is no doubt that the two athletes were fierce competitive rivals on the ice, for each, lurking just behind the scenes, were other kinds of pressures. For Witt, there were the demands of the East German government and the need to demonstrate through her performance the superiority of that political system. For Thomas, it was being a representative of a minority group and at the same time becoming someone who was mainstreamed; she was competing in a white sport and entering the medical profession. Perhaps the greatest rival each needed to overcome was the pressure, within themselves and from their respective cultures, that placed so many demands on two women who just wanted to skate.

II
Team Games

The Red Sox's Eric Hinske colliding with the Yankee's Jorge Posada at home plate during a 2007 game at Boston's Fenway Park. *Courtesy of Getty Images.*

— seven

Bitter Foes,
but Marketing Pros
The Red Sox–Yankees Rivalry

RYAN KING-WHITE —

Red Sox Nation? What a bunch of shit that is. That was a creation of the Red Sox and ESPN, which is filled with Red Sox fans. Go anywhere in America and you won't see Red Sox hats and jackets, you'll see Yankee hats and jackets. This is a Yankee country. We're going to put the Yankees back on top and restore the universe to order.

—Hank Steinbrenner, 2008

As I write this chapter in the fall of 2008 the baseball world seems asunder. The Tampa Bay Rays lead the American League East, a division dominated over the past fifteen seasons by the struggling third-place New York Yankees. Hank Steinbrenner's aforementioned quote reflects the recent frustrations felt by the most successful American sporting franchise over the past few years. For despite winning seven of the past eight division titles, and going to the playoffs in every season in the new century, the Yankees have not tasted World Series success since 2000. Conversely, their longtime rival, the Boston Red Sox, has made huge gains on the Yankees (inter)national prominence in terms of fan following and on-field success.[1] In fact, they have celebrated World Series victories in 2004 and 2007, while *USA Today* ran a front-page article in September 2007 entitled "Red Sox Nation: New King of the Road," which made the argument that they had overtaken the Yankees in terms of baseball fan popularity.[2]

This reversal in fortune is shocking, considering that until 2004 the Yankees had captured twenty-six World Series titles while the Red Sox had endured eighty-six years of poor performances and legendary near misses.

The Red Sox struggle, often attributed to a farcical "curse of the Bambino,"[3] more likely based on the team's management, ownership, and, indeed, fans covert racism,[4] was finally overcome when they shockingly became the first team to rally from a 3-0 deficit in the 2004 American League (AL) Championship Series against the Yankees on their way to a sixth World Series title. Three seasons later, in 2007, the Red Sox took their first division title in twelve years and once again won the World Series. With their recent run of success, coupled with a wildly loyal fan base,

> baseball continues to be the number one sport in greater Boston. At any time of the year, fan interest in the Red Sox outweighs the aggregate tonnage of that accorded the Celtics, Patriots, and Bruins. . . . The Red Sox are the team that never goes out of fashion. They can be stupid, boring, and contemptuous of their consumers. They can finish last three years in a row. They can be on strike for six months. They still have a choke hold on New England sports fans.[5]

The new Red Sox ownership triumvirate of John Henry, Tom Werner, and Larry Lucchino (the majority owners of Fenway Sports group) has adeptly taken advantage of this fierce loyalty and, through the combined efforts of Dr. Charles Steinberg (vice president of Public Affairs)[6] and Sam Kennedy (senior vice president of Sales and Marketing), has ushered in a new age in which there actually is a rivalry between the Red Sox and Yankees, where both teams are competing on a fairly even level. Simultaneously, the national sports media has been keen on perpetuating the competition between the two teams on and off the field. As Steinbrenner noted, the Entertainment and Sports Network (ESPN) runs year-round coverage of the two teams on their various television, Internet, and radio programs. Moreover, the teams have their own local cable channels, YES (Yankees Entertainment and Sports Network) and NESN (New England Sports Network), that flood fans with information and public-interest stories about the two teams and their relationship to one another. Interestingly, these mediated accounts have provided what I believe are superficial engagements with the rivalry by merely focusing on a few popularly remembered events throughout each team's history (ie., the sale of Babe Ruth, the 1949 season, the 1978 season, and the team's recent meetings in the AL playoffs) which serve to popularize a largely one-sided and un-eventful relationship between the Red Sox and Yankees.

Throughout the following then, I intend to outline how the Red Sox–Yankees "rivalry" began and grew through a historical rendering of the relationship's early days. Within this historical account, this project will discount and confirm some of the dominant mythologies surrounding the rivalry. In so doing the chapter will position this form of remembering as largely a media creation which overlooks the historical and contextual realities of their contentious relationship, but simultaneously (re)creates and perpetuates hatred between the fans of both teams. Finally, this project will outline how, in the present day, this rivalry has been a means for the ownership of both teams to exploit their fan's passion in order to garner more capital—even if it puts those fans at risk to personal bodily injury and, in a recent case, even death.[7]

The Beginnings of a Rivalry, 1903–1920

In 1903 the original Baltimore Orioles migrated north to become the New York Highlanders (changed to the Yankees in 1913) of the American League (AL) and, within a year, challenged the Boston Americans (renamed the Red Sox in 1908) for the AL title. Glen Stout and Richard Johnson, two sportswriters who have written extensively on the history of both the Yankees and Red Sox,[8] argue that from the very first series the two team's players were at odds on the field, as were their fans off the field. To put it briefly:

> From the very first game several factors combined to transform a simple sporting contest into something more. Throughout the nineteenth century, Boston was considered the Hub of American culture, her most sophisticated and refined city. But the future was New York. The city had grown exponentially since the Civil War. It had taken over as the nation's commercial center and was quickly usurping Boston's cultural advantage.[9]

Moreover, in the second game of their initial three-game set a collision between New York outfielder Dave Fultz and Boston pitcher George Winter solidified an animosity that already existed between the Americans and the Orioles while simultaneously buttressing the newer issues between the people of Boston and New York. In short, the rivalry, one that was initially dominated by the American's/Red Sox, began. Over the course of the next fifteen years the team from Boston took four more World Series titles and even defeated the Highlander's in the season's last series for the AL title in 1904—it would be the last time that the Boston franchise beat the New York franchise with similar stakes on the line until 2004.

During the first two decades of the twentieth century Boston was clearly the class of the American League and, indeed, Major League Baseball. Conversely, the Highlanders/Yankees followed their upstart 1904 season with two more second-place finishes (1906 and 1910) but never seriously challenged for American League supremacy until the early 1920s. Despite the early dominance of the Yankees by the Red Sox, near the end of the century's second decade the balance of power in the American League was beginning to shift, thanks to a rift between AL ownership and league president Ban Johnson.[10]

Red Sox owner Harry Frazee, Yankee owners Colonels Jacob Rupert and Tillinghast L'Homedieu Huston, and Chicago White Sox owner Charlie Comiskey teamed together, as the "Insurrectos," against Johnson in a joint effort to undermine his power over the league.[11] The battle with Johnson most prominently played out when the Red Sox initiated a seemingly several-year de facto talent dump to the Yankees by trading the rights to pitcher Carl Mays, who had walked out on the team in July, for $40,000 and two players—Allan Russell and Bob McGraw. However, because Mays had walked out on the Red Sox, Johnson attempted to suspend him and ultimately tried to stop Mays from signing and playing with the Yankees through a series of failed court injunctions.

Eventually, Johnson gave way, but the Red Sox, Yankees, and White Sox had created an atmosphere whereby no one else in the eight-team American League was willing to make trades with them. As such, most of the teams' transactions had to be with one another. Further, following the 1919 Black Sox scandal, which put the White Sox off-limits to anybody for a time, the Yankees were all the Red Sox had and vice versa.[12]

The beginning of the Yankees–Red Sox rivalry is instructive in many ways. First, it is clear from their very first meeting that something was a little different when the two teams played against one another. Second, for the most part, although there has always been a certain level of on-field animosity, only one of the two teams is usually successful during a particular season. As such, the idea of a historic rivalry between the Red Sox and Yankees has almost always been more a creation of the media and fans than any real hatred between the two franchises. In fact, following the 1904 season-ending series, the two teams did not compete again so closely for the league title until the late 1940s.[13] Finally, the two team's ownership has always been willing to forge business alliances despite their supposed rivalry, and this clearly carried over in the early 1920s.

The Rise of the Yankees and the Tumultuous Red Sox, 1920–1949

Building on their trade of Mays, the Red Sox and Yankees ownership continued their symbiotic relationship when the two Colonels gave Frazee $125,000 for disgruntled superstar Babe Ruth.[14] This trade provided further evidence of the connection between the Red Sox and Yankee ownership, given the fact that the Sox had a better trade offer from the St. Louis Browns.[15] The transaction, which was initially received in the Boston and New York press with mixed reviews, morphed over the course of the century into "the curse of the Bambino."[16] Since that trade the Yankees turned into Major League Baseball's most powerful franchise and provided the most lasting mythology in the two team's rivalry. This is a story, however, that conveniently overlooks the fact that Ruth was often drunk, was seemingly unwilling to play for the Red Sox, and was later tied to a false idea that the money used to buy him was for a failed play named No-No Nanette (it was, in fact, a huge success).[17]

As time wore on Frazee seemingly turned the Red Sox into a minor league team of sorts for the Yankees, sending them key players like Waite Hoyt, Herb Pennock, Harry Harper, Wally Schang, Mike McNally, Everett Scott, Sam Jones, Joe Bush, Joe Dugan, and Elmer Smith, which helped the Yankees become the preeminent franchise in Major League Baseball.[18] Though this is often referred to as "the rape of the Red Sox,"[19] in all but one case each of the trades were justifiable;[20] they all just happened to benefit the Yankees in the end. Moreover, in the immediate period thereafter the Red Sox became one of the worst teams in Major League Baseball, while the Yankees rose to power.

The Yankees built the league's premier stadium (Yankee Stadium) in 1923 and won their first of twenty-six World Series that season. With a collection of hitting stars like Babe Ruth, Lou Gehrig, and Tony Lazzeri, as well as a formidable pitching staff, the Yankees dominated the 1920s and early 1930s by winning five American League titles and four World Series. Meanwhile, the Red Sox floundered in the American

League second division, continued to play in Fenway Park even though it burned twice,[21] and essentially became an afterthought to Yankees fans in terms of any rivalry.

This began to change in 1933 when the Red Sox were bought by Tom Yawkey, whose wealth largely came from a South Carolina rice plantation, and the team was willing and able to purchase high-priced players around the league. Moreover, Yawkey spent $1.5 million to purchase the team and repair and update Fenway Park as a more modern baseball attraction.[22] Unfortunately, along with the money, Yawkey also brought his southern racist values to the team, which contributed to the country-club atmosphere that the team and its fans have yet to completely overcome.[23]

Under new ownership the Red Sox once again became relevant by the late 1930s and early 1940s. However, as the Red Sox were beginning to gather great Major League talent, albeit often on the downside of their careers, the Yankees were still continuing to taste success on the field. For example, the Red Sox built their success primarily around the hitting of Jimmy Foxx and Ted Williams, while the Yankees countered with great hitters like Joe DiMaggio, Charlie Keller, and Tommy Henrich and a wealth of talented pitching. Moreover, the Yankees created the most formidable minor league system in baseball with which to continuously stock the team with young talent.[24]

Following the hiring of manager Joe McCarthy in 1931, the Yankees took eight of the next twelve AL titles and seven more World Series championships, giving them a total of ten in twenty-one seasons. The rivalry began to heat up again when the Red Sox contended for American League supremacy by finishing second to the Yankees four times between 1938 and 1942. However, the World War II conflict took away the Red Sox best players, Ted Williams, Bobby Doerr, and Johnny Pesky. When the trio returned from the war in 1945, the real "curse" of the Red Sox franchise became apparent—racism.[25]

Prior to the 1945 season, the team held a tryout for three black players, Sam Jethroe, Marvin Williams, and future superstar Jackie Robinson.[26] During the tryout, one member of team management uttered the unforgettable phrase, "Get those niggers off the field."[27] This type of thinking prevented the Red Sox from breaking the color barrier and signing Jackie Robinson and/or Willie Mays, whom the Red Sox relinquished their rights to in 1949 (two players who would have surely helped the team be more successful);[28] and it laid the foundation for the team to be referred to as "the plantation" well into the 1980s.[29]

Instead of years of prolonged success, bolstered by the signing of top talent regardless of race and ethnicity, the Red Sox created a lily-white atmosphere that haunts the team and its fans to this day. Notwithstanding this fact, the Sox captured the 1946 AL title (losing the World Series in seven games) and maintained a high level of on-field play through the rest of the decade. Conversely, by their standards, following a World Series triumph in 1943, the Yankees struggled through the mid-1940s until reaching and winning the World Series again in 1947. Finally, both franchises were successful at the same time again, and by 1949 the rivalry had its second close pennant chase.

Following their close second-place finish to the Cleveland Indians (losing in a one-game playoff) the Red Sox entered the 1949 season confident that they could take the AL title. The Yankees were predicted to finish third behind the Red Sox and Indians in the popular press.[30] However, as the season got underway oft-injured Yankee outfielder Joe DiMaggio was finally healthy and helped carry his team to a successful season. His longtime competitor Ted Williams, a player DiMaggio was almost traded for in 1947 in a drunken night out by Red Sox and Yankee ownership, was doing likewise for the Red Sox.[31] Moreover, "Joltin Joe's" brother, Dom DiMaggio, was also playing well for the Red Sox and helped temper any animosity Red Sox fans would generally hold for a top player on another team.

As the season came to a close Joe DiMaggio suffered with a bout of pneumonia, and the Red Sox took the division lead with five games to play. They could not take advantage of the lead and put the season away by the time the two teams had a two-game series to finish the season. Ahead by a game, all the Red Sox had to do was defeat the Yankees in New York one time, and DiMaggio was still sick.[32] Miraculously, Joe DiMaggio recovered enough from his affliction and had a huge series at the plate. Meanwhile, time and again the Red Sox would struggle at several key moments at the plate and in the field, which ultimately led to their season's demise.[33]

Yankees Take the Power Back, 1949–1964

Following their devastating loss in 1949 to the Yankees, the Red Sox again went into a tailspin and it took them another eighteen years to reemerge as contenders for the AL crown. Owner Tom Yawkey was so disgusted by their four-year run of near-misses that he would not return to Yankee Stadium for nineteen years.[34] During this period the Red Sox finished no higher than third place, often battled not to finish last, and even had the franchise looking to move to another city or at least replace Fenway Park.[35] Moreover, the racism that permeated the franchise prevented the club from signing black players and resulted in the Sox being the last Major League Baseball team to integrate in 1959.[36]

Though by many accounts no less racist, the Yankees were able to benefit from their extensive minor league system to combat the influx of talented black players in the Major Leagues.[37] Between 1949 and 1960, Casey Stengel led the Yankees to ten AL titles, and seven World Series Championships. He left the team following the Yankees devastating 1960 loss to the overmatched Pittsburgh Pirates. Under the direction of Ralph Houk and Yogi Berra, the Yankees continued to dominate the American League, winning four consecutive AL titles between 1961 and 1964 and captured two more World Series championships. Following their unprecedented run of fourteen AL titles and nine Word Series champ-ionships in sixteen years, the Yankees slumped over the course of the next decade. This was precipitated by the incursion of the draft, limits on minor league systems, and, of course, their own poor history with racism, which allowed the rest of Major League Baseball to compete with their impressive juggernaut.[38] In other words, since the Yankees could no longer purchase the best talent in the Major Leagues and saw their minor league program decimated, they too had to face the fact that the only way forward was through integration.

Impossible Dreams and an Ownership Change, 1964–1973

Importantly, while the Red Sox always had the money to compete with the Yankees, throughout the aforementioned period for various reasons (continued racism, poor management, and key injuries) they were never able to challenge them on the field. As such, the rivalry became dormant as fans of Major League Baseball saw new franchises begin to challenge for supremacy. More specifically, despite the fact that the Yankees were not very competitive between 1964 and 1975, because of their outstand-ing on-field success over the previous forty-five years, they were better equipped to handle a dry spell of success than the Red Sox—particularly in terms of maintaining fan popularity. Conversely, because the Red Sox had been so bad for so long their fan base dwindled and offered no challenge to the Yankees in regards to fan following.

Meanwhile, Minnesota, Baltimore, Detroit, and Oakland each took turns representing the American League in the World Series between 1964 and 1974 in every season except for one—1967. In fact, the 1967 season, when the Red Sox finally captured the American League title, has as much to do with the perpetuation of the Red Sox–Yankees rivalry as any other. Quite interestingly, it was during this campaign that the Yankees finished ninth place at 72-90 and twenty games out of first place. However, the Red Sox franchise, which was struggling to get fans to come to Fenway Park, overcame 100 to 1 odds of winning the division and embarked on the "impossible dream" season—thereby reenergizing a fast-dwindling fan base. Dan Shaughnessy wrote:

> On Friday, July 14, (1967) the Red Sox bashed the Orioles, 11–5. It was the first of 10 straight victories, a winning streak that legitimized Boston's contender status. It was the longest local winning streak in 10 years, and when the conquerers [sic] returned from Cleveland the night of July 23, there were 15,000 fanatics at Logan Airport. This was the first gathering of what today is known as Red Sox Nation. Airport officials said the crowd was bigger than the one that greeted the Beatles. There would be no more crowds of 461 fans (September 1965). There would be no more battles for the basement with the likes of the Washington Senators. From this point forward, the Red Sox would be annual contenders, wildly popular at the gate and on the airwaves.[39]

As the 1967 season came to a close, the Red Sox benefited from several key breaks on the field and bore the fruits of General Manager Dick O'Connell's labor. Despite an early setback regarding black pitcher Earl Wilson,[40] O'Connell understood that to have a competitive team in Boston he was going to have to sign minority talent. During his tenure as team director (1965–1977) O'Connell did just that, signing or trading for Reggie Smith, George Scott, Joe Foy, Jose Tartabull, Elston Howard, and later Jim Rice, Luis Tiant, and Cecil Cooper. Further, the impossible dream season captured the hearts and imagination of the New England region.

The Red Sox's struggle with race and always having a fatal flaw helped the city, which was struggling with its own race and class issue,[41] identify closely with the team. Moreover, though the Red Sox would ultimately lose to the St. Louis Cardinals in the World Series (which conveniently allowed for the mythological curse of the Bambino to continue), they were revived as a franchise.[42] Quite literally, following the 1967 season, going to Fenway Park, which was a few seasons from being razed, became a special event for fans of the Red Sox.[43] Young sportswriters Peter Gammons and Will McDonough, who started at the Boston Globe in the 1960s, helped perpetuate interest in the team by providing some of the most respected sports journalism in the nation.[44] Thus, in future seasons where the Red Sox faded, their fans could count on the media to provide incisive information about the team to keep them interested regardless of on-field success.

Further, under General Manager Dick O'Connell's direction the newly integrated (at least on the field) Red Sox organization became a force. Though fans still favored white players like Carl Yazstremski, Fred Lynn, and Jim Lonborg while shouting racial epithets at the team's black players, for a time the Sox were now competitive.[45] Soon thereafter the New York Yankees experienced a franchise renaissance when George Steinbrenner purchased the team from CBS corporation in 1973. Under his leadership, the Yankees also became an on-field success, which, consequently, helped set the context for how the rivalry is experienced today. In other words, "the Yankee pinstripes would come to represent the detached upper-class who had caused issues like 'forced busing' in Boston" that many fans of the Red Sox so despised, and they could act out this dislike by supporting their team intensely.[46]

Conflict Renewed: Part I, 1973–1980

To this point, however, though there were brief moments of intense competition, any rivalry between the two teams was relatively understated. The Red Sox had (in)advertently stocked the Yankees early World Series teams, joined forces with their ownership to undermine the AL president, then essentially struggled on the field with the notable exceptions of 1946–49 and 1967. However, as both franchises attempted to overcome their on-field struggles, largely revolving around racist management and/or fans, the two teams simultaneously rose to power in the American League during the 1970s. More importantly, led by a feud between their talented and passionate catchers (Thurman Munson of the Yankees and Carlton Fisk of the Red Sox), extreme hatred between the two teams boiled over for the first time.

Late in the 1973 season Munson and Fisk started a bench-clearing brawl following a collision at home plate.[47] There had been fights between players on the two teams before, notably, in 1952 when rookie Red Sox outfielder Jimmy Piersall and Yankee second baseman Billy Martin fought under the Fenway Park stands before the game even started, but this was the first time that it seemed as if both teams hated each other.[48] Perhaps part of it was that Piersall was later diagnosed with bipolar syndrome,[49] whereas the more recent fight stemmed from Fisk's and Munson's genuine dislike for one another. The other aspect is that now the Red Sox had come to represent the people of Boston.[50] The Yankees continued to be a very popular team and both teams were relatively competitive on the field, so this dislike would be played out on a national stage, in pressure situations, for the next few seasons.

In 1974 the Yankees caught and passed the Red Sox to finish in second place in the AL East, and the competition kept the two teams' aggressive attitude toward one another simmering. The next season the Red Sox captured the AL East and lost in the World Series in seven games to the Cincinnati Reds, while the Yankees fell to a third-place finish. Though there were no notable on-field incidents in 1975, there was no love lost between these two franchises, and their contentious relationships exploded again in 1976—with serious consequences.[51]

Following their World Series appearance in 1975 the Red Sox were confident that they could contend again the following season and, with Tom Yawkey's deep pockets, compete with the Yankees on the free agent market. Unfortunately, they got off to a poor start when they traveled to Yankee Stadium for a four-game series in late May. To illustrate the rise of the rivalry, this was the highest attended four-game series in Yankee Stadium since 1947.[52] In the opening game Fisk again got into a fight, this time with Yankee outfielder/designated hitter Lou Pinella. Their scuffle set off another bench-clearing brawl as within "seconds both dugouts emptied and there were a dozen fights going on all over the field. Players on both sides quickly punched each other out and stood in knots around home plate, grappling with each other."[53] In the end, the Red Sox only left-handed starter, Bill Lee, tore a ligament in his shoulder, causing him to miss two months of the season.

If the initial fight between Fisk and Munson had helped (re)ignite the rivalry, then the 1976 brawl sent it to new heights. Bill Lee started a trend of political referencing in between the Red Sox and Yankees when he called Yankee manager Billy Martin a "Nazi" and his players "Steinbrenner's Brown Shirts."[54] The Red Sox promptly struggled to a third-place finish, while the Yankees took their first AL Title since 1964 in Billy Martin's first full year as manager. Interestingly, many Red Sox players and fans blamed the Yankees for their poor showing during the 1976 season and looked forward to turning the tables against their rivals.[55] More devastating for the Red Sox, however, was the death of owner Tom Yawkey on July 9, 1976. Following Yawkey's passing, his wife, Jean, took over the team along with friends James Curran and Joseph LaCour, and much upheaval in terms of roster and management within the Red Sox was soon to follow.[56]

As such, in terms of competitiveness, the 1977 season had as much to do with the Red Sox continued failure to succeed in winning the World Series and the Yankees continued success as any other. With free agency in full swing, and Jean Yawkey's and George Steinbrenner's deep pockets, there was an opportunity again for rich teams to buy a competitive advantage over less wealthy clubs. Boston signed pitcher Bill Campbell as well as trading for pitcher Mike Torrez and position players George Scott and Bernie Carbo. The Yankees countered by purchasing Reggie Jackson, for $2.96 million over five years, and pitcher Don Gullett, while also trading for key players Mickey Rivers and Bucky Dent. The two teams were now stocked with talent and competed late into September. However, yet again, the Yankees took control of the division, captured the AL East title, and defeated the Los Angeles Dodgers for the World Series.[57]

The post-1977 season is important in that it contributed to stunting the Red Sox future while giving the Yankees another competitive advantage. More specifically, when Tom Yawkey hired Dick O'Connell to be general manager there was an influx of diversity on the Red Sox roster. Thus, though Yawkey, by many accounts, was an outright racist, through hiring O'Connell he helped the franchise overcome some of the problems that come with having such a regressive owner. Jean Yawkey and her friends believed otherwise. At the conclusion of the season Jean Yawkey decided to retain manager Don Zimmer, who had lost the respect of his entire pitching staff, and fired O'Connell.[58] In so doing, the Red Sox commitment to some semblance of diversity (they did have a habit of trading away black stars) reverted to a past of near-racial exclusion. Although they always had the money to compete on the free agent market, it would take the Red Sox until 1992 (the year after Jean Yawkey died) to sign a black free agent—a full seventeen years after free agency was introduced in Major League Baseball.[59]

On the other hand, in terms of forming a roster, George Steinbrenner could care less about the racial and ethnic background of his players. As long as they performed well on the field he would sign and keep them, and Reggie Jackson was a perfect example of his philosophy. When he first joined the Yankees in 1977, a report in *Sport* magazine surfaced in which Jackson claimed to be "the straw that stirs the drink."[60] While his claim infuriated teammates and his manager, it turned out to be prophetic as he hit three home runs in the decisive sixth game of the World Series.

Regardless of their seemingly different attitudes about race and ethnicity, both teams entered the 1978 season primed to compete for AL East supremacy. Behind sluggers Jim Rice, Dwight Evans, and Fred Lynn, coupled with the strong pitching of Dennis Eckersley, Mike Torrez, and Luis Tiant, the Red Sox raced out to an early lead in the division. Conversely, the Yankees, who were aptly titled the "Bronx Zoo" by third baseman Greg Nettles, nearly fell apart.[61]

As the season wore on the Red Sox kept pulling away from the AL teams. On July 19, the Red Sox were 61-28, nine games ahead of the Milwaukee Brewers and a whopping fourteen and a half games ahead of the fourth-place Yankees. In an effort to calm the "Bronx Zoo," five days later Steinbrenner fired Martin and replaced him with Bob Lemon. With renewed focus, the Yankees made an improbable run, and the Red Sox, which sustained key injuries to Jery Remy and Dwight Evans, collapsed.

Though they would ultimately recover from the "Boston Massacre,"[62] an early-September four-game series sweep to the Yankees by a combined score of 42–9, and even a three-and-a-half-game deficit to the Yankees in mid-September, the Red Sox struggled to a force a playoff with their nemesis. This would be the first playoff game between the two teams since 1949, and the game's result helped solidify the competition between the two into a rivalry—albeit one clearly dominated by the Yankees. Though the Yankees trailed 2–0 in the sixth inning, they remained within striking distance for light-hitting Bucky Dent to smack a three-run, two-out, home run in the seventh inning to give the Yankees a lead they would never relinquish.

Once again the Yankees would go on to win the World Series and prove that they dominated their rivalry with the Red Sox because they had not lost a meaningful game to them since 1904. Further, Bucky Dent's home run was added to Red Sox lore as another reason they were cursed, and it also solidified their fans' hatred of the New York Yankees—while simultaneously providing Yankee fans with confidence that they would never lose to the Red Sox. However, 1978 proved to be the beginning of the end of this incarnation of the Red Sox–Yankees rivalry since neither team would compete so closely for AL supremacy for another twenty-one seasons.

In 1979 both the Red Sox and Yankees struggled to third and fourth finishes, respectively. However, in terms of perpetuating the rivalry, 1979 proved to be an important year. On September 9, the Entertainment and Sports Network (ESPN), based in Bristol, Connecticut, aired on cable for the first time. Situated between Boston and New York and focused on New England–based sports (at least early on), the twenty-four-hour sports broadcasting channel would come to provide year-round information on the Red Sox–Yankees rivalry—particularly as the former's futility continued.

Rivalry with Whom? 1980–1996

As the 1980s began, both teams found it difficult to repeat their success of the previous decade. The Yankees returned to the playoffs in 1980 and 1981 but lost in the American League Championship Series and World Series. Meanwhile, the Red Sox struggled during the first half of the 1980s. Once again new teams began to challenge for AL East supremacy as the Baltimore Orioles, Milwaukee Brewers, Detroit Tigers, and Toronto Blue Jays took turns representing the division in the playoffs—capturing two World Series between them.

Following their World Series loss to the Los Angeles Dodgers, the Yankees would not return to the playoffs for another fourteen seasons. However, led by fan favorite Don Mattingly and the talent of a bevy of high-priced free agents like Dave Winfield and Rickey Henderson, the Yankees compiled the highest winning record for any Major League franchise in the 1980s; but they consistently fell just short of the division title. Conversely, in 1986 the Red Sox were finally able to put together a steady effort and captured their first division and AL title since 1975.[63]

Though the Yankees were not involved, 1986 added to Red Sox fans' desperation and provided yet another key media moment in the rivalry. Having miraculously overcome a 3–1 deficit against the Angels in the AL Conference Series, the Red Sox carried that momentum into the World Series against another New York team—the Mets. Vastly over-matched in terms of talent, the Red Sox were able to position themselves within one out of a World Series title in the tenth inning of game six. However, in an unlikely turn of events, the Sox blew the lead, the game, and, two days later, the World Series.

Once again, the devastating loss provided further evidence that the team was under a curse, and winning the World Series was their only way out of it. In terms of the rivalry, beating the Yankees on the way to the World Series was still not part of it. Yet 1986 was a key year in the future perpetuation of the rivalry between the two franchises. More specifically, *Boston Globe* writer Nathan Cobb was sent to Bobby Valentine's Sports Gallery Café in Millford, Connecticut, to write a story on the World Series. In the article Cobb invented the term "Red Sox Nation" in reference to the team's fans.[64] Four years later, in his book *The Curse of the Bambino*, Dan Shaughnessy popularized the phrase, thereby providing the media with a simple reference and the fans with a seeming united front to compete with the wildly popular New York Yankees.

Throughout the rest of the 1980s the Yankees continued to be successful enough to keep the interest of their fans, but never quite good enough to earn AL East supremacy. Perhaps emblematic of the Yankees decade of frustration, in 1990 the tumultuous reign of George Steinbrenner as Yankee owner briefly came to a close as he was forced to resign for trying to disparage outfielder Dave Winfield.[65] Conversely, the Red Sox were able to perform at a high level. In 1988 and 1990 they captured the AL East title only to lose eight consecutive playoff games to the newly dominant Oakland Athletics. Yet again, however, the poor history Boston and the Red Sox had with racism reared its ugly head. As mentioned previously, the franchise did not sign a black free agent until after Jean Yawkey passed away.

For years, the Red Sox had maintained a roster with a minimum of minorities, and the atmosphere in the clubhouse was referred to as "the plantation" around the league.[66] By the early 1990s, when the Sox were finally ready to start signing minorities, their history of organizational racism proved devastating. Great black players like Joe Carter, Dave Winfield, Tim Raines, Kirby Puckett, Ken Griffey Jr., Barry Bonds,

Marquis Grissom, and David Justice refused to sign with the team. In fact, the latter two actually had it written into their contract that they were not to be traded to Boston.[67] Eventually, as in the 1950s and '60s, bad luck coupled with the Red Sox unwillingness/inability to sign minority stars prevented the team from actually capturing their elusive World Series title.

In the mid-1990s, the Red Sox began to struggle once again, while the Yankees began a new rise to dominance. George Steinbrenner was allowed to return to his role of owner of the Yankees in 1993 with a new strategy in mind. Instead of constantly stocking his team with high-priced free-agent talent and/or trading future stars for great players, he was also willing to allow his minor leaguers develop.[68] By 1995 this new mixture of young and old proved successful as the Yankees returned to the playoffs for the first time since 1981 and marked the only time wildly popular first baseman Don Mattingly would ever play in the post season.

Though the team would fall to the Seattle Mariners in a decisive fifth game, the newest incarnation of the Yankees dynasty began anew. In 1996 the team's mixture of young homegrown talent (Andy Pettitte, Mariano Rivera, Derek Jeter, Ramiro Mendoza, and Bernie Williams), veteran leadership (Wade Boggs, Joe Girardi, and Paul O'Neill), and, of course, high-priced free agents (Tino Martinez, Dwight Gooden, Jimmy Key, David Cone, and Kenny Rodgers) provided New York with their first World Series since 1978. Moreover, with their newfound strategy, the Yankees were poised to compete at a high level for years to come.

Conflict Renewed: Part II, 1998–2003

Following a disappointing loss to the Cleveland Indians in game five of the AL Division Series (ALDS) in 1997, in which Mariano Rivera would suffer his only blown save in the playoffs for the next three years, the Yankees came into the 1998 season looking for their second World Series in three years. Meanwhile, the new ownership of the Red Sox, operating under the moniker "Jean Yawkey trust," was actively seeking to reverse the connection of the team to racism. According to Howard Bryant, Mo Vaughn, who joined the team in 1992, openly worked to change the perception from a player standpoint.[69] And by 1998 Vaughn was joined by arguably the most important free-agent signing in team history, Pedro Martinez.

Though Mo Vaughn opened the door for change in the franchise, it was the young Dominican pitcher who kicked it down. Quite literally, on days that Martinez pitched, the previously all-white cultural landscape of Fenway shifted as Dominican (im)migrants populated the park, waving flags, beating drums, and chanting loudly for the brash young star.[70] Unfortunately, though the Yankees started the year 0-4, they staked their claim as the greatest baseball team ever assembled and finished on an incredible 114-44 run to take the division by a staggering twenty-two games. Still, the Red Sox took second with a better record than the Central Division champion Cleveland Indians and West Division titleholder Texas Rangers and clinched their first birth into the playoffs in eight seasons.

In the 1998 playoffs, the Red Sox easily fell to the Cleveland Indians three games to one as the Yankees swept through to the AL Championship Series. The Yankees continued their new run of dominance by defeating Cleveland in six games and sweeping the San Diego Padres for the World Series. Importantly, for the Yankees, this playoff run offered more evidence of their legendary mystique that seemingly carried the team through tense moments in the playoffs. Building from Derek Jeter's fan-aided home run in the AL Championship Series against the Orioles and Jim Leyritz's improbable home run in game three of the 1996 World Series, in 1998 the Yankees enjoyed the benefit of home runs hooking foul (against Texas), being held up by the wind (Cleveland), and a terrible call in game one of the World Series, which led to Tino Martinez's momentum-shifting grand slam.[71] When juxtaposed with the Red Sox's historically based bad luck, the stage was set for their first playoff meeting since 1978.

In 1999, the Yankees, using their now tried-and-true method of mixing homegrown talent and high-priced free agents, were poised to repeat their World Series win. Conversely, the Red Sox, using a mixture of good hitting and perhaps the greatest season ever by a pitcher in the modern era (Pedro Martinez), once again reached the playoffs as the Wild Card—finishing four games behind the AL East champion Yankees. The rivalry between the two teams got its first jolt in several decades when, following his incredible season, Pedro Martinez was up for season-ending individual honors.

Though his 23-4 record, 2.07 ERA (earned run average), and 313 strikeouts won the pitching triple crown and a Cy Young award, Martinez fell short of the AL Most Valuable Player (MVP). That Martinez did not win the MVP was of little surprise given that the last pitcher to earn the honor was Dennis Eckersley in 1992. It was the reason he came up short, which infuriated Red Sox fans and essentially restarted the Boston–New York rivalry. Martinez captured the most first place votes (eight of twenty-eight) but was omitted from Minnesota's LaVelle Neal's and New York's George King's ballot, causing him to fall thirteen points short of the award. Most infuriating for Martinez supporters was King's contention that he would not vote for a pitcher under the principle that they are not everyday players even though one year prior he had voted for pitchers David Wells (New York Yankees) and Rick Helling (Texas).[72]

With the MVP controversy fresh in their minds, and the media constantly reminding the general public of their past failures against the Yankees, the Red Sox and Red Sox Nation desperately wanted to exact a measure of revenge. The Yankees attitude was much different and could be characterized by former catcher Yogi Berra's statement to Bernie Williams: "Relax, we've been playing these guys for 80 years—they're never gonna beat us."[73] Building on their history of good luck, particularly on their two recent World Series runs, the Yankees opportunistically took advantage of a few questionable calls throughout their five-game series victory.

Further perpetuating the rivalry, however, was the behavior of the Red Sox and their fans coupled with the Yankee reaction to their boorish behavior. The Red Sox and their fans' frustration with constantly coming up short to the Yankees particularly came to a head in game four of 1999 ALCS. During that contest the fans taunted Yankee pitcher Andy Pettitte, chanted "Just Say No" to outfielder Darryl Strawberry (who had a long history of drug abuse), and, following Red Sox manager Jimmy Williams' ejection, began showering the field with debris—even hitting outfielder Paul O'Neill with a beer bottle.[74] Following the game, some of the upset Yankee players commented on the lack of class exhibited by Red Sox fans; and, as pitcher Jeff Nelson asserted, "They better lose tomorrow. I think 56,000, 57,000 [spectators] will appreciate what they did to us today."[75] As mentioned previously, the Red Sox did lose the series in five games, sending the Yankees to the World Series and, consequently, their second straight world title.

Following the 1999 season, casual baseball fans were increasingly attracted to the Yankee–Red Sox rivalry. Apparently, the desperation of

Red Sox fans juxtaposed with the justifiable confidence of Yankees fans was appealing to a national audience. Dan Shaughnessy now had the 1999 season to write about in the third printing of *The Curse of the Bambino*, and many braced for the next collision between these two teams. At a new fever pitch, the Red Sox–Yankees rivalry was about to become a phenomenon that has now far exceeded what the rivalry was at any point in the previous century.

Once again Pedro Martinez was a key contributor in moving the rivalry forward. For all of their overwhelming accomplishments over the course of the previous two seasons, the Yankees struggled at only one thing, defeating Pedro Martinez. In a sense, he gave the Yankees and their fans reason to care about playing a team "they never lost to" because they almost always lost to him. In other words, following his outstanding 1999 regular season outing against the Yankees (seventeen strikeouts and one hit) and subsequent playoff performance, Martinez was a Red Sox player with the confidence of a Yankee.[76] At the end of spring 2000, the second coming of this rivalry received another huge jolt.

On May 28, 2000, the Red Sox traveled to Yankee Stadium to play a nationally televised game that was a reprise of the pitching matchup from game three of the 1999 ALCS—Roger Clemens versus Pedro Martinez. In addition, the two teams were tied atop the AL East standings, and, thus, the winner took an early lead in the division. Coming off of the controversial 1999 ALCS, ESPN took advantage of the interest of the game and marketed it as "Cy Young vs. Cy Old." In what proved to be a brief peak in the rivalry, Martinez and the Red Sox won a memorable pitching duel 2–0.[77]

However, the Yankees were able to shift their fortunes against Martinez by winning twice against him later during the season, and they took a commanding nine-game division lead with twenty-two to play at the end of the 2000. Despite going 3-16 to end the season, the Yankees held off the Red Sox and clinched the AL East title with an 87-74 record—fifth best in the American League. Even with their terrible finish the Yankees would defeat Oakland, Seattle, and the New York Mets to clinch their third consecutive World Series.

Over the course of the next two seasons, the media attention surrounding the Yankees–Red Sox rivalry again died down, save for the constant questions about the curse of the Bambino. In 2001 Martinez, frustrated with having to answer questions about the mythical curse, famously stated, "Wake up the Babe, and I'll drill him in the ass."[78] He promptly injured his arm, and the 2001 season was essentially lost for the Red Sox. The Yankees, on the other hand, would cruise to another division title, and Mike Mussina would counter Pedro's recent performances with a near-perfect game in September. More importantly, though, they would eventually fall in seven games to the Arizona Diamondbacks, who were led by the outstanding pitching of Randy Johnson and Curt Schilling.

In 2002, despite their loss to the Anaheim Angels in the ALDS, the Yankees still had little to concern themselves with in terms of the Red Sox. However, at the end of that season, the next key moment in the rivalry took place. The Yawkey Trust sold the Red Sox to a group headed by John Henry (former minority owner of the Yankees), Larry Luchinno, Tom Werner, and the *New York Times* for $700 million.[79] Further, despite struggling for success during the 2001 and 2002 seasons, the Yankees and Red Sox were stockpiling their teams with young talent and high-priced players who would make the teams the two most talented in baseball during the 2003 and 2004 seasons. The Red Sox, benefiting from Dan Duquette's (who would be fired following the 2002 season in favor of twenty-eight-year-old Theo Epstein) struggle to combat the charges of racism still swirling around the team, were now able to attract top minority players like Manny Ramirez.[80]

Conversely, the Yankees were able to use their immense wealth and name value to continue the run of dominance over their rival. This famously came to the fore once again as they countered the Red Sox's incredible effort to sign Cuban pitcher Jose Contreras and signed him to a free-agent contract worth $32 million over four years. Larry Lucchino, already frustrated by finishing second to the Yankees, referred to the Yankees as "the Evil Empire"—a terminology from Ronald Reagan's Cold War claims toward the Soviet Union.[81] George Steinbrenner took the response as a charge that he was communist and angrily replied that Lucchino was "a chameleon who knew nothing about baseball."[82] For the 2003 season, then, the competition between the two teams had begun in December.

As the regular season started the Yankees boasted a pitching staff of six strong pitchers (Roger Clemens, Andy Pettitte, Mike Mussina, David Wells, Jeff Weaver, and Jose Contreras) and a slugging offense that would score 877 runs and hit 230 home runs. The Red Sox had a more potent offense (961 runs scored and 238 home runs) but were less than stellar on mound after the duo of Pedro Martinez and Derek Lowe. Despite their lack of consistent starting pitching, the Red Sox chased the Yankees throughout the course of the 2003 season but finished second to them for the sixth straight season.

During the season the Yankees established themselves as the class of the American League and confidently marched into the playoffs. If the Yankees were symbols of professionalism, then the 2003 Red Sox were their antithesis. General Manager Theo Epstein built the team using a form of Billy Bean's Moneyball style, which is based in finding statistical edges that often overlook personality differences and body types typical of athletic baseball players.[83] The result was a roster of interesting characters whose personalities did not necessarily mesh, but all rallied behind first baseman Kevin Millar's country-music-inspired mantra, "Cowboy Up." Given the recent renewal of the rivalry, and the two teams' personality differences, the popular media frothed at the mouth in hopes of another ALCS meeting between the two teams.

Neither team disappointed the press, and both made it to the ALCS using their distinctive styles. The Yankees quietly defeated the Twins in four games, taking the last three straight, and were primed for a return visit to the World Series. Meanwhile, the Red Sox fell behind the Athletics two games to none (marking ten straight playoff losses to the Athletics). Upon their return to Boston the Red Sox, perhaps taking a cue from their fans, taunted the Athletics throughout the final three games on their way to another matchup with the Yankees in the ALCS.[84]

Following their struggle through five arduous games against the Athletics, the Red Sox's starting pitching staff was decimated. However, they were able to forge a split in the first two games at Yankee Stadium, leading to another Pedro Martinez versus Roger Clemens matchup. To date, in four starts against one another, Martinez (2-0, 0.93 ERA) had dominated Clemens (0-2, 4.50 ERA), but the Yankees were determined to take the lead in the ALCS at Fenway Park. From the beginning it was clear that Clemens and Martinez did not have their best stuff but were able to keep the opposition off balance enough to keep their respective teams in the game. The Sox took a 2–0 lead in the first, but the Yankees battled back to tie the game at 2–2 after three innings. In the top of the fourth Jorge Posada started the Yankees off with a walk, followed by Nick Johnson's single and Hidecki Matsui's tie-breaking double. With runners on second and third and no one out, a frustrated Martinez once again stirred the rivalry by uncorking a 93 mph fastball at Karim Garcia that just missed his head but hit him in the back. The result was a shouting match between Martinez and the entire Yankee bench.

Re-energized, Martinez would not allow a hit to his final eleven batters (he gave up a run on a double play), but the conflict was just getting started. As Clemens returned to the mound in the bottom of the fourth, the tone of the game had definitely changed. Manny Ramirez led the inning off and, after a high pitch from Clemens that was nowhere near him, started pointing to the mound and yelling at the Yankee pitcher. The dugouts quickly emptied, and Yankee bench coach Don Zimmer (manager of the Red Sox in 1978) charged after Pedro Martinez. Martinez, seeing the seventy-two-year-old lumbering after him, side-stepped and pushed him aside. Zimmer hit the ground and rolled a few times, and, as Grady Little later commented, the ALCS was "upgraded from a battle to a war."[85]

As the dust settled, so did the pitching, and the Yankees held on for a 4–3 victory. The fighting, however, did not stop. In the ninth inning, Yankee reliever Jeff Nelson, right fielder Karim Garcia, and Boston groundskeeper Paul Williams threw punches in the bullpen that resulted in a hand laceration for Garcia. The three were later charged criminally with assault and battery for their participation in the fight.[86] The embarrassing behavior by all parties earned national attention as the ALCS was garnering great television ratings.[87]

With millions of people watching, the Yankees would, once again, take the series in seven games on the back of third baseman Aaron Boone's dramatic walk-off home run in extra innings. Though the Yankees would fall in six games to the Marlins, in many ways, the World Series had become inconsequential to the media and general public. More to the point, following their exciting playoff battle, there was a sense that both teams had more to offer; and, unlike in 1950, 1979, and 2000, the Red Sox did not come apart at the seems. In fact, starting with the off-season, they got stronger.

2004: Rivalry Finally

Two days after the 2003 baseball season came to a close the Red Sox fired manager Grady Little and looked to improve a team that was more than likely going to break up after the 2004 season.[88] Initially, the Red Sox started talking with the Texas Rangers about trading for superstar short-stop Alex Rodriguez and also tried to discern who to re-sign for the following year. While continuing trade talks with the Rangers, the Red Sox also looked to improve their pitching staff. In the end they traded for and signed Arizona Diamondback ace (and noted Yankee killer) Curt Schilling and Oakland Athletics closer Keith Foulke.[89]

The Yankees, on the other hand, lost Roger Clemens to semi-retirement (he would later come back with the Houston Astros the following season) and Andy Pettitte, who signed with the Houston Astros. To make up for the loss of the two star pitchers, the Yankees traded Nick Johnson, Juan Rivera, and reliever Randy Choate for Montreal Expos pitcher Javier Vazquez. In addition to signing Vazquez, the Yankees were also able to trade Jeff Weaver for pitcher Kevin Brown and signed relievers Tom Gordon and Paul Quantrill, slugger Gary Sheffield, and Kenny Lofton. Meanwhile, they stood by and watched as the Red Sox attempted to make a deal for Alex Rodriguez.

As the trade talks commenced between the Red Sox and Rangers for Rodriguez's services, Commissioner Bud Selig intervened and placed a deadline on the possible trade for 5 PM on December 17. Initially, the trade would have included beloved Red Sox shortstop Nomar Garciaparra for Rodriguez, but it eventually morphed into a three-team deal involving the Chicago White Sox. The deal which would have the Red Sox send left fielder Manny Ramirez, minor league pitcher John Lester, and cash to the Rangers for Alex Rodriguez, then Garciaparra to the White Sox for left fielder Magglio Ordonez was blocked by the Major League Baseball players union because Rodriguez would have had to take a pay cut for the trade to be accepted by the Red Sox.[90] Any talk of Rodriguez joining the newest incarnation of the Red Sox–Yankee rivalry was hushed until a month later when Yankee hero Aaron Boone seriously injured his knee playing basketball.

With no third baseman for the upcoming season, the Yankees now entered into trade talks with the Rangers for Rodriguez. With more money to spend and an absolute need to fill the position, the Yankees were prepared to take all the steps to acquire the superstar. On February 16, 2004, they did just that, sending second baseman Alfonso Soriano to the Rangers for Rodriguez and cash to help alleviate the huge addition to their already bloated payroll. Now Aaron Boone had not only beaten the Sox in game seven of the ALCS, but precipitated a trade for the player that was going to help the Red Sox finally beat the Yankees. For Yankees fans this was yet another sign of their never-ending superiority over the Red Sox, while Red Sox Nation fumed over another potential lost season.[91]

The media used the opportunity to push the notion of a Red Sox–Yankee rivalry to new heights as the Alex Rodriguez acquisition provided more evidence for "the curse of the Bambino." In early April of 2004, Dan Shaughnessy used the recent turn of events to update and publish his book *The Curse of the Bambino* for a third time as fans of both teams prepared for another competitive season. Still, to this point, the Red Sox had not defeated the Yankees in an important game since 1904. Thus, while the media used the opportunity to strengthen ratings by claiming that there was a rivalry, under the strict definition of a rivalry, whereby both teams defeat one another, the Red Sox and Yankees had still not met that requirement.[92] 2004 would forever change that.

Throughout the season the two teams battled back and forth for the division, but by the end of July the Yankees had surged to a ten-and-a-half-game lead. However, a fight-filled slugfest late in the month, in which the Red Sox came back to beat the Yankees 9–8,[93] coupled with the Sox trading their popular but oft-injured and unhappy Nomar Garciaparra and minor leaguer Henri Stanley for Orlando Cabrera, Doug Mientkiewicz, and Dave Roberts, helped galvanize the team.[94] Though the Red Sox fell short of winning the division by three games, as the playoffs began, the media, general public, and two teams looked forward to a rematch of the 2003 ALCS; but, again, they would both have to survive the first round of the playoffs.

Neither team disappointed as the Yankees defeated the Twins in four games, while the Red Sox swept the Angels in three. In the 2004 ALCS the Yankees took advantage of an injury Curt Shilling sustained in the first round of the playoffs, utilized a great pitching performance by John Lieber, and outslugged their rivals in Boston to take the first three games of the series. However, the Red Sox showed resolve by coming back to take the next three games, getting Yankee ace reliever Mariano Rivera to blow two consecutive playoff saves for the first time ever and getting timely hitting and base running from David Ortiz and Dave Roberts, respectively. With the momentum clearly on their side the Red Sox jumped out of the gates against the Yankees Kevin Brown in game seven and never looked back. When it ended, the Red Sox had officially discarded the curse of the Bambino and left a silenced Yankee

Stadium, save for a few raucous Red Sox fans, as American League Champions. Once again, the World Series seemed inconsequential, but this time the AL champion would prevail, and the Red Sox took their first World Series in eighty-six years following a four-game sweep of the St. Louis Cardinals.

Now that they had defeated the Yankees, won the World Series, and proven that they had similar spending power, the Red Sox had officially arrived as a true rival to the Yankees. That off-season the team began selling official membership in Red Sox Nation, transitioning the moniker into an "absolute corporate marketing monster."[95] Given their recent success, and with the help of never-ending media coverage, the Red Sox were becoming as popular as the Yankees.[96] Moreover, aided by ESPN, YES, and NESN (the latter two being the Yankees and Red Sox local television channels, respectively) the Yankees–Red Sox rivalry had achieved a new level of media saturation.[97]

Yet perhaps in part because of this market saturation since 2004, the rivalry has continued, but clearly without the same qualitative and quantitative level of meaning. In 2008 ratings for baseball have dropped as the Red Sox and Yankees have not fielded the most competitive teams in baseball.[98] Though the general excitement over the rivalry has died down, the hatred between the fans and their two teams has boiled over a few times. In 2005, for example, Yankee outfielder Gary Sheffield was punched in the face by a Red Sox fan while trying to retrieve a ball in the outfield at Fenway Park.[99] During my research (on Red Sox Nation) in 2007, I personally witnessed several hundred fans fighting at Yankee Stadium, resulting in a large amount of ejections. More recently, a Yankee fan ran over and killed a Red Sox fan outside a bar in Boston.[100] So while the hatred between the teams may be in a dormant state today, it is always a heated series away from reigniting.

Coda: Consistent Rivalry or Dependence on Success?

Looking back at the course of history, the recent dip in general public interest for the Yankees–Red Sox rivalry should come as little surprise. In baseball, over a season that takes 162 games, teams must endure injury, roster and management upheaval, as well as (unrealistic) fan expectations, and for one team to maintain a highly successful run atop the standings is rare. For two to be continuously dominant, in the same division, is nearly impossible. This is perhaps why there are so few continuously meaningful Major League Baseball rivalries.

More to the point, what is to be understood then about the unique nature of the Red Sox–Yankee rivalry is that, unlike historic college or professional football rivalries, where teams can look forward to playing each other once or twice a season, the Red Sox and Yankees now face each other no less than nineteen times a year. Thus it is difficult to have this rivalry be meaningful game after game, season after season. This year the success of upstart teams like the Tampa Bay Rays and Milwaukee Brewers, as well as the historically underperforming Chicago Cubs, has provided much more compelling story lines for the general baseball-watching public to really care about a rivalry between second- and third-place teams in the American League East. More importantly, over the course of Major League Baseball history, seasons like this one occur more often than those in which the Red Sox and Yankees are competing for the playoffs and/or World Series.

Thus I believe that that the most recent rise in general public importance between the Yankees and Red Sox has more to do with the two clubs holding the record for most consecutive finishes in first and second place in the AL East Division, respectively, between 1997 and 2005. Moreover, this general run of success for both teams has taken place in an era where most people in the United States have access to twenty-four-hour-media coverage on the sport and the relationship between the two teams, which serves to constantly remind them that a rivalry does, in fact, exist.

Therefore, I would argue that the Red Sox–Yankees rivalry has always conveniently overlooked or ignored the historical fact that the two teams' managements have often been friends and/or worked together—which is true even today.[101] At the same time, throughout baseball history, there have been short periods of time (early 1900s, 1940s, late 1970s, and the present) when both teams have been successful, with highly competitive players on their roster who have captured the interest and imagination of both cities. Moreover, the success (and post-9/11 resolve) of New York City and the Yankees and the social struggles of Boston and the Red Sox have helped the fans of these teams ally themselves a bit more closely and/or seek to have their identity represented by their respective clubs more than other cities' fans.[102]

Given this context then, when the Yankees and Red Sox do have successful teams in the same season, as evidenced by the (recent) past, these games seem to mean more to more people—perhaps buttressed by the constant media attention.[103] They also have a history of exciting postseason meetings with which to rekindle the rivalry when it becomes dormant. Conversely, if, for example, the Chicago Cubs and Milwaukee Brewers were to play in this season's playoffs, though they are only ninety miles apart, the series does not contain the same historical, mythological, and media-generated ingredients to create the same sense of intense hatred between the two clubs' fans.

In closing, a rivalry between the Red Sox and Yankees does exist. It may not be as historically based as members of the media or the two teams' ownership and fans would like the general public to believe, but there is a qualitatively and quantitatively different relationship between the two ball clubs in comparison to other competing Major League Baseball franchises. However, given the Red Sox's ability to finally defeat the Yankees in 2004 and then win another World Series in 2007, the relationship between the two ball clubs and their fans has changed. The dynamic between the two franchises has been altered in that the historically dominated Red Sox is now the most recently successful team in Major League Baseball. Only time will tell how the recent run of success against the Yankees will affect the rivalry. In other words, will people stop being interested because the Red Sox finally beat the Yankees, or will it be more exciting now that the Yankees are looking for their first taste of success in nearly a decade? I am not quite sure yet, but will be watching to find out.

Owen Nolan of the Toronto Maple Leafs skating ahead of Joe Juneau of the Montreal Canadiens in a 2003 game at Air Canada Center in Toronto. *Courtesy of Getty Images.*

eight

A Tale of Two Cities

The Toronto Maple Leafs versus the Montreal Canadiens

BRIAN P. SOEBBING
AND DANIEL S. MASON

The Montreal Canadiens and Toronto Maple Leafs remain two of the most successful and enduring franchises in the National Hockey League (NHL). The two teams have won the most Stanley Cup Championships and have a rivalry that dates back over ninety years. Just as the two franchises have vied for hockey supremacy over the years, Montreal and Toronto have also contended for status as Canada's premier city. The purpose of this chapter is to review the historic relationship between the two franchises and cities. Following a brief overview of both cities, we explore the competitive relationship between the two teams. The development of new facilities to replace the Forum in Montreal and Maple Leaf Gardens in Toronto is then discussed in the context of these broader changes. In doing so, the evolving rivalry between the two teams will be revealed.

Toronto and Montreal

Although the two cities have at various times vied for economic and cultural dominance, Toronto and Montreal have very different reputations. Basic comparisons have typically considered Toronto as a "good" city, or "city that works," while Montreal is more associated with its European-influenced cultural elements.[1] As a result, some have considered that the two cities have developed identities that are rooted in their differences from one another.[2] From its earliest days, Montreal was clearly the hub of Canadian culture, industry, and sport.[3] For the first seventy years or so of the twentieth century, Montreal remained Canada's financial center.

However, starting in the 1970s the out-migration of Anglophone Canadians in Montreal, specifically—and the province of Quebec, more generally—began to occur. Meanwhile, Toronto continued to grow in size and influence.

Deep-seated Anglophone-Francophone tensions also provided a backdrop for the post–World II shift in prominence of the two cities, and hockey's cultural significance in Montreal and Quebec has been linked to the broader changes that occurred during the 1950s and 1960s. For example, the "Richard Riot" of 1955—when Canadiens' star, Maurice "Rocket" Richard, was suspended for the remainder of the regular season and playoffs for an on-ice incident—is widely considered a turning point in Quebec's Quiet Revolution.[4] Pent-up anger and frustration manifested itself in the riot, where Montrealers rebelled against their local Francophone hero's punishment by the NHL. While Francophones held a population majority in Montreal since the 1870s, the French-speaking population only gained power in the province and city in the 1960s and 1970s.[5] During the last decades of the twentieth century, "widespread changes in the economy and culture of Montreal have occurred against the backdrop of postwar struggles for Quebec independence, the election of pro-sovereignty governments and significant changes in Quebec's socioeconomic and demographic composition."[6] This also led to the emergence of partitionism, where in the aftermath of the 1995 referendum—which saw Quebec remain a part of Canada by a very narrow margin —arguments were put forth that Quebec could secede from Canada but give citizens the choice to remain in Canada and not leave the territory.[7]

At the same time, the City of Montreal has aggressively pursued a strategy to position itself as a tourist city. The first major foray into creating the city as an event destination occurred during the 1960s through the mid 1970s, when the city hosted two mega-events: Expo '67 and the 1976 Summer Olympic Games. Expo '67 attracted 50 million visitors, and $1.5 billion was invested in infrastructure. The Olympic Games, originally projected to cost $121 million, eventually required an investment of $922 million. By itself, Olympic Stadium cost an additional $537 million after the games were over, and the total cost of the games, including debt, was in excess of $3 billion.[8] As one observer noted, "Montreal is caught in this double bind between striving to become a 'world class city' and preserving and cultivating specificity, or distinctiveness."[9]

Since the 1970s, Toronto has surpassed Montreal in terms of population and economic influence. Immediately following the Second World War, Toronto witnessed rapid growth in manufacturing, housing, and significant public spending on infrastructure.[10] Many foreign business interests chose to locate their Canadian operations in the city. "By 1971, Toronto was acknowledged as having eclipsed Montreal as the headquarters and financial-service capital of Canada."[11] Meanwhile, the city was lauded as "one of the few metropolitan areas in North America whose social environment did not decline with rapid expansion."[12]

Rivalry Background

A constant through all of the growth and change in Montreal and Toronto was the rivalry between its two NHL teams, the Canadiens and Maple Leafs, which both joined the NHL in its inaugural season in 1917. The 2009–2010 NHL season marked the ninety-fourth year of the storied rivalry, although many acknowledge that the rivalry began in earnest in 1946. That year Frank Selke Sr. quit his position in the Toronto Maple Leafs organization due to friction with Managing Director Conn Smythe. Selke then became the general manager of the rival Montreal Canadiens and lead the Canadiens to six Stanley Cups and transformed Montreal into a powerhouse in the NHL. Although the rivalry has cooled somewhat in recent years, in March 2006 the Canadiens eliminated the Maple Leafs from the playoffs. The following season, the Maple Leafs returned the favor to the Canadiens.[13]

Through the years, no two NHL teams have been more successful than the Canadiens and the Maple Leafs. The Canadiens and Maple Leafs are number one and two, respectively, in most Stanley Cup Championships. The Canadiens have won twenty-three Stanley Cups compared to thirteen Stanley Cup titles for Toronto. Table 1 and table 2 illustrate the Stanley Cup Championship years for each franchise while also listing the rival's season points and finish within the conference for that season. As one can see from table 2, six times in Toronto's Stanley Cup Championship seasons, Montreal has been the best team in the conference for that season. However, the rivalry has been decidedly one-sided in recent decades as Toronto has not captured a Stanley Cup Championship since the 1966–1967 season. In contrast, Montreal has won ten championships since then. In addition, the 1976–1977 Montreal Canadiens team is considered the greatest hockey team of all time and was voted the second-greatest team

TABLE 1: Montreal Stanley Cup Championships

M. S. CUP YEARS	1924	1930	1931	1944	1946
Toronto points	20	40	53	50	45
Toronto Conf. finish	3	3	2	3	5
Total games	24	44	44	50	50

M. S. CUP YEARS	1966	1968	1969	1971	1973
Toronto points	79	76	85	82	64
Toronto Conf. finish	3	5	4	4	6
Total games	70	74	76	78	78

Note: "NA" signified that Toronto was not in same conference as Montreal. From the 1982–1983 season through the 1997–1998 season, Toronto was in Clarence Campbell Conference (currently known as the Western Conference) while Montreal was in the Prince of Wales Conference (Eastern Conference).

TABLE 2: Toronto Stanley Cup Championships

T. S. CUP YEARS	1918	1922	1932	1942	1945
Montreal points	26	25	57	39	80
Montreal Conf. finish	1	3	1	6	1
Total games	22	24	48	48	50

in any sport of the twentieth century, behind only the 1927 New York Yankees of Major League Baseball (MLB).[14]

Not only are Montreal and Toronto the two most successful NHL franchises in the NHL in terms of Stanley Cup Championships, the two clubs boast a long list of NHL Hall of Fame players. According to the Legends of Hockey Web site (which operates in conjunction with the Hockey Hall of Fame), there are fifty-two Hall of Fame inductees who have played for Montreal, with Patrick Roy and Dick Duff being the two most recent players inducted in 2006. Toronto closely trails with fifty, with Brian Leetch most recently inducted with the 2009 Hall of Fame class.[15]

The two rivals have enjoyed success defined not only by Stanley Cup titles and legendary players, but also through their competitiveness during the regular season. Different from the other three North American sports

1953	1956	1957	1958	1959	1960	1965
67	61	57	53	65	79	74
5	4	5	6	4	2	4
70	70	70	70	70	70	70

1976	1977	1978	1979	1986	1993
83	81	92	81	57	99
5	5 Tied	4	5	NA	NA
80	80	80	80	80	84

1947	1948	1949	1951	1962	1963	1964	1967
78	51	65	65	98	79	85	77
1	5	3	3	1	3	1	2
60	60	60	70	70	70	70	70

leagues that use winning percentage as a performance measure, the NHL uses points as its performance measure. Points are obtained from both winning the game and tying the game. Since the inception of the shootout starting in the 2005–2006 season, ties have been eliminated and replaced with overtime losses. In addition, due to the different number of regular season games played throughout NHL history, it is difficult to compare on-ice performance purely from points awarded in a given season. Therefore, points per game provides a useful performance measure to show regular season performance for the two rival clubs from the 1917–1918 season through the 2007–2008 season. Figure 8.1 shows the comparison of the two clubs throughout NHL history. The performance of both franchises rivaled each other through the early portion of the NHL. Beginning around 1970, Montreal experienced a drastic increase in performance in comparison to the rival Maple Leafs, when the Canadiens captured six Stanley Cup Championships through 1979. Montreal's success continued until the early 1990s. The mid to late 1990s showed the reemergence of the Maple Leafs' performance on the ice while the Canadiens experienced a decline in on-ice performance. However, over the past few seasons the Canadiens have reemerged as one of the top teams in the NHL while the Maple Leafs' performance has fallen back to around one point per game.

Not surprisingly, the teams have established an extensive head-to-head record against one another. Through the end of the 2008–09 season, the two teams had met 696 times during the regular season, with Montreal holding a 328-275 win-loss edge (with 88 ties).[16] In addition, the two teams have met 15 times in the Stanley Cup Playoffs, with the Canadiens holding the all-time edge with eight wins (and an overall record of 71-42). Six of those playoff meetings have been for the Stanley Cup championship (1917–1918, 1946–1947, 1950–1951, 1958–1959, 1959–1960, and 1966–1967). Despite an overall losing record against Montreal, Toronto has won four of the six meetings when the Stanley Cup was on the line.[17]

Fans of the two teams have enjoyed many historic confrontations over the ninety plus years of the rivalry. To illustrate, five memorable match-ups are reviewed. On March 23, 1944, Maurice "the Rocket" Richard scored all five goals as the Canadiens defeated the Maple Leafs 5–1. For his effort, Richard earned the first, second, and third star of the game.[18]

In 1951, the two clubs met in the Stanley Cup Final. Each game in the five-game series went into overtime, with the Canadiens' Richard scoring in all five games. However, the Maple Leafs overcame Richard's heroics to capture the cup. Leafs' defenseman Bill Barilko scored the series' clinching overtime goal. That moment, featuring Barilko flying through the air as he shot the puck on net, remains one of hockey's most enduring images. The song "Fifty Mission Cap," performed by a popular Canadian band, the Tragically Hip, later celebrated Barilko and his final NHL goal.[19]

The franchises met again in the 1960 Stanley Cup Final. This time, the Canadiens swept the Maple Leafs in four straight games, winning the cup at Maple Leaf Gardens and setting an NHL record with their fifth consecutive Stanley Cup victory. It also marked the final game of "Rocket" Richard's NHL career. The Maple Leafs' fans expressed their appreciation of one of the greatest players to ever play, giving him a warm farewell after the game.[20]

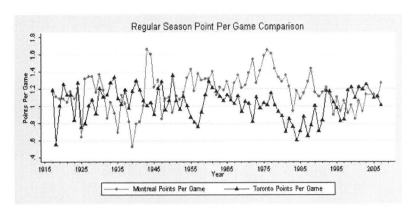

Fig. 8.1. Regular season points per game (1917–1918 through 2007–2008)

Montreal was a heavy favorite to win the 1967 Stanley Cup Final as it again faced off against Toronto. A rumor circulated that the mayor of Montreal had already ordered the trophy case to display the Stanley Cup for the upcoming World Exposition, Expo '67. However, with a roster of aging veterans, Toronto captured the Stanley Cup in six games.

The 1967 Stanley Cup was the last cup victory for Toronto.[21] However, the teams continue to play critical games against one another. On April 7, 2007, Montreal held the eighth and final playoff spot with Toronto in ninth place, only two points behind the rival Canadiens. The game played at the Air Canada Centre was the regular season finale for both teams. Reports said the crowd of over nineteen thousand was on its feet for the entire game. Toronto jumped out to an early two-goal lead (3–1) only to see Montreal lead by two goals in the middle of the second period on a hat trick by Michael Ryder and a goal by Christopher Higgins (5–3). Toronto scored a late second-period goal to cut Montreal's lead to one (5–4) and netted the equalizer early in the third period. The Leafs' Kyle Wellwood scored the game winner less than four minutes into the third period as Toronto held on to win the game 6–5 and eliminated the Canadiens from the playoffs. The win gave the Maple Leafs sole possession of eighth place with one day left in the NHL season.[22]

Urban Revitalization and the New Arenas

Both teams have developed significant followings both within their respective communities and elsewhere. With the onset of CBC radio (and later television) coverage of games in the 1930s, and the absence of any other Canadian-based NHL teams until the 1970s, hockey fans throughout the country continue to maintain long-standing ties to either the Leafs or Canadiens.[23] However, despite their enduring popularity, by the early 1990s both franchises were feeling pressures from changes to the industry and broader economic climate that would influence team and league strategies. First, with the hiring of Gary Bettman as the league's first commissioner, the NHL pursued an aggressive expansion strategy that sought to increase the profile of the league in non-traditional hockey markets in the southern United States.[24] Second, several Canadian teams were in financial jeopardy due to the declining value of the Canadian dollar, small market sizes, and antiquated facilities. By the mid 1990s, two Canada-based franchises—the Winnipeg Jets and Quebec Nordiques—succumbed to these pressures and relocated to Phoenix, AZ, and Denver, CO, respectively.

Unlike the Quebec City and Winnipeg markets, Toronto and Montreal were not likely a threat to relocate. However, the ability of the two franchises to generate revenues was limited by their existing facilities. In Montreal, the Forum was built in 1924 and had been the host arena for the Canadiens since 1926. Originally seating under ten thousand, it was renovated over the years and eventually held nearly eighteen thousand for hockey games (including standing-room only).[25]

Maple Leaf Gardens opened in 1931, built by Conn Smythe. Like the Forum, it was the site of many historic NHL and international hockey games and had been expanded and renovated over the years. It seated less than sixteen thousand fans and had no club seats. As a result, both the Forum and Maple Leaf Gardens were not likely candidates for further renovation as there was now demand for more spacious luxury seating and more luxury boxes. However, given the cultural significance of each building, team owners would have to carefully move through the process of exploring any new arena construction.[26]

In Montreal, team president Ronald Corey had conducted several feasibility studies during the late 1980s that explored adding luxury seating and corporate suites. However, on August 24, 1989, he announced that the team would need a new, as opposed to renovated, arena.[27] In order to gain public acceptance—they would be leaving a historic and treasured facility—the team positioned the transition in terms of a new facility conferring world-class city status on the city of Montreal.[28] In

Toronto, similar concerns about the viability of Maple Leaf Gardens had led to speculation of that arena's replacement. Not long after joining the Leafs as team president, Cliff Fletcher was quoted as saying, "'The facts of life . . . are that we have to provide our fans with the same amenities as fans are getting in other North American cities with new facilities.'"[29] Thus, the need for a new facility was often framed in terms of the need for the teams to establish amenities and comforts that would bring the arenas on par with the facilities that existed in other leading "world-class" urban centers.

Before examining the construction of the Bell Centre and the Air Canada Centre (ACC), it is important to examine arena construction and funding for arena construction within the North American professional sports industry during this time period. The 1990s fell within two sports facility construction-funding eras. According to John Crompton, Dennis Howard, and Turgut Var, the period of major league sports facility construction between 1985 through 1994 is considered the transitional era, a time when the percentage of public funding for a new facility was decreasing. The public's portion of funding for a new facility in the previous era (from 1970 to 1984), termed the public subsidy era, was 93 percent. During the transitional era, the percentage of public funds used for facilities decreased to 64 percent of total facility costs. The authors also differentiated arenas from stadiums. The public funded the entire arena project during the public subsidy era. During the transitional era, the public funding for new arenas decreased to 49 percent.[30]

The second funding era began in 1995 and was termed the fully loaded era. This era was characterized by an even further decrease in the percentage of public funding to the overall cost of new facilities. Total public funding for all facilities was at 51 percent of the total cost. In examining arenas specifically, public funding decreased from 49 percent in the transitional era to 39 percent in the fully loaded era. The authors commented, "The increased contributions from the franchises reflects the growing unwillingness of taxpayers to wholly fund these projects."[31] This was the case for both facilities in discussion here, which were privately financed.

Crompton, Howard, and Var listed several factors that led to a decrease in the use of public spending throughout the two eras. One was the increased revenue streams available to North American professional sports teams. These streams came from items such as lease agreements, national and regional broadcasting rights, merchandise, and sponsorship agreements. Another factor was a general increase in private funding for public programs and services. The final factor was an increasing public animosity toward fully funding professional sports facilities with public funds.[32]

The fully loaded era was the era in which the Molson Centre (now called the Bell Centre) and the Air Canada Centre (ACC) opened. This era represented the construction of 45 percent of the entire population of major league professional sport facilities in North America.[33] Crompton, Howard, and Var observed that for the most part, "facilities from which teams moved were not physically obsolete, rather they were commercially obsolete."[34] The new facilities built in this era had many similar characteristics. These characteristics include an increased number of luxury boxes, wider concourses, improved sightlines, and increased number of concession options. Table 3 provides an overview of the Bell (Molson) Centre and the ACC.

The Molson Centre, opened in 1996 to replace the Montreal Forum, was constructed specifically as a hockey facility. It was and remains the largest venue (defined by stadium capacity) in the NHL. The facility was constructed to provide revenue streams to the Canadiens that the old Forum could not. When completed, the Molson Centre had over 2,600 club seats, 135 luxury boxes, and four restaurants. The new arena "offered a way to pay growing salaries and still deliver a profit."[35]

The ACC opened in 1999 for both the Maple Leafs and the National Basketball Association's (NBA) Toronto Raptors. Embracing the boosterism-driven competition for a state-of-the-art facility, Maple Leafs forward Tie Domi said, "This [ACC] is the best in the whole league, the best ever. . . . [T]here's no comparison to any of the new places around the National Hockey League."[36] This was echoed by one local journalist,

TABLE 3: Air Canada Centre and Bell (nee Molson) Centre

ARENA	YEAR BUILT	COST	DESIGN
Air Canada Center	1999	265C	HOK; Brisbin, Brook and Beynon
Centre Bell	1996	230C	Various

who noted that "sports and entertainment fans in Toronto and Southern Ontario would watch their favourite activities in one of the best facilities in the world."[37]

However, the development, construction, and transition process for the new arenas did not occur without conflict. For the Canadiens, dealing with abandoning the Forum was an issue. For the Maple Leafs, a major issue related to its relationship with the Toronto Raptors. The ACC was originally planned to be constructed for the Raptors alone. Toronto was awarded an NBA franchise in 1993 and began its first season of play in 1995. The belief in 1993 was that a group formed by Larry Tannebaum would be awarded the franchise by the NBA owners. Tannebaum and Steve Stavro, the majority owner of the Maple Leafs, planned on building a joint facility that would have the spirit of Maple Leaf Gardens, but with the "fully loaded" features seen for this time period. The NBA owners, however, accepted an alternative bid by John Bitove. Bitove and Stavro had previous conflicts with each other; thus, the idea of a joint facility between the two seemed unlikely.[38] In the meantime, the Raptors needed to begin construction on a new arena immediately or face a financial penalty under an agreement between the Raptors, the NBA, and the Ontario government, signed in 1994.[39] In addition, the Maple Leafs would only accept the Raptors as a tenant to a new arena and not a partner in an arena plan.[40] As a result, the Raptors began construction of the Air Canada Centre on their own as a basketball-only facility.

However, the Maple Leafs still wanted a new hockey facility to replace Maple Leaf Gardens, now the oldest facility in the NHL. Due to the rift between the owners of the two franchises, a jointly held facility was not possible even though it made the most economic sense for both teams and the city of Toronto. As a result, the Maple Leafs forged ahead with its own arena plans and bought the Union Station building a few

CONSTRUCTION	CAPACITY	SUITES	CLUB SEATS	NAMING RIGHTS (AMOUNT/YEARS)
PCL	18,800	152	1,020	$40M/20Y
Hunt	21,273	135	2,656	$64M/20Y

short blocks from the Air Canada Centre construction site. A plan in 1997 called for the construction of a nineteen-thousand-seat arena on top of Union Station. Even though the Raptors were already constructing the ACC, the Maple Leafs "reached out" to the Raptors in hopes of the Raptors becoming part of its arena plan. Raptors officials rebuffed the plan and described the Maple Leafs' plan as abstract.[41] However, a unique change occurred which brought the two rival franchises together.

In October 1996, the minority owner of the Raptors, Allan Slaight, triggered a clause in the ownership contract to become majority owner of the franchise. Bitove could not come up with the matching funds and, as a result, Slaight became majority owner. In a November 1996 column, journalist James Chrisitie wrote that Slaight would probably add Larry Tannebaum as part of his ownership group. Recall that Tannebaum had competed with the Bitove group for the bid to be the original owner of the Raptors. The result was a possible partnership between the two franchises on an arena project.[42] Two years later, Slaight put the Raptors franchise up for sale and it was bought by Stavro and the Maple Leaf Gardens Limited group, the parent company of the Toronto Maple Leafs.[43] With a new arena ready to open, Stavro altered the arena plans slightly in order for the arena to accommodate both the Raptors and the Leafs. In the end, the ACC was constructed with both franchises operating under the same arena and the same ownership group. As explained by Gunderson, "The acquisition of Union Station was important to the Leafs/Raptors alliance because it provided them with the opportunity to construct, first, a 'gateway' to the ACC and the waterfront commercial sector, and secondly, possible future corporate spaces, such as office towers and hotels. This was something that the acquisition of the ACC alone would not have allowed the Maple Leaf corporation to do."[44]

The conflict was different for the Montreal Canadiens. The economic climate in the 1990s was difficult for all Canadian NHL franchises. The Quebec Nordiques and the Winnipeg Jets would relocate to the United States during this time. One reason for the relocation of these franchises was the securing of more favorable arena funding deals that had significant public funding included. Provincial and the national governments in Canada did not provide as much public funding compared to their United States counterparts.

Another critical factor that increased the need for a new facility was the weakening of the Canadian dollar (CAD) against the United States dollar (USD). Figure 8.2 illustrates the nominal Canadian to U.S. exchange rate from 1990 through 2007. The exchange rate was high in 1997, reflecting the problems that all Canadian franchises had to face. A weakening CAD made it more expensive for Canadian franchises to pay players who were being paid in USD. In addition, since tickets were paid in CAD, teams were finding it difficult to generate additional revenue to compensate for the deflating CAD. This would influence team payrolls and, potentially, on-ice performance. Figure 8.3 illustrates the on-ice performance (measured by points per game) of the Maple Leafs and the Canadians beginning in the 1990–1991 season through the 2007–2008 season, where it appears that teams were able to weather the storm regarding on-ice performance (see fig. 8.3). The exchange rate reached its lowest point in 2002 and has been on a steady increase ever since, giving relief to the Canadian NHL franchises.

The Montreal Canadians had an additional challenge, the substantial government taxes paid by the team. As shown in table 3, the Molson Centre was built for 265 million CAD, all of which was privately financed. In an article appearing in April 1999, the Canadiens' president, Ronald Corey, stated that his team's tax bill was 9.6 million CAD for that

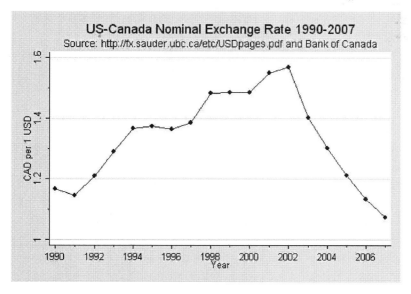

Fig. 8.2. U.S.–Canadian nominal exchange rate (1990–2007)

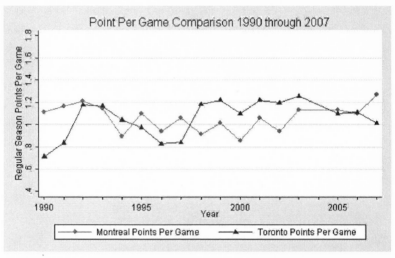

Fig. 8.3. Points per game comparison (1990–1991 season through 2007–2008 season)

year. This figure was higher than the taxes paid by all of the U.S.-based NHL teams combined.45 Corey sought relief from the high tax burden; however, he did not receive any relief from the city. This made maximizing revenues for the Canadiens even more critical.

Both the Canadiens and Maple Leafs were poised to increase team revenues through the new revenue-generating amenities in their respective facilities. However, the transfer from the Forum and Maple Leaf Gardens to the new arenas was a delicate one. Although the moves would clearly improve the financial positions of both franchises, the two arenas that were being left behind had evolved into important social spaces in their respective communities.[46] As explained by Belanger, "Markers of memory are powerfully encoded into popular cultural practices in general—such as sports teams—and the buildings that have housed these teams. But few sports teams and few buildings have been as culturally significant as the Montreal *Canadiens* and the Montreal Forum."[47] In order to make a seamless transition from the Forum to the Molson Centre, the team had to find a way to symbolically transport the team to its new environs. To do so, a parade, called "le Grand Demenagement" (the great move) was organized the day before the opening game in the Molson Centre. The parade featured retired players and moved relics from the Forum, including Stanley

Cup banners. Over 200,000 spectators attended the parade.[48] In addition, both cities held elaborate closing ceremonies in order to honor the team's past and celebrate the move to the new facilities.

The building of the new arenas in both Montreal and Toronto allowed both clubs to reemerge as prominent franchises in the NHL from both a business perspective and an on-ice perspective. Figure 8.4 illustrates the point per game breakdown beginning in the 1995–1996 season through the 2007–2008 season. The 1995–1996 season represented the one season prior to the opening of the Molson Centre in Montreal. Montreal's points per game were relatively stable. However, in the 2007–2008 season, Montreal reemerged as a contending team in the Eastern Conference. Toronto, on the other hand, illustrated a jump in its points per game when the ACC opened in 1999. The club jumped from approximately 0.8 points per game in 1997–1998 season to approximately 1.2 points per game in the 1998–1999 season. Toronto remained at that level until the past few seasons, when its points per game has diminished.

The teams' reemergence from a business perspective is also important to examine. Figure 8.5 illustrates the real franchise valuation, expressed in 2006 USD, of the two rival franchises. In examining figure 8.5, one notices the dramatic increase in the value of the Canadiens

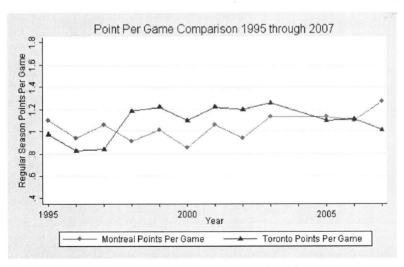

Fig. 8.4. Points per game comparison (1995–1996 season through 2007–2008 season)

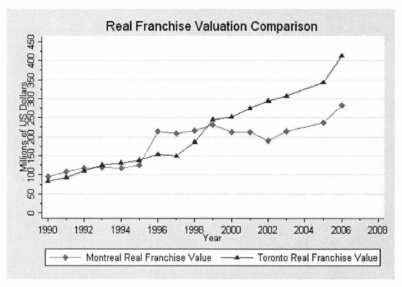

Fig. 8.5. Real franchise valuation comparison (1990–2006)

franchise with the opening of the Bell Centre in 1996. The value decreased until 2002 and this was probably due to the weakening Canadian Dollar. However, due to the strengthening of the dollar and better on-ice performance, the value of the franchise has risen again. The Maple Leafs franchise experienced its own increase in the first full season of the ACC in 1999. Unlike the Canadiens, the Maple Leafs did not experience a decline in the franchise value. The franchise value has been increasing and the Maple Leafs franchise is now the highest valued franchise in the NHL at over 400 million USD.

Conclusion

The Toronto Maple Leafs and Montreal Canadiens have had a storied rivalry since the teams entered the NHL over ninety years ago. As this chapter has shown, the rivalry has not been limited solely to on-the-ice activities, but reflects broader competitive forces that have witnessed Toronto and Montreal vie for status as Canada's preeminent economic and cultural center. In addition, both cities witnessed the closing of long-standing facilities in the 1990s that reflected the economic demands of a new NHL. In developing these new facilities, and building on the estab-lished hockey cultures within their cities, both franchises have emerged as economic powerhouses as the Canadian dollar has strengthened. Despite a relative lack of competitive success in recent years, both teams seem poised to improve their standing among NHL teams and return to the status that has made them the two dominant franchises in NHL history and the sport's greatest rivalry.

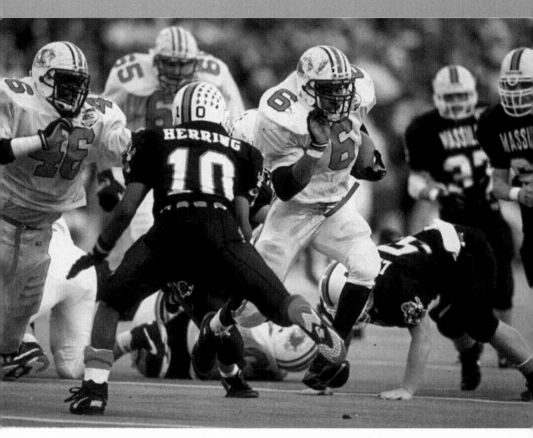

Canton McKinley's Adrian Brown breaking through the Massillon defensive line in a 1994 game at Massillon. *Courtesy of Getty Images.*

nine

Like Cats and Dogs
The Massillon–Canton McKinley Football Rivalry

LAWRENCE W. HUGENBERG
AND BRIAN C. PATTIE

For many of us, high school was about much more than just attending classes and making new friends. Most of us remember Friday or Saturday nights during the fall because it meant the varsity school football team was scheduled to play. Throughout the day, you heard chatter about the upcoming game and whom your school was playing. The big question was, were you playing against your big rival or were you just playing another game? In Ohio, everyone knows of the rivalry between the Canton McKinley Bulldogs and the Massillon Tigers. Thomas Maroon, Margaret Maroon, and Craig Holbert captured the mythic reason why this rivalry is important to local citizens, writing:

> Route 21 and Interstate 77 are the Tigris and the Euphrates Rivers of today's modern football. Route 21 leads to the Tigers, and Interstate 77 will send any football fan into euphoria. Interstate 77 connects Cleveland, Akron, and Canton, the hottest bed of football in the history of mankind. Route 21 connects Massillon to this group. To the people of this region, the Tigris and Euphrates are the start of human civilization, but Route 21 and Interstate 77 are the start of life.[1]

Wherever you went to high school in Ohio, if they have a football team and a primary rival, you understand all facets of the long-standing football rivalry between the Canton McKinley Bulldogs and the Massillon Tigers.

In this chapter, we explain the importance of high school football in Ohio, specifically, northeastern Ohio. We explore reasons for the

Canton McKinley Bulldog–Massillon Tiger high school football rivalry, including its roots in the first days of professional football in the United States. We also explore the history and current importance of this rivalry. Another section of this chapter explores the two cities: Canton and Massillon. We explain their population decline as it relates to their industrial decline as part of a larger regional economic malaise. We also mention some of the dynamic personalities who coached both teams and later became famous for their college and/or professional football coaching successes. Finally, we make observations of the 2007 rivalry game at Fawcett Stadium in Canton, Ohio, the home field of the Canton McKinley Bulldogs and the annual National Football League's Hall of Fame Game that concludes the induction ceremonies.

The Importance of High School Football

High school football is an important part of the American landscape in small towns and urban centers, in farm towns and manufacturing towns, and in affluent suburbs and economically challenged suburbs. To many loyal and emotional fans, high school football provides weeks of enjoyment when their team wins or weeks of dejection when the team loses. The emphasis placed on high school football in communities can be dramatic. Occasionally, this emphasis results in misguided behaviors. For example, *USA Today* reported on Hoover (Alabama) High School which was being investigated for changing grades of football players, pressuring teachers to "give" grades to the school's football players, and giving preferential treatment to football players.[2] The pressure to succeed increased at this high school when it started the 2006 season as the number-one-ranked high school team in *USA Today*'s Super 25 ratings. The pressures to succeed in high school football, the Pop Warner league, or the local city football association reflect the values of our culture and rival the pressures to win at the college and professional levels. One fan, discussing the importance of football in Ohio, wrote on myespn.go.com, "A lot of people underestimate the pride and tradition of Ohio football as a whole. From pee-wee to the Browns the integrity that Ohio football is based on cannot be matched."

Seemingly, Vince Lombardi, legendary coach of the Green Bay Packers and winning coach of the first two Super Bowls, was right:

"Winning isn't everything, it is the only thing." In trying to explain our nation's compulsion with winning at any cost, Robert Samuelson, a columnist for the *Washington Post,* wrote, "For a subset of Americans, ambition becomes unmoored from anchors of good judgment, widely accepted social norms or ethical values."[3]

In 2007, the Ohio High School Athletic Association commissioned a study to determine the percentages of adults attending sporting events in Ohio.[4] The results indicated that 26.3% of adults in Ohio attend high school sports—more than reported attending Major League Baseball games (21.8%), National Football League games (8.4%), college football games (5.7%), National Basketball Association games (3.7%), and college basketball games (2.8%). The preference for high school football is intriguing because Ohio has two professional baseball teams (Cleveland Indians and Cincinnati Reds), two professional football teams (Cincinnati Bengals and Cleveland Browns), one professional basketball team (Cleveland Cavaliers), and dozens of large and small colleges (The Ohio State University, Kent State University, University of Cincinnati, Xavier University, Mount Union College, University of Dayton, Ohio Northern University, Marietta College, etc.) fielding teams in football and basketball. One reason for the higher reported attendance at high school football games might be the proximity of alumni to their high school—people who live in the same or neighboring community support their team. A second reason could be the alumni's logical emotional attachment to their high school, resulting in their return on the weekends to attend a game. Finally, another reason might be the blue-collar, hard-working nature of people throughout the Buckeye State. In support of this premise, one fan noted on ESPN.go.com, when discussing the Titletown competition, "There are four things that will always be in Massillon. There will always be pride, courage, hard work and Massillon football. Go Tigers." Related to the hard-working nature of fans, the economics of entertainment dollars becomes a more central issue in many households. Because of the high cost of attending many college and professional sporting events, high school football has clear economic value. For one or a combination of the reasons noted above, sports fans in Ohio report their preference for attending high school football games. For many fans of their local high school team, but specifically for fans of the Massillon Tigers, football "is a cult, a religion."[5]

The Importance of the Canton-Massillon Rivalry

The importance of high school football in Canton and Massillon, Ohio, cannot be underestimated. On Friday and Saturday nights, Canton McKinley and Massillon football games draw thousands of fans from their schools and local communities—whether playing home or away. Families plan their social calendar for the weekend around their team's games. For example, a family will meet for dinner, hurriedly eat, organize what to wear to the game, and arrive at the stadium to watch their team warm up before the game. Parents and children wear their team's colors: sweatshirts, stocking caps, T-shirts, jackets, ball caps, etc. Each piece of clothing bears their team's colors and frequently their team's mascot. Young boys and girls will find a small football or put on small cheerleading uniforms so they can pretend they are representing their schools at the game. Teenagers will paint the family car with the team's colors and mascot. In Massillon, families drive down city streets throughout the season identifying the houses of team members because of the large placards indicating where Tiger football players live. During the week leading up to the Canton McKinley game, anyone driving through downtown will notice the large banners hanging from the lampposts saying, "Beat McKinley." Store owners hang the "Closed" signs on their shops so they, too, can attend the game—after all, they know few people will be shopping during their community's high school game.

Massillon and Canton McKinley have booster associations with hundreds of members supporting athletics—specifically football—financially and emotionally. For both schools, rivalry week starts as soon as the referee's whistle blows ending the previous week's game. One fan likened the week of preparation and anticipation for the Massillon–Canton McKinley game like getting ready for "Christmas, birthdays, weddings," and any other large event in our lives.[6] It is this emotional attachment to their local schools, whether alumni or not, that draws them to the weekly games. Until their team's next game, fans in local restaurants, shops, bars, barber shops, and beauty salons sit or stand around discussing how well or badly their team played. Fans recount every play, starting with the kickoff, and each mistake the high school players make and criticize the coaches unmercifully for each offensive and defensive play call made during a win or loss. Rick Shepas, former Tiger coach, in discussing the importance of winning in Massillon, noted, "Unless you win the state title in Massillon, nothing is ever good enough."[7] The mayor of Massillon, Francis H. Cicchinelli, noted that Massillon Tiger football is "part of our history, part of the fabric of this city."[8] In the movie about Massillon Tiger football, *Go Tigers!* head coach Shepas stated, "The identity of the town is what takes place at the high school."[9] Businesses in Massillon have a history of celebrating with the team. In the 1951 documentary, *Touchdown Town,* businesses flew flags on poles in front of their shops to celebrate the team's state championships, downtown streets were closed for part of Friday afternoons so that the marching band and students from the high school could march through the streets to a pep rally, and there were displays in all the windows. One such display highlighted the "best" players from last week's game by placing their pictures and statistics in the window.[10] The city's team spirit and fan pride in the Tigers is a consistent theme regardless of how well the team is doing in a particular season. Recently, a fan wrote on myespn.co.com, defending Massillon's selection as one of the finalists for the Titletown crown, "Remember the history that our town holds in football history. Name another school that has as much tradition or history that our town has. this [*sic*] is why Massillon should be Titletown USA or at least deserves to be in the running."

Rivalry Roots in Professional Football

One reason the Canton-Massillon rivalry is so important lies in the early days of professional football, which was founded in northeastern Ohio. Importantly, two of the teams in professional football were the Canton Bulldogs and the Massillon Tigers. In the early days of the professional game, these two teams representing Canton and Massillon, Ohio, played against each other. Both high school teams took their mascot names from the early professional teams.[11] According to Kimberly Kenney, "Akron was the first city in the area to add a professional football franchise in 1903. Canton and Massillon soon followed, and football became a major pastime for both communities. Annual matches between rival teams attracted large audiences and captured the attention of almost everyone in town."[12] Thomas Maroon, Margaret Maroon, and Craig Holbert reported, "The first documented Canton team played Massillon for the Ohio League Championship in 1905 and 1906, losing to them twice."[13] The Canton Bulldogs won the World Championship in 1919, 1922, and 1923. After winning the third championship, the team was sold and moved to Cleveland, Ohio.[14] This rich professional football history led the National Football League (NFL) to place the Professional Football Hall of Fame (HOF) in Canton, Ohio, in the early 1960s. To commemorate this link to the Canton Bulldog and Massillon Tiger past, the HOF opened with Jim Thorpe's Canton Bulldog blanket and Knute Rockne's Massillon Tiger pro team helmet. Henry Timken of the Timken Company donated $250,000 to bring the HOF to Canton and "renew the city's tarnished reputation as a haven for gangsters, gambling, and prostitution."[15] Other Canton business leaders raised almost $380,000 for the construction of the HOF.

History of the rivalry

The Canton McKinley and Massillon high schools have been competing against each other on the football field since 1894.[16] In explaining the importance of the longevity of the New York Yankee–Boston Red Sox rivalry, Sean Deveney, noted, "There's more than a century of history and animosity between the teams, of course, but history alone cannot carry a rivalry. . . . A true rivalry must contain some element of relevance in the present."[17] Deveney's observations explain the importance of history to a rivalry, but he emphasizes the need for relevance to the current fan. This statement certainly applies to the long-standing rivalry between the Massillon Tigers and Canton McKinley Bulldogs. According to the *Massillon Tigers Cyber Review,* from 1894 to 2006 there have been 115 games, with Massillon winning 61, Canton McKinley winning 49, and 5 games ending in ties. Fans at the early games at the turn of the twentieth century had to stand to watch the game, and admissions were collected by passing the hat during each game.[18]

The length of time Canton McKinley and Massillon have competed against each other contributes to the rivalry. However, in noting Deveney's emphasis on current relevance for the fans, it is the annual importance of the game that adds to the intensity of the rivalry. Every year the two teams compete late in the season—usually the last game on both team's schedule. In addition, almost every year there are state rankings and playoff implications at stake—frequently with the winning team entering the playoffs and the losing team not qualifying for the playoffs. As a result of this relevance to the team's fans, attendance at these rivalry games is very high. For example, when the two teams played in the Akron Rubber Bowl in 1994, attendance exceeded 32,200 fans. From 1894 to 2006, a total of 1,648,686 fans have attended Massillon–Canton McKinley football games.[19]

In addition to their loyalty to one of the high schools, Canton McKinley and Massillon fans share additional characteristics. According to Garry Crawford, "Sport fan communities, and in particular audiences at 'live' sport events, tend to have identifiable demographic profiles."[20] This is certainly true of the fans following the Massillon Tigers and Canton McKinley Bulldogs. Many of their demographic similarities are based on their environment—either from Massillon or Canton. For example, Maroon, Maroon, and Holbert noted, "The love of football in this region starts from birth, such as in Massillon where every boy receives a football and every girl a set of pom-poms."[21] The 1951 film *Touchdown Town* reported that the boosters gave every baby boy a football before they left the hospital.[22] This story was reiterated as the film *Go Tigers!* opens with a member of the boosters arriving at a local hospital, placing a small orange Tiger football in the crib next to a newborn baby boy, and telling the mother that he hopes he grows up to play for the Tigers.[23]

Larry Kovak reiterated the importance of high school football in this part of Ohio, writing, "High school football is hugely popular in northeast Ohio and still is today."[24] The emotional ties to these two high schools were also noted by Wilbur Arnold, citing Ron Maly, writing in the *Des Moines Sunday Register*: "In the beginning when The Great Creator was drawing plans for this world of ours, He decided there should be something for everyone. He gave us the mountains to reach the sky, deep blue seas, green forests, dry deserts, gorgeous flowers, and gigantic trees. Then he decided there should be football and he gave us Massillon. He created only one Massillon. He knew that would be enough."[25] Bob Commings, a former head coach at Massillon, recognized the importance of the football team to the community, noting, "If anyone wants to get anything worthwhile done they should come to Massillon and see how they do football. Nothing ever suffered from football and much has improved because of football."[26] To incite the already high emotions associated with the rivalry game, the mayor of Massillon gives the Massillon Tiger Marching Band unlimited access to the city on the Friday before the Canton McKinley game. This unlimited access means the Marching Tigers can march down any street, through any municipal building, and stop at any city park at any time during the day.[27]

Success of the Football Programs

The intensity of the rivalry between Canton McKinley and Massillon is largely a result of the historic successes of the two football programs. Francis H. Cicchinelli, mayor of Massillon, noted that the Canton McKinley–Massillon football rivalry is not just about the schools; "it is about attacking our business community and industries."[28] The fans, citizens, and business communities of both cities take the rivalry between Canton McKinley and Massillon personally. In *Touchdown Town*, the Massillon Chamber of Commerce proclaimed Massillon to be the "Number One Grid City in America." The chamber highlighted the fact that they had the largest high school stadium in the United States and had produced more players and captains in college football than any other high school in the United States.[29]

The Massillon Tigers have the most wins of any high school football team in Ohio (754)—the Canton McKinley Bulldogs have the second most wins (739). The Tigers have been voted state champion twenty-two times. although they have not won a championship since Ohio instituted a playoff system. The Bulldogs were voted state champion seven times and also won the championship three times during the playoff era (1981, 1997, and 1998). The Tigers were also named Associated Press National Champions nine times (1935, 1936, 1939, 1940, 1950, 1952, 1953, 1959, and 1961). Canton McKinley was named *USA Today* National Champion in 1997. Although both teams have encountered enormous and similar successes, it is the Massillon Tigers that receive most of the notoriety in the rivalry—at the expense of the Bulldogs.

This fact was never more evident than in 2008 when ESPN included Massillon, Ohio, as one of the twenty cities pursuing the title of "TitleTown."[30] Other nominees for this award included renowned cities like New York, Chicago, Dallas, Boston, Columbus (Ohio), Los Angeles, and Detroit, whose teams have won multiple sports championships. The staff writer for the *Independent* went on to note that some of the criteria used by ESPN to select the finalists included "a community's pride, passion, performance, history and tradition." In making the announcement, ESPN noted that it considered the Massillon Tigers a "national high school powerhouse."[31] Nothing will add intensity to an already prominent rivalry than sole national media attention. From the chamber of commerce film in the 1950s, to the *Sports Illustrated* story in the 1990s, to the 2001 documentary, to the 2008 ESPN "TitleTown" competition, Massillon has received national recognition. Nothing makes Canton McKinley Bulldog football fans happier than beating their "nationally recognized" high school football powerhouse in their annual rivalry game.

Perhaps another reason why Massillon has received more attention is due to the fact that, although it is an economically depressed steel mill city, the fanaticism of the school cannot help but draw attention. In the 1980s, the varsity football team of Massillon had a booster club of 2,700 members, a lighted stadium that held 20,000 spectators, and a 109-page *Official Football Media Guide*.[32] The school also hired a statistician, a trainer, and a football information director, all of whom were full-time employees.[33] The school also had ten assistant coaches along with a head coach.[34]

The Cross-County Rivalry

The intensity of the rivalry between Massillon and Canton McKinley also had to do with the fact that the two schools represented relatively small industrial cities (Massillon with a population of approximately 30,000 and Canton with a population of approximately 80,000) in Stark County, Ohio, separated by only a few miles. Both towns are blue-collar, Midwestern, middle-class cities struggling to maintain their economic strengths, keep local unemployment low, and avoid excessive property foreclosures. Both cities were hit hard during each economic down cycle since the late 1970s, when the steel industry collapsed in the United States. According to the U.S. Census Bureau, Massillon's median household income in 1999 was $32,734 with 10.7 percent of its citizens living below the poverty line.[35] The economic statistics are worse for Canton, according to the Census Bureau. In 1999, the median income in Canton was $28,730 with 19.2 percent of its population living below the poverty line. Through all the economic cycles, both good and bad, on Friday nights and Saturday afternoons fans of the Tigers and Bulldogs pack up their children and distant relatives in cars, SUVs, and buses to attend the football game—whether the game is home or away. This loyalty is even higher when game day arrives for the Tiger-Bulldog football game. No one living in Canton, Massillon, Stark County, or northeastern Ohio believes that this is "just another football game." For home games, the streets of Massillon are lined with Tiger mascot flags flying on telephone poles, front porches, and flag poles in almost every yard—celebrating Tiger football past and present. This display of community loyalty and support for the Tiger football team reveals the importance of the rivalry game. City government, city businesses, and city residents demonstrate their loyalty and spirit though these displays.

Throughout history, these two schools have remained two of the best high school teams in Ohio—at any time either or both could contend for the state football championship. One of the most significant games in the Canton-Massillon rivalry was played in 1994, which was the 100th meeting between the two schools. The notoriety of the game became national when it was featured in the November 14, 1994, issue of *Sports Illustrated*. Both teams that year had a record of 8-1 and were preparing to enter the state playoffs. Hall of Fame quarterback Bart Starr of the Green Bay Packers flipped the coin at midfield. Massillon beat McKinley 42–41, due to a missed extra point in overtime by McKinley. To better understand the importance of the 1994 victory to the Tiger fans, the *Independent* (Massillon, Ohio) printed extra copies as a result of the win. The managing editor at the time, Kevin Coffey, stated, "We were going to print 7,500 copies of the paper, but after Massillon won, we kicked it up to 10,000. In this town, if it has to do with the Tigers, people will buy it."[36]

To illustrate the importance of winning this cross-county rivalry game, all one has to do is witness a victory celebration. Winning bragging rights for an entire year adds to the fans' sense of community with their fellow fans. After all, sports fans agree—winning is better than losing. For example, in 2001, the season portrayed in *Go Tigers!* the Massillon Tigers won the heated rivalry game on Canton McKinley's home field. After the game was over, the scene shifted immediately to downtown Massillon, where the streets were closed as the entire town partied, awaiting the arrival of their conquering heroes. The victory parade included dozens of cars honking horns in celebration, police cars with their lights flashing, and school buses with the Tiger football team. As the buses drove slowly to a stop, fans were beating on the sides of the buses and players were hanging out of the windows shaking hands and giving "high fives" to their adoring fans, consisting of all diverse demographic categories. When the players exited the buses, they were mobbed by their classmates, fans, families, and children.

Of course, to understand the pride of the Tiger fans, all one needs to do is visit www.Massillonproud.com. The Web site, launched in 1996, is dedicated to the fans of Massillon Tiger football. It is a place where Tiger fans can relive the glory days of the past, talk about current or future Massillon squads, and, perhaps most importantly, show their sheer enthusiasm for their team. On the message boards, some of the more notable members include user names such as Big Cat, Tiger forever, and TigerBob75. One of the threads, I am MASSILLON, was created in order for the Tiger faithful to explain what it means for them to be Massillon Tiger fans. Tiger Embalmer stated, "Often times I'm asked why am I a Massillon fan? I tell them all the same thing. If you went to a game you would understand. I can guarantee that for 10–15 weeks a year there isn't a town in the world that could shake a stick at Massillon."[37]

Characteristics of the Two Cities

Although the economies of both cities are similar, they differ in population. In the 1950s Canton was almost four times larger than Massillon; currently, Canton is only two-and-a-half times the size of Massillon. Due to the disparity in population, one might expect that Canton McKinley would field the better team. Although the Massillon community is smaller, the Tigers have won more games in this rivalry, as noted previously.

Canton and Massillon have not escaped the collapse of traditional industries in northeastern Ohio. Beginning in the late 1970s when the steel industry collapsed to today's financial issues surrounding the subprime mortgage crisis, the economy of northeastern Ohio has been eroded to its current distressing, weak economic level. Today, few steel mills operate in the triangle known as the Rust Belt. The pattern of losing higher-paying, industrial jobs and replacing them with service jobs has occurred throughout northeastern Ohio. The result has been a steady decrease in per capita income, housing prices, and the standard of living in the area.

Population Statistics

Conversely, according to the U.S. Census Bureau, since 1950 the population of Massillon, Ohio, has remained constant.[38] Data in each ten-year census recording period shows that the population of Massillon has remained close to 30,000 people. In 1950 the population was 29,594, and in 2000 the population was 30,557 (1960 population was 31,236; 1980 was 31,325; and 1990 was 30,969).[39]

On the other hand, according to the Census Bureau (1961, 2003), in the same time period Canton has experienced a dramatic loss of population (30.9 percent). In 1950 the population of Canton was 116,912, and in 2000 the population was 80,806 (1960 population was 113,631; 1980 was 93,077; and 1990 was 84,161). As the population of Canton decreased, so did the number of housing units (in 1980 there were 38,556 units, and in 2000 there were 35,502 units).[40] Like many other cities in Northeast Ohio (Akron, Cleveland, and Youngstown), Canton was victim of the economic problems associated with multiple factory and manufacturing plant closures in the rubber, automotive, and steel industries. Plants and factories closed, support industries collapsed, homes were foreclosed, and people moved away in search of work. Like the other cities above, when plants close and population leaves, community leaders struggle to find new and diverse industrial and manufacturing facilities to replace lost jobs.

It should also be noted that the rivalry continues to be so important to each community not only because of the history of the rivalry or the proximity of the two communities. There are many high schools in Ohio and around the country that have played each other in football for decades or who are in close proximity but do not have the intense rivalry that exists between Canton McKinley and Massillon. The rivalry is extraordinarily significant to the Canton McKinley and Massillon fans today, in part, because it reminds people of the *glory days*—days of economic prosperity, growth, and football teams that won Ohio and national football championships. This rivalry in particular reminds fans of their glory days when they attended Canton McKinley or Massillon high schools.

For the fans of Massillon, the 1970s and 1980s could be considered such glory years. During these two decades, from 1970 to 1989, the Tigers had a winning season every single year. On game days during these years, the streets of Massillon were lined with orange and black flags and banners as well as handwritten signs urging the team on to victory.[41] In 1985, Massillon won its 600th game, becoming the first high school team in the United States to achieve this level.[42]

Industry and the Rivalry

Part of what makes the Canton-Massillon rivalry so intense is the industrial and blue-collar worker rivalries established early in the twentieth century. As Edward Heald pointed out, in Massillon during the 1940s and 1950s, one of the largest and most influential companies was the Tyson Bearing Company, a division of SKF Industries, Inc.[43] During this period, SKF Industries was one of the largest roller-bearing companies in the United States. The company was incorporated in Delaware in 1929 and moved to Massillon. The new plant was dedicated on August 9, 1942. Due to the company's involvement in supplying the U.S. military in World War II, their dedication read, "Today-Production, Tomorrow-Victory." Not only was the company influential in creating jobs in the Massillon area, it also had a special link with the Massillon football team. At the height of the high school football season in October 1943, the company purchased $500,000 worth of war bonds to build two bombers, named after the Massillon Tiger football team and the school's marching band. S. Robert Weirich, the mayor of Massillon at the time, presented the company the All-American "M" citation, which was awarded by the Tiger Booster Club Committee in recognition of the company's generous donation in the school's name.[44]

In 1901, the Timken Roller Bearing Company moved from St. Louis, Missouri, to Canton. The company initially employed just fifty people. By 1919, the company had grown to six thousand employees. In 1966, the company opened a new centralized research and development facility in North Canton, which was the first of twelve technology centers it would open globally.45 In the early 1960s, the Timken Corporation was instrumental in raising necessary funds to bring the National Football League Hall of Fame to Canton—in part recognizing the importance of the original Canton Bulldogs to the development of professional football.

The Canton-Massillon area has been appropriately called the "Cradle of Alloy Steel" for it was in both of these cites where the first large-scale production of alloy steel for automobiles and other applications began. During World War II, the Republic Steel plants in Canton and Massillon became a primary production center of alloy steels for armor plate, shells, rifle barrels, aircraft engines, and airplane bombs. By 1951, Republic Steel employed 9,524 people in Canton and 5,445 in Massillon.[46] When the steel industry collapsed in the late 1970s, the fortunes of both Massillon and Canton changed dramatically.

As influential as the steel and bearing companies were in both Canton and Massillon, they were by no means the only industries which influenced the economic fortunes of these two cities. The 1950s saw a great expansion in the diversity of companies that came to both Canton and Massillon. The Harrison Paint and Varnish Company, the Canton Elevator and Manufacturing Company, and the Mercier Tool and Die Company were new companies in Canton which, like the bearing and steel companies, also epitomized the blue-collar nature of the city.[47]

The Canton business community has a long history of recognizing their beloved Bulldogs. In November 1919, the Canton Rotary Club initiated the custom of recognizing the McKinley Bulldog football team the day before the Canton-Massillon game. The next year, in recognition of the tremendous season of the 1920 McKinley team (which went undefeated and was not scored upon in eight games), seventeen players and the lone cheerleader were each given a football with a gold letter.[48]

The communities compete for industries to locate buildings in their cities. The proximity of the two cities adds to the competition of "their" teams; thousands of alumni remain in the local area, attending weekly games. These plus the economy of attending local sporting events have contributed to the development of the rivalry between Canton McKinley and Massillon. These are just some of the elements that are part of the fabric of the rivalry. Another component to the rivalry is the list of great coaches and players who have participated in the Canton McKinley Bulldog–Massillon Tiger games.

The Cradle of Coaches

Miami University in Oxford, Ohio, is referred to as the "Cradle of Coaches" because some of the most legendary collegiate and/or professional football coaches attended or coached at the university. These names include Bill Arnsparger, Earl "Red" Blaik, Paul Brown, Dick Crum, Weeb Eubank, Sid Gillman, John Harbaugh, Woody Hayes, Bill Mallory, Ara Parseghian, John Pont, Bo Schembechler, Jim Tressel, Randy Walker, and Ron Zook.[49] If Miami University is the "Cradle of Coaches," Massillon High School is the "Cradle of Coaches II."

Massillon High School Coaching Legends

Tim Rogers wrote about the 2008 appointment of a new football coach at Massillon High School: "Massillon, regarded as one of the premier high school coaching jobs in the country."[50] The new coach follows a long line of coaches who coached the Massillon Tigers and went on to renowned careers in college and professional coaching—Paul Brown, Earl Bruce, Leo Strang, Bob Commings, and Lee Tressel.

As Wilbur Arnold noted, "Coach Paul Brown put Massillon on the national map."[51] Everyone is familiar with Paul Brown's career *after* his nine years coaching the Massillon Tigers (1932–1940) because he went on to coach The Ohio State University team, founded and coached the Cleveland Browns, and later founded, owned, and coached the Cincinnati Bengals. During his tenure with the Massillon Tigers, his coaching record was 80-8-2. His teams won six state titles and four national championships. In discussing the importance of the Massillon Tigers to the city, Brown wrote: "We had a sign in our locker room: 'You represent the best football town in the United States. Never disappoint your people by the way you represent it.' That feeling was shared by the townspeople, and I knew immediately if our players went astray because every waitress in town knew them, and they were not shy about naming anyone who did not observe the spirit of our rules."[52]

In addition to his coaching successes at Massillon, Brown started the Booster Club that continues to support the Massillon Tiger football program both financially and emotionally.[53] Many years after his departure from Massillon, the high school named the stadium in his honor—Paul Brown Tiger Stadium. As faithful Tiger fans walk to the west entrance of the stadium on game day, they come face-to-face with a life-size statue memorializing Paul Brown.

Another famous coach at Massillon was Lee Tressel (1956–1957). Perhaps not as famous as his son, Jim Tressel, who won four national championships while coaching Youngstown State University and one national championship at The Ohio State University, Coach Lee Tressel had an outstanding record at Massillon (16-2-1). He coached at Massillon for only two years before leaving to coach his alma mater, Baldwin Wallace in Berea, Ohio.[54] He is a member of the College Football Hall of Fame due to his successes at Baldwin Wallace.

Following Coach Tressel as head coach was Leo Strang (1958–1963). Strang understood the importance of high school football to the citizens of Ohio. He coached successful programs at Caldwell High School, Upper Sandusky High School, and East Cleveland Shaw High School. During his tenure at Massillon, his teams won three state championships and two national championships. His coaching record was 54-8-1. He left Massillon High School in 1964 to become head football coach at Kent State University.[55]

Another notable coach at Massillon who also had an outstanding college coaching career was Earl Bruce (1964–1965). Bruce understood the focus on high school football in northeast Ohio because of his successes at Salem High School (near Youngstown, Ohio). Bruce is the only undefeated coach in the history of Massillon Tiger football (20-0-0). Coach Woody Hayes hired Bruce as an assistant coach at The Ohio State University. When Hayes was fired by the university, Bruce was elevated to head coach. After a distinguished career at Ohio State, Bruce went to Colorado State University and rebuilt a lackluster football program.[56]

Another Massillon coach who later excelled coaching football in the Big Ten was Bob Commings (1969–1973). Commings also understood the importance of high school football in Northeast Ohio. He came from Struthers High School, from the strong Steel Valley Conference in

Youngstown, Ohio. His record as coach at Massillon was 43-6-2, winning one state championship in 1970 and going undefeated in 1971 but losing in the inaugural year of the state playoffs in 1972. In 1974, Commings left Massillon to become the head football coach at his alma mater, the University of Iowa.[57]

Canton McKinley High School Coaching Legends

As memorable as many of the Massillon coaches have been, Canton McKinley has also had its share of successful coaches. Perhaps the most well known of these coaches is Don Nehlen. Nehlen only coached Canton McKinley for one season in 1964, leading the Bulldogs to a 9-1 season. Nehlen left Canton McKinley to become the quarterback coach at the University of Michigan, working with the legendary Bo Schembechler (from the Cradle of Coaches, Miami University). Later, Nehlen became head coach at Bowling Green University (now Bowling Green State University in Bowling Green, Ohio). He coached the Falcons to eight winning seasons in nine years. Nehlen's most memorable coaching stop, however, was at West Virginia University from 1980 to 2000. Nehlen compiled a 149-93-4 record, as well as leading the Mountaineers to twelve bowl appearances in his twenty-one seasons at the university.[58] In 1988, Nehlen led his team to the National Championship game against Notre Dame. He also coached the Mountaineers to an undefeated regular season in 1993, before losing to the University of Florida in the Sugar Bowl. In 2005, Nehlen was inducted into the College Football Hall of Fame.

Another prolific coach with a McKinley connection was Ben Schwartzwalder, head coach in 1941. Later, Schwartzwalder was head coach at Syracuse University from 1949 to 1973, where he compiled a 152-91-3 record.[59] He coached one of the greatest running backs in the history of the National Football League—Jim Brown. His Orangemen won the National Championship in 1959, led by another outstanding running back—Heisman Trophy Award winner Ernie Davis. Schwartzwalder was elected into the College Football Hall of Fame in 1982.

Wayne Fontez is a familiar name to fans of the National Football League. Although Fontez never coached at Canton McKinley, he played for the Bulldogs in the late 1950s. Fontez was head coach of the Detroit

Lions from 1988 to 1996. Fontez has the most wins and losses of any coach in the history of the Lion franchise, with a 67-71 record.[60] During the 1991 season, Fontez coached the Lions to their first playoff victory since 1957, defeating the Dallas Cowboys 38–6.

From a Canton McKinley Bulldog fan perspective, the most successful coach has to have been Thom McDaniels. During his tenure as the head coach from 1982 to 1997, the Bulldogs won 134 games and captured the state championship title in 1997. In 1997, which was McDaniels last season as head coach at McKinley, the team was also ranked number one in the nation by *USA Today*.[61]

Conclusion

There is something uniquely different about high school athletics. There are no scholarships, no big money contracts, and no endorsement deals. Instead, the student-athletes at Massillon and Canton McKinley not only play for the love of the game, but play to be part of something larger. It is about being part of and representing their community. Above all else, to the players, the fans, and the communities, it is about bragging rights —it is about winning "the game." Paul Brown said it succinctly: "The public is interested in only one thing—whether you win or lose."[62]

The goal of this chapter was to provide insight into one of the most heated high school rivalries in the United States: the Massillon Tiger–Canton McKinley Bulldog rivalry. As illustrated, the rivalry between the two schools is deeper than just football—it is about community, pride, and winning. From the people in Northeast Ohio who love high school sports, to the demographics of the two cites, to the industries who support their respective communities and teams, to the many famous coaches and players, these two schools provide a unique and unparalleled experience for fans today and have provided that same unique experience for more than a century.

If anyone doubts the importance of the Canton McKinley–Massillon rivalry and its position in national folklore, one just has to note what one Massillon Tiger fan reported: this is the only high school football game for which a person interested in placing a legal wager can get odds from Las Vegas.[63] Richard Natale, writing in the *Los Angeles Times*, noted that the Bulldog-Tiger rivalry "is offered for online betting in Las Vegas."[64] The social significance of this fact elevates the Massillon–Canton McKinley football rivalry to national prominence. This fact makes the annual fall battle on the field an important cultural event reflecting the importance of community, family, rivalry, winning, and, oh yes, high school football.

Diana Taurisi of the University of Connecticut fighting over a loose ball with the University of Tennessee's Tasha Butts at the NCAA Women's Final Four Tournament at the New Orleans Arena in 2004. *Courtesy of Getty Images.*

ten

A Rivalry for the Ages

Tennessee-UConn Women's Basketball

JAIME SCHULTZ

> It has become women's basketball version of the Hatfields and McCoys. The Connecticut-Tennessee women's basketball rivalry is being compared to the Yankees–Red Sox or Celtics-Lakers. Whether the coaches like it or not—and they do not—it has become the Lady Vols' Pat Summitt vs. UConn's Geno Auriemma.
>
> —Kristie Ackert, "Geno's Pique Reaches Summitt: Huskies, Vols Still Fuss, Fight"

In June 2007, the sports world buzzed with speculation as to why Pat Summitt, coach of the University of Tennessee Lady Volunteers basketball program, declined to sign the contract that would continue their regular-season contests with the University of Connecticut. Since the two teams first met in 1995, theirs has been alternatively framed as "the meanest rivalry in sport," "the greatest rivalry in women's team sports," and "the best rivalry in women's basketball." Over the years, competition between the two has "elevated and expanded the sport" and "revolutionized the women's game," yet without explanation the series came to a halt. When asked about her refusal, Summitt would only reply "Geno knows." In response, Geno Auriemma, coach of the UConn Huskies, told his local newspaper, "I think she should just come out and say she's not playing us because she hates my guts." The best fans could hope for was that the two would meet in the 2008 NCAA championship, where the animosity between these storied programs could be played out on the hardwood.[1]

There are general elements, often in combination with one another, that go into the construction and perpetuation of sporting rivalries. Those on either side of the conflict typically share a common history that, over time, is spun into a narrative that transcends athletic competition. There must be regular contact and a sense of parity between two factions. Often times, coaches or standout athletes possess polarizing personalities that induce others to take sides in brewing feuds. There might also be some type of positional disparity—either physical or ideological—between the athletes and their followers that contributes to a sense of partisanship. And while there are myriad small-scale rivalries about which the majority of people will never learn (which is not to say that those antagonisms do not matter), to be a capital-R, grade-A, big-deal Rivalry, the public has to care about it, which means the public has to hear about it, which means the sport-media-commercial complex has to promote it.[2]

The importance of media coverage may go a long way toward explaining the lack of women on top rivalry lists from authoritative outlets like the *Sporting News,* the *New York Times, Sports Illustrated,* and ESPN. At a time when women's athletics receives less than 10 percent of all television and print coverage devoted to sports, it is understandable that the general public knows little about the hostilities between the American and Norwegian soccer teams or the Canadian and U.S. hockey teams or the UCLA and USC volleyball squads. Moreover, disproportionate attention is paid to female athletes in individual and "gender appropriate" sports so that when women's sporting rivalries are mentioned, they typically do not go beyond the Martina Navratilova–Chris Evert or Nancy Kerrigan–Tonya Harding pairings. This is part of what makes the rivalry between the Tennessee Lady Vols and the UConn Huskies so intriguing: not only does the matchup pit the two best teams in the sport against one another, people pay attention when they meet. In fact, their contest for the 2004 NCAA national championship earned the highest television ratings on ESPN for *any* basketball game—men's or women's.[3]

In this chapter I "read" the rivalry between Tennessee and UConn by analyzing pertinent media texts published between 1995 and 2008.

The sources I surveyed began with the student newspapers affiliated with the University of Tennessee (the *Daily Beacon*) and the University of Connecticut (the *Daily Campus*). Then, consulting the most recent information from the Audit Bureau of Circulations, a not-for-profit organization that tracks North American media distributions, I reviewed the most geographically relevant and widely read local, regional, and national newspapers associated with the two schools. Finally, I examined stories about the teams and their rivalry in sports-related outlets, including both print and online versions of *Sports Illustrated, ESPN the Magazine* and its online partner ESPN.com, and *Women's Basketball,* as well as autobiographies and biographies about Summitt and Auriemma, media guides put out by their respective institutions, and secondary sources on women's college basketball.[4]

Based on these examinations, I identified three main components involved in creating and sustaining the Tennessee-UConn rivalry. First, and perhaps most simply, the two teams have enjoyed a relative dominance in Division I women's intercollegiate basketball. Every time the two teams meet, commented Summitt, "There's always something significant on the line." They are consistently among the top-ranked teams, boast the nation's best players, battle for the top recruits, and the games between the two—both during the regular season and, frequently, during the NCAA tournament—are fiercely competitive and unpredictable. The second component involves the success and personalities of Tennessee's Pat Summitt and UConn's Geno Auriemma, who have served as head coaches of their programs since before the rivalry emerged. Between them, the two coaches have won thirteen of the last twenty-two national championships and scores of coach-of-the-year honors, making them among the very best in the history of the game. At the same time, their personal and professional styles of conduct have led to several public conflicts that the media both reports and stokes. As such, the popular press constitutes both primary source material and the third major agent in the antagonism between UConn and Tennessee. Print and electronic forms of media have been inextricably involved in nearly every aspect of the rivalry: its initiation, perpetuation, and, most recently, its suspension.[5]

The Big Enchilada

A bit of history is necessary to understand the significance of the Tennessee-UConn rivalry, for although college women began playing basketball almost immediately after James Naismith invented it in the winter of 1891–1892, their path has been neither smooth nor direct. Senda Berenson Abbott, director of Physical Training at Smith College, introduced a modified version of "basket ball" to her students, and its popularity quickly spread across the country. By 1896, the first women's intercollegiate contest took place between students at Stanford University and those attending the University of California, Berkley. In 1899, a group of women physical educators met to standardize the game; and two years later, the Spalding Athletic Library published the first set of women's rules that would, among other things, eliminate "undue physical exertion" and "star playing." The number of participants fluctuated between five and nine, and officials eventually settled on six—three offensive and three defensive—confined to their assigned halves of the court and additional strategies were implemented to limit physical strain and contact between participants.[6]

Intercollegiate competition was eventually deemed anathema to women physical educators' philosophy of moderation, participation, and play for play's sake. "There is no Vassar-Smith basketball game," commented famed sportswriter John R. Tunis in 1929, "because the authorities in the colleges believe sport as a form of recreation rather than as a means of establishing athletic authority." As Paula Welch shows, intercollegiate competition declined drastically by 1930. Instead, "women in colleges and universities engaged in low key playday, sportsday, and interclass competition. Collegiate physical educators had, through rule changes and standards, bred a game that was nearly immune to highly competitive play." In the schools, basketball became a fitness activity, but outside the cloistered women's gymnasiums, it retained its sporting profile, primarily organized by the Amateur Athletic Union.[7]

According to historian Joan S. Hult, "basketball's most dramatic changes for girls and women actually occurred between 1966 and 1970" as rules began to conform to the male model of the sport. The first national tournament took place in 1969 and "ushered in the modern era of women's intercollegiate basketball" and in 1972, the newly formed

Association of Intercollegiate Athletics for Women (AIAW) introduced national college championships. In the early 1980s, however, officials in the NCAA voted to host several Division I tournaments in a clear effort to take over the governance of women's college sports. Women's athletic departments were given a tough choice: remain loyal to the organization that had provided for and cultivated their programs or side with the powerful NCAA, whose annual budget and lucrative television contracts dwarfed those of the AIAW. Eighteen of the previous year's top twenty basketball programs opted to join the NCAA's 1982 inaugural tournament, including the University of Tennessee. "I almost felt like we were stabbing people in the back that had made our dreams possible at a very young age in women's sports," Pat Summitt later stated.

> Yet, I knew realistically that the only way the sport could grow to the level we enjoy today was under the umbrella of the NCAA. That brought instant credibility to women's athletics. It gave us that name attachment; it gave us championships in a first-class arena, and we needed that. I thought that without that we may never have the opportunities to make the strides that are necessary for women to have what they have today.

That year there were two national champions: one from the AIAW tournament and a second crowned by the NCAA. It was the demise of the women's organization.[8]

One wonders what Senda Berenson Abbott and the other foremothers of women's basketball might think of today's highly mediated, commercialized, and spectacularized game, for it was precisely the type of game they strove to avoid. It was also the type of game that Tennessee and UConn typified from the first time they met in 1995. Summitt had been at Tennessee since 1974, compiling an impressive dossier that included three national championships. Auriemma had been at Connecticut since 1985 and in the late 1980s and early 1990s had impressed the nation by taking the historically hapless Huskies to the top of the Big East Conference and their first of many trips to the NCAA national tournament. Their success took place amidst several significant events in U.S. women's basketball during the mid to late 1990s, including a gold-medal performance at the 1996 Olympic Games, the addition of sixteen teams to the NCAA Division I tournament (making a total of

sixty-four, the same as the men), the establishment of two women's professional leagues, and the opening of the Women's Basketball Hall of
Fame in Knoxville, Tennessee; and in 1994, Nike introduced the "Air
Swoopes," a tribute to Sheryl Swoopes and the first basketball shoe
named for a woman athlete. "It was," said Auriemma, "the right time,
with women's basketball becoming popular." Yet the college game still
needed a hyped-up, marquee rivalry to get the public's attention; as history began to unfold, the most obvious choice became UConn versus
Tennessee.[9]

Before the 1994–1995 season the two teams had never met. Summitt
and Auriemma shared the belief that to be the best team by the March
tournament, they needed to play the best teams in the regular season.
Connecticut was slated to play an ESPN-televised game on Martin
Luther King Day and needed an opponent. According to Auriemma, he
suggested, "Call Pat," and she responded, "Absolutely." At the time of
the game, Tennessee boasted a number one ranking and a 16-0 record.
Positioned just behind the Vols at 12-0, UConn nipped at their heels.[10]

The media paid unprecedented attention in the days leading up to
what many speculated would be the "game of the year in women's basketball." Scalpers were reportedly demanding—and getting—as much
as two hundred dollars for tickets that originally sold for eight dollars.
The more than eight thousand fans who packed Connecticut's Gampel
Pavilion witnessed Tennessee get off to an early 4–0 lead, but within
minutes, UConn upended the score by 15–6, and the Lady Vols never
got closer than 4 points behind the Huskies, who stunned the odds-on
favorite 77–66. As the *Boston Globe's* Bob Ryan reported, it "was more
than just a very good women's college basketball matchup . . . more
than just a battle of No. 1 vs. No. 2, a game of such surpassing importance that the national poll voting was delayed until the game's conclusion." It was, he wrote, "the biggest women's sports event in the history
of New England. . . . This was the Big Enchilada."[11]

Ten weeks later, the sixty-four teams in the NCAA tournament had
been whittled down to two: the Vols and the Huskies. Over eighteen
thousand fans crowded Minneapolis's Target Center to witness the best
teams in the game battle one another for the national title. At halftime,
Tennessee was on top, 38–32. In the final five minutes of play, the teams

rallied back and forth at a fevered pitch, swapping the lead, and with just over two minutes remaining, UConn was behind. But with 1:51 to go in the game, the Huskies captured the lead and did not let go, finishing with 70 points to the Vols' 64 and becoming only the second women's team in history to go undefeated en route to the national title. As Summitt would later write, the rivalry had "grown up overnight with the rapidity of a brushfire." By 1996, UConn was already being called Tennessee's "old nemesis."[12]

From their initial January 15, 1995, meeting, the regular-season games between Tennessee and Connecticut became a staple in women's college basketball. In 1996, UConn traveled to Tennessee for the first time and snapped the Vols' sixty-nine-game winning streak on their home court. The teams met again that year in the semifinals of the NCAA tournament, where the Vols were finally able to reverse the order of things in a dramatic overtime victory against the Huskies on the way to their fourth national title. The pattern continued the following year, with Connecticut besting Tennessee in January and the Vols ousting the Huskies from the NCAA tournament while working toward their second of three consecutive national championships.

By the 1999–2000 season, the teams had agreed to play each other twice during the regular season. CBS, which had a contract with the Big East Conference, televised the first contest in January. ESPN televised the second a month later, making it the first time the channel aired a regular-season women's basketball game in prime time as part of its "Rivalry Week" package. UConn traveled to Knoxville and defeated the Vols on their home court. The Vols returned the favor in Storrs. The 2000 NCAA national championship game provided the rubber match. As the *New York Times* reported, "The bracket builders planned it. Television prayed for it. Fans wanted it. The players anticipated it. They all got it." In the end, UConn won their second national title by a lopsided score of 71–52 and took the edge in the all-time series against Tennessee by 6–5. It seemed impossible that the teams had met just eleven times, for theirs had already been cemented as the "best rivalry in women's basketball." They continued their two-game series the following season, but many wondered if the Tennessee-UConn rivalry would suffer from overexposure. By the 2002–2003 season the teams scaled back their matchups to one before Summitt opted to discontinue their regular-season games.[13]

As of the end of the 2007–2008 season, the teams have met twenty-two times in thirteen years, each game airing on national television. Fifteen of those encounters have been during the regular season. The other seven occurred in the context of the NCAA tournament, including a regional final, two Final Four matchups and, on four occasions, Tennessee and UConn have squared off for the national title. In each of those capstone events, the Huskies have bested the Lady Vols, earning coach Auriemma a total of five national championships to Summitt's eight; and, in total, UConn leads the rivalry by a score of 13–9. More often than not, the teams are ranked number one and two at tip-off, positions that might certainly be traded when the final buzzer sounds.

The two programs boast tremendous success. In addition to eight national championships (two shy of UCLA's record under John Wooden), Tennessee has garnered thirteen Southeastern Conference (SEC) tournament titles and an overall record of 983-182 (.844 winning percentage), with Summitt at the helm for the past thirty-four years. When Summitt reached 800 wins in 2003, she joined an elite fraternity of just three other coaches in Division I basketball, and her 880th victory two years later put her at the top of the list of all-time winningest coaches in the college game. Tennessee is the only team to appear in every NCAA tournament since its advent in 1982 and has reached the "Sweet 16" each time. There have been eighteen Final Fours, making it such that every woman who has completed her eligibility under Summitt has been to at least one semifinal game.[14]

Auriemma's twenty-three-season run at Connecticut is also impressive. Under his tutelage, the Huskies have recorded a record of 657-122 (.843 winning percentage) that includes fifteen consecutive Big East titles and appearances in the Sweet 16 of the NCAA national tournament as well as nine Final Four appearances. On December 31, 2006, Auriemma recorded his 600th win with the Huskies, making him the fastest coach in NCAA Division I women's basketball history to reach that milestone. He got there in just 716 games, outpacing the previous record holder, Pat Summitt, who took 734 games to accomplish the task.

Based on the success of these coaches, it comes as no surprise that they also top the charts in terms of salaries in women's college basketball. In 2006, Summitt became the sport's first "million dollar coach," inking a contract with Tennessee that made her salary comparable to Tennessee's men's coach Bruce Pearl's salary and would also "enable Summitt to surpass Connecticut coach Geno Auriemma," according to the *Knoxville News Sentinel*. Not to be outdone, Auriemma recently signed a five-year, $8 million contract that reseated him on top of the college women's basketball pay scale. As of July 3, 2008, the *Knoxville News Sentinel* reported, "Discussions regarding UT women's basketball coach Pat Summitt's new contract are ongoing, but a deal has yet to be finalized." The rivalry between the two extends beyond the confines of the basketball court.[15]

Another set of numbers indicates the importance and popularity of basketball at Tennessee and UConn: game attendance. While average attendance for all Division I women's basketball teams during the 2006–2007 season totaled only 1,586, Tennessee topped the charts, with 14,678 fans typically filling the Thompson-Boling Arena (where the court is named for Summitt), and UConn was a close second at 10,802. Individually, then, the two teams generate a tremendous amount of interest. Together, it is difficult to quantify just how important they are to women's basketball.[16]

Summitt and Auriemma could not have reached their places of prominence without the tremendous list of athletes they have been fortunate to coach, and over the years their rosters read like a veritable who's who in women's college basketball. Names like Diana Taurasi, Jennifer Rizzotti, Tamika Catchings, Chamique Holdsclaw, Semeka Randall, Svetlana Abrosmova, Swin Cash, Sue Bird, Rebecca Lobo, and Candace Parker tend to resonate even with those who do not claim to be fans of the women's game. Year after year, either UConn or Tennessee boasts the best recruiting class in the nation, consistently adding the top high school prospects to their squads and contributing to the two teams' dominance in the sport.

Since Auriemma's arrival, eleven Connecticut players have been named to the All-American first team, six have been National Players of the Year, and eight have gone on to compete in the Olympic Games. Beginning in 1976, fifteen Tennessee players have made the U.S. Olympic team, there have been numerous All-Americans, and in 2000, Chamique

Holdsclaw was named Naismith's Player of the Century. At the same time, commented a former Lady Vol, "The players are coming and going," but Summitt and Auriemma remain "the staples of the program." When analyzing the rivalry between the University of Tennessee and the University of Connecticut, it is impossible to avoid a discussion about the two coaches.[17]

Clash of the Titans

The relationship between Summitt and Auriemma provides a "compelling subplot" to the Tennessee-UConn rivalry, one that often develops into the main storyline. The typical narrative about the two goes something like this: he goads her, she takes the high road; she needs to lighten up, he needs to grow up; he's all talk, she's all business. In the end, the press usually concludes that their antagonism generates greater exposure for their contests and the women's game in general and that the final outcome of the on-court competition justifies their off-court behavior. Following some verbal sparring that went on around UConn's 2003 NCAA tournament victory, for example, *USA Today* reported, "In the end, Auriemma got the last jab. The one that really counted."[18]

Undoubtedly, Auriemma and Summitt are more complicated than such facile statements as "He's a cranky Yankee, she's a Southern lady" imply, and those who know them both speculate that they are more alike than different. Friends, peers, and former players describe the two as passionate, intense, competitive, demanding, abrasive, dedicated, unrelenting perfectionists. In the same breath, those acquainted with the duo also call them caring, compassionate, generous, talented, brilliant, and witty mentors. Nevertheless, journalists tend to characterize Summitt by "her trademark intensity." When it comes to Auriemma, "arrogant is the word that's bandied about the most." *Sports Illustrated*'s Lars Anderson commented that to be near Summitt, "you know you're in the presence of a legend." She has been called a "steely-eyed firebrand" and an "ambassador for the game" while concomitantly criticized as "too serious" and, according to the *Hartford Courant,* "one of the pettiest figures in the history of college athletics." Depictions of Auriemma, on the other hand, veer toward the smarmy. Journalists refer to his "effusive big-brother style," his "matinee idol looks" and "perfect hair," and his "puke-invoking grin." He has been called a "spellbinding salesman," "slick and ambitious," "jealous and paranoid," "a one-man fraternity of glibness and gamesmanship," and "ultimately endearing." Even their physical affectations are set in contradistinction to one another: Summitt is known for "The Stare"; Auriemma for his "cock-of-the-walk gait," both of which are presented as manifestations of their clashing personalities. This type of characterizational shorthand makes it easier for journalists to draw battle lines and readers to choose sides, which generates further hype around the Tennessee-UConn matchups.[19]

Lest one think that Summitt is depicted more favorably—somehow more deserving of success and praise than Auriemma (who feels the press gives her "preferential treatment")—consider their biographies at the Naismith Memorial Basketball Hall of Fame. When it comes to Auriemma, a 2006 inductee, the blurb wends its way through his humble beginnings to "building a program" that would "redefine dominance in the sport of basketball."

> He is one of the most charismatic individuals in the sport of women's basketball and one of the game's most engaging personalities. His dedication and passion have been primary factors in the dramatic rise of popularity of the women's game.[20]

Conversely, Summitt, enshrined in 2000, is lauded as one who "has created a legacy of success and integrity unparalleled in women's basketball." Yet the entry is little more than a compilation of her coaching accomplishments, coming off a bit dry and striking a distinctly different tenor than the one dedicated to Auriemma. No author is connected to either piece and there are a host of possible explanations regarding the imbalance between them. Regardless of the reason, the end result is the same: he infuses life and personality into an otherwise dull game, epitomized by the no-nonsense approach of Summitt. Inaccurate, unmerited, and subjectively decoded to be sure, but nonetheless there for public consumption.[21]

Another element that factors into the public personas of the two coaches is that they offer two versions of the American Dream narrative. Summitt, born to a tobacco and dairy farming family in Tennessee, grew up "cash poor . . . hard pressed" and was raised like "a combination of a fourth son and an extra field hand. If I made a mistake," she wrote, "I got whipped. If I cried, I got whipped harder." The media has latched onto this image, representing Summit as the hardworking country girl who, with pluck and perseverance, reached the highest echelon of women's basketball. One author records,

> According to *Successful Farming* magazine, Summitt developed her skills as a fierce competitor in the hayloft of the family barn where she and her three brothers did "basketball battle" after the chores were done. The family unit instilled teamwork and hard work ethics that she holds for her athletes today.

She is the local hero who made good—one so invested in her Tennessee roots (and her job) that when she went into labor on a recruiting trip to Pennsylvania, she not only finished the visit, but insisted the pilot fly her back to Tennessee. She simply could not give birth to her son outside the state. Such tales have become the stuff of Summitt lore.[22]

Auriemma's, on the other hand, is offered as the quintessential immigrant tale. Born in Montella, Italy, he came to America at age seven with little money, uneducated parents, and no grasp of the English language. While the Auriemmas "were awed by the running water, electricity, automobiles, and legal tender," little Luigi (his birth name) was determined to succeed and unafraid to apply gumption, grit, and perhaps a bit of guile to that end. "Because of my background," he writes, "because of where I come from, I have this feeling that I have to constantly prove myself—over and over again, just like when I was seven years old, trying to fit in, trying to show everyone I was just as good as they were." As such, he grew up "tough" and "street-smart." His cocky self-assuredness, he explains, only masks the deep insecurities he felt as a foreigner and that continue to gnaw at him whenever he feels he does not get the respect he deserves. With an admitted "chip on [his] shoulder," he feels he will "never be treated" as well as the press and the public treat Summitt, "no matter what our team accomplishes."[23]

Auriemma uses his past to explain his character and behavior in the present. Indeed, the two coaches share a don't-forget-where-you-came-from philosophy and often pepper their coach-speak with anecdotes from their respective backgrounds. On his persistent jabs at Summitt and others, Auriemma wrote, "Growing up in the neighborhood, there was only one thing you could do, one way to survive: You had to make fun of people. You could make fun of anything: how someone looked, how they dressed, what their nationality was, what their religion was, who their girlfriends were, whether they could throw or hit or pitch. You just had to find something to make fun of them." After Auriemma slung several of his arrows in Summitt's direction, she remarked, "If I said the things that Geno does, even today, my 80-year-old father would probably take me out behind the shed and whip me with a tobacco stick." These types of accounts make for good copy, adding richness to the characters around which journalists like to build the Tennessee-UConn rivalry.[24]

An additional difference between them that is emphasized in reports of their rivalry concerns the paths each have taken to the halls of fame. Again, their success stories are boiled down to accessible, though somewhat misleading nuggets: she is the "grande dame of the women's game" while he is "the newcomer." In reality, Summitt has just two years more coaching experience and two years of age on Auriemma, but one area in which they do differ is in playing experience. Summitt's career, according to the dominant story line, is one that "began . . . as an evening diversion in a hayloft." Originally assigned to a high school without a girls' basketball team, her father moved the seven-member household "six miles down the road," so his daughter would have the chance to play. She became an All-American point guard at the University of Tennessee–Martin in the days that there "were no athletic scholarships for women, no money for decent uniforms, or hotels. On the road," wrote Summitt, "we slept on mats in the gym of whatever campus we visited." She continued her athletic career as a member of the U.S. national team, playing in the 1975 Pan Am Games and as co-captain at the 1976 Olympics, the first time basketball had been offered for women, earning a silver medal in the process. She would later coach the squad to its first gold medal in the sport at the 1984 games.[25]

Meanwhile, up north, Auriemma "kept getting cut" from his high school team. He later earned a spot on the squad as a backup point guard. He "wasn't a great basketball player," in the words of one biographer, but he "prided himself on being a great teammate." He joined the team at Montgomery County Community College and, upon matriculating to West Chester State University, transitioned into coaching, beginning with a junior varsity girls' program, a boys' team at his old high school in Norristown, Pennsylvania, and as an assistant at St. Joseph's College in Philadelphia. In 1981, he accepted an assistant position at the University of Virginia, one of the top twenty teams in the nation, with head coach Debbie Ryan. Four years later, Auriemma found himself interviewing for the head position at the University of Connecticut. As he recollects, he was unceremoniously offered the $29,000 job "over a cup of coffee at Dunkin' Donuts."[26]

By Auriemma's account, it was an inglorious beginning. A team that had just one winning season since its inception in 1974, the Huskies shared less-than-ideal facilities, wore "hideous" uniforms, and had "no equipment." They concluded 1985–1986 with a 12-15 record; the following year, UConn finished 14-13; then 17-11, and by 1989, the Huskies compiled a record of 24-6, a Big East Conference championship, and bid for the NCAA tournament for the first time in the school's history. Auriemma was crowned Big East Coach of the Year and the University of Connecticut seemed well on its way to becoming a national powerhouse.[27]

A simple formula accounts for Auriemma's quick turnaround of a team once considered the "Big East doormats": equal parts brilliant coaching and aggressive recruiting. By 1991, the team was making regular appearances in the Final Four of the NCAA tournament, but it was in 1995 that the Huskies truly arrived. With a perfect 35-0 record, UConn stung the near dynastic Lady Vols not once, but twice, en route to the national championship, earning their coach all the deserved accolades that accompany such a feat.[28]

By the time Auriemma had taken over at UConn, Summitt had been at Tennessee for seven years. Rehabilitating her knee, which had sidelined her at the beginning of her senior season at UT-Martin, the twenty-two-year-old Summitt took the reins at the University of Tennessee in Knoxville while simultaneously teaching classes and working toward a graduate degree. At the time, the program had "no scholarships and few fans; they weren't even called the Lady Vols yet. In addition to teaching her players rebounding, blocking out and man-to-man defense, Summit drove the team van, washed uniforms and taped ankles." Because the AIAW forbade off-campus recruiting, she put the team together by holding open tryouts, teaching the full-court college game to women who grew up with the six-player version. That first season, the Lady Vols finished with a 16-8 record, averaging around fifty fans at each home game.[29]

Returning from the 1976 Olympics, Summitt set the wheels in motion to become the premiere program in women's college basketball, convincing two of her Olympic teammates to play for the Vols and the Tennessee high schools to abandon the six-player game for the full-court version played in colleges and universities. Since that first 1974–1975 season, when Summitt took over a "glorified intramural program," she has become the winningest coach in the college game, amassing an unparalleled record. It is an accomplishment not likely to be broken, in part, as critics argue, because of her longevity in the position.[30]

She is the only woman coach to make the coveted *Sports Illustrated* cover; the banner reads, "The Wizard of Knoxville" and asks, "Is Tennessee's Pat Summitt the best college basketball coach since John Wooden?" Others have answered in the affirmative, naming both Summitt and UCLA's Wooden—the venerated "Wizard of Westwood"—as the Naismith Coaches of the Century. The honors pile on. Journalists comment that she is "considered the undisputed queen of coaching in the women's game," and, as one writer puts it, "Summitt is living, breathing, walking women's college basketball history." While one can certainly not dispute the changes to the game she has both passed through and inspired, it is little wonder that Geno Auiremma feels that she is the "untouchable . . . golden girl" who enjoys a privileged status long denied to him.[31]

The Gendered Politics of Coaching

Although both Summitt and Auriemma have tried to deflect attention away from the conflicts between them, they each play a crucial role in their teams' contrariety. As reported in the *Washington Post*, it is "the personality differences between these two coaching greats—her Southern charm and his blatant arrogance"—as well as their on-court successes, that make such a compelling story. But it also goes beyond what has been referred to as "the emerging cult of personality in women's hoops," stretching into personal affronts, individual resentments, and the gendered politics of coaching. At one point, the two were on friendly terms, but as time and the rivalry progressed the cordialness was replaced by coolness and a "relationship that Geno has worked very had to create," according to Summitt. There have been several high-profile skirmishes between them that have fanned the fires, and to say Auriemma instigated these incidents is, perhaps, unfair. What does seem fair, however, is to acknowledge that he has become increasingly antagonistic, publicizing several of their behind-the-scenes skirmishes and repeatedly assailing Summitt's character. Arguably, she has done the same to him in what he has characterized as a "passive-aggressive" style.[32]

While there have been multiple controversies between the coaches, there are four in particular that seem to mark turning points in their relationship or, at the very least, seem to be repeated in subsequent stories about them. The latest of these was Summitt's refusal to sign the contract that would continue their regular-season meetings. Another borders on the inane. At a press conference in 2004, a reporter asked Summitt, "If Auriemma were stranded with a broken-down car on a dark highway in Tennessee, would you stop?" Amidst laughter from the crowd, she replied, "I would stop and say, 'Geno, you need any help here?'" The press subsequently relayed the scenario to Auriemma, who brusquely responded, "I would walk." This exchange illustrates the ways in which the popular media not only reports on the rivalry between the coaches and their teams, but continually stokes it as well. The melodrama between Summitt and Auriemma, whether real, imagined, or somewhere in the middle, adds dimension to the game and makes for undeniably good press.[33]

The other two defining moments in their public rivalry, both initiated by Auriemma, came during the 2003 NCAA tournament. Significantly, this marked the first year that all of the women's games would be televised, and whether his actions had any effect or not, or whether it was some type of promotional strategy on his part, the public tuned in. Ratings were 32 percent higher than they had been the previous year. It began with Auriemma referring to Tennessee as the "Evil Empire," a jeer he later defended, asserting the allusion was to Boston Red Sox president Larry Lucchino's reference to the New York Yankees as such, and not to the film *Star Wars* or to insinuate that Summitt was akin to the nefarious Darth Vader.

A later collection of comments was arguably more damaging. A year earlier, Summitt approached Harry Perretta, coach of the Villanova women's basketball team, and asked if he would share his offensive strategies and insights with her. Perretta, admittedly flattered, graciously consented and spent some time counseling the Vols' staff and teaching them his motion offense. Such interactions are common in sports, but what made this especially contentious was Perretta's longtime friendship with Auriemma. Moreover, it was that offense which Tennessee used to hand UConn their first loss that season, though the Huskies were able to exact revenge in the finals of the national tournament later that year.

Clearly annoyed by the relationship Perretta and Summitt had forged, Auriemma sexualized the barbs he directed toward them: "He left me for an older woman," the Huskie coach bemoaned. Upon learning that the two had shared several phone conversations, Auriemma quipped, "Pat thinks he is going steady with her." On another occasion, he facetiously griped that Summitt had given Parretta a "bubble bath" and then played the role of a lover scorned: "I am jealous, Harry and I used to be in the hot tub together." Reiterating the former gibe, he continued, "He dumped me for the Evil Empire." Summitt responded: "I agree with Geno that he's jealous. But I think you could also put paranoid in there. I think you learn more about Geno from this than you do about Pat or Harry." Yes, but we also learn about the gendered nature of athletics. Rather than crediting Summitt for her ability to identify a weakness in her coaching and the best strategy with which to correct it, the press framed her as doing something underhanded. And rather than chastising Auriemma for being sexist, demeaning, and for trivializing Summitt's wherewithal to improve her team, journalists reported Auriemma's comments with a wink and a nod. One journalist went so far as to write that "Poor Harry" was caught in the middle of a "gender conflict." But does the fact that Summitt is a woman and Auriemma a man automatically make the conflict between them gendered? It unfortunately seems so.[34]

Amidst these types of comments, Auriemma has often expressed that being a male coach in women's basketball has put him at a disadvantage. He explains that many women in the profession dislike him because, "You know, like, I'm a man. . . . Ever heard of gender equity? It's when everyone is treated equally. . . . Those women don't like the male influence in women's basketball." Articles bearing titles like "He's The Man," "Auriemma, Man among Women," and "Boys on the Side: Reverse Discrimination?" bolster his position, as do the writings of such renowned journalists as Frank Deford, who comments that Auriemma "got in under the wire" when hired at Connecticut: "Nowadays a man would have no shot at a high-profile women's college basketball job."[35]

This perception of an "antimale process," as Deford labels it, may have some semblance of merit, for women's collegiate basketball, offered at 98.8 percent of Division I, II, and III schools with women's athletic programs, is somewhat unique in that women have consistently coached the majority of these teams. While women currently make up 42.8 percent of head coaches for all women's teams and just 20.6 percent of all teams (women's and men's), women coach 59.1 percent of women's basketball teams. It must be acknowledged, though, that this number is among the lowest in the sport's history, down from 64.6 percent in 1998 and 79.4 percent in 1978. At just the Division I level alone, women comprise 64.1 percent of head basketball coaches (and none of men's team, yet no one decries an "antifemale process" in the men's game), down from 69.0 percent in 2002 and 72.2 percent in 1992. So while Auriemma laments the difficulty of being "a man trying to break into the old girls' network" women's coaching prominence in the sport is steadily eroding.[36]

There have been a number of attempts to explain the simultaneous increase in women's athletic participation and decrease in their percentage at key functionary positions. Some speculate that athletic directors tend to hire those from the male-dominated network of which they are a part. Others argue that the lack of female coaching mentors, the increasing money and prestige that women's sports offer, the gradual separation of athletics from physical education departments, women's "work-family conflicts," and other gendered roles and biases contribute to the relatively few women in collegiate coaching. Additionally, many female athletes express a preference for male coaches, which, as scholars contend, is evidence of the "ideology of masculine superiority" in sports as well as a manifestation of homophobia. Explaining her decision to choose UConn, former standout Diana Taurasi told *Sports Illustrated*, "I know this will irritate a lot of coaches . . . but I wanted to play for a man." While Auriemma may feel as if his sex puts him at a disadvantage in the world of women's basketball, there are undoubtedly those who see it as an asset.[37]

Auriemma has accused the organizers of the NCAA women's basketball tournament of colluding to minimize the number of male coaches who reach the Final Four, an allegation Summitt and members of the committee have separately called "ridiculous." He became especially suspicious in 2001, when three top teams, all coached by men, were placed in the same bracket. He argues that "it *is* different being a man coaching the woman's game. There are always going to be certain people who don't want you to succeed, just because you are a man." Yet, he also seems to lack reverence for the game that gives him his livelihood. In his autobiography, for instance, he derides female basketball players, confessing his initial reluctance to coach them and their lack of "offensive innovation." Perhaps the difficulties he allegedly experiences as a man coaching a women's game have something to do with the opinions he expresses about that game.[38]

In another example, he contends that women do not warrant salaries equal to their male counterparts: "A lot of women's coaches badger their athletic director to be paid the same as the men's coach. Their feeling is, 'I do the same job as the men's basketball coach, therefore, I want the same money.' Bullshit. You don't have the same job. They are two different animals."[39] In contrast, a perusal of Summitt's writings and publicized comments reveals a consistent, though subtle, advocacy for gender equity. In response to male coaches protesting that they do not receive equal opportunity in women's basketball, she countered,

> [Women] don't get as many opportunities. We're second-class citizens. . . . Some of the men in the game—not all—need to get over this. If I'm an athletic director, I'm going to hire the most qualified person. If their credentials are the same, I'm going to hire a woman. Women haven't had the same opportunities. They can't

coach men, with the rare exception. I don't think, sometimes, men
appreciate what we've gone through.[40]

As Summitt prepared for the 1976 Olympic Games, she recollected, "I
knew I wanted to make a difference for women. So I think that's when
I found my real calling. Sports, it struck me, could be a vital avenue to
self-worth for women." And while Auriemma writes that he would "love
to give the men's game a try," Summitt has twice declined the chance
to coach the Tennessee men's program, stating, "I don't consider that a
step up." She makes a good point. No matter how far women's basketball has come since its early days at Smith College, most people still consider men's basketball the normalized, dominant form of the game
—that to which any coach should logically aspire. In this way, women's
basketball continues to be seen as somehow inferior, rather than being
judged on its own progress and merits.[41]

Mediating the Rivalry

It is difficult to think about the Tennessee-UConn rivalry and not implicate
the two coaches, for without the "animosity between Pat and Geno," commented former Huskie Rebecca Lobo, "the rivalry wouldn't be what it is
today, which is the premier matchup in the women's game." Auriemma,
especially, draws attention to himself and the game with a seemingly endless supply of controversy; and over the years, journalists have called him
a "walking soundbite" and observed that his "discourse is the stuff of headlines." Certainly, such comments speak to his personality, but they also
point to the symbiotic relationship between sport and the media. The frequently one-dimensional representations of Auriemma, particularly when
diametrically opposed to those of Summitt, are likely to capture con-
sumers' attention, which helps sell the product of the Tennessee-UConn
rivalry. It is a rivalry that would not exist, at least on the same national
level that it does today, without the influence of the media to encourage
and maintain it.[42]

There have been a number of other rivalries in the history of women's
college basketball. Before Connecticut, for instance, Tennessee frequently
struggled with Louisiana Tech; and since the 1980s, a handful of other
teams have vied for the top spot in the nation, including the University of

Texas, Stanford, the University of Southern California, and Old Dominion University, to name a few. "We had all these rivalries," Summitt said. "We just didn't have the television exposure or the amount of press. People were not as familiar across the country with us as they are now." Rarely, if ever, were teams from the northeastern United States contenders for basketball's top honors, so the influential northeastern media paid little attention to the sport. That was, of course, until the University of Connecticut began to turn things around.[43]

Connecticut is a relatively small state, but it is ideally situated at the epicenter of several powerful media outlets. The University of Connecticut, then, was almost assured substantial media coverage if it could produce a successful team. ESPN, in particular, with its headquarters in nearby Bristol, Connecticut, had been a supporter of Husky athletics since its 1979 inception; and the initial Tennessee-UConn meeting was not just broadcast by ESPN, but was orchestrated by the cable juggernaut. In addition to the television exposure, print media and, especially, newspapers located in the Northeast contributed to the extraordinary coverage of the game. The *New York Times* "treated UConn like a local team," write Pamela Grundy and Susan Shackelford, providing almost daily coverage in the period leading up to the event. Connecticut's Sports Information department issued 135 media credentials—at the time, the most for any men's or women's game in the history of the institution.[44]

It was, in the words of Mike Soltys, ESPN's vice president of domestic network communications, "the dawn of a new, more popular era of women's basketball." When the teams met a second time that season in the final of the NCAA tournament, the number of viewers who tuned in to see it on CBS was a strong indication of what lay ahead. The Nielsen ratings for the broadcast showed that almost three times as many people watched the Tennessee-UConn championship game than tuned in to Fox's coverage of the National Hockey League, airing at the same time, and 14 percent more people watched the women's final than they did NBC's broadcast of professional men's basketball.[45]

The two teams involved, as well as women's basketball in general, felt an immediate impact after those first two meetings. As one journalist wrote, since the beginning "every game has become a showdown, a showcase, on national television." Before the start of the next season,

Connecticut Public Television signed a three-year, $2.8 million deal to broadcast the Huskies' games. ABC jumped on the bandwagon, airing several women's college games after showing just one in 1995. ESPN agreed to a seven-year, $19 million deal with the NCAA to televise forty-one more women's contests than it had the previous year. The popular media has also influenced regular-season scheduling. Because of a contract with the Big East Conference, for example, CBS traditionally had the broadcast rights to UConn's games, but ESPN's desire to air the matchup with Tennessee contributed to the addition of a second in-season matchup in 2000 and 2001.[46]

The association between the Tennessee and UConn women's basketball teams is more than a succession of one game after the next, one season after another. Each matchup becomes a significant plot point in a complicated story arc with no predictable or foreseeable resolution. A host of literary allusions have been used to describe the relationship between the two teams that provide "good theater," "drama," and "sub-plots galore," in which "Pat and Geno" become "The Game's Favorite Soap Opera." Thus, the rivalry between them is mass communicated as a serialized production. It is the first time in the history of sports that the popular press used audience-building techniques typically associated with men's sports and applied them to sustain coverage of a women's team sport. Each time Tennessee and UConn meet, concentration on the teams' standout personalities, histories, and achievements are every bit as important to the broadcast as the game itself.[47]

Without the traditional Tennessee-UConn game to publicize, the popular media searched for answers as to why their favorite rivalry had been so abruptly cancelled. Summitt, for her part, avoided the questions, saying only that its discontinuation would allow women's basketball to cultivate other rivalries. Auriemma contended that her ability to get away with calling off the series and to stay silent on her reasons were further proof of the privileged status she had long enjoyed: "This game is bigger than any individual," he declared. "I could understand [the decision] if the game had suddenly become irrelevant. But it hadn't. There aren't many relevant games played in women's basketball each season." The word "relevant" is a tricky one, but if Auriemma meant it in the sense that other contests failed to generate the same widespread excitement as the annual Tennessee-UConn games, it seems as though he was right.[48]

As the 2007–2008 season wore on, no team or storyline proved compelling enough to supplant the Vol-Husky status. If any school had captured national attention in the previous year, it was Rutgers University, which suffered the racist and sexist remarks of radio shock jock Don Imus following their loss to Tennessee in the finals of the 2007 national tournament. The dignity, grace, and integrity with which the athletes and, in particular, their coach, C. Vivian Stringer, handled the aftermath of Imus's comments was widely admired. Stanford University and their longtime, highly decorated coach, Tara VanDerveer, offered another option to which both basketball fans and casual observers might be drawn. But the media continued to chase after the story behind the Tennessee-UConn cancellation, rather than focus efforts on promoting other teams or building other rivalries.

In March 2008, newspapers across the country revealed that the University of Connecticut had self-reported a recruiting violation to the NCAA. The violation concerned Maya Moore, who, in 2005, was hotly pursued by the top programs in the country (including Tennessee) before deciding to sign with the University of Connecticut. UConn admitted that school officials had arranged for Moore, a two-time national high school player of the year, to tour the ESPN studios, which constituted a secondary NCAA rules violation or an "improper benefit" —one that is offered to an athletic recruit, but not available to all potential students. The penalties for a secondary violation are typically minor, often resulting in little more than a letter in the offending school's file. After the self-report, UConn officials declared that they "now consider this matter closed," while journalists persisted after the larger story.[49]

ESPN then uncovered that the University of Tennessee had registered a complaint with Southeastern Conference officials against the University of Connecticut. Tennessee and SEC representatives refused to comment on the nature of the grievances and Auriemma questioned ESPN's timing, "nine months after the fact. You've got the NCAA tournament going on and you've got 64 teams playing and [ESPN journalist] Trey Wingo wants to talk about Geno and Pat." Indeed, in all the time that had elapsed since the cancellation was announced, the timing of the investigation seemed suspicious, for it would certainly cause viewers to pay greater attention to the tournament, which was, unsurprisingly, broadcast on ESPN.[50]

As one school after the next was eliminated from the 2008 NCAA tournament, leaving just Rutgers, Stanford, Tennessee, and Connecticut in the Final Four, it was clear that most viewers hoped for a grudge match between the Vols and the Huskies. It was not to be. Stanford ousted UConn, Tennessee captured its eighth national championship, and ESPN filed a Freedom of Information request that would force Vols' officials to make public their charges against Connecticut. In compliance, Tennessee released a thirty-four-page document, including a letter from Tennessee athletic director Joan Cronan, to the SEC Commissioner dated 2006 stating,

> From time to time we have encountered situations related to the University of Connecticut's women's basketball program that would seem to be a violation of the rules. . . . This information comes as a result of discussion among basketball coaches at the SEC spring meeting, information shared by AAU and high school coaches, prospective student athletes, as well as numerous other individuals.

In all, they levied eight charges against Connecticut for recruiting violations of eleven NCAA bylaws, including illegal contact between former UConn athletes and recruits and media involvement with prospective players. Of the violations, an official statement from UConn read, there was "only one highly publicized result," a point that Auriemma clarified in an end-of-season press conference: "She accused us of cheating in recruiting, but she doesn't have the courage to say it in public." "She," of course, was Summitt, and the "one highly publicized result" had to do with Maya Moore.[51]

With the tournament over and the reason for the end to their series made public, one journalist characterized the rivalry between the University of Connecticut and the University of Tennessee women's basketball teams as the "cold war." It is an apt analogy, for although there is no direct contact or conflict between the two superpowers, there remains a sense of tension and hostility as each struggles for the ultimate, elusive ascendancy in women's college basketball. At the same time, there is always a threat that the two might meet again on the hard-wood of the NCAA national tournament. It is the anticipation for that occurrence—that itchy expectation for a reunion—that sustains and per-haps enhances the rivalry between them. Players will come and go, records will rise and fall, but so long as Summitt and Auriemma are coaching these teams, the media will pay attention and the country will watch. The cancellation of the regular-season play between these two amazing programs does not mean the end of their rivalry. It just means we have to wait a little longer.[52]

Ohio Stadium dedication game between Ohio State and Michigan on October 21, 1922. *Courtesy of The Ohio State University Archives.*

eleven

Three Yards and a Pool of Blood

Ohio State versus Michigan

BRAD AUSTIN ——

Regardless of what you might think personally of football at Ohio State remember that on October 21, your football team was in the spotlight. I do not know how many hundreds of college football games there were that day. I do know that your team, my team, the team representing the Ohio State University was good enough to participate in a game that dimmed every other college game in the country. We were all crushed by the Michigan defeat. We were stunned. We thought we would win because we wanted to win. It meant so much to us. Football does that to you.

—Ohio State University Monthly, 1933

Woody would get you ready [for Michigan] all year. We used to say that Michigan was a separate season, a season in itself. He prepared for Michigan all year. Spring practice we'd be getting ready for Michigan defense. It was constant preparation for that game— the whole season every Monday.

—Archie Griffin

A book on sports rivalries would seem tragically incomplete to most readers without a chapter on the University of Michigan–Ohio State University football rivalry. Certainly, intrastate games such as Oregon–Oregon State, Auburn-Alabama, and California-Stanford have rich and distinguished histories, just as interconference rivalries such as Tennessee-Alabama, Texas-Oklahoma, and USC-UCLA do. Intersectional rivalries, most often featuring Notre Dame, have long inspired interest and deep passions on a national scale. Nonetheless, looking at the span of college football history from the vantage point of the early twenty-first century, the Ohio State–Michigan rivalry easily distinguishes itself as the most interesting and significant of them all.

While other traditional college football games make claims to being "the Big Game," Ohio State–Michigan has been the most consistently meaningful game for the longest span. This meaning both includes and transcends the importance of the game to title races. Pitting two of the nation's largest universities against each other (along with two of the largest alumni bases) in season-ending games that usually have Big Ten conference and often national championship implications, this November game seems tailor-made for drama, intrigue, and, above all, passion. Just as importantly, the outcome of the game helps much of the population of both states define themselves, marking them as "winners" or "losers" just as much as the actual participants of the game.

The participants, however, are those that do win or lose the game. Many of the men involved in this rivalry helped to create and personify the nation's college football landscape: Fritz Crisler, Bo, Woody, Paul Brown, Archie Griffin, Charles Woodson, Hopalong Cassady, Desmond Howard, and Eddie George. Together, these universities have claimed eighteen national championships and have won outright or shared seventy-three Big Ten titles. Moreover, the individual talent on display in this rivalry has been astounding: ten Heisman Trophy winners, 322 All-American players, and 112 first-round draft picks. While it took some athletes years to establish their reputations, others gained notoriety almost solely because of their brilliant performances on college football's biggest stage, in a game where even the stadia have personalities and nicknames: the "Big House" and the "Horseshoe." Ohio State fans still have nightmares about Tim Biakiabuta's 313-yard explosion against the Buckeyes in 1995, and Wolverine fans cannot yet believe that Troy Smith produced almost 400 total yards against them in 2004.

The use of a possessive pronoun in the preceding sentence was no accident. This game's meaning stems in large part from the ways it has personalized and crystallized a larger statewide rivalry over the past 110 years. The emergence of the most storied and heated rivalry in college athletics has its roots in the economics and politics of the nineteenth and early twentieth century. With Michigan producing automobiles in the early 1900s at an even greater rate than Ohio produced presidents in the late 1800s, these states were among the most important and exciting places to be during the formative years of modern American and college football history. It shouldn't be a surprise that their universities also craved and created a similar place in the athletic spotlight.

The intensity of the Ohio State–Michigan rivalry is a product of both nature and nurture. Two neighboring states competing for prominence in all aspects of intellectual, economic, and political life created the conditions for a heated rivalry, but the passions associated with this game would have never spread to the extent that they did without the active encouragement of specific people from both universities throughout the course of the rivalry or without the good fortune of having the rivalry's most meaningful transitions coincide with the advent of new mass communication capabilities. Because these technologies have allowed millions to witness (and participate in) the rivalry, the story of the Michigan–Ohio State series is the story of just how much "Big-Time" college sports can mean to both participants and partisans.

Founded in 1817, the University of Michigan was one of the first public universities in the new nation, and it was certainly one of the first in the old Northwest Territory. It was, unfortunately, more of a university in name than in operation, and the "in name" part deserves scrutiny. The original name for the institution was the "Catholepistemiad, or University, of Michigania." Originally housed in Detroit, the university never really found success or students and existed in theory only from 1827 to 1837. At that point, with Michigan a newly organized state, the state constitution reinvigorated the university ideal and relocated it to Ann Arbor. By 1841, the university had enrolled its newest cohort of undergraduates and was on its way to earning a national reputation for academic excellence. By 1866, the University of Michigan had become the largest university in the country, with more than twelve hundred undergraduate students.[1]

In contrast to Michigan, Ohio State got a much later start on its road to academic excellence, a pattern that would be repeated on the athletic field. Public education had existed in Ohio from the beginning, with the Land Ordinances of 1785 and 1787 making clear provisions for the "maintenance of public schools" and the encouragement of "schools and the means of education." During the ensuing decades, as anyone familiar with the modern educational landscape of Ohio would attest, liberal arts colleges began sprouting up all over the state. By the 1840s Kenyon, Denison, Oberlin, Marietta, and several other colleges provided an avenue for higher education within Ohio. By 1859, there were twenty-two small colleges operating in Ohio, but no public institution of higher learning.[2]

The Ohio State University owes its existence to the 1862 Morrill Act, the educational legislation that mandated the use of proceeds from the sales of federal land grants to support public higher education. While its wording allowed a relatively broad interpretation of the types of education that the new colleges and universities might provide, it did mandate instruction in "such branches of learning as are related to agriculture and the mechanic arts." Accordingly, in September of 1873, the institution now known as the Ohio State University opened its doors as the Ohio Agricultural and Mechanical College, even though it offered a wider range of courses and degrees than this name indicates. This "A and M" beginning led contemporaries to refer to the school as the "Agricultural College" and helped launch lingering stereotypes of Ohio State fans as rubes and hayseeds, at least in the eyes of Michigan supporters.[3]

The college's first president, Edward Orton, almost immediately began a campaign to rectify the situation, positing that "if a shorter and less misleading designation should be adopted, we shall perhaps reap some immediate advantage."[4] After convincing the board of trustees to adopt its new name in 1878, Orton started tackling the much more difficult challenges of making the newly renamed Ohio State University a leader in the region and the nation, in the classroom and on the athletic fields.

If the University of Michigan enjoyed a head start in the race to academic excellence, it also enjoyed similar advantages in the quest for athletic supremacy in the late nineteenth and early twentieth centuries. In fact, it is important to note that even though Ohio State and Michigan first met on the football field in 1897, the "rivalry" did not commence for another twenty-two years. It is, after all, difficult to consider an opponent a rival if you never lose to them. Until 1919, that was the case in the Michigan–Ohio State series. Until that point, with the exception of a single tie, Michigan won and Ohio State lost.

American colleges had long used their athletic programs to garner prestige and to link themselves with established and more elite institutions. This phenomenon began with Harvard and Yale seeking to emulate the crew competitions between Oxford and Cambridge with their 1852 crew meet, an event that marked, as Ronald Smith has explained, not only the advent of intercollegiate competition, but also the commercialization of intercollegiate competition. Other institutions soon followed suit, so that by the late 1800s, private eastern colleges and universities had established themselves as the elites of American intercollegiate athletics, most particularly in college football.[5]

In an imaginative phrase, historian John Watterson has compared the growing popularity of college football in the 1890s to a "computer virus;" seemingly every institution that came into contact with the sport had its student body infected by its popularity. Neither the University of Michigan nor Ohio State was immune to the football bug. Ohio State first played intercollegiate football in 1890, going 1-3, by beating Ohio Wesleyan 20–14 and losing to the College of Wooster, Kenyon College, and Denison College by a combined 96–10.[6]

The University of Michigan fared better. The late nineteenth and early twentieth centuries were a good time to be a booster of Michigan, the state or the university. As the auto industry made the state the heart of the American industrial boom, the university maintained its reputation for academic excellence and expanded it to include athletic superiority as well. It did so exceedingly well[7]

With its first intercollegiate football game in 1879, the University of Michigan began creating a tradition that would bring notoriety to the school and help create a reputation for distinction. (Michigan has the records for both the most wins and the highest winning percentage in college football history.) As their fight song, "The Victors," indicates, Michigan enjoyed early success in the Western Conference and proclaimed its team "the Champions of the West" after its first conference championship in 1898. Others shortly followed in 1901, 1902, 1903, 1904, and 1906. Although this claim remained disputed, largely by Michigan's chief rivals at the University of Chicago and the University of Minnesota, the self-characterization stuck, as did, in some observers' minds, a reputation for self-promotion and haughtiness.[8]

Although it may surprise contemporary observers, Ohio State was not close to being the most important game on Michigan's schedule throughout the first two decades of the twentieth century. The Ohio State–Michigan series began just as Michigan was establishing itself as a legitimate force in college football and the self-proclaimed champion of a region. This was not good timing for Ohio State. In the first contest, held in Ann Arbor in October of 1897, the Wolverines outscored the Buckeyes 34–0 in the first half, and while the Ohio State fans could claim a moral victory because of the scoreless second half, that would be just about their only consolation for the next two decades. It would certainly have to be for the next three years because the two schools didn't even schedule each other again until 1900, when they played a scoreless tie in Ann Arbor.[9]

What is now an annual rivalry, therefore, was initially neither annual nor a rivalry, at least not at the same time. After 1900, the schools played each other for twelve consecutive years, with Michigan winning eleven of the twelve games by a combined score of 318–18, with the remaining game a 3–3 tie. To its credit, Ohio State did manage to score against Michigan in a full third of the contests, even though this accomplishment is diminished by the fact that it never reached double digits and gave up 86 points in the 1902 game. To put the one-sided nature of the early series in additional perspective, in six of the twelve games, Michigan scored more than Ohio State did in all twelve combined.[10]

The series was not yet a true rivalry from Michigan's perspective; for the Wolverines the most important games were the contests against Minnesota and Chicago. For an example of this, one needs only to read a 1901 article in the *Michigan Alumnus,* "The Most Satisfying Moment in My Athletic Experience at Michigan." The former athletes profiled in the magazine recall football games against Harvard, Cornell, and Chicago, track meets, and baseball games, but not a single alumnus mentions Ohio State. The Buckeyes simply didn't matter to the Wolverines.[11]

The same could not be said from the Ohio State perspective, and the legacy of Ohio State's frustration can be heard at the conclusion of every home football game today. In their 1902 meeting ("contest" doesn't seem quite accurate), Michigan destroyed Ohio State by the score of 86–0. This was when Fielding Yost's teams were at the height of their power, and the game left the OSU student newspaper to report that "Ohio had expected to be beaten, but 86 to 0 was so far beyond the thought of the most pessimistic, that the 1800 loyal rooters were fairly shocked into dumbness."

One member of the team, however, could still find his voice, or at least his pen, during the long train ride home. During that undoubtedly difficult trip a freshman player, Fred Cornell, wrote the words to Ohio State's Alma Mater: "O come let's sing Ohio's praise, and songs to Alma Mater raise!"[12]

Michigan withdrew from the Western Conference in 1908 in order to continue playing more than five games, including contests against the powerful eastern schools that helped establish its reputation, and it maintained its series with Ohio State. This lasted until 1912, when Ohio State joined the Western Conference and, accordingly, could not play Michigan anymore. The two schools did not resume their series until 1918, the year after Michigan returned to the fold, and also a year after Ohio State had won its first Western Conference crown. Absence had not made the Buckeyes' hearts grow any fonder of the Wolverines, and even though the old pattern initially continued, with Ohio State losing 14–0, the Buckeyes were starting to emerge as a sincere threat to Michigan's dominance.[13]

Until Ohio State actually won a game, however, Michigan continued to discount the significance of the game. In 1910, the Case Western matchup received much more notice than the Ohio State game, and the Ohio State game received equal press attention with Michigan freshmen contests in 1911. As late as 1918, Michigan actually wanted to cancel the Ohio State game, so it could quickly schedule a meeting with Illinois to settle the conference championship. After the seemingly inevitable Michigan victory over OSU that year, the local newspapers devoted two columns to the story. Beating Ohio State simply wasn't surprising or newsworthy in 1918, even if the ritual beating caused great consternation to the Buckeye faithful.[14]

It *would* be newsworthy in the 1920s, though, as the series benefited from an almost perfect confluence of competitive balance, the construction of mammoth stadia, and the advent of national radio broadcasts. These combinations of forces and events were the key to this rivalry claiming an increasing level of importance at the local, regional, and national levels.

More precisely, the series became a rivalry in 1919 when All-American running back Chic Harley led the Buckeyes as they "accomplished that which made the heart of every alumnus joyous—the defeat of Michigan at football."[15] Ohio State alumni and fans had been ready to celebrate a victory, with the "greatest crowd in school history" attending the pre-game rally. Afterwards, the student newspaper could proclaim that "the 'jinx' is banished. Ohio State spirit and claims of prowess [could] roam unrestrained by fears of unconquered foes."[16]

The student columnist continued explaining the greater significance of the landmark victory to the state and university, noting that "the entire country was interested in the outcome of the struggle on Ferry Field," and when the team won "the reputation of the institution it represented was likewise elevated to a higher level." This was because the "faith of the University's followers in the standing of their institution rose with a force equal to that of a skyrocket yell," and readers should have recognized that the supporters' "faith is not going to descend. It is going to stay up and continue mounting higher."[17]

From the Ohio State perspective, this was clearly a monumentally meaningful victory, one that would inspire the entire state to greater deeds; but those reporting on Michigan football did not seem to believe that a single defeat to an exceptionally talented Ohio State team was much cause for concern. They did, however, begin to care a little more about the series when Ohio State repeated the feat the following year. By 1921, there was a noticeable increase in Michigan's pre-game press, with headlines focusing on how "Former Stars Return to Help Yost Groom Team for Ohio State Game." It didn't help: Michigan lost again, leading to such delightfully derisive headlines from Columbus as "'Hurroo for 'The Amaized and Blue.'" This linguistic mockery of Michigan's "Maize and Blue" would become standard fare for Ohio State fans and reporters over the coming decades. So would the increasing pressure on coaches who had the misfortune of losing to their rivals too often. In 1921, immediately after the Ohio State loss, an editorial entitled "Yost Has Seen His Day" appeared in the Michigan student newspaper.[18]

Because of this emergence of competitive balance, the rivalry continued to grow in stature and significance, so much so that before the 1922 game Michigan newspapers began printing mocking cartoons and poems about Ohio State. It is not clear whether or not a literature professsor at either university would have approved of H. C. Cherrington's "In the Bluish Haze," but by this point in the emerging rivalry, many Michigan fans surely applauded:

> A bluish haze o'er the fields of maize
>
> Turned scarlet, then gray, our hopes.

And then we knew that the Maize and Blue

    Had upset the Buckeye dopes.

    'Twas a hard old day

    For Scarlet and Gray

    And a sunset trailed with mopes.

(3rd Stanza)

The big horseshoe was a mass of blue

    Of the mental sort, as no harbor

The Yost-men left to the "O's" bereft,

    In the game that rejoiced Ann Arbor.

    But no close shave

    That they ever gave

    Could surpass our three-year barber.

After those lean years we can dim our tears,

    And say it's no idle boast,

That the Wolverines may its proud fur preen,

    For it has a host in Yost

    And for Wilce's boys

    We wish you new joys:

"To the future"—that's our toast.[19]

Although the 1922 victory had, in some Michiganders' eyes, rendered "Ohio's Repudiation . . . Complete," it was clear that the series would never be the same again. Ohio State had gotten the attention of the Michigan players and supporters, so much so that 1923 newspaper articles highlighted the fact that Ohio State represented the "hardest and most important game" on the schedule and that this game was the seniors' "last chance at Ohio," language conspicuously absent for the previous two decades in Michigan circles.[20] As the rivalry became more heated and competitive, the crowds kept growing. For the 1923 game, for example, more than 55,000 ticket applications were rejected because Michigan's Ferry Field could accommodate only 44,000.[21] The enormous amount of public interest in this game, coupled with the inability to satisfy more than 50,000 customers, helps explain the next stage of these universities' rivalry.

With ever-increasing interest in their athletic offerings, universities across the country launched ambitious stadium drives during the 1920s, with Ohio State and Michigan constructing two of the nation's largest. From this point forward, what was becoming the nation's biggest game would literally have access to two of the nation's biggest stages. The universities needed the larger stadia because the rivalry had also become the focus of a great deal of community interest. This can be seen, for example, in the eleven special trains carrying 5,500 supporters from Columbus to Ann Arbor for the 1921 game and real-time scoreboards updating crowds exceeding 3,000 that remained on campus.[22]

Just like the teams and games themselves, the stadia had larger meanings for their respective states and other constituencies. In a fundraising pamphlet for its planned stadium, which illustrated perfectly Ohio's continuing quest for outside validation, Ohio State claimed, "The Stadium will be for all Ohio. . . . [A]s an architectural triumph, it will lend prestige to the city of Columbus and the State."[23] During the parade before the stadium's 1922 dedication, a banner communicated a similar sentiment: "COLUMBUS DISCOVERED AMERICA, THE STADIUM WILL HELP AMERICA DISCOVER COLUMBUS."[24]

If, however, Ohio State's leaders wanted the 70,0000 fans at the stadium's dedication ceremony to witness an actual and not just an architectural triumph, they should have scheduled an opponent other than Michigan. The *Columbus Sunday Dispatch*'s headline, stretching across the top of the front page, said it all, "Ohio's Great Stadium Is Dedicated; Michigan Avenges Defeat of 1921." Six years later, when Michigan All-American Benny Oosterbann threw three touchdown passes against Ohio State, the dedication of Michigan Stadium left its crowd of 87,000 feeling more satisfied.[25] In a rivalry so immense that even the stadia have names, those from the "Big House" were 2-0 versus the representatives of "the Horseshoe" in dedication games.

It is entirely appropriate to focus on the newspaper coverage of the games and the stadium dedications because the rivalry gained national attention and achieved national significance only by having newspaper columnists and, increasingly, radio broadcasts tell the stories of the games and the personalities of those who competed in them. The 1920s were, as Frederick Lewis Allen noted, the "Ballyhoo Years," a time of great excitement over seemingly trivial events and an era that witnessed the rise of syndicated columnists and national circulation magazines to help shape a national culture. The Ohio State–Michigan rivalry had every possible advantage in the race to establish a national profile: neighboring states with nine of the fifty largest cities in the country (with the media centers to match), combined student populations exceeding 24,000, two enormous stadia, and a combined fifteen conference championships between them by 1930.[26]

While the games of the 1920s were consistently competitive and would have warranted attention on their own merits, officials at both schools did almost everything within their powers to attract even more notice for the rivalry. This impulse explains the reasons for each school "dedicating" its stadium with games against the other after the buildings had already opened for business, and it also explains the unfortunate decision to add fireworks when Columbus hosted the annual spectacle in 1926. The fact that the documents related to this event are kept in an archival folder entitled "Bomb Explosion: Michigan Game, 1926" captures the essence of the mistake. It seems that the appropriately named Pain's Fireworks was unable to keep all of the explosives out of the assembled crowd of 90,000, leading to Ohio State paying thousands of dollars to injured patrons as compensation for their burned arms and legs, lacerated scalps, broken bones, ruined clothes, and, in one instance, dropped binoculars.[27] The archives don't include bills for the thousands of broken Buckeye hearts after the Michigan victory.

While the "Bomb Explosion" seems to have been an isolated case of administrative exuberance and pyrotechnological incompetence, newspaper and radio reporters spent much of the 1920s providing their own rhetorical fireworks to both generate and describe the rivalry's passion and meaning to their audiences. This was certainly evident in the decade's student reporting, as the young protégées were learning to mimic their professional counterparts' rhetorical excesses. A *Michigan Alumnus* description of the 1926 game neatly epitomizes the trend in reporting:

> So close was the fight, so desperate and thrilling the fashion in which it was waged, so overpowering the setting and the sheer bulk of the multitude that watched and showed, that it is difficult to write of it in the commonplace terms of a game between vigorous young undergraduates, the temptation is to employ Homeric verse

or at least the more virile terminology of the war-correspondent. When two evenly-matched teams are pitted against each other in a game as inherently exciting as football and the spectacle is staged in a structure whose proportions suggest the looming bulks of ancient Thebes, and which holds a howling, shrieking human mass thrice as large as the entire population of Ann Arbor, the affair assumes epic proportions, and one who witnessed it and who suffered the agonies and the ecstasies of those nerve-twisting hours is tempted to write in language born of his emotions.[28]

Throughout the decade, prominent newspapers from around the country continued to make their readers aware of the huge crowds attending, and high stakes attached to, the Michigan–Ohio State game. Readers of the *New York Times,* for example, had at least 359 opportunities to read about Ohio State and Michigan football during the 1920s. Increasingly, however, the American audience was taking advantage of radio broadcasts to vicariously experience the games themselves rather than reading about them the following morning. The Ohio State–Michigan rivalry was at the center of this new national trend.[29]

The Ohio State–Michigan game was first broadcast in 1924 on Detroit's WWJ radio station, making this one of the first Big Ten games to be broadcast, and the universities would continue to benefit and profit from commercial broadcasts from this point forward. Despite concerns that broadcasts might reduce attendance and fan interest, the regional and national notoriety these broadcasts provided seems to have only generated more enthusiasm throughout the 1920s as the teams attracted their largest crowds ever.[30]

The increased success of the rivalry and its attached spectacle served the universities well during the Great Depression. During this most difficult decade, the rivalry persevered, maintaining the public's interest level and, in a related measure, the game's relative prosperity throughout. This, however, was not inevitable; the universities' leaders showed great imagination in their efforts to create and feed public interest in their games.

Despite frequently voiced concerns about the potential for radio broadcasts to dampen attendance totals, the schools responded to public pressure to keep providing access to the games, even to those who could not afford tickets. In 1932, the Ohio State alumni magazine identified the

OSU-Michigan game as "big news to the rest of the United States" and identified the broadcasters who "told the world" how the game unfolded. Again in 1934, the *Ohio State University Monthly* informed OSU's alumni that three different stations, using three different announcers and six "strategically placed microphones," would broadcast Ohio State's games. Alumni could listen to Red Barber and others call the game as it happened, vicariously participating in the (presumed) victories by listening to the "blare of the bands" and the "cheers of the crowds."[31]

One measure of the importance of the rivalry to the general population of both states was the schools' continued ability to charge relatively high ticket prices for these games, even if it was *only* for these games. In 1930, Ohio State offered no Michigan tickets for less than $3.00, and the university sold 54,251 tickets for $3.00 and 4,560 for $4.00. Two years later, while almost twenty-two thousand spectators paid $3.00 or more for their tickets, single-ticket sales for the Michigan game fell from 58,811 to 35,533, even though Ohio State also offered $2.20 and $1.50 tickets. By the 1934 home game, Ohio State sold only 2,079 tickets at $3.00. In contrast, 75 percent of the fifty thousand fans paid either $2.50 or $2.00 for their tickets, and 20 percent paid less than $2.00. In other words, four years after the minimum ticket price for the Michigan game was $3.00, 95 percent of the paying customers got in for less than that. These were still the most expensive ticket prices Ohio State dared to present for its games (excepting its first home game against Notre Dame), and during a time when the Michigan football revenue fell from $400,000 in 1929 to $152,000 in 1935, the revenue from this single game annually represented more than 35 percent of the annual revenue, and as much as 65 percent.[32] This was clearly a rivalry worth paying to see.

Until the mid-1930s the rivalry had a place on the map (two places, actually) but not one on the calendar. The fact that this changed during the depths of the Depression is the best indicator of the importance both schools and their fans placed on the rivalry by this point. Faced with plummeting athletic revenues, the Ohio State Athletic Board began discussing the possibility of moving the Michigan game back to the last game of the season as early as May 1932, but they realized that they could not possibly adjust the schedule before 1934 at the earliest.[33] An extended excerpt from the *Ohio State University Monthly* provides ample evidence to understand why the universities agreed to make this the last game of each season. The stakes, financial and otherwise, were simply too high to do otherwise. The description of the October 1933 game reads like this:

> Neither Michigan nor Ohio State had played a single Big Ten foe and yet the winner of the game was heralded from coast to coast as the likely champion. More than 85,000 people found reason to be in the Michigan Stadium that afternoon. The great broadcasting networks, hundreds of leased telegraph and telephone wires and hundreds of newspaper men were ready to send the news of the great struggle to the awaiting millions of sport loving people of the country.
>
> You already know the score; you knew as soon as the final gun ended the game that Michigan won 13–0.
>
> Regardless of what you might think personally of football at Ohio State remember that on October 21, your football team was in the spotlight. I do not know how many hundreds of college football games there were that day. I do know that your team, my team, the team representing the Ohio State University was good enough to participate in a game that dimmed every other college game in the country. We were all crushed by the Michigan defeat. We were stunned. We thought we would win because we wanted to win. It meant so much to us. Football does that to you.[34]

This quote almost perfectly illustrates the state of the rivalry by the early 1930s. The national press was transmitting descriptions to all corners of the country; it was the most important game of the season, even though it was the first Big Ten game that year; and a loss had the ability to "stun" and "crush" disappointed fans of "my team" and "your team" because "football does that to you."

Losing such an important game early in the season could do more than crush spirits; it could also diminish fan interest in the rest of the season and diminish ticket sales for later games. By 1935 Michigan and Ohio State officials would be able to guarantee that this scenario would never happen again. During the middle of the Depression, when they desperately needed to maximize fan interest and ticket revenue, the universities agreed to permanently move the game to the last weekend of the season. Doing so served them well in the 1930s, and it has continued to do so ever since, giving passionate fans the possibility of redemption during a troubled season and providing casual football fans with a regular date on the calendar.

Even though the rivalry had become more balanced and competitive by the 1930s, it always seemed as if Ohio State was still trying to catch up to Michigan, placing more emphasis on the game than even rabid Wolverine fans. This was not only true for the Buckeyes' legions of supporters, but also true for the coaches and players themselves. This emphasis on beating Michigan found its most perfect expression in the words of Coach Francis Schmidt and in the rituals of the Pants Club.

When Francis Schmidt was hired in 1934, after OSU had lost nine of the last twelve to Michigan, he got the question that seemingly all Ohio State coaches immediately get: What are you going to do about Michigan? His answer, if unoriginal, was memorable: "Michigan? They put their pants on one leg at a time, don't they?" This unintimidated and unimpressed attitude inspired Buckeye fans, and the fact that his team backed up his bravado with a 34–0 victory led to the first fan assaults on Ohio State's goalposts and to one of the more interesting and telling aspects of the rivalry: the Pants Club.[35]

Begun in 1935, the Pants Club was a way for Ohio State to continue focusing attention on the Michigan game long after the season's conclusion. According to Article One of its constitution, the Pants Club exists "to foster the most casual type of attitude toward an institution of higher education somewhat north of the Ohio line, whose colors shall habitually be, as far as we are concerned, amaized and blue." The club would meet after each Michigan victory ("annually as often as possible," according to the constitution), and each member of victorious teams would receive "golden pants" jewelry as an emblem of their victory.[36]

Even though the club constitution proclaimed a desire to generate a "most casual attitude" toward Michigan, the club's effect was certainly the opposite. Ohio State athletic director Lynn St. John clearly recognized this when he wrote to his Michigan counterpart, H. O. Crisler, in 1942. St. John referenced earlier conversations about how to "develop a cooperative arrangement whereby we might add something to the tradition and mutual importance of the Ohio State–Michigan game." So, what was St. John's idea? He thought it would be nice if the Michigan football captain, George Ceithaml, and a prominent Michigan alumnus would attend OSU's victory celebration the following month, a gesture that would "really serve to strengthen the traditional rivalry" between the schools. Not surprisingly, the Michigan captain declined this generous offer, but he did graciously send his game pants to Columbus, just as "the losing general turns over his sword to the victor." Ceithaml summarized the state of the rivalry when he noted, "We are honored that your boys will wear gold replicas of our pants on their watch chains, for you must respect a competitor around which you build so unique and interesting a tradition."[37]

With competitive balance, school songs, unflattering stereotypes, and "pants clubs" firmly in place, the Michigan–Ohio State game had established itself as one of the premier rivalries in the nation by the late 1940s, but it would grow in both stature and significance during the 1950s and 1960s because of another fortunate convergence of personalities, performance, and press capabilities. Just as the nation's football fans were gaining the ability to watch college football games from the comfort of their living rooms, Ohio State hired a football coach whose personality and list of achievements were both substantial enough to command their attention. Once Michigan hired a worthy counterpart, the popularity and intensity of the rivalry went to new heights, and the stakes of the games seemingly always involved championships and Rose Bowl berths. The fact that a national audience could observe the action on network television did nothing but amplify the emotions of the Ohio and Michigan fans.

In the early 1950s, the confluence of two seemingly otherworldly forces transformed Ohio State football and its relevance to the state and nation. The first was the arrival of network television cameras in college football stadia; the second was the power of Woody Hayes's personality and will. As early as 1948, the university was considering broadcasting one or two football games, and this was no surprise considering the level of interest in OSU football across the state. That same year, more than twenty thousand attended the spring scrimmage.[38]

A much larger number of Ohio and Michigan citizens wanted to see "their" teams play more meaningful fall games and felt no reluctance about communicating their demands to university officials and their elected representatives. By 1949, the debate in the Big Ten revolved around live telecasts, with almost everyone agreeing that delayed broadcasts were acceptable. The University of Michigan came out in favor of live telecasts earlier than Ohio State did, in large part because Ohio State feared losing a substantial percentage of its gate revenue since fans would have the option to see the game without a ticket.[39]

This line of reasoning did not convince all of the universities' constituents. One rural Ohioan, someone who testified to the power of broadcasts to generate "interest in our University in a manner never approached before," worried that the Big Ten's ban on live telecasts would only serve to make the "99 [out of 100] who can't get away [to the game] for one reason or another who follow the broadcasts and talk about the events for the following week" to become, gasp, Notre Dame supporters after watching that university's televised games. This correspondent was sure that the "gentlemen living in towns do not as yet fully appreciate what television means to the rural family" and compared them to the Luddites of the 1800s who destroyed farm equipment in fear of personal obsolescence.[40]

Scores of similar letters appeared in the mailboxes of newspaper editorial boards, congressmen, and various university and athletic officials throughout the 1949 and 1950 seasons. Based on these letters, it is apparent that the citizens of Ohio felt like their natural rights to Big Ten football were being violated. The collected employees of the Curtis Art Glass Company asked their congressman if Big Ten officials had "forgotten that it is the little guys like us (we are also taxpayers) that helped to build their stadiums and send our kids to their schools, or there wouldn't be any Big Ten?"[41]

While Ohio State athletic director Richard Larkins expressed sympathy for rural folks who wanted to witness live games from their homes (as well as "shut-ins, wounded veterans, or anyone else who is not able to attend the games"), he consistently defended the Big Ten's ban because he did not want to jeopardize football gate receipts, the funds that provided for all of the other sports at most universities. He gently reminded all of his correspondents that no tax dollars went to the university's athletic programs and that, at its core, the "program exists for the benefit of the university student."[42]

The outcry following the 1950 Snow Bowl game against Michigan helped create the conditions for live football broadcasts and the arrival of a new Ohio State coach who would cause plenty of storms in Big Ten stadia on his own. With Ohio State assured of at least tying for the Big

Ten Championship if the game was declared a draw, Larkins agreed to
play Michigan in the middle of a ferocious blizzard. The resulting game
was almost too ugly to watch, which was fortunate because the fifty
thousand fans who made it to the stadium could barely see the field
because of the swirling snow. The two teams managed just three first
downs, punted forty-five times, and combined for sixty-eight total yards.
Ultimately, the numbers on the scoreboard are the most important, and
there Michigan had a 9–3 victory, scoring on a safety and a touchdown
off a blocked punt.[43]

Larkins received scores of letters which, in his own estimation, went
about ten to one against his decision to play the game. Not only did
Michigan get a surprise Rose Bowl berth and Big Ten championship, but
Larkins and the other "dumb-heads" responsible for the game had given
Ohio State fans another year of misery. According to a Springfield, Ohio,
correspondent, "Ohio State really fell to zero in prestige in addition to
14th place in National rating for what [Larkins] did. The Michigan
Alumni here in this area are really giving it to the Ohio State alumni."
Other letters came from those who had been stuck on the side of the
road or who were among the "33 odd thousand who thot [sic] Ohio State
University had some Common Horse Sense," horse sense enough not
to play Michigan games in blizzards or, at least, to allow television broadcasts so that fans would only risk high blood pressure, and not pneumonia, during the games.[44]

Looking for a fresh start, Ohio State hired Wayne Woodrow
"Woody" Hayes in 1951 as its head football coach; for the next twenty-
eight years he would epitomize Ohio State's loathing for all things associated with "the state up north." Hayes reportedly refused to contribute
anything to Michigan's economy, leading to apocryphal stories of him
pushing his out-of-gas car across the Michigan-Ohio state line in order
to buy fuel back home. Later in his career he refused to even utter the
word "Michigan," so distasteful was it to him.[45]

That wasn't always the case though. In his first press conference, when
he was predictably asked, "What about Michigan?" he surprisingly
responded, "We'll consider Michigan a little later. Right now I'm beginning
to think about our opener against Southern Methodist and Michigan
State." While this seeming lack of concern about the Buckeyes' traditional
rival must have concerned some of the alumni, they would soon realize

that they did not need to worry about Woody. He wanted to beat Michigan worse than any fan ever would.[46]

Throughout the 1950s and 1960s, fans would repeatedly get the chance to witness Woody's teams doing exactly that, and he would do it almost entirely with players from the state of Ohio, further intensifying the rivalry's sense of "us" versus "them." In 1962, Hayes could point out that of his three teams invited to the Rose Bowl, 128 of the 132 players were from Ohio (this might help explain the OSU song detailing why "we don't give a damn about the whole state of Michigan"). Over the next eighteen years, Hayes's Ohio State teams and his Ohio players beat Michigan eleven times, winning five conference championships and three national championships, while featuring seventeen All-Americans. Hayes used this abundant homegrown talent to stoke the rivalry whenever he could. For example, during the 1961 game, Ohio State received a kick-off with thirty-four seconds left, while leading 42–20. Eschewing the "three yards and a cloud of dust" philosophy that was his trademark, Hayes's team threw the ball on four consecutive plays, scoring with five seconds left to make the score 48–20. Hayes then elected to go for two because, he allegedly remarked, he couldn't go for three. The final score of 50–20 is a telling testament to the power of a rivalry game to overcome basic rules of sportsmanship, with Michigan fans not forgetting how the Ohio State team "added further insult to injury" at the end of the game.[47]

The 1968 showdown was the game that caused Michigan to look for a coach equal to Hayes. It was a massacre, a 50–14 demolition of fourth-ranked Michigan in a game that clinched another Rose Bowl trip for the second-ranked Buckeyes and led to another national championship, a game that George Vescey described as "perhaps the most significant meeting between the old rivals" to his *New York Times* readers.[48] On top of the competitive significance of the game, this contest provided another ripe opportunity to humiliate a rival, and the Buckeyes took it. This time, Hayes got his 50 points even without converting the attempted last-second 2-point conversion; but, to fans on both sides of the rivalry, it was the thought that counted. It appeared that Hayes had finally, and permanently, tipped the rivalry's balance of power in Columbus's direction.[49]

Appearances were, in this case, deceiving, for in 1969 a former Buckeye assistant named Bo Schembechler took over the reigns at

Michigan and inaugurated the most competitive and publicized era of the
rivalry: the ten-year war. Over the next ten years, only Ohio State and
Michigan won or shared the Big Ten title; the league had truly become
the Big Two and Little Eight, which meant that the rivalry had become
even more meaningful to all concerned.

This stretch began with about as big an upset as could be imagined
in such an intense rivalry. As the Michigan game approached, the 1969
Buckeyes had already established themselves as legends in their own
time. With five All-Americans on the roster, the defending national
champions had steamrolled their opposition, extending their existing
fourteen-game winning streak by winning all eight 1969 games by an
average of 37 points, with no games closer than 27 points. They were a
juggernaut, and they were prepared to cap another perfect season with
a second straight demolition of Michigan.[50]

It was not to be. Schembechler had promised his first team that
"those who stay will be champions," and he began establishing his own
legacy for that day, denying his mentor and the Buckeyes a claim for
immortality and another national championship while claiming a Big
Ten championship and Rose Bowl trip for Michigan. In front of 103,588
ecstatic fans in Michigan Stadium and a national television audience, the
Wolverines destroyed the Buckeyes' dream season, 24–12.[51]

After losing with what he always claimed was his best team ever,
Hayes promised his players that "we will start preparing for those guys
on the way back home." While we have no archival record of Ohio State
coaches' game planning on the ride back to Columbus, we do have evidence that they wanted to be sure that their players did not forget what
had transpired. The coaches had the players walk every day, as they
entered and exited the locker room, over a rug displaying the Michigan
score. The players got the message, as quarterback Rex Kern acknowledged when he explained that he thought "about Michigan every morning when I [got] up for a whole year." Nothing, it seems, intensifies a
rivalry more than losing to your rival with everything on the line.[52]

The next year, tensions could not have risen higher. The *Ohio State
University Monthly* explained the state-wide atmosphere preceding the
game in this way:

> BEAT Michigan Week in Columbus, 1970, had been a week like no
> other. The hearts of Buckeye fans had pulsed 24–12 for a year—and

now it all focused on Columbus. Ohio State boosters fidgeted all week, biting their nails and drinking their coffee strong and black. Cigarette and tranquilizer sales must have jumped 50 percent.

Saturday's tension hung in the air, obliterating vision of everything but Scarlet and Gray. The students rallied 'til the wee hours most of the week, beating a path down High Street to the Statehouse and back. The Buckeye Battle Cry resounded and the shouts "Yea, Ohio" and "Go Bucks" were heard almost any hour of the day or night—in almost every gathering.

People have called Columbus a football crazy town before, but never has that description had more meaning.

In front of 87,331 "howling fans" Ohio State won, in the "awesome, aggressive style that ha[d] become the trademark of Ohio State football teams for two decades."[53]

With television networks making this rivalry a staple of the nation's late November diet, Bo Schembechler and Woody Hayes and the two institutions they represented continued to loom large over the landscape of college football. For the next eight years, these coaches personified what it meant to be a "Michigan Man" or an "Ohio State" man to their universities, their states, and the nation.

They did so, however, with a level of respect for each other that the fan bases were often unable to match. While they certainly played minds games with each other and, in Schembechler's words, "In those ten years we coached against each other, I never dialed the phone to call him [Hayes], and he never dialed the phone to call me," these giants of the profession respected each other and the other's accomplishments. This is perhaps best demonstrated by the fact that Schembechler later asked Hayes to address his team and that Hayes asked Schembechler to introduce him before he gave an important speech. The principle participants in the rivalry could admire and respect each other, even if the Michigan and Ohio State fan groups could not always do the same.[54]

The rivalry that competitive balance and national print and radio coverage built and that passionate fan bases, television, and dynamic personalities maintained has continued to thrive in the years after the ten-year war. Without the importance placed on the Michigan game, Ohio State's John Cooper would be celebrated as a legend in Columbus, and without the benefits of a sterling start to the rivalry, Lloyd Carr might not have been able to survive a series of otherwise disappointing (by

Michigan standards) seasons. For many people, however, the Big Two of the Big Ten continue to play a one-game season, and a defeat in that game can nullify greatness in the rest of the schedule.

Ohio State coach John Cooper's career epitomizes the ways that the rivalry game record could virtually nullify all other accomplishments. Cooper's career-winning percentage of .715 was slightly greater than the program's overall mark and, while lower than Hayes's .761 mark, was considerably higher than Paul Brown's .685 percentage. Moreover, the seven-season period between the 1992 and 1998 seasons was one of the more successful stretches in Ohio State's history. During that era, Cooper's teams shared three Big Ten Championships and finished second in the other four years. How could anyone have possibly been upset with that, especially when Ohio State's main rival had four different four-loss seasons and one three-loss season during the same period?[55]

The answer, of course, was Cooper's record in the Michigan game. The reason for Cooper's downfall was the same reason for Gary Moeller's and Lloyd Carr's extended tenures. After Cooper lost his first three games to Michigan, the Ohio State University president proclaimed the 1992 13–13 tie "one of our greatest wins."[56] That's setting the bar pretty low, and Ohio State fans weren't ready to celebrate this "victory," especially after they thought the Tennessean Cooper had not displayed enough Ohio-style fight by going for two points after a late touchdown. After another loss in 1993, Cooper's Buckeyes finally broke the jinx with a 1994 victory, but they were unable to maintain any momentum in the rivalry. In fact, Cooper's teams beat Michigan only once more during his time at Ohio State, during the 1998 season when the Buckeyes were as talented as any team in the nation.[57]

During this stretch, Michigan's teams were able to consistently "save" their seasons by beating Ohio State, with the additional pleasure of derailing Ohio State's title chances at the same time. In 1993, a 7-4 Michigan team ended Ohio State's undefeated season in their traditional final game, and in 1995 and 1996, they did it again. In 1997, Ohio State had the opportunity to return the favor and destroy Michigan's perfect season and national title hopes, but the Wolverines prevailed 20–14. Whether it was a Wolverine running back breaking loose for 313 yards, an Ohio State defensive back slipping to the ground at the most inopportune moment, or a Michigan punt return breaking the Buckeyes' backs, the breaks seemed to go the Wolverines' way during the 1990s, to the continuing consternation of Buckeyes everywhere.[58]

Cooper finished his career with a record against Michigan of 2-10-1, or one could reasonably see this the other way: Cooper's 2-10-1 record against Michigan ended his career. It was not a surprise, then, that the coach hired to replace Cooper, Jim Tressel, made sure Michigan was at the center of his first public pronouncement of his Ohio State career. Standing at mid-court during an Ohio State basketball game, Tressel famously assured the rapt crowd that they would "be proud of their team in the classroom, in the community and, most especially, in 310 days in Ann Arbor, Michigan, on the football field."[59]

This focus on Michigan was not simply a publicity stunt; when asked a year later how many days until the Big Game, Tressell knew the precise number. Now, all Michigan and Ohio State fans are familiar with a few more numbers as well: 6-1, Tressel's record against Michigan, numbers that have established his legacy and helped lead to the 2007 retirement of Lloyd Carr, his Michigan counterpart, who started his career 5-1 against Ohio State but ended it 6-7.[60]

However one perceives the relationship between Cooper's and Carr's rivalry records and their retirements, no one could dispute the impact of yet another new technology in communicating and escalating fans' passionate attachment to these teams and this game: the Internet. With the rise of fan sites, message boards, and chat rooms, fans from across the nation and the world can participate in the types of conversations that require fellow zealots and lots of free time. In short, thanks to the Internet, the entire world has access to the local sports bar, for better or worse.

For Ohio State fans wanting up-to-the-minute recruiting updates in June or wanting to revisit the agony of Ohio State's worst loss ever (the 1969 game was the consensus choice in an extended late May 2008 discussion), the "Ozone" is the place to go (www.the-ozone.net). There, on every football game day, fans from around the world report that the "Block O" flag is flying in their new hometowns, and seemingly every day a poster will update the number of days left before the season opener and the Michigan game. Woody Hayes would surely approve of this continual focus on "The School Up North" ("TSUN" in chatroom shorthand).

As for Michigan, it certainly has its Web sites for devotees as well.

TheWolverine.com is just one of dozens of sites devoted to explaining which Arizona high school tight end is considering playing football for Michigan and, in great detail, how Ohio State is a lesser institution than Michigan. To visit these fan-centered Web sites is to get a real sense of the passion thousands of supporters feel for their teams and of the meaning this rivalry has to their lives and in constructing their self identities. The view (and the frequent vitriol) isn't always pretty, but it is certainly illuminating.

For rivalries to exist, they need several key ingredients, and the Ohio State–Michigan rivalry has them all. First and foremost, the games must have athletic meaning. Simply put, important two-way rivalries do not exist when one of the foes is comparatively inconsequential. For example, almost no one would have referred to the Notre Dame–Naval Academy annual game as a "rivalry" during Notre Dame's recently ended winning streak of over 40 games. It was certainly a meaningful game, full of pageantry and history, but it was not a rivalry. In comparison, it is exhausting to list the ways the Ohio State–Michigan games have had clear consequences on conference and national title races. Rose Bowl and, more recently, BCS (Bowl Championship Series) title game berths have continually been on the line when these two teams met, and it has been that way since the 1920s.

Secondly, to be meaningful, rivalries must be personal; one needs to be able to put a face on the opposition. For Ohioans, Michigan and its flagship university seemingly spent the entire twentieth century looking down on Ohio and Ohio State, and not just on a map either. The jokes the fans of both teams tell about each other reveal a great deal about their relative perceived status, just as the fact that such categories as "Michigan" and "Ohio State" jokes exist tell us about the intensity of the rivalry. To Ohio State fans, Michigan represents misplaced elitism and snobbery. To Michigan fans, "OSU" still equals "A & M": Ohio State is a school of, by, and for country bumpkins and unsophisticated rubes. Consequently, Ohio State fans love to disprove Michigan's constantly proclaimed superiority, just as Michigan fans love proving the accuracy of their claim

Finally, for a rivalry to have real meaning, others have to notice. Sustained media attention is not a sufficient cause, but it is a necessary one for this rivalry. By the 1970s, Keith Jackson had become the voice of the game as much as Bo and Woody were the faces. Over the decades, a variety of new media was there to escalate the gridiron battles into full-fledged cultural and institutional wars. Through national newspaper coverage, radio and television broadcasts, and the rise of decentralized Web sites, the Michigan–Ohio State rivalry has acquired national meanings, and the games have become "appointment viewing" for generations of sports fans. Legions of sports fans, especially but not exclusively from the represented states, want to participate because the game matters in almost every measurable and intangible way. It has become *the* rivalry game of college football.

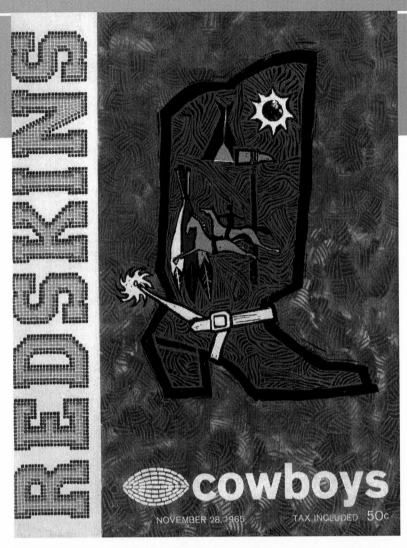

Program cover of the famous November 28, 1965, Redskins-Cowboys game. The Redskins, riding the arm of Sonny Jurgeson, who passed for 411 yards, overcame a 21–0 deficit to defeat the Cowboys 34–31. *Provided by Stephen Norwood.*

twelve

Corporate Cowboys and Blue-Collar Bureaucrats

The Dallas-Washington Football Rivalry

STEPHEN H. NORWOOD

The longest sustained rivalry in U.S. professional sports, between the Dallas Cowboys and the Washington Redskins, evoking the violent conflict associated with westward expansion, a central theme in American history, is unusual in that it involves cities that are neither regional nor economic competitors. No other professional sports rivalry of this duration, lasting from 1960 until the present, has been sustained between teams so geographically distant. The few involving widely separated cities, notably, between baseball's New York Giants and Chicago Cubs in the first decade of the twentieth century and the Brooklyn Dodgers and St. Louis Cardinals during the 1940s, lasted only a few years.

In professional sports, fans take rivalries much more seriously than players. Practitioners of an elite craft, the players associate rivalries with the immaturity of collegiate "rah rah" culture. Professional football players' views of opponents are shaped by a strong respect for their abilities, which can offset the bitterest competition between teams.[1]

The power of such mutual respect is reflected in a letter written to Washington Redskins quarterback Sonny Jurgensen after his team suffered a stinging 42–37 defeat against the Cleveland Browns in November 1967. The Redskins were trailing badly for much of the game, by margins of 28–10 and 42–24; Jurgensen had rallied the Redskins with a spectacular performance, completing thirty-two of fifty passes for 418 yards and three touchdowns, despite noticeably poor protection from a porous offensive line. The *Washington Post* commented that even the Browns' five sacks of Jurgensen do "not tell the whole story of how roughly he was worked over." Having led the Redskins to the Browns 26-yard line with only twenty-eight seconds remaining on the clock, Jurgensen's valiant effort came to naught when defensive end Bill Glass "hand-fought his way through blockers" and hurled the quarterback for a game-ending loss.[2]

Shortly afterward, Jurgensen received a letter from Cheryl Meredith, who had watched the Washington-Cleveland game on television with her husband, Dallas Cowboys quarterback Don Meredith. Cheryl Meredith explained that at the start she and Don had been rooting for the Browns, because a Redskins defeat would increase the Cowboys' chances of winning the National Football League's (NFL) Capitol Division against rival Washington. "However," Cheryl Meredith continued, "you played such an outstanding game—always coming from behind and never losing your spirit—that by the end of the game we were jumping up and down, screaming and yelling, really pulling for you to make that last touchdown." Then she described her husband's reaction when Glass sacked Jurgensen to end the Redskins' final drive: "Don turned to me, looking sick and hands perspiring. He said, 'You don't know how he feels . . . it's something you'll never understand . . . I feel sick!' Sincerely, Cheryl Meredith (Mrs. Don Meredith)."[3]

Significantly, Dallas's legendary head coach, Tom Landry, who directed the Cowboys from the time they entered the NFL as an expansion team in 1960 until 1989, did not mention the rivalry with the Redskins in his autobiography, published in 1990. Joe Gibbs, Redskins head coach from 1981 to 1992 and again from 2004 until 2007, gave it very little attention in his autobiography, published the same year as Landry's. Noting that "self-proclaimed experts" reminded him when he became Redskins head coach that his job security depended on his beating the Dallas Cowboys, he suggested that the Washington-Dallas rivalry was primarily the concern of fans and sportswriters.[4]

Still, even fans' emotional investment in the rivalries between franchises is relatively limited, in part because American professional sports teams include players from similar ethnic and religious backgrounds. Americans do not perceive games as symbolic ethnic or religious conflicts, unlike the case in European and South American soccer matches.[5] In the United States, regional animosities in professional sports are mitigated by the mixing of players from different regions on each team's roster, which is not the case in college athletics. Indeed, the two Washington Redskins players whom the press identified as most antagonistic to the Dallas Cowboys, defensive tackle Diron Talbert and linebacker Jack Pardee, were both Texans.

During the 1960s, when the Cowboys-Redskins rivalry developed, Dallas and Washington were very different kinds of cities, located in regions that distrusted each other. Dallas had long been renowned as an open shop city and a center of right-wing extremism. It had a thriving Ku Klux Klan during the 1920s. Rodeo performers had appeared at Dallas's Texas State Fair in Klan regalia.[6] During the 1930s, labor organizers in Dallas met fierce and often violent resistance from employers. Several organizers were seriously injured in beatings by company thugs, and one was even tarred and feathered.[7] Dallas earned its reputation as the "city of hate" even before the assassination of President John F. Kennedy there on November 22, 1963. It was the base of one of the nation's most prominent right-wing extremists, General Edwin Walker, and the John Birch Society had a strong following there.

The national press gave wide attention to the vicious attacks against Adlai Stevenson, U.S. ambassador to the United Nations (UN) and former Democratic presidential candidate, after he gave a speech in Dallas in October 1963. Outside the auditorium, anti-UN demonstrators repeatedly shoved him, two men spat in his face, and a woman struck him over the head with her picket sign. Stevenson was forced to stop several times during his address because of catcalls. The *Washington Post,* in an editorial, accused the Dallas demonstrators of behaving like "creatures from a jungle swamp," and compared them to "Baluba tribesmen in the Congo."[8]

The assassination of President Kennedy the next month reinforced Dallas's reputation for violence and right-wing extremism. Posters mounted along Dallas streets in anticipation of the president's visit accused him of treason. An advertisement placed in the November 22, 1963, Dallas *Morning News* charged that President Kennedy had "scrapped the Monroe Doctrine in favor of the 'Spirit of Moscow,'" and suggested that he was "systematically pro-communist."[9] Arthur M. Schlesinger Jr. suggested that Dallas contained many "distraught and rootless people" who had been drawn to the city by its "climate of alienation and anger." They detested President Kennedy as the incarnation of "reason and poise." Schlesinger reported in his Pulitzer prize–winning study of the Kennedy administration, *A Thousand Days,* that schoolchildren in Dallas had applauded when they learned of the president's assassination.[10] That President Kennedy's accused assassin Lee Harvey Oswald was shot dead while in Dallas police custody confirmed to many Americans that the city was uncivilized.

Fans irate about President Kennedy's assassination expressed strong antagonism toward the Dallas Cowboys for a long time afterward, blaming the city for the tragedy because of its reputation for violence and intolerance. Dallas's All-Pro defensive tackle Bob Lilly recalled that when the Cowboys arrived at Cleveland's Municipal Stadium to play the Browns two days after the assassination, the fans were so hostile that "we didn't know whether we were going to get shot or what." From the stands, spectators yelled that the Cowboys were "murderers." Lilly declared, "We never got over the stigma when we played other teams. . . . We'd go on the road, and people booed us because of that."[11] Head coach Tom Landry stated that the Kennedy assassination "tainted everything having to do with Dallas" and recalled that in Cleveland the Cowboys "were booed with a bitterness we had never encountered before." The lusty booing continued everywhere the Cowboys played that season and into the next.[12]

Roger Staubach, the Cowboys quarterback during the 1970s, recalled that Ethel Kennedy expressed considerable disappointment in him when they met at a social gathering because his Naval Academy team had lost the 1963 Cotton Bowl to the University of Texas Longhorns. She lectured Staubach that he had been "representing the Navy and the country" at the game, "as if Texas wasn't part of the country."[13]

The involvement of multimillionaire oil baron Clint Murchison Sr., father of the team's owner, Clint Jr., in Far Right causes reinforced the antagonism of many northern liberals toward the Dallas Cowboys. One of Texas's four wealthiest oil men, the senior Murchison was a close friend and prominent supporter of Senator Joe McCarthy, so contemptuous of President Harry S Truman that he insisted on spelling his surname with a lower case "t." When McCarthy made a mysterious trip to Texas in 1953 to confer with Far Right oil barons, including Clint Sr. and H. L. Hunt, Clint Jr. and his brother John flew him in their luxury DC-3 to the Murchison ranch in Mexico's Sierra Madre Mountains. Robert DePugh, leader of the extremist Minutemen, claimed that the senior Murchison had donated money to American Nazi Party leader George Lincoln Rockwell.[14]

Dallas also had a long-standing reputation for cultural philistinism, which influenced perceptions of the Cowboys outside the region. The coarseness of Dallas's rising oil elite, which had assumed the city's economic leadership by the 1940s, gave rise to the remark, "Crude oil produces crude people."[15] In 1956, the Dallas County Patriotic Council, a coalition of civic groups, attracted national attention by launching a well-publicized attack on the Dallas Museum of Fine Arts for displaying the work of artists they deemed "Communist." They targeted four works in a forthcoming show called "Sports in Art," organized by *Sports Illustrated* magazine: a drawing of a baseball game by Ben Shahn, a depiction of skating by Yasuo Kuniyoshi, a winter scene by Leon Kroll, and a painting of a fisherman by William Zorach. The Dallas County Patriotic Council also demanded the removal from the museum of works by John Sloan, a leading painter of the Ash Can school. A *New York Times* reporter denounced the council as "esthetic vigilantes" contemptuous of "reason, decency, and real Americanism."[16]

Although Dallas was primarily involved with the oil industry, banking, and insurance and was not a cattle town like neighboring Fort Worth, it was surrounded by ranch country, and its population embraced the masculinist, individualist, and laissez-faire values associated with the Old West. Dallas provided the highest proportion of votes of any major U.S. city for Republican candidate Richard M. Nixon, a Californian, when he ran against the Harvard-educated Bostonian John F. Kennedy in 1960. The owners of Dallas's NFL expansion franchise in 1960 considered only names associated with the western frontier for the team. Starting with the Steers and the Rangers, they finally settled on the Cowboys.[17] Unlike some Houston teams, which selected futuristic names—the baseball Astros, the basketball Rockets—Dallas's sports franchises all identified themselves with the nineteenth-century frontier: the baseball Rangers, the football Cowboys and Texans, and the basketball Mavericks.

The Cowboys' predominantly conservative fans managed to displace their hostility toward what they perceived as an intrusive, liberal federal government onto the Redskins, who represented the nation's capital. Dallas residents, many of whom attended Cowboys games wearing the ten-gallon hats and high boots of a mythic West and arrived in pickup trucks, derided Washingtonians as pallid bureaucrats confined to cubicles, lacking any connection to the great American outdoors. By contrast, Washington Redskins fans, a significant proportion of whom were federal employees, tended to view Dallas as culturally unsophisticated, populated by crass and garish, newly rich oil barons and western rubes.

Both cities used professional football to compensate for underlying

fears of inadequacy. Dallas's principal industry, oil, was endemically inse-
cure, and those who invested in it, or depended on it for a living, constantly worried about losing everything in an economic downturn. With
a population of less than 700,000 in 1960, Dallas was the NFL's smallest
city, ahead of only Green Bay. There were no other major league sports
franchises in Dallas when the Cowboys were formed. Many questioned
whether it was capable of supporting professional football. Its previous
NFL team, the Dallas Texans, had drawn such low attendance during its
only season of operation in 1952 that its owners returned the franchise
to the league before the season ended. The team had then left Dallas,
playing its remaining five games on the road.[18]

Washington, D.C., during the 1960s, although populated by many
transplanted northern professionals, and boasting cultural facilities vastly
superior to those of Dallas, suffered from its lack of night life and an image
as a city of dull government bureaucrats and ponderous national monu-
ments. Washington had been a major league sports city since the nineteenth century, but its teams had generally fared poorly. The sorry records
of the baseball Senators gave rise to the slogan: "Washington—First in
War, First in Peace, and Last in the American League." The football
Redskins had fielded strong teams between 1937 and 1945, a period when
they won two NFL championships and five Eastern Division titles, but at
that time professional football had only a marginal following. After World
War II, the Redskins had been perennial losers, enjoying only three winning seasons from 1946 until 1969.[19]

From the beginning there was antagonism between the Dallas and
Washington franchises because George Preston Marshall, Washington
Redskins owner from 1937 until his death in 1969, had tried to block the
NFL's expansion during the late 1950s. He feared that awarding a team
to Dallas would cut into the Redskins' lucrative television and radio market in the southeastern United States, which had no professional football
team besides Washington. Marshall identified the Redskins as the team
of the South, having his band play *Dixie* before games. Almost alone,
Marshall vigorously opposed awarding Dallas a franchise.[20]

Once the Cowboys had been admitted into the NFL, however,
Marshall was instrumental in establishing a necessary precondition for a
rivalry with the Redskins. In 1961, when the NFL added a second expansion franchise, the Minnesota Vikings, Marshall lobbied to have Dallas,

rather than Minnesota, placed in the Eastern Conference with the Redskins. This guaranteed that the Cowboys would play the Redskins twice every year. The Dallas ownership also wanted the Cowboys in the Eastern Conference, in part because it included the New York Giants, located in the NFL's most glamorous city and biggest market. Marshall believed that Eastern Conference attendance would benefit from adding a warm weather city, especially in November and December. Moreover, Dallas's Cotton Bowl seated seventy thousand, whereas the Vikings were slated to play in a stadium whose capacity was only forty thousand. The Vikings also shared their stadium with major league baseball's Minnesota Twins, which made scheduling games more difficult.[21]

Contributing to the development of a Washington-Dallas rivalry was the strong commitment of each franchise to pageantry, traditionally far more associated with college than professional football, as a means of heightening fans' emotional commitment to the team. In such an environment the notion of an intense rivalry with a particular opponent, an almost universal feature of the college game, uncommon in the NFL, appeared more legitimate to fans. Redskins owner George Preston Marshall, married to a movie starlet, introduced the halftime show and the marching band to professional football. His halftime shows, produced by the Capitol Theatre's Joel Margolis, might feature movie stars, circus acts, or the National Symphony Orchestra. Drawing on another collegiate custom, Marshall referred to the Redskins by their uniform colors, "the burgundy and gold," and gave them a team fight song, "Hail to the Redskins," a rarity at the time.[22]

In 1962, Marshall brought female cheerleaders, another major feature of college football, into the NFL. Marshall's Redskinettes, however, were more erotic than college cheerleaders. Aged eighteen to thirty-five, they dressed in short skirts and black wigs with long pigtails to resemble Indian maidens. Unlike their college counterparts, they did not lead cheers, but danced evocatively along the sidelines in flesh-colored tights after Redskins touchdowns, during time-outs, and at halftime. One Redskinette noted in 1969, "All you need is a good pair of legs . . . and no matter what the team is doing, the whole stadium turns."[23]

Tex Schramm, Dallas's general manager from 1960 to 1989, was very much drawn to George Preston Marshall's use of pageantry and hoopla to stimulate fan interest in his club. In 1972 he established the Dallas

Cowboys Cheerleaders, who became almost as well known as the team itself. They replaced Dallas's initial cheerleading squad, the conservatively dressed Cow Belles, recruited from area high schools. More eroticized than the Redskinettes, the Dallas Cowboys Cheerleaders resembled Las Vegas showgirls, scantily clad in silvery blue satin halters above bare midriffs, pushup bras, white hot pants, and go-go boots. Their skimpy outfits remained almost unchanged into the early twenty-first century. At games they "wildly sh[ook] their breasts and their comely rear ends" to the accompaniment of pulsating rock music. Dallas sportswriter Skip Bayless called them the Leerleaders. The Cowboys weekly newspaper featured centerfolds of Dallas Cowboys Cheerleaders in seductive poses.[24]

The Dallas Cowboys Cheerleaders highly eroticized presentation suggested a difference in cultural outlook between the competing cities that contributed to their rivalry. Many Washingtonians considered Dallas residents much less enlightened on women's issues. In Dallas, the Cowboys Cheerleaders were held up as models for little girls, which was not the case in Washington with the Redskinettes. Every year, forty thousand girls competed in the Little Miss Dallas Cowboys Cheerleaders contest. Feminists condemned such beauty pageants for small children for inculcating traditional sex roles at an early age and for sexually exploiting young girls. Dallas-area clothing stores marketed a special line of Dallas Cowboys Cheerleaders outfits for little girls. In the Dallas area, the Cowboys Cheerleaders never drew protests as demeaning to women, as was sometimes the case outside the region.[25]

In Washington, by contrast, there were numerous public complaints when the Redskinettes in 1978 donned more revealing costumes. Joel Margolis declared, "We're not gonna be left behind." The new Redskinettes' red-fringed, crocus-yellow uniforms contained a "diamond-shaped panel which unleashes the navel."[26] Letters to the *Washington Post* complained about the "tacky costumes," calling them "downright disgusting," and noted specifically the "vulgar exposure of the belly."[27]

Dallas management also employed heavily made-up young women attendants known as Texettes. Dressed in short skirts, they waited on sportswriters in the press box at Texas Stadium, to which the Cowboys moved in 1971. These "highly skilled flirters" were "even available to give shoulder rubs to ease deadline tension."[28] There was nothing remotely equivalent at Washington's Robert F. Kennedy (RFK) Stadium.

Although the Dallas Cowboys were established only in 1960, a noticeable rivalry with the Washington Redskins developed after only a few years, dramatized in four consecutive games between 1965 and 1967 that are often included in lists of the NFL's most thrilling contests. These games drew particular attention because they were staged during the decade when professional football replaced baseball as the nation's most popular sport. All four games were decided by three points or less, and each team won two of them. Although at that time both teams were still mediocre, they were led by two of the era's most accomplished and charismatic quarterbacks, Washington's Sonny Jurgensen and Dallas's "Dandy" Don Meredith. Both quarterbacks were masters of the two-minute drill.[29]

The excellence of the quarterbacks on both sides fueled the rivalry for decades. Besides Jurgensen, one of the greatest passers in football history, Washington fielded Billy Kilmer, much less proficient mechanically but an outstanding motivator, and Joe Theismann. Dallas boasted Roger Staubach, arguably the greatest quarterback of the 1970s, Danny White, and Troy Aikman. Legendary coach Vince Lombardi considered the very disproportionate importance of the quarterback position a glaring flaw in an otherwise perfectly balanced team sport.[30] Bert Jones, one of the NFL's premier quarterbacks during the 1970s, maintained that a great quarterback can make his team leap ahead more than any other player. A great quarterback can drive an average team to a higher level, but an average quarterback can never do so.[31]

The Dallas-Washington rivalry, which became particularly intense during the 1970s, was shaped by a multitude of factors besides the teams' names: the sharp contrast between the cities; clashing team identities; the quality of quarterbacks; and the opposing alignment of the teams during the NFL players' strikes of 1974, 1982, and 1987. The Redskins head coach from 1971 through 1977, George Allen, was especially antagonistic to the Cowboys. Several of his players fueled the rivalry by persistently taunting particular Cowboys, notably, quarterback Roger Staubach and running back Tony Dorsett, whom they called "bug eyes."

The Dallas Cowboys developed a national following during the 1970s, which focused more attention on the rivalry with the Redskins. The Cowboys were denominated "America's Team" because of excellent performance on the field and their own skillful marketing. The label glamorized the Cowboys, but also elicited the resentment of other teams, including the Redskins, who considered it arrogant. As Raiders safety Mike Davis asked, "What are we, Guatamalans?"[32] During this period Cowboys' souvenirs accounted for over a quarter of those that NFL Properties sold, far more than any other team's. Their radio network was the league's largest, consisting of almost two hundred stations in fourteen states. The tabloid *Dallas Cowboys Weekly* reached a circulation of about one hundred thousand, a significant portion of it outside Texas, the second largest of any weekly sports publication in the United States.[33]

Fueling the Cowboys' arrogance, according to some Redskins, was what linebacker Jack Pardee called "this superior-being type thing." Complaining that the Cowboys constantly boasted of their "superior scouting, superior coaching, superior talent," Pardee declared, "That's what makes it more gratifying to knock them off."[34] The Cowboys played in five Super Bowls during the 1970s and compiled a .729 winning percentage in regular-season games for the decade, the best of any NFL team. The Redskins were also regularly in the playoffs and went to their first Super Bowl in 1973, although their national fan base was not as large as Dallas's. The Redskins thrashed the Cowboys in the National Conference championship game to qualify for that Super Bowl, a contest remembered for the "constant string of Cowboys being helped off or carried off the field."[35]

The enormous nationwide popularity of the Dallas Cowboys Cheerleaders, football's "first pinups," solidified Dallas's identity as "America's Team," particularly among those with a more traditional conception of women. In 1977 the Dallas Cowboys Cheerleaders "cheesecake posters" even outsold Farrah Fawcett's.[36]

The Redskins identified as a blue-collar, physical team and considered their Dallas rivals emotionless and machine-like, emasculated by their austere and authoritarian head coach Tom Landry. This view was shared by some dissident Cowboys players. Tony Dorsett described Landry as unfeeling, "more like a computer than a human being." He complained that Cowboys management dispensed with players it thought had "too much personality." Sportswriters and fans noted that the Cowboys never seemed to be really fired up: "The team plays like Tom Landry looks."[37] When Cowboys running back Walt Garrison was asked whether he had ever seen

Landry smile, he replied, "No, I only played nine years."[38] Sportswriter Skip Bayless referred to Landry as "Stoneface," and Cowboys running back Duane Thomas called him "Plastic Man."[39]

The Cowboys' image as a cold and dehumanized organization was reinforced by its pioneering use of computers in drafting players and developing game strategies. Duane Thomas claimed that the Cowboys used the computer to create "Landry's Humanoids." Landry himself remained remote from his players. Dorsett declared that never once during his years with the Cowboys had he ever had the opportunity to talk football with Landry over dinner. Even Roger Staubach, a Landry favorite who worked with him in the Fellowship of Christian Athletes, recalled that he had once played eighteen holes of golf with Landry, during which his coach did not say fifteen words to him. Staubach stated that Landry was not close to any player on the Cowboys.[40]

The Redskins, living up to their rough, working-class image that belied that of the city of bureaucrats they called home, repeatedly impugned the Cowboys' masculinity in an effort to disrupt their ability to focus. They referred to Roger Staubach as a "little boy quarterback" because Coach Landry did not allow him to call the plays.[41] Diron Talbert taunted that Staubach wore "skirts" and slept with a night light on.[42] Landry himself recalled "Staubach's anger rising with each personal taunt from the Redskins' camp."[43] Washington quarterback Joe Theismann declared that when Dallas defensive end Ed "Too Tall" Jones gave him his best shot on the field, "it felt like getting hit by a little child."[44] The Redskins' heralded offensive line, fittingly dubbed "the Hogs," nucleus of four Super Bowl teams between 1983 and 1992, reinforced the team's tough, unrefined image. Washington fans delighted in attending games wearing plastic pig snouts strapped to their faces.[45]

Dallas sportswriter Skip Bayless put a negative spin on the Redskins' roughneck image, depicting them as barbaric. He claimed that the Redskins "don't play football, they mud wrestle. They get you in that frozen slop they call grass, and they hold and bite and gouge your eyes until you give." He continued: "Their scouts only time prospects in marshes or snowstorms. They don't care how fast you cover 40 yards, just if you can survive." Bayless concluded with a swipe at the Cowboys' most vocal tormentor: "I believe I saw [Diron] Talbert deliver a soliloquy—'ug' in 'Conan the Barbarian.'"[46]

Paradoxically, while Washingtonians looked down on Dallas as unrefined, they passionately embraced a team of roughnecks, reveling in their physicality. The Dallas Cowboys, by contrast, although invoking frontier symbols and backed by fans contemptuous of effete easterners, projected a modern corporate image. Dallas played in a stadium that Cowboys receiver Pete Gent called "ultramodern to the point of perversity."[47] While real cowboys rode the grassy plains, the football Cowboys strode on artificial turf. Many perceived the team as "without emotion." "Cold and mechanically precise," the Cowboys "could be beaten by those whose blood ran hotter, by the teams that could simply knock the hell out of them." Gent observed, "In Dallas, you saw the future. Corporate America."[48] This suggests that rooting for their teams in part satisfied fans' compensatory needs, allowing them to embrace attributes and entertain fantasies denied them in real life.

Landry's aggressive public highlighting of his strong evangelical Christian beliefs created an image of the Cowboys as "goody-goody boys." This was reinforced by the public perception of Dallas quarterback Roger Staubach, the team's most famous player during the 1970s, as very straight-laced. Don Meredith remarked, "I wouldn't want my kid to grow up like Roger Staubach. I'd want my kid to have more fun."[49] Walt Garrison claimed that Staubach just could not relax: "Even when he's laughing he's at attention." Garrison once persuaded Staubach to try snuff, but neglected to tell him he was supposed to spit. Staubach swallowed the chaw instead, turned green, and "puked his guts out."[50] When *Sport* magazine awarded Staubach a sports car as the most valuable player in Super Bowl VI in 1972, he asked if he could have a station wagon instead.[51] Like Landry, Staubach, a Naval Academy graduate, was prominent in the Fellowship of Christian Athletes.

Staubach himself described how some of his teammates exploited his naiveté and innocence to play a training camp prank on him. One of them called him over to meet a striking young redhead wearing a low-cut blouse and miniskirt, whom he introduced as "Sister Teresa." Staubach recalled his surprise at meeting a nun who resembled "one of those sexy Hollywood types." But he swallowed her story that she was just temporarily on leave from the convent. Although the redhead was "living it up" with several of the Cowboys, throughout the summer Staubach acted "very reverent" toward her, always addressing her as "Sister Teresa." The situation provoked much amusement among his teammates.[52]

Tony Dorsett noted that the Cowboys' stylish silver and "fantasy blue" uniforms with big stars on the shoulders and helmets made them appear "squeaky clean." Tex Schramm videotaped a male model in the uniform to determine whether it looked right on television. The pants were made from a material with "greater light reflexivity," which gave them a "true silver glow." Dorsett felt they made the Cowboys appear effeminate: "They kinda look like ladies' satin pants."[53] A journalist commented that whereas Pittsburgh's colors brought to mind a steel mill, Dallas's "remind you of a jewelry store."[54]

Exploiting the Redskins' image as the tougher and grittier team, a Washington fan mocked the Cowboys for never getting their "shiny uniforms" dirty on their home field artificial turf. He boasted that when they came to Washington and played the Redskins on real grass, "we mess them up." Smearing the Cowboys in dirt and mud, the Redskins made them "pay for the laundry."[55]

Dallas receiver Butch Johnson complained that by 1983 the Cowboys players off the field were so absorbed in displaying their expensive apparel in public that they resembled androgynous rock stars more than football players or workingmen. He recalled that the "biggest competition" among Dallas players was "dressing for the team plane." According to Johnson, "If you didn't have a mink or an Armani or something really sharp, other players would really talk bad about you."[56] To be sure, there were some Cowboys players who rejected anything that suggested androgyny. When many Cowboys pushed to have the team wear white shoes instead of black, Bob Lilly expressed his opposition by declaring, "White shoes are for fags."[57]

Coach Landry himself had early in his coaching career determined to dress in such a way as to look "successful and businesslike along the sideline." Disdaining the informal attire many football coaches favored, Landry always wore well-tailored jackets and trousers and a fashionable fedora hat at the stadium. Butch Johnson noted that in cold weather, Landry would dress for a game in a "full-length cashmere coat. . . . No sweatshirt for him."[58]

The contrast between the two teams became more pronounced

after the Cowboys moved in 1971 from the Cotton Bowl into the new, luxurious Texas Stadium in the upscale north Dallas suburb of Irving. The dilapidated Cotton Bowl, where the Cowboys had played since their first season in 1960, was located on the much less fashionable south side of Dallas, near some of the city's most impoverished African American neighborhoods. During the early 1960s, African Americans composed a significant proportion of the attendance at Cowboys home games, although they were concentrated disproportionately in the least desirable end zone sections. Spectators at the Cotton Bowl were crowded into uncomfortable, splintery wooden seats.[59]

Texas Stadium, by contrast, "the Taj Mahal" of football arenas, featured vast numbers of luxury suites. It embodied Washington's image of Dallas. Wealthy Dallas residents brought their own bartenders to games. Not surprisingly, sportswriters labeled the new stadium "Millionaires' Meadows" and "The House of Greed."[60] Writer Dan Jenkins observed at a Cowboy game that "up and down the carpeted halls of the complex, people milled about with their cocktails, as if they were at a convention in a hotel."[61] Cowboys defensive back Cornell Green complained that Texas Stadium resembled a country club more than a football field. Mel Renfro, an African American Cowboys player like Green, opposed the move to Texas Stadium because its distance from south Dallas's working-class and minority neighborhoods, along with its higher ticket prices, made attending games prohibitive for less affluent fans.[62]

At the games, the wealthy fans appeared more interested in being seen and in making business connections than in football, and crowd enthusiasm diminished significantly. They could only identify with a winner and tended not to support the team when it was losing. CBS broadcaster Tom Brookshier, a former NFL player, commented that Dallas fans "don't know football, they just know something's wrong if the Cowboys aren't winning by two touchdowns."[63] Bert Jones, NFL quarterback from 1973 to 1982, considered Dallas fans less attentive than those in eastern seaboard cities.[64] Tony Dorsett recalled that he saw so many people in the stands dressed in mink coats and expensive suits that he sometimes wondered whether he was at a football game or a fashion show. Dallas fans disappointed him because they were not boisterous enough. Mel Renfro similarly described Texas Stadium fans as "a bunch of rich people who couldn't get excited about anything."[65]

By contrast, the Washington Redskins played until 1997 at RFK Stadium, which lacked luxury boxes but was packed with frenzied fans who made it a "madhouse." New York Giants linebacker Steve DeOssie stated that fans at RFK were heavily involved in the game and made it difficult for opposing teams to hear signals.[66] Roger Staubach said that Redskins fans at RFK made the earth shake.[67]

Much of the Redskins players' antagonism toward the Cowboys was rooted in their contempt for Dallas management, notorious for paying low salaries and aggressively opposing the demands of the NFL Players Association. Dallas fans, residing in a conservative open-shop city, strongly approved of the Cowboys management's hard line against the Players Association. In 1987, Dallas fans strongly backed a Cowboys team largely composed of strikebreakers recruited by management, a policy the NFL owners adopted to break the players' strike. This provided a sharp contrast with the lack of fan support for strikebreaking teams in northern cities more sympathetic to organized labor.[68]

The Dallas Cowboys enjoyed a reputation as one of the teams least supportive of the Players Association. During players' strikes in the 1970s and 1980s, many Dallas players, including stars, crossed picket lines. In the 1987 strike, twenty-one Cowboys did so, a number surpassed only by the Raiders and Cardinals among NFL teams.[69] Cowboys player representative Doug Cosbie called his team "a league-wide joke" and commented, "Our guys are just too afraid of management to take part in a strike."[70]

Dallas management was notorious around the NFL for paying low salaries to its players, despite the excellent records the team compiled. Dallas linebacker D. D. Lewis recalled seeing this highlighted in "a great cartoon": a Cadillac facade was attached to the front of a "beat-up" Volkswagen, captioned "Cowboys salaries." At the beginning of the 1987 season, thirty-three NFL defensive ends, according to Duane Thomas, were making higher salaries than Dallas's Ed "Too Tall" Jones, who had played twelve years and twice been selected for the Pro Bowl. Many Cowboys resented being underpaid. All-Pro receiver Drew Pearson, who played in three Super Bowls, exclaimed: "I'd go around the league and find out these sons of bitches were making twice as much as me, and they weren't even winning." Cowboys middle linebacker Lee Roy Jordan, who starred on several Super Bowl teams, stated that after eleven seasons in the NFL and four Pro Bowls, he was only making about $50,000 a year. He noted that teammate Bob Lilly, arguably the greatest defensive tackle of his era and a Hall of Famer, was never paid $100,000 a year.[71]

Duane Thomas, the hero of Dallas's victory in Super Bowl VI in 1972, stated that after ten years with the Cowboys, Lilly was making "a peon's wage." Lilly had been selected for the Pro Bowl eight times. Thomas explained that Dallas management kept salaries down by locking players into long-term agreements under unfavorable terms and keeping them ignorant of what other teams were paying. He recalled that Dallas management once instructed Lilly, then making about $27,000 a year, not to speak about his salary when he went to the Pro Bowl because he would only make other players jealous. At the Pro Bowl, Lilly discovered that the Los Angeles Rams were paying their defensive tackle, Merlin Olsen, $80,000 a year.[72]

Many NFL players considered Dallas quarterback Roger Staubach and his successor Danny White, both team leaders, too cozy with management. Both Staubach and White denounced the NFL Players Association as excessively militant. Staubach claimed that it was "trying to revolutionize football, instead of taking steps to improve it." He was disturbed to see players during the 1974 strike picketing in T-shirts proclaiming "No Freedom, No Football" that displayed a clenched fist, which Staubach called "the sign of revolution." He also suggested that some of the African American pickets were using the clenched fist symbol to express "a kind of black separatism." Staubach crossed the picket line in 1974, although he remained a dues-paying member of the Players Association. In his autobiography, he declared that the players should have entered the bargaining sessions with the owners "very humble" and told them "the NFL had been good to us all."[73]

Danny White, who described himself as "almost ultraconservative," similarly expressed displeasure with what he called "hard-line revolutionary attitudes" that he associated with Players Association activists during the 1982 strike. White charged that the union's salary demands were "way out of line." He crossed the picket line to play with a Dallas team consisting largely of strikebreakers.[74]

Dallas general manager Tex Schramm's prominence as spokesman and negotiator for the NFL owners reinforced the Cowboys anti-labor image. When the Players Association staged its first significant con-

frontation in 1970, the owners selected Schramm to head their negotiating committee. According to Schramm's friendly biographer, Bob St.
John, the player representatives assumed they could use their youth to
advantage and wear down their middle-aged management adversaries
during bargaining sessions. But in the fifty-year-old Schramm they more
than met their match. Just as the veteran Minnesota Fats outlasts cocky
young Fast Eddie Felson in their all-night pool game in *The Hustler,* playing ever more vigorously until his exhausted opponent collapses,
Schramm, "sipping Scotch," never tired as his young counterparts, one
by one, left the table in the wee hours of the morning, physically unable
to continue.[75]

The Redskins, by contrast, were among the NFL teams most committed to the union. Joe Washington, who participated in the 1982 NFL
players' strike, described the Redskins as "definitely pro-union." Defensive
back Tony Peters recalled that the Redskins strike vote that year was
"nearly unanimous." Many of the higher salaried players, such as quarterback Joe Theismann and Peters himself, were determined to help their
less-compensated teammates. Linebacker Steve Zabel, who helped lead a
wildcat strike with the New England Patriots in 1975, noted that the
Washington Redskins was among the first teams to join it.[76] The Redskins
location in Washington, where the NFL Players Association was head-
quartered, helped solidify the team's commitment to the union.

Washington Redskins defensive tackle Diron Talbert explained that
he was antagonistic toward Dallas because he resented its labor policy,
not its players. He found it outrageous that Cowboys management paid
only two or three key players a decent salary "and that was about it."
Several Cowboys players consulted Talbert to learn how much they were
underpaid.[77] Dallas's Lee Roy Jordan claimed that Washington center
Len Hauss, an early Players Association supporter, "hated my guts"
because Jordan was anti-union.[78]

The Redskins strong pro-union orientation developed when George
Allen was their head coach during the early 1970s. Allen disdained rookies
and believed that a winning team had to be built around veterans. He
traded away many of the Redskins high-level draft choices to acquire
them. The Redskins high age profile when Allen was coach caused sportswriters to name them the "Over the Hill Gang." Many of the veterans
Allen traded for were disgruntled when they were with their former

teams, often because of salary disputes, and were predisposed to support the Players Association.

George Allen took the Redskins' rivalry with the Cowboys more seriously than anyone else on either side. He referred to games against Dallas as Super Bowls and World War III and once even smashed a block of wood with a karate chop to dramatize his antipathy toward the Cowboys. During Allen's years as Redskins head coach the two teams were evenly matched, with the Cowboys and Redskins each winning about half the games.[79]

Allen encouraged some of his players to bait the Cowboys in an effort to give his team a psychological edge. Football requires intense concentration, and anger in a player can affect his ability to focus. Taunting is widely used in football for this purpose, as it is in warfare among primitive peoples. A New Guinea Highlander who participated in the incessant combat between his own Handa clan and the rival Ombals explained to anthropologist Jared Diamond that a warrior cannot fight well unless his mind is clear. Uncontrolled anger makes a warrior less disciplined and more careless, undermining his effectiveness.[80] Suggesting the persistence of the primitive perspective in the most modern of sports, defensive tackle Diron Talbert threatened to take off quarterback Roger Staubach's ears as souvenirs. Staubach recalled that Talbert refused to shake his hand when they met as team captains for the pre-game coin toss.[81]

Bob Lilly claimed that George Allen succeeded in driving even Coach Landry to distraction by spying on Cowboys practices from a nearby hotel. Landry determined to put a stop to this by having the Cowboys rent the hotel's top floors two weeks before each game against the Redskins. Lilly concluded, "We let it bother us."[82]

The Dallas-Washington rivalry lost a little of its edge after the evangelical Christian Joe Gibbs became the Redskins head coach in 1981 because Tom Landry, a "fellow believer," was a good friend.[83] Both men lectured frequently for the Fellowship of Christian Athletes and were prominently involved in the Billy Graham Crusade.[84] In 1984, Gibbs and Landry teamed up to lobby the U.S. Senate for a Constitutional amendment to permit prayer in the public schools. They were joined by Roger Staubach. At a pep rally for their cause in Washington, Landry blamed the U.S. Supreme Court for taking God "out of the marketplace," allowing "humanism" to enter the resulting void. Gibbs complained that

"Marxist doctrine and pornographic presentation" were protected in society as freedom of speech, while school prayer was prohibited.[85]

Indeed, the Cowboys and Redskins had much in common, as both sponsored organized Christian prayer in their locker rooms, even before Gibbs arrived on the scene. Many liberals and civil libertarians recoiled in shock when, after thrashing the Cowboys in the 1972 NFC Championship game, George Allen had team chaplain Tom Skinner lead the Redskins in Christian prayer on national television, the first time in NFL history this had ever occurred. When Redskins backup quarterback Sam Wyche noticed that a sportswriter present was not kneeling, he became enraged and tore up his notepad.[86] In 1988, the Redskins joined their Super Bowl opponents, the Denver Broncos, coached by Landry protegé and former Cowboy Dan Reeves, in the first prayer meeting involving opposing NFL teams prior to a game.[87]

Similarly, the Cowboys displayed a strong and near unanimous commitment to the team prayer services held before each game, led by a minister. Running back Don Perkins stated in 1966 that some players who were not Protestants did not participate, but described attendance as "pretty general."[88] In his muckraking novel about the Cowboys and professional football, *North Dallas Forty* (1973), former Dallas receiver Pete Gent described half the team immediately falling to one knee when Coach B. A. (based on Landry) calls on them to pray before a game, while almost all the rest sit or stand with head bowed and eyes closed. Only two players, Phil Elliott (Gent) and quarterback Seth Maxwell (based on Don Meredith), do not participate. Emphasizing Landry's stern control and insistence on conformity, Gent has Elliott keep his eyes open and look around the locker room to make sure he "didn't get caught not praying." Elliott notices smoke rising from behind an equipment trunk: "It was Maxwell sitting on the floor, smoking a cigarette and watching the smoke drift aimlessly upward." The two non-participants go undetected by their coach because he keeps his eyes tightly shut while praying.[89]

One cannot reliably assess the impact of racism and the treatment accorded African American players on the Washington-Dallas rivalry, although it may have influenced the perceptions of some liberal fans. Initially, there was not much difference between the franchises on racial issues. The Washington Redskins had long been attacked as racist for refusing to employ or draft black players and was the last NFL team to desegregate. Owner George Preston Marshall dropped the color bar only after years of intense public pressure from the African American press, civil rights groups, and *Washington Post* sports columnist Shirley Povich, and a warning from President Kennedy's secretary of the interior, Stewart Udall, that the team would be denied the use of the new D.C. Stadium, built with federal funds, unless it desegregated.[90] Marshall relinquished ownership of the Redskins in 1963, and within a few years the Redskins' racial composition did not differ appreciably from that of other NFL teams.

Some African American players on the Redskins in later years did harbor feelings about racial insensitivity and discrimination on the team, but the situation appears to have been worse on the Cowboys. The Redskins' star running back and receiver Charley Taylor during the 1960s "boiled from within at black-excluded cliques in the clubhouse." When George Preston Marshall died in 1969, many of the Redskins' African American players balked at attending his memorial service, but management forced them to go.[91] Tony Peters complained that the Redskins employed no African Americans in positions of real responsibility in the front office and overlooked qualified blacks for major coaching positions. After about thirty years in the Redskins organization and election to the Hall of Fame, Charley Taylor was unceremoniously discharged from an untitled minor coaching position without ever being considered as an offensive coordinator or head coach. Bobby Mitchell, another African American Redskins Hall of Famer, served as assistant general manager, which Peters identified as a figurehead position, and was assigned only insignificant tasks.[92]

Dallas's African American players, however, seemed to have more complaints about the racial atmosphere on their team and in their city. Duane Thomas, who played for both Dallas and Washington, said that blacks and whites mixed more easily on the Redskins.[93] Tony Dorsett noted that the lack of racial intermingling on the Cowboys was strikingly different from what he had been used to in high school and college in western Pennsylvania. He also stated that Dallas management strongly disapproved of black players dating white women. Dorsett was struck when he arrived in Dallas that whites openly uttered racial insults to him. Dallas police, suspicious of a young black man driving a fancy car, pulled him over more times than he cared to remember. In what he called his "welcome to Dallas," Dorsett was arrested on two counts of assault for fighting with a white bartender whom he claimed had hurled racial epithets at him, although the charges were dropped.[94]

On occasion, racial tension on the Cowboys team precipitated violence. According to Duane Thomas, when black Cowboy Margene Adkins called out to some of his teammates to look at a white woman they passed walking down Bourbon Street in New Orleans, white running back Walt Garrison threw a drink at him and slashed his jacket with a hook knife. When Garrison refused to pay for the jacket, Adkins "cold cocked him" in the shower.[95]

Throughout the 1960s, Dallas remained residentially very segregated, and African American Cowboys were restricted to living in south Dallas, a great distance away from the team's practice facilities in Irving. For two years Mel Renfro tried unsuccessfully to find housing in north Dallas. After President Johnson signed open housing legislation in 1968, Renfro filed an anti-discrimination suit in court. He emphasized that general manager Tex Schramm tried to persuade him not to go to court and, when he did, retaliated by denying him money at contract time. Renfro declared that Coach Landry condoned segregation by remaining indifferent to the racial discrimination his black players experienced in Dallas. Pete Gent recalled that because Dallas's black players were confined to undesirable, crime-ridden neighborhoods, some of them removed personal belongings from their homes when the team went on the road and stored them at Gent's for safekeeping.[96]

The names of the Dallas and Washington football clubs–Cowboys and Redskins–which any American schoolchild could relate to the bitterly fought conflict over domination of vast expanses of the continent, established a basis for a rivalry, especially in football, the most violent of team sports. The fighting between white frontiersman and settlers ("Cowboys") and Native Americans ("Redskins") both reflected and shaped American views of independence and manliness. The images of the lone cowboy riding on the open range and the proud and ungovernable Indian brave who roamed the plains and resisted confinement symbolized an autonomy that modern bureaucratic society denied to most men, but for which many still longed, at least unconsciously.

Both the frontiersman and the Indian had long been invoked as symbols of American freedom and even as the model American. The western

High Noon, a personal favorite of President Eisenhower, "topped the play-bill" of films shown in the American pavilion at the 1958 Brussels World's Fair, which the United States used to define itself to foreign countries. The film celebrates a frontier marshal with the courage to disregard the community's wishes and stand alone against outlaws. Eisenhower considered the western novelist Zane Gray his favorite writer. Patriots often invoked Indian symbolism to illustrate their commitment to freedom. The men who staged the Boston Tea Party dressed as Indians, and the minutemen who confronted the redcoats at Lexington and Concord fought them "in the Indian manner." In 1794, men participating in the Whiskey Rebellion donned Indian war paint.[97] Early in the twentieth century, an Indian's head appeared on both the penny and the nickel, along with that of Liberty on the quarter.

Nonetheless, naming alone is not sufficient to sustain a sports rivalry. Teams must encounter each other regularly (twice a year in the NFL), as the Redskins and Cowboys have since being placed in the same conference in 1961. The quality of the teams must be similar enough to excite the fans' interest in the games' outcomes. The Redskins and Cowboys were fairly evenly matched for long periods of times, particularly during the first three decades of their existence. Indeed, it was not until 1968 that one team won both of the year's matchups. Even when fielding mediocre teams in the mid-1960s, both Dallas and Washington possessed explosive offenses and outstanding quarterbacks capable of achieving dramatic, come-from-behind victories.

The rivalry also benefited from the reputations coaches Tom Landry and George Allen enjoyed from activities outside football, which heightened their celebrity. Head coaches receive more attention in football than in other less complex sports because they have a greater impact on the game. The plays that they design and impart to the team in tightly supervised practices require careful coordination among several players and split-second timing.[98] Landry was prominent in the religious arena, and Allen gained much attention as a personal friend of President Richard M. Nixon, who visited Redskins practices and even recommended plays. Nixon invited Allen to attend a state dinner for Prince Juan Carlos and Princess Sophia of Spain.[99] During the Reagan years, the Republican Party similarly exploited Landry's prestige as a coach by having him preside at a prayer breakfast at its national convention in 1984.[100]

The Dallas-Washington rivalry included some of professional football's most memorable games and moments, beginning with the dramatic Jurgensen-Meredith passing duels of the mid-1960s. Arguably the most famous tackle in football history occurred in a nationally televised Cowboys-Redskins Monday night game on October 8, 1973, that George Allen called "one of the greatest games of all time." Unlike the usual high-scoring Dallas-Washington matchups, this game was dominated by defense and special teams. Trailing 14–7, with fourth down and goal on the Redskins' four-yard line, Cowboys running back Walt Garrison caught a pass from quarterback Craig Morton about a foot from the end zone. The highly capable Morton entered the game in the third quarter after the Redskins' front four had sacked Roger Staubach seven times. Garrison, a rodeo cowboy during the off-season, a "bronco buster," was considered "one of the hardest men in the league to bring down single-handed," according to the *Washington Post*'s David DuPree. But Redskins strong safety Kenny Houston met Garrison inches from the goal line and did not yield, bringing the game to a dramatic finish. Allen was amazed at Houston's tackle, commenting: "I haven't seen many guys tackle that guy alone. He twists. He fights. You can't tackle him low."[101]

George Allen pioneered in developing highly proficient special teams, and they performed spectacularly in the game. He even had his kickoff receiving team introduced prior to the game, rather than the offense or defense. The numerous turnovers the Redskins special teams effected added a further dimension of unpredictability and excitement to their games with the Cowboys. In the first quarter of the October 8, 1973, game, Bill Malinchak, a leader on special teams, leapt on the Dallas punter "like Dracula out of the night," blocking his kick. Tom Landry declared that the Redskins' blocking the punt and two field goals was a principal reason for Dallas's defeat.[102]

The rivalry persists to this day, but diminished in intensity after 1992, in part because the Redskins ceased to field consistently outstanding teams and employed a succession of undistinguished quarterbacks and coaches, except for Joe Gibbs (2004–07). Even Gibbs, whose first term as Redskins coach (1981–1992) earned him election to the Hall of Fame, compiled a mediocre won-loss record during this second term. Having won seventeen of their past twenty-four games against Washington through 2007, Dallas assumed a commanding 56-38-2 lead in the series.[103]

Serious scandals involving drugs and sexual battery, well publicized by the mass media, tarnished the Dallas Cowboys' image and detracted from their appeal. *New York Times* columnist George Vecsey wrote in 1997 that "America's Team lost its steam partly because decades of crude behavior, a legacy of debauchery and drug abuse, had caught up with the Cowboys."[104] Dallas sportswriter Skip Bayless commented the same year that the Cowboys "have long been among the worst role models in sports." In separate incidents during the 1970s and early 1980s, three Cowboys were arrested for sexually abusing young girls, two of whom were only ten years old. Superstar receiver "Bullet" Bob Hayes, once known as "the World's Fastest Human," was sent to prison for drug trafficking after he retired. As early as 1983, an FBI drug investigation of several Cowboys resulted in a new nickname: "South America's Team."[105]

During the 1990s, there was a torrent of negative publicity surrounding the Cowboys concerning felonious drug use and debauchery. This gave rise to the joke: "If two Dallas Cowboys are in a car, who's driving? The police." In the most widely publicized case, superstar receiver Michael Irvin in 1996 pleaded guilty to second-degree felony cocaine possession. Irvin epitomized the wealthy, narcissistic contemporary athlete who caused many fans to lose interest in professional sports. He often appeared in public wearing a mink coat, lavender suit, gilt-edged sunglasses, a diamond watch, gold chains, and gaudy rings. When Irvin purchased a new BMW, he instructed the dealer not to tint the windows, so that people could recognize him when he was driving. The NFL twice suspended Pro Bowl defensive tackle Leon Lett for violating NFL drug policy, the second time for an entire year. In 1999, Mark Tuinei, an offensive lineman who played for the Cowboys from 1983 to 1998 and was on three Super Bowl teams, died after injecting heroin. The press learned that several Cowboys rented a "Party House" for liaisons with women not their wives or regular girlfriends, and some players were often seen at topless dance bars in Dallas. Others pleaded guilty or no contest to drunk driving.[106]

Even Cowboys head coach Barry Switzer was arrested at Dallas–Fort Worth International Airport in 1997 when a loaded gun was found in his carry-on luggage. Cowboys owner Jerry Jones imposed on Switzer the largest fine an NFL coach had ever been required to pay. He declared that the arrest had "brought pain and embarrassment to a team trying to improve its image."[107]

By the early twenty-first century, the nation's increasingly homogenized character had eroded the regional distinctions on which team rivalries depended. This process was stimulated by television; the rise of chain stores, motels, and other enterprises; the building and expansion of the interstate highway system; the proliferation of tract suburbs; and a physically mobile population that increasingly moved between regions. The long-standing success of the Dallas Cowboys, "America's Team," itself diluted the rivalry with the Washington Redskins by helping to transform Dallas's image from forbidding "city of hate" to glitzy capital of a modern, dynamic Sunbelt. Dallas, a major international airline hub, had become a metropolis that more closely resembled the NFL's other large cities.

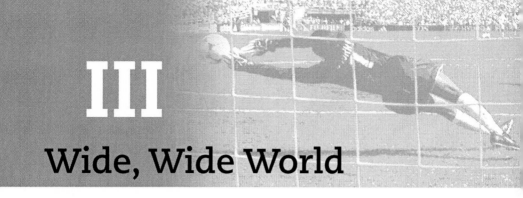

III

Wide, Wide World

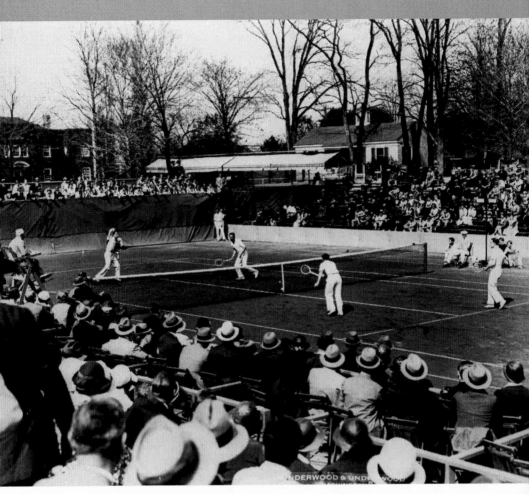

America versus Canada in a doubles match in the 1932 Davis Cup. *Courtesy of the Library of Congress.*

thirteen
Imperial Rivalries
America versus Britain for the Davis Cup

S. W. POPE

During the summer of 1899, four members of the Harvard University tennis team competed in a Monterey, California, tournament and they were chuffed (happily encouraged) by the level of play (beyond the East Coast) in the new game of lawn tennis. Having keenly followed the America's Cup competition earlier in the summer (during which time a Scots tea baron, Thomas Lipton, made his first of five unsuccessful challenges in yachts named *Shamrock*), Dwight Davis had a hunch that an international competition might do for tennis what the America's Cup had done for yachting. "If team matches between players from different parts of the same country arouse such great interest and promote such good feeling," Davis wondered, "would not similar international contests have even wider and more far-reaching consequences?"[1]

Just three years earlier, of course, the modern Olympics had been launched by Frenchman Pierre de Coubertin—followed in 1899 by the Paris Exposition. Clearly, interest in international sporting competition was in the air. The modern Olympics and World's Fairs emerged within the context of raging imperial rivalries and, as such, provided a prominent venue for Western imperialist powers to symbolically contest and validate their respective national and sporting prowess. Davis, a Harvard student, drafted the tournament format of what would later be called the Davis Cup with the advice of Richard Olyney, who served as secretary of state under President Grover Cleveland. Davis, a twenty-year-old man of considerable inherited wealth, commissioned and donated a sterling silver bowl—purchasing it out of his own funds. He was later appointed secretary of war in 1924 (a post which he served until 1929) and then governor-general of the Philippines (1929–32).[2] No doubt his eastern patrician and government connections would only elevate the status of the Davis Cup (in 1924 President Calvin Coolidge agreed to draw the contestants' names out of a bowl at the White House)—which, obviously, delighted the young American tennis establishment.[3]

The Davis Cup (first played in 1900) was the first attempt to stage a grand, annual competition between the two leading tennis powers of the day—an early effort by Americans to challenge the mother country of modern sport, Britain. For the American hosts, the first competition in 1900 was a spectacular success, proof of how far the country's tennis had progressed. An unabashedly jingoistic drawing in one Boston paper showed a giant silver bowl being towed off the tennis court by two tiny American players while the third player sat on the rim waving an American flag. Three other players, bowing slightly in apparent obeisance, stood on the sidelines watching it go, a limp Union Jack at their side.[4]

The turn of the century context is enormously significant in understanding this emergent international sporting competition. With an imperial sense of destiny, the United States challenged Britain on various cultural and political fronts. Between the Spanish-American War and World War II, the United States not only achieved a sprawling empire with colonial possessions and protectorates in the Far East and in the Caribbean, but also emerged after 1945 as a bona fide superpower. Although one can find numerous protestations within American discourse about the "evils" of European empire, by the late nineteenth century it became clear to the American ruling interests that the United States could not be left behind in securing markets for expanded foreign trade as well as in procuring key resources for industrial production.

The long-revered anti-imperialist national mythology hailed as evidence of the nation's "exceptional" place in the world was eclipsed by an openly imperial rhetoric and an "open door" foreign policy bolstered by a global police presence—in short, a growing recognition that the nation was increasingly embracing the ideology and practices it had long denounced. Thomas Bender explains how the United States entered the twentieth century "well experienced in taking territory and in the affairs of empire. The United States was, thus, part of a larger history of the European or Western economic and cultural domination of the planet . . . that began in the fifteenth century."[5] Although territorial acquisition and military intervention would be less extensive than what characterized the British empire, a new-styled American neo-imperialism emerged based upon financial hegemony—a slightly kinder and gentler and perhaps softer type of empire (although one might assess the experience of American muscle in the Caribbean and Latin America prior to World War II before simply going along with this generalization).

Analyzing how just as the United States was in the process of supplanting Britain as the leading global power (which would be accomplished after World War I), Mark Dyreson writes that Americans also "assume[d] that their sporting traditions would make the globe more American—precisely as the British had believed about their sport and culture a generation earlier." Dyreson notes the irony of such American efforts to spread national culture through sport prior to (and even after) World War II: "Just as the United States had borrowed from Great Britain the idea of using sport as a tool to construct national identity while at the same time rejecting the British notion that the tool would inevitably spread British-style culture around the world," he writes, "so too did other nations accept the American notion of defining nationhood through sporting prowess but rejected Americanization in favor of their own nationalisms."[6]

In his excellent recent book on the topic, Gerald Gems documents the myriad ways in which Americans sought to evangelize and export their games (and attendant values) abroad as part of a broader imperialist effort based upon a presumed position of superiority (to the peoples whose trade and natural resources they coveted). Gems shows how American imperialists found many rational uses for sport in "the cultural interplay that transpired in colonialism," and although the colonials readily warmed to American sporting practices and proved themselves quick learners in beating their Yankee masters at their own games (especially in baseball and basketball), the colonials did not particularly warm to the cultural, religious, and ideological packaging which accompanied these sports.[7]

American sporting imperial visions were also on display outside the colonial context. One such pre-twentieth-century (and immediately pre–Spanish American War) illuminative example is Albert Spalding's 1888 world tour of professional baseball players. Spalding, in his efforts to market baseball as a global game (and thereby extend his sporting goods empire abroad), exuded a fledgling American imperialist mentality. Thomas Zeiler argues that Spalding's band of baseball adventurers functioned as imperial diplomats who carried the dominant nationalistic and

296 S. W. POPE

racial values (e.g., a general cultural ordering of races and societies) and combined what he characterizes as "an entrepreneurial spirit with principles as well as imperial intentions" and, thus, played a part (however small) in "reshaping the world in the coming century under American leadership."[8]

Although the game probably dates back to the early fourteenth century, when it was first played in French monasteries, lawn tennis is a quintessentially modern sport dating back to 1874 with the publication of a friend of the Prince of Wales (late Edward VII), Major Walter Wingfield's British patent office license for "A Portable Court of Playing Tennis." It was Wingfield who codified and marketed tennis as a suitable game—a gentle diversion and an alternative to croquet and bowls—for upper-class ladies and gentlemen (replete with a handy kit containing net, balls, and racquets for play on most large English country home gardens).[9] In 1877 the rules and conventions were established by the All England Croquet Club in the London suburb of Wimbeldon, which hosted the first tennis tournament.

The game diffused quickly. Tennis arrived in the United States within months of Wingfield's patent, where early tournaments were held in 1876 and 1880 (in Massachusetts and Staten Island); and the first official national championship was held at the Newport, Rhode Island, Casino in 1881—the same year that the U.S. National Lawn Tennis Association (later simply the USTA) was formed (and would serve as the country's governing body). Lawn tennis spread quickly beyond its Anglo-American hub as clubs were established in France, Brazil, Scotland, Ireland, and India during the mid to late 1870s; and by 1890, it was also played in South Africa, Denmark, Switzerland, Holland, Finland, Greece, Turkey, Lebanon, and Egypt. Yet, despite its international diffusion, the sport was dominated for the first half century by England, the United States, France, and Australia.[10]

The key venue for early lawn tennis was the country club—a late nineteenth-century development which derived from elite male city clubs wherein leisure traditions and customs were created as a form of social status and networking. As James Mayo writes, commuting advances and suburban development "enabled elites to create a lifestyle that integrated their desire for club life, outdoor and leisure activities, and suburban living. . . . [T]he combination of these conditions played an essential role in the formation of the country club."[11] While the international diffusion of the country club ideal has yet to attract its historians, as the three leading tennis powers in the late nineteenth and early twentieth centuries, it is reasonably clear that elite, private clubs in Britain, the United States, and Australia hatched the first two generations of elite tennis players internationally. In Australia, the competitive version reached its greatest heights at the Melbourne Cricket Club in the 1880s,[12] although tennis at club level was still primarily a Protestant pursuit surrounded by the business ethic and the concomitants of the Masonic Lodge.[13] The movers and shakers of this emergent international tennis culture had the habit of bumping into each other in various and sundry places—at the Pyramids, along the French Riviera, and at Henley, Wimbledon, and Lords in London.[14] As such, fin de siècle tennis, like most sports, was "based on a fraternity of elites, among both the athletes who garnered public adulation and the officials who wielded power behind the scenes," Barbara Keys writes—a "world oddly poised between modernity and tradition, embracing technology, quantification, and progress even while grasping outdated ideals of amateurism and the purity of play. It mediated between nationalism and internationalism, strengthening both simultaneously."[15]

With elite backgrounds and imperial aspirations, the Anglophile Americans and Australians exhibited similar class and ideological characteristics as their former colonial masters. For the Australians, according to Graeme Smith, those included financial security; an emphasis on high or privileged birth, family, social acceptability, and contacts; often a sense of colonial swagger that harked back to the well-bred jackaroo, even the new chum colonial experience; connections with the Colonial Service, with Empire, possibly with the Indian Colonial Service or other areas of experience such as Public School; often an informal link with the occupiers of the Vice Regal office; a membership holding in common private schooling and a calling to the professions; an ascendancy, in Australia at least, of the landed, the squatter, the entrepreneur; and an assumption of common ground with the officer class in the armed services, who were to be welcomed as social or playing guests, even if not skillful at either of the games.[16] With this in mind, it should not be surprising that the leading Australasian players in the early Davis Cup competitions hailed from privileged backgrounds. Both Anthony Wilding (New Zealand) and Norman

Brookes hailed from privileged English migrant families. Wilding did his prep schooling in England and studied law at Cambridge. He became intimate friends with statesmen, European aristocrats, and royalty, frequently being a house guest in palaces and stately homes.[17] Brookes (described by Bill Tilden as "the greatest tennis brain of the twentieth century"), the son of a wealthy ship owner and bridge builder, took to the game at age five and would go on to dominate the administration of Australian tennis until the mid 1950s. Brookes was also a skilled cricketer, adept at billiards, and won several national golf titles.

Underpinned by a healthy faith in social Darwinism as an ideological rationale for Anglo-American-Australian gentlemen's destiny to run the world (and in so doing, preserve class exclusivity), the tennis establishment perpetuated a Victorian-era amateur code until the 1930s.[18] According to historian E. Digby Baltzell, the amateur sporting code was an aspect of a class code of honor which was uniquely characteristic of the Anglo-American social systems between the Civil War and World War II—which dominated the tennis world until the early 1960s but which died a slow death during the late 1960s.[19] Most of the scholarship on amateurism has depicted its spread as an example of British cultural imperialism—an ideology concocted by headmasters, clergymen, and editors that diffused from Britain to the "rest" of the sporting nations. Murray Phillips's analysis of sporting amateurism in Australia at the turn of the twentieth century suggests that "the accepted definition was interpreted differently and selectively or was modified . . . which effectively differentiated within sporting activities and in different locations." In the case of Australia, amateurism "overwhelmingly favoured the version that did not explicitly discriminate along occupational or class lines" (as had been the case in Britain); and thus, when discussing amateurism in sport, Phillips argues, "It is more accurate to talk about 'amateurisms,' in the plural [which] reflects the selective, fluid and dynamic dimensions of the amateurism as it was interpreted in the context of local, regional and national historical traditions."[20]

The creation of the Davis Cup was the greatest achievement of American tennis. The Europeans regarded its "round robin" structure as indicative of an American competitive spirit and a distinctly American method—which obligated all contestants to contest each of the opposing team's singles players (rather than evading particular players by virtue of a lucky draw).[21] There is substantial evidence to suggest that the Davis Cup profoundly stimulated interest in the game within the United States.

Originally only America and Britain contested the trophy, but by World War I France, Belgium, Austria, Australasia, Germany, and Canada had entered teams. Up to 1927 the only three nations to win the Davis Cup were the United States, Great Britain, and Australasia. The French dominated competition between 1927 and 1933, led by Rene Lacoste and the so-called Three Musketeers after the Bill Tilden–dominated era of 1920 to 1926, when America had its first "golden" hero of the sport. France has since won the cup just once, and Britain has not held it since 1937. For twenty-seven years after World War II the Davis Cup was won by either the United States or Australia, until South Africa won it by default in 1974. Indeed, during the 1950s and early 1960s—the "golden age" of Australian tennis—the staging of the Davis Cup became a fixture on the Aussie sporting calendar, and Aussie players dominated. By the mid 1980s sixty-two nations played in the competition; the field has doubled during the past twenty years, as 137 teams competed in 2007.[22]

So long as the Davis Cup remained primarily a U.S.-British affair, relations were cordial, if not culturally contentious at times. Once the English players returned home from the first Davis Cup competition held at Longwood Country Club, they unloaded their frustrations about the conditions under which they were forced to compete for the new trophy: American balls were too soft, the grass on courts was too long, the nets sagged, etc. Davis's biographer noted how "several of the elements that had been factors in the outcome of the first Davis Cup competition would surface again and again in future challenges. Overconfidence, for instance, and dissatisfaction with the conditions of the host country's courts, and possibly most important, the inability of a country to convince its leading players that they were needed and that patriotism outranked personal convenience."[23]

The geopolitical dynamics changed after Australia's (and New Zealand's) 1907 triumph, which was the first time that the trophy had been won by a country other than United States or Britain and meant that the world tennis powers would have to travel south if they were to regain the Davis Cup. The Aussie defense in 1908 on its own turf, in

November's 100+ F temperatures, proved to be a decisive home court advantage over their American and British rivals, but the competition also laid to rest any enduring notions that tennis was a namby-pamby sport (associated with afternoon teas)—and, in the process, the 1908 Cup Challenge was the key watershed in legitimizing lawn tennis as a major modern, masculine, and decidedly "Australian" sport.[24] Mabel Brookes, wife of Australia's leading tennis figure, noted in her autobiography the way in which Australian tennis victories unified the athletes with their fellow countrymen: the victorious player "belongs to his country. . . . [H]e has fought a battle, done a job for the people who now see themselves with him as one and indivisible."[25] For the Americans and Britons, the discursive script between the mother country of modern sport and the emergent world power would follow similar lines as those which unfolded during the controversial 1908 London Olympics that summer.[26]

After the 1908 competition, the financial logistics of the British and Americans sending teams "down-under" created tensions within the various national associations, as such a journey required considerable time, expense, and acclimatization for the players. The trip from the American eastern seaboard via the Suez Canal required six weeks, and for the U.S. Lawn Tennis Association (USLTA) it cost $2,400, a princely sum, roughly the cost of a three-bedroom house.[27] Four years later, the Americans remained by the struggle of having to contend for "their" tournament in faraway Christchurch. Harry Waidner, secretary of the Western LTA, suggested that the United States should withdraw from participation unless Australasia agreed to defend the Davis Cup on American soil. Having become used to the trophy residing in Melbourne, Norman Brookes's response to such American threats was curt—if another team really wanted the Davis Cup, they would jolly well have to come and get it. For the Aussies, Davis Cup triumphs were savored not merely for their own sake—matches played in a strongly nationalistic climate with national flags, uniforms, anthems, and civic receptions—the event was presented as a celebration of nationalism. Success in the Davis Cup was taken by many Australians as indicative of much more than a mere sporting achievement. The victories seemed to symbolize Australia's recent shift away from Britain and outward to the world in general, and the United States in particular.[28]

In 1912, the Americans failed to enter a team in the Challenge Round, although, to their relief, the Brits won and brought the Davis Cup back to England.[29] That year, Maurice McLoughlin, a young Scotch-Irish lad who perfected his game on the public courts of San Francisco, won the Men's LTA Championship, which signaled to Baltzell an interesting omen not only in the American class system but also in the world of tennis.[30] Yet in spite of hopeful prospects for a new generation of tennis, the Americans refused to attend the inaugural meeting of the newly formed International Lawn Tennis Federation due to the fact that their English rivals wanted to claim exclusive ownership in holding the lawn tennis championships (i.e., Wimbeldon). Americans thought that the only truly world championship was the Davis Cup, and only in 1923, after considerable wrangling, were the Americans persuaded to become members of the international federation—only after England relinquished, calling the All England Championships the "world championships."

The end of World War I represented an important watershed in American imperial thinking with regard to sport. Americans emerged from World War I with a newfound sense of confidence in their ability to exert cultural and political muscle with other European powers as well as within the nation's established spheres of influence in the Caribbean and the Far East. This invigorated cultural swagger derived from the fact that after World War I the United States had eclipsed Britain and had become the new center of economic power.

During the interwar years Americans achieved the most significant and longest-lasting impact on international sport. While modern, competitive sport was a British invention, by the interwar years the leading edge of international sport management was increasingly identified with the United States. In addition to eclipsing Britain as the world's foremost "sporting nation," Americans played the key role in commercializing and democratizing international sport, imbuing it with moral and technocratic impulses (rigorous training, an achievement-oriented ethos, and the celebration of individual heroes)[31] and expanding its connections to the worlds of entertainment and mass culture. Like jazz, Hollywood movies, and Ford's mass-production techniques, American sport techniques and styles inspired emulation and envy (as well as derision) as male-oriented spectator sport became a central component of national life during the

1920s, based upon the celebrity of athletes such as Bill Tilden—perhaps the leading light of the "golden people" (another key story line in this larger history of the Davis Cup). For large swaths of the American public, the nation's stars and international victories—garbed in heavy layers by the self-designated sport ambassadors—influenced the way they perceived the country's role and destiny in world history: a supposedly benevolent, benign, exceptionalist role in the world, a force for peace, as well as proof of the superiority of democracy as a political and social system.[32]

According to Baltzell (who has written probably the best single-volume work on American tennis history), whose principal concern is with the rise and decline of upper-class dominance in both American tennis and politics more generally, the last and greatest period of American prowess was between the mid 1930s and late 1940s. During this time the United States produced a talented generation of players (Ellsworth Vines, Donald Budge, Robert Riggs, Richard Gonzalez, and Jack Kramer, all born and bred on the public courts in California) who represented the most democratic one to play for glory on the clean-cut lawns of the staid and snobbish cricket and tennis clubs along the eastern seaboard. It was also during the 1930s that Britain won its last Davis Cup victories (in 1933, 1967, and 1937) led by the stellar play of Fred Perry.

To conclude, then, although largely neglected by sport historians, the Davis Cup provides a fertile and suggestive case study for better understanding American sporting imperial initiatives at the turn of the century (and throughout the twentieth century). The promotion of the Davis Cup contains elements of an imperialist mentality alongside a much longer Anglo-American dynamic within sports history. The Davis Cup (in particular, and sport more generally) is a prime example of the longer historical pattern of American imitation and absorption of British models and then the gradual reversal of the process to a later, more reciprocal interrelationship within popular culture. During colonial and antebellum times, Americans imported various British sports and games and, subsequently, transformed them with newly invented rules, conventions, traditions, and meanings after the Civil War. After the mid-nineteenth century, American-styled entertainment such as the minstrel and Wild West shows eclipsed the British theater and English popular music within American popular culture and paved the way for the export of jazz and blues—as well as Hollywood film—to Britain after World

War I and a broader range of consumerist trends (such as fast food, supermarkets, and household appliances) after World War II.[33] In short, the Davis Cup competition is an example of the way in which Americans indigenized a cultural sporting import, namely tennis; created a nationalistic, international sporting competition; and effectively exported it back to Britain within the wider context of a burgeoning imperial rivalry on the world stage between these two rival sporting nations.

Bernhard Langer of Europe (*left*) walking with the United State's Hale Irwin on the final day of singles competition of the 1991 Ryder Cup at Kiawah Island, South Carolina. *Courtesy of Getty Images.*

fourteen

This Has Nothing to Do with Money

The Ryder Cup and International Rivalry in Golf

JOHN NAURIGHT

The atmosphere is something I cannot explain. We would play 100 holes and we would not be tired because the spectators would carry us in their arms.

—*Ignacio Garrido, Spanish Ryder Cup European team member*

Grown men wept. The jubilant crowd overflowed onto the green. Fans waved huge American flags and sang The Star-Spangled Banner. What played out that Sunday afternoon on the venerable fairways of The Country Club may go down in history as the greatest victory the golf world has ever seen.

—*Bob Bubka and Tom Clavin, The Ryder Cup: Golf's Greatest Event*

We have seen in this volume many cases of rivalries in sport, but within individual sports such as golf and tennis we often think of personal rivalries such as Arnold Palmer versus Jack Nicklaus or Roger Federer versus Rafael Nadal, Chris Evert then Steffi Graf versus Martina Navratilova, etc. While golf is primarily an individual sport, the Ryder Cup has become perhaps the most hotly contested golf event both in terms of players and of spectators. Unlike the Davis Cup and other cup competitions in team sports, the Ryder Cup is a single event pitting the same two teams against each other in alternate years. The Ryder Cup is unique in that it also provides the first instance of a pan-continental identity which centers on the European team. Indeed, the Ryder Cup is the only competition in which

Europeans unite in a common cause in sport. Can you imagine any other place where English and German sports fans would be on the same side?[1] This is a fairly recent phenomenon, however, as for much of its history the Ryder Cup was a rather low-key gentlemanly affair between American golfers and their British and Irish counterparts. The competition became so lopsided in favor of the Americans, however, that Jack Nicklaus suggested, after the 1977 event, that the British and Irish team should be expanded to include the rest of Europe. Indeed, other than 1957, the British and Irish team had not held the Ryder Cup since 1933. The European Tour, Nicklaus argued, was gaining in quality players, and the addition of stars such as Seve Ballesteros of Spain would both expand the competition and interest in it and make it more competitive. In its first iteration, the European team in 1979 only added British Open champion Ballesteros and Antonio Garrido, both of Spain, to the usual cache of British and Irish players. The U.S. team continued its success in 1979 and 1981. The 1983 competition at Palm Beach Gardens in Florida, however, went down to the wire with the United States winning only by 14½ to 13½. Since that time the European team has won or retained the Ryder Cup in 1985, 1987, 1989, 1995, 1997, 2002, 2004, and 2006, with the 2004 and 2006 events being won by large margins.[2] Since 1985 the American team has only won in 1991, 1993, 1999, and 2008. The score line since 1985 reads thus: seven wins to Europe, one draw in which Europe retained the Ryder Cup, and only four wins for the United States.[3]

This chapter examines the history of the Ryder Cup with particular focus on the period since 1983, when the new European team became more competitive, and then perhaps even dominant over the America team, the 2008 result notwithstanding, and how this heated battle has emerged as one of the most intense rivalries in international sport and certainly the most intense in golf. Despite the individual dominance of Tiger Woods and the high ranking of teammates such as Phil Mickelson and Jim Furyk, the European team appears to coalesce better as a team and among fans. Perhaps surprisingly, Woods, Mickelson, and Furyk each rank among the worse players based on record among Americans who have played fifteen or more matches in the Ryder Cup. Indeed, the American triumph in 2008 was achieved while Woods was out of competition due to injury. Why this apparent anomaly should be the case will be explored, and it may allude to much more than mere friendly sporting rivalry as was originally intended. The chapter runs from the initial origins of the Ryder Cup in 1926 and 1927 through the 2006 Ryder Cup held in Ireland, with brief discussion of the 2008 competition in Louisville, Kentucky.

Early History of Transatlantic Golf

Originally a purely Scottish pastime and only initially played in England by Scottish transplants, by the 1880s golf was popular throughout the British Isles. The first club founded by English golfers was Royal North Devon at Westward Ho! which was established in 1864. Indeed, Royal North Devon produced two of the leading golfers of the late nineteenth and early twentieth centuries, amateur Horace Hutchinson and professional J. H. Taylor, who began as a caddie for Hutchinson.[4] By the 1890s two of the three leading professional players of the day were English, Taylor and the great Harry Vardon, who between them won eleven Open Championships between 1894 and 1914. Along with Scotsman James Braid, who won five Open Championships himself, this "Great Triumvirate" dominated golf in the British Isles and golfing headlines internationally.

In the United States the game had not really taken off despite evidence that colonial planters near Charleston, South Carolina, may have played for a time. In 1786 there was a clubhouse on Harleston's Green in present-day downtown Charleston. Three years earlier in 1783 a shipment of ninety-six golf clubs and 432 golf balls had been sent to Charleston from Leith in Scotland, though there is no record of a course being created or of formal golf holes. John Deas, who received the equipment, died in 1790, and perhaps the interest died with him. Printed dinner invitations discovered in Savannah, Georgia, suggest a golf club was present there as early as 1796; but it seems to have disappeared by 1818, again with no evidence of a course layout.[5] The first recorded golf course in the United States appeared at White Sulpher Springs in West Virginia in 1884, though it fell into disrepair and disuse by 1900, only to be resurrected in the 1990s.[6] It was in and around the major cities of New York, Boston, and Chicago that the game finally took off in the United States as country clubs began to be established.[7] These clubs were staffed primarily with Scottish professionals brought over to teach locals the game. Indeed, the leading professional golfers in the United States were Scottish expatriates who won most tournaments and all sixteen U.S. Open championships prior to 1911, except for the victory by Harry Vardon in 1900. The United States Golf Association was founded in 1894 to coordinate rules and development of the game, and by 1898 there were 103 member clubs, though just a year later the total number of known golf clubs had reached 887, with 154 of these already west of the Mississippi River. By 1910 there were at least twenty major tournaments being held each year in the United States.[8]

As golf became established in the United States, amateur and open championships were created on both sides of the Atlantic. It was not long before discussions turned to the comparative qualities of golfers on each side of the ocean. In order to capitalize on the emerging mass market in golf and to promote its own products, the Spalding Company funded a tour of the United States by Harry Vardon in 1900, which culminated in Vardon winning the U.S. Open. The same year, J. H. Taylor also toured America, finishing second to Vardon in the U.S. Open. Vardon, in particular, highlighted the vast differences in quality of leading professional golfers between Britain and the United States as he won all but two of his singles matches (both to the transplanted Scot Bernard Nicholls) and won most of the matches where he played the best ball of two other golfers.[9]

The first chink in the British golfing armor occurred in 1904 when Australian-born, but naturalized American, Walter Travis won the Amateur Championship in Britain. Travis learned his golf at a late stage as an adult in the United States and was known to be the best putter of his era. He caused a stir when he used a center-shafted putter, unheard of to that time, and one later banned by the Royal and Ancient Golf Club, the rule makers for golf around the world, except for the United States, where the United States Golf Association (USGA) made the rules.[10] The win by Travis fueled great speculation about the relative state of American golf in comparison with that in Britain, speculation that volleyed back and forth across the Atlantic for several years. The victories by John J. McDermott, the first by a native-born American, in the 1911 and 1912 U.S. Opens led to moves to get Harry Vardon back to contend for the 1913 championship. By that time Vardon had won the Open Championship in Britain five times and was still considered the greatest golfer in the world. Vardon and fellow Jersey-born Ted Ray embarked on a mission to reclaim the U.S. Championship at the Country Club at Brookline near Boston. In the most amazing golf result to that time and perhaps ever, unknown amateur Francis Ouimet defeated Vardon and Ray in a playoff (after Vardon had missed a six-inch putt) to win outright.[11] Ouimet's victory sparked belief in the United States that American golfers could hold their own against the best Britain had to offer. This belief was perhaps strengthened after Vardon won the Open Championship for the sixth time in 1914 on the eve of World War I. Vardon made one last tilt at the U.S. Open in 1920, at the age of fifty, when he finished second to Ted Ray. Vardon's and Ray's performance quieted American bravado, though only temporarily. After 1925, no British player won in the U.S. Open until Tony Jacklin took the title in 1970. American dominance of British championships during the 1920s began to turn the tide of confidence in the superiority of the American tournament system and the American golfer. Travel difficulties meant that only a few golfers crossed the Atlantic to compete each year, but American professional Walter Hagen and amateur Bobby Jones demonstrated repeatedly during the 1920s that U.S. excellence in golf was a reality and was at the minimum on a par with the best Britain had to offer. Their successes sparked an increasing number of American-based professionals to make the voyage across the Atlantic. Hagen became the first American-born player to win the Open Championship in 1922, winning a total of four times between 1922 and 1929. In 1930, Jones, Open champion in 1926 and 1927, won all four major championships of the day, including the Amateur and Open Championships in Britain. In fact, American players won the Open Championship each year between 1924 and 1933. In this climate, it is not surprising that the two enduring team competitions in men's golf, the Walker Cup and the Ryder Cup, were established.

The Establishment of the Ryder Cup

Unlike natural team sports such as soccer and rugby, international team competition in golf was slow to emerge. While a series of challenge matches between English and Scottish golfers took place as early as the 1890s, the first truly international professional team match did not occur until 1913 when the U.S. team of four players was defeated by a French team led by Arnaud Massy at Versailles. World War I interrupted the opportunity for further competitions until the 1920s. Credit for the idea that led to the Ryder Cup lies with Ohio businessman S. P. Jermain, who was instrumental in inviting Ted Ray and Harry Vardon to play in the 1920 U.S. Open at his home club of Inverness. As a result of Ray's and Vardon's first and second place finishes, respectively, Jermain believed that international competition between the United States and Britain should be encouraged. Later that year, Jim Harnett, circulation manager of *Golf Illustrated* magazine in New York, sought to boost his readership through asking readers to contribute to a fund to send a team of American professionals over to play a British team. Though he came up short of raising his targeted funds, the U.S. Professional Golf Association (PGA) decided in December 1920 to advance the balance to Harnett. Determining player eligibility for the U.S. team was a thorny issue as many professionals in the United States were foreign born, many from Scotland.[12] It was decided that players had to be resident in the United States for at least five years and that they intended to become U.S. citizens in order to play for the United States.[13]

The match took place at Gleneagles in Scotland in June 1921 with a strong U.S. team of Walter Hagen, Tommy Armour, Wild Bill Melhorn, Wilfred Reid, Jock Hutchison, Fred McLeod, Tom Kerrigan, and Jim Hackney, led by captain Emmett French. The American team was so humbled by the British golfers that it is reported the U.S. ambassador departed in "a distinct huff." The only consolation was that Jock Hutchison stayed on to win the Open Championship at his birthplace of St. Andrews.[14] The match was not well supported and, indeed, it was widely thought that the U.S. team would be whitewashed. The British team won nine matches, the United States only three, with three matches halved. Little enthusiasm for a repeat match appeared at the time, though Walter Hagen remained convinced it was a good idea.[15] Indeed, Hagen did much to fan the flames of possible future competition by winning the Open Championship in 1922 and 1924, becoming the first native-born American to take away the top prize in British professional golf, reigniting the debate about the relative merits of golf in each country. British golf was also in transition in the early 1920s as the old great champions such as Vardon, Taylor, and Braid came to the end of their competitive careers. A new generation led by George Duncan, Arthur Havers, Abe Mitchell, and, eventually, Henry Cotton emerged in their place, though failing to fully replicate the success of the Great Triumvirate.

The final foundation for the Ryder Cup was laid in 1926 during an informal match between British and American golfers at Royal Wentworth in England. The match was organized due to the fact that the Open Championship was so oversubscribed that the Royal and Ancient Golf

Club announced in 1925 that they would hold regional qualifying. Over a dozen top American golfers were scheduled to play at Sunningdale in England, including Bobby Jones. As a result an invitation was presented to American professionals to play a match nearby at Wentworth prior to the qualifying tournament. Hagen, of course, led in accepting the challenge. Due to the General Strike in May, several American players' travel plans were disrupted and the U.S. team had to be supplemented with English players and Australian-born Joe Kirkwood. Samuel Ryder, a wealthy merchant who came to golf at the age of fifty, sponsored the event and offered a trophy, but withheld it due to the weakened opposition. The British team won easily again by 13½ to 1½, after which the players "retired to the clubhouse for champagne and sandwiches." Ryder funded a trophy to the tune of £100, supported by the same amount from *Golf Illustrated* and £50 from the Royal and Ancient Golf Club, to be presented at a formal competition between the two nations at Worcester, Massachusetts, in 1927.[16]

The Ryder Cup in the Era of the United States versus Great Britain and Ireland

The first four Ryder Cups were split evenly with the United States winning at home in 1927 and 1931 and the British team doing the same in 1929 and 1933. After those four events, the United States won each Ryder Cup match until 1957 (no matches were held between the 1937 one and the resumption of competition in 1947 after World War II) and then each one again until 1969, when Jack Nicklaus conceded a Tony Jacklin putt to ensure a tie, though the United States retained the cup under the competition rules.[17] The United States won every other Ryder Cup contested until 1985. By the end of the 1930s it was clear that the United States had eclipsed Britain in production of golfing talent with players such as Walter Hagen, Bobby Jones, and Gene Sarazen dominating the game. While British players occasionally won the Open Championship through the 1930s and 1940s (the most successful of whom was Henry Cotton, the Open winner in 1934, 1937, and 1948), no British golfer won the U.S. Open between Willie Macfarlane's win in 1925 and Tony Jacklin's win in 1970. No British player won the Masters or PGA championship in the United States either prior to the 1980s. Indeed, American dominance was so great by the end of the 1940s that the United States won the 1947 Ryder Cup by eleven matches to one, though the return match at Ganton in Yorkshire was a much closer 7–5 win for the Americans.

The British team was hamstrung in the early years by the refusal of the British PGA to take a flexible attitude to player participation, deciding to reward loyalty and to make selection more of an honor rather than deciding to place the strongest team on the course. Indeed, in 1931 the top British player, Henry Cotton, was omitted as he wished to stay and play some tournaments in the United States after the Ryder Cup was completed. PGA rules stated that players selected had to travel to and from the matches together as a team. For taking what was seen as an individualistic attitude, Cotton was vilified in the British press. Two other top golfers, Percy Alliss and Aubrey Boomer, were also omitted due to the fact that they were based on the Continent. Thus the British team of 1929 sailed to the United States without three of its best golfers, with a team whose age averaged over forty.[18] Typical of many cases in international sporting competition, the British were shackled by the lead boots of tradition and viewed such competitions as "sporting" rather than do-or-die events. As a result, in many sports that the British invented, their early dominance was rapidly eclipsed in the twentieth century.[19]

A second handicap faced by British golfers was the nature of professional golf there compared to the United States before the 1950s. In Britain few regular tournaments existed and a professional's primary means of earning a living was through his position as a club professional. A major part of his duties was to be present at the club on weekends to play with the members. In the United States, by contrast, a regular series of tournaments appeared by the 1920s, which allowed leading PGA golfers to subsist on tournament winnings without the necessity of being tied to a particular club. Leading young British professional Henry Cotton realized this and competed in the United States during the 1928–29 season. It was Cotton who promoted what was to become the European tour through participating in national championships throughout Europe in the 1930s and again after World War II. Indeed, Cotton did much to almost single-handedly prop up British golfing fortunes in the 1930s, though a steady decline was evident. He won famous challenge matches against the American champion of the British Open, Densmore Shute, and the great Walter Hagen in 1933 after his British team had narrowly lost the Ryder Cup to the United States.[20]

The American team was not without its controversies, however. The most significant issue was whether a player had to be born in the United States in order to play for the United States in the Ryder Cup. Walter Hagen spoke out against the requirement that U.S. players had to be American born as this excluded Tommy Armour, Macdonald Smith, Jim Barnes, and Jock Hutchison, all born in Scotland, and Australian-born Joe Kirkwood, all of whom had become naturalized American citizens. Other players such as U.S. Open Champion Johnny Farrell argued that foreign-born professionals "really developed the fundamentals of their games before coming to the states." The British supported the ban, believing that many of their top players had been lured by potential financial reward to the United States and to include them would amount to the U.S. team "buying" the Ryder Cup. This argument had little basis in fact since the excluded players mentioned were part of the 1926 U.S. team that was thoroughly routed at Wentworth.[21] Nevertheless, the U.S. team was to remain an exclusively homegrown one.

The American team took nothing for granted in the 1949 match held not long after Captain Ben Hogan's near fatal automobile crash. On the meaning of the Ryder Cup, Hogan stated, "We care about who is selected, but we care more about winning."[22] Hogan trained the U.S. team hard, scheduling early practices, and engaged in gamesmanship aimed at upsetting the British team through protesting the legality of the grooves in their irons. All of this was a calculated effort to gain the upper hand for a U.S. team missing Hogan, Byron Nelson, and U.S. Open champion Cary Middlecoff.[23] Though the British put up a valiant effort, Hogan's determination helped secure the American victory. The United States continued to win easily at home in 1951 and 1955, though the situation was far different on British soil in 1953 and 1957.

The U.S. team had become so successful in Ryder Cup matches that it was becoming difficult to convince all of the best players of the need for them to travel for the match at Wentworth in 1953. Hogan and Harrison were selected but did not travel, and experts felt this was the weakest team the United States had fielded to date. Despite this, the American team held on to win 6½ to 5½.[24]

In 1955 the British and Irish team won four points for the first time in a match held in the United States, so a concerted effort was mounted to finally regain the Ryder Cup in 1957. The Americans were hampered by Hogan and Sam Snead declining invitations and by the PGA refusing to select Cary Middlecoff or Julius Boros after they would not play in the PGA Championship. Middlecoff and Boros chose to play in a lucrative exhibition match rather than the PGA, which did not endear them to the selectors.[25] Still the United States fielded a team of ten, including Captain Jack Burke Jr., eight of whom won major championships during their careers. The United States led after the opening day by four balls but were soundly beaten in the singles for a stunning 7½ to 4½ win to the British and Irish side. Captain Dai Rees stated, "It was the most thrilling day of my life. I was so proud of captaining a winning side that it probably made up for all those disappointments I endured in many British Open Championships."[26] The British public savored the win; and for his efforts, Rees was named BBC Sports Personality of the Year for 1957 and in 1958 was made a commander of the British Empire by Queen Elizabeth.[27]

In 1961 several changes were made to the Ryder Cup which intended to make it more competitive. Prior to that time singles matches were held over thirty-six holes, which provided a stronger chance of the best overall player winning the match. British players had often held a lead at lunchtime only to lose it in the afternoon round. For all future Ryder Cups, singles matches were to be held over eighteen holes. The overall format was changed so that there would be eight foursomes and sixteen singles matches all played over eighteen holes. Despite the changes, the American team won 14½ to 9½ to keep the cup they had won at home in 1959. The 1961 team included three Ryder Cup rookies, Arnold Palmer, Billy Casper, and Gene Littler, who between them had won the three previous U.S. Open championships.

A third day of competition was added in 1963 with additional four-ball matches played. The American team easily demonstrated their superiority, winning by a massive score of 23 to 9. The Americans were so strong in 1965 that they could still afford to leave out a young Jack Nicklaus, who, despite four major championships to his credit, had not completed his PGA apprenticeship period. Indeed, Nicklaus was also left out in 1967 as he did not have enough time after his apprenticeship was over to earn enough points to qualify, though he was the world's best golfer and held seven major titles. The exclusion of Nicklaus did not seem to hurt the Americans as they won convincingly at home again by 23½ to 8½.

Transforming the Ryder Cup into a Pan-European versus U.S. Event

With rare exceptions, such as the first tied match in 1969, American dominance meant that the Ryder Cup risked losing interest, particularly among American golfers and fans. The U.S. team dominated the 1970s, winning each event comfortably. In an effort to rekindle interest and balance in the competition, Jack Nicklaus championed the inclusion of European players into the event for 1979. He recounts in his autobiography: "By the time of the 1977 contest at Royal Lytham . . . it had become clear to me that the imbalance inherent in pitting a nation that then possessed about fifteen million golfers against two countries, Britain and Ireland, with barely a million between them was turning the match into a non-event, at least as far as the American public was concerned, and also to some extent for its top players."[28]

Though only Spaniards Seve Ballesteros and Antonio Garrido qualified for the 1979 European team, the course was in motion for the future. The United States won 17 to 11 that year and again easily by 18½ to 9½ at Walton Heath in Surrey, England, in 1981, with two Spaniards and Bernard Langer of Germany on the European squad. In 1983, however, things began to change as the United States narrowly held the Ryder Cup with a 14½ to 13½ win at Palm Beach Gardens in Florida. The European team included Ballesteros, Jose Maria Canizares (Spain), and Langer as well as a new cadre of British stars including Nick Faldo, Ian Woosnam, Sandy Lyle, and Sam Torrence, most of whom debuted in 1981 or 1983. More importantly perhaps, Tony Jacklin, a longtime critic of the way in which British and European teams were handled, was named as captain. Jacklin insisted that the team would be run under his terms and in a professional manner.[29] With the match tied 8–8 going into the final day, Nicklaus exhorted his players not to make him the first U.S. captain to lose the Ryder Cup on U.S. soil! The players responded, though it took a last-match victory by Tom Watson over Bernard Gallagher to secure the victory.[30] Still, the performance of the European team was the best to that time in the United States and bode well for the future.

The 1985 match at the Belfry in England brought the Ryder Cup to Europe for the first time since 1957, which was the only time the British and Irish team had won since the first four Ryder Cups were split between 1927 and 1933. The more experienced European team won by 16½ to

11½, again captained by Tony Jacklin. While many fancied Europe's chances, most still thought the United States had enough muscle to win. The evenness of the competition was ensured when the Europeans won in 1987 for the first time ever in the United States at Jack Nicklaus's own course at Muirfield Village in Ohio. Nicklaus captained the U.S. team and Jacklin once again led the Europeans behind the scenes while Seve Ballesteros won four points from his five matches to lead on the course, including the victory over Curtis Strange in the singles that won the Ryder Cup for Europe. Thus, in a stunning upset, the European team won 15–13 to keep the cup. For the first time, a major American television network, ABC, televised the event live over the three days of action.[31] With a dramatic 14–14 tie, where eight of the twelve singles matches reached the final green, in 1989, again at the Belfry, the Europeans under Jacklin retained the Ryder Cup for a third consecutive time, thus setting the stage for a major American effort in 1991 to reclaim the cup.

The 1991 Ryder Cup provided perhaps the greatest drama in American golf history, at least since Ouimet's 1913 victory over Varden and Ray. The match at Kiawah Island in South Carolina entered the final day all square at 8–8 as the singles loomed. The United States traditionally has been stronger in singles, so hopes were high for an American victory. Prior to play, Steve Pate, who was injured, was unable to compete and ½ point was given to each side, reducing the number of singles matches on the final day by one. As millions watched on television, the day began with a dramatic rematch between Nick Faldo and Raymond Floyd, who had battled through a playoff in the 1990 Masters. Again Faldo came out ahead; and with David Feherty already besting Payne Stewart in the second match, Europe had the start it needed to have a chance, leading 10½ to 8½. Americans feared the worst when, amazingly, Mark Calchavecchia lost the last four holes to turn a certain victory into a tie with Colin Montgomerie. Now it was 11–9 to Europe. Corey Pavin scored the first American victory of the day as chants of "USA, USA" roared from the crowd. Soon after, Paul Azinger held off Jose Maria Olazabal to again level the score with six matches still in progress. Ballesteros, again proving a master of team competition with 4½ out of a possible 5 points, won his match over Wayne Levi. Matters were again even as Chip Beck upset Europe's top-ranked player, Ian Woosnam. It was all square with only four matches to complete. Then Paul Broadhurst returned the favor, upsetting Mark O'Meara and leaving Europe 1 point away from retaining the Ryder

Cup, 13–12, with only three matches to complete. With Fred Couples taking out Sam Torrence, though, scores were again level at 13–13 with only the Lanny Wadkins versus Mark James match and Hale Irwin against Bernard Langer left to complete. Wadkins took the United States within ½ point of victory, finishing off James 3 and 2, and a U.S. lead of 14–13. It was all down to the final match between two famous champions. Irwin played well and took a one-up lead to the seventeenth tee. This meant that Langer needed to win both holes for Europe to retain the cup. The seventeenth hole was as dramatic as any hole ever was with Langer holing a vital four footer to take the match to the final hole all square. Left with a six-foot putt to win the match and retain the cup for Europe, Langer, who had holed courageous putts on the fifteenth, sixteenth, and seventeenth holes, just missed, giving the United States the most dramatic win in the history of the Ryder Cup. Peter Allis, anchor of the BBC's coverage, put it best: "I've been in golf all my life, and my father before me, but I think this will stay in my memory: The sadness of Langer's putt, on the final hole, having played so well. The mistakes of Calcavecchia, the braveness of the players. . . . It really has been an incredible event."[32]

The return match in 1993 at the Belfry also went to the final hole on the final match as Davis Love III held off Constantino Rocca for a 15–13 U.S. victory. As eight-time major championship winner Tom Watson held the Ryder Cup aloft for the American team, he stated, "This is the finest experience I have had in the game of golf."[33]

After the dramatic American victories of 1991 and 1993, it was now clear that the Ryder Cup had become the most significant event in a sport usually dedicated to individual achievement. That this happened at a time between the last professional major victory by Jack Nicklaus in 1986 and the first by Tiger Woods in 1997, thus falling at a time when there was for the first time since the 1910s no dominant American golfer on the world stage, only further heightened the position of the Ryder Cup in American and European imaginations. Indeed, for the first twelve years of global golf rankings, which began in 1986, no American finished the year at number one while Greg Norman, Nick Faldo, Ian Woosnam, Seve Ballesteros, and Nick Price, three of the five members of the European Ryder Cup team, each topped the list at least once. The 1991 U.S. victory was perhaps made sweeter since the four top-ranked golfers in the world were all on the European team (Woosnam, Faldo, Olazabal, and Ballesteros), while Bernhard Langer was ranked seventh. The United

States repeated its 1991 win in 1993 with a close and hard fought 15–13 victory at the Belfrey.

With the momentum apparently shifting slightly back toward the United States, the 1995 host at Oak Hill, questions were raised as to whether the temporary period of European success was over. With the United States heading into the final day with an unusual lead of 9–7, a third successive victory appeared likely. As the closing singles matches came in, Nick Faldo took Europe within a point of victory, 13½ to 12½ with two matches remaining on the course. Philip Walton defeated Jay Haas to secure a European victory in a fashion nearly as dramatic as the U.S. win in 1991, squeaking it out by 14½ to 13½. In 1997 the Ryder Cup was held on the continent of Europe for the first time at Seve Ballesteros's home course of Valderrama. Again Europe won in dramatic fashion that could not have been dreamt up by a Hollywood scriptwriter. With a Rockyesque name, Constantine Rocca of Italy upset the heavily favored Tiger Woods 4 and 2. As Dan Jenkins put it in *Golf Digest,* "Tiger wasn't alone in his frustration. Other . . . stars like Lehman, Couples, and Mickelson also took lumps from guys with v's and z's in their names, guys whose names end in vowels, guys who sound like waiters. A Dane, for God's sake! Bjorn. Guy with a j wandering around in his name."[34] While Jenkins was asleep or focused narrowly on U.S. golfers and the U.S. tour, the game of golf rapidly globalized. Many of Europe's top players and much of its newly emerging talent came from "new" golfing territory such as Denmark and Sweden. As recently as 1981, a German and a Spaniard or two was exotic enough; but by the mid-1990s, the European team looked more like a truly representative team and not just the old British and Irish team with a sprinkling of assistance from the likes of Ballesteros, Langer, and Olazabal. Again, it all came down to the last few closely fought matches. Bernhard Langer, with great poetic justice, secured the point that ensured Europe would retain the Ryder Cup with a 14–11 lead. Two additional losses, though, meant that the score was 14–13 as the final match headed for a dramatic conclusion. Europe's leading player, Colin Montgomerie, the only European in the singles matches who outranked his American opponent in the World Golf Rankings, fought back twice to gain the ½point Europe needed to secure another 14½ to 13½ win, conceding Scott Hoch's twelve-foot par putt at the last hole in sporting fashion.[35] Though they came up short, the Americans nearly pulled off an amazing comeback as they won 8 out of a possible 12 points in the singles. Unfortunately for the United States, Europe continued its tradition of building leads during the first two days of four-ball and four-somes competitions. Another telling fact was that between 1987 and 1997, 114 matches had gone as far as the seventeenth hole, but the United States only won forty of those matches, thus making Europe the better clutch team. The Ryder Cup had, in one decade, become one of the closest fought and dramatic events on the global sporting calendar in no small part due to the grit and determination of the European team. From 1987 through the 1999 Ryder Cup neither team had won by more than 15–13, and the total points for all of these cups combined was 97½ points for the United States and 97½ points for Europe.[36] It appeared that Jack Nicklaus was right in predicting that including all of Europe would make the Ryder Cup the most exciting event in all of professional golf. This was certainly a far cry from the U.S. dominance of the event between World War II and the early 1980s.

Shifting the Balance to Europe?

With losses in 1995 and 1997, the United States hosted the 1999 Ryder Cup in Boston, symbolic in American history for its historic role in resisting foreign, particularly British, dominance. The American team was one of the strongest ever fielded, at least on paper. Tiger Woods, fresh off his dramatic PGA win over a young Sergio Garcia, led the team along with world number two David Duval, still near the height of his success. They were supported by several major championship winners, including Payne Stewart, Mark O'Meara, Justin Leonard, and Tom Lehman. Other players, including future major champions and multiple tournament winners Phil Mickelson, Jim Furyk, and Davis Love III, were also part of the team. By contrast, the European team fielded only four members of their 1997 win-ning team and seven Ryder Cup rookies. The U.S. team had ten of the top twenty players in the world, while the Europeans only had four. Despite this disparity, the European team was led by two gritty and highly com-petitive veterans in Jose Maria Olazabal (14-8-3 prior to 1999) and Montgomerie. The Europeans also fielded several up-and-coming stars such as Padraig Harrington, Lee Westwood, and Darren Clarke. However, team captain Mark James left several veterans on the sidelines, including Faldo, Langer, Woosnam, and Sam Torrance. Ballesteros had tried to qualify for the team but fell far short and knew his best playing days were now behind him. Thus, the European team appeared to be one in transition while the American team was as formidable a group as any Ryder Cup team in history and certainly since Nicklaus and Watson led the 1981 team.[37] Despite their apparent handicap, the Europeans fought valiantly only to go down to a miraculous putt by Leonard on the seventeenth hole of his match with Olazabal, which enabled him to halve the match, giving the United States a 14½ to 13½ win. Leonard's celebration was a bit premature and, though not a surprising reaction, a bit unsporting as Olazabal had a twenty-five-foot putt to halve the hole. Had he made that putt and gone on to win the eighteenth (which, in fact, he did), then the result would have been 14–14, allowing the Europeans to retain the Ryder Cup.[38] Even some of the American media condemned the actions of the U.S. team as many of them ran across the line of Olazabal's putt as they rushed to embrace Leonard on the green. The European players were outraged: "The Americans will look back often on the moment. And the Europeans will not forget it either, all of them because of the defeat and some for the Americans' reaction." European player Sam Torrance stated, "It's about the most disgusting thing I've ever seen. This is not sour grapes. . . . Tom Lehman calls himself a man of God. His behavior today has been disgusting."[39]

One key difference in the new breed of American players and their European counterparts appeared in the lead up to the Ryder Cup, however. Tiger Woods had referred to the cup as a mere "exhibition," which was echoed more forcefully by David Duval in the lead up to the match. Officials took it very seriously, however. With the American team trailing 10–6 heading into the singles matches on the final day, then Texas governor George W. Bush, whose great-grandfather had donated the trophy for the amateur Walker Cup competition between the United States and Britain and Ireland when he was president of the USGA in 1920, was summoned to talk to the players. Bush inspired the players by reading from the memoirs of a soldier who was killed at the Alamo.[40]

Explaining European Success

It is hard to draw a single conclusion as to why the European team appears to overachieve and its fans take perhaps more interest in the results. First, this is the one time that a pan-European team is produced to challenge the United States; and thus the Ryder Cup provides a locus for European identity from Spain to Sweden and from Ireland to Italy, where Ryder Cup golfers have originated and where golf is now widely played. Unlike other sports, where players such as Christian Ronaldo compete for Manchester United in England but for Portugal in the European and World championships, in golf Jose Maria Olazabal can be Spanish and heralded in England for his exploits on behalf of Europe. Second, this is the only competition of its type for the European team. With the exception of 2001, since 1994 the Ryder Cup and Presidents Cup have been held in alternate years.[41] The Presidents Cup pits the United States against a Rest of the World team, excluding Europe, so that the top American golfers compete every year while the European team has two years between events. It also could be argued, however, that this also focuses the American team more clearly on the team competition format given that they compete against the likes of Ernie Els, Vijay Singh, Adam Scott, Retief Goosen, and Mike Weir on the off year. Success in the Presidents Cup has not translated into better performances against the European team, however. Indeed, the United States won five of the seven Presidents Cups held between 1994 and 2007, while the Rest of the World won only in 1998. The American team won the Presidents Cup handily in 2005 and 2007, but it was thrashed by the Europeans in 2004 and 2006 in the Ryder Cup.

Furthermore, European success cannot be explained based on a loaded team as could be done when Ballesteros, Faldo, Langer, Woosnam, and Olazabal were mainstays of the team between 1985 and 1995. Before Padraig Harrington's win in the 2007 Open Championship, the last European to win a major championship was Paul Lawrie in 1999, and before that Jose Maria Olazabal's victory in the 1994 Masters. In the time since Olazabal's win American players have won seventeen majors while Tiger Woods and Phil Mickelson have easily outranked Europe's top golfer. Individual dominance does not necessarily translate into Ryder Cup success. As of 2008 Woods had an all-time record of 10 wins, 13 losses, and 2 halves, while Mickelson had won 10, lost 14, and halved 6 and Jim Furyk's record was 8 wins, 13 losses, and 3 matches halved.[42]

Another possible explanation may lie in the differing spectating cultures of the United States and Europe, particularly as those have infiltrated golf since the mid 1980s. The Ryder Cup has moved from a garden tea party atmosphere to a raucous affair more in line with an American football game for U.S. fans and a soccer match for the Europeans, replete with boisterous singing and chanting by the European faithful known most recently as Faldo's Barmy Army. "Barmy Army" is a term normally attached to English fans who exuberantly support the English national soccer and cricket teams. Related to this is the tendency of non-Americans to unite as much *against* the United States as for their own team, a fact caused by American global preeminence post–World War II. Many Europeans have a love-hate relationship with the United States and Americans. Similar problems have been faced by the American Davis Cup team in tennis, especially if they draw a match against a Central or South American nation, where U.S. interference was prevalent throughout the twentieth century. Thus, it only takes a small incident such as the premature celebration surrounding Leonard's putt in 1999, or the post–Gulf War camouflage hats of 1991, to fan the flames of a European jingoism that in this case is focused squarely *against* the United States. American fans, by contrast, have no particular reason to unite in a hatred of Europe, particularly when the majority of Americans are of European descent. Even when there have been moments of heated drama, such as the backlash against France at the beginning of the wars in Iraq and Afghanistan, another European country, such as the United Kingdom, sided with the United States. While a German American could easily cheer on the German soccer team against Italy (or even quietly against the United States), a European team is more amorphous and Europeans, particularly western and northern Europeans who have played in the Ryder Cup, are generally from the more "friendly" nations.

American players have admitted to struggling against the changed nature of spectating at Ryder Cups, particularly when they are held in Europe. Indeed, Lee Trevino remarked that he would not play in present-day Ryder Cups as the climate has changed from when he participated in the 1970s. Trevino remarked in 2001, "I remember when the Ryder Cup was friendly. We ate dinner with the players from the opposite team. The wives went shopping together. The fans gave me just as much applause when I lost as when I won. I don't like what I see now. It's almost like a contest of who can treat the other side the worst."[43] Curtis Strange marked the change as occurring at the Belfry: "1985 was also the first time I'd ever played in front of fans that weren't rooting for you real hard. Know what I'm saying? They were rooting like hell for their own team and didn't give a rat's ass about you. So that was an eye-opener too. I was fine with it, but it was troubling to some of the players on the team."[44] Peter Jacobson, whose views were echoed by his U.S. teammates, complained: "All the cheering when we missed shots. I've never known anything like it before, especially from British crowds. You expect so much more from them."[45] Justin Leonard echoed Jacobson in 1999, "It's an experience you really can't prepare for, playing your first Ryder Cup on foreign soil. It can be a little bit intimidating, especially when you step on the first tee Friday, hit a poor shot, and you hear people cheering. That's something you don't hear too much on a golf course."[46] Tiger Woods, keenly aware of the environment in Europe, took the U.S. rookies out prior to the 2006 match. In an interview with the British press prior to the event he remarked that the players would never face an environment in golf such as they were about to see (and hear) in Ireland. Woods stated:

> Well, they won't have played in front of fans like that, and an atmosphere that way. It's different playing in the Ryder Cup versus a regular tour event. It's bipartisan versus the fans cheering for 156 different other individuals. So you have basically one or the other. It's very different. All these guys love college football, pro football and basketball so obviously they understand the atmosphere being that way, they just have never played in it before. But as I have always said, last time I checked, lowest score still wins.[47]

In contrast to U.S. team concerns over boisterous crowds, the European players seem to draw energy from them, especially on their home turf. In 2001, Jesper Parnavik, Swedish veteran of the 1997 and 1999 Ryder Cups stated: "I want the crowds to be as rowdy as they can. I like the chaos, the energy that comes with the Ryder Cup. But there's a very small line between doing that and stepping over the line. It should be right on top of that line."[48] Having said that, there are times when the American team and fans were viewed as taking things too far, particularly in 1991 and 1999, along with the continuous heckling of European players by American fans at Brookline.[49] The European successes in the Ryder Cup awakened the American audience to the need for strong support. The crowd in 1999 at the Country Club in Brookline near Boston was as loud a force as had ever been heard on an American golf course. Alan Campbell in the *Sunday Herald* called that crowd "a hostile and jingoistic crowd prepared to stop at nothing to ensure a home victory."[50] However, it is the European fans

who are the more boisterous, a far cry from the early days of British gentlemanly gentility. In 2008, the European spectating culture of innovative
and impromptu singing and chanting throughout a sports event, creating
a carnivalesque atmosphere, was prevalent amid the more predictable,
though thunderous, "U-S-A, U-S-A" that erupted from the American fans.
The European fans responded tauntingly by singing, "You only chant
when you are winning."[51] Though surely sung in jest, there is a large element of truth in the statement. American fans often go very quiet when
things are turned against them, while British fans are used to poking fun
at themselves and the opposition when they are up or down. This attitude
translates to the players, who feel the passion, but also feel under less pressure to win. Additionally, it may be as simple as the Europeans having a
better ability to understand the team approach and how to lift themselves
up as a group, which goes hand in hand with their supporters, who have
fun in victory or defeat and provide the European team with a small,
though not insignificant, advantage every time the two teams tee it up.

Conclusion

The Ryder Cup has come a long way from the more genteel days of the
1920s to the heated rivalry of the 1990s and 2000s. Intended as a competition to foster friendly interaction and fellowship between the two
main golf-playing nations of the world, the competition has expanded
and now is followed globally via television and the Internet. The Ryder
Cup now receives more attention than golf's major championships.
Other than the Olympic Games, the American public does not take
many international sporting competitions too seriously, ignoring the fortunes of American teams. Rather, the focus tends to be on domestic
competitions. In Europe, the Ryder Cup has taken on a unique dimension. Europeans are used to international competitions. The best soccer
teams play in the European Champions League; national teams compete
in the World Cup, the Union of European Football Associations (UEFA)
Championships, and qualifiers for each virtually every year. In the Ryder
Cup, however, a European-wide audience can unite behind a single
team. While there have been moments of American jingoism during
the Ryder Cups held on U.S. soil, the cup has come to mean more to
Europeans and, arguably, to the European players. Take the examples

of Colin Montgomerie, European Order of Merit winner from 1993 to 1999 and again in 2005; Tiger Woods, the world's dominant player since 1997; and Phil Mickelson, world number two for much of that period. Montgomerie, five-time runner-up in major championships but never a winner, has an amazing Ryder Cup record of 20-9-7, and through 2006 had never lost a singles match in eight Ryder Cup appearances. By contrast, Woods, Mickelson, and Furyk, the top American players between 1996 and 2008, barely won 40 percent of their matches between them, hardly inspiring performances in comparison with their seventeen major championships to Montgomerie's zero. For Montgomerie and his European colleagues, the Ryder Cup means as much or more than a major championship victory. Perhaps that is why the 2008 U.S. team performed better than any other for at least twenty years, winning by 16½ points to 11½. Woods was out due to injury; and a group that one journalist labeled a "Redneck, white and blue squad," with a host of younger players and Ryder Cup newcomers, held off a spirited European challenge at home at Valhalla in Louisville, Kentucky. The United States dominated the singles matches 7½ to 4½, despite Phil Mickelson continuing to under-perform in losing his singles match.[52]

The 2004 and 2006 Ryder Cups demonstrated that the Europeans had mastered the art of playing as a team much more consistently than the Americans even though they don't represent their own countries in the competition. The U.S. team appears to respond best at home when their backs are against the wall, as they did in 1999 and 2008; however, there appears to be a lack of consistency in the intensity that top American players bring to the competition. Having said all of this, we must remember that golf is a fickle game, and on a given day any top-ranking player may beat another. Indeed, the difference in the 2008 Ryder Cup was still slim enough that if Sergio Garcia had attained his usual winning percentage, the result would have been different (Garcia failed to win a point in 2008). The Ryder Cup has shown that, while Tiger Woods may be the best individual player the golfing world has ever seen, in team competition he is human after all, at least when judged one day at a time.

American Hayes Jones (*left*) eclipses Lee Calhoun at the finish of the 110-meter hurdles at the 1959 meet in Philadelphia. Anatoly Mikhailov and Nikolai Berezutsky finished third and fourth, respectively. *Courtesy of National Archives.*

fifteen
The Match of the Century
The U.S.-USSR Rivalry in Sports

CHRIS ELZEY

On July 27, 1958, the day the Soviet Union was to compete against the United States in the very first head-to-head track meet between the two nations in Moscow, an article about the two-day competition was published in the Soviet newspaper *Trud*. "Who Will Win?" the headline asked. Surprisingly, the article's author, Yuri Vanyat, praised the American team and the capitalist nation's decades-long domination of the sport. Yet victory for the visitors was no sure thing. Acknowledging that "the men's team of the guests is stronger," Vanyat believed that the meet "[would] be determined by" the country whose women athletes performed the best. That edge, claimed Vanyat, rested with the Soviets. "The team of the USSR could win this match," but only if the Soviet women lived up to their billing, he wrote.[1]

Five and a half weeks earlier an American sportswriter had offered his take on the meet. Previewing the United States national track championships, from which a team of more than forty men was to be selected for the meet in Moscow, Arthur Daley of the *New York Times* began his column by describing the unusually high level of excitement surrounding the trials. Evidently, American athletes wanted to do well in the nationals so they could compete against the Soviets and beat them. In his piece, Daley explained that the Moscow meet would be divided into two different competitions, one for the men and one for the women. He predicted the Americans would win the men's meet, and the Soviets the women's. "Keeping ahead of the Russians," he observed, "is just as much of an unrelenting man-size job in sports as it is in everything else." But differences in format—Was the meet one or two competitions? Were men's scores and women's scores to be combined or kept separate?—

would throw the outcome of the meet into a state of confusion. The Cold War rivalry in sports was about to heat up.[2]

The 1958 American-Soviet track meet, dubbed the "Match of the Century" by the Soviet press, was a significant moment in the sporting relationship between the two countries. Never before had the superpowers directly squared off in a sport that was so popular on both sides of the Iron Curtain. Track and field was the great common denominator of two great athletic traditions, and American and Soviet sports fans loved it. Its popularity ensured that both nations would recognize the Match of the Century for what it was: a clash of sporting titans in which neither side held an inherent advantage.[3]

In addition, the meet featured all of the contentiousness that would characterize future Soviet-American sporting events. There were controversies, protests, accusations, sniping and inflammatory language. Most of the hostility surrounding the 1958 meet drew upon the mutual suspicion and distrust created by the Cold War, and American and Soviet fans alike reacted according to the divergent worldviews that were formed during the turbulent years of the immediate post–World War II era.

As would be the case whenever the two superpowers competed in athletic events, the 1958 track meet transcended sports. What mattered most was defeating one's ideological foe. Looking back upon the 1952 Olympic Games in Helsinki, the first Olympic Games in which the Soviet Union competed, two-time gold medal winner Bob Mathias said, "There were many more pressures on American athletes because of the Russians than in 1948. They were in a sense the real enemy. You just loved to beat 'em. You just had to beat 'em. It wasn't like beating some guys from a friendly country like Australia. This feeling was strong down through the whole team, even members in sports where the Russians didn't excel."[4]

By gaining the upper hand in sports competitions, both the United States and the Soviet Union attempted to prove the advantages of their economic and social systems. They were not just games and contests pitting the United States against the Soviet Union. They were capitalism against communism, West against East, us against them. The athletic rivalry that developed would become one of the fiercest the sports world ever witnessed. The Match of the Century reflected the intensity of the rivalry and intensified it.

The Early Years of the U.S.-USSR Rivalry in Sports

The roots of the U.S.-USSR sports rivalry extend back to the late 1940s. At the very moment political discord was dividing Western Europe from Eastern Europe the Soviet Union altered its isolationist athletic policy and began entering teams in international competitions. The timing of this shift was no coincidence. Prior to the onset of the Cold War, international sport had failed to warrant even an afterthought from Communist Party leaders. It was judged to be corrupt, elitist, and antithetical to the teachings of Marxism. But after World War II, the Kremlin increasingly recognized sports' propaganda potential, especially after Soviet athletes began returning home with championships. A Soviet authority on sport in late 1949 boasted, "The increasing number of successes achieved by Soviet athletes . . . is a victory for the Soviet form of society and the socialist sports system; it provides irrefutable proof of the superiority of socialist culture over the moribund culture of capitalist states."[5]

Declaring such pronouncements was one thing, backing them up another. But from the start the Soviets displayed remarkable proficiency in most competitions they entered. In 1947, for instance, they won the European title in men's basketball. Two years later they claimed the world title in men's volleyball. The next year a combined women's and men's track team surprised many by taking the European championships in Brussels. And in 1954 the Soviet Union captured the world hockey championship, after having only played the winter sport seriously for a handful of years.[6]

The first post–World War II competition pitting Americans versus Soviets occurred in chess. Compared to later events, this first match, played in 1945 with moves reported over the radio (the Soviets won easily, 15½ to 4½), exhibited little hostility (proceeds went to Russian War Relief). The same was true the following year when an American team traveled to Moscow (again the Americans lost, but not as badly, 12½ to 7½). In these early years the win-at-all-costs attitude had yet to take hold, mostly because relations between the United States and the Soviet Union were relatively cordial. But by the early 1950s, with the souring of American-Soviet relations, chess became like other sports, an East-West proving ground. After the Soviet Union won the 1950 women's world championship in chess, the *Moscow Bolshevik,* a Soviet paper, cast the victory in a chauvinistic light. "Thanks to the party, the government and the beloved leader of the people, [Joseph] Stalin," announced the *Bolshevik,* "the Soviet chess players by their deeds added luster to our beloved country."[7]

Burnishing the country's international image was part of the master plan put in motion by postwar Soviet leaders, and sports became a valuable tool in achieving this aim. Calls for new athletic world marks immediately rang forth. In an address fittingly given on Physical Cultural Day in 1947, Nicolai Romanov, the Soviets' chief sports administrator, pronounced, "Our goal is to unceasingly develop physical culture and sport. It is a mass, popular movement with the goal of establishing the capacity of Soviet athletes to struggle for national and world records for the glory of our homeland." A Communist Party pronouncement the next year similarly urged sports associations and affiliates in every Soviet republic "to raise the level of skill, so that Soviet sportsmen might win world supremacy in the major sports in the immediate future."[8]

To ensure such athletic achievement, Soviet leaders upped the government's involvement in sports. Furthermore, financial support for athletic pursuits came directly from the Kremlin's coffers. As early as October 1945, Soviet authorities had begun offering "monetary prizes" of up to twenty-five thousand rubles to individuals "for outstanding sports results." The offer was smartly rescinded two years later when the Soviet Union started to enter teams in international amateur events. Nevertheless, the Kremlin quietly maintained the practice of supporting top-notch athletes with governmental funds and other perks, much to the dismay of the United States. To Americans, the Soviet system smacked of professionalism. In contrast, American amateur athletes received no government funds, and the nation's top amateur sports organization, the Amateur Athletic Union (AAU), operated on a comparatively shoestring budget financed by private donors.[9]

The issue of professionalism in amateur athletics brought the sports rivalry to a boiling point. United States authorities felt that the Soviet sports system placed American athletes at a disadvantage, a claim Soviet officials brushed off by denying that professional sports existed in their country. The dispute flared after the Soviets announced they would take part in the 1952 Olympic Games in Helsinki—their first Olympic Games. In the United States pleas went out far and wide asking citizens to send money to the cash-strapped United States Olympic Committee (USOC).

Bob Hope and Bing Crosby entertained as hosts of a special USOC telethon. Making his pitch, the *New York Times'* Arthur Daley wrote, "The Communist propaganda machine must be silenced [in Helsinki] so that there can't be even one distorted bleat out of it in regard to the Olympics. In sports the Red brothers have reached the put-up-or-shut-up stage. Let's shut them up. Let's support the United States Olympic team." Indiana senator Homer Capehart was so moved by Daley's piece that he had it included in the *Congressional Record.*[10]

Yet even before the start of the Helsinki Games, serious strains in the U.S.-USSR sporting relationship were being felt. The Soviets' un-Olympic attitude was partly to blame. For one, the Kremlin had prohibited the Olympic torch relay from passing through parts of its Baltic republics, forcing Helsinki organizers to redirect the relay a great distance. Then, instead of housing their delegation in the Olympic Village, the Soviets and their Eastern European counterparts created a separate Socialist camp on the outskirts of Helsinki, better known to Westerners as the "Little Iron Curtain." The Soviets eventually opened up their camp, even holding elaborate receptions for American team members. That display of goodwill later prompted two writers for *Literaturnaya Gazeta* to imply that the real Iron Curtain compound had been the regular Olympic Village, since American authorities had failed to host even a single gathering for foreign teams. To many, the two Olympic camps symbolized the two ideological camps of the Cold War.[11]

The competition in Helsinki was spirited, and for their first ever Olympic Games, the Soviets performed surprisingly well—so well, in fact, that for virtually the entire span of the games they were able to maintain a sizeable lead over the United States in unofficial points. As could be expected, the Soviet press happily circulated the news, printing the number of Soviet and American medals and overall point totals. Authorities at the Soviets' Olympic camp even raised an enormous scoreboard that kept track of American and Soviet tallies.[12]

Since the Soviet Union held such a large lead for most of the competition, the different scoring systems employed by the two superpowers never became much of an issue. But as the Americans mounted a comeback toward the tail end of the sixteen-day competitions, the way in which each country kept score became almost as important as counting the number of atomic bombs in each other's nuclear arsenal. Both formats awarded the same number of points for second through sixth place—five, four, three, two and one, respectively. However, the systems differed in the number of points given for first place. The Soviets, adhering to the European system, awarded seven points. The Americans, following a format used in the United States, awarded ten. That small three-point differential would spark one of the first great controversies in the U.S.-USSR sports rivalry.[13]

Still, as the Helsinki Olympics drew to a close, the Soviets had a firm grip on the lead; victory appeared to be theirs. But on the penultimate day of the games, American victories in boxing, swimming, and basketball catapulted the United States in front, 610–553½, as Americans calculated it. Then, on the final day a bronze medal in equestrian gave the United States four more points. The Americans had won, 614–553½. Yet Soviet calculations showed no corresponding American victory. In fact, the system would show no victory for the Soviets either. What it would come to show was a result only a few could have imagined: a draw, 494–494. But nobody knew that yet because the Soviets had not announced it.

Incredibly, the following day Soviet papers reported that the Soviet Union had won the rivalry. Moscow radio repeated the news. *Izvestia* informed readers that a Finnish newspaper had also crowned the Soviets as the Olympic winners. *Sovetski Sport* went a step further, attributing the triumph to the core principle of the communist nation. "The victory of the Soviet sportsmen in the Olympic Games," the sports newspaper observed in a front-page article, "is an outstanding demonstration of our great movement ahead, of the development of our national culture and the flourishing of our talents, which is impossible in any capitalistic country."[14]

Americans were shocked. Had not the United States won? Had not the score placed the United States ahead? What really rankled Americans was the Soviets' self-righteous attitude that insisted: We won. Victory was ours. Our point system said so. But Americans athletes, officials, and fans had their doubts.[15]

To Nicolai Romanov tumbled the unenviable task of explaining why the Soviets had erroneously declared victory. In an interview with Soviet journalists, the Soviet Olympic chief offered only a short, terse sentence as explanation: "The press reported earlier that U.S. athletes scored 490 points but revised figures now show that they also scored 494." Apparently, the Americans' final four points had not been counted—thus, the tie. Romanov then blamed biased refereeing against Soviet athletes, particularly in boxing, for undermining the Soviet Union's chances. Worse, there had been Olympic arbiters who had "credited some American athletes with undeserved victories, especially toward the end of the competitions." All of it added up to one thing: "There can be no doubt," Romanov said, "that if the judging had been correct . . . the athletes of the Soviet Union and certain other countries would have won considerably more prizes." To Romanov, the Soviets had not lost so much as they had had victory snatched from them.[16]

But the Olympics were never meant to be an in-your-face competition placing one country versus another. Hence, no authorized Olympic point-scoring system existed. To have one would only invite country-to-country comparisons, thus intensifying nationalistic fervor. Ever one to keep the Olympic Games pure, International Olympic Committee (IOC) president Avery Brundage went out of his way to denounce all formats of scoring. Even so, his harsh words carried little influence with American and Soviet fans. They kept and followed Olympic tallies religiously.[17]

Despite Brundage's voluble preachments, the rancor engendered by the 1952 scoring dispute would find various outlets at the next Olympic Games in Melbourne, Australia. The U.S.-USSR sports rivalry was about to enter a more tempestuous phase.

The Rivalry Intensifies:
The 1956 Melbourne Olympic Games

The Soviets' surprising achievements in 1952 caused great consternation both in United States sports circles and in the halls of Congress, particularly during the months preceding the 1956 Olympic Games. How had the Soviets achieved such rapid success? What were their training methods? And most important: What could the United States do to deflect the propaganda that was certain to result from other Soviet athletic feats? All of these questions derived from the same essential concern: Soviet professionalism in sport disadvantaged American amateurs. With determination and spirited commentary, U.S. political and sports authorities attacked the Soviet athletic system.[18]

Wielding the largest cudgel was Senator John Butler of Maryland.

To be sure, the Maryland senator was just one of many Soviet bashers. But Butler was sui generis. He took the practice of flaying the Soviets to new heights. He gave impassioned speeches on the issue of Soviet professionalism. He discussed the matter on the floor of the Senate. In short, he was a tireless foot soldier in the war against the Soviet national sports program.

In an April address to a local Knights of Columbus group, Butler led a frontal assault. Drawing upon magazine and newspaper articles critical of the Soviet system, and using venomous language, he denounced the Soviets' program and railed against the athletes who benefited from its services. As he saw it, Soviet athletes were "athletic Frankenstein monsters." They were "animated beasts of propaganda." They were "unprincipled disciples of the devil." They were "just one more devilish weapon in the Communist cold-war arsenal to be used in their relentless drive for superiority in every phase of human existence." Butler's sharp tongue drew comment. Two days after the enlivened address, *Washington Post* sports columnist Shirley Povich wrote that the Maryland senator not only had "[made] a strong bid for the Olympic name-calling title," but had "broke[n] at least a couple of local records for purple descriptives."[19]

Purple descriptives aside, the senator had floated a radical suggestion during his Knights of Columbus speech. In language that was classic Butler, he said that since the Soviets' national sports program stood in clear infringement of Olympic amateur codes, Americans "should do everything humanly possible to ban Russia and her barbaric goon squads from participation in the 1956 summer Olympics at Melbourne, Australia." Roughly six weeks after his Maryland address, Butler introduced a congressional resolution calling on all U.S. amateur sports bodies to support an Olympic ban of the Soviet Union.[20]

The Soviets were unmoved. Their cool demeanor resulted in part from knowing that IOC president Avery Brundage considered their sports program to be in line with amateur sports standards. Even so, Soviet sports officials often took an active role in defending their program. One way was to issue counteraccusations, frequently contending that the American practice of awarding athletic scholarships was not unlike the professional model of compensating athletes. Another way was to deny all charges of professionalism. One Soviet commentator in the mid-1960s wrote, "We have amateur sportsmen and no professionals as understood in the West . . . because professional sports is imbued with a spirit of profit and corruption, which is alien to socialist society." Still another way was to accuse the United States of political skullduggery. After the American Brundage rebuked Polish officials in 1953 for holding a four-month-long training camp for boxers, *Sovetski Sport* dismissed the reprimand as being nothing more than a devious scheme "of American imperialism and intelligence organs of the United States to help . . . undermine the bases of European national sovereignty."[21]

Americans were having none of it. There was just too much evidence to the contrary, much of which came from reliable sources—respected journalists, scholars, even an erstwhile Soviet spy. Such mainstream articles as "Reds Hope to Rule Sports Too" and "Red Amateurs Are Pros" presented the damning information. Readers learned that many so-called amateur athletes received bogus jobs, government payments, and expensive automobiles. Most important, Soviet athletes were able to devote much more time to training than their U.S. rivals. In the American court of public opinion, the Soviets were guilty as charged.[22]

All the talk of professionalism in athletics only heightened the anticipation for the 1956 Summer Olympic Games in Melbourne, which ran from late November to early December. As it turned out, the 1956 games proved to be just the reverse of the Olympic competitions held four years earlier. Unlike in Helsinki, in Melbourne it was the Americans who dashed out to a quick lead (in each nation's scoring format nonetheless), and the Soviets were the ones who came storming back. The Soviet Union's brutal repression of the Hungarian insurrection in November and the Suez Canal crisis in late October and early November ensured that the theme of political discord would form a central story line in many Olympic narratives, including the unofficial contest for points between the American and Soviet teams.

For much of the Melbourne Olympic Games the Americans were able to maintain a wide margin over the Soviets, with the United States benefiting from some friendly scheduling. Olympic organizers had placed events favorable to American contestants at the beginning of the competitions, and midway through the games the United States looked to be out of reach. *U.S. News and World Report* even issued a celebratory whoop after American athletes had dusted their Soviet counterparts in the track-and-field segment of the competitions. "Red 'Supermen'

Lose," shouted a headline in the news magazine, the subhead adding, "In Olympics, U.S. Tops Subsidized Russians." To some, it seemed like the United States had already won.[23]

But then the Soviets began amassing points in events that suited them. With six days remaining, the United States held nearly a seventy-five-point advantage, following the American format. Then the race tightened significantly. The next-to-last day of the Olympics, a Thursday, the tide turned in the Soviets' favor. To *Komsomolskaya Pravda,* the day would be known as "the Golden Thursday of Soviet Sport." And it truly was. Competing in such events as wrestling and gymnastics, Soviet athletes earned a dozen gold medals, while U.S. competitors failed to garner even a single one. By the end of Golden Thursday, both nations' scoring formats showed that the Soviets had seized the lead, and two days later the games finished with the Soviets ahead, according to both nations' figures. The Soviet Union was the new Olympic king.[24]

Soviets rejoiced. "Glorious victory for Soviet sport," headlined *Pravda* on page 1. "Soviet team strongest at Olympic Games," enthralled a width-of-the-page *Sovetski Sport* headline. "No country," crowed *Trud,* "ever won with such an overwhelming advantage, with such a record amount of points in the history of the Olympic Games." To Soviet fans, their nation's win was history in the making.[25]

There was more. In newspapers Soviet illustrators depicted the triumphant Olympians with victory wreaths around their neck or standing atop a victory podium. A drawing in *Komsomolskaya Pravda* showed a Soviet athlete breaking a finish tape made of gold medals. Two steps behind was an American runner. For its part, *Sovetski Sport* chose to extol the virtues of the national sports system: "The victory of the Soviet Union at the Olympic Games was the result of the consistent nurturing of the development of physical culture and sport by the Communist Party and the Soviet government, as well as the result of the development of mass sport in our country." The 1956 Olympic Games were clearly a proud moment for the Soviets.[26]

The same could not be said for Americans. Their team had been trounced, and they knew it. In all categories—points, number of gold medals, number of total medals—the Soviets had come out on top. Yet even amid such doom and gloom Americans found reason for solace. For instance, commentators played up the fact that during the games almost three dozen Hungarian athletes, not wanting to return to a

Soviet-controlled Hungary, had contacted a writer from *Sports Illustrated* about obtaining political asylum, which they eventually received. The message was clear: A communistic Soviet Union might have won, but a democratic United States was the country of choice. In addition, journalists noted that many of the Soviets' successes had come in events Americans knew or cared little about, as opposed to U.S. athletes who had controlled the more popular sports. As *Newsweek* put it, "American had won the big events; Russia had won the big prize." Seen in the politically charged context of the times, the United States won some of the major battles but not the war.[27]

The antagonism surrounding the Melbourne Olympic Games lingered. Four days after the Olympics, a contingent of eighteen Soviet officials, coaches, and journalists landed at the Los Angeles international airport. Their intent was to fly to New York and then home. However, in Los Angeles immigration authorities blocked their passage, claiming "security reasons." Left with little choice, the Soviet delegation was forced to fly around the United States and over the Arctic Circle. Two days after the incident, an *Izvestia* headline asked, "Why Was This Done?" Responding, the newspaper blamed State Department officials and their double-dealing shenanigans.[28]

Roughly three and a half months later the athletic antagonism made headlines again. In early April the Soviet newspaper *Literaturnaya Gazeta* accused American intelligence agencies of attempting to distract Soviet athletes with alluring temptresses during the Olympic Games in Melbourne. The Soviet paper contended that the United States' recent decision to halt the limited number of Soviet-American athletic contacts was payback for the ineffectiveness of the seductress stratagem. In reality, U.S. sports officials had been forced by the Eisenhower administration to suspend the contacts because of the Soviet crackdown in Hungary.[29]

As the *Literaturnaya Gazeta* article made clear, staging head-to-head athletic events between the two superpowers would not be easy. Politics always seemed to play a role. But when an agreement was finally reached, a classic battle ensued.

Background to the Match of the Century

During the spring and early summer of 1958, as the Match of the Century drew near, sports fans could not be completely certain that it would even take place. They had good reason. Since 1953, the idea of a dual meet had been discussed, but financial and political exigencies always seemed to intrude, scrapping plans. As far as the Soviets were concerned, the stickiest of points was the United States' 1952 Immigration and Nationality Act, familiarly called the McCarran-Walter Act, so termed for Nevada senator Patrick McCarran and Pennsylvania representative Francis Walter, both of whom sponsored the legislation. A product of an era in which loyalty oaths were demanded of government workers and Senator Joseph McCarthy's communist witch hunt was creating fear and panic among those who were subpoenaed to appear before his Senate subcommittee, the McCarran-Walter Act mandated the fingerprinting of unregistered visitors from communist nations. However, Soviet authorities were not about to comply with a measure they detested, and American officials were equally stubborn in heeding calls to suspend the law. So, year after year prospects for the meet died a death of diplomatic intransigence.[30]

New life was breathed into these prospects with the signing of the American-Soviet Cultural Exchange Agreement in late January 1958, three months after the fingerprinting regulation was eliminated. For the first time American and Soviet scientists, musicians, dancers, artists, students, teachers, doctors, journalists, and athletes could officially travel to each others' country under the auspices of a bilateral program. The exchanges were wildly successful, and citizens on both sides of the Iron Curtain were treated to artistic and musical performances. In 1958 the agreement oversaw the exchange of eighty-two American programs and sixty-eight from the Soviet Union. A new agreement was to be signed every two years.[31]

For sports fans, the cultural exchanges offered something unique: Soviet and American teams in direct competition. There were basketball and hockey games, wrestling and weightlifting matches, even crew races. The track-and-field section of the athletic exchanges, in particular, whetted the appetite of Soviet authorities. They loved the sport. As Soviet sports historian Robert Edelman has noted, Communist Party leaders embraced track and field because it jibed so well with their political philosophy. Edelman suggests that much like a five-year economic plan, the sport could be analyzed and quantified, its results compared. Moreover, party officials appreciated the sport for what it offered militarily. Embodying this sport-military link was the Soviet fitness program, Gotov k Trudu i

Oborone (GTO), or Ready for Labor and Defense. Begun in the early 1930s, GTO promoted physical fitness among all citizens. Badges could be earned based on how fast participants ran or swam, how well they skied, how far they jumped. Also included were activities with a distinct military flavor: the hand grenade toss and rifle marksmanship, among others.[32]

As supportive of track as Communist Party leaders were, the goal of attaining leadership in the sport went largely unmet. During the early to mid-1950s, the United States dominated track and field, especially men's. At the 1952 Olympic Games in Helsinki, American athletes (men and women) won fifteen track-and-field gold medals; the Soviets, just two (both by women). At the Melbourne Olympics in 1956, the United States earned sixteen gold track medals; the Soviet Union, five. By early 1959, the United States held almost a 3:1 advantage in the number of men's world records in international distances (meters as opposed to yards and miles). In track and field the United States ruled.[33]

The American men's team for the Match of the Century—to be held in Moscow—reflected this superiority. The roster included U.S. champs and Olympic gold medalists. No fewer than eight world records were held or shared by American team members. *Track and Field* listed many of them in its coveted top-ten list in the world in various events for 1957 and 1958. Track aficionados were impressed. Writing in the *Pittsburgh Courier,* retired half-miler and two-time Olympic champion Mal Whitfield predicted the United States would win easily. Two weeks before the meet, U.S. assistant track coach Payton Jordan, who would go on to coach the phenomenal U.S. team at the 1968 Olympic Games in Mexico City, rated the squad among the greatest in American track-and-field history.[34]

Aware of the Americans' strength, the Soviets responded by assembling as fine a squad as they could, even altering their national team selection process to resemble that of the United States. Still, they recognized it would take a miracle for the Soviet men to come out ahead. But if the United States were number one in the world, the Soviets were runners-up. Despite their relatively brief experience with the sport, they had developed world-class talent, and their squad for the Moscow meet reflected this point: it too had Olympic medalists and world record holders, only they were fewer in number.[35]

Where the Soviets excelled was in women's track. They were the world's dominant power, particularly in field events. During the 1950s they won multiple Olympic medals, four of which were gold. In 1957 a select team of Soviet women humiliated their British counterparts in a dual meet in London, 73–40. Several of the athletes who distinguished themselves in the Olympics and in London were picked to compete against the Americans. Given the Soviets' experience and past successes, it was widely believed that they would continue what had become routine whenever Soviet women entered international meets: they would win, and win handily.[36]

Facing such odds, the American women were not given much of a chance. They were young (teenagers, mostly), inexperienced, and largely untested in international competition. Whereas the Soviets had a roster filled with world-ranked athletes, the American team had none. But lost in all the prognostications was this: the American women had talent, lots of it, and they had heart. Eight of the women on the team ran for the predominantly black college of Tennessee State, a powerhouse in women's intercollegiate track, and they were not used to losing. Moreover, boosting the Tennessee State students' confidence was the fact that their college coach, Ed Temple, would be coaching the women's team in Moscow.[37]

American team members prepared for the Match of the Century as if they were going to war. All realized the seriousness of their mission. In his autobiography, women's coach Temple recalled the intense mood: "We trained at Montclair State, and we were going [to Moscow] for business." The men's squad trained at West Point, where a boot camp–like atmosphere prevailed. "We do nothing here but eat, sleep and work on the field and track," University of Texas quarter-miler Eddie Southern told a reporter from the *New York Times*. "Everyone is keen and determined to do his best." The U.S. men's coach, George Eastment, a serious man who coached track and lectured in law at Manhattan College in New York, sounded like a four-star general addressing nervous troops before combat. "To win," he declared, "our best men will need to be at their very best, but we will do it."[38]

American sports journalists added to the militaristic overtones. A picture of an American athlete and official in the *Chicago Daily Tribune* two weeks before the meet carried the caption, "They're Ready to Invade Russia Now." Headline writers especially had a field day. The *New York*

Times headlined one piece, "U.S. Girls' Team Drills for Meet in Russia." An article in *Sports Illustrated* was tersely titled, "A Shot at the Russians." A headline in the *Los Angeles Times* on the opening day of the meet read, "Yankee, Soviet Track Forces Collide Today." Interestingly, Soviet commentary was largely devoid of such militaristic comparisons.[39]

Given the political significance of the meet, it is surprising that American and Soviet track officials were able to agree even on a single detail. Negotiations for the United States had been handled by the privately funded Amateur Athletic Union (AAU). In contrast, Soviet negotiators had direct links to the Kremlin; indeed, they *were* the government, apparatchiks who worked for the All-Union Physical Culture Council, an agency with ministerial status. Surprisingly, the two nation's divergent sports systems rarely interfered with the organization of the meet.[40]

The format was straightforward enough: twenty-two events for the men, ten for the women. Each event was to feature two entrants per team, and athletes were to receive points based on where they finished. First place was to get five; second, three; third, two and fourth, one. Relay events were to have two teams, with points awarded in descending order: first place, five; second, three.

The thorniest issue during the planning phase had centered on the system of scoring, not the point values themselves, but the way in which points were to be counted. Knowing that the Soviet Union had the upper hand in women's events, the Americans pushed for a meet in which women's tallies and men's tallies would be scored apart. The Soviets, of course, wanted just the opposite: points from the men's competition and points from the women's competition applied to a cumulative score. Victory for both countries turned on the way points would be counted.

Squabbles arose. In early April, Daniel Ferris, head of the U.S. delegation to Moscow, tried to allay American concerns over the issue of scoring. Speaking at the New York Athletic Club in New York, Ferris told an audience that a Soviet authority had all but ensured him that the meet would be scored as two distinct competitions. The Soviets disagreed. In an Associated Press article published just before the meet, Soviet coach Gavril Korobkov left no room for ambiguity, stating, "We're counting this as one dual meet." The Soviet press repeated Korobkov's sentiments. International sporting prestige seemed to hinge on whether the meet was gender neutral or gender specific.[41]

Displaying patriotic fervor, Americans got behind their team. Hundreds cheered on the squad during a practice meet at Randall's Island Stadium in July. Sportswriters offered words of encouragement. American businesses gave team members cartloads of products. Hershey donated chocolate. Borden provided enriched powdered milk. Noxzema distributed facial and shaving creams.[42]

As the date of the meet approached, everything seemed to be going smoothly. Then politics intruded. On June 27, exactly one month before the start of the meet, a U.S. Air Force cargo plane accidentally strayed into enemy airspace. Two Soviet MIG jets intercepted the Douglas DC-6 and opened fire, sending the plane to the ground in a fiery, smoking wreck. The nine crewmen aboard survived but were quickly seized by Soviet authorities and detained for eleven days.[43]

Cold War passions flamed. Diplomats issued protests. Newspapers ran stories about the crisis on page 1. Elevating American ire, crew members revealed upon release that they had been hit and punched by locals just after landing. Worse, one crewman said that he had almost been hanged. Although the crisis never seriously threatened to cancel the meet, it reaffirmed Cold War assumptions.[44]

Then a much graver crisis occurred. On July 15 American president Dwight Eisenhower ordered American troops into Lebanon in response to a request from Lebanon's president, Camille Chamoun, who feared that opposition forces were poised to topple his government. Washington was afraid a pro-communist regime would assume power. Three days after Eisenhower's orders, roughly fourteen thousand U.S. troops were in Lebanon.[45]

The military response drew howls of protests from the Soviets. Tass, the official news agency of the Soviet Union, labeled it an "act of open aggression." An editorial in *Pravda* declared, "The world has moved to the brink of catastrophe." The Kremlin even went so far as to suggest that war threatened. In Moscow, just a week and a half before the Match of the Century was to begin, a crowd of some fifty thousand converged in front of the American embassy. Hand-painted placards screaming "Hands off Lebanon!" dotted the throng. Agitated demonstrators even attacked the embassy, breaking windows, splattering paint on walls. There was also a report that "several windows were apparently broken by air gun slugs." Anything American became a target. A *Seattle Post-*

Intelligencer sportswriter in Moscow to cover an American-Soviet crew race wrote, "One woman approached us, hissing and spitting." All the while Soviet security forces stood by, letting the bedlam run its course.[46]

No one was sure how the crisis in the Middle East would impact the Moscow track meet. Given that plenty of sporting events between the superpowers had fallen prey to politics before, the outlook did not appear bright. Matters seemed to worsen after Eisenhower denied a request from Soviet ruler Nikita Khrushchev to convene a special summit with the United States and three other nations that, in Khrushchev's mind, would help defuse the touchy situation—and simultaneously bolster his image as a beneficent diplomat. For their part, American athletes remained hopeful. But there was no escaping the inescapable: the tense mood added a new dimension to the meet. In the meantime, a decision had to be made soon, since the American team was scheduled to depart shortly. AAU officials anxiously waited, dreading a phone call from Washington informing them that the meet had been called off.[47]

But the call never came. State Department authorities had mulled over the situation, concluding that if the Soviets protested during the Americans' visit, it would backfire, painting the Soviets in a bad light. Ironically, critical of the Soviets' usage of sport to score political points, the State Department had used sport to score points of its own. By July 19, track officials in both countries knew that the meet was on. The Americans were going to Moscow. And the Soviets were waiting.[48]

On July 20, seventy-three American athletes, coaches, and officials left Idlewild Airport in Queens, New York. The team was to fly to Moscow via Helsinki, where the Americans would board three smaller planes for the last leg to the Soviet capital. The team's attire reflected the professionalism with which they had approached the meet. Men were dressed in coats and ties, women in blue blazers and white berets. Arriving in Helsinki after fifteen long hours, the group met up with three other American athletes who had been competing in Europe for part of the summer. Tired, a bit disoriented, and uncertain of exactly what to expect, the Americans touched down in Moscow more than twenty-four hours after departing New York. It was 1:00 AM.[49]

The first out the plane door was longtime AAU official Eddie Rosenblum, swinging a big U.S. flag above his head. If the large contingent of more than five hundred Soviet officials, athletes, and average citizens was offended by the patriotic display, the Americans never sensed it. As team members disembarked, the crowd began to clap, politely at first then increasingly louder. Flowers, handshakes, smiles, and kisses of greetings followed. It all made for a warm scene. What diplomats had spent years trying to accomplish was momentarily achieved in the wee hours of the morning at an airport near Moscow.[50]

Until the start of the meet, the warm relations continued, even as the turbulent situation in the Middle East dominated headlines. But the niceties were merely a façade. Ever since the early days of the Cold War the two superpowers had been locked in a fierce struggle. In all areas—technology, weaponry, space exploration, cultural affairs, even food production—the United States and the USSR strove to outdo each other. It was no different in sports. The Moscow meet, however, presented the Soviets an unprecedented opportunity. To the Kremlin, it was a chance to score propaganda points. To individual Soviet athletes, it was a chance to prove themselves against the best—and perhaps even more. If successful, they might garner special privileges normally reserved for Communist Party bigwigs and Politburo members.

The Americans wanted to defeat their rivals just as much. Recent U.S. setbacks in other endeavors—the Soviets' successful launch of Sputnik some ten months earlier, for example—only increased their desire to win. U.S. athletes saw the meet as an opportunity to reclaim Cold War bragging rights lost in the Melbourne Olympics and uplift the sagging spirits of their fellow countrymen. In a way, the Match of the Century was America's athletic response to Sputnik.

The Match of the Century

A gray sky hung ominously over Moscow on the afternoon of July 27, 1958. The air was heavy and warm. For much of the afternoon it looked like it might rain. But by 5 PM, the time the meet was slated to begin, none had fallen. In the stands of Moscow's giant Lenin Stadium sat more than 55,000 spectators, although organizers had predicted that the meet would sell out—an impressive feat, given that the stadium held more than 103,000. No doubt the chance of rain had kept some people away. Too, the price of entry was unusually high—between twelve and fifteen rubles. Russian sports fans were accustomed to spending just a fraction of that. In addition, the meet was to be broadcast on Moscow television, and many probably decided to watch it at home.[51]

Anxious athletes from both nations were itching to start. As if his team did not already have enough motivation, American coach George Eastment tried to wring out a little more by playing to his men's sense of patriotism. In a pre-meet address Eastment told the team, "You are representing 170 [million] Americans." He continued, "What you do here today . . . will be watched throughout the world." And then he reminded the team, "There are international tensions in the world and today is very important." Doubtless, Soviet athletes heard something similar from their coach.[52]

The Match of the Century began with the parade of athletes. Members of each team marched behind a standard bearer holding either an American or Soviet flag. The Americans were garbed in plain AAU sweats; the Soviets wore warm-ups with CCCP printed across their chest. Along the upper deck of the stadium a gigantic red sign with white letters declared, "Glory to the Communist Party of the Soviet Union." While the American national anthem played, no discourteous behavior was detected. But once the competition started it became obvious who the crowd favored.[53]

Ten men's events and five women's events were scheduled for the first day. The Americans did not disappoint. Five-foot-four speedster Ira Murchison, dubbed the "Human Sputnik" by Soviet admirers, nearly tied his own world record to claim the 100 meters. Glenn Davis, a twenty-three-year-old Ohio State University student, easily took the 400 meters in 45.6 seconds. The American's 400-meter relay squad beat the Soviet team by an impressive seven-tenths of a second, and nearly broke the world record. Shot putter Parry O'Brien of Los Angeles outdistanced his closest Soviet competitor by more than seven feet. At the end of the day, the American men held a sizeable margin, 61–45.[54]

The American women gave a solid account of themselves, even surpassing expectations. Much success was owed to the performance of the Tennessee State women, the Tigerbelles. Tennessee State student Barbara Jones captured the 100 meters; and the 400-meter relay squad, comprised solely of Tigerbelles, blitzed the Soviet squad in 44.8 seconds, setting a new U.S. mark. But, as had been expected, the Soviets controlled the field events, winning all three decisively. Only Earlene Brown, a young,

bespectacled, African American homemaker, salvaged some respect for
the visitors, finishing second in the discus. At the end of the day, the Soviet
women outperformed the American women, 30–22, but combined with
the men's results, the United States still led.

Americans celebrated. "U.S. LEADS RUSSIANS IN TRACK, 83–75,"
shouted a banner in the *Los Angeles Times*. "Russians Sulk as U.S. Stars
Take Lead," headlined the *Chicago Daily Tribune*. Taking joy in wounded
Soviet pride, newspapers nationwide reported that after the Americans
had scored victories in the first three contests Moscow television cut its
transmission of the meet and ran a film instead.[55]

Day two, a Monday, featured several longer races. And since the
Soviets excelled in distance events, the meet looked like it might belong
to the home team. Even the weather seemed to portend Soviet success,
the mild temperatures and dip in humidity suiting endurance runners. Yet
it was the American men who began quickly, winning the first four events.
But then the Soviets captured five of the next eight, including the triple
jump, which Oleg Ryakhovsky won with a world record leap of almost
54 feet 6 inches. The men's competition closed with a sensational performance by the United States' Rafer Johnson, who outscored his Soviet rival,
Vasily Kuznetsov, to win the decathlon. Johnson's triumph was all the
sweeter since he had broken the world mark set earlier that summer by
Kutznetsov. After two days of competition, the American men had over-
powered their rivals, 126–109.[56]

As many had predicted, the women's meet would decide the overall
champion. The American women tried mightily—homemaker Earlene
Brown captured the shot put, beating world record holder Galina
Zabina—but in the end they could do little against the Soviet juggernaut.
The home team won four of five events and placed both first and second
in three of them. The women's totals for two days showed the Soviets
with a wide lead, 63–44. Adding the result to the men's score gave the
Soviet Union a razor-thin margin, 172–170, and the Match of the Century.

Now it was the Soviets' turn to rejoice. "Bravo, Soviet Track Team!
Our Team Won the Competition with the Americans," a *Komsomolskaya
Pravda* headline exulted. *Izvestia* announced, "Match of the best—Soviet
athletes are victorious in stubborn struggle between U.S. and U.S.S.R.
track and field athletes." *Sovetski Sport* devoted almost its entire front
page to the news, with a subhead in big, bold letters proclaiming,

"172:170." *Pravda,* for its part, bragged that the Soviet's victory "was the first defeat of an American track team in many decades."[57]

Americans saw things differently. The meet that mattered was the men's, not the women's. Therefore, the United States had won. Headlines told the story. One in a West Coast paper declared, "U.S. Men's Team Defeats Russians." A Midwest daily announced, "U.S. Men Top Russia; Girls Lose." Referencing the much discussed plans for a five-nation summit, a *Chicago Daily Defender* headline ignored the women's competition altogether, exclaiming, "U.S. Captures Summit Meet from Russians." Mixed with a deeply pervasive anticommunism, chauvinistic attitudes about women's sports clouded Americans' vision.[58]

In a wire-service story printed two days after the meet, men's coach George Eastment gave voice to this view. In the article, Eastment hotly disputed the claim by Soviet coach Gavril Korobkov that the next Soviet-American track meet in 1959 would similarly combine men's results with women's. "We never pool them in the United States," Eastment said, explaining, "I don't think we've got more than 200 women training over the whole country." The American coach then voiced displeasure over the way in which Soviet organizers had handled the Moscow meet. "When we meet next year it will be two dual meets—one women's and one men's counted separately, just as this one was supposed to be."[59]

Americans refused to believe the Soviets had won. Some argued that the scoring system in Moscow had unduly favored the home team. By comparison, results derived from scoring in traditional dual meets showed that the Soviet Union had actually lost. More, a writer for *Track and Field News* argued that even with the Soviets using the non-traditional method of scoring, the United States still had defeated their rivals; points for defeated relay squads should have been worth two points and not three, as head-to-head meets in Europe typically scored relay races at the time. A sports columnist for the *Boston Globe* suggested that the United States had been the real winner since the American team had the greatest number of first-place finishers. "We lost no athletic face in Moscow," the *Globe* columnist wrote in bolded text. "Who won the most gold medals? We did."[60]

Inflaming passions even more, American officials insisted that Soviet planners had duped them. The proof was a Soviet letter sent to American delegation head Daniel Ferris. According to Ferris, the letter was a contract of sorts, an agreement that ensured the meet was to be scored as two competitions. To American officials, such assurances were essential. American coach Eastment observed, "Without that letter we wouldn't have left the United States."[61]

One day after the meet Ferris made public a communication between Soviet and American authorities. It appears to have been a telegram. The Associated Press article that printed a passage from it never clarified its origins. "Considered your proposal concerning scoring track and field athletics USA-USSR match," the communication read. "We suggest publish scores of men and women points and total scores as traditional. Regards Andrianov." Andrianov was Konstantin Andrianov, IOC delegate and chair of the Soviet National Olympic Committee, whose imprimatur on the passage gave the communication, and thereby Ferris's assertion, an air of authenticity.[62]

Interestingly, Soviet authorities had publicly maintained throughout that scoring was to consist of combined totals. Equally persistent, the Americans had maintained that the meet was to be just the reverse, even though in late November 1957 the AAU had voted down the suggestion of tying the demands for separate scoring to plans of sending an American team. Nevertheless, Americans believed that it was the Soviets who had reneged on their word, which only reaffirmed negative perceptions about the communist nation. As the opening sentence of a *U.S. News and World Report* article entitled "How to Win a Track Meet—the Soviet Way" put it, "Even in sports, Americans are finding that the Soviet Union has a strange way with the rules of the game."[63]

Thus to Americans, the Soviets were swindlers, not winners. "REDS KEEP SCORE, WIN TRACK MEET," the *Atlanta Journal* headlined in capital letters. Sportswriter Jerry Nason of the *Boston Evening Globe* complained in text highlighted in bolded type, "The scoring was rigged in such a way it was difficult for [the Soviets] to lose, although they almost did." A sports columnist for the *Boston Herald* offered a folksier assessment, bemoaning that "if we just weren't so afraid of the Russians, we could have a lot of fun laughing at them. Even in sports, they're simply so dadburned obvious. And what's obvious is that they're invariably going to cheat if they can."[64]

Criticism came not just from the sports page. Editorials chimed in as well. One in the *Chicago Daily Tribune* castigated the Soviets while simultaneously tying sports to politics. "The track meet just concluded in Moscow . . . provides a simple lesson in what the Communists seek to accomplish in getting together with Americans. That goes for 'summit' conferences or anything else," the editorial grumbled. "What the Russians want is to win at our expense, however it can be done. They want to look better than we do, not only to feed their own self-esteem but to preen before the world."[65]

The Soviets fired back. They claimed that the system of scoring could not have been manipulated because American officials and sports journalists had known about the system well before the meet started. As *Sovetski Sport* saw it, the controversy resulted from the efforts of anticommunist forces in the United States. These haters of the Soviet Union, claimed the paper, had attempted to distract attention away from a well-earned Soviet victory by miring the achievement in charges of cheating. "To recognize the entire defeat of the American team is to lose another chance to talk about the advantages of the American way of life," the sports paper argued.[66]

Despite all the squabbling, the idea of a U.S.-USSR track meet would develop into a permanent fixture. Over the course of roughly the next three decades, American and Soviet athletes faced off in what became known as the U.S.-USSR track series. As could be expected, each meet contained its own Cold War drama, replete with heated commentary, disputes over scoring, fierce rivalries between individual competitors, and political quarrels. But it was the Match of the Century that had set the pattern.[67]

It would not be until 1964 that the United States claimed its first overall win in the series. At the meet in Los Angeles, with Attorney General Robert Kennedy in attendance, American men and women posted the second largest margin of victory up to that time. In the men's category, the Soviets would finally defeat the American squad in 1965 in Kiev. As for the American women, their first win would have to wait a few more years. In 1969, at the meet in Los Angeles, the women eked out a three-point win over their Soviet rivals. But no matter the score, athletes from both nations competed with a ferocity that belonged in the gladiatorial arena.

One incident at the 1959 meet in Philadelphia illustrates this competitive spirit. Bob Soth was a gangly distance runner who, most commentators felt, would finish no higher than third in the 10,000 meters. But to the amazement of many, during much of the long race he was able to keep pace with the two favored Soviet runners, even surging ahead of both, then moving back into second place, where he stayed within striking distance of the Soviet lead runner until about a quarter of the grueling race remained.[68]

Then it happened. He hit the proverbial runner's wall. His legs became rubbery. His vision blurred. Disorientation consumed him. As the second and trailing Soviet runner sped past him, he battled the urge to stop. Seen from the stands, the twenty-six-year-old Soth teetered. Mustering all his might, he managed to stagger on for several more torturous laps. Finally, it was too much. His body gave out and he crashed to the cindery track, unconscious. Soth had literally run himself into the ground. Later, after receiving intravenous fluids, he confessed, "I wasn't running to get a point or two," adding, "I was running to beat the Russians. That was the best race I've ever run until I fell out." Perhaps fellow teammate Eddie Southern, a swift twenty-year-old quarter-miler who captured the 400 meters in Philadelphia, was thinking of Soth when he offered his views on the just completed American-Soviet meet. Remarked Southern, The superpower sports rivalry "made [the meet] all bigger, somehow. You would nearly rather die than lose."[69]

The U.S.-USSR Rivalry beyond the Match of the Century

Soviet and American track athletes would compete next at the 1960 Olympic Games in Rome. Although the combined U.S. men's and women's track team earned one more gold medal than their Soviet rivals, the U.S. Olympic squad was soundly beaten by the Soviet team in the total number of first places. Similarly discouraging results occurred in the silver and bronze medal categories. Such a performance pushed some very important Americans to reevaluate the nation's sports program. And they did it with the Soviets in mind.

John F. Kennedy was one of the first to sound the alarm. As president-elect, Kennedy in late 1960 penned an article for *Sports Illustrated* in which he bemoaned the apparent dip in American physical fitness. Given the recent spike in Cold War tensions, the implications were plain. "We face in the Soviet Union," wrote Kennedy, "a powerful and implacable adversary. . . . To meet the challenge of this enemy will require determination and will and effort on the part of all Americans. Only if our citizens are physically fit will they be fully capable of such an effort." To Kennedy, sport was a much-needed weapon of defense against Soviet advances.[70]

In late July 1964, also in *Sports Illustrated,* Kennedy's brother, Robert F. Kennedy, sounded a similar message. For RFK the issue turned on the need to bolster amateur athletics. Again the Soviets drew a Kennedy's barbs, if only by inference. RFK wrote that "in this day of international stalemates nations use" athletic triumphs "to prove their superiority over the 'soft and decadent' democratic way of life." As the attorney general saw it, the matter required overturning past defeats. "It is thus in our national interests that we regain our Olympic superiority—that we once again give the world visible proof of our inner strength and vitality."[71]

RFK's words hardly changed matters. The Soviet Olympic squad achieved yet another unofficial victory over its American rival at the notorious 1972 Summer Games in Munich, where Israeli athletes and officials were kidnapped and massacred by a radical Palestinian group.[72]

But just as the Kennedy brothers politicized the U.S.-USSR sports rivalry, so too did the Soviet Union. Following the 1972 games, and focusing on the Soviet team's achievements, an athletic journal editorialized, "The success of Soviet athletes in [Munich] resulted from the superiority of sport development in a socialist state." The magazine *Sport in the USSR* claimed, "The mounting impact of socialist sport on the world sports movement is one of the best and most comprehensible means of explaining to people . . . the advantages which the socialist system has over capitalism."[73]

Not only did the Soviet team outperform the American squad in the number of medals and in the number of first places in Munich, Soviets athletes and their Eastern European counterparts won track gold medals in events U.S. athletes had dominated for decades. Two of the biggest victories occurred in the men's 100- and 200-meter dashes. The fleet-footed Valery Borzov, a Ukrainian, shocked Americans by scoring the double victory himself. Borzov's dual wins represented an athletic coup for the Soviet Union. No Soviet man had ever won an Olympic gold medal in the sprints. The drubbing at Munich convinced American authorities that the long-standing practice of never mixing amateur athletics with governmental support had to come to an end. The resulting federally mandated Amateur Sports Act of 1978 provided, for the first time, real government assistance to the nation's top-flight athletes.[74]

But Munich was yet to offer even a bigger coup for the Soviets—and it would become one of the most contentious games in the annals of sports. The United States and the Soviet had two of the strongest teams in the 1972 Olympic basketball competition. Everyone knew, however, that the Americans dominated the sport. In fact, they had never lost an Olympic basketball game—something the Soviets understood all too well. Between the Olympic years of 1952 and 1964, they had played the United States in every Olympic final. And every time the United States had finished ahead.

In the gold-medal contest in Munich, it was the Soviets who got off to a swift start, and they maintained their advantage for nearly the entire contest. However, with just three seconds to play, and the Soviet Union in front, 49–48, Doug Collins of the United States stepped to the foul line for two shots. America's perfect Olympic record at stake, he made one, then another, nudging the Americans ahead. Deafening cheers from American fans filled the Olympic *basketballhalle*. It was the United States' first lead of the game.[75]

Following Collins's second shot, a Soviet player hastily retrieved the ball and fired an inbounds pass to a teammate. But then the referees halted action. Just one second appeared on the clock. The Soviet coach had apparently requested a timeout just before Collins had released his second free throw. After a brief delay, in which it was decided to set the clock back to three seconds, a Soviet player again tossed the ball to a teammate, who quickly turned and launched a long-distance shot. But the shot missed, the horn going off. The game appeared to be over.

From the American bench burst jubilant bedlam. On the other bench, the Soviets slumped, dejected. But then in a bizarre turn of events, Olympic officials informed both teams that the game was not finished. Apparently, play had resumed before the official timer had had a chance to change the clock from one second to three seconds. The sounding of the horn was meant to inform the referees that the time on the scoreboard was incorrect—not that the game had concluded. So for a third time a Soviet player readied himself to make the last pass of the game.

This time the clock was correct, as was the full-court toss hurled by the Soviet passer. Its recipient, the long-armed Alexander Belov, soared over two U.S. players and grasped the ball. Meanwhile, the two Americans, jumping into each other, tumbled to the court, momentarily exposing the basket. With the carefree nonchalance of a seventh-grader shooting baskets alone in a driveway, Belov dropped the ball into the goal as the final horn blew a second time. The game was over.

Wild, celebratory madness now shifted to the Soviets' end of the floor. Euphoric players bear hugged and jumped up and down. A bottle of vodka appeared. At the other end of the court the American bench was a welter of emotion. Some players were dazed. Others were angry. Still others were confused. Near the scorer's table, a red-faced Hank Iba, the American coach, pleaded his case. His arguments were turned away. For the first time in Olympic basketball history the United States had lost.

But one final affront was awaiting the Americans. Following the game, U.S. officials filed an official protest. The next day an Olympic Jury of Appeals announced its verdict. In front of a crowded press room crammed with sports reporters and Olympic officials, the jury chairman said that the panel had voted against the Americans, 3–2. Few were surprised. On the jury panel sat delegates from Poland, Hungary, and Cuba, as well as Italy and Puerto Rico. Cold War loyalties had sealed the Americans' fate. The United States had now lost twice in two days.

Americans decried the maltreatment. A New England sportswriter called the basketball game "the biggest robbery since the famous Brinks job in Boston." On the CBS Sunday News Dan Rather labeled it a "theft by stopwatch result." Telegrams and missives from surly Americans flowed into Munich. An editorial cartoon in the *Dayton Daily News* showed four stern-faced U.S. basketball players at the airport just before leaving the games with enormous screws bored through their chests. A TV reporter asks them, "Other Than That, Did You Enjoy the Olympics?"[76]

Americans foisted much of the blame onto the Soviets. ABC newsman Howard K. Smith called the game "a blatant theft by the Russians." *Washington Post*'s Shirley Povich upped the vitriol. "In the basketball finals . . . our Russian brothers browbeat the Brazilian referee, and demanded and got what amounted to three final whistles," Povich wrote. "They used Russian terror mathematics to stretch the one remaining second on the electric clock into a useful six, then said they just come from behind to beat the American team by one point." For

their part, the Soviets denied any wrongdoing and, in fact, would maintain that the game's closing moments had been in complete accordance
with the rules. Once again, a U.S.-USSR athletic event had finished with
both sides claiming victory.[77]

There would be other Soviet-American Olympic matchups that
stirred similarly fervent passions—the U.S. hockey triumph at the 1980
Lake Placid Winter Games, for one. That semi-final game contained all
the drama one might suspect in such a David (the United States) versus
Goliath (the Soviet Union) contest. Surprising even their most ardent
fans, the Americans would go on to defeat Finland in the gold-medal
game. But what made the semi-final win over the Soviets so monumen-
tal was the meaning Americans derived from it. During the late 1970s
and early 1980s, there was a prevailing sense that the nation seemed to
be slipping—both economically and militarily. To make matters worse,
the invasion of Afghanistan by the Soviet Union in late 1979 had set the
two superpowers on edge, and among the reprisals urged by the United
States was a boycott of the upcoming Summer Olympic Games in
Moscow. Thus, the U.S.-USSR hockey game in Lake Placid occurred
amidst national self doubts and elevated Cold War tensions.

It was in this context that Americans interpreted victory. Boisterous
cries of "USA! USA! USA!" reverberated throughout the otherwise
sleepy hamlet of Lake Placid, delirious fans celebrating until well after
the game was finished. Down state, full-throated renditions of "God
Bless America" broke out in New York City drinking establishments after
patrons received the stunning news. Papers nationwide reported the
upset on page 1. The *Philadelphia Inquirer*'s front-page headline succinctly
read, "USA!" Congressmen praised the American team on the floor of
the House. Addressing the crowd at a New York rally, U.S. coach Herb
Brooks remarked, "Each of the players [has] a gold medal and it's
theirs—they've earned it. But in so many ways that gold medal is yours,
too. The medal stands for our system and our way of life, a system that
stresses talent, enthusiasm and the work ethic." For Americans, the victory represented a political and ideological victory over the nation's arch-
enemy, while letting loose years of pent-up frustration.[78]

Meanwhile, President Carter's threat of a U.S. boycott was stimulating an impassioned debate among many Americans. Some felt politics
and sport should never mix, while others believed that sport was a legit-

imate diplomatic tool. Either way, anti-Soviet attitudes abounded. Following President Carter's January announcement of a possible boycott, multiple Olympic gold medalist Al Oerter, who finished second in the discus in the Match of the Century some two decades earlier, declared, "The only way to compete against Moscow is to stuff it down their throats in their own backyard." But boycott supporters had popular backing—as high as 74 percent, according to one poll—and the backing from American politicians and sports officials too. In the U.S. House of Representatives the vote endorsing Carter's boycott was a whopping 386 to 12; in the Senate, 88–4. U.S. Olympic Committee (USOC) delegates in April similarly gave their blessing: for every vote cast against the boycott, two votes were cast for it. In late May the United States formally withdrew from the Summer Games in Moscow.[79]

The Soviets, to say the least, were angry. In response, propagandists claimed that the United States was staying away to avoid suffering yet another embarrassing Olympic loss. The newspaper *Sovetskaya Rossia* charged the Carter administration with bribing several countries to skip the Olympic Games in Moscow. The paper also warned that American saboteurs, whose devious methods consisted of using "false bottomed suitcases, panties, and other underwear with secret pockets, confectionery packs, crackers, candies, and cookies and coffee jars filled with leaflets and pamphlets printed on tissue paper," had plans to undermine the Moscow Olympics. Soviet and American authorities even differed on the number of nations that intended to boycott the games.[80]

The Soviets would retaliate with an Olympic boycott of their own, withdrawing from the Los Angeles Summer Games in 1984. Again, accusations, half-truths, and fallacies were bandied about. For example, Soviet papers claimed that the U.S. government had ties to an anti-Soviet faction in California whose aim was to harass Soviet team members during the Olympic Games—or possibly even worse. The stone-faced Marat Gramov, head of the Soviet Olympic committee, levied the strange charge that American intelligence officers planned to abduct Soviet athletes after giving "them . . . psychotropic preparations that destroy the nervous system." According to *Izvestia*, the Reagan administration had forced the Soviets' hand so that the president and his men could ride the wave of patriotism generated by a strong American Olympic showing to reelection later that fall. On the other side of the Iron Curtain a writer in the conservative *Human Events* believed that the boycott had actually been a blessing, since it kept Soviet secret agents who doubled as Olympic athletes off American soil. Illinois representative Philip Crane had the *Human Events* article entered into the *Congressional Record*.[81]

Mikhail Gorbachev's reordering of Soviet society in the mid to late 1980s was the beginning of the end for the U.S.-USSR sports rivalry. Without question, athletic competitions between the two superpowers during the *glasnost* years still exhibited much of the rawness and rancor that defined earlier events. The Goodwill Games in Moscow in 1986, for example, the first summer Olympic-like competition involving the two countries since the Montreal Olympic Games in 1976, featured overt political symbols—a gigantic image of Lenin during the opening festivities, for instance—and testy American accusations that Soviet schedulers had rigged the competition against U.S. athletes. There was also the Soviets' victory over the United States in the basketball final at the 1988 Seoul Olympic Games, which produced euphoric celebrations in Soviet sports circles, while U.S. supporters sulked. But with the opening up of the Soviet Union and a general warming of relations between the two countries, the sports rivalry began to lose some of its vitality.

When the Soviet Union dissolved in 1991, the Cold War rivalry in sports evaporated too. For decades both superpowers had used sport as a yardstick to measure the successes of one society against the setbacks of the other. Such was the competitive nature of the Cold War, and it cut across all fields. But when the Soviet Union ceased to exist, the life force of that cutthroat struggle drained away.

For citizens of the former Soviet Union, sport in the post–Cold War era took the form of a once-great emperor now clad in nary a stitch of clothes. Athletic success offered little consolation to a citizenry struggling to survive. As *Sovetski Sport,* the former mouthpiece of Soviet athletic excellence, queried in the spring of 1992, "What does the small group of athletes on the medal stand, who are often more concerned with their own winnings than with the prestige of Russia as a great power, give to a hungry and destroyed country?" That question was unfathomable during even the warmest years of the Soviet-American athletic rivalry.[82]

Back in 1958, on the eve of the Match of the Century, Americans and Soviets too were concerned over issues of survival. But the threat of thermonuclear war at the time ensured that it was of a much greater order. As a result, sport became both a literal and metaphorical battleground. Athletes were soldiers, coaches and officials were colonels, explaining a victory in ideological terms the rallying cry. As California representative Harlan Hagen said in his extended remarks in Congress after Rafer Johnson broke the world record in the decathlon at the 1958 meet, "Mr. Speaker, a splendid young Negro athlete from California has again demonstrated to the Soviet Union and other critics of our country that we produce the best, under a system of incentives and freedom which they would label inefficient and decadent." It was not unlike the elation Soviets expressed of their achievements on the track. Victory over one's ideological opponent was the be-all and end-all of the U.S.-USSR athletic rivalry in sports.[83]

U.S. goalkeeper Brianna Scurry lunging to stop the penalty kick of China's Liu Ying in the shootout of the final game of the 1999 Women's World Cup Soccer in Pasadena, California. *Courtesy of Getty Images.*

sixteen

Dare to Dream
U.S. Women's Soccer versus the World

LINDSEY J. MEÂN —

The U.S. women's soccer team is a winner on the world's stage, earning them a consistent number one ranking. Yet, with the notable exception of the China-U.S. rivalry, women's soccer and its international team rivalries have been overlooked by the media and, consequently, remain unfamiliar to the wider U.S. audience. In this chapter I discuss the virtual invisibility of U.S. women's soccer and its key rivalries as a significant topic in mediated sport, arguing that this oversight arises from a number of interconnected reasons linked to the ideological significance of sport, of soccer, and women's sport in America.

In the United States, both soccer and women's sport have a problematic social, cultural, and ideological existence. Soccer itself sits in rivalry and contrast to American sports and the way sport is "done," while women's sporting presence remains a challenge to sport as a male domain. Consequently, the United States has provided a relatively unique sociopolitical setting for soccer as women's sport, yet one that is ultimately dilemmatic. U.S. women's soccer has been a major international success but a domestic failure, its successes inconsistently celebrated and largely ignored by the sporting media and, hence, traditional sport audiences. This contradictory positioning can be usefully understood if soccer and women's soccer are examined within the system of ideological rivalries that comprise sport and its inextricable links with nation, masculinity, and the media. My intention, therefore, is to outline some of the broader commercial and ideological rivalries that have contributed to both the success and failure of women's soccer in the United States before focusing on how these have shaped the circumstances and mediated constructions of the American team's international rivalries.

Outside the United States soccer is commonly known as football, and the U.S. game known as football is relegated to being referred to as *American football,* linguistically marked as the outsider. In further contrast, across the globe soccer comprises the essence of hegemonic masculinity and embodies the nation as *the* national sport. Given the global popularity of soccer alongside concerted efforts to popularize it as a men's game in the United States, America's continued resistance to soccer as a top sport remains complex and multifaceted. However, a brief consideration of the significance of sport as highly mediated and crucial for constructing nation and masculinity offers some insights into this resistance, providing an underlying account of the socio-ideological, commercial, and economic rivalry between both U.S. and non-U.S. sports and men's and women's sports. Exploring these different levels of ideological and commercial rivalry contributes to a wider account of how and why the U.S. women's team found the actual and ideological space to develop to a high standard and international acclaim, yet still failed to win the media exposure it needed to succeed in the domestic sphere.

Sport as Ideology

Sport plays a major ideological role in the construction of nation, key identities, and social categories as a major site for the demarcation of gender and the construction of masculinity.[1] This power, together with its intertextual embeddedness with other key discourses (such as politics),[2] means sport comprises a powerful foundational discourse crucial for constructing understandings of the world.[3] But sport is also increasingly significant given its predominance as a media site in an increasingly mediated world. Indeed, the mediated context of sport and its commodification for consumption (termed *mediatization*) has rendered it even more ideologically and commercially powerful given the global economic imperatives that dominate U.S. sports media and its power to influence identities and meanings, reflected in the increasing business links between sport, media, entertainment, and merchandising corporations, such as Disney.[4] Consequently, these ideological and commercial imperatives are inextricably linked to ways in which the United States "does" sport (i.e., the ways in which sport is practiced, produced, and reproduced) and why soccer sits as an ideological and commercial rival.

American Sport: Soccer Is Not U.S.

In the United States, soccer is somewhat of an anathema for a number of reasons. Soccer is, ultimately, a game which contradicts the basic American ideological tenet that there is always a winner; that is, someone is always number one. (Penalty kicks are only used in finals or other circumstances that require a definitive winner, otherwise a *draw* is normal.) Most American sports are structured to ensure there is a winner, (re)producing winning as having special ideological significance for competition. As such, the possibility that teams can come out "equal" may contribute to the American notion that soccer is about fair play, whereas in other parts of the world it is the epitome of aggressive, competitive, masculinity.[5] (The prevalence of women and children playing soccer in the United States is also likely to contribute to the "fair play" positioning of soccer.)

It has also been observed that the United States likes to be *the* winner. Certainly the U.S. media has been observed as predominantly focusing on sports at which it dominates; and, while it certainly does not stand alone amongst all nations as possessing such a selective lens, the number of sports at which the United States is dominant can make it appear to be focused heavily on its own success. But if the United States likes a winner so much, then why has the significant success of U.S. women's soccer never transformed it into a "main event"?

The most noted arguments for why soccer has had great difficulty establishing itself in the United States stem from the positioning of soccer as an immigrant sport and a women's sport.[6] Sport constructs and embodies nation as an imagined and shared interpretative community, manifesting nation politically, emotionally, psychologically, metaphorically, and figuratively.[7] Thus, during the Cold War, it was not simply the athletes who were competing when the USSR and the United States met. Indeed, the ideological and political significance of sport is apparent in the significance of the 1998 Iran versus U.S. soccer game, a sporting event that would usually have gone relatively unremarked upon in the media and been of little interest to most Americans.[8] Equally, the mediated construction of nation, gender, competition, and rivalries has become a significant part of the spectacular mediatization of sport,[9] making these national and political narratives a significant element of the media's commodification of sport for audience consumption.[10]

As noted earlier, sport is also significant for the construction of masculinity and male identity, no real surprise given the interlinking of nation and masculine identities. Thus sport remains a site in which masculinity is dominant and remains *the* standard, making women's presence ideologically problematic, particularly given the link between masculinity and heterosexuality and their literal embodiment within the male body in sport.[11] Consequently, sport has been highly resistant to the entry of women, particularly into male-typed sports, and men resist participation in feminized sports. However, male sport as the standard renders it the significant site for nation, politics, etc., with women's sports typically second tier and largely ignored or symbolically erased;[12] the exception being hegemonically feminized sports that are usually individual events (rather than team), emphasize aesthetics, and have athletes that "fit" predominant beauty discourses.[13] Thus the U.S. positioning of soccer as a women's and/or foreigners' sport arguably foregrounds why U.S. women's soccer was given the ideological space to develop to such a high standard, in contrast to nations in which it is a male-typed sport. However, it also accounts for the lack of media support or interest, alongside the failure to use the international success of the team for political and nation-building imperatives. The impact and implications of these issues are returned to later in the direct discussion of the U.S. women's soccer team.

The Competition for Global Significance

While sport has a strong history as nation-building, its ideological elements also make it an important colonizing tool that conveys political and cultural ideals and creates spheres of influence, more recently overtly recognized as merchandizing potential. Thus, the United States continues to make efforts to export its "big three" sports throughout the world, with comparatively limited success compared to the continued major global expansion of soccer.

The colonizing and economic importance of sport is evident in the recognition of the Fédération Internationale de Football Association (FIFA, soccer's regulating body) as a major sociocultural and economic global force.[14] FIFA's cultural and ideological impact has been observed in many places, in countries to which it has comparatively recently introduced soccer (such as China) as well as places in which it has increased its influence through developmental and educational initiatives (for example, in many African countries). Indeed, the commercial benefits of teaming up with FIFA are apparent in the multimillion-dollar business arrangement that exists between Coca-Cola and FIFA and their ambitious (and ultimately unsuccessful) attempt to popularize soccer in the United States by staging FIFA's flagship tournament, the (men's) World Cup, in America in 1994.[15] But while the ideological challenges of soccer as an American men's sport are important, there is no question that one of the major rivals to soccer's success in the United States—as a sport and as a women's sport—is the media.

Soccer Versus Television

There are two key elements that require consideration in addressing the role of the media in the failure of soccer, and women's soccer in particular. First, soccer is not suited to current U.S. broadcast practices that permit frequent commercial breaks and TV timeouts, dictated by the television producers rather than the sports officials, practices that can impact audience experience at televised live events as well as while viewing on television. Second, and directly related to the issues outlined above, soccer, generally, and women's soccer, specifically, comprise an ideological challenge which requires them being positioned and constructed in ways that do not challenge the predominant U.S. male sporting hegemony. How this manifests in poor production values and problematic representational practices is outlined below.

American TV and the Commercial Imperative

In terms of U.S. practices, soccer appears to be a commercially unfriendly sport that has not been amenable to alteration to meet the commercial requirements of television. Soccer is a game of two forty-five-minute halves (or periods) of continuous play during which there are *no* commercial breaks (and in many countries no commercials of any form).[16] Indeed, in negotiating to bring FIFA's World Cup to the United States, FIFA was apparently lobbied to change the structure of the game (into smaller periods or permit "TV timeouts") to enable more commercial breaks.[17] FIFA refused, but if FIFA had "played ball" with the U.S. media imperative by conceding some changes it is possible that soccer might have been furnished with higher television production values (discussed below) in the United States, substantively increasing its likelihood of successful entry into the U.S. sport market.

Nonetheless, the request to change a historic and global game itself demonstrates the power of U.S. media and its commercial imperative. But it also demonstrates the power and economic security of FIFA to be able to refuse. In the symbiotic relationship between sport and media, many scholars argue that the power now lies firmly in the hands of the media, particularly the U.S. media that has both the financial power and will to shape the scheduling of the most significant global sporting events (e.g., the Summer Olympics) to accommodate U.S. primetime television commercial imperatives. Thus soccer and FIFA provide a rival and challenge to America's position as number one in terms of media power and sociocultural significance.

Soccer as a Media Construction

Deborah Cameron's notion that people, not organizations, "do" things is crucial in understanding the role of the sport media, which is first and foremost a collection of people.[18] With this acknowledgment comes the understanding that sport is mediated by practices shaped by the ideological values and identities of those who produce sport media, reproducing sport for consumption. Given the significance of sport as a masculine discourse, it is not surprising that research reveals the predominance of white male hegemony in sport media.[19] Thus, women's sports and soccer are ideological rivals to traditional sport as well as rivals for airtime and attention, challenging the same predominant discourses about gender and nation from which identities arise. The common view in the United States that *soccer just doesn't make good television* is contradicted by the fact that there is a huge audience for soccer on television outside the United States. Consequently, if we consider the research showing the impact of the differential representational practices and production values used for different sports, typically used to differentially frame men's and women's, we can start to appreciate that it is soccer on *American* television that isn't good.

No sport is intrinsically televisual or newsworthy, rather sport is con-structed or commodified for consumption. Narratives and other pro-duction techniques (soundtracks, camera angles, commentary, graphics, replays, etc.) construct the event and the athletes. Valued sports are typ-ically given high production values, meaning multiple production tech-niques and narratives are used to construct the event as important, exciting, and spectacular, thus building audiences and creating spectac-ular television. In contrast, less-valued sports (like women's sports and soccer) have low production values. Lower production value means fewer cameras, less technical wizardry (e.g., slow-motion, replays, graphics and statistics), less narrative content (e.g., interviews, analysis), basically, less of the features that make sport into interesting, spectacular, hypermasculine television—features that sports audiences have come to expect.[20]

The impact of this is that sports with low production values look slow and boring, particularly compared with the spectacular production of other sports, which in turn confirms popular perceptions, part of the cycle of power that reproduces definitions and social categories.[21] It is through such differential production values that the big American sports are reproduced as exciting and spectacular; "othered" sports, as slow and untelevisual; and men as the sporting standard, women as the "other." Commentators with little or no interest and knowledge of the sport which they are broadcasting exacerbate this problem.

As such, the double whammy of U.S. women's soccer as female and foreign account for why it has been comparatively ignored and has suf-fered from poor production values. The power to construct meaning in sport is significant, and Jean Williams observes that "the cynicism of sports writers and pundits [has] remained bitterly enduring" toward women's soccer.[22] Williams argues that the sports media predicted the 1999 Women's World Cup in Los Angeles would be a failure and then subsequently referred to its success as a "one–off." This prediction has arguably been made real by an actively disinterested media that has failed to provide media coverage or a consistently compelling narrative about U.S. women's soccer. Indeed, adopting the revenge narrative usually deployed for other teams, John Haydon's *Washington Times* article on September 9, 2007, was entitled "U.S. Looks for Revenge" and positioned the struggle as being between the U.S. women's team and a disinterested nation, stating, "The U.S. national team is on a mission to put the women's game back in the spotlight at the 2007 FIFA World Cup that begins in China tomorrow." Such a statement serves to overlook the role of the media as the "spotlight."

In fact, the American media remains one of the most enduring and major rivals for the U.S. team as recognized in the 2007 Nike media campaign promoting itself, the U.S. women's soccer team, and the impending FIFA Women's World Cup. The Nike campaign played on the team's lack of recognition and celebrity contrasted with its success, referring to them as "the greatest team you've never heard of." But the enduring nature of the media's neglect of women's soccer was most evident in the lack of coverage of the Women's United Soccer Association professional league (WUSA). WUSA was started using the momentum of the 1999 Women's World Cup, an event that had unexpectedly mobilized the American nation to become fans of women's soccer, a momentum and fandom lost to the transience of the media spotlight.[23]

U.S. Women's Soccer

The role of the media needs to be addressed to understand the context of women's soccer in the United States. The media plays a role in making sport commercially successful, hence the U.S. media has impacted structurally and culturally on the actual and perceived performance of the U.S. team (especially regarding in the failure of WUSA), but also as the major site for the representation (or not) of the team's competitive rivalries. As such, there are rivalries that the U.S. team's fans share as an interpretative community and rivalries that exist as mediated narratives across a wider range of interpretative communities. However, since most international competition is mediated for even dedicated fans, the media has a considerable impact on emerging rivalries as constructed narratives, alongside and interlinked with historical and ideo-political national narratives. Consequently, in considering the competitive and mediated rivalries of the U.S. women's team, it seems ideologically relevant to consider why certain rivalry narratives have not emerged, given which teams have emerged as significant competitors to U.S. dominance. Nonetheless, a wider appreciation of the specific context of U.S. women's soccer and the role of the media warrant some consideration before the team rivalries are discussed.

The historical growth and success of U.S. women's soccer can be directly linked to the issues of nation and gender in sport and the lack of ideological value placed on soccer as an American male sport. In the 1980s, colleges and universities were struggling to meet federal legislation ruling that sport be included under the remit of Title IX. Suddenly, women had to be provided with equivalent access to sport, and soccer was a cost-effective way to achieve this, given that it requires limited specialized equipment. As a sport constructed as outside the American male's realm of interest and unrelated to masculinity, soccer as a female sport was not as ideologically threatening as their incursion into other sporting arenas, despite the potential ideological dilemma arising from soccer as a team sport (although the lack of available professional progression and wider competition in women's soccer at the time are also likely to have rendered their presence less threatening). The lack of men's soccer as an established national sport also meant that the women players were less restricted by a historical tradition about style of play.[24]

U.S. Women's Soccer versus the Media

Ranked first in the world, the U.S. women's soccer team is a remarkable success. As noted by Michael Lewis in the *New York Daily News* on July 29, 2008, "Championships are always expected of the Americans. . . . The Americans are the Brazil of women's soccer. Anything less than a championship is considered a failure."[25] But despite this success, the U.S. domestic soccer game has severely suffered from an absence of substantive support from the media, sponsors, and the American public. The failure of the women's league (WUSA, 2001–2003) may not initially seem relevant for the national team; after all, many athletes who represent the nation are not professional.[26] But as a team sport, soccer requires a context in which the elite level of players can compete and train together, a context which has only existed in U.S. colleges, outside of WUSA's two-year duration (pending the success of the new U.S. Women's Professional Soccer league [WPS] launched in March 2009).

The failure of WUSA in 2003 meant that the careers of elite women soccer players returned to being effectively over on leaving college, unless they were willing and able to join professional leagues in countries like Norway. As such, the failure of WUSA left a huge hole in the continued participation, development, progress, experience, and match fitness of players comprising the U.S. women's team (especially given the significant recent progress of women's soccer in other countries). Indeed, the psychological and emotional impact of the announcement of WUSA's demise immediately prior to the 2003 Women's World Cup (moved to the United States due to SARS) was rarely considered in the analysis of the team's "poor" performance (they came in third).

In contrast to the United States, the (professional) development of women players in many other countries has been improving; and, as a result, the women's international game is beginning to change. Many teams from countries steeped in the tradition of male soccer (such as Germany, Brazil, and England), in which women's soccer had previously been disenfranchised (and even banned), have benefited from the success of U.S. women's soccer both directly (foreign players in WUSA) and indirectly (as inspirational and pioneering). The pioneering narrative of the U.S. women's soccer context is widely mediated in the U.S. media. For example, Barry Svluga wrote in the *Washington Post,* "There is no overstating the impact this group of women [the U.S. team] had on women's athletics in the United States and beyond,"[27] a narrative that works up the greatness of the United States as a place where women's soccer has progressed without addressing the actual challenges and failures epitomized by the demise of WUSA. Indeed, the impact of the demise of WUSA remains unaddressed in most commentaries about the national team's performance.

The increased mediatization of sport means that media coverage and good audience-building techniques are essential for sponsors and events. Indeed, the assumption, despite the diversity of audiences for the 1999 Women's World Cup tournament, that the main audience for women's soccer is and will always be young girls can be seen as part of the problem for WUSA. Without a media strategy to construct the sport as relevant and interesting to traditional sporting audiences, ratings and sponsorship are problematic. Failure of the major networks to broadcast WUSA games outside late-night hours (some afternoon games were on "non-major" channels), combined with poor media production, ensured little audience outside the most dedicated of fans.

Since Mia Hamm, Julie Foudy, etc., the 1999 "girls of summer," have now retired,[28] the current U.S. team media narrative appears to be one of less consistent success and even less media attention. During the highly successful 1999 Women's World Cup, the media narrative heavily emphasized the heterosexuality of key members of the U.S. team, a dominant strategy in reporting on women's sport.[29] Previous key U.S. team players, such as Mia Hamm, fitted traditional hegemonic femininity with both implicit and explicit indications of their heterosexuality apparent in mediated narratives about their personal relationships and their ponytails (as iconic symbols of American sporting femininity) and participation in their sexualization (e.g., Brandi Chastain posing nude with two soccer balls). In contrast, a key player in the new U.S. team, Abby Wambach, is a tall, powerful player (without a ponytail) whose style arguably appears harder and more aggressive than that of previous U.S. players (perhaps a reflection of a changing game). The media narrative about Wambach positions her as a key player while consistently mentioning her height and size, effectively positioning her as outside the normative female category but without combining it with other linguistic descriptors that overtly position her outside heterosexuality.

Wambach has appeared in the media but, unlike the more cooperative "girls of summer," has not participated in reproducing herself within the boundaries of traditional hegemonic femininity. Instead, Wambach has frequently appeared in the media; and when she has, she is typically shown in unglamorized and unsexualized poses and has not spoken widely about her relationships outside of those with her team and on the field. In contrast, the more traditionally heterosexually feminine and "media friendly" Hope Solo has been prominently featured in the U.S. media; but, despite initial media attempts to position her as "the new face of U.S. women's soccer," she became and remains somewhat problematic for audiences given her contentious history within the team. Thus, it could be argued that—despite their 2008 Olympic gold medal—the current U.S. team lacks players that are both pivotal and traditionally feminine (enough) to warrant major media attention; i.e., there is a lack of key players that fit the narrow hegemonic discourse of feminine beauty reproduced in, and preferred by, the sport media.

U.S. Women's Soccer Rivals

There are two main international tournaments for women's soccer: FIFA's Women's World Cup and the Summer Olympics. Compared to the men's game, the small size and recency of the women's tournaments reflect the limited number of women's national teams and the lack of financial support for them to attend. The Women's World Cup started in 1991 and has no qualifying competition, changing from a 12- to 16-team competition in 1999. In contrast, the men's inaugural World Cup was in 1930, and the upcoming 2010 World Cup involves 204 teams currently competing in six strongly contested world regional qualifying competitions to reach the tournament "final" of 32 teams. The men's 2010 tournament was heavily promoted on FIFA.com during 2007, building an audience for the tournament years in advance, in contrast to the lack of promotion for the 2007 Women's World Cup.[30] However, the women's Olympic soccer (started in 1996) is a significant competition, while the men's Olympic soccer (started in 1900) is considered to be relatively irrelevant by many "male" soccer nations. The U.S. women are three-time Olympic gold medalists (of four tournaments, including 2008) and have won two of the Women's World Cup tournaments (1991 and 1999). Yet the 2008 NBC Olympic coverage broadcast limited *prime-time* coverage (even as "news") of the American women's soccer despite their history, their potential, and, ultimately, their gold medal.

As the two key events in the women's international soccer calendar, the Olympics and the Women's World Cup have a shared history of participants, winners, and competitive rivalries limited by the number of national teams. But the media narratives used to commodify the rivalries for consumption also inform us about the development of women's soccer, the ideological and political issues relevant to the representation of rivalries, and how mediated practices typically used for women athletes have intersected with the construction of nation. As such it is of interest to consider which rivalries have emerged and which have been commodified or overlooked by the media.

Table 1 shows the results of all the women's Olympic and World Cup competitions, revealing the United States' main competition. The consistent presence of Norway from 1991 to 2007 indicates why many older and dedicated fans consider Norway a key rival. But probably most familiar to the general (sporting) public is the highly mediated rivalry with China, although table 1 reveals the short-lived nature of the Chinese challenge (1995, 1996, and 1999). Equally, a rivalry with Brazil has only slowly and more recently begun to consistently emerge in a mediated

TABLE 1: Women's World Cup and Olympic Soccer Results

| | WOMEN'S WORLD CUP | | | | WOMEN'S OLYMPICS | | |
	1ST	2ND	3RD	4TH		GOLD	SILVER	BRONZE
1991	U.S.	Norway	Sweden	Germany				
1995	Norway	Germany	U.S.	China	1996	U.S.	China	Norway
1999	U.S.	China	Brazil	Norway	2000	Norway	U.S.	Germany
2003	Germany	Sweden	U.S.	Canada	2004	U.S.	Brazil	Germany
2007	Germany	Brazil	U.S.	Norway	2008	U.S.	Brazil	Germany

form despite its competitive emergence in 2004 (and arguably earlier). But the failure of a U.S.-German rivalry to emerge as a major media narrative is especially puzzling given the ways in which the German team has actually challenged the United States' dominance. Indeed, the ousting of U.S. hero Mia Hamm as FIFA's (female) Player of the Year (2001 and 2002) by German star Birgit Prinz (2003, 2004, and 2005) and Germany's consistent contention for number one world ranking provide a good indication of just how Germany has rivaled the United States.

United States versus Norway

Norway has remained a consistently strong presence in women's soccer. Norway's early and continued presence as one of the best national teams alongside the United States means that this rivalry is somewhat pragmatic, originating from a time when the United States and Norway were each other's main obstacle at a time of little media interest in the U.S. women's soccer. Indeed, an Associated Press report on Norway beating the United States in the 2000 Olympics noted the historic rivalry:

> It also gave [Norway] the right to claim a spot next to the United States as the top team of the past decade in major international women's soccer. "Maybe we are the best team in the world now," Norway coach Per-Matthias Hagmo said. "We have beaten the United States four times this year, China three times." With the victory, Norway adds the 2000 Olympic title to its 1995 World Cup championship. The United States can claim the 1991 and last year's thrilling World Cup triumph in front of U.S. fans at the Rose Bowl

plus the gold medal at the 1996 Atlanta Games. The victory also
means Norway is still the only nation with an all-time winning
record (15-13-2) against the United States. The Norwegians are also
the only team to defeat the Americans in a World Cup or Olympic
tournament, the other victory coming in the 1995 World Cup
semifinals.[31]

Yet while the Norwegians were a major rival for the fans and "on paper,"
the U.S. media predominantly and consistently failed to commodify this
into a compelling narrative.

This failure can be attributed to two key issues. First, the lack of
ideological or political difference between the United States and Norway
that would otherwise warrant commodification into an imaginative or
compelling nation-building media narrative for U.S. audience consumption. Second, the Norwegian women's team players are not known as
"outside" hegemonic femininity; that is, they are not perceived as big
and unfeminine, nor as reproducers of hegemonic beauty since they are
not widely considered a bunch of "Babes" (the description used for the
U.S. team on July 5, 1999, in the *Independent,* a British newspaper).[32]
Thus, in terms of typical representational practices of women athletes,
the Norwegian team lacks the qualities to make the players significant
to the media since they neither fulfill the cultural disciplinary functions
of being constructed as "butch,"[33] nor warrant representation to repro-
duce hegemonic femininity.[34] As such, the rivalry has been rendered
invisible—or symbolically erased—by the media.

Consequently, while the Norway-U.S. rivalry lacks the criteria that
would make it "newsworthy" or significant for mediatization, for U.S. fans
the rivalry has remained competitively significant and enduring. Thus,
when the U.S. media reported the Norwegian victory over the United
States in the first game of the 2008 Olympics as a "shock,"[35] this news was
arguably a greater reflection of the consistent media narrative of the
Americans as the only team to beat and a disregard of the history of close
competition and rivalry between the two teams. In fairness, the article did
position Norway as medal contenders but accounted for the U.S. defeat
by suggesting that the Americans were off their game. The report also
referred to a Norwegian player as having "outmuscled" her U.S. counterpart, a linguistic choice typically deployed to "other" women in sport by
dismissing them as outside acceptable femininity. Indeed, the language of

muscularity, which should be appropriate for the discussion of women in sport, remains problematic given its potential to be discursively deployed in ways that can undermine, rather than promote, women's athleticism.[36]

Norway has also become a rival for the unofficial title of most female-friendly soccer nation given its successful professional women's league that has attracted some of the world's top players, particularly since the demise of WUSA. As in other nations, the institutional development and cultural expansion of women's soccer in Norway did not really gain momentum until the 1980s. Norway does have a history of men's soccer, but until the 1990s the Norwegian men had achieved little international success (having failed to reach the World Cup final tournament until 1994 and 1998). The lack of international Norwegian male soccer success, alongside other cultural factors—such as a less powerful link between soccer, masculinity, and, hence, sexuality than has been observed in other nations—is likely to account for why the women's game in Norway developed more quickly and strongly than in other countries in which soccer has been a predominantly male game.[37] Equally, the Norwegian men's game has a particular style which is somewhat reflected in the women's style, making them a strong, tenacious, and defensive team, but without the flair and style typically associated with nations such as Brazil and Italy, which are more easily fitted to traditional hegemonic femininity.

United States versus the People's Republic of China

The lack of media narrative about the United States' rivalry with Norway sits in contrast to the mediated rivalry with China. Despite a relatively short-lived history as serious competition to the U.S. team, the rivalry with China remains one of the key mediated and commodified narratives in U.S. women's soccer.

China's history as an international soccer nation is comparatively new, with no substantive history as a masculinized or feminized sport. While the game in the modern global form was introduced early in the twentieth century as a men's game, a professional league was not formed until 1994. Although soccer could be seen as a foreign sport, it is considered akin to a long-established Chinese game and has been overwhelmingly and enthusiastically embraced. A skilled and attacking style of play has been developed by both the Chinese men's and women's teams. The women have reached an impressive international standard fast, particularly compared to the men's team, although the extensive histories, standard, and sheer volume of competition in men's soccer make equivalent achievement on the international stage a substantively greater challenge.

The lack of a gendered history combined with great enthusiasm for soccer accounts, to a large extent, for the relatively quick international success of the women's team and the domestic success of the Women's World Cups hosted by China. Indeed, the marketing potential and enthusiasm for (even) women's soccer arguably accounts for why FIFA has twice awarded the Women's World Cup to China (in 1991, the inaugural competition, and in 2007, after the 2003 tournament was transferred to the United States at short notice due to SARS). Since the U.S. team won the 1991 (inaugural) and 1999 Women's World Cups and has consistently won Olympic gold medals, it is clear why China would view the United States as the team to beat. Equally, China emerged as a serious competitor to the United States as the opposing team in the final game of the 1996 Olympics and the 1999 World Cup, the 1999 final being significant as the tournament (held in the United States) in which the American women's soccer team captured the American imagination. Consequently, while the familiar and ideologically significant wider sporting narrative of Chinese-American rivalry provided an established discourse for commodification, the media's assurance that the interest in women's soccer was only fleeting provides some account for why a wider historical perspective or narrative of this rivalry was not constructed.[38]

The ideological and political differences between China and the United States have provided a powerful context and media narrative for a rivalry recently played out in the sporting arena. Since sport provides core discourses for identities, nation is constructed and enacted through sport, which provides a public arena for the ideological and political battle between contraposed nations. This includes representational practices that construct the other nation as "other"; that is, to build nation requires a (derogatory) positioning of opposed nations as different and outside of normative actions and attitudes. Thus the U.S. media narrative about China and its sport programs relies heavily on narratives that construct the opposition as products of a heartless, militarized, bureaucratic, and automated production line. Such narratives are already familiar to U.S.

audiences due to their common usage as part of the previous Cold War battle played out in sport. Consuming the "enemy" as a faceless, militarized machine is therefore already part of the accepted action for the interpretative community of sport as well as part of the process of shared meaning-making for wider American interpretative communities.

Consequently, the U.S. media narrative about the rivalry with China constructs it as a clash of both political and cultural ideologies and styles. A classic example of this is available in a commercial from the sponsor of the 2003 Women's World Cup, Adidas, promoting both their product and the tournament. Viewable on YouTube, the commercial was made by a Dutch advertising agency (unsurprising, since the Netherlands is the corporate home of Adidas).[39]

The narrative sequence of the commercial commences with a uniform and uniformed squad of Chinese women, in regimented lines, performing synchronized martial arts exercises, visibly integrating soccer balls in some of the (edited) action. Seen at a distance, they are a faceless and uniform unit mobilizing familiar discourses that position the Chinese as homogenous and interchangeable. The use of a martial drill as the action, rather than using soccer drills, serves to work up familiar iconic and stereotypical ideas about Chinese forms of action and knowledge while simultaneously emphasizing the aggression of the Chinese challenge (as the martial form in the United States is widely associated with fighting rather than promoting health and balance, for example). The regimented form of the squad further contributes to the perceived threat and aggression of China, mobilizing discourses of Chinese militarism and its potentially overwhelming size of population. This contrasts with the positioning of the (substantially fewer) U.S. women who, awoken by the Chinese, individually emerge to respond to the Chinese challenge by forming a group that is cohesive yet remains strongly individualized through the non-uniformity of their stances and sporting attire. One member of the Chinese squad, an actual member of the Chinese team, steps forward to issue a direct challenge to the U.S. team by performing a series of soccer skills completed by passing the ball to the feet of the Americans. The challenge is symbolically accepted by one of the key U.S. players (Aly Wagner), who places her foot on the ball (discursively owning the ball in soccer terms) with her team surrounding her, arms folded, heads high, staring down the Chinese team.

The commercial enacts the ideological differences between China and the United States and their familiar cultural embodiment, mobilizing ideas that position China as an overwhelming, de-individuated, homogenous threat and aggressor (as they lay down the challenge to the docile, sleeping Americans). The United States is in contrast constructed as the established power to be challenged (as a soccer team and as a nation), yet as a power that is not overtly aggressive but responsive and ready for any challenge (emerging from slumber yet ready for action in sporting apparel rather than sleeping attire). Equally, the coming together of the American women into one grouping to respond to the challenge of the Chinese, while wearing non-uniform (but themed) clothing, constructs them as a cohesive team of unique individuals through which we can consume the United States as a coherent nation of unique individuals coming together under one flag.

While the commercial was apparently designed to be shown in both the United States and China, its narrative and representational practices appear to come from a very Western perspective, as could be expected from a text designed by a Western European agency and corporation. Equally, I have no information on responses to or use of the text within China. However, prnewswire.com notes that the narrative itself comes from "the American players' perspective." The article later states, "The commercial captures the subtleties of each culture—on the one hand you have the Chinese, who are very uniform and regimented, and on the other hand there are the U.S. women with their individuality and unique personalities."[40] The implicit suggestion that the Chinese do not have unique personalities seems redolent of Western media narratives about China and Chinese athletes and evident in the media narrative about the U.S.-China women's soccer rivalry.

In terms of representations of femininity, it is interesting to note how, contrary to typical mediated sport practices, the explicitly sexualized femininization of the women athletes is missing from this text. Unusually, the main narrative is of action—albeit not the action of playing sport. However, it is the faceless mass of the Chinese who are in action, rather than the more familiarly heterosexualized Americans. Indeed, the distance from which the Chinese are viewed makes their gender somewhat ambiguous, and their dissimilarity from the popularly heterosexualized female athletic form in Western media makes the narrative of their difference and "otherness" more compelling.[41] Nonetheless, the action remains somewhat feminized and graceful, "a mixture of wu-shu, tai chi and soccer moves which pay tribute to the beauty of women's soccer."[42] Thus the Chinese players are not commodified for consumption as typical heterosexual femininity, while the American players remain representative of the traditional values of American athletic femininity with their familiar iconic ponytails, whiteness, predominant blondness, and slender physiques, along with their comparative lack of action. In this mediated narrative China and the Chinese women are clearly "othered," positioning the American women as the standard.

United States versus Brazil

The "Samba Queens," as a major U.S. competitor and rival, has taken some time to come to the attention of the media.[43] The media's relative failure to pay attention to this rivalry can be explained by a lack of attention and interest in women's soccer as a mediated sport, alongside the lack of political and ideological conflict with Brazil around which to build a narrative. Brazil's key players fit the traditional feminine athletic form, being variously described as "lithe" and their style described as a metaphorical and actual dance, meaning Brazil has offered the media a great opportunity to cover women's soccer using the traditional representational practices for women athletes. The Brazilian team is also highly skilled and comes from a great men's soccer nation. Yet these positives also comprise part of the problem of commodifying the U.S.-Brazil rivalry, since the media emphasis on the hegemonic heterosexual appeal, petiteness, and athletic skill of the Brazilian team means the comparative action of a rivalry narrative might be ideologically problematic, potentially "othering" the U.S. team from central membership in heterosexual femininity.

Equally, the Brazilian women have achieved great success despite the extreme masculinity of the sport in the country and the powerful resistance that still faces them in their own nation. This remains a powerful U.S. media narrative about the Brazilians, but too much comparative attention could also raise some ideological issues about the position of women's sport in the United States. Media narratives consistently position the U.S. women's team as coming from an envious national context, only superficially addressing the issue of exclusion in Brazil and in ways that do not address issues in the American context. For example, in 2004, Scott Pitoniak reported: "[The Brazilians] would love to take a page from [the United States] and attempt to establish women's soccer in their country the way the Americans have in theirs. They believe a gold medal would help them popularize the game among Brazilian females. It would help them begin to crawl out of the enormous shadow cast by their men's national team, which has won a record five World Cups."[44] This narrative fails to address the systematic and extreme resistance to women's soccer in Brazil, suggesting the failure is in women's interest rather than the institutional and cultural bar on women playing what remains predominantly viewed as a sport for men only. It also infers the women's game is well established in the United States, glossing over the issues raised by the previous year's demise of the women's professional game.

But a mediated rivalry narrative between Brazil and the United States is increasingly prominent, at least on FIFA.com's Olympic report, where titles of posted articles built up the 2008 Olympic final as "Revenge" (August 19, 2008) and the teams as "foes" (August 18, 2008).[45] Indeed, as is increasingly being noted in some of the sporting media, the Brazil-U.S. rivalry is actually quite antagonistic and bitter, with accusations from both teams of intentionally dangerous physical play. This form of intentionally aggressive and combative play does not fit well within sporting ideologies that reserve such forms of play for men, providing a further account of why the Brazil-U.S. rivalry continues to be somewhat overlooked by the media. The idea that women are naturally aggressive is very problematic for predominant sporting discourses. Consequently, the familiar strategy of using male coaches to account for women's sport success can be observed in accounting for the apparent U.S.-Brazil antagonism. This strategy is clearly adopted in a further extract from Scott Pitoniak's 2004 Olympic report, alongside an explanation that dismisses the claim about the U.S. team as simply sour grapes: "Still peeved about his team's 2–0 loss to the United States in an early round match 12 days ago, [the male Brazil coach] continues to tell Brazilian reporters that the Americans are dirty players. . . . To their credit, it doesn't appear the Brazilian players have adopted their coach's motivational ploy. They talk as if they have great respect for the Americans."[46]

What about Germany?

During the time in which China emerged as the United States' major rival, and before Brazil emerged as a serious threat, Germany stood as the clear heir apparent to the United States and prime candidate as major U.S. rival for many titles. Germany has won the last two Women's World Cups and taken the Olympic bronze in the last three competitions. However, in line with the issues discussed so far, Germany lacks a number of features that render it ideal for media consumption. First, there is no political ideological clash with Germany as a democratic and majority Christian nation. Second, there is no major sporting history with the current German nation to make it a sporting rival that threatens U.S. national identity. Third, while the German women's team is considered to be excellent and includes some of the world's greatest current individual players, such as Birgit Prinz, the key German players do not fit the hegemonic ideals of women athletes who receive media attention. But unlike the Chinese and Brazilians, whose femininity can be constructed as comparatively unchallenging to Western notions of masculinity, the German women pose a direct threat to masculine sporting discourses as tall, powerful, aggressive women who do not perform traditional heterosexualized femininity.

The contrast between the traditionally feminized U.S. team and the alternative femininity of the German team could have been a powerful mediated narrative, particularly given the culturally disciplining potential of this narrative.[47] Indeed this narrative has been widely used by the media for the Brazil-Germany rivalry, often personified by contrasting the petite, "lithe" Brazilian Marta with the German "juggernaut" Birgit Prinz.[48] The common narrative constructing the German women as masculine emerges from the lack of traditional hegemonic femininity and style perceived in their form of play and the ways in which this is ideologically threatening. This narrative serves to "other" the German team and negate their success, providing a disciplinary function. This narrative also serves a similar function for the opposition's fans, particularly after a defeat. Consequently, just as a Brazilian-U.S. rivalry narrative could raise ideological problems for the U.S. women's femininity, a comparison to the already mediatized masculinity of the Germans could be problematic given the comparative size and style of the United States' key player, Abby Wambach, and the media's attention to the details that emphasize her above-average size.

To a great extent, Abby Wambach matches up in size and style to Birgit Prinz (although Wambach arguably has not yet shown the brilliance that has led to Prinz's three titles as FIFA Player of the Year). Consequently, the popular media narrative of the Germans as problematically masculine, often personified by Prinz, becomes ideologically challenging when used in relation to the U.S. team and its personification through Wambach (as a key player/striker). Indeed, like Prinz, Wambach is (as noted earlier) already subject to consistent media comments about her height.

Concluding Comments

Overall, the ideological significance of sport and soccer has been argued to account for the lack of media attention on, or emergence of, U.S. women's soccer rivalries. The focus of the U.S. media on sports that construct nation, national identity, and masculinity has meant that quintessentially male American sports and those which it can win on the world stage against nations of opposing political ideologies are emphasized, while soccer, women's soccer in particular, has been ignored and rendered invisible. As such, the highly successful U.S. women's soccer team has been overlooked because, even though they win, their competition has been mainly against ideologically unchallenging nations in a sport that challenges American sporting ideologies surrounding gender, nation, and the nature of competition. The ideological exception offered by China, both politically and in terms of femininity, accounts for why this of all the potential rivalries captured the media's attention and, hence, the nation's. Basically, China was the ideal candidate for a mediated "othering" that simultaneously positioned the U.S. women as appropriate representatives of national pride, American ideology, and femininity.

Of course it could be argued that the U.S.-China rivalry emerged because of the success of the 1999 U.S.-based Women's World Cup tournament and China's position as the opposing team in the final. But failure to build subsequent media narratives provides support for the assertion that this narrative was an exceptional occurrence, rather than a narrative that simply reflected a historic point in time. Equally, the success of a sporting event lies in its mediated representation. This is essentially the major rival to U.S. women's soccer since it can be argued that the lack of consistent narrative construction, audience-building, and primetime scheduling, along with low production values, has systematically undermined the position of women's soccer. These elements continue to thwart any chance of capturing the popular imagination of the nation, largely because other sports remain key rivals for the attention, interests, and identities of the people who produce mediated sport.

NOTES

1. The Purest of Rivalries—*Joseph M. Turrini*

1. Although Yang Chuan-Kwang was his correct name in his native Taiwan, he was known in the West as C. K. Yang. For the sake of consistency this chapter will refer to him as C. K. Yang throughout. Trevor Slack, Hsu Yuan-min, Tsai Chiung-tzu, and Fan Hong, "The Road to Modernization: Sport in Taiwan," *International Journal of the History of the Sport* 19, no. 2 (2002): 348.

2. Hal Bateman, "Johnson Outlasts Yang," *Track and Field News,* September 1960, 16.

3. The chapter epigraph is from an interview with Elvin "Ducky" Drake, "The Decathlon Videorecording: Rafer Johnson and C. K. Yang, 1960, Rome," Olympiad Series (from Bud Greenspan documentary), 7:56, LA84 Foundation Library, Los Angeles, California, videocassette.

4. Frank Zarnowski, *The Decathlon: A Colorful History of Track and Field's Most Challenging Event* (Champaign: Leisure Press, 1989), 95.

5. Rafer Johnson (with Philip Goldberg), *The Best That I Can Be: An Autobiography* (New York: Doubleday, 1998), 1–21.

6. "To Do a Little Better," *Time,* August 29, 1960, 54.

7. Johnson, *The Best That I Can Be,* 22–33.

8. Ibid., 27.

9. Ibid., 33–35.

10. Ibid., 35–42.

11. The prep decathlons included all ten events and were scored like a regular decathlon, but they also included significant differences that make it impossible to compare scores with collegiate, Olympic, or other international competitions. The first decathlon in San Francisco, for example, included an 800-meter race instead of the 1,500. All of the competitions used lighter high school implements in the weight events, such as a 12-pound shot put and a 3.9-pound discus. Johnson, *The Best That I Can Be,* 42–43.

12. "New Decathlon Star," *Track and Field News,* June 1954, 3.

13. Johnson, *The Best That I Can Be,* 43.

14. This was the first decathlon that Rafer Johnson competed in that did not use the lighter high school implements or the shorter 800-meter race. Thus, many consider it his first true decathlon. Michael Strauss, "Richards Regains Decathlon Crown," *New York Times,* July 3, 1954; Johnson, *The Best That I Can Be,* 42–43.

15. Craig Dixon, interview by Dr. Margaret Costa, March 25, 1991, transcript, An Olympian's Oral History Project, LA84 Foundation Library, 10.

16. Johnson, *The Best That I Can Be,* 58–59.

17. "Rafer Johnson Elected President; Ellis, Gamer, Kerns, Vargas Won," *UCLA Daily Bruin,* April 24, 1958, 1; Johnson, *The Best That I Can Be,* 111–112.

18. "Athletic Department to Get Non-Discrimination Plaque," *UCLA Daily Bruin,* February 25, 1955, 1.

19. Johnson, *The Best That I Can Be,* 62.

20. "Jones of U.S. Lowers World Mark in 400-Meter Run at Pan-American Games," *New York Times,* March 19, 1955; "Miranda Defeats Santee in Upset for 1,500 Crown," *New York Times,* March 20, 1955; "Johnson Wins Decathlon," *UCLA Daily Bruin,* March 21, 1955, 4; "Bruin Sets World Record: Rafer Johnson Breaks Decathlon Standard in Kingsburg Meet," *UCLA Daily Bruin,* June 17, 1955, 7; "Johnson in Record 7985," *Track and Field News,* June 1955, 1, 5.

21. For a few examples, see Ralph Seligman, "30 Point Performance Recorded by Johnson," *UCLA Daily Bruin,* March 28, 1955, 7; Ralph Seligman, "Brubabes Lose: Rafer Still Hot," *UCLA Daily Bruin,* March 30, 1955, 6; Ralph Seligman, "Johnson, Batonmen Sparkle as Frosh Spikers Down Taft," *UCLA Daily Bruin,* April 18, 1955, 7.

22. "Brubabes Tops SC 73–58, Johnson, Cook Star in Win," *UCLA Daily Bruin,* May 11, 1955, 7.

23. "Bruin Track Squad Takes PCC Crown," *UCLA Daily Bruin,* May 23, 1956, 10; "UCLA Edges So. California," *Track and Field News,* May 1956, 5.

24. "College Track Summaries," *New York Times,* June 17, 1956.

25. "Rafer Gets Top Awards," *UCLA Daily Bruin,* February 28, 1957, 3.

26. "Olympic Predictions," *Track and Field News,* November 1956, 8; Judd Swarzman, "Johnson, Drummond Give UCLA Hope for World Track Honors," *UCLA Daily Bruin,* September 11, 1956, 27.

27. Rafer Johnson, quoted in Zarnowski, *The Decathlon,* 89.

28. Johnson, *The Best That I Can Be,* 101.

29. Milt Campbell holds a significant amount of resentment at the lack of appreciation and limited financial opportunities he received despite having won a silver and a gold medal in the decathlon in 1952 and 1956. Campbell thinks that his opportunities were limited because he was an African American. He also seems to hold some resentment over the fact that most think Johnson would have won in 1956 if he was healthy. Zarnowski, *The Decathlon,* 79; Bert Nelson, "Campbell Beats Johnson," *Track and Field News,* December 1956, 18; Dave Anderson, "The Olympic Time Capsule," *New York Times,* April 25, 1976; Merrell Noden, "Best Athlete You Never Knew," *Sports Illustrated,* August 5, 1996, http://vault.sportsillustrated.cnn.com/vault/article/magazine/MAG1008475/index.htm (accessed July 9, 2008); Flip Bondy, "Milt Campbell, One of the Best Athletes You've Ever Known," *New York Daily News,* May 18, 2008, http://www.nydailynews.com/sports/more_sports/2008/05/17/2008-05 17_milt_campbell_one_of_the_best_athletes_y.html (accessed July 9, 2008).

30. Elvin "Ducky" Drake, interview by Joel Gardner, January 24, 1979, March 7, 1979, and March 5, 1980, transcript, UCLA Oral History Program, Charles E. Young Research Library, Department of Special Collections, UCLA, Los Angeles, California, 58.

31. "Amateur Athletic Foundation Lifetime Achievement Award Honoring Rafer Johnson and C. K. Yang," hosted by Dwight Stones, April 10, 1997, LA84 Foundation Library, unedited videocassette.

32. Allison Danzig, "Campbell Takes Decathlon Title with Record 7,937-Point Total," *New York Times,* December 1, 1960.

33. Ibid.; Bert Nelson, "Campbell Beats Johnson," *Track and Field News,* December 1956, 19.

34. "1957 World List: Decathlon," *Track and Field News,* January 1958, 10; "Records in LH, Decathlon," *Track and Field News,* May 1958, 1, 2.

35. Pincus Sober, "U.S. Track and Field Teams Compete in Moscow, Warsaw, Budapest, Athens," *Amateur Athlete,* September 1958, 5.

36. Johnson, *The Best That I Can Be,* 114.

37. R. L. Quercetani, "Decathlon, HSJ Records," *Track and Field News,* August 1958, 4; Max Frankel, "Soviet Defeats U.S. Track Team," *New York Times,* July 29, 1958; Ralph Colson, "The Report from Moscow," *Amateur Athlete,* April 1959, 28.

38. Colson, "The Report from Moscow," 28.

39. Johnson, *The Best That I Can Be,* 69.

40. "People," *Time,* January 19, 1959.

41. "Whatever It Takes," *Time,* July 18, 1960, 48.

42. Bill Becker, "Rafer Johnson: A Goodwill Ambassador," *New York Times,* May 3, 1964.

43. Johnson, *The Best That I Can Be,* 115.

44. Ibid., 113.

45. Slack et al., "The Road to Modernization: Sport in Taiwan," 348.

46. Robert Creamer, "The Cobra and C. K. Yang," *Sports Illustrated,* December 23, 1963, 76.

47. Zarnowski, *The Decathlon,* 98; Bob Mathias (with Robert Mendes), *The Bob Mathias Story* (Champaign: Sports Publishing LLC, 2001), 95–96; Don Holst and Marcia Popp, *American Men of Olympic Track and Field: Interviews with Athletes and Coaches* (Jefferson: McFarland & Company, Inc., Publishers, 2005), 88; "C. K. Yang Determined to Win Decathlon for China in 1964," *Los Angeles Times,* March 15, 1961.

48. Yang spoke fluent Japanese as well as Chinese, a result of Japanese involvement in Taiwan during his youth.

49. Fan Hong, "Communist China and the Asian Games, 1951–1990: The Thirty-Nine Year Struggle," *Sport in Society* 8, no. 3 (September 2005): 480; Gerald Chan, "The 'Two-Chinas' Problem and the Olympic Formula," *Pacific Affairs* 58, no. 3 (Autumn 1985): 473–474.

50. Xu Guoqi, *Olympic Dreams: China and Sports, 1895–2008* (Cambridge: Harvard University Press, 2008), 77.

51. Ibid., 87.

52. Ibid., 76.

53. The name was changed to the Olympic Committee of the People's Democratic Republic of China in 1957.

54. Hong, "Communist China and the Asian Games," 481.

55. Guoqi, *Olympic Dreams,* 85.

56. Chan, "The 'Two-Chinas' Problem," 474–475; Richard Espy, *The Politics of the Olympic Games: With an Epilogue, 1976–1980* (Berkeley: University of California Press, 1981), 43–45.

57. Slack et al., "The Road to Modernization: Sport in Taiwan," 346.

58. Zarnowski, *The Decathlon,* 97.

59. "1957 World Rankings: Decathlon," *Track and Field News,* December 1957, 12; "1957 World List: Decathlon," *Track and Field News,* January 1958, 10; "1958 World Rankings: Decathlon," *Track and Field News,* December 1958, 14; "1958 World List: Decathlon," *Track and Field News,* January 1959, 11.

60. Drake interview by Gardner, 62.

61. Ibid.; "Amateur Athletic Foundation Lifetime Achievement Award Honoring

Rafer Johnson and C. K. Yang," LA84 Foundation Library; Johnson, *The Best That I Can Be,* 133.

62. Rafer Johnson, interview with Peter Gambaccini, *Runner's World,* April 30, 2007, http://racingnews.runnersworld.com/2007/04/a_brief_chat_wi_13.html (accessed May 23, 2008).

63. The best testament to their lifetime friendship is the 1997 Amateur Athletic Foundation Lifetime Achievement Award event, where both Yang and Johnson spoke at length about each other in glowing terms. "Amateur Athletic Foundation Lifetime Achievement Award Honoring Rafer Johnson and C. K. Yang," LA84 Foundation Library; "C. K. Yang, 74, Decathlon Silver Medalist, Is Dead," *New York Times,* February 1, 2007.

64. Joseph M. Sheehan, "Ten N.C.A.A. Track Meet Records Tumble," *New York Times,* June 19, 1960.

65. "Redskins Select Notre Dame End," *New York Times,* January 22, 1959; Johnson, *The Best That I Can Be,* 138.

66. Johnson, *The Best That I Can Be,* 134; *Sportlook,* "Rafer Johnson Interview with Roy Firestone," episode 412, April 25, 1983 (recorded and aired), videocassette, LA84 Foundation Library.

67. "Amateur Athletic Foundation Lifetime Achievement Award Honoring Rafer Johnson and C. K. Yang"; Johnson, *The Best That I Can Be,* 134.

68. Dixon interview by Costa, 11; "Amateur Athletic Foundation Lifetime Achievement Award Honoring Rafer Johnson and C. K. Yang."

69. Johnson, *The Best That I Can Be,* 250.

70. "Rafer Johnson Ailing," *New York Times,* June 21, 1959.

71. "Kuznetsov Betters Decathlon Record," *New York Times,* May 18, 1959.

72. "Yang Wins Decathlon," *Track and Field News,* July 1959, 13.

73. "Yang Sweeps Opening of AAU Decathlon," *Los Angeles Times,* August 28, 1959; "Yang Breaks AAU Record," *Los Angeles Times,* August 29, 1959.

74. Joseph M. Sheehan, "Johnson to Get U.S. Team Berth If He Is Ready for Competition," *New York Times,* June 22, 1959; "Soviet Union Names Squad of 57 for Track Meet with U.S. in Philadelphia," *New York Times,* July 9, 1959; "Johnson on Sidelines," *New York Times,* July 11, 1959; "59 Russian Track Stars Depart for U.S. Amid Publicity Burst," *New York Times,* July 13, 1959; "59 Soviet Track Athletes Arrive for Week-End Meet Against U.S. Teams," *New York Times,* July 14, 1959.

75. "USA-USSR Meet," *Track and Field News,* August 1959, 3; Joseph M. Sheehan, "U.S. Men Beat Soviet in Track; Russian Women Are Victorious," *New York Times,* July 20, 1959.

76. "European Report," *Track and Field News,* September 1959, 13; "1959 World Rankings: Decathlon," *Track and Field News,* December 1959, 19.

77. Johnson, *The Best That I Can Be,* 142; "Mulkey Selected for Trip to Rome," *New York Times,* July 18, 1960, 37.

78. "To Do a Little Better," *Time,* August 29, 1960, 55.

79. Ibid.

80. Drake interview, 67–68; Hal Bateman, "On Your Marks," *Track and Field News,* August 1960, 18; Al Wolf, "Rafer Believes All-Time Best Needed for Olympic Decathlon," *Los Angeles Times,* May 3, 1960.

81. Drake interview by Gardner, 67.

82. Allison Danzig, "Rafer Johnson Picked to Carry U.S. Flag in Olympic Opening-Day Parade" *New York Times*, August 23, 1960; "Whatever It Takes," *Time*, July 18, 1960, 52.

83. "To Do a Little Better," *Time*, August 29, 1960, 52.

84. Danzig, "Rafer Johnson Picked to Carry U.S. Flag in Olympic Opening-Day Parade."

85. Guoqi, *Olympic Dreams*, 87.

86. Ibid., 90.

87. Espy, *The Politics of the Olympic Games*, 63–66.

88. Ibid., 63.

89. "Yang May Miss Decathlon Over Games Taiwan Issue," *Los Angeles Times*, August 22, 1960.

90. Guoqi, *Olympic Dreams*, 90–92.

91. Dave Anderson, "The Gray Suitcase on the Bunk," *New York Times*, July 17, 1976.

92. Guoqi, *Olympic Dreams*, 93.

93. Robert Daley, "The Parade: History, Tragedy and Politics," *New York Times*, August 26, 1960.

94. The quote was in a letter from Avery Brundage and Otto Mayer to the Taiwan delegation. Quoted in Guoqi, *Olympic Dreams*, 93.

95. Daley, "The Parade: History, Tragedy and Politics."

96. For examples, see Hal Bateman, "Johnson Outlasts Yang," *Track and Field News*, September 1960, 18; "Yang of Taiwan Wins Decathlon," *Los Angeles Times*, June 28, 1959; "Yang Wins, But Misses Record," *Los Angeles Times*, July 2, 1962.

97. For examples, see "Davis' Shot-Put Is Best on Coast," *New York Times*, April 24, 1960; "Yang Gets 2 Awards at Track Dinner," *Los Angeles Times*, June 2, 1962; Arnold Lester, "UCLA Track Gets a Foreign Flavor," *UCLA Bruin*, February 2, 1960, 19; Art Spander, "Two Bruins Eye Olympic Decathlon," *UCLA Bruin*, May 18, 1960, 1; Mort Salzman, "Johnson Back Home Now, History's Best Wins Again," *UCLA Daily Bruin*, September 13, 1960, 31; Dick Drake, "Yang Scores Brilliant 9,121," *Track and Field News*, May 1963, 1.

98. Robert Creamer, "The Cobra and C. K. Yang," *Sports Illustrated*, December 23, 1963, 67–68.

99. "European Report," *Track and Field News*, June 1960, 14; Hal Batemen, "Johnson Outlasts Yang," *Track and Field News*, September 1960, 16–17; Braven Dyer, "Johnson Takes Slim Lead Over Yang in Decathlon," *Los Angeles Times*, September 6, 1960; "Soviet Coach Calls U.S. Team Standout," *New York Times*, August 9, 1960; Allison Danzig, "Decathlon Lead Goes to Johnson," *New York Times*, September 6, 1960.

100. Although the Soviet star earned his second Olympic bronze medal when he finished a distant third.

101. Drake interview by Gardner, 69; Bateman, "Johnson Outlasts Yang," 16.

102. Allison Danzig, "Decathlon Lead Goes to Johnson," *New York Times*, September 6, 1960.

103. Braven Dyer, "Johnson Takes Slim Lead Over Yang in Decathlon," *Los Angeles Times*, September 6, 1960.

104. Bateman, "Johnson Outlasts Yang," 16.

105. Drake interview by Gardner, 69.

106. Zarnowksi, *The Decathlon*, 88.

107. Drake interview by Gardner, 68.

108. Journalist quoted in Johnson, *The Best That I Can Be*, 69.

109. "The Champion," *Time*, September 19, 1960, 75.

110. Interview with Ducky Drake, "The Decathlon Videorecording: Rafer Johnson and C. K. Yang, 1960, Rome," Olympiad Series, 7:56 (from Bud Greenspan documentary), LA84 Foundation Library, videocassette.

111. Coach Drake quoted in Zarnowski, *The Decathlon*, 89.

112. Drake interview by Gardner, 71–72.

113. Hal Bateman, "Johnson Outlasts Yang," *Track and Field News*, September 1960, 17.

114. "Johnson Retires From 2-Day Grind," *New York Times*, September 7, 1960.

115. Johnson, *The Best That I Can Be*, 156.

116. "Johnson Retires From 2-Day Grind."

117. Bateman, "Johnson Outlasts Yang," 16–17.

118. "Johnson Retires From 2-Day Grind."

119. On the pole-vaulting phenomenon and the incredible increase in the heights vaulted, see "Indoor Report: Pole Vault," *Track and Field News*, February 1963, 12–13; Dick Drake, "13 Vaulters Over 16 Feet," *Track and Field News*, May 1963, 22–23; "Nikula Soars into Oribt, Hits 16–8¾," *Los Angeles Times*, February 3, 1963; Al Wolf, "Vaulters on Way to Moon," *Los Angeles Times*, January 11, 1964; Tex Maule, "He Could Do It on Bamboo," *Sports Illustrated*, February 26, 1962.

120. "Yang Zooms to 16' 3¼,'" *Track and Field News*, January 1963, 3.

121. For example, see "Yang Stars in UCLA-SC Relay Meet," *Los Angeles Times*, February 26, 1961; "Yang Sparks UCLA with Five Firsts," *Los Angeles Times*, March 18, 1962; "Bruins Rout Cal Spikers, 99–32," *Los Angeles Times*, April 22, 1962; "Johnson of California High Jumps Seven Feet," *New York Times*, April 22, 1962; Al Wolf, "Only 1,284 Fans on Hand to See USC Win Big 5 Meet," *Los Angeles Times*, May 27, 1962.

122. For example, see "Upsets in Track Paced by Grelle," *New York Times*, February 11, 1963; "Pole Vault Stars Await Santa Barbara Meet Today," *New York Times*, March 30, 1963; "Crothers's 1:50.2 Sets 880 Record in Track on Coast," *New York Times*, December 28, 1963; "Pennel Shatters Pole-Vault Mark," *New York Times*, January 19, 1964; "Kidd Will Oppose Two Strong Foes in 3-Mile Tonight," *New York Times*, January 24, 1964; "World Trackmen Hit Stride Early," *New York Times*, January 27, 1964; "O'Hara Seeks Mark Tonight," *New York Times* March 6, 1964; "O'Hara Breaks His World Indoor Record Mile Record with 3:56.4 Chicago Victory, *New York Times*, March 7, 1964.

123. Craig Dixon, UCLA assistant coach when Yang started at UCLA, claimed years later that "C. K. could have been a great decathlete, but he lost focus." Dixon does not elaborate how he thought Yang lost focus, but his devotion to the pole vault could very well be what Dixon was thinking of. Dixon interview by Costa, 11.

124. Al Wolf, "Yang Given a Chance to Top Decathlon Mark at Mt. SAC," *Los Angeles Times*, April 23, 1963.

125. "9,121-Point Total Erases Old Mark," *New York Times*, Aril 29, 1963.

126. "New Table Hurts Yang," *Track and Field News*, September 1964, 24.

127. Dick Drake, "Holdorf Edges Aun," *Track and Field News*, October/November 1964, 32–33.

128. Robert Creamer, "The Cobra and C. K. Yang," *Sports Illustrated,* December 23, 1963, 77.

129. Frank Litsky, "C. K. Yang: A Continent Rests on His Shoulders," *New York Times,* May 16, 1963.

130. Ibid.

131. "Amateur Athletic Foundation Lifetime Achievement Award Honoring Rafer Johnson and C. K. Yang," LA84 Foundation Library.

132. Taiwan's difficulties with China continued to pose challenges to Yang between 1961 and 1964. For example, Taiwan was barred from the 1962 Asian Games held in Indonesia. "C. K. Yang Not Bitter About Being Barred," *Los Angeles Times,* August 31, 1962; "On Edge for the Games," *Time,* July 19, 1976, 54; Espy, *The Politics of the Olympic Games,* 147–155.

133. Rick Chu quoted in Slack et al., "The Road to Modernization: Sport in Taiwan," 349.

134. Ibid.

135. "Rafer Johnson in Movie Role," *New York Times,* September 20, 1960.

136. For the most comprehensive Rafer Johnson filmography, see *The Internet Movie Database,* "Rafer Johnson," http://www.imdb.com/name/nm0426020/ (accessed May 27, 2008); Johnson, *The Best That I Can Be,* 162–165.

137. Johnson, *The Best That I Can Be,* 172–178.

138. Ibid., 228–232.

139. Ibid., 168–170, 183; "The Newest Frontier," *Time,* March 10, 1961, 18, 20; David Halberstam, "Recruits Flocking to Join Corps," *New York Times,* March 2, 1961; "Robert Kennedy Target of Sit-In," *New York Times,* March 14, 1962.

140. Johnson, *The Best That I Can Be,* 198–201; Wallace Turner, "The Shooting: A Victory Celebration That Ended with Shots, Screams and Curses," *New York Times,* June 6, 1968; Terry Robards, "Relatives Kept Vigil at the Hospital," *New York Times,* June 6, 1968.

141. Johnson, *The Best That I Can Be,* 232–234.

142. For example, see *Sportlook* interviews where Rafer was promoting Special Olympics and the Hershey Track and Field for Youth Program. *Sportlook,* "Rafer Johnson Interview with Roy Firestone," episode 412, April 25, 1983 (recorded and aired), videocassette, LA84 Foundation Library; *Sportlook,* "Rafer Johnson Interview with Ted Green," episode 617, June 24, 1986 (aired), March 28, 1986 (recorded), videocassette, LA84 Foundation Library.

143. Al Wolf, "Rafer Predicts Win for Pupil," *Los Angeles Times,* March 1, 1961; Hal Bateman, "On Your Marks," *Track and Field News,* March 1961, 11.

144. "Yang Earns 3 Bruin Awards," *Los Angeles Times,* May 29, 1963; Bateman, "On Your Marks," 7.

145. Johnson, *The Best That I Can Be,* 225.

146. Drake interview by Gardner, 72.

147. Dixon interview by Costa, 11.

148. Lisa Dillman, "C. K. Yang, 74: Decathlete Won Taiwan's 1st Olympic Medal at 1960 Rome Olympic Games," *Los Angeles Times,* January 30, 2007.

149. Johnson, *The Best That I Can Be,* 172.

150. Ibid., 144.

2. The King and the Bear—*George B. Kirsch*

1. Jack Nicklaus quoted in Steve Hershey and Jerry Potter, "Palmer, Nicklaus Renew Friendship, Rivalry, at Memorial," *USA Today*, June 3, 1993; Reid Hanley, "Fellow Pros Pay Tribute to Palmer," *Chicago Tribune*, June 3, 1993.

2. Arnold Palmer with James Dodson, *A Golfer's Life* (New York: Random House, 1999), chapters 1–7.

3. Herbert Warren Wind, "Gasps for a Fabulous Finish," *Sports Illustrated* 12 (April 18, 1960): 12–15; Herbert Warren Wind, "Destiny's New Favorite," *Sports Illustrated* 12 (June 27, 1960): 24–25, 65.

4. Ray Cave, "Sportsman of the Year: Arnold Palmer," *Sports Illustrated* 14 (January 9, 1961): 23–31.

5. Jack Nicklaus quoted in Tom Callahan, "How Much Did They Really Love Each Other?" *Golf Digest* 44 (August 1993): 58.

6. Palmer, *A Golfer's Life*, 165–166, 205.

7. Jack Nicklaus with Ken Bowden, *My Story* (New York: Simon & Schuster, 1997), 79; Palmer, *A Golfer's Life*, 317.

8. Palmer, *A Golfer's Life*, 207–208; Howard Sounes, *The Wicked Game: Arnold Palmer, Jack Nicklaus, Tiger Woods, and the Business of Modern Golf* (New York: Harper Collins, 2004), 82; Nicklaus, *My Story*, 75.

9. *New York Times*, June 18, 1962, 29, December 26, 1962, 10.

10. Palmer, *A Golfer's Life*, 166.

11. Ibid., 318–321.

12. *New York Times*, April 13, 1964, 36.

13. Frederick C. Klein, "Arnold Palmer, Inc.," *Wall Street Journal*, July 8, 1966, 1, 14.

14. Oscar Fraley, "Lonesome Jack," *Golf* 6 (January 1964), 16, 46–47; Dr. Bruce C. Ogilvie, "Why Fans Pull Against Nicklaus," *Golf Digest* 17 (October 1966), 29–30.

15. Nicklaus, *My Story*, 85–87.

16. Ibid., 144.

17. Ken Bowden, "Why Nicklaus Is Back on Top," *Golf Digest* 22 (July 1971), 49.

18. Gary Player quoted in Ian O'Connor, *Arnie and Jack: Palmer, Nicklaus, and Golf's Greatest Rivalry* (Boston: Houghton Mifflin, 2008), 290–291.

19. Klein, "Arnold Palmer, Inc.," 1; see also Al Laney, "The Age of Palmer," *Golf* 11 (December 1969): 51–54, 92–96; "Arnold Palmer: Man of the Silver Era," *Golf Digest* 26 (August 1975): 34–39.

20. Interview with Mark McCormack quoted in Howard Sounes, *The Wicked Game*, 55.

21. Callahan, "How Much Did They Really Love Each Other?" 60.

22. Jack Nicklaus quoted in Sounes, *The Wicked Game*, 105.

23. John S. Radosta, "Nicklaus Impresario of New Tournament," *New York Times*, July 27, 1975.

24. Jack Nicklaus quoted in *New York Times*, July 22, 1978.

25. Jaime Diaz, "Arnie and Jack, Jack and Arnie," *New York Times*, March 18, 1999.

26. Palmer, *A Golfer's Life*, 256–272; Nicklaus, *My Story*, 240.

27. *New York Times*, August 20, 1968, August 21, 1968, September 25, 1968; Mark Mulvoy, "The Revolt of the Touring Pros," *Sports Illustrated* 29 (September 2, 1968): 20–

21; Jack Nicklaus, "Rebuttal to a Searing Attack," *Sports Illustrated* 29 (September 16, 1968): 30–31.

28. *New York Times,* December 14, 1968, January 23, 1969.

29. Palmer, *A Golfer's Life,* 282–285.

30. Nicklaus, *My Story,* 324–326; Sounes, *The Wicked Game,* 131–133.

31. Sounes, *The Wicked Game,* 3, 134–136, 151, 214–215, 256–257.

32. Arnold Palmer and Jack Nicklaus quoted in Brian Callahan, "The King and Bear," *Golf Magazine* 43 (November 2001): 80–81.

33. Arnold Palmer quoted in "Nicklaus-Palmer Draws Crowd," *New York Times,* April 14, 1980.

34. Arnold Palmer, "What Jack Meant to Me," *Golf Magazine* 47 (September 2005): 116; Callahan, "How Much Did They Really Love Each Other?" 58–63.

35. Callahan, "How Much Did They Really Love Each Other?" 58–63.

36. Nicklaus, *My Story,* 236–237.

37. Palmer, *A Golfer's Life,* 321–323.

38. Jack Nicklaus quoted in *Atlanta Journal-Constitution,* April 11, 1996, E8.

3. The Mortality of Kings—*Gerald Early*

1. Mark Kram, *The Ghosts of Manila: The Fateful Blood Feud Between Muhammad Ali and Joe Frazier* (New York: HarperCollins, 2001), 53.

2. Joe Frazier and Phil Berger, *Smokin' Joe: The Autobiography* (New York: Macmillan, 1996), 19.

3. Frazier and Berger, *Smokin' Joe,* 7

4. Joe Martin quoted in Thomas Hauser, *Muhammad Ali: His Life and Times* (New York: Simon & Schuster, 1991), 19.

5. Hauser, *Muhammad Ali,* 22–23.

6. Cassius Clay, *The Greatest: My Own Story* (New York: Random House, 1975), 76.

7. David Remnick, *King of the World: Muhammad Ali and the Rise of an American Hero* New York: Random House, 1998), 89, 90–91.

8. Cassius Clay quoted in Remnick, *King of the World,* 103–104.

9. Cassius Clay quoted in Hauser, *Muhammad Ali,* 42.

10. Remnick, *King of the World,* 74.

11. Kram, *The Ghosts of Manila,* 24–25.

12. Frazier and Berger, *Smokin' Joe,* 67.

13. Kram, *The Ghosts of Manila,* 151, 153–154.

14. Frazier and Berger, *Smokin' Joe,* 196.

15. Kram, *The Ghosts of Manila,* 1.

4. "We Were about Winning"—*Daniel A. Nathan*

It is with great pleasure that I thank Greg Pfitzer and David Wiggins for their constructive criticism of this chapter and for their support, patience, and good cheer.

1. Jack McCallum, "Perfect Ending," *Sports Illustrated,* April 21, 2008, 40.

2. Harvey Araton, "Throwback Finals? That's Wishful Thinking," *New York Times,* April 20, 2008, Sports.

3. Pat Riley quoted in Bob Ryan, "The Two and Only," *Sports Illustrated,* December 14, 1992, 55.

4. Magic Johnson quoted in Ryan, "The Two and Only," 55.

5. Grant Farred, *Phantom Calls: Race and the Globalization of the NBA* (Chicago: Prickly Paradigm Press, 2006), 4–5.

6. Johnette Howard, *The Rivals: Chris Evert vs. Martina Navratilova: Their Epic Duels and Extraordinary Friendship* (New York: Broadway Books, 2005), 10.

7. Ryan, "The Two and Only," 50.

8. Ryan, "The Two and Only," 50.

9. Magic Johnson and Larry Byrd quoted in Ryan, "The Two and Only," 53.

10. Gordon S. White Jr., "Michigan State Defeats Indiana State for N.C.A.A. Title," *New York Times,* March 27, 1979.

11. Actually, the 1979 NCAA championship game was not the first time that Bird and Johnson had been on the same court, for they were teammates before they were adversaries, if briefly. In April 1978, after Bird's junior and Johnson's freshman years, they both played for the U.S. team in the World Invitation Tournament, a round-robin competition played in the United States, featuring the Soviet Union, Yugoslavia, and Cuba. Bird reminisces in his autobiography, *Drive* (1989): "The big thing in between my junior and senior years was participation on an All-Star team with such players as Magic Johnson, Sidney Moncrief, James Bailey and a bunch of guys from [the University of] Kentucky," which had just won the NCAA championship. A precursor to the 1979 Pan American and 1980 Olympic Games, the World Invitation Tournament should certainly be understood in a Cold War context, but also in terms of laying a foundation of admiration and sportsmanship for the Bird-Johnson rivalry. See "U.S. Five Beats Soviet Team, 107–82," *New York Times,* April 10, 1978; Larry Bird (with Bob Ryan), *Drive: The Story of My Life* (New York: Bantam Books, [1989] 1990), 60. Oddly, in one of his autobiographies, Johnson discusses playing with Bird and says that "playing on the same team with him was sweet." Earvin "Magic" Johnson and Rich Levin, *Magic* (New York: Viking Press, 1983), 109. In another book, Johnson says, prior to the game in Salt Lake City, "I'd seen him [Bird] play on television but never in person." Earvin "Magic" Johnson and Roy S. Johnson, *Magic's Touch* (Reading, MA: Addison-Wesley Pub. Co., 1989), 3.

12. Bird was not a one-man team; Indiana State was a talented, disciplined, cohesive, and well-coached squad. See Malcolm Moran, "Indiana State Story: Implausible Success," *New York Times,* March 25, 1979; Jack Rohan, "N.C.A.A. Final Preview," *New York Times,* March 26, 1979.

13. Larry Keith, "He's Gone to the Head of His Class," *Sports Illustrated,* November 27, 1978, 50.

14. Keith, "He's Gone to the Head of His Class," 49.

15. Rohan, "N.C.A.A. Final Preview," C6.

16. Malcolm Moran, "Johnson: Magical by Nature," *New York Times,* March 26, 1979.

17. Moran, "Johnson: Magical by Nature," C6.

18. Sam Goldaper, "Knicks Draft a Guard, as Big Men Get Away," *New York Times,* June 10, 1978.

19. Ralph Wiley, "Saviors," in *The Gospel According to ESPN: Saints, Saviors & Sinners,* ed. Jay Lovinger (New York: Hyperion, 2002), 180, 182.

20. Frank DeFord, "A Rare Bird Bows Out," *Newsweek,* August 31, 1992, 60.

21. Peter Bonventre, "Big Bird," *Newsweek,* February 26, 1979, 99.

22. Bonventre, "Big Bird," 99.

23. Rohan, "N.C.A.A. Final Preview," C6.

24. Ryan, "The Two and Only," 49.

25. Frank DeFord, "A Rare Bird Bows Out," *Newsweek,* August 31, 1992, 60.

26. Quoted in "Pure Gold in The Corn Belt," *Time,* February 26, 1979, 74.

27. Moran, "Johnson: Magical by Nature," C6.

28. Larry Bird quoted in Keith, "They Caged the Bird," *Sports Illustrated,* April 2, 1979, 19.

29. White, "Michigan State Defeats Indiana State for N.C.A.A. Title," 13.

30. Larry Bird quoted in Craig Hilsop, "Earvin's Merry Magic Show Mesmerizes Brilliant Bird," *The Sporting News,* April 7, 1979, 60.

31. Kathryn Jay, *More Than Just a Game: Sports in American Life since 1945* (New York: Columbia University Press, 2004), 201.

32. Earvin "Magic" Johnson (with William Novak), *My Life* (New York: Random House, 1992), 83–84.

33. In addition to being the first game in the Bird-Magic rivalry, the 1979 championship was a defining moment in NCAA tournament history. It certainly captivated much of the nation, earning a 24.1 share on television, the highest rating ever for a college basketball game. Ten years later, *Sport* magazine described it (hyperbolically?) as "probably the most memorable game in college basketball history." On the game's twentieth anniversary, sports columnist Hal Bock suggested that the first Bird-Johnson game thrust the NCAA tournament permanently into the national spotlight. More recently, ESPN's senior college basketball writer Andy Katz contends that the 1979 championship game "helped set the tone for a 20-year period where players actually grabbed equal billing with the head coaches" and that "the Bird-Magic showdown was a turning point for the NCAA Tournament, which became one of sports hottest properties." To Bird and Johnson, the game endures. For Johnson, who loves to talk about it, it was the pinnacle of his brief but brilliant college career. Bird does not like to discuss it. William Ladson and Raymond Harper, "Glory Days: Magic Vs Bird," *Sport,* April 1999, 76; Hal Bock, "'Magic' meets Bird—the game that changed the tourney," *The Saratogian,* March 29, 1999, 3C; Andy Katz, "From coast to coast, a magical pair," http://espn.go.com/endofcentury/s/ century/katz.html (accessed March 4, 2007).

34. Paul Boyer, *Promises to Keep: The United States since World War II* (Lexington: D. C. Heath and Company, 1995), 424–425.

35. Tom Wolfe, "The 'Me' Decade and the Third Great Awakening," *New York,* August 23, 1976; Nicholas Lemann, "How the Seventies Changed America," *American Heritage,* July/August 1991, 49.

36. Haynes Johnson, *Sleepwalking Through History: America in the Reagan Years* (New York: Doubleday, 1991), 77.

37. Edward D. Berkowitz, *Something Happened: A Political and Cultural Overview of the Seventies* (New York: Columbia University Press, 2006), 53–70.

38. Bruce J. Schulman, *The Seventies: The Great Shift in American Culture, Society, and Politics* (New York: Free Press, 2001), xi.

39. Schulman, *The Seventies,* xi.

40. John Feinstein, *The Punch: One Night, Two Lives, and the Fight That Changed Basketball Forever* (Boston: Little, Brown, and Co., 2002).

41. Jack McCallum, "Larry Bird & Magic Johnson," *Sports Illustrated,* September 19, 1994, 67.

42. E. M. Swift, "From Corned Beef to Caviar," *Sports Illustrated,* June 3, 1991, 80; Peter C. Bjarkman, *The History of the NBA* (Avenel, NJ: Crescent Books, 1992), 118–119. For more on the NBA in the 1970s, see Todd Boyd, *Young, Black, Rich and Famous: The Rise of the NBA, the Hip Hop Invasion, and the Transformation of American Culture* (New York: Doubleday, 2003), 19–43.

43. David L. Andrews, "Whither the NBA, Whither America?" *Peace Review* 11 (1999): 505.

44. The Celtics selected Bird with the No. 6 pick in the 1978 NBA draft. Bird had just completed his junior year at Indiana State and had made it clear that he would return for his senior season. Nonetheless, Celtics president and general manager Red Auerbach thought Bird was worth the wait and gamble, since if he was not under contract before the 1979 NBA draft, the Celtics would lose his signing rights. Meanwhile, the Lakers selected Johnson with the No. 1 pick in the 1979 NBA draft, despite having a 47-35 record and making the playoffs that year. Los Angeles held the first pick in the draft because the New Orleans (soon to be Utah) Jazz had sent its 1979 first-round pick to the Lakers in 1976 as compensation for the free agent signing of guard Gail Goodrich, and the Jazz had won a coin flip against the Chicago Bulls, the team with the worst record in the Eastern Conference. (At the time, the NBA used a coin flip between the last-place finishers in each of its conferences to determine which team would receive the first pick in the draft, a system that existed until 1985.) All of which makes me wonder what would have become of the Bird-Johnson rivalry if the Golden State Warriors had selected Bird with the No. 5 pick in the 1978 draft, instead of forward Purvis Short? What if the Celtics had been unable to sign Bird before the 1979 draft, thus losing his rights? What if the Bulls had called "tails" during the coin flip to determine who would have the first pick in the 1979 draft? Jackie MacMullan, "He was worth the wait," September 30, 1998, http://sportsillustrated.cnn.com/basketball/nba/1998/bird/perspective/macmullan.html (accessed June 1, 2008); Roland Lazenby, *The Show: The Inside Story of the Spectacular Los Angeles Lakers in the Words of Those Who Lived It* (New York: McGraw-Hill, 2006), 187; http://www.nba.com/history/draft_evolution.html (accessed June 2, 2008).

45. See http://www.nba.com/history/finals/champions.html (accessed June 3, 2008).

46. For an excellent article on Russell, see Aram Goudsouzian, "Bill Russell and the Basketball Revolution," *American Studies,* 47, no. 3/4 (Fall–Winter 2006): 61–85.

47. Peter May, *The Big Three* (New York: Simon and Schuster, 1994), 176.

48. Because the Celtics and Lakers were (and remain) in different conferences, Eastern and Western, the teams only played each other twice during the regular season. For box scores of all of these games, see Ryan, "The Two and Only," 47–52.

49. Larry Bird with Jackie MacMullan, *Bird Watching: On Playing and Coaching the Game I Love* (New York: Warner Books, [1999] 2000), 67.

50. Bird, *Drive,* 74.

51. In 2007–08, the Celtics broke the record for the best single-season turnaround in NBA history by improving from 24 wins in 2006–07 to 66 wins, a total of 42 games.

52. Sam Goldaper, "76ers Oust Celtics," *New York Times,* April 28, 1980.

53. Bird, *Drive,* 86.

54. Jeffrey Lane, *Under the Boards: The Cultural Revolution in Basketball* (Lincoln: University of Nebraska Press, 2007), 114.

55. See http://www.nba.com/history/this_date_may.html (accessed June 3, 2008).

56. Sam Goldaper, "Celtics Beat Rockets, 102–91, and Win a 14th N.B.A. Title," *New York Times*, May 15, 1981.

57. John Papanek, "Once More, with a Lot of Feeling," *Sports Illustrated*, May 25, 1981, 39.

58. Jamaal Wilkes quoted in Lazenby, *The Show*, 191.

59. Bjarkman, *The History of the NBA*, 123.

60. See http://www.nba.com/historical/playerfile/index.html?player= magic_johnson (accessed June 1, 2008).

61. Magic Johnson quoted in Sam Goldaper, "Lakers Down 76ers, 123–107, and Capture N.B.A. Crown," *New York Times*, May 17, 1980.

62. Doug Collins quoted in Lazenby, *The Show*, 200.

63. Jerry Buss quoted in Goldaper, "Lakers Down 76ers," 20.

64. Garry Wills, *Reagan's America: Innocents at Home* (Garden City, NJ: Doubleday & Company, 1987), 1.

65. Cornel West, "The '80s: Market Culture Run Amok," *Newsweek*, January 3, 1994, 48; Swift, "From Corned Beef to Caviar." Michael Jordan, who entered the league in 1984, helped too, of course, but despite his sensational play and success as a corporate spokesperson, his team, the Chicago Bulls, did not win its first NBA championship until after Bird and Johnson's prime.

66. Steven Travers, *The Good, the Bad, and the Ugly: Heart-Pounding, Jaw-Dropping, and Gut-Wrenching Moments from Los Angeles Lakers History* (Chicago: Triumph Books, 2007), 156.

67. See http://www.nba.com/history/players/bird_stats.html (accessed May 1, 2008); http://www.nba.com/history/players/johnsonm_stats.html (accessed May 1, 2008); and Ryan, "The Two and Only," 47.

68. May, *The Big Three*, 176.

69. Bruce Newman, "Together at Center Stage," *Sports Illustrated*, June 4, 1984, 36.

70. John Taylor, *The Rivalry: Bill Russell, Wilt Chamberlain, and the Golden Age of Basketball* (New York: Ballantine Books, 2006).

71. Larry Bird quoted in Newman, "Together at Center Stage," 36.

72. Magic Johnson quoted in Newman, "Together at Center Stage," 40.

73. When the series was over, Bird said: "Gerald's steal in Game 2 definitely was the biggest play of the series. If he didn't make that steal, we would have been down 2–0, and it would have been very tough to come back on their court." Quoted in George Vecsey, "Bird Was Heart of the Celtics," *New York Times*, June 13, 1984.

74. Chuck Klosterman describes Rambis as "a role player who seemed artless on purpose, going so far as refusing to purchase contact lenses." Chuck Klosterman, *Sex, Drugs, and Cocoa Puffs: A Low Culture Manifesto* (New York: Scribner, [2003] 2004), 98.

75. Bjarkman, *The History of the NBA*, 133; Sam Goldaper, "Celtics Beat Lakers and Win 15th N.B.A. Title," *New York Times*, June 13, 1984.

76. See http://www.nba.com/history/finals/19831984.html (accessed June 15, 2008).

77. Brent Musberger and Larry Bird quoted in Jim Podhoretz and Larry Weitzman, *Larry Bird: A Basketball Legend* (New York: NBA Entertainment, [1991] 2004), DVD.

78. Bird, *Drive*, 137.

79. Ibid., 188.

80. Leigh Montville, "Friends, Foes for Life, Bird's and Magic's Relationship Always Something Special," *Boston Globe*, June 12, 1987, 61.

81. Johnson, *My Life*, 204.

82. Bird, *Drive*, 188.

83. Johnson, *My Life*, 204–205.

84. See http://www.nba.com/history/awards_mvp.html (accessed June 15, 2008)s.

85. Alexander Wolff, "The 'Movie Stars' Changed Their Act," *Sports Illustrated*, June 10, 1985, 36.

86. That is, the first two games were in Boston and the next two were in Los Angeles, with game 5 in Los Angeles if necessary, and the final two games in Boston, if necessary. Chris Colston, "Celtics had role in Finals format switch," *USA Today*, June 11, 2008.

87. Sam Goldaper, "Abdul-Jabbar Leads Way," *New York Times*, June 10, 1985.

88. Alexander Wolff, "Finally, a Happy Laker Landing," *Sports Illustrated*, June 17, 1985, 24.

89. Larry Bird quoted in Goldaper, "Abdul-Jabbar Leads Way," C11.

90. Magic Johnson quoted in Roy Johnson, "Lakers Erase the Pain," *New York Times*, June 10, 1985.

91. Johnson, *My Life*, 199.

92. Bird, *Drive*, 152.

93. Leigh Montville, "Sixth Sense," *Boston Globe*, May 16, 1986.

94. Bird finished fourth in the league in points (25.8 ppg), seventh in rebounds (9.8 rpg), and ninth in steals (2.02 per game). He also led the league in free throw percentage (.896), finished fourth in three-point field goal percentage (.423), and led the Celtics in assists with 6.8 per game.

95. Jack McCallum, "When Push Came to Shove . . . ," *Sports Illustrated*, June 2, 1986, 26.

96. Red Auerbach quoted in Thomas Boswell, "Bird and the '85–'86 Celtics: They May Not Get Better Than This," *Washington Post*, June 9, 1986.

97. Larry Bird quoted in Boswell, "Bird and the '85-'86 Celtics."

98. Larry Bird quoted in Jack McCallum, "The Cruelest Thing Ever," *Sports Illustrated*, June 30, 1986, 20.

99. Jack McCallum, "The Mystique Goes On," *Sports Illustrated*, June 8, 1987, 37.

100. Sam Goldaper, "Kite Unlikely Hero in Victory by Celtics," *New York Times*, June 8, 1987.

101. Magic Johnson quoted in Sam Goldaper, "It's Magic! Shot with :02 Left Gives Lakers 3–1 Lead," *New York Times*, June 10, 1987.

102. Johnson, *My Life*, 200.

103. Larry Bird quoted in Jack McCallum, "Your Ball, L.A.," *Sports Illustrated*, June 22, 1987, 19.

104. Roy S. Johnson, "Johnson Leads Lakers to 4th Title since '80," *New York Times*, June 15, 1987.

105. Larry Bird quoted in Mark Heisler, "Ghost Stories," *Los Angeles Times*, June 10, 2008.

106. Larry Bird quoted in Ryan, "The Two and Only," 55.

107. Bird, *Drive*, 212–214.

108. Pico Iyer, "'It Can Happen to Anybody. Even Magic Johnson,'" *Time*, November 18, 1991, 26.

109. Robert McG. Thomas Jr., "News Reverberates Through Basketball, and Well Beyond It," *New York Times*, November 8, 1991, B13; Tom Callahan, "Stunned by Magic," *U.S. News & World Report*, November 18, 1991, 82–84.

110. Richard W. Stevenson, "Basketball Star Retires on Advice of His Doctors," *New York Times*, November 8, 1991.

111. "Magic's Show," *The Nation*, December 2, 1991, 691.

112. Magic Johnson with Roy S. Johnson, "I'll Deal with It," *Sports Illustrated*, November 18, 1991, 21.

113. Bird, *Bird Watching*, 258.

114. Ibid., 258.

115. Steve Springer, "An Off-the-Wall Retirement? Ceremony," *Los Angeles Times*, February 17, 1992.

116. Johnson, *My Life*, 305.

117. Larry Bird quoted in Springer, "An Off-the-Wall Retirement? Ceremony."

118. "No. 32 Is Lifted to the Rafters as Magic Johnson Is Honored," *New York Times*, February 17, 1992.

119. As I have written elsewhere, "Thanks to a 1989 FIBA rule change (and the vote was not close, 56–13), the Barcelona games was the first in which professionals were allowed to compete. The effect was perceived to be explosive. 'Those Olympics and that first Dream Team were an international powder keg that created a revolution that affected the far most reaches of the earth,' according to Donny Nelson, the current General Manager of the NBA's Dallas Mavericks and, since 1990, a volunteer assistant coach for the Lithuanian national basketball team. Why? Conventional wisdom has it that the original 'Dream Team,' comprised as it was of NBA superstars who obliterated the competition on its way to winning the gold medal, was a watershed media event that catapulted basketball to global recognition and inspired athletes and basketball federations all over the world." Daniel A. Nathan, "Travelling: Notes on Basketball and Globalization; or, Why the San Antonio Spurs Are the Future," *International Journal of the History of Sport* 25, no. 6 (May 2008): 742–743.

120. The Dream Team included Larry Bird, Magic Johnson, Charles Barkley, Clyde Drexler, Patrick Ewing, Michael Jordan, Karl Malone, Chris Mullin, Scottie Pippen, David Robinson, John Stockton, and Christian Laettner, the squad's lone collegian.

121. Frank Deford, "Team of Dreams," *Newsweek*, July 6, 1992, 26–28.

122. Chuck Daly quoted in "The Original Dream Team," http://www.nba.com/history/dreamT_moments.html (accessed July 1, 2008).

123. Tom Callahan, "The Lopsided Dream," *U.S. News & World Report*, August 10, 1992, 37.

124. Bird, *Bird Watching*, 24, 33.

125. Jack McCallum, "Dreamy," *Sports Illustrated*, August 17, 1992, 19.

126. Johnson, *My Life*, 321.

127. David Halberstam, *Playing for Keeps: Michael Jordan and the World He Made* (New York: Random House, 1999), 298.

128. Harvey Araton, "Theme Comes True: The Dream Team Captures the Gold," *New York Times*, August 1992, S1.

129. Jack McCallum, "Larry Bird & Magic Johnson," *Sports Illustrated*, September 19, 1994, 68.

130. For more on the Dream Team, see Jack McCallum, *Dream Team: The Inside Story of the 1992 U.S. Olympic Basketball Team* (Boston: Little, Brown, 1992); Michael Ralph, "Epilogue: It Was All a Dream (Wasn't It?)," *International Journal of the History of Sport* 24, no. 2 (February 2007): 311–316.

131. Larry Bird quoted in Harvey Araton, "With Gold in Hand, Johnson and Bird Chart Their Futures," *New York Times*, August 10, 1992.

132. Michael Wilbon, "Artistry Spun from Conceit and Passion," *Washington Post*, August 19, 1992.

133. "A Garden Bereft of Bird," *Boston Globe*, August 19, 1992.

134. Pat Riley quoted in Clifton Brown, "Bird Unlaces His Sneakers and Says Goodbye," *New York Times*, August 19, 1992, B9.

135. Magic Johnson quoted in "Boston's Bird man set new standards in court procedure," *Toronto Star*, August 19, 1992.

136. Araton, "Theme Comes True: The Dream Team Captures the Gold."

137. Mike Dodd, "'Larry Legend' Closes Career," *USA Today*, August 19, 1992. Also see David DuPree, "Bird Made Most of His Athletic Gifts," *USA Today*, August 19, 1992.

138. "Boston's Bird man set new standards in court procedure."

139. DeFord, "A Rare Bird Bows Out," 60.

140. May, *The Big Three*, 277.

141. Dan Shaughnessy, "Perfect Ending to a Legendary Tale," *Boston Globe*, February 5, 1993.

142. Ibid.

143. Magic Johnson quoted in Shaughnessy, "Perfect Ending to a Legendary Tale," 65.

144. Larry Bird quoted in Michael Madden, "Encore . . . Magic and Bird Celebrate the Times of Their Lives," *Boston Globe*, February 5, 1993.

145. Ibid.

146. Harvey Araton, "A Worthy Bird Has an Unlikely Night," *New York Times*, February 5, 1993.

147. Magic Johnson quoted in Madden, "Encore . . . Magic and Bird Celebrate the Times of Their Lives," 70.

148. Larry Bird quoted in Shaughnessy, "Perfect Ending to a Legendary Tale," 65.

149. Peter May, "As Sure as His Shot, Bird Is In," *Boston Globe*, June 30, 1998.

150. Mike Wise, "With Big Assist from Bird, Johnson Enters Hall of Fame," *New York Times*, September 28, 2002.

151. Bob Ryan, "Bird, Hall of Fame: It's Truly a Perfect Fit," *Boston Globe*, June 30, 1998.

152. Harvey Araton, "A Player Who Was Truly Exceptional," *New York Times*, October 4, 1998.

153. Wilbon, "Artistry Spun from Conceit and Passion.".

154. Wise, "With Big Assist from Bird, Johnson Enters Hall of Fame.".

155. Ibid.

156. Magic Johnson quoted in Wise, "With Big Assist from Bird, Johnson Enters Hall of Fame."

157. Ibid.

158. Larry Bird quoted in Mark Heisler, "A Great Standard of Living," *Los Angeles Times,* September 28, 2002.

159. Heisler, "A Great Standard of Living."

160. John Currin quoted in Peter Plagens, "Brilliance or Bust," *Newsweek,* December 22, 2003, 51.

161. Too much can be made of basketball statistics, at least as they are commonly understood. According to Michael Lewis, author of *Moneyball: The Art of Winning an Unfair Game* (2003), "It turns out there is no statistic that a basketball player accumulates that cannot be amassed selfishly." Michael Lewis, "The No-Stats All-Star," *New York Times Magazine,* February 15, 2009, 31.

162. Jack McCallum, "Walking Tall," *Sports Illustrated,* August 31, 1992, 14.

163. Harvey Araton, *Crashing the Borders: How Basketball Won the World and Lost Its Soul at Home* (New York: Free Press, 2005), 54. Writer Nelson George agrees with McCallum and Araton: "At times during their first six years in the pros Bird definitely had the edge. But over the course of their entire careers when you consider championships won (Magic five, Bird three), the impact of injuries (Magic has never missed more than a quarter of Laker games any season, while Bird has seen his last three seasons haunted by back and foot problems), and the ability to improve (Bird's outside shooting has grown erratic, while Magic has become a better free throw and three-point shooter), Johnson, over all, has to be given the edge. That he broke Oscar Robertson's all-time NBA assist record in 1991, while Bird will probably hold no all-time league records, makes one lean toward this future Hall of Famer. That still means Bird was better than 99 percent of the NBA most of his career. Not bad for a white boy. Or anyone else." Nelson George, *Elevating the Game: Black Men and Basketball* (New York: HarperCollins, 1992), 224.

164. This is one reason that the former competitors, along with sportswriter Jackie MacMullan, are "teaming up to write a book together, chronicling their rivalry and friendship." Matthew Thornton, "Bird, Johnson to Write Book for HMH," *Publishers Weekly,* May 27, 2008, http://www.publishersweekly.com/article/CA6564162.html (accessed May 29, 2008).

165. Visual artists, such as Leroy Neiman, Stephen Marotta, and Edgar J. Brown, have also been drawn to Bird and Johnson.

166. Leigh Montville, "Friends, Foes for Life, Bird's and Magic's Relationship Always Something Special," *Boston Globe,* June 12, 1987.

167. John Edgar Wideman, *Hoop Roots: Basketball, Race, and Love* (Boston: Houghton Mifflin Company, 2001), 167–168.

168. Ibid., 168.

169. Ibid.

170. David Halberstam, "The Stuff Dreams Are Made Of," *Sports Illustrated,* June 29, 1987, 40.

171. Ibid., 44.

172. Boyd, *Young, Black, Rich and Famous,* 53.

173. Perhaps Chuck Klosterman takes the racial politics of the Celtics-Lakers and, by implication, the Bird-Johnson rivalry too far: "To say that the 1980s rivalry between the Celtics and the Lakers represents America's racial anguish is actually a short-sighted understatement. As I have grown older, it's become clear that the

Lakers-Celtics rivalry represents absolutely *everything*: race, religion, politics, mathematics, the reason I'm still not married, the Challenger explosion, Man vs. Beast, and everything else. There is no relationship that isn't a Celtics-Lakers relationship." Klosterman, *Sex, Drugs, and Cocoa Puffs*, 97.

174. Scoop Jackson, "1980s vs. Today: Lakers-Celtics," June 5, 2008, http://sports. espn.go.com/espn/page2/story?page=80vstoday/lakerscltics (accessed June 5, 2008).

175. Halberstam, "The Stuff Dreams Are Made Of," 40.

176. Boyd, *Young, Black, Rich and Famous*, 51.

177. Carlo Rotella, "The Stepping Stone: Larry Holmes, Gerry Cooney, and *Rocky*," in *In the Game: Race, Identity, and Sports in the Twentieth Century*, ed. Amy Bass (New York: Palgrave Macmillan, 2005), 239.

178. Ibid.

179. Michael Omi and Howard Winant, *Racial Formation in the United States: From the 1960s to the 1990s*, 2nd ed. (New York: Routledge, [1986] 1994), 135. Also see Andrew Hacker, *Two Nations: Black and White, Separate, Hostile, Unequal* (New York: Charles Scribner's Sons, 1992); and Benjamin G. Rader, *American Ways: A History of American Cultures, 1865–Present*, vol. 2, 2nd ed. (Belmont, CA: Thomson Wadsworth, 2006).

180. Boyd, *Young, Black, Rich and Famous*, 67.

181. Sportswriter Jackie MacMullan claims, "As far as he [Bird] was concerned, he and Magic Johnson were the same; he really never made a distinction between race, and I think most of his teammates would tell you the same thing." Quoted in Lane, *Under the Boards*, 116.

182. Araton, *Crashing the Borders*, 53.

183. George, *Elevating the Game*, 223. Isiah Thomas, the Detroit Piston's perennial All-Star guard, was at the center of a controversy about Bird's racial identity that drew attention to some of these issues. After game 7 of the 1987 Eastern Conference Finals, which the Celtics won, beating the Pistons, 117–114, a frustrated (and not yet infamous) Detroit rookie, Dennis Rodman, told reporters, "Larry Bird is overrated in a lot of areas. I don't think he's the greatest player. He's way overrated." Rodman explained that the media hyped Bird "because he's white." Learning about Rodman's comments, Thomas added, "I think Larry is a very, very good basketball player. An exceptional talent, but I'd have to agree with Rodman. If Bird was black, he'd be just another good guy." Thomas later said he was "joking." Bird accepted Thomas's explanation: "If the statement doesn't bother me, it shouldn't bother anybody. If Isiah tells me it was a joking matter, it should be left at that. The N.B.A. is sometimes not the easiest thing to be in, and after a game like that, in the heat of the locker room, it's probably not the best time to talk to us." Months later, Rodman said: "If we had won the game, I wouldn't have said anything like that. I was hurting, and I wanted to hurt those people back. But I shouldn't have said what I said. Larry Bird proved to me he's one of the best, and they were the better team that day. I made a mistake." Quoted in Bruce Newman, "Black, White—And Gray," *Sports Illustrated*, May 2, 1988, 58, 69. Quoted in Ira Berkow, "The Coloring of Bird," *New York Times*, June 2, 1987, D27. Quoted in Roy S. Johnson, "Thomas Explains Comments on Bird," *New York Times*, June 5, 1987, D20.

184. Lane, *Under the Boards*, 116.

185. Magic Johnson quoted in Wilbon, "Artistry Spun from Conceit and Passion," D1.

186. Magic Johnson quoted in Ryan, "The Two and Only," 46.

187. Callahan, "Stunned by Magic," *U.S. News & World Report*, November 18, 1991, 83.

188. May, *The Big Three*, 176.

189. Bjarkman, *The History of the NBA*, 6.

190. Jack McCallum, "Leaving a Huge Void," *Sports Illustrated*, March 23, 1992, 20. More recently, McCallum has written: "It is an exaggeration to conclude that the rivalry saved the league, but without a doubt it ushered in an era of unprecedented prosperity." Jack McCallum, "The Rivalry," *Sports Illustrated*, June 9, 2008, 39.

191. David Hackett Fischer, *Historians' Fallacies: Toward a Logic of Historical Thought* (New York: Harper & Row, Publishers, 1970), 166.

192. Araton, *Crashing the Borders*, 52–53.

193. Andrews, "Whither the NBA, Whither America?" 505–506.

194. Bjarkman, *The History of the NBA*, 120.

195. Mark Starr, "My Favorite Year," *Newsweek*, August 14, 2006, 52.

196. Jack Craig, "NBA Needed Time to Cash in on Rising Stars," *Boston Globe*, February 5, 1993. Craig quotes one television executive: "They [Bird and Johnson] were the bedrock, along with Erving, early in the '80s, when the league was emerging from a down period on TV. They were players on key teams that could be relied upon to deliver national audiences. They helped broaden interest."

197. "Parasocial relationship" refers to the phenomenon of developing intimate-imaginary relationships with public figures (e.g., politicians, celebrities, athletes) that one does not in fact know; see Richard Jackson Harris, *A Cognitive Psychology of Mass Communication* (Mahwah, NJ: L. Erlbaum Associates, 2004). For more on basking in reflected glory, see Edward R. Hirt, Dolf Zillmann, Grant A. Erickson, and Chris Kennedy, "Costs and Benefits of Allegiance: Changes in Fans' Self-Ascribed Competencies after Team Victory versus Defeat," *Journal of Personality and Social Psychology* 63, no. 5 (1992): 724–738.

198. Bob Ryan reports that Bird "never laid any claim to inventing the sport, and he went out of his way to reject any notion that he and Magic Johnson deserve credit for reviving the NBA. 'Two guys did not turn the league around,' [Bird] said firmly. 'There were a lot of great players before us and after us.'" Bob Ryan, "Fans Won't Let Legend Go Quietly," *Boston Globe*, October 3, 1998, G9.

199. Jackie MacMullan, "A Jewel of a Duel," *Sports Illustrated*, November 29, 1999, 134.

200. DeFord, "A Rare Bird Bows Out," 60.

201. Robert Lipsyte and Peter Levine, *Idols of the Game: A Sporting History of the American Century* (Atlanta: Turner Publishing, 1995), 326–327.

202. Peter Newmann, "Top 10 moments in Celtics-Lakers postseason history," June 1, 2008, http://sports.espn.go.com/nba/playoffs2008/news/story?page=top10-bosvslal (accessed June 1, 2008).

203. Jon Saraceno, "A Classic Rivalry Revisited," *USA Today*, June 5, 2008, 1E.

204. Bob Hohler, "The Legendary Rivalry Resumes," *Boston Globe*, June 5, 2008, A1.

205. Jack McCallum, "Road to Redemption," *Sports Illustrated*, June 16, 2008, 34.

206. Magic Johnson Quoted in Michael Lee, "Wrapped Up in Present," *Washington Post*, June 5, 2008, E1.

207. "The Playoffs: Where Amazing Happens," April 27, 2008, http://www.nba.com/features/only_be_one_080410.html (accessed April 27, 2008).

208. The ad can be seen on YouTube at http://www.youtube.com/watch?v= PWHEv5yH2qU (accessed April 27, 2008).

5. Friendly Rivals—Mary Jo Festle

1. Mary Jo Festle, *Playing Nice: Politics and Apologies in Women's Sports* (New York: Columbia University Press, 1996), 142–150.

2. Chris Evert, with Neil Amdur, *Chrissie: My Own Story* (New York: Simon and Schuster, 1982), 193.

3. Ibid., 40.

4. Quoted in Ibid., 85.

5. Chris Evert Lloyd and John Lloyd with Carol Thatcher, *Lloyd on Lloyd* (New York: Beaufort Books, 1985), 44. Early career records are included in Evert, *Chrissie*, 227–238.

6. Evert, *Chrissie*, 59–61.

7. Evert Lloyd and Lloyd, *Lloyd on Lloyd*, 34; L. John Wertheim, "My Three Sons," *Sports Illustrated*, September 3, 2006.

8. Dave Anderson, "The Chris and Jimmy Romance Revival," *New York Times*, September 6, 1975.

9. Mary Carillo and Sally Jenkins quoted in Nancy E. Spencer, "'America's Sweetheart' and 'Czech-Mate,' A Discursive Analysis of the Evert-Navratilova Rivalry," *Journal of Sport and Social Issues* 27, no. 1 (February 2003): 18–37.

10. Evert Lloyd and Lloyd, *Lloyd on Lloyd*, 54.

11. Frank Deford, "Love and Love," *Sports Illusrated*, April 27, 1981, 68–84.

12. B. J. Phillips, "Not Cinderella—Just the Best," *Time*, September 14, 1981, 77–80.

13. Evert, *Chrissie*, 76.

14. Johnette Howard, *The Rivals: Chris Evert vs. Martina Navratilova, Their Epic Duels and Extraordinary Friendship* (New York: Broadway Books, 2005), 78.

15. Chris Evert quoted in Sally Jenkins, "I've Lived a Charmed Life," *Sports Illustrated*, May 25, 1992, 62.

16. Chris Evert quoted in Howard, *Rivals*, 78–9.

17. Evert, *Chrissie*, 105.

18. Evert Lloyd and Lloyd, *Lloyd on Lloyd*, 32; Evert, *Chrissie*, 171.

19. Festle, *Playing Nice*, 45–52, 289.

20. Evert, *Chrissie*, 164; Festle, *Playing Nice*, 152–153. She later claimed that the quote was misinterpreted.

21. Evert, *Chrissie*, 169.

22. Chris Evert quoted in Grace Lichtenstein, *A Long Way Baby: Behind the Scenes in Women's Pro Tennis* (New York: Morrow, 1986), 86.

23. Chris Evert quoted in Jenkins, "I've Lived a Charmed Life," 63.

24. Lloyd and Lloyd, *Lloyd on Lloyd*, 102. See also Donna Doherty and Mark Preston, "Evert Newest Hall of Famer," *Tennis* 31, no. 5 (September 1995): 19.

25. Evert, *Chrissie*, 128–129, 147.

26. Ibid., 44.

27. Ibid., 169; Deford, "Love and Love."

28. Chris Evert quoted in Festle, *Playing Nice*, 234; Deford, "Love and Love."

29. Martina Navratilova with George Vecsey, *Martina* (New York: Knopf, 1985), 18.

30. Ibid., 31, 52.

31. Billie Jean King quoted in Adrianne Blue, *Martina: The Lives and Times of Martina Navratilova* (Secaucus, NJ: Birch Lane Press, 1995), 14.

32. Navratilova, *Martina*, 91.

33. Ibid., 114–127.

34. Howard, *Rivals*, 114.

35. Navratilova, *Martina*, 16.

36. Howard, *Rivals*, 65.

37. Chris Evert quoted in Ibid., 120.

38. Evert, *Chrissie*, 148–150.

39. Chris Evert quoted in Howard, *Rivals*, 124.

40. Nancy Lieberman quoted in Howard, *Rivals*, 172–3.

41. Navratilova, *Martina*, 145.

42. Ibid.

43. Ibid., 261–267.

44. Mary Carillo quoted in Howard, *Rivals*, 206.

45. Chris Evert Lloyd, "In Defense of Billie Jean," *World Tennis*, July 1981, 8. For a more detailed treatment of the incident, see Festle, *Playing Nice*, 235–240.

46. George Vecsey quoted in Howard, *Rivals*, 176–7.

47. Martina Navratilova quoted in Blue, *Martina*, 106.

48. Donna Lopiano quoted in Larry Schwartz, "Martina was alone on top," ESPN.com, ESPN Top Athletes of the Twentieth Century, espn.go.com/sports century/features/00016378.html (accessed July 10, 2007).

49. Martina Navratilova quoted in Howard, *Rivals*, 270.

50. Spencer, "'America's Sweetheart' and 'Czech-Mate,'" 19.

51. Frank Deford, "The Day Chrissie Reclaimed Paris," *Sports Illustrated*, June 17, 1985, 37.

52. Spencer, "'America's Sweetheart' and 'Czech-Mate,'" 20.

53. Curry Kirkpatrick, "Nine's so Fine," *Sports Illustrated*, July 16, 1990, 21–s22.

54. Navratilova, *Martina*, 249; Howard, *Rivals*, 195.

55. Navratilova, *Martina*, 55.

56. Ibid., 255.

57. Chris Evert quoted in Howard, *Rivals*, 195–196.

58. Grace Lichtenstein quoted in Howard, *Rivals*, 195.

59. Navratilova, *Martina*, 268.

60. Martina Navratilova quoted in Spencer, "'America's Sweetheart' and 'Czech-Mate,'" 26.

61. Navratilova, *Martina*, 97–98.

62. Martina Navratilova quoted in Blue, *Martina*, 215–216.

63. Chris Evert quoted in Howard, *Rivals*, 243.

64. Evert Lloyd and Lloyd, *Lloyd on Lloyd*, 182–183.

65. Ibid., 194.

66. Martina Navratilova quoted in Frank Deford, "The Day Chrissie Reclaimed Paris," *Sports Illustrated*, June 17, 1985, 28–37.

67. Mike Lupica, "Martina Was Second to One," *Tennis* 31, no. 2 (June 1995): 48–49.

68. Chris Evert quoted in Billie Jean King with Cynthia Starr, *We Have Come a Long*

Way (Regina Ryan Publishing Enterprises, 1988), 176; L.J.W., "Martina Navratilova and Chris Evert," *Sports Illustrated for Women* 1, no. 4 (Winter 1999/2000): 84.

69. Navratilova, *Martina*, 145.

70. Evert, *Chrissie*, 222.

71. Sally Jenkins, "I've Lived a Charmed Life," *Sports Illustrated*, May 25, 1992, 63.

72. Navratilova, *Martina*, 96, for other tensions, see also 148, 135, 221; Chris Evert as told to Curry Kirkpatrick, "Tennis Was My Showcase," *Sports Illustrated*, August 28, 1989, 78.

73. Martina Navratilova and Chris Evert quoted in Howard, *Rivals*, 253.

74. Evert, "Tennis Was My Showcase," 78.

75. Howard, *Rivals*, 255–258.

76. Martina Navratilova quoted in Howard, *Rivals*, 254.

77. Czech player Hana Mandlikova noted, "Martina was the gutsy one. She opened the door for a lot of other players and made things loosen up for us. She paid the price and that's why I respect her so much." Quoted in Cindy Shmerler, "The End of an Era," *Women's Sports and Fitness* 16, no. 8 (November/December 1994): 23.

6. The Battle of the Carmens—Alison M. Wrynn and Annette R. Hofmann

We would like to thank Jutta Braun, University of Potsdam in Germany, for all her support in understanding and gaining access to sources about German Democratic Republic (East Germany) sports.

1. E. M. Swift, "Cashing in on the Collywobbles," *Sports Illustrated*, March 31, 1986, 28–35.

2. James R. Hines, *Figure Skating: A History* (Urbana and Chicago: University of Illinois Press, 2006).

3. Ibid.

4. Ibid.

5. Gina Daddario, *Women's Sport and Spectacle: Gendered Television Coverage and the Olympic Games* (Westport, CT: Praeger, 1998).

6. Christine Brennan, *Inside Edge: A Revealing Journey into the Secret World of Figure Skating* (New York: Anchor Books, 1996).

7. Headline in an article of *Bild Hamburg*, February 27, 1988, 12. The German original: Sex Komma Null für Kati, would be translated into Sex Comma (or, in this case, point) Zero. In Germany the number 6 (*sechs*) is pronounced almost like "sex."

8. Ellyn Kestnbaum, *Culture on Ice: Figure Skating and Cultural Meaning* (Middletown, CT: Wesleyan University Press, 2003).

9. "Skater Cuts a Fresh Figure," *New York Times*, March 5, 1985. Another article claims that Thomas began skating lessons at age five. The discrepancy could be related to when she began general skating lessons and when she engaged an elite professional coach. See "The Nation's No. 1 Skating Sensation, Debi Thomas," *Ebony* 41 (1986): 147–148, 150–152.

10. Other African Americans who had won U.S. figure-skating titles by 1986 included Atoy Wilson, who won the novice men's division in 1966; Richard Ewell, 1970 junior men's champion; Richard Ewell and Michelle McCladdie, 1972 junior

pair's champions; Reggie Stanley, novice men's champion in 1975; and Joan Campbell, 1980 novice ladies' champion. "The Nation's No. 1 Skating Sensation, Debi Thomas."

11. Thomas was not the first woman to remain a full-time pre-med student while pursuing her skating career as this is the path that Tenley Albright took as well. See Hines, *Figure Skating*.

12. "Debi Thomas to Retire to Attend Medical School," *Jet*, May 25, 1992, 47.

13. Thomas is particularly proud of her post-figure-skating accomplishments as a physician. See her Web site, "Debi Thomas Online," at http://docdebithomas.com/ (accessed October 16, 2008).

14. "The prettiest face of socialism," German original: "Das schönste Gesicht des Sozialismus."

15. Katarina Witt with E. M. Swift, *Only with Passion. Figure Skating's Most Winning Champion on Competion and Life* (New York: Public Affairs, 2005), 22–24, cover of the book.

16. "Katarina Witt," *Wer, wie, wo, was in Chemnitz*, February 2006, http://www.members.futureprojects.info/chemnitz09114/c06.8.htm (accessed February 25, 2008).

17. "Debi Thomas Wins World Skating Title," *Los Angeles Times*, March 22 1986.

18. "Boitano, Thomas in Good Shape," *New York Times*, January 11, 1988.

19. Kestnbaum, *Culture on Ice*.

20. "Pressure Ahead for Debi Thomas," *New York Times*, September 23, 1986.

21. Frank Litsky, "Thomas Toppled by Witt in Showdown," *New York Times*, March 15, 1987.

22. Michael Janofsky, "Thomas Leads Skating; Witt Second," *New York Times*, February 26, 1988.

23. Kestnbaum, *Culture on Ice*.

24. "Witt-Thomas a TV Hit," *New York Times*, March 2, 1988.

25. George Vecsey, "The 15-Second Career," *New York Times*, February 29, 1988.

26. Gerald Eskenazi, "Camera's Scrutiny May Add to Stress," *New York Times*, February 29, 1988.

27. Michael Janofsky, "Thomas is 3d after Canadian," *New York Times*, February 28, 1988.

28. "Debi Thomas Loses Gold, but Wins Bronze and Now Takes Aim at World Title," *Jet*, March 14, 1988, 52.

29. "Debi Thomas Wins Bronze, Gets Diamond in Marriage," *Jet*, April 11, 1988, 52–53.

30. Michael Janofsky, "Style Distinguishes Top Figure Skaters," *New York Times*, February 23, 1988.

31. Frank Litsky, "What's What, Who's Who, Where It Happens," *New York Times*, February 7, 1988.

32. German quote: "Ständige Bemühen ihres Staates um die Erhaltung des Friedens und die Garantie des Rechts auf Arbeit."

33. "Ich finde unsere Politik richtig," *Deutsches Sportecho*, February 18, 1988, 3.

34. Hans Joachim Teichler, "Herrschaft und Eigensinn im DDR-Sport," in *Transformationen des deutschen Sports seit 1939*, ed. Michael Krüger (Hamburg: Czwalina, 2001), 233.

35. Kai Reinhart, "Herrschaft und Widerständigkeit im DDR-Sport. Eine Analyse

des staatlichen und des informellen Sports vor dem Hindergrund der Theorie Michel Foucaults" Unpublished (PhD thesis, University of Münster, Germany, 2007), 136.

36. Reinhart, "Herrschaft und Widerständigkeit," 182.

37. German original quote: "Es drückt eine enge Verbindung zwischen den Sportlern und der Partei der Arbeiterklasse, zwischen den Sportlern und unserer DDR, unserem sozialistischen Vaterland, aus." "Festlicher Empfang für unsere Olympioniken im Hotel 'Stadt Berlin'," *Deutsches Sportecho*, February 22, 1984, 3

38. "Ich finde unsere Politik richtig," *Deutsches Sportecho*, February 18, 1988, 3.

39. Witt, *Only with Passion*, 103.

40. E. M. Swift, "Another Miracle on Ice," *Sports Illustrated*, March 17, 1986, 54–61.

41. "The Nation's No. 1 Skating Sensation, Debi Thomas."

42. Kestnbaum, *Culture on Ice*.

43. Richard Goldsberry, "Skate Queen to Hollywood: Mabel Fairbanks May Be Cast in Ice Film," *Chicago Defender*, February 2, 1946, 16.

44. Bob Ottum, "He Did a Bang-up Job," *Sports Illustrated*, February 11, 1985. 84–85; Bob Ottum, "Guaranteed to Keep the Chin Up," *Sports Illustrated*, February 4, 1985, 28–38.

45. Pat Cannon, "Debi Thomas Wants Only to Be the Best," *Los Angeles Times*, July 29, 1985, C9.

46. "Debi Thomas Wins World Skating Title," 12.

47. "The Nation's No. 1 Skating Sensation, Debi Thomas."s

48. German originals: "Jubel um Katarina, die Große" and "Kati or Debi—welche kriegt Gold."

49. German original: "Debi gegen Kati—ganz privat. Männer, Mode und Musik."

50. Witt, *Only with Passion*, 104–105.

51. German original: "Kampf zweier Welten."

52. Dieter Wales, "Tagebuch," *Deutsches Sportecho*, February 29, 1988, n.p.

53. Dave Anderson, "Olympics Take a First Step on the Road to Reality," *New York Times*, February 7, 1988.

54. German original: "Auf die DDR und die Partei der Arbeitsklasse singt Katarina Witt bei Gelegenheit Lobeshymnen. Schließlich ist sie Genossin in spe, seit November 1985 Kandidatin für die SED."

55. German original: "kapitalistisch getönter Sonderstatus und sozialistisch gefärbtes (extra-) Klassenbewusstsein"

56. German original: "Werbeträger darf sie nur in eigener Sache und zum höheren Wohl ihres Mäzens, der DDR, sein. Katharina Witt—zum Greifen nahe und doch so fern, eine Märchenfigur des Sports. Verführerisch, 'westlich' im Habitus, unverkrampft—und doch an den ehernen Spielregelns ihrer Gesellschaft immer dann gebunden, wenn das nach außen behauptende Selbstverständnis sozialistischer Ideale auf dem Spiel steht. Dabei ist sie eine Märchenfigur auf Abruf. Beendet sie ihre Karriere, womit jährlich zu rechnen ist, muss sie vielleicht für immer in das Provinz-Amiente von Karl-Marx-Stadt zurückkehren. Selbst für sie ist die Freiheit nicht grenzenlos. " Roland Zorn, "Eine Märchenfigur auf Abruf: Sozialistisches Leitbild und privilegierter Star," *Frankfurter Allgemeine Zeitung*, March 19, 1986, 22.

57. Thomas Fetzer, "Die gesellschaftliche Akzeptanz des Leistungssports-systems," in Hans-Joachim Teichler, ed., *Sport in der DDR. Eigensinn, Konflikte, Trends* (Köln, Germany: Spunrt und Buch Strauß, 2003), 358–422.

58. Michael Janofsky, "Capturing the Fire of 'Carmen' on Ice," *New York Times,* October 30, 1987.

59. E. M. Swift, "To Witt, the Victory," *Sports Illustrated,* March 7, 1988, 46–55.

60. Robert Helmick quoted in Michael Janofsky, "Americans Measure Their Performance," *New York Times,* March 1, 1988.

7. Bitter Foes, but Marketing Pros—Ryan King-White

1. Rob Bradford. "The Transcontinental Courtship of Daisuke Matsusaka," *Red Sox Annual 2007* 11 (2007): 25–28.

2. Paul White, "Red Sox Nation: New King of the Road," *USA Today,* August 23, 2007.

3. Glenn Stout, "A Curse Born of Hate," *ESPN.com,* October 3, 2004, http://sports.espn.go.com/mlb/playoffs2004/news/story?page=Curse041005 (accessed May 29, 2008).

4. For a more critical explanation of this see Howard Bryant, *Living It: Boston and Sports,* ed. Emily Heistand and Ande Zellman (Boston: Beacon Press, 2004), 117–131; *Shut Out: A Story of Race and Baseball in Boston* (New York: Routledge, 2002); Glen Stout and Richard Johnson, *Red Sox Century* (New York: Houghton Mifflin, 2004); Ryan King-White, "Playing Their Part: Red Sox Nation 2007," *Journal of Contemporary Ethnography,* forthcoming.

5. Dan Shaughnessy, *At Fenway: Dispatches from Red Sox Nation* (Boston: Penguin Press, 1996), 54.

6. Charles Steinberg left this post on December 31, 2007, for a similar position with the Los Angeles Dodgers.

7. Bob Underwood, "Cop: Sox Fan Hit, Killed over Yankee Rivalry," *Boston Herald,* May 6, 2008.

8. Glen Stout and Richard Johnson, *Yankees Century: 100 Years of New York Yankees Baseball* (New York: Houghton Mifflin, 2002); Stout and Johnson, *Red Sox Century.*

9. Stout and Johnson, *Red Sox Century,* 28.

10. See, for example, "Yanks and Red Sox Close Big Trade," *New York Times,* December 16, 1920; "Owners of New York Yankees Start Suit Against Ban Johnson for $500,000 Damages," *New York Times,* February 3, 1920; "Yankees Swing Big Deal with Red Sox," *New York Times,* December 21, 1921; "Yankees Not Worried about a Triple Play," *New York Times,* April 29, 1922.

11. For a summary of this relationship and primary sources, respectively, see Stout and Johnson, *Yankees Century,* 79; "May Appeal to Law for Yankees' Share," *New York Times,* November 19, 1919; "New Board Gives Yankees a Shock," *New York Times,* December 17, 1919; "Yank's Owners Are Sustained by Court," *New York Times,* October 26, 1919.

12. Stout and Johnson, *Red Sox Century,* 144–151.

13. See David Halberstam, *Summer of '49* (New York: HaperCollins, 1989).

14. "Ruth Tells Tales of His Boston Days," *New York Times,* January 16, 1920.

15. Stout and Johnson, *Red Sox Century,* 151.

16. "Huggins Story of Luring Babe Ruth," *Boston Globe,* January 22, 1920; "Babe Ruth Accepts Terms of Yankees," *New York Times,* January 7, 1920; Dan Shaughnessy, *The Curse of the Bambino* (Boston: Penguin Press, 1990), 22.

17. Leah Montville, *The Big Bam: The Life and Times of Babe Ruth* (New York: Doubleday, 2005), 17.

18. Shaughnessy, *The Curse of the Bambino*, 34–35

19. Burt Whitman quoted in Stout, "A Curse Born of Hate," 66.

20. Stout and Johnson, *Red Sox Century*, 137–152.

21. Philip Lowry, *Green Cathedrals: The Ultimate Celebrations of All 273 Major League and Negro League Ballparks Past and Present* (New York: Addison Wesley Publishing, 1993), 25.

22. Lowry, *Green Cathedrals;* Stout and Johnson, *Red Sox Century*, 22–26

23. Bryant, *Shut Out* (New York: Routledge, 2002), 171; King-White, "Playing Their Part."

24. Stout and Johnson, *Yankees Century*, 148–149.

25. Robert Barney and David Barney, "Get Those Niggers off the Field: Racial Integration and the Real Curse of the Boston Red Sox," *Nine* 16, no. 1 (2007): 1–9.

26. Bryant, *Shut Out*, 28–34.

27. Barney and Barney, "Get Those Niggers off the Field"; Keane quoted in Bryant, *Shut Out*, 41.

28. Halberstam, *Summer of '49*, 175–176, 260.

29. Bryant, *Shut Out*, 139.

30. Stout and Johnson, *Yankees Century*, 225.

31. Stout and Johnson, *Yankees Century*, 263.

32. John Drebinger, "Yanks Whip Red Sox in Season Finale to Win 16th American League Pennant," *New York Times*, October 3, 1949.

33. John Drebinger, "Reynolds to Face Newcombe (Maybe) in Series Opener Today," *New York Times*, October 5, 1949; Halberstam, *Summer of '49*, 175–176, 260; Stout and Johnson, *Red Sox Century*, 269–272; Stout and Johnson, *Yankees Century*, 227–229.

34. Stout and Johnson, *Red Sox Century*, 272.

35. Glen Rifkin, "How the Red Sox Touch All the Branding Bases," *Strategy+Business*, 4th quarter, 1999.

36. Bryant, *Shut Out*, 94.

37. Stout and Johnson, *Yankees Century*, 50–51.

38. Bryant, *Shut Out*, 50–51; Stout and Johnson, *Yankees Century*, 291.

39. Dan Shaughnessy, "The Impossible Dream," *Boston Globe*, April 3, 1992, 40.

40. Bryant, *Shut Out*, 76–80.

41. Ronald P. Formisano, *Boston against Busing: Race, Class, and Ethnicity in the 1960s and '70s* (Chapel Hill: University of North Carolina Press, 1991), x.

42. Bryant, *Shut Out*, 87–89; Shaughnessy, *The Curse of the Bambino*, Stout and Johnson, *Red Sox Century*, 215–340; Shaughnessy, *At Fenway*, 145.

43. Rifkin, "How the Red Sox touch all the branding bases."

44. Bryant, *Shut Out*, 94–98.

45. Ibid., 135–146.

46. John Bracey, professor of Afro-American History at the University of Massachusetts–Amherst, in discussion with the author, July 2007.

47. Joseph Durson, "Yanks Lose, 3–2, in 9th and Drop Out of Lead," *New York Times*, August 2, 1973, 43.

48. Harvey Frommer, *Red Sox vs. Yankees: The Great Rivalry* (Champaign, IL: Sports Publishing, 2005), 130–132.

49. Jimmy Piersall, *Fear Strikes Out: The Jimmy Piersall Story*, Alan Parkula, Paramount Pictures, 1957.

50. Bryant, *Living It: Boston and Sports*, 121.

51. Parton Keese, "Dineen, Newest Yankee, Gets Hit in 12th to Top Red Sox, 6–5," *New York Times*, May 22, 1976, 41.

52. Stout and Johnson, *Red Sox Century*, 370.

53. Ibid., 371.

54. George Plasketes, "The Rebel Hero in Baseball: Bill "Spaceman" Lee in an Orbit All His Own," *Journal of Popular Culture* 21, no. 1 (1987): 121–138.

55. Stout and Johnson, *Red Sox Century*, 378.

56. Bryant, *Shut Out*, 137.

57. Stout and Johnson, *Yankees Century*, 355–360.

58. Stout and Johnson, *Red Sox Century*, 391.

59. Bryant, *Shut Out*, 170.

60. Robert Ward, "Reggie Jackson in No-Man's Land," *Sport*, June 1977.

61. Stout and Johnson, *Yankees Century*, 338.

62. Shaughnessy, *The Curse of the Bambino*, 138.

63. Larry Whiteside, "That Clinches It, Red Sox Rap Blue Jays, Wrap Up East," *Boston Globe*, September 29, 1986.

64. Nathan Cobb, "Baseball Border War in Milford, Conn. Geography Brings Sox and Mets Fans Cheek to Jowl," *Boston Globe*, October 20, 1986.

65. See, for example, Steve Burkowitz, "Commissioner Orders Steinbrenner to Resign," *Washinton Post*, July 31, 1990; Mark Heisler, "Finally Piece Comes to the Zoo," *Los Angeles Times*, August 5, 1990.

66. Bryant, *Shut Out*, 139.

67. Ibid., 207–208.

68. Ira Berkow, "Sports of the Times; Yankee Chieftan Returns," *New York TImes*, September 15, 1993.

69. Bryant, *Shut Out*, 219–234.

70. Alan Klein, "Latinizing Fenway: Examining Media, Race, and Fans of Pedro Martinez," *Sport Sociology Journal* 17, no. 4 (2000): 403–429.

71. Kieran Darcy, "No Four-Leaf Clover Here," *ESPN.com*, http://sports.espn.go.com/espn/page2/story?page=tortured/sandiego (accessed September 21, 2007).

72. Dan Shaughnessy, "NY Writer Throws Curve on MVP Pick," *Boston Globe*, November 21, 1999.

73. Ian O'Connor, "Yankee Pride Returns," *USA Today*, October 5, 2003.

74. Buster Olney, "Pettitte Comes Through Loud and Clear as the Yankees Drown Out the Sox," *New York Times*, October 17, 1999; sJoe Lapointe, "Williams Says Bad Calls Incited Fenway Fans," *New York Times*, October 18, 1999.

75. Jeff Nelson quoted in Olney, "Pettitte Comes Through Loud and Clear as the Yankees Drown Out the Sox."

76. Those who watched the game suggest that, given the Yankees' immense talent, and this being the height of the steroid era, Martinez fell one pitch (a home run to Chilli Davis) shy of throwing the greatest game of all time. As Paul O'Neill later said, "We didn't get beat by the Red Sox, we got beat by Pedro Martinez." Quoted from Buster Olney in the *New York Times*, September 11, 1999.

77. Mike Berman, "Pedro Wins Pitchers Duel," *USA Today.com*, May 29, 2000,

http://www.usatoday.com/sports/baseball/roost/year2/rst0529.htm (accessed January 23, 2008).

78. Brian McGrory, "Taking Teeth out of Curse? Teen Hit by Ramirez Foul Ball Lives in Babe Ruth's Former House," *Boston Globe,* September 2, 2004.

79. John Dobosz, "Remaking the Red Sox." *Forbes.com,* October 22, 2004, http://www.forbes.com/ceonetwork/2004/10/22/1022bookreview.html (accessed May 17, 2008).

80. Seth Mnookin, *Feeding the Monster: How Money, Smarts, and Nerve Took a Team to the Top* (New York: Simon and Schuster, 2006), 74.

81. Gordon Edes, "Steinbrenner Returns Salvo," *Boston Globe,* December 30, 2002.

82. Ibid.

83. Ron Borges, "'Boy Wonder' Becomes 'The Man': Epstein Defied Conventional Wisdom to Build Winner," *MSNBC.com,* October 28, 2004, http://nbc sports.msnbc.com/id/6241541/ (accessed September 21, 2007).

84. Tim Casey, "A's Fans Felt Lost after Weekend," *Boston Globe,* October 7, 2003; Jackie MacMullen, "Sweet Success for This Pair," *Boston Globe,* October 5, 2003; Bob Ryan, "Ain't Misbehavin': It's a Show," *Boston Globe,* October 10, 2003.

85. Michael Holley, "They May Go Down Swinging," *Boston Globe,* October 12, 2003.

86. Katie Zezima,"2 Yankees and Worker Charged IN Fight," *New York Times,* December 19, 2003.

87. Rudy Martzke, "Red Sox, Yankees Prove Baseball Can Be a Ratings Hit," *USA Today,* October 20, 2004.

88. Several key players' contracts, including Nomar Garciaparra, Pedro Martinez, Derek Lowe, and Jason Varitek, would conclude at season's end. As such, it was understood that this would be the last time this particular group of players would play for the Red Sox.

89. Mnookin, *Feeding the Monster,* 244–246.

90. Ibid., 248–254.

91. Bill Simmons, *Now I Can Die in Peace: How ESPN's Sports Guy Found Salvation, with a Little Help from Nomar, Pedro, Shawshank and the 2004 Red Sox* (New York: ESPN Books, 2005), 228.

92. Simmons, *Now I Can Die in Peace,* 183–186.

93. Nick Cafardo, "Finally They Show Signs of Life," *Boston Globe,* July 25, 2004.

94. Simmons, *Now I Can Die in Peace,* 333–342.

95. Dan Shaughnessy, author and columnist for the *Boston Globe,* in conversation with author, July 2007.

96. Mnookin, *Feeding the Monster,* 373.

97. Leanne Schreiber, "Viewers Held Hostage by 'Tyranny of the Storyline,'" *ESPN.com,* June 7, 2007, http://sports.espn.go.com/espn/print?id=2897260&type= story (accessed August 24, 2008).

98. John Ourand, "MLB Ratings Down, but Network Looks Ahead," *Street and Smith's Sport Business Journal,* July 7, 2008, 6.

99. Tyler Kepner, "Red Sox, Fans, Batter Yankees," *New York Times,* April 15, 2005.

100. Mike Underwood, "Cops: Sox Fan Hit, Killed over Yankees Rivalry," *Boston Herald,* May 6, 2008,.

101. Melissa Trujillo, "Buried David Ortiz Jersey Nets $175K for Jimmy Fund

Charity," *ESPN.com*, April 24, 2008, http://sports.espn.go.com/mlb/news/story?id=
3365119 (accessed May 29, 2008).

102. Bryant, *Living It: Boston and Sports*, 127.

103. Simmons, *Now I Can Die in Peace*, 333–342.s

8. A Tale of Two Cities—Brian P. Soebbing and Daniel S. Mason

1. Kevin Dowler, "'To Squeeze a Single Sentence Out': Estrangement and
Disenchantment in Benjamin's Marseilles," in *Urban Enigmas: Montreal, Toronto and the
Problem of Comparing Cities*, ed. Johanne Sloan (Montreal: McGill-Queen's University
Press, 2007), 92.

2. Alan Blum, "Comparing Cities: On the Mutual Honouring of Peculiarities," in
Urban Enigmas: Montreal, Toronto and the Problem of Comparing Cities, ed. Johanne Sloan
(Montreal: McGill-Queen's University Press, 2007), 19.

3. See Alan Metcalfe, *Canada Learns to Play: The Emergence of Organized Sport,
1807–1914* (Toronto, McClelland & Stewart, 1987), for an overview of Montreal's
importance in the development of sport in Canada.

4. Anouk Belanger, "Urban Space and Collective Memory: Analyzing the
Various Dimensions of the Production of Memory," *Canadian Journal of Urban
Research* 11, no. 1 (2002): 70.

5. Julie-Anne Boudreau, "The Politics of Territorialization: Regionalism,
Localism, and Other isms . . . the Case of Montreal," *Journal of Urban Affairs* 25, no. 2
(2003): 187.

6. Anouk Belanger, "Sport Venues and the Spectacularization of Urban Spaces in
North America," *International Review for the Sociology of Sport* 35, no 3 (2000): 389.

7. Boudreau, "The Politics of Territorialization," 179. "The 1995 referendum on
sovereignty came as a slap in the face for Anglo-Montrealers. When Franco-national-
ists came close to winning (the results were 50.6% against sovereignty and 49.4% in
support), language politics came back forcibly in daily life" (Ibid., 193).

8. Marc V. Levine, "Tourism-Based Redevelopment and the Fiscal Crisis of the
City: The Case of Montreal," *Canadian Journal of Urban Research* 12, no. 1 (2003):
102–123.

9. Belanger, "Urban Space and Collective Memory," 73.

10. Betsy Donald, "Spinning Toronto's Golden Age: The Making of a 'City That
Worked,'" *Environment and Planning A* 34 (2002): 2132.

11. Ibid., 2137.

12. Ibid.

13. TSN.ca, "The Rivalry: The Toronto Maple Leafs vs The Montreal Canadiens,"
http://www.tsn.ca/nhl/feature/?fid=10912&hubname (accessed May 14, 2008).

14. ESPN.com, "The 10 Greatest Teams," http://espn.go.com/endofcentury/s/
other/greatteams.html (accessed May 14, 2008).

15. Legends of Hockey.net, "The Legends: Players," http://www.legendsof
hockey.net/html/legendsplayer.htm (accessed September 18, 2009).

16. Record generated from Montreal Canadiens 2008–2009 media guide plus the
2007–2008 season results from ESPN.com.

17. TSN.ca, "The Rivalry."

18. Ibid.

19. Ibid.

20. Ibid.

21. Ibid.

22. Associated Press, "Leafs Stay Alive, Send Home Habs with Third-Period Rally," http://sports.espn.go.com/nhl/recap?gameId=270407021 (accessed July 10, 2008).

23. See Richard Gruneau and David Whitson, *Hockey Night in Canada: Sports, Identities, and Cultural Politics* (Toronto: Garamond Press, 1993).

24. See Daniel S. Mason, "Expanding the Footprint? Questioning the NHL's Expansion and Relocation Strategy." In *Artificial Ice: Hockey, Culture, and Commerce,* ed. David Whitson and Richard Gruneau (Toronto: Garamond Press, 2006), 181–199.

25. Paul Munsey and Cory Suppes, "Montreal Forum," http://hockey.ballparks. com/NHL/MontrealCanadiens/oldindex.htm (accessed July 15, 2008).

26. Paul Munsey and Cory Suppes, "Maple Leaf Gardens," http://hockey.ball parks.com/NHL/TorontoMapleLeafs/index.htm (accessed July 15, 2008).

27. Lisa Gunderson, "Memory, Modernity, and the City: An Interpretive Analysis of Montreal and Toronto's Respective Moves from Their Historic Professional Hockey Arenas" (Master's thesis, University of Waterloo, 2004), 57.

28. Ibid.

29. Ibid., 56.

30. John L. Crompton, Dennis R. Howard, and Turgut Var, "Financing Major League Facilities: Status, Evolution and Conflicting Forces," *Journal of Sport Management* 17 (2003): 156–184.

31. Ibid., 167.

32. Ibid., 156–184.

33. Ibid., 156–184.

34. Ibid., 167.

35. Michael Grange, "U.S., unlike Canada, eager to pay price for sports facilities American governments often turn to the taxpayer to raise money while Canada relies on private sector, leaving one country at a disadvantage Montreal Canadiens," *Globe and Mail,* October 30, 1998, Proquest, via Canadian Newsstand, http://www. proquest.com (accessed May 15, 2008).

36. David Shoalts, "Toronto fans will take Centre stage Toronto's newest sports and entertainment complex is set to open. It's the Air Canada Centre, the home for hockey's Maple Leafs and basketball's Raptors. It marks a new era in stadium construction in the city—a facility built for the fans first," *Globe and Mail,* February 17, 1999, Proquest, via Canadian Newsstand, http://www.proquest.com (accessed May 15, 2008).

37. Ibid.

38. Jim Proudfoot, "Centre Stage; New arena debuts by presenting the greatest rivalry in pro sports: Leafs vs. Habs," *Toronto Star,* February 20, 1999, Proquest, via Canadian Newsstand, http://www.proquest.com (accessed May 15, 2008).

39. James Christie and Robert MacLeod, "Raptors Pay Hefty Penalty for Arena Construction Delay," *Globe and Mail,* September 29, 1995, Proquest, via Canadian Newsstand, http://www.proquest.com (accessed May 15, 2008).

40. "Hockey: Maple Leafs look to ride the rails: NHL team talking about building

new arena on top of Union Station," *Standard,* April 18, 1997, Proquest, via Canadian Newsstand, http://www.proquest.com (accessed May 15, 2008).

41. James Christie, "Slaight wins Raptor bidding Sources say Bitove unable to secure $88-million needed to block bid from fellow club owner," *Globe and Mail,* November 15, 1996, Proquest, via Canadian Newsstand, http://www.proquest.com (accessed May 15, 2008).

42. Rod McQueen, "Stavro Buys Raptors and Air Canada Maple Leafs' owner plans sports, entertainment and retail complex at Toronto's historic Union Station," *Financial Post,* February 13, 1998, Proquest, via Canadian Newsstand, http://www.proquest.com (accessed May 15, 2008).

43. Gunderson, "Memory, Modernity, and the City," 60.

44. Ronald Corey, "A Taxing Burden: The Molson Centre isn't looking for a special break, it's just seeking relief from a property assessment that it considers unfairly high," *Gazette,* April 20, 1999, Proquest, via Canadian Newsstand, http://www.proquest.com (accessed May 15, 2008).

45. Gunderson, "Memory, Modernity, and the City," 67.

46. Belanger, "Sport Venues and the Spectacularization of Urban Spaces," 392.

47. Ibid., 389.

48. Ibid., 392.

9. Like Cats and Dogs—*Lawrence W. Hugenberg and Brian C. Pattie*

1. Thomas Maroon, Margaret Maroon, and Craig Holbert, *Akron-Canton Football Heritage* (Charleston, SC: Arcadia Publishing, 2006), 2.

2. "Alabama School Investigated: Management, Control of Hoover Football Team at Issue," *USA Today,* July 30, 2007.

3. Robert L. Samuelson, "Ambition's Curse: Winning at Any Cost," *Plain Dealer,* October 18, 2007.

4. Shaheen Samavati, "OHSAA Rejects Bid to Broadcast Tournaments," *Plain Dealer,* August 10, 2007.

5. *Touchdown Town,* newsreel, directed by Andre Baruch (Massillon, OH: Chamber of Commerce, 1951).

6. *Go Tigers! Massillon Ohio Where They Live, Breathe and Eat Football,* DVD, directed by Kenneth Carlson (New York: New York Video Group, 2001–2002).

7. Rick Shepas quoted in Bill Lubinder, "Memories to Kick Around: Playoff Games Rekindle Max Shafer's Thrill, Then Agony," *Plain Dealer,* October 27, 2007.

8. Francis H. Cicchinelli quoted in *Go Tigers! Massillon Ohio Where They Live, Breathe and Eat Football.*

9. Rick Shepas quoted in *Go Tigers!: Massillon Ohio Where They Live, Breathe and Eat Football.*

10. *Touchdown Town,* newsreel.

11. Wilbur Arnold, "Massillon Tigers Football History," http://www.massillontigers.com/history.htm (accessed April 15, 2008).

12. Kimberly A. Kenney, *Canton: A Journey through Time* (Charleston, SC: Arcadia Publishing, 2003), 107.

13. Maroon, Maroon, and Holbert, *Akron-Canton Football Heritage,* 8.

14. Kenney, *Canton,* 108.

15. Ibid., 146.

16. John E. White, *The Massillon Tigers Story: The First Hundred Years* (Lake Forest, CA: Class Press, 1994); Scott H. Shook, *Massillon Memories: The Inside Story of the Greatest Show in High School Football* (Massillon, OH: Massillon Memories Publishing Company, 1998).

17. Sean Deveney, "Bad Blood," *Sporting News,* August 27, 2007, 18.

18. Wilbur Arnold, "Massillon Tigers Football History," http://www.massillon-tigers.com/history.htm (accessed June 1, 2008).

19. "Massillon-Canton Series Historical Facts," Massillon Tigers Cyber Review, http://www.massillontigers.com/mckinley/massillon%20canton%facts.htm (accessed April 15, 2008).

20. Garry Crawford, *Consuming Sport: Fans, Sport and Culture* (New York: Routledge, 2004), 54.

21. Maroon, Maroon, and Holbert, *Akron-Canton Football Heritage,* 103.

22. *Touchdown Town,* newsreel.

23. *Go Tigers! Massillon Ohio Where They Live, Breathe and Eat Football.*

24. Larry Kovak, *Seriously, It's Just High School Football* (Baltimore, MD: Publish America, 2006), 10.

25. Ron Maly quoted in Wilbur Arnold, "Massillon Tigers Football History," http://www.massillontigers.com/history.htm (accessed June 1, 2008).

26. Bob Commings quoted in Arnold, "Massillon Tigers Football History."

27. *Go Tigers! Massillon Ohio Where They Live, Breathe and Eat Football.*

28. Ibid.

29. *Touchdown Town,* newsreel.

30. "Massillon Preparing to Rally for Its TitleTown Close-Up," *Independent,* http://www/indeonline.comn/sports/x390625094/Massillon-preparing-to-rally-for-its—TitleTown-Close-Up (accessed June 1, 2008).

31. Ibid.

32. Benjamin B. Rader, *American Sports: From the Age of Folk Games to the Age of Televised Sports* (Upper Saddle River, NJ: Prentice Hall, 1999), 330.

33. Ibid.

34. Ibid.

35. U.S. Census Bureau, *2000 Census of Population and Housing: Population and Housing Unit Counts* (Washington D.C.,: U.S. Government Printing Office, 2000).

36. Kevin Coffey quoted in Leigh Montville, "The Centurians," *Sports Illustrated,* November 14, 1994, 44.

37. "I Am Massillon," Massillon Proud, http://massillonproud.com/forum/showthread.php?t=5151 (accessed April 15, 2008).

38. U.S. Census Bureau, *2000 Census of Population and Housing: Population and Housing Unit Counts* (Washington, D.C.,: U.S. Government Printing Office, 2000).

39. Ibid.

40. Ibid.

41. Richard O. Davies, *Sports in American Life: A History* (Malden, MA: Blackwell, 2007), 413.

42. Ibid., 414.

43. Edward T. Heald, *The Stark County Story: The American Way of Life, 1917–1959* (Columbus: Stoneman Press, 1959), 65.

44. Ibid., 66.

45. "Timkin History," Timkin, http://www.timken.com/en-us/about/Pages/History.aspx (accessed May 1, 2008).

46. Heald, *The Stark County Story,* 64.

47. Ibid., 116, 122.

48. Ibid., 574.

49. Bob Kurz, *Miami of Ohio: The Cradle of Coaches* (Troy, OH: Troy Daily News), 140.

50. Tim Rogers, "Massillon Gets Hall as Coach," *Plain Dealer,* April 11, 2008.

51. Wilbur Arnold, "Massillon Tigers Football History," http://www.massillon tigers.com/history.htm (accessed June 1, 2008).

52. Paul Brown, *PB: The Paul Brown Story* (New York, Atheneum, 1979), 52.

53. Arnold, "Massillon Tigers Football History."

54. Ibid.

55. Ibid.

56. Ibid.

57. Ibid.

58. "WVU Sports Hall of Fame," West Virginia University Athletics, http://www.wvu.edu/~sports/hall_fame/don_nehlen.htm (accessed April 15, 2008).

59. "College Football Hall of Fame," College Football Hall of Fame, http://www.collegefootball.org/famersearch.php?id=50027 (accessed June 1, 2008).

60. "Detroit Lions History and Records," Detroit Lions, http://detroitlions.com/section_display.cfm?section_id=8&top=1&level=3 (accessed June 1, 2008).

61. Dennis Tuttle, "National Rankings Alter Football," *USA Today,* August 20, 2002, http://www.usatoday.com/sports/preps/football/2002-08-20-maindata_x.htm (accessed June 1, 2008).

62. Brown, *PB: The Paul Brown Story,* 61.

63. *Go Tigers! Massillon Ohio Where They Live, Breathe and Eat Football.*

64. Richard Natale, "In His Ohio, Tigers Rule the Earth: Documentarian Kenneth A. Carlson's Hometown Is Obsessed with the High School Football Team, and so is He," *Los Angeles Times,* September 16 2001, http://www.gotigersfilm.com/latimes.htm (accessed April 15, 2008).

10. A Rivalry for the Ages—*Jaime Schultz*

1. Frank Deford, "This Year Is Truly the Year of Women in Sports Headlines," *Sports Illustrated,* May 28, 2008, http://sportsillustrated.cnn.com (accessed June 1, 2008); Jeff Jacobs, "Tennessee's Allegations Don't Amount to Much," *Hartford Courant,* April 27, 2008, www.courant.com (accessed June 1, 2008); Liz Robbins, "N.C.A.A. Basketball Tournament," *New York Times,* April 2, 2000, 8.2; Lars Anderson, "The Face-Off," *Sports Illustrated, Commemorative Huskie Edition,* 2003, 12; Kelli Anderson, "Tennessee and UConn Call Off the War," *Sports Illustrated,* December 31, 2007, 61. Summitt's comments were broadcast on the ESPN program "Rome Is Burning," quoted in Shelley Smith, "Geno and Pat Headed for a Championship Showdown," March 21, 2008, ESPN.com (accessed April 15, 2008).

2. Michael A. Messner, *Taking the Field: Women, Men, and Sports* (Minneapolis: University of Minnesota Press, 2002), 77.

3. See, for example, Joe Buck, "The Last Word on the Best Rivalries," *Sporting News,* September 22, 2003, 38; Richard Sandomir, "Warmth Is Found in a Heated Rivalry," *New York Times,* November 13, 2007; "The 10 Greatest Rivalries," January 3, 2000, http://espn.go.com (accessed February 8, 2008); "Rivals," *Sports Illustrated,* April 24, 2004, 6–10; Frank Deford, "A Pair Beyond Compare," *Sports Illustrated,* May 26, 1986, 70–84. On page 95 of *Taking the Field,* for instance, Messner notes that in sports reporting on televised network news, women's sports garnered 8.2 percent coverage; on average, women's sports comprised just 2.2 percent of the total broadcast of ESPN's *SportsCenter.* About 13 percent of newspaper space is devoted to women's sports, based on a study by Susan Tyler Eastman and Andrew C. Billings, "Gender Parity in the Olympics: Hyping Women Athletes, Favoring Men Athletes," *Journal of Sport & Social Issues* 23 (1999): 140–170. Only 12 percent of magazine advertisements featuring celebrity athlete endorsers depicted women, according to Stacy Landreth Grau, Georgina Roselli, and Charles R. Taylor, "Where's Tamika Catchings? A Content Analysis of Female Athlete Endorsers in Magazine Advertisements," *Journal of Current Issues & Research in Advertising* 29 (2007): 55–65. See also Ronald Bishop, "Missing in Action: Feature Coverage of Women's Sports in *Sports Illustrated,*" *Journal of Sport & Social Issues* 27 (2003): 184–194.

4. To borrow from Michael Oriard, I analyze the "'secondary texts' of sports journalism that have always interpreted the 'primary text' of the game itself." Michael Oriard, *Reading Football: How the Popular Press Created an American Spectacle* (Chapel Hill: University of North Carolina Press, 1993), 10. See also Susan Birrell and Mary G. McDonald, *Reading Sport: Critical Essays on Power and Representation* (Boston: Northeastern University Press, 2000); Mary G. McDonald and Susan Birrell, "Reading Sport Critically: A Methodology for Interrogating Power," *Sociology of Sport Journal* 16 (1999): 283–300. For local outlets, I selected the *Knoxville News Sentinel* and, because Storrs, Connecticut, is a relatively small town, opted for the *Hartford Courant,* published just over twenty miles away, with the largest readership in the state. Expanding my search, I reviewed most widely circulated papers in the northeastern and southeastern United States, using the *Boston Globe* and the *Atlanta Journal-Constitution,* respectively. For a national perspective, I looked to *USA Today,* the *New York Times,* and the *Washington Post,* eliminating those papers based in the western United States because of the locations of the two universities.

5. Throughout this project, I have struggled with which school to list first when identifying the rivalry and whether such designation demonstrates a personal bias. I will list the University of Tennessee first, but only for the sake of consistency and because the school's women's basketball team has a longer history than the University of Connecticut's. Wendy Parker, "Clash of the Titans," *Atlanta Journal & Constitution,* January 3, 1998.

6. Alice W. Frymir, *Basket Ball for Women: How to Coach and Play the Game* (New York: A. S. Barnes & Co., 1930), 8. On the six-player game, see Shelley Lucas, "Courting Controversy: Gender and Power in Iowa Girls' Basketball," *Journal of Sport History* 30 (2004); Janice Beran, Six-on-Six to Full Court Press: A Century of Iowa Girls' Basketball (Ames: Iowa State University, 1993); Max McElwain, *The Only Dance in Iowa* (Lincoln: University of Nebraska Press, 2004).

7. See Lynne Emery, "The First Intercollegiate Contest for Women: Basketball, April 4, 1896," in *Her Story in Sport: A Historical Anthology of Women in Sports,* ed. Reet

Howell (West Point, NY: Leisure Press, 1982), 417–423; John R. Tunis, "Women and the Sports Business," *Harper's Magazine* 159 (1929), 213; Paula Welch, "Interscholastic Basketball: Bane of Collegiate Physical Educators," in Howell, *Her Story in Sport,* 426.

8. Joan S. Hult, "The Saga of Competition: Basketball Battles and Governance War," in *A Century of Women's Basketball: From Frailty to Final Four,* ed. Joan S. Hult and Marianna Trekell (Reston, VA: American Alliance for Health, Physical Education, Recreation and Dance, 1991), 234; Jill Hutchison, "Women's Intercollegiate Basketball: AIAW/NCAA," in Hult and Trekell, *A Century of Women's Basketball,* 309; Summitt quoted in Pamela Grundy and Susan Shackelford, *Shattering the Glass: The Remarkable History of Women's Basketball* (New York: New Press, 2005), 180.

9. Leigh Montville, "Dynamic Tension," *Sports Illustrated,* March 8, 1999, 64.

10. Geno Auriemma with Jackie MacMullan, *Geno: In Pursuit of Perfection* (New York: Warner Books, 2006), 272.

11. Frank Litsky, "At UConn, the Women Take on High Court," *New York Times,* January 16, 1995; Debbie Becker, "Tenn.-UConn translates into Tough Ticket," *USA Today,* January 16, 1995; Bob Ryan, "This One Ranks Right Up There," *Boston Globe,* January 17, 1995.

12. Wendy Parker, "UConn Ends Lady Vols' Win Streak," *Atlanta Journal & Constitution,* January 7, 1996.

13. Liz Robbins, "UConn-Tennessee: Game 3 Today Is What Counts," *Atlanta Journal and Constitution,* April 2, 2000; Wendy Parker, "Tennessee, UConn Play Rivalry Down," *Atlanta Journal and Constitution,* February 1, 2001.

14. This includes Summitt's 175-48 record during the AIAW era. Since then, two other women have reached 800 wins: University of Texas's Jody Conradt and Rutgers's C. Vivian Stringer.

15. Dan Fleser, "Summitt Will Be First Women's $1M Coach," *Knoxville News Sentinel,* March 11, 2006, http://www.knoxnews.com (accessed February 8, 2008); Dan Uhlinger and John Altavilla, "Geno Auriemma Signs with UConn through 2013," *Hartford Courant,* June 25, 2008, www.courant.com (accessed July 1, 2008). See also Dick Patrick, "Rising Salaries Increase Pressure on Top Women's Coaches," *USA Today,* March, 7, 2007, http://www.usatoday.com (accessed April 24, 2008).

16. Statistics reported by the NCAA, available at http://www.ncaa.org/stats/w_basketball/attendance/2006–07/2006–07_w_basketball_attendance.pdf (accessed February 8, 2008).

17. Dan Fleser, "More than Geno vs. Pat," *Knoxville News Sentinel,* January 7, 2005, http://www.knoxnews.com (accessed February 8, 2008).

18. Kelly Whiteside, "UConn Holds off Tennessee," *USA Today,* April 9, 2003, 1C; L. Anderson, "The Face-Off."

19. Mark Bechtel, "He Hate Me," *Sports Illustrated,* January 31, 2005, 18; Kent Garber, "Showing How the Game Is Played," *US News and World Reports,* November 19, 2007, 60; Frank Deford, "Geno Auriemma + Diana Taurasi = Love, Italian Style," *Sports Illustrated,* November 24, 2003, 124; L. Anderson, "The Face-Off"; Mel Greenberg, "Summitt Used to Life at the Top," *Philadelphia Inquirer,* November 4, 2005, D1; Dick Patrick, "Rivals Summitt, Auriemma Two of a Kind," *USA Today,* April 8, 2003; Jeff Jacobs, "Tennessee's Allegations Don't Amount to Much," *Hartford Courant,* April 27, 2008, www.courant.com (accessed June 1, 2008); Deford, "Geno Auriemma + Diana Taurasi," 124; Christine Brennan, "Auriemma, Man among Women," *USA Today,*

NOTES TO PAGES 223–29

418

April 7, 2004; Ira Berkow, "N.C.A.A. Tournament: Auriemma Helps Pave the Way at UConn," *New York Times*, April 2, 1995; "Auriemma Sticks His Foot in His Mouth," *Daily Beacon*, February 4, 2004, http://dailybeacon.utk.edu/s (accessed February 8, 2008); Jere Longman, "Always Pursuing Perfection," *New York Times*, March 18, 2002; Grundy and Shackelford, *Shattering the Glass*, 122; L. Anderson, "The Face-Off," "Dick Patrick, "Rivals Summitt, Auriemma Two of a Kind," *USA Today*, April 8, 2003, 3C; Harvey Araton, "Sports of the Times; Friend Gets Tangled in Coaches' Rivalry," *New York Times*, April 8, 2003.

20. Auriemma, *Geno*, 281, 27; Naismith Memorial Basketball Hall of Fame, http://www.hoophall.com/halloffamers/bhof-geno-auriemma.html (accessed February 8, 2008).

21. Ibid.

22. Pat Summitt with Sally Jenkins, *Raise the Roof* (New York: Broadway Books, 1998), 73–74; Rosemarie Skaine, *Women College Basketball Coaches* (Jefferson, NC: McFarland, 2001), 148.

23. "Spell of the UCONN," *Coach & the Athletic Director* 70 (2001): 62; Auriemma, *Geno*, 18, 239, 270, 281.

24. Patrick, "Rivals Summitt, Auriemma," 3C; Angela Watts, "One-Upsmanship for the Women," *Washington Post*, April 8, 2003.

25. Grundy and Shackelford, *Shattering the Glass*, 241; Jere Longman, "Summitt and Tennessee Roll to Another Title," *New York Times*, April 9, 2008; Pat Summitt with Sally Jenkins, *Reach for the Summit* (New York: Broadway Books, 1998), 21; Summitt, *Raise the Roof*, 75.

26. "Spell of the UCONN," *Coach & the Athletic Director* 70 (2001): 63; Richard Kent, ed., *Inside Women's College Basketball: Anatomy of Two Seasons* (Lanham, MA: Taylor Trade Publishing, 2002), 127; Auriemma, *Geno*, 23.

27. Auriemma, *Geno*, 25.

28. Hank Hersch, "At the Summitt Again," *Sports Illustrated*, April 8, 1991, 36. For a complete list of Auriemma's coaching honors, see the official UConn Huskies' Web site at http://www.uconnhuskies.com.

29. Andrew Lawrence, "A Whole New Ball Game," *Sports Illustrated*, April 12, 2007, 10.

30. Lawrence, "A Whole New Ball Game."

31. For a complete list of Summitt's coaching honors, see the official Tennessee Lady Vols' Web site at www.utladyvols.com; Amy Shipley, "U-Conn in a Laugher," *Washington Post*, April 3, 2000; Bob Ryan, "Summitt, Tennessee Still Pull Rank on Rivals," *Boston Globe*, December 30, 2000; Auriemma, *Geno*, 273.

32. Watts, "One-Upsmanship"; Brennan, "Auriemma, Man among Women"; Summitt quoted in Lynn Zinser, "N.C.A.A. Women's Final Matchup," *New York Times*, April 6, 2004; Auriemma quoted in "Auriemma Explains Why Summitt Ended Series," *New York Times*, April 24, 2008.

33. Summitt and Auriemma quoted in Dick Patrick and Kelly Whiteside, "UConn vs. Tennessee in Title Game, Take 4," *USA Today*, April 6, 2004.

34. Araton, "Sports of the Times"; L. Anderson, "The Face-Off," 13; Kristie Ackert, "Geno & Pat Got at It Again," *New York Daily News*, April 8, 2003; quoted in Viv Bernstein, "Lady Vols Top Villanova to Reach Final Four," *New York Times*, April 1, 2003; Araton, "Sports of the Times."

35. Auriemma quoted in Jackie MacMullan, "He's the Man," *Sports Illustrated for Women* 1 (Spring 1999), 70; Brennan, "Auriemma, Man among Women"; Deford, "Geno Auriemma + Diana Taurasi," 124. See also Ailene Voisin, "UConn's Auriemma Takes Honors, Snubs in Stride," *Atlanta Journal & Constitution*, April 11, 1995; Wendy Parker, "Gender Gap: Legion of Male Coaches Dwindling," *Atlanta Journal & Constitution*, March 25, 2000; John Walters, Albert Kim, and Mark Marvic, "Boys on the Side: Reverse Discrimination?" *Sports Illustrated*, April 2, 2001, 26.

36. R. Vivian Acosta and Linda Jean Carpenter, "Women in Intercollegiate Sport: A Longitudinal, National Study, Thirty-One Year Update, 1977–2008," http://web pages.charter.net/womeninsport/2008%20Summary%20Final.pdf (accessed February 8, 2008); Auriemma, *Geno*, 274.

37. Marlene A. Dixon and Jennifer E. Bruening, "Work-Family Conflict in Coaching I: A Top-Down Perspective," *Journal of Sport Management* 21 (2007): 377–406; Jolinda J. Ellis and Gerald Masterson, "Gender Variations in Coaching Jobs," *Coach & the Athletic Director*, October 2007, 60–61; Nancy Theberge, "The Construction of Gender in Sport: Women, Coaching, and the Naturalization of Difference," *Social Problems* 40 (1993): 301–313; Pat Griffin, *Strong Women, Deep Closets* (Champaign, IL: Human Kinetics, 1998); Diana Taurasi quoted in Deford, "Geno Auriemma + Diana Taurasi," 126.

38. Longman, "Always Pursuing Perfection." See especially, Walters, Kim, and Marvic, "Boys on the Side," 26; Auriemma, *Geno*, 270–271; see, for example, Auriemma, *Geno*, 216.

39. Auriemma, *Geno*, 148.

40. Summitt quoted in Jere Longman, "Debating the Male Coach's Role," *New York Times*, March 29. 2002.

41. Summitt, *Reach for the Summitt*, 23; Auriemma, *Geno*, 144; Summitt quoted in Harvey Araton, "Money Race: Will Women Follow Men?" *New York Times*, March 28, 1997.

42. L. Anderson, "The Face-Off," 61; Ailene Voisin, "1995 NCAA Women's Basketball Championship," *Atlanta Journal & Constitution*, April 2, 1995; Fleser, "More than Geno vs. Pat."

43. Summitt quoted in Bob Ryan, "Summitt, Tennessee Still Pull Rank on Rivals," *Boston Globe*, December 30, 2000.

44. Grundy and Shackelford, *Shattering the Glass*, 218.

45. Mike Soltys quoted in John Altavilla, "ESPN Tried to Save Vols Series," *Hartford Courant*, June 10, 2007, E11; Richard Sandomir, "Women's Sports Get a Boost," *New York Times*, April 9, 1995.

46. Robbins, "N.C.A.A. Basketball Tournament," 8.2; Dick Patrick, "UConn Stirs New Interest," *USA Today*, November 17, 1995; Sandomir, "Women's Sports Get a Boost," 7.

47. See, for example, Watts, "One-Upsmanship"; Dick Patrick, "Rivals Summitt, Auriemma"; Susan Bickelhaupt, "Bird, Lawson: Young Guns Are Old Reliables," *Boston Globe*, April 2, 2000; Dick Patrick, "UConn Favored Vs. Nemesis Tenn.," *USA Today*, March 29, 2002; "Pat and Geno: The Game's Favorite Soap Opera," *Women's Basketball* 7 (November 2007): 8.

48. Auriemma quoted in John Altavilla and Lori Riley, "Geno Putting Press on Pat," *Hartford Courant*, September 25, 2007.

49. Shelley Smith, "Sources Say Moore's visit to ESPN Was Secondary Rules Violation," March 14, 2008, http://sports.espn.go.com (accessed April 24, 2008); "Connecticut Self-Reported Moore's Tour of ESPN to NCAA," ESPN.com, March 19, 2008, http://sports.espn.go.com (accessed June 1, 2008).

50. Quoted in "Auriemma: Lady Vols Quit UConn Series Over Recruiting Gripe," ESPN.com, 23 April 2008, http://espn.go.com/ (accessed June 1, 2008).

51. Auriemma quoted in John Altavilla, "Tennessee Releases Allegations Against UConn," *Hartford Courant*, April 27, 2008, www.courant.com (accessed June 1, 2008).

52. Kevin Meacham, "Auriemma Wraps Up Season," *Daily Campus*, April 23, 2008, www.dailycampus.com (accessed June 1, 2008).

11. Three Yards and a Pool of Blood—Brad Austin

1. Howard E. Peckman, *The University of Michigan, 1817–1992*, 175th Anniversary Edition, edited and updated by Margaret L. Steneck and Nicholas H. Steneck (Ann Arbor: University of Michigan Bentley Historical Library, 1994), 6, 18, 24, and 63.

2. James E. Pollard, *History of The Ohio State University: The Story of Its First Seventy-Five Years, 1873–1948* (Columbus: The Ohio State University Press, 1952), 1.

3. Ibid., 2–3 and 31.

4. Edward Orton quoted in ibid., 40.

5. Ronald A. Smith, *Sports and Freedom: The Rise of Big-Time College Athletics* (New York: Oxford University Press, 1988), 26–34.

6. John Sayles Watterson, *College Football: History, Spectacle, Controversy* (Baltimore: The Johns Hopkins University Press, 2000), 41; *Ohio State University Monthly* 40 (June 1949): 28.

7. See Chapter 6, "Angell: The Golden Years," in Peckman, *The University of Michigan*.

8. Peckman, *The University of Michigan*, 106–111.

9. Bill Cromartie, *The Big One* (Atlanta: Gridiron Publishers, 1979), 1–15.

10. "Ohio State Football Record," *Ohio State University Monthly* 40 (June 1949): 28.

11. "The Most Satisfying Moment in My Athletic Experience at Michigan," *Michigan Alumnus* 8 (November 1901).

12. "Building of the Library," *Ohio State University Monthly*, 40 (October 1948): 47.

13. Cromartie, *The Big One*, 59–63.

14. "Yosts Must Play Scheduled Tilt with Ohio State," November 1918, "Sports Information Office 1860—Scrapbooks," Box 1, Reel 2, Bentley Historical Library, University of Michigan. See the rest of this reel to get a sense of the relative lack of importance the Ohio State game had to Michigan students and fans in the 1900s and 1910s.

15. Steve White, *One Game Season: Ohio State vs. Michigan* (Collegeville, MN: One Game Season, 1995), 49; William Bach, "The Michigan Game and Other Athletics Notes on the Sport Situation," *Ohio State Monthly* (November 1919), viewed online at http://library.osu.edu/sites/archives/OSUvsMichigan/news/1919.htm (accessed September 14, 2009).

16. "Greatest Crowd in School History Present at Rally," *Ohio State University Lantern*, October 24, 1919, 1; "Everybody Happy?" *Ohio State University Lantern*, October 27, 1919, 2.

17. "Everybody Happy?" *Ohio State University Lantern,* October 27, 1919.

18. "Has Yost Seen His Day?" Letter to Editor of *Michigan Daily,* October 1921, "Sports Information Office, 1860—, Scrapbooks," Box 1, Reel 2, Bentley Historical Library, University of Michigan. See the rest of the reel for additional examples of escalating coverage in Michigan in the early 1920s.

19. H. E. Cherrington, "In the Bluish Haze," October 1922, "Sports Information Office, 1860—, Scrapbooks," Box 1, Reel 1, Bentley Historical Library, University of Michigan.

20. Harry Bullion, "Ohio's Repudiation Regarded Complete," October 1922, "Sports Information Office, 1860—, Scrapbooks," Box 1, Reel 1; "Varsity Squad Lets Up Intensive Training for Ohio State Game," October 1923, "Sports Information Office, 1860—, Scrapbooks," Box 1, Reel 1; and "Last Chance at Ohio," October 1923, "Sports Information Office, 1860—, Scrapbooks," Box 1, Reel 1, Bentley Historical Library, University of Michigan.

21. "55,000 Applications Returned, 44,000 Filled at Ann Arbor," *New York Times,* October 20, 1923.

22. *Ohio State Monthly* 8 (December 1921): 15.

23. Ohio State quoted in Raymond Schmidt, *Shaping College Football: The Transformation of an American Sport, 1919–1930* (Syracuse: Syracuse University Press, 2007), 49.

24. Cromartie, *The Big One,* 78.

25. Ibid., 103. This wasn't the first game played at Michigan Stadium, but it was the first one with a crowd this size. Only 17,483 (out of 50,000) paid to see the first game against Ohio Wesleyan, and 27,864 attended the second game, a victory over Michigan State.

26. Frederick Lewis Allen, *Only Yesterday: An Informal History of the Nineteen-Twenties* (New York: London, Harper & Brothers, 1931), 161; U.S. Bureau of the Census, "Population of the 100 Largest Urban Places, 1930," http://www.census.gov/population/www/documentation/twps0027/tab16.txt (accessed September 14, 2009); Peckman, *The University of Michigan,* 198; Pollard, *History of The Ohio State University,* 266.

27. See letters in "Athletics, Director of" (RG 9/e 1–5), "Bomb Explosion: Michigan Game: 1926," The Ohio State University Archives, hereafter cited as TOSUA.

28. *Michigan Alumnus,* http://bentley.umich.edu/athdept/football/umosu/rnalrep/1926osu.htm (accessed September 14, 2009).

29. This figure is the result of a database search of the *New York Times* digital archives. See http://query.nytimes.com/search/query?srchst=p#top to replicate the search, using "Ohio State" and "Michigan" and "football" as the search terms.

30. Cromartie, *The Big One,* 92; see also Ronald A. Smith, *Play-by-Play: Radio, Television, and Big-Time College Sport* (Baltimore: The Johns Hopkins University Press, 2001).

31. "Photo Caption," *Ohio State University Monthly* 24 (November 1932): 42; "Games Being Broadcast," *Ohio State University Monthly* 26 (October 1934): 28.

32. "Number of Tickets Sold," in "The Ohio State University Athletic Department: Financial Statements," April 27, 1936 ("Athletic Board: Minutes: September 1934–June 1940," 9/e-1/1), Director of Athletics, TOSUA; Ralph W.

Aigler, "Financial Aspects of the University's Athletic Program" ("Addresses and Articles: 1931–1941," 9/e-1/1), Director of Athletics, TOSUA.

33. See "Football Guarantees Received and Paid, 1928–1936," in "Athletics: Director of (RG 9/e-1/1)," Athletic Board Minutes: Jul 1927–Jun 1934," TOSUA; and, for a Michigan perspective, see Ralph Aigler, "Financial Aspects of the University's Athletic Program," in "Athletics: Director of (RG 9/e-1/1)," "Addresses and Articles: 1931–1941," TOSUA.

34. Larry Snyder, "Drubbing by Michigan Clouds What Seems Likely to Prove to Be an Otherwise Prefect Record for 1933 Grid Squad," *Ohio State University Monthly* 25 (November 1933): 51.

35. "A Brief History," "Athletics: Director of (RG 9e-1/12), "Michigan Pants Club: 1943–44," TOSUA; Greg Emmanuel, *The 100-Yard War: Inside the 100-Year-Old Michigan–Ohio State Football Rivalry* (Hoboken, NJ: John Wiley and Sons, 2004), 78.

36. Emmanuel, *The 100-Yard War*, 78; "Constitution of the Pants Club," "Athletics: Director of (RG 9e-1/12), "Michigan Pants Club: 1953," TOSUA.

37. Lynn St. John to H. O. Crisler, December 26, 1942, "Athletics: Director of (RG 9e-1/12), "Michigan Pants Club: 1943–44," TOSUA; "Pants," January 22, 1943, "Athletics: Director of (RG 9e-1/12), "Michigan Pants Club: 1943–44," TOSUA.

38. Oscar L. Thomas to Dwight W. Martin, April 23, 1948," "Television: 1947–1950," Director of Athletics (RG 9/e-1/20), TOSUA; "20,000 at Spring Game," *Ohio State University Monthly* 40 (June 1949), 29.

39. Howard L. Bevis to Edgar Dale, March 2, 1949, "Television: 1947–1950," Director of Athletics (RG 9/e-1/20), TOSUA.

40. G. G. McIlroy to Richard Larkins, April 21, 1950, "Television Ban on Live Television: 1950," Director of Athletics (RG 9/e-1/20), TOSUA.

41. The Employees of the Curtis Art Glass Company to Hon. John M. Vorys, May 1, 1950, "Television Ban on Live Television: 1950," Director of Athletics (RG 9/e-1/20), TOSUA.

42. Richard Larkins to G. G. McIlroy, April 24, 1950, and May 10, 1950, "Television Ban on Live Television: 1950," Director of Athletics (RG 9/e-1/20), TOSUA.

43. White, *One Game Season,* 173.

44. Richard Larkins to Frank Mead, December 1, 1950, "A Loyal Fan" to Richard Larkins, November 27, 1950, and Carl Trautman to Richard Larkins, December 5, 1950, "Snow Bowl Game: November 25, 1950," Director of Athletics (RG 9/e-1/9), TOSUA. For a fuller sampling of the letters, see entire folder.

45. Emmanual, *The 100-Yard War,* 71–72,

46. "Football Coach Woody Hayes Appointed," *Ohio State University Monthly* 2 (February 26, 1951): 19.

47. Roy Terrell, "You Love Woody or Hate Him," *Sports Illustrated,* September 24, 1962, in Mike Bynum, ed., *Woody Hayes: The Man and His Dynasty* (Gridiron Football Properties, 1991), 41; "Ohio State 50, Michigan 20," *Ohio State University Monthly* 53 (December 1961), http://library.osu.edu/sites/archives/osuvs.michigan/news.1961.htm (accessed September 14, 2009); Cliff Marks, "Crippled Team Falls to OSU Power, 50–20," *Michigan Daily,* November 26, 1961, found on Bentley Historical Library Web page: http://bentley.umich.edu/athdept/football/umosu/rivalrep/1961osu.htm (accessed September 14, 2009).

48. George Vecesy, "Michigan Routed by Buckeyes," *New York Times*, November 23, 1968, in Bynum, *Woody Hayes*, 150.

49. Bynum, *Woody Hayes*, 197 and 199.

50. White, *One Game Season*, 250.

51. Cromartie, *The Big One*, 268–274.

52. Rex Kern quoted in Emmanuel, *The 100-Yard War*, 96–97.

53. Neil Amdur, "Buckeyes Get Revenge on Michigan," *New York Times*, November 21, 1970, in Bynum, *Woody Hayes*, 157.

54. Schembechler, *Tradition: Bo Schembechler's Michigan Memories* (Ann Arbor, MI: Clock Tower Press, 2003), 168 and 171; Bob Hunter, "Bo-Woody Kinship Survived Rivalry," *Columbus Dispatch*, November 18, 2006.

55. *Ohio State Spring Football Media Guide* (Columbus, 2008), 106–107; "University of Michigan—Football All-Time Record" available at http://bentley.umich.edu/athdept/football/misc/fbrecord.htm (accessed September 14, 2009).

56. White, *One Game Season*, 341.

57. "OSU vs. Michigan," Bentley Historical Library Web site: http://bentley.umich.edu/athdept/football/umosu/results.htm (accessed September 14, 2009).

58. See "Biakabutuka's 313 yards ruin Ohio State's title hopes," *Michigan Daily*, November 26, 1996, available at "OSU vs. Michigan," Bentley Historical Library Web site: http://bentley.umich.edu/athdept/football/umosu/rivalrep/1995osu.htm (accessed September 14, 2009).

59. Jere Longman, "College Football; In Columbus, It's That Perilous Time of Year," *New York Times*, October 26, 2002.

60. Longman, "College Football; In Columbus, It's That Perilous Time of Year;" "UM vs. OSU Coaches," http://bentley.umich.edu/athdept/football/umosu/coaches.htm (accessed September 14, 2009).

12. Corporate Cowboys and Blue-Collar Bureaucrats— Stephen H. Norwood

1. Redskins and Cowboys often expressed the highest regard for their opponents' abilities. Washington All-Pro safety Tony Peters, whose team beat the Cowboys in the National Conference championship in 1982 to reach the Super Bowl, told me, "Our rivalry with Dallas was somewhat exaggerated by the press." He emphasized, "The players had mutual respect for one another." Stephen H. Norwood, *Real Football: Conversations on America's Game* (Jackson: University Press of Mississippi, 2004), 322. Peters considered Dallas's Roger Staubach probably the best quarterback he played against in an eleven-year NFL career: "The guy just had no quit in him, and I think he felt he could win any game he was in." Tony Peters, interview by Stephen H. Norwood, Norman, OK, July 19, 1993. Dallas coach Tom Landry praised Redskins quarterback Sonny Jurgensen as the most accurate passer in the National Football League since Norm Van Brocklin. *Washington Post*, November 22, 1967. In 1981, Redskins quarterback Joe Theismann called Dallas's front four "the best in football." *New York Times*, November 22, 1981. Dallas quarterback Danny White said he developed "a new respect" for Theismann after watching him throw five interceptions against the Cowboys: He did not "crawl back into his shell. . . . He just kept firing." *Dallas Morning News*, July 26, 1986.

2. *Washington Post,* November 27, 1967.

3. Ibid., December 10, 1967.

4. Tom Landry with Gregg Lewis, *Tom Landry: An Autobiography* (Grand Rapids, MI: Zondervan, 1990); Joe Gibbs with Jerry Jenkins, *Joe Gibbs: Fourth and One* (Nashville: Thomas Nelson Publishers, 1991), 141.

5. Steven A. Riess, *City Games: The Evolution of American Urban Society and the Rise of Sports* (Urbana: University of Illinois Press, 1989), 226.

6. Kenneth T. Jackson, *The Ku Klux Klan in the City* (New York: Oxford University Press, 1967), 67–77.

7. Stephen H. Norwood, *Strikebreaking and Intimidation: Mercenaries and Masculinity in Twentieth-Century America* (Chapel Hill: University of North Carolina Press, 2002), 171–172, 186.

8. *Washington Post,* October 26–27, 1963; *New York Times,* October 25 and 26, 1963; David Talbot, "Warrior for Peace," *Time,* July 2, 2007, 50.

9. Arthur M. Schlesinger Jr., *A Thousand Days: John F. Kennedy in the White House* (Greenwich, CT: Fawcett Publications, 1965), 930, 933–934; Talbot, "Warrior for Peace," 50.

10. Schlesinger, *A Thousand Days,* 935–936.

11. Peter Golenbock, *Cowboys Have Always Been My Heroes: The Definitive Oral History of America's Team* (New York: Warner Books, 1997), 194.

12. Landry, *Tom Landry,* 147.

13. Roger Staubach with Sam Blair and Bob St. John, *First Down, Lifetime to Go* (Waco, TX: Word Books, 1974), 93.

14. Jane Wolfe, *The Murchisons: The Rise and Fall of a Texas Dynasty* (New York: St. Martin's Press, 1989), 192, 194–196; *Washington Post,* May 31 and June 18, 1953; Frederick J. Simonelli, *American Fuehrer: George Lincoln Rockwell and the American Nazi Party* (Urbana: University of Illinois Press, 1999), 41. Simonelli states that DePugh's claim, "while possible, cannot be verified." Simonelli, *American Fuehrer,* 41.

15. Wolfe, *Murchisons,* 106–107.

16. Ibid., 202–203; *New York Times,* February 12, March 4, and May 27, 1956.

17. Talbot, "Warrior for Peace," 50; Golenbock, *Cowboys,* 32.

18. Bob St. John, *Tex! The Man Who Built the Dallas Cowboys* (Englewood Cliffs, NJ: Prentice Hall, 1988), 177; Donald Chipman, Randolph Campbell, and Robert Calvert, *The Dallas Cowboys and the NFL* (Norman: University of Oklahoma Press, 1970), 11, 30; Golenbock, *Cowboys,* 15, 17–18; *New York Times,* November 15, 1952.

19. George Solomon, *The Team Nobody Wanted: The Washington Redskins* (Chicago: Henry Regnery, 1973), 20; "Sammy Baugh," *Coffin Corner* (Early Fall 1996): 15.

20. Chipman, Campbell, and Calvert, *Dallas Cowboys and NFL,* 22; Jack Clary, *Washington Redskins* (New York: Macmillan, 1974), 169. Because of serious illness, Marshall gave up actual control of the Redskins in 1963. Solomon, *Team,* 23.

21. *Washington Post,* January 22, 1961, and November 30, 1966. There was no necessary geographical logic to an NFL team's conference assignment: the Baltimore Colts and later the Atlanta Falcons were placed in the Western Conference.

22. St. John, *Tex!* 184; Thomas G. Smith, "Civil Rights on the Gridiron: The Kennedy Administration and the Desegregation of the Washington Redskins," *Journal of Sport History* 14 (Summer 1987): 191; Obituaries of George Preston Marshall, *New York Times,* August 10, 1969, and Washington *Post,* August 10, 1969; Clary, *Redskins,* 6, 62, 152–153.

23. *Washington Post,* August 31 and November 23, 1969.

24. St. John, *Tex!* 185; Wolfe, *Murchisons,* 257; Pamela Colloff, "Flipping Out," *Texas Monthly,* October 2005, 139; Skip Bayless, *God's Coach: The Hymns, Hype, and Hypocrisy of Tom Landry's Cowboys* (New York: Simon and Schuster, 1990), 23–24, 179; Golenbock, *Cowboys,* 677; *San Diego Union-Tribune,* September 22, 2002.

25. Bayless, *God's Coach,* 182–183.

26. *Washington Post,* September 12, 1978.

27. Ibid., September 16, 1978.

28. Bayless, *God's Coach,* 39.

29. Jack Clary, *Pro Football's Great Moments* (New York: Bonanza Books, 1987 [1983]), 104–109. Jurgensen was elected to the Pro Football Hall of Fame in 1983.

30. David Maraniss, *When Pride Still Mattered: A Life of Vince Lombardi* (New York: Simon and Schuster, 1999), 255. Staubach was elected to the Pro Football Hall of Fame in 1985 and Aikman in 2006.

31. Norwood, *Real Football,* 68–70.

32. Duane Thomas and Paul Zimmerman, *Duane Thomas and the Fall of America's Team* (New York: Warner Books, 1988), 122.

33. Golenbock, *Cowboys,* 644; Landry, *Tom Landry,* 218; *Washington Post,* December 14, 1979.

34. *Washington Post,* September 26, 1978.

35. Thomas, *Duane Thomas,* 118.

36. Colloff, "Flipping Out," 142.

37. Tony Dorsett and Harvey Frommer, *Running Tough: Memoirs of a Football Maverick* (New York: Doubleday, 1989), 80, 125–126.

38. Walt Garrison with John Tullius, *Once a Cowboy* (New York: Random House, 1988), 60. Garrison included a photograph of a smiling Landry in *Once a Cowboy,* captioned "The only known picture of Tom Landry smiling."

39. Bayless, *God's Coach,* 55; Golenbock, *Cowboys,* 465.

40. Dorsett, *Running Tough,* 181; Staubach, *First Down,* 254.

41. *Washington Post,* November 22, 1986, and December 4, 1973.

42. Michael Richman, *The Redskins Encyclopedia* (Philadelphia: Temple University Press, 2008), 113; *Washington Post,* September 2, 1983. Paradoxically, Staubach was part of the very small minority of NFL players who were war veterans, having served in the navy in Vietnam.

43. *Dallas Morning News,* August 30, 1992.

44. Ibid., September 7, 1985.

45. *Minneapolis Star-Tribune,* January 27, 1992.

46. *Washington Post,* January 22, 1983.

47. Pete Gent, *North Dallas Forty* (New York: Ballantine Books, 1973), 208.

48. Thomas, *Duane Thomas,* 117, 123.

49. Dorsett, *Running Tough,* 98–99.

50. Garrison, *Once a Cowboy,* 188–189.

51. Staubach, *First Down,* 218.

52. Ibid., 226–227.

53. Dorsett, *Running Tough,* 104; Bayless, *God's Coach,* 174.

54. Paul Zimmerman, "Dallas Can Have 'em," *Sports Illustrated,* September 1, 1982, 171.

55. *Washington Post,* September 9, 1985.

56. Bayless, *God's Coach,* 197.

57. Garrison, *Once a Cowboy,* 191.

58. Landry, *Tom Landry,* 219; Obituary of Tom Landry, *New York Times,* February 13, 2000; Bayless, *God's Coach,* 197.

59. Wolfe, *Murchisons,* 298–299; Chipman, Campbell, and Calvert, *Dallas Cowboys and NFL,* 144; Golenbock, *Cowboys,* 468.

60. Solomon, *Team,* 189–190; Bayless, *God's Coach,* 157.

61. Dan Jenkins, "The Cowboys Had the Horses," *Sports Illustrated,* December 22, 1975, 31.

62. Golenbock, *Cowboys,* 468–469.

63. Bayless, *God's Coach,* 177.

64. Norwood, *Real Football,* 64.

65. Dorsett, *Running Tough,* 200–201; Golenbock, *Cowboys,* 469.

66. *New York Times,* October 28, 1990.

67. Staubach, *First Down,* 296.

68. St. John, *Tex!* 149.

69. Thomas, *Duane Thomas,* 171.

70. Bayless, *God's Coach,* 258.

71. Ibid., 126, 149, 202; Thomas, *Duane Thomas,* 167.

72. Thomas, *Duane Thomas,* 69, 71.

73. Staubach, *First Down,* 290–291.

74. *Washington Post,* December 2, 1982.

75. St. John, *Tex!* 139.

76. Norwood, *Real Football,* 206, 250–251, 319.

77. *Washington Post,* September 27, 1978.

78. Golenbock, *Cowboys,* 561.

79. *Washington Post,* September 3, 1981; *Dallas Morning News,* October 9, 1986, and April 22, 1989.

80. Jared Diamond, "Vengeance Is Ours," *New Yorker,* April 21, 2008, 80–81.

81. *Dallas Morning News,* November 23, 1990, and August 30, 1992. For insight into how anger can disturb a football player's concentration, see conversations with Bert Jones and Ken Mendenhall, both ten-year NFL veterans, in Norwood, *Real Football,* 76, 369. Jones talks about the "weird psychological games" in which players engage on the field.

82. *Dallas Morning News,* August 30, 1992.

83. Gibbs, *Fourth and One,* 170; *Dallas Morning News,* August 30, 1992.

84. Landry, *Tom Landry,* 175; Bayless, *God's Coach,* 19, 156; *New York Times,* January 26, 1988.

85. *Washington Post,* February 25 and March 1, 1984.

86. Solomon, *Team,* 230; *Washington Post,* November 14, 1973.

87. *New York Times,* January 26, 1988.

88. *Washington Post,* December 31, 1966.

89. Gent, *North Dallas Forty,* 232–233.

90. Smith, "Civil Rights on the Gridiron," 189, 194, 197–199, 203–204; *Chicago Defender,* January 10 and October 15, 1957, and March 29, June 8, and August 3, 1961; *Pittsburgh Courier,* February 9 and October 19, 1957, and January 4, 1958; Shirley

Povich, *All These Mornings* (Englewood Cliffs, NJ: Prentice-Hall, 1969), 88–89; *Washington Post,* August 3 and December 8, 1961.

91. Solomon, *Team,* 23, 61.

92. Norwood, *Real Football,* 342–343.

93. Thomas, *Duane Thomas,* 147.

94. Dorsett, *Running Tough,* 49–52, 83.

95. Thomas, *Duane Thomas,* 146.

96. Golenbock, *Cowboys,* 284, 347–348; Chipman, Campbell, and Calvert, *Dallas Cowboys and the NFL,* 139–140.

97. Karal Ann Marling, *As Seen on TV: The Visual Culture of Everyday Life in the 1950s* (Cambridge, MA: Harvard University Press, 1994), 47; Richard Slotkin, *Regeneration through Violence: The Mythology of the American Frontier, 1600–1860* (Middletown, CT: Wesleyan University Press, 1973), 241, 347; Winthrop D. Jordan, *White over Black: American Attitudes toward the Negro, 1550–1812* (Baltimore: Penguin, 1968), 90–91.

98. Norwood, *Real Football,* 10. Baltimore Colts quarterback Bert Jones noted: "Everything in the NFL was much more complex than in college. Today in a college game, you can look out on the field and tell what defense they're in. Whereas in the pros, you never knew. You saw so many different coverages and so many different fronts. You really had to be adept at understanding them." Norwood, *Real Football,* 62.

99. *Washington Post,* January 28, November 24, and December 28, 1971, October 14, 1972, and January 2, 1973.

100. Ibid., August 18, 1984.

101. *Washington Post,* October 9–10, 1973. Kenny Houston was elected to the Pro Football Hall of Fame in 1986.

102. *Washington Post,* October 9–10, 1973.

103. *Dallas Morning News,* December 13, 2005. The Redskins enjoyed only three winning seasons from 1993 to 2006. Richman, *Redskins Encyclopedia,* 112, 185.

104. *New York Times,* January 12, 1997.

105. Bayless, *God's Coach,* 208; Skip Bayless, "Boys Will Be Boys," *Sports Illustrated,* January 13, 1997, 90; *New York Times,* October 18, 1974, July 9 and 11, 1983, April 1, 1984, July 22, 1990.

106. *New York Times,* April 2 and 28, July 14 and 25, December 4, 1996, August 3, 1997, and May 11–12, 1999; Golenbock, *Cowboys,* 702.

107. *New York Times,* August 5 and 7, 1997.

13. Imperial Rivalries—S. W. Pope

1. Dwight Davis quoted in Nancy Kriplen, *Dwight Davis: The Man and the Cup* (London: Ebury Press, 1999), 37.

2. For early biographic information on Dwight Davis, see Kriplen, *Dwight Davis,* 1–32.

3. Alan Trengove, *The Story of the Davis Cup* (London, Stanley Paul, 1985), 20, 125, 126.

4. Ibid., 63.

5. Thomas Bender, *A Nation among Nations: America's Place in World History* (New York Hill & Wang, 2006), 191.

6. Mark Dyreson, "Globalizing the Nation-Making Process: Modern Sport in World History," *International Journal of the History of Sport* 20 (2003): 97.

7. Gerald Gems, "Sport, Colonialism, and United States Imperialism," paper delivered at the Chicago Seminar on Sport, 32–33, copy in author's possession.

8. Thomas Zeiler, *Ambassadors in Pinstripes: The Spalding World Baseball Tour and the Birth of American Empire* (Lantham, MD: Rowan & Littlefield, 2006), ix–x.

9. For the authoritative work, see Heiner Gillmeister, *Tennis: A Cultural History* (New York: New York University Press, 1998).

10. David W. Galenson, "Tennis," in *Encyclopedia of World Sport: From Ancient Times to the Present*, ed. D. Levinson and K. Christensen (New York: Oxford University Press, 1999), 392.

11. James M. Mayo, *The American Country Club: Its Origins and Development* (New Brunswick, NJ: Rutgers University Press, 1998), 65.

12. E. Digby Baltzell, *Sporting Gentlemen: Men's Tennis from the Age of Honor to the Cult of the Superstar* (NY: Free Press, 1995), 134, 137–138.

13. Ibid.

14. According to Baltzell, the more Anglophilic families had their daughters presented at the Court at St. James (along with the British debutantes and dignitaries of the year). Baltzell, *Sporting Gentlemen*, 85. For more on the early expansion of tennis and its bourgeois origins, see ibid., 39–81.

15. Barbara Keys, *Globalizing Sport: National Rivalry and International Community in the 1930s* (Cambridge: Harvard University Press, 2006), 14.

16. Graeme Smith, "Privilege in Tennis and Lawn Tennis: The Geelong and Royal South Yarra Examples But Not Forgetting the Story of the Farmer's Wrist," *Sporting Traditions* 3, no. 2 (May 1987): 210; and Graeme Smith, "Lawn Tennis," in *Sport in Australia: A Social History*, ed. W. Vamplew and B. Stoddart (Cambridge University Press, 1994), 133–153.

17. Trengove, *The Story of the Davis Cup*, 38.

18. Ibid., 21, passim.

19. Baltzell, *Sporting Gentlemen*, 34–35.

20. Murray G. Phillips, "Diminishing Contrasts and Increasing Varieties: Globalisation Theory and 'Reading' Amateurism in Australian Sport," *Sporting Traditions* 18 (2001): 25, 28, 24.

21. Gillmeister, *Tennis*, 213.

22. For an overview of the Davis Cup's history, see Richard Evans, *The Davis Cup: Celebrating 100 Years of International Tennis* (London, Ebury Press, 1998).

23. Kriplen, *Dwight Davis*, 64.

24. June Senyard, "The Tennis Court: A Country Woman's Window to the Modern World," *Sporting Traditions* 13 (1996), 27–28.

25. Mabel Brookes quoted in Trengove, *The Story of the Davis Cup*, 70.

26. For a brief synopsis of this Olympiad, see S. W. Pope, *Patriotic Games: Sporting Traditions in the American Imagination, 1876–1926*, 2nd ed. (Knoxville: University of Tennessee Press, 2007), 45–49.

27. Trengove, *The Story of the Davis Cup*, 50.

28. Kevin Fewster, "Advantage Australia: Davis Cup Tennis, 1950–1959," *Sporting Traditions*, 62.

29. Ibid.

30. Baltzell, *Sporting Gentlemen,* 85.

31. Keys, "Globalizing Sport," 89.

32. Ibid., 15, 89.

33. "John Bull and Uncle Sam: Four Centuries of British-American Relations," Library of Congress exhibition, http://www.loc.gov/exhibits/british/brit-7.html.

14. This Has Nothing to Do with Money—*John Nauright*

1. Indeed, English soccer fans are notorious for chanting, "Two world wars and one world cup" in reference to their 1966 victory over West Germany in the FIFA World Cup (though the Germans have been far more successful at winning World Cups and European Championships than have the English).

2. Match statistics through 1997 are drawn primarily from Colin M. Jarman, *The Ryder Cup: The Definitive History of Playing Golf for Pride and Country* (Chicago: Contemporary Books, 1999). Under Ryder Cup rules, should the result end in a tie (today 14–14) then the cup holders retain the cup. The Ryder Cup has only ended in a tie in 1969 and 1989.

3. This chapter was completed just after the 2008 Ryder Cup in which the U.S. team, minus Tiger Woods, won the cup at Valhalla Country Club in Louisville, Kentucky.

4. Robert Browning, *A History of Golf* (London, 1955; reprinted edition in The Classics of Golf series, London: Dent & Sons, n.d.), 90–93.

5. Paula Diperna and Vikki Keller, *Oakhurst: The Birth and Rebirth of America's First Golf Course* (New York: Walker Publishing, 2002), 21–22.

6. See Diperna and Keller, *Oakhurst,* for a discussion of the history of the course and its restoration.

7. For a discussion of this process, see Richard J. Moss, *Golf and the American Country Club* (Urbana and Chicago: University of Illinois Press, 2001).

8. Figures outlined in S. W. Pope, *Patriotic Games: Sporting Traditions in the American Imagination, 1876–1926,* new ed. (Knoxville: University of Tennessee Press, 2007), 6.

9. For a detailed account of Vardon's tour, see Bob Labbance with Brian Siplo, *The Vardon Invasion: Harry's Triumphant 1900 American Tour* (Ann Arbor: Sports Media Group, 2008). The tour was covered extensively in the British weekly *Golf Illustrated.*

10. For more on Walter Travis and his victory, see Bob Labbance, *The Old Man: The Biography of Walter J. Travis* (Chelsea, MI: Sleeping Bear Press, 2000), 81–101. Travis, now often forgotten in American golfing history, was a key figure both on and off the course in the first decades of the twentieth century.

11. The Ouimet victory has entered American golfing folklore, spurred on in recent times by Mark Frost, *The Greatest Game Ever Played* (New York: Hyperion, 2002) and the subsequent motion picture of the same name, for which Frost wrote the screenplay. The cultural meaning of the Ouimet victory and its retelling has been analyzed by John Ramfjord and John Nauright, "The Greatest Game Ever Played? Francis Ouimet and the 1913 U.S. Open in History and Memory," paper presented to the Popular Culture Association Annual Conference, Boston, MA, April 7, 2007.

12. My ongoing research on professional golfer migration between the 1890s and 1930s has found that two hundred American-based professionals between 1900 and

1930 came from the Scottish golfing town of Carnoustie alone, while many others were from famous golfing locales such as St. Andrews and North Berwick.

13. Dale Concannon, *Complete Illustrated History of the Ryder Cup: Golf's Greatest Drama* (Chicago: Triumph Books, 2006), 10–11.

14. Peter Dobereiner, *Maestro: The Life of Henry Cotton* (London: Hodder & Stoughton, 1992), 113–114.

15. Concannon, *Complete Illustrated History of the Ryder Cup,* 11.

16. Ibid., 14–15; Robin McMillan, *Us against Them: An Oral History of the Ryder Cup* (New York: HarperCollins, 2004), 7–9.

17. No Ryder Cups were held after 1937 until 1947 due to World War II.

18. Dobereiner, *Maestro,* 32.

19. From initial views of superiority, the British ultimately began to participate more fully in international competition, though with mixed success. England did not participate in the FIFA World Cups prior to World War II and only won when it hosted the competition in 1966, even losing to the United States in 1950. In 1905 and 1906 the English national rugby team was famously defeated by New Zealand and South Africa, which dominated the sport for most of the twentieth century. In cricket, Australia rapidly caught up with the "mother" country, while by the 1950s the West Indies and India were also successful. Early British prowess in track and field was quickly eclipsed by the United States. Many other examples abound. In each case, it was other countries that took an innovative approach to developing sporting excellence. For a detailed discussion of this see John Nauright, "Colonial Manhood and Imperial Race Virility: British Responses to Colonial Rugby Tours," in *Making Men: Rugby and Masculine Identity,* ed. John Nauright and Timothy J. L. Chandler (London: Routledge, 1996), 121–139.

20. Dobereiner, *Maestro,* 107–109.

21. Stephen R. Lowe, *Sir Walter and Mr. Jones: Walter Hagen, Bobby Jones, and the Rise of American Golf* (Chelsea, MI: Sleeping Bear Press, 2000), 235.

22. Ben Hogan quoted in Jarman, *The Ryder Cup,* 87.

23. Jarman, *The Ryder Cup,* 87–88.

24. Ibid., 105.

25. Concannon, *Complete Illustrated History of the Ryder Cup,* 65.

26. Dai Rees quoted in Jarman, *The Ryder Cup,* 134. Rees was runner-up in the Open Championship in 1953, 1954, and 1961. He played on nine Ryder Cup teams between 1937 and 1961 with a very respectable 7-9-1 record in a time when his teams nearly always lost the Ryder Cup matches.

27. Nick Faldo in 1989 is the only other golfer to have won the award since its inception in 1954.

28. Jack Nicklaus with Ken Bowden, *My Story* (New York: Simon & Schuster, 1997).

29. Jarman, *The Ryder Cup,* 406.

30. Ibid., 424.

31. Ibid., 466.

32. Peter Allis quoted in Jarman, *The Ryder Cup,* 579.

33. Tom Watson quoted in Bob Bubka and Tom Clavin, *The Ryder Cup: Golf's Greatest Event* (New York: Three Rivers Press, 1999), 96, 100.

34. Dan Jenkins quoted in Jarman, *The Ryder Cup,* 708.

35. Jarman, *The Ryder Cup,* 708–718.

36. Bubka and Clavin, *The Ryder Cup*, 224; Jarman, *The Ryder Cup*, 722.

37. Bubka and Clavin, *The Ryder Cup*, 3–5.

38. Ibid., 22–23.

39. Sam Torrance quoted in CNNSI.com, "Unbridled Celebration: Decorum Breaks Down with Leonard's Winning Putt," September 26, 1999, http://sports illustrated.cnn.com/golf/1999/ryder_cup/news/1999/09/26/celebration_sidebar_ ap/ (accessed November 8, 2008).

40. Concannon, *Complete Illustrated History of the Ryder Cup*, 179. (Of course, no one dared mention that the U.S. soldiers were routed at the Alamo!)

41. The 2001 Ryder Cup was postponed after the September 11 attack on the United States, moving each competition back a year and switching the Ryder Cup from odd- to even-numbered years.

42. A complete list of Ryder Cup player records can be found online at http:// golf.about.com/od/rydercup/a/rydercuprecords_2.htm (accessed October 12, 2008).

43. Lee Trevino quoted in Mike Stachura, "Civility vs. Hostility: The Ryder Cup Has Become Golf's Biggest, Most Boisterous Event, Is It Time to Turn Down the Volume?" *Golf Digest*, September 2001, http://findarticles.com/p/articles/mi_ m0HFI/is_9_52/ai_77453562 (accessed July 12, 2008).

44. Curtis Strange quoted in McMillan, *Us against Them*, 108.

45. Peter Jacobson quoted in Concannon, *Complete Illustrated History of the Ryder Cup*, 124.

46. Justin Leonard quoted in Bubka and Clavin, *The Ryder Cup*, 5.

47. Tiger Woods quoted in Kevin Mitchell, "American Mortal: Tiger Shows His Tender Side," *London Observer*, September 17, 2006, 12.

48. Jesper Parnavik quoted in Stachura, "Civility vs. Hostility."

49. Concannon, *Complete Illustrated History of the Ryder Cup*, 180–182; Stachura, "Civility vs. Hostility."

50. Alan Campbell, "Europe on Home Straight," *Sunday Herald* (Scotland), September 24, 2006.

51. Michael Gibbons, "European Fans Winning the Battle of the Song," Europeantour.com reporting on the official Ryder Cup, http://www.rydercup.com/ 2008/rydercup/2008/europe/09/20/fanssong/index.html (accessed October 28, 2008).

52. Dave Shedloski, "Redneck, White and Blue Squad Exemplifies American Spirit," PGATour.com's senior correspondent reporting on the result of the Ryder Cup on the official Ryder Cup Web site, http://www.rydercup.com/2008/rydercup/ 2008/usa/09/21/shedanalysis/index.html (accessed October 28, 2008). In all fairness to Mickelson though, Europe's top two players, Padraig Harrington and Sergio Garcia, also lost their singles matches.

15. The Match of the Century—*Chris Elzey*

The author would like to acknowledge the help of Adrienne Chafetz, Joseph Gokhberg, and Ekaterina Perfilieva in the preparation of this chapter.

1. *Trud*, July 27, 1958, 4.

2. *New York Times*, June 19, 1958, 42.

3. The phrase "Match of the Century" can be found in several publications. See

Izvestia, July 29, 1958, 4; *Legkaia Atletika,* September 1958, 2; *Sovetski Sport,* July 29, 1958, 1; *Moscow News,* July 30, 1958, 8; and *USSR Illustrated Monthly,* October 1958, 59. *Pravda* also referred to the 1959 U.S.-USSR meet as the "Match of the Century." See *Current Digest of the Soviet Press* 11, no. 29 (August 19, 1959): 35.

4. Bob Mathias quoted in William O. Johnson Jr., *All That Glitters Is Not Gold: The Olympic Games* (New York: G. P. Putnam's Sons, 1972), 221.

5. Quoted in James Riordan, *Sport, Politics and Communism* (Manchester, UK: Manchester University Press, 1991), 138. The literature on sports in the USSR is extensive. For example, see James Riordan, *Sport in Soviet Society: Development of Sport and Physical Education in Russia and the USSR* (Cambridge, UK: Cambridge University Press, 1977); Robert Edelman, *Serious Fun: A History of Spectator Sports in the USSR* (New York: Oxford University Press, 1993); James Riordan, "The U.S.S.R.," in *Sport Under Communism: The U.S.S.R., Czechoslovakia, the G.D.R., China, Cuba,* ed. James Riordan (London: C. Hurst & Co., 1978), 13–53; Victor Louis and Jennifer Louis, *Sport in the Soviet Union* (1964; repr., Oxford, UK, and Elmsford, NY: Pergamon Press, 1980); and N. Norman Shneidman, *The Soviet Road to Olympus: Theory and Practice of Soviet Physical Culture and Sport* (Toronto: Ontario Institute for Studies in Education, 1978).

6. Valeri Shteinbakh, *The Soviet Contribution to the Olympics* (Moscow: Novosti Press Agency Publishing House, 1980), 36; Riordan, *Sport in Soviet Society,* 367; and *New York Times,* August 28, 1950, 22.

7. 1945 chess match in *New York Times,* September 2, 1945, 32; September 3, 20; and September 5, 27. For an account of the 1946 match, see *New York Times,* August 31, 1946, 11; September 10, 10; September 12, 10; September 15, 5; September 16, 9; September 17, 4. *Moscow Bolshevik* quoted in Barrett M. Reed, Memo to Department of State, January 23, 1950, File 861.453/11–1450, Box 5167, Decimal File, 1950–54, Department of State Records, RG 59, National Archives at College Park, College Park, MD.

8. Nicolai Romanov quoted in Edelman, *Serious Fun,* 122; Communist Party pronouncement in Riordan, *Sport in Soviet Society,* 165.

9. Financial incentives quoted in Riordan, *Sport in Soviet Society,* 162.

10. *New York Times,* June 10, 1952, 32; *Congressional Record,* Vol. 98, 82nd Congress, 2nd Session, 1952, A3697-A3698. For an examination of the Soviets' decision to compete in the Olympic Games, see Jennifer Parks, "Verbal Gymnastics: Sports, Bureaucracy, and the Soviet Union's Entrance into the Olympic Games, 1946–1952," in *East Plays West: Sport and the Cold War,* ed. Stephen Wagg and David L. Andrews (New York and London: Routledge, 2007), 27–44.

11. Decathlete Bob Mathias remembered that the Soviet's camp was called the "Little Iron Curtain." See Myron Tassin, *Bob Mathias: The Life of the Olympic Champion* (New York: St. Martin's Press, 1983), 77. *Literaturnaya Gazeta* article in *Current Digest of the Soviet Press* 4, no. 31 (September 13, 1952): 27–28.

12. For Soviet papers, see *Sovetski Sport,* July 24, 26, 29, 31, 1952, pages 5, 3, 1, 1, respectively; *Izvestia,* July 23, 25, 26, 30, 1952, all page 4; *Trud,* July 23, 24, 25, 26, 30, 1952, all page 4; and *Pravda,* July 23, 25, 26, 29, 30, 1952, all page 4. Once the Americans started to cut into the lead, the Soviet press stopped printing scores and medal counts.

13. For a good overview of the U.S.-USSR rivalry in the Olympics Games, especially between 1952 and 1964, see, William J. Baker, *Sports in the Western World*

(Totowa, NJ: Rowman and Littlefield, 1982), 263–282. Also worthwhile is James Riordan, "The USSR and the Olympic Games," *Stadion* 6 (1980): 219–313.

14. The Soviet newspapers were *Izvestia*, August 4, 1952, 4; *Trud*, August 4, 1952, 4; and *Pravda*, August 4, 1952, 4. *Komsomolskaya Pravda* and *Sovetski Sport* carried the news two days after the Olympic Games. See *Komsomolskaya Pravda*, August 5, 1952, 3; and *Sovetski Sport*, August 5, 1952, 1. Radio Moscow information in Foreign Broadcast Information Service, *Daily Report, Foreign Radio Broadcasts, USSR and Eastern Europe*, August 6, 1952, CC13. Information on Finnish papers in *Izvestia*, August 4, 1952, 4, and *Sovetski Sport*, August 5, 1952, 1.

15. A United Press story published two days earlier reported that the Americans had defeated the Soviet team, "even under the Russian system of scoring 7–5–4–3–2–1 for first through sixth [place]," a point that would later prove to be erroneous. See *Washington Post*, August 3, 1952, C1.

16. Nicolai Romanov quoted in *Current Digest of the Soviet Press* 4, no. 30 (September 6, 1952): 10.

17. No sooner had Avery Brundage been chosen IOC president then the Olympic organization issued a resolution condemning point keeping. See Allen Guttmann, *The Games Must Go On: Avery Brundage and the Olympic Movement* (New York: Columbia University Press, 1984), 121.

18. For American views about the Soviets' use of athletics as propaganda, see John Washburn, "Sport as a Soviet Tool," *Foreign Affairs* (April 1956): 490–499.

19. John Butler quoted in *Congressional Record*, 84th Congress, 2nd Session, Vol. 102, 5986–5987; *Washington Post*, April 5, 1956, 53.

20. *Congressional Record*, 84th Congress, 2nd Session, Vol. 102, 5987, 8334–8335.

21. Among the places Avery Brundage expressed his views was in a *Saturday Evening Post* article, "I Must Admit—Russian Athletes Are Great!". See *Saturday Evening Post*, April 30, 1955, 28; Soviet commentator quoted in Nikolai Tarasov, *Soviet Sport Today* (Moscow: Novosti Press Agency Publishing House, 1964), 42. In 1960 IOC member Konstantin Andrianov wrote a letter to the *IOC Bulletin* in which he stated, "*There are simply no conditions for existence of professionalism* in Soviet sport" (Andrianov's italics). See *Bulletin of the International Olympic Committee*, November 1960, 71–72; quote is from page 71. *Sovetski Sport* quoted in Richard Espy, *The Politics of the Olympic Games: With an Epilogue, 1976–1980* (Berkeley: University of California Press, 1981), 51.

22. *U.S. News & World Report*, August 20, 1954, 35–37; and *Life*, June 6, 1955, 93–94, 97–98, 101–102, 105–106.

23. "Red 'Supermen' Lose," *U.S. News & World Report*, December 7, 1956, 106.

24. *Komsomolskaya Pravda*, December 7, 1956, 4; figures in *Time*, December 17, 1956, 80.

25. *Pravda*, December 9, 1956, 1; *Sovetski Sport*, December 8, 1956, 1; and *Trud*, December 9, 1956, 1.

26. *Komsomolskaya Pravda*, December 9, 1956, 4; and *Sovetski Sport*, December 8, 1956, 1. Other illustrations in *Trud*, December 9, 1956, 4; and *Vecherniaia Moskva*, December 8, 1956, 1.

27. The writer, Andre Laguerre, wrote an article about the Hungarians' defection. See *Sports Illustrated*, December 17, 1956, 14–18. The Hungarians' story was also mentioned in *Life*, December 17, 1956, 96; and *New York Times*, December 22, 30,

1956, 6, 1(S); *Newsweek*, December 17, 1956, 96. For other publications discussing the emptiness of Soviet victories, see *Life*, December 17, 1956, 95–96; *Time*, December 17, 1956, 80; and *Washington Post*, December 9, 1956, 2C.

28. *Izvestia* in *Current Digest of the Soviet Press* 8, no. 50 (January 23, 1957): 23. For American articles about the incident, see *Los Angeles Times*, December 12, 13, 1956, 1C; and *New York Times*, December 13, 1956, 5.

29. *Literaturnaya Gazeta* information in *Washington Post*, April 3, 1957, 5B. The accusations also included unsuccessful "kidnappings, sneak-thievery and frame-ups on espionage charges." See W. Johnson, *All That Glitters Is Not Gold*, 228–229.

30. Patrick McCarran also sponsored the 1950 Internal Security Act, which, as its name implies, dealt with communist activities inside the country. For more on the McCarran-Walter Act, see Walter L. Hixson, *Parting the Curtain: Propaganda, Culture, and the Cold War, 1945–1961* (New York: St. Martin's Press, 1998), 102–103; Yale Richmond, *Cultural Exchange and the Cold War: Raising the Iron Curtain* (University Park: Pennsylvania State University Press, 2003), 215; and J. D. Parks, *Culture, Conflict, and Coexistence: American-Soviet Cultural Relations, 1917–1958* (Jefferson, NC, and London, UK: McFarland & Company, 1983), 127–128, 140–141.

31. The exchange program was officially called "Agreement between the United States of America and the Union of Soviet Socialist Republics on Exchanges in the Cultural, Technical and Educational Fields." For more on the agreement, see *United States Treaties and Other International Agreements*, Vol. 9, *1958*, TIAS 3975 (Washington, DC: United States Government Printing Office, 1959), 13–39. Performers included the Bolshoi Ballet, the Philadelphia Symphony Orchestra, the pianist Van Cliburn, and the Moiseyev Dancers. Figure for number of agreements in Committee on Foreign Relations, 86th Congress, 1st Session, *United States Exchange Programs with the Soviet Union, Poland, Czechoslovakia, Rumania, and Hungary* (Washington, DC: United States Government Printing Office, 1959), 3. For more on the 1958 cultural agreement, see Yale Richmond, *U.S.-Soviet Cultural Exchanges, 1958–1986: Who Wins?* (Boulder, CO: Westview Press, 1987); Victor Rosenberg, *Soviet-American Relations, 1953–1960: Diplomacy and Cultural Exchange during the Eisenhower Presidency* (Jefferson, NC: McFarland & Co., 2005); Richmond, *Cultural Exchange and the Cold War;* and Parks, *Culture, Conflict, and Coexistence.*

32. Edelman, *Serious Fun*, 75. Edelman discusses the militaristic purpose of track and field on page 76. The *Great Soviet Encyclopedia* described the sport as being "one of the most important and popular sports." See N. G. Ozolin, "Track and Field Athletics," in *Great Soviet Encyclopedia: A Translation of the Third Edition*, Vol. 14, ed. A. M. Prokhorov (Moscow: Sovetskaia Entsiklopedia Publishing House, 1973; New York: Macmillan, 1977), 779. For more on GTO, see Riordan, *Sport in Soviet Society*, 128–129; Louis and Louis, *Sport in the Soviet Union*, 4. For a Soviet interpretation of the program, see *Soviet Sport, Questions and Answers* (Moscow: Novosti Press Agency Publishing House, 1974), 21–22.

33. Of the fifteen American gold medals in 1952, fourteen were won by men. The scenario repeated itself in 1956, with fifteen of sixteen medals going to men. Medal count compiled from Associated Press and Grolier, *Pursuit of Excellence, the Olympic Story* (Danbury, CT: Grolier Enterprises Inc., 1983), 382–386. For world records, see Association of Track Statisticians, *International Athletics Annual—1959* (London, UK: World Sports, 1959), 6–7.

34. World records included events in yards and meters. See Association of Track Statisticians, *International Athletics Annual—1959*, 6–7; *Track and Field News,* December 1957, 7–12, and December 1958, 8–14; *Pittsburgh Courier,* July 12, 1958, 19; Jordan in *Christian Science Monitor,* July 14, 1958, 11.

35. Instead of picking a team based on athletes' past performances, they opted to follow the U.S. practice of holding national trials. See *Washington Post,* July 16, 1958, 22A; and *Track and Field News,* August 1958, 4. The Soviets' world record holders included high jumper Yuri Stepanov and distance walker Leonid Spirin.

36. 1957 meet in *New York Times,* August 25, 1957, 185. Included were Galina Zybina, 1952 Olympic gold medalist and world record holder in the shot put; Tamara Press, discus winner at the 1957 London meet and future Olympic gold medalist (1960 and 1964); Nina Ponomareva, 1952 discus gold medalist, 1956 discus bronze medalist and future Olympic gold medalist (1960); and Nelli Eliseeva, winner of the eighty-meter hurdles at the London meet.

37. Roster information in *New York Times,* July 7, 1958, 32. Temple said about his 1958 Tennessee State squad, "Out of all of the teams I had as far as depth, nineteen fifty-eight was the greatest team." See Louise Mead Tricard, *American Women's Track and Field: A History, 1895 through 1980* (Jefferson, NC: McFarland & Company, 1996), 422.

38. Ed Temple with B'Lou Carter, *Only the Pure in Heart Survive* (Nashville, TN: Broadman Press, 1980), 112. Eddie Southern quoted in *New York Times,* July 17, 1958, 22; George Eastment quoted in *Washington Post,* July 19, 1958, 12A.

39. *Chicago Daily Tribune,* July 13, 1958, 3S; *New York Times,* July 16, 1958, 34; *Sports Illustrated,* July 28, 1958, 14–15; and *Los Angeles Times,* July 27, 1958, 4C. Militaristic references also discussed in Victor Peppard and James Riordan, *Playing Politics: Soviet Sport Diplomacy to 1992* (Greenwich, CT; London, UK: JAI Press, 1993), 77–78. The use of Cold War metaphors was not unique to the 1958 meet. Prior to the meet, American journalists made use of them. For an interesting analysis of how the Cold War influenced the coverage of *Sports Illustrated,* see John Massaro, "Press Box Propaganda? The Cold War and *Sports Illustrated,* 1956," *Journal of American Culture* 26 (September 2003): 361–370.

40. For more on the All-Union Council, see Riordan, "The U.S.S.R.," 23–24.

41. Ferris reference from *New York Times,* April 8, 1958, 36; Gavril Korobkov quoted in *Washington Post,* July 27, 1958, 3C. The *Moscow News,* for instance, carried this description: "The result of the match will be decided on the combined scores of women and men." See *Moscow News,* July 23, 1958, 8.

42. *New York Times,* July 20, 1958, 1(VI), 3(VI); American companies in *Amateur Athlete,* August 1958, 8.

43. *Washington Post,* June 29, 1958, 1; and *Los Angeles Times,* June 29, 1958, 1. The crisis overlapped with a hostage situation involving American military personnel and communist authorities in East Berlin. See *Department of State Bulletin,* July 14, 1958, 50–54, and July 28, 1958, 147.

44. Front-page coverage included *Washington Post,* June 29, 1958, 1; *Los Angeles Times,* June 29, 1958, 1; *Washington Post,* July 7, 1958, 1; and *New York Times,* July 11, 1958, 1.

45. Salim Yaqub, *Containing Arab Nationalism: The Eisenhower Doctrine and the Middle East* (Chapel Hill: University of North Carolina Press, 2004), 226–228, 238–239;

436   NOTES TO PAGES 343–46

Robert A. Divine, *Eisenhower and the Cold War* (New York: Oxford University Press, 1981), 97–104; and Alan Dowty, *Middle East Crisis: U.S. Decision-Making in 1958, 1970 and 1973* (Berkeley: University of California Press, 1984), 60–76.

46. Tass and *Pravda* quoted in Foreign Broadcast Information Service, *Daily Report, USSR & East Europe,* July 16, 1958, BB1, and July 21, 1958, BB32. Soviet threats of war included the staging of military exercises near the Middle East but inside the Soviet Union. See *Current Digest of the Soviet Press* 10, no. 29 (August 27, 1958): 3. Protest signs in *Current Digest of the Soviet Press* 10, no. 29 (August 27, 1958): 3, 4. Damage to embassy in *Seattle-Post Intelligencer,* July 19, 1958, 1. Air gun information in telegram from American embassy to State Department in Washington, July 18, 1958; File 570 Incidents—1958—tab—Demonstrations—June 24-July 17–18; Box 9; Records of the Foreign Service Posts of the Department of State, Union of Soviet Socialist Republic, Moscow Embassy; Classified General Records, RG 84; National Archives at College Park, College Park, MD. *Seattle Post-Intelligencer,* July 22, 1958, 3.

47. The three nations were Great Britain, India, and France. Eisenhower believed that the United Nations was a more appropriate venue to discuss geopolitical differences in the Middle East, and that, unlike Khrushchev's suggested summit, Israel should be involved in any discussion about the Middle East. See Dwight D. Eisenhower, *The White House Years: Waging Peace, 1956–1961* (Garden City, NJ; New York: Doubleday & Company, 1965), 283. See also Dowty, *Middle East Crisis,* 75. Khrushchev was also motivated by his intense desire to reduce Cold War tensions by having an official meeting with the United States. See William Taubman, *Khrushchev: The Man and His Era* (New York: W. W. Norton & Company, 2003), 399–402.

48. Dan Ferris, the point man for the American delegation, was the one who learned that State Department officials would not scrap the meet. See *New York Times,* July 20, 1958, 1(V).

49. For information on the Americans' departure and flights, see *New York Times,* July 21, 1958, 29; Rafer Johnson with Philip Goldberg, *The Best That I Can Be: An Autobiography* (New York: Doubleday, 1998), 116; and Temple, *Only the Pure in Heart Survive,* 112. A picture in *Amateur Athlete* shows the team just before their departure. See *Amateur Athlete,* August 1958, 5. The three athletes were Rink Babka, Glenn Davis, and James Brewer. See *Amateur Athlete,* September 1958, 33.

50. *New York Times,* July 22, 1958, 22; *Sports Illustrated,* August 4, 1958, 8; R. Johnson, *The Best That I Can Be,* 116; and Temple, *Only the Pure in Heart Survive,* 112.

51. *New York Times,* July 28, 1958, 17. Ads for the meet listed the price of tickets. See *Vecherniaia Moskva,* July 18, 1958, 4; and *Moscow News,* July 23, 1958, 8.

52. George Eastment quoted in *New York Times,* July 28, 1958, 17.

53. Picture of sign in *Pravda,* July 28, 1958, 4; and *Soviet Weekly,* August 7, 1958, 4; *New York Times,* July 28, 1958, 17.

54. For events of the first day, see *Track and Field News,* August 1958, 4–5.

55. *Los Angeles Times,* July 28, 1958, 1(II); and *Chicago Daily Tribune,* July 28, 1958, 1B. For Soviet television transmission, see *New York Herald Tribune,* late city ed., July 28, 1958, 1(III); and *Chicago Daily Tribune,* July 28, 1958, 1B.

56. For more on the actual competition, see *Track and Field News,* August 1958, 4–6; *New York Times,* July 29, 1958, 1, 27; *Amateur Athlete,* September 1958, 5–7. Rafer Johnson discussed the decathlon in Moscow in his autobiography, *The Best That I Can Be,* 119–123.

57. *Komsomolskaya Pravda*, July 29, 1958, 4; *Izvestia* quoted in *Current Digest of the Soviet Press* 10, no. 30 (September 3, 1958): 40; *Sovetski Sport*, July 29, 1958, 1; and *Pravda*, July 29, 1958, 2.

58. *Seattle Post-Intelligencer*, July 29, 1958, 16; *Chicago Daily Sun-Times*, July 29, 1958, 56; and *Chicago Daily Defender* (Daily ed.), July 29, 1958, 24.

59. George Eastment quoted in *New York Times*, July 30, 1958, 25.

60. First through fourth places were usually scored 5, 3, 1, 1, respectively; and only relay squads that were victorious earned points. Argument for an American victory in *New York Times*, July 29, 1958, 27; *Track and Field News*, August 1958, 4; *Boston Globe* (Morning ed.), July 29, 1958, 23.

61. George Eastment quoted in *San Francisco Examiner*, July 29, 1958, 12(II).

62. Associated Press article in *San Francisco Examiner*, July 30, 1958, 15(II).

63. *New York Times*, November 30, 1958, 28; *U.S. News and World Report*, August 8, 1958, 37.

64. *Atlanta Journal*, July 29, 1958, 15; *Boston Evening Globe*, July 29, 1958, 37; and *Boston Herald*, July 28, 1958, 9. The swindler idea was prevalent as early as 1951. See Richard B. Walsh, "The Soviet Athlete in International Competition," *Department of State Bulletin* 25 (December 24, 1951): 1007–1010.

65. *Chicago Daily Tribune*, August 1, 1958, 12.

66. *Sovetski Sport*, August 5, 1958, 7.

67. For more on the U.S.-USSR track series, see Joseph M. Turrini, "'It Was Communism versus the Free World': The USA-USSR Dual Track Meet Series and the Development of Track and Field in the United States," *Journal of Sport History* 28 (Fall 2001): 427–471; and Peppard and Riordan, *Playing Politics*, 75–94. Turrini's article is an excellent and thorough examination of the series. Of noted interest is his argument regarding not only the way in which the series helped popularize women's track in the United States, but the way in which it convinced American government officials to involve themselves more in the area of amateur sports. For a Soviet perspective, see "Rostislav Orlov, "Twenty-Four Rounds of the 'Match of the Giants,'" in *USSR-USA Sports Encounters*, ed. Victor Kuznetsov and Mikhail Lukashev (Moscow: Progress Publishers, 1977), 33–55.

68. For more on the 10,000 meters, see *Amateur Athlete*, August 1959, 9–10; *Track and Field News*, August 1959, 4; and *Sports Illustrated*, July 27, 1959, 15–17, 20–21.

69. Bob Soth and Eddie Southern quoted in *Sports Illustrated*, July 29, 1959, 23.

70. John F. Kennedy in *Sports Illustrated*, December 26, 1960, 16.

71. Robert F. Kennedy in *Sports Illustrated*, July 27, 1964, 13.

72. The exception was the 1968 Olympic Games in Mexico City in which the U.S. team outperformed the squad from the Soviet Union. The Americans earned forty-five gold medals to the Soviets' twenty-nine. The overall medal count also went to the United States, 107–91.

73. Soviet editorial quoted in Shneidman, *The Soviet Road to Olympus*, 14; *Sport in the USSR* quoted in James W. Riordan, "Politics of Elite Sport in East and West," in *Sport and Politics*, ed. Gerald Redmond (Champaign, IL: Human Kinetics Publisher, 1986), 38.

74. These events included the pole vault, the high jump, the shot put, the discus, and the decathlon. For the role of Munich in helping establish the Amateur Sports Act of 1978, see Thomas H. Hunt, "Countering the Soviet Threat in the Olympic Medals

Race: The Amateur Sports Act of 1978 and American Athletics Policy Reform," *International Journal of the History of Sport* 24 (June 2007), 796–818.

75. Description of the game in this paragraph and the four that follow is from ABC videotape coverage of the final.

76. *Manchester Union Leader,* September 12, 1972, 19; *CBS Sunday News with Dan Rather* transcript, September 10, 1972, 11; telegrams and letters in Box 185, File: Games—XXth Olympiad, Munich, Germany 1972—USA-USSR Basketball Game, Avery Brundage Collection, University of Illinois, Champaign, Illinois; *Dayton Daily News,* September 12, 1972, 18.

77. Howard Smith in WHCA VTR #5771, Tape 2 of 2, National Archives at College Park, College Park, MD; *Washington Post,* September 11, 1972, 1D.

78. Chanting in *Atlanta Constitution,* February 23, 1980, 3C; "God Bless America" information in *New York Times,* February 23, 1980, 16. For front-page coverage (all on February 23, 1980), see *San Francisco Chronicle, Boston Globe, Philadelphia Inquirer, Washington Star, Chicago Tribune, New York Times, Washington Post,* and *Los Angeles Times. Philadelphia Inquirer,* February 23, 1980, 1. For congressmen's remarks, see *Congressional Record,* Vol. 126, 96th Congress, 1980, 3610–3612, 3648, 3650, 3654–3655, 3658. Brooks quoted in Tim Wendel, *Going for the Gold: How the U.S. Won at Lake Placid* (Westport, CT: Lawrence Hill & Company, 1980), 47.

79. Al Oerter quoted in *Newsweek,* January 28, 1980, 27; poll figure in *Chicago Tribune,* March 28, 1980, 1B; and *Track and Field News,* March 1980, 37; congressional vote in Allen Guttmann, *The Olympics: A History of the Modern Games* (Urbana: University of Illinois Press, 1992), 150; USOC delegate vote in *New York Times,* April 13, 1980, 1.

80. Soviet propaganda in Derick L. Hulme Jr., *The Political Olympics: Moscow, Afghanistan, and the 1980 U.S. Boycott* (Westport, CT: Praeger, 1990), 118; *Sovetskaya Rossia* accusation in *Current Digest of the Soviet Press* 32, no. 14 (May 7, 1980): 19; *Sovetskaya Rossia* quoted in Barukh Hazan, *Olympic Sports and Propaganda Games: Moscow 1980* (New Brunswick, NJ: Transaction Books, 1982), 178. The State Department in late May estimated the number of boycotting nations to be more than sixty, while the Soviets placed the number at twenty-nine. See *New York Times,* May 28, 1980, 10A.

81. Anti-Soviet faction in *Current Digest of the Soviet Press* 36, no. 19 (June 6, 1984): 4; Gramov in *Current Digest of the Soviet Press* 36, no. 19(June 6, 1984): 6; *Izvestia* in *Current Digest of the Soviet Press* 36, no. 21 (June 20, 1984): 19–20; *Human Events,* August 11, 1984, 10; *Congressional Record,* 98th Congress, 2nd Session, Vol. 130, 1984, 24171.

82. *Sovetski Sport* quoted in *Sports Illustrated,* July 13, 1992, 48.

83. *Congressional Record,* 85th Congress, 2nd Session, Vol. 104, 1958, A6926.

16. Dare to Dream—Lindsey J. Meân

1. Michael A. Messner, "Sports and Male Domination: The Female Athlete as Contested Ideological Terrain," *Sociology of Sport Journal* 5 (1988): 197–211.

2. Michael J. Shapiro, "Representing World Politics: The Sport/War Intertext," in *International/Intertextual Relation,* ed. J. Der Derian and M. J. Shapiro (Lexington, MA: Lexington Books, 1989): 69–96.

3. Lindsey J. Meân, "Identity and Discursive Practice: Doing Gender on the Football Pitch," *Discourse & Society* 12 (2001): 789–815. Using Dominique Maingueneau's criteria for foundational discourses.

4. André Jansson, "The Mediatization of Consumption: Towards an Analytical Framework of Image Culture," *Journal of Consumer Culture* 2 (2002): 5–31.

5. John Sugden and Alan Tomlinson, "Soccer Culture, National Identity, and the World Cup," in *Hosts and Champions: Soccer Culture, National Identity, and the World Cup*, ed. John Sugden and Alan Tomlinson (Aldershot, UK: Arena, 1994): 3–12.

6. Ibid.

7. Ingar Mehus, "Distinction through Sport Consumption," *International Review for the Sociology of Sport* 40 (2005): 321–333.

8. Fernando Delgado, "The Fusing of Sport and Politics: Media Constructions of U.S. versus Iran at France '98," *Journal of Sport & Social Issues* 27 (2003): 293–307.

9. Garry Crawford, *Consuming Sport. Fans, Sport, and Culture* (London and New York: Routledge, 2004).

10. Hugh O'Donnell, "Mapping the Mythical: A Geopolitics of National Sporting Stereotypes," *Discourse and Society* 5 (1994): 345–380.

11. Patricia Vertinsky, "Time Gentlemen Please: The Space and Place of Gender in Sport History," in *Deconstructing Sport History: A Postmodern Analysis*, ed. Murray G. Phillips (Albany: SUNY Press, 2006): 227–243.

12. Mary J. Kane and Helen J. Lenskyj, "Media Treatment of Female Athletes: Issues of Gender and Sexualities," in *Mediasport*, ed. Lawrence. A. Wenner (London: Routledge, 1998): 186–201.

13. Neal Christopherson et al., "Two Kicks Forward, One Kick Back: A Content Analysis of Media Discourses on the 1999 Women's World Cup Soccer Championship," *Sociology of Sport Journal* 19 (2002): 170–188.

14. Leslie Sklair, *Sociology of the Global System* (London: Harvester Wheatsheaf, 1991).

15. Sugden and Tomlinson, "Soccer Culture, National Identity, and the World Cup," 3–12.

16. In the United States, (invasive) on-screen advertisements during play and commentator "promotional content" have become part of televising soccer in the absence of commercial breaks; although this limits commercial potential. However, it is unlikely that such practices would be acceptable or condoned in other countries.

17. Sugden and Tomlinson, "Soccer Culture, National Identity, and the World Cup," 3–12.

18. Deborah Cameron, "'Is There Any Ketchup, Vera?' Gender, Power, and Pragmatics," *Discourse and Society* 9 (1998): 437–455.

19. Marie Hardin, "Stopped at the Gate: Women's Sports, 'Reader Interests,' and Decision Making by Editors," *Journalism & Mass Communication Quarterly* 82 (2005): 62–77.

20. Garry Crawford, *Consuming Sport: Fans, Sport, and Culture* (London and New York: Routledge, 2004); Mary J. Kane and Helen J. Lenskyj, "Media Treatment of Female Athletes: Issues of Gender and Sexualities," in *Mediasport*, ed. Lawrence. A. Wenner (London: Routledge, 1998): 186–201.

21. Michel Foucault, *The Order of Things: An Archeology of the Human Sciences* (New York: Vintage/Random House, 1970) and *The Archaeology of Knowledge* (London: Tavistock, 1972).

22. Jean Williams, *A Beautiful Game: International Perspectives on Women's Football* (Oxford and New York: Berg, 2007), 46.

23. The temporary or fair-weather nature of the 1999 world cup fans could be blamed for the subsequent failure of WUSA, but the lack of media attention, audience building, and commercial imperative are significant given the role of these in mediatization and, thus, success. The failure of the NHL to fully recover (status, fan base, and financially) from the loss of one season of play in the media spotlight is indicative of the power of media and commercial interests over fan loyalty and commitment.

24. The advantages and disadvantages of this are complex and mixed. For example, women's play may be less restricted by having to be different from the men's game, yet a cultural history that provides a highly competitive, established style to form the discursive framing and content of the way the game is played may also be beneficial.

25. Michael Lewis, "U.S. Women's Soccer Team Will Miss Abby Wambach's Golden Touch," *NYDailyNews.com,* July 29, 2008, http://www.nydailynews.com/sports/more_sports/2008/07/29/2008-07-29_us_womens_soccer_team_will_miss_abby_wam.html (accessed July 29, 2008).

26. As in many industries, two years is not enough time to become profitable (the model adopted by the WNBA allowed for a longer period to become financially self-sustaining). Equally, many argue that senior appointees to WUSA reflected a paternalistic and hobbyist framing of the endeavor, rather than WUSA as a serious sporting enterprise.

27. Barry Svrluga, "U.S. Women Win Soccer Gold Medal: Era Ends Joyously for Pioneering Team," *Washington Post,* August 26, 2004, A01, http://www.washingtonpost.com/ac2/wp-dyn/A36021-2004Aug26?language=printer (accessed August 1, 2008).

28. Jere Longman, *The Girls of Summer* (New York: Harper Collins Publishers, 2000).

29. Neal Christopherson et al., "Two Kicks Forward, One Kick Back: A Content Analysis of Media Discourses on the 1999 Women's World Cup Soccer Championship," *Sociology of Sport Journal* 19 (2002): 170–188; Jayne Caudwell, "Women's Football in the United Kingdom." *Journal of Sport and Social Issues* 23 (1999): 390–402.

30. Lindsey J. Meân, "Making Masculinity and Framing Femininity: FIFA, Soccer, and World Cup Websites," in *Examining Identity in Sports Media,* ed. Heather Hundley and Andrew Billings (New York: Sage Publications, 2010).

31. Associated Press, "Norway Scores in Overtime to Win," ESPN.com, September 28, 2000, http://espn.go.com/oly/summer00/news/2000/0928/785251.html (accessed July 19, 2008).

32. Andrew Marshall, "Babes' Stir Football Fever," *London Independent,* July 5, 1999, Sport, 7. Like most British newspapers, this newspaper is not known for its coverage of women's soccer (or women's sports per se).

33. Judith Butler, *Gender Trouble: Feminism and the Subversion of Identity* (New York: Routledge, 1990).

34. Jayne Caudwell, "Women's Football in the United Kingdom." *Journal of Sport and Social Issues* 23 (1999): 390–402.

35. Associated Press, "Norway Scores Early to Shock U.S.," ESPN.com, August 6,

2008, http://soccernet.espn.go.com/news/story?id=560383&cc=5901&campaign=
rss&source=ESPNHeadlines (accessed August 22, 2008).

36. Lindsey J. Meân and Jeffrey W. Kassing, "'Would Just Like to Be Known as an
Athlete': Managing Hegemony, Femininity, and Heterosexuality in Female Sport,"
Western Journal of Communication 72 (2008): 126–144.

37. Jayne Caudwell, "Women's Football in the United Kingdom," *Journal of Sport
and Social Issues* 23 (1999): 390–402.

38. Jean Williams, *A Beautiful Game: International Perspectives on Women's Football*
(Oxford and New York: Berg, 2007).

39. Adidas commercial, thirty-second version at http://www.youtube.com/
watch?v=g7YIWuZaozw and sixty-second version at http://www.youtube.com/
watch?v=pRg-di-EWLw (accessed August 2, 2008).

40. Prnewswire.com, "Adidas Rekindles US-China Women's Soccer Rivalry,"
http://prnewswire.com/mnr/adidas/11260 (accessed August 2, 2008).

41. Neal Christopherson et al., "Two Kicks Forward, One Kick Back: A Content
Analysis of Media Discourses on the 1999 Women's World Cup Soccer Championship," *Sociology of Sport Journal* 19 (2002): 170–188.

42. Prnewswire.com, "Adidas Rekindles US-China Women's Soccer Rivalry,"
http://prnewswire.com/mnr/adidas/11260 (accessed August 2, 2008).

43. "Samba Queens" has been used to refer to the Brazilian team in a number of
media texts. For example, William Gildea, "At the Big Jack, a Match Made for
History," *Washington Post*, June 28, 1999, D1.

44. Scott Pitoniak, "Women's Soccer Final Could Get Rough," *Gannett News
Service,* August 25, 2004, http://argusleader.gannettonline.com/gns/olympics/
20040825-50998.html (accessed July 17, 2008).

45. Fifa.com, "Familiar Foes Set Up Final Repeat," Fifa.com, August 18, 2008,
http://www.fifa.com/womensolympic/news/newsid=854724.html#familiar+foes+
final+repeat (accessed August 22, 2008); and "Revenge on the Menu in Beijing,"
Fifa.com, August 19, 2008, http://www.fifa.com/womensolympic/news/newsid=
855247.html#revenge+menu+beijing (accessed August 22, 2008).

46. Pitoniak, "Women's Soccer Final Could Get Rough."

47. Judith Butler, *Gender Trouble: Feminism and the Subversion of Identity*
(Routledge: New York, 1990).

48. Lindsey J. Meân, "Framing Athletes as Women: Sex, Soccer, and the 'Miss
World Cup,'" paper presented at the annual National Communication Association
Convention, Chicago, November 15–18, 2007.

CONTRIBUTORS

DAVID K. WIGGINS (co-editor) is a professor and director of the School of Recreation, Health, and Tourism at George Mason University. He received his AB and MA from San Diego State University and PhD from the University of Maryland. His research has focused on the history of American sport, particularly as it relates to the African American experience in sport and physical activity. Among his numerous publications are *Out of the Shadows: A Biographical History of African American Athletes; The Unlevel Playing Field: A Documentary History of the African American Experience in Sport* (with Patrick B. Miller); *Sport and the Color Line: Black Athletes and Race Relations in Twentieth-Century America* (with Patrick B. Miller); and *Glory Bound: Black Athletes in a White America.*

R. PIERRE RODGERS (co-editor) is an associate professor of sport management and co-coordinator of the graduate program in the School of Recreation, Health, and Tourism at George Mason University. He received his BA from the University of Alabama, MA from Memphis State University, and PhD from The Pennsylvania State University. He is a former associate editor for *Communication Teacher.* His research interests focus on the interrelationship between race, sport, popular culture, and communication. He has published in journals such as *World Communication, Psychological Reports,* and the *Journal of the Collegiate Forensic Association.*

BRAD AUSTIN is an associate professor of history at Salem State College, Massachusetts. He received his BA from Lyon College, his MA from the University of Tennessee, and his PhD from The Ohio State University. His research focuses on the history of American intercollegiate athletics, particularly on the meanings of men's and women's college sports during the Great Depression. He has published essays in the *Journal of Sport History,* the *Journal of East Tennessee History,* and the *American Historical Association's Perspectives on History.* He also served as the chairperson of the American Historical Association's Teaching Prize Committee.

GERALD EARLY is Merle Kling Professor of Modern Letters at Washington University in St. Louis. He received his BA from the University of Pennsylvania and MA and PhD from Cornell University. He is the author or editor of a number of works, including *Tuxedo Junction; Daughters: On Family and Fatherhood; One Nation under A Groove: Motown and American Culture; The Muhammad Ali Reader; This Is Where I Came In: Black America in the 1960s;* and *The Culture of Bruising: Essays on Prizefighting, Literature, and Modern American Culture.*

CHRIS ELZEY is an adjunct professor of American history in Washington, DC. He earned a BA from the University of Pennsylvania, an MA from the University of Alabama, and a PhD from Purdue University. His research interests include ethnicity and the Olympic Games and the Cold War and sport. He has published articles on American Jewish Olympians and on basketball.

MARY JO FESTLE is a professor of history at Elon University. She received her BA from Knox College and her MA and PhD from the University of North Carolina–Chapel Hill. Her scholarly interests include recent U.S. history, particularly as related to social movements, oral history, organ transplantation, and the intersections of sex, race, class, and culture. She is the author of a number of articles on those topics as well as *Playing Nice: Politics and Apologies in Women's Sports.*

ANNETTE R. HOFMANN is a professor of sport science at the Ludwigsburg University of Education, Germany. She received her MA and PhD from the University of Tübingen. Her research has focused on the history of German Americans in sports and physical education and on gender studies in sports. Among her publications are *Aufstieg und Niedergang des deutschen Turnens in den USA; Turnen and Sport: Transatlantic Transfers; International Perspectives on Sporting Women in Past and Present* (with Else Trangbæk); *Historical Perspectives on Gender, Body, Movement, and Sport* (with Susan Bandy and Arnd Krüger).

LAWRENCE W. HUGENBERG (1953–2008) was a nationally renowned scholar in the field of communication studies. He received his BSSW, MA, and PhD from the The Ohio State University and was a professor in the School of Communication Studies at Kent State University. His interests included sports communication, media and popular culture, organizational communication, and communication pedagogy. Among his numerous publications are "NASCAR Fans in Their Own Words: Motivation Expressed in Narrative" (with Barbara Hugenberg); "The NASCAR Fan as Emotional Stakeholder: Changing the Sport, Changing the Fan" (with Barbara Hugenberg); and *Sports Mania: Essays on Fandom and the Media in the Twenty-First Century* (with Adam C. Earnheardt and Paul M. Haridakis).

RYAN KING-WHITE is an assistant professor in the Department of Kinesiology at Towson University. He received his BS from Ithaca College and MA and PhD from the University of Maryland. His research has focused on the various ways the bodily performance is informed and evaluated in and through the contemporary (American) sociopolitical context, particularly as it relates to the interrelationship of the George W. Bush presidency and various forms of nationalism. Among his publications are "Revisiting the Networked Production of the 2003 Little League World Series: Narrative of American Innocence" (with Michael Silk and David Andrews); "The Little League World Series: Spectacle of Youthful Innocence or Specter of the New Right" (with Michael Silk and David Andrews); and "Beyond the Stadium and into the Street: Sport and Anti-Americanism in South Korea" (with Eunha Koh and David Andrews).

GEORGE B. KIRSCH is a professor of history at Manhattan College. He received his BA from Cornell University and his MA and PhD from Columbia University. He specializes in the history of sport in the United States, especially ethnicity, nineteenth-century baseball, and golf. He is co-editor of the *Encyclopedia of Ethnicity and Sports in the United States* and author of *Baseball and Cricket: The Creation of American Team Sports; Baseball in Blue and Gray: The National Pastime during the Civil War;* and *Golf in America.*

DANIEL S. MASON is a professor with the Faculty of Physical Education and Recreation and an adjunct professor with the School of Business at the University of Alberta. He received his BPE and MA from the University of British Columbia and PhD from the University of

Alberta. Mason's research takes an interdisciplinary approach and focuses on the business of sport and the relationships between its stakeholders, including all levels of government, sports teams and leagues, the communities that host teams, agents, and players' associations. His research has been published in such journals as the *American Behavioral Scientist, Contemporary Economic Policy, Economic Development Quarterly, International Journal of Sport Finance, Journal of Sport Management, Journal of Urban Affairs, Managing Leisure,* and *Urban History Review.*

LINDSEY J. MEÂN is an assistant professor in communication studies in the Division of Social and Behavioral Sciences at Arizona State University. She received her BSc (Hons) from Plymouth Polytechnic and PhD from the University of Sheffield, both in the United Kingdom. Her primary research focuses on identities, discourses, language, and representational practices in interaction, media, and organizations, with a particular interest in sport, gender, race, and diversity. She is the author (with Angela Goddard) of *Language and Gender* and the forthcoming *Sport: Language, Culture, and Everyday Discourses* (with Kelby Halone). Her work has been published in journals such as *Discourse and Society, Communication Yearbook, Sex Roles, International Journal of Sport Communication, Western Journal of Communication,* and *American Behavioral Scientist.*

DANIEL A. NATHAN is an associate professor of American studies at Skidmore College. He received his BA from Allegheny College and his MA and PhD from the University of Iowa. The author of the award-winning *Saying It's So: A Cultural History of the Black Sox Scandal,* Nathan has also published essays and book, film, and exhibition reviews for *Aethlon: The Journal of Sport Literature, American Quarterly, Journal of American Studies, Journal of Sport History,* the *OAH Magazine of History,* and the *Sociology of Sport Journal.* He has also served as the film, media, and museum reviews editor for the *Journal of Sport History* and is on the editorial board of the *International Journal of the History of Sport.*

JOHN NAURIGHT is a professor of sport management and heads the Academy of International Sport at George Mason University. He is also Visiting Professor of Sports Studies at Aarhus University in Denmark. He received his BA and MA degrees in history from the University of South

Carolina and his PhD in history from Queens University in Canada. His research has focused on gender and race in sport and on the political economy of sport in the English-speaking world. His publications include *Sport, Cultures, and Identities in South Africa* and edited volumes, including *Making Men* and the *Routledge Companion to Sports History*.

STEPHEN H. NORWOOD is professor of history at the University of Oklahoma. He received his BA from Tufts University and his MA and PhD from Columbia University. His most recent book is *The Third Reich in the Ivory Tower: Complicity and Conflict on American Campuses*. He is editor (with Eunice G. Pollack) of the two-volume *Encyclopedia of American Jewish History*, which won the *Booklist* Editor's Choice Award. Norwood is the winner of the Herbert G. Gutman Award in American Social History and co-winner of the Macmillan / SABR Award in Baseball History. His most recent sports history publications are *Real Football: Conversations on America's Game* and "American Jewish Muscle: Forging a New Masculinity in the Streets and in the Ring, 1890–1940" in *Modern Judaism*.

BRIAN C. PATTIE is a graduate assistant in the School of Communication Studies at Kent State University. He received his BA from Oakland University and his MA from Wayne State University. His research interests include sports communication, interpersonal communication, conflict management, and cognition.

S. W. POPE is director of the International Center for Performance Excellence at West Virginia University. He received a BA from Hope College, MA from the University of Connecticut, and PhD from the University of Maine. In addition to various articles, reviews, and book chapters, he is co-editor (with John Nauright) of the *Routledge Companion to Sports History*; author of *Patriotic Games: Sporting Traditions in the American Imagination, 1876–1926*; editor of *The New American Sport History: Recent Approaches and Perspectives*; and co-editor (with John Nauright) of *The New Sport Management Reader*.

JAIME SCHULTZ is an assistant professor in the Department of Kinesiology at the University of Maryland, College Park. She received her BA from Luther College and MA and PhD from the University of

Iowa. Her research centers on issues of gender, race, and cultural memory in relation to the history of sport and physical culture. She has published several book chapters and articles in journals such as the *Journal of Sport History, Stadion, International Journal of the History of Sport, Sociology of Sport Journal, Journal of Sport and Social Issues,* and *Sport and Society.* She is currently completing a book, to be titled "From Sex Tests to Sports Bras: Gender, Technology, and U.S. Women's Sport."

BRIAN P. SOEBBING is a PhD student in the Management Research Group within the Faculty of Physical Education and Recreation at the University of Alberta. Soebbing received his BBA from Saint Louis University and a MS from the University of Illinois at Urbana-Champaign. His main research interest focuses on both the uncertainty of game outcomes and competitive balance in professional and collegiate sport leagues. His secondary interests include examining gambling behavior, specifically sports betting, and investigating the relationship between coaching and organizational performance. His research has been published in the *International Journal of Sport Finance* and in several book chapters. He has also presented his research at various conferences, including the North American Society for Sport Management, Western Economic Association, and the International Conference on Gambling and Risk Taking.

JOSEPH M. TURRINI is an assistant professor and coordinator of the Archival Administration Program in the School of Library and Information Science at Wayne State University. He received a BA from San Francisco State University and an MA and PhD from Wayne State University. His research has focused on sport, labor, archival history, and archival education. He has published articles in a number of journals, including *Journal of Sport History, Sport History Review, American Archivist, Perspectives,* and *Labor History.* His book, *The End of Amateurism in American Track and Field,* is being published by the University of Illinois Press.

ALISON M. WRYNN is a full professor and associate chair for the Department of Kinesiology at California State University, Long Beach. She received her BS from Springfield College, her MA from California State University, Long Beach, and her PhD from the University of

California, Berkeley. Her research is focused on the history of sport, physical education, and exercise science, particularly on women's roles in these arenas. She is co-editor of the textbook *Women, Sport, and Physical Activity: Challenges and Triumphs*, second edition, and her research has been funded in the past by the Olympic Studies Centre of the International Olympic Committee and the Women's Sports Foundation.

INDEX